The Loneliness of the Black Republican

POLITICS AND SOCIETY IN TWENTIETH-CENTURY AMERICA

SERIES EDITORS
William Chafe, Gary Gerstle, Linda Gordon, and Julian Zelizer

*The Loneliness of the Black Republican: Pragmatic Politics and
the Pursuit of Power* BY LEAH WRIGHT RIGUEUR

*Don't Blame Us: Suburban Liberals and the Transformation
of the Democratic Party* BY LILY GEISMER

*Relentless Reformer: Josephine Roche and Progressivism
in Twentieth-Century America* BY ROBYN MUNCY

Power Lines: Phoenix and the Making of the Modern Southwest BY ANDREW NEEDHAM

*Lobbying America: The Politics of Business from Nixon
to NAFTA* BY BENJAMIN C. WATERHOUSE

*The Color of Success: Asian Americans and the Origins
of the Model Minority* BY ELLEN D. WU

The Second Red Scare and the Unmaking of the New Deal Left BY LANDON STORRS

Mothers of Conservatism: Women and the Postwar Right BY MICHELLE M. NICKERSON

*Between Citizens and the State: The Politics of American Higher
Education in the 20th Century* BY CHRISTOPHER P. LOSS

Philanthropy in America: A History BY OLIVIER ZUNZ

The Loneliness of the Black Republican

PRAGMATIC POLITICS AND THE
PURSUIT OF POWER

Leah Wright Rigueur

PRINCETON UNIVERSITY PRESS

Princeton and Oxford

press.princeton.edu

Jacket art: Photograph of Jewel Lafontant taken during the 1960 Republican National
Convention. Courtesy of the Oberlin College Archives.

Library of Congress Cataloging-in-Publication Data
Wright Rigueur, Leah, 1981–
    The loneliness of the Black Republican : pragmatic politics and the pursuit of power /
Leah Wright Rigueur.
        pages cm — (Politics and society in twentieth-century America)
    Includes bibliographical references and index.
    ISBN 978-0-691-15901-0 (hardcover : acid-free paper)
        1. African Americans—Politics and government—20th century.   2. African
American politicians—History—20th century.   3. African American political activists—
History—20th century.   4. Republican Party (U.S. : 1854–)—History—20th century.
5. Conservatism—United States—History—20th century.   6. Politics, Practical—United
States—History—20th century.   7. Power (Social sciences)—United States—History—
20th century. 8. United States—Politics and government—1933–1945.   9. United
States—Politics and government—1945–1989.   I. Title.

E185.615.W85 2015

323.1196'0730904—dc23

                                            2014013056

British Library Cataloging-in-Publication Data is available

This book has been composed in Sabon

Printed on acid-free paper. ∞

Printed in the United States of America

10 9 8 7 6 5 4 3 2 1

For Austin Vladimir

Contents

Acknowledgments

FINDING THE PERFECT WAY TO SAY "THANK YOU" TO EVERYONE THAT helped me with this project has been a difficult task because words cannot fully capture the extent of my gratitude. Still, it's important for me to articulate how thankful I am to be surrounded by the vibrant intellectual and creative communities that ultimately shaped this book, by guiding me through the process and encouraging me, every single step of the way.

The bones of this project first emerged during my tenure as a graduate student at Princeton University. To call my time there challenging would be an understatement; the invigorating intellectual environment was crucial to my development as a writer and scholar. I benefited tremendously from the mentorship and wisdom of the faculty members in the History Department and at the Center for African American Studies, particularly Margot Canaday, Joshua Guild, Hendrik Hartog, Tera Hunter, Emmanuel Kreike, Nell Painter, Robert Tignor, Christine Stansell, and Sean Wilentz. I want to extend a special thank you to Daniel Rodgers, whose advice and moral support always provided clarity at precisely the right moment throughout my graduate career. I continued to be awed by Karen Jackson-Weaver; while at Princeton, she served as my mentor and advocate and was truly an inspiration. And even now, though I am years removed from the university, she continues to help me develop as a scholar and leader. The members of my dissertation committee devoted a generous amount of time, energy, and resources to my work (and still do!). Eddie Glaude offered shrewd direction and continues to advocate on my behalf. From day one, Timothy Thurber served as both a friend and scholarly adviser. His groundbreaking research motivates me to push the boundaries of my own scholarship. I was extremely fortunate to have an opportunity to work with Julian Zelizer before I left New Jersey—his outlook on politics and history completely reshaped the way that I thought about multiple scholarly fields. He consistently pushed me to develop abstract ideas into rigorous and thoughtful arguments. He's also quick to lend a helping hand and provide candid advice (and he's always right). Julian's intellectual determination and dedication to his craft are dazzling to watch and have greatly influenced my own scholarly drive.

Trying to summarize what Kevin Kruse's friendship and mentorship means to me is an impossible charge. From my first day of graduate school, when he sent me a cheerful "Welcome!" e-mail, Kevin has been steadfast in his support. He was an exceptional dissertation adviser and advocate, reading multiple draft chapters (including the truly terrible ones), painstakingly combing through every line of my dissertation, offering line-by-line feedback, and providing dozens of pages of notes and comments. Part of Kevin's brilliance is his gift for language and the written word; he has the ability to help you turn a clunky underdeveloped concept into a sophisticated and complex idea—and he does it all effortlessly. He was involved with the production of this book, every step of the way—assessing project proposals, fellowship applications, and chapters. He was, and still is, good for a much-needed pep talk, which I appreciate for so many hard-to-articulate reasons. I'm so grateful that I have such a magnificent mentor and friend who refuses to let me doubt my work or myself.

Wesleyan University warmly welcomed me as I transitioned from graduate student to professor. During my first year on campus, all of the faculty members in the History Department and the Program in African American Studies went out of their way to dole out sage wisdom about the inner workings of academia. It was (and still is) excellent advice that helped me forge an ambitious path at the university and beyond. To the entire faculty in History and African American Studies, especially Lois Brown, Paul Erickson, Demetrius Eudell, Nat Greene, Courtney Fullilove, Patricia Hill, Cecilia Miller, Vijay Pinch, Laurie Nussdorfer, Ashraf Rushdy, Gary Shaw, Victoria Smolkin-Rothrock, and Ann Wightman—thank you. I am also grateful for the wise counsel and friendship of Erness Brody, Alex Dupuy, Renee Johnson Thornton, Rashida Shaw, Gina Ulysse, and Krishna Winston. Ann duCille is the model of intellectual prowess; she is also one of the kindest people I know. I am fortunate to call her my friend. I am indebted to Rick Elphick, who read book proposal drafts, offered general feedback on the project, and once spent more than six hours with me, on a hazy summer evening, discussing the framework of the book. Likewise, Ronald Schatz and Magda Teter both generously offered constructive suggestions on the manuscript on multiple occasions, while the spring 2012 cohort at the Wesleyan Center for the Humanities offered sharp insights into the third chapter of this manuscript. Joan Chiari, Lori Flannigan, and Ann Tanasi are at the cusp of sainthood. They have endured nonstop questions and requests from me with patience, grace, and, of course, humor. My undergraduate research assistants, Spencer Hattendorf, Christian Hosam, Hannah Korevaar, CaVar Reid, and Amber

Smith did a tremendous amount of work on my behalf, showcasing their scholarly thoughtfulness and impressive work ethic.

Sarah Mahurin deserves an extra special thank you for bringing so much fierceness and joy into the monotony of everyday academic life. I love that her passion for all things pop culture is outweighed only by her untiring commitment to social justice. Equal parts brilliant, caring, and fabulous (and so clearly my work twin!). I also owe a debt of gratitude to Claire Potter who has been a fantastic mentor and friend. Claire's feedback was instrumental as I was revising my manuscript; her advice has always been clear, frank, and constructive. I appreciate her pointed observations and guidance. Her unshakable belief in my skills has helped me develop into a more confident scholar and intellectual. Tehama Lopez-Bunyasi, my writing partner and lovely, compassionate friend, has offered me nonstop encouragement since the day we first met in her adviser's living room in New Jersey. Our marathon brainstorming sessions (and, really, watching the fascinating way she mulls over ideas and works through difficult concepts) remind me why I love the profession. Chin Jou and Dov Weinryb Grohsgal both have been terrific and supportive friends since our early days at Princeton. They read dozens of versions of my dissertation and book manuscript (among many, many, many other favors), and for that I am so grateful. Dov also helped me reconceptualize the two longest and most difficult chapters of the book—a vital breakthrough. Without his assistance, the project would have been stuck in writing-block limbo indefinitely.

My beautiful CPC writing family was such a big part of the successful completion of this book. At our first session in 2010, we detailed our respective scholarly aims; less than five years later, we've each hit those goals—time to set some new ones! Thank you for giving me structure, holding me accountable, speaking plainly, pushing me to be the best, and making me laugh to the point of tears. Working with David Lobenstine was such a delight—he made revision fun! David, thank you for helping me find my voice and helping my manuscript "sing." Additionally, I am appreciative of a broader community of scholars who helped mold this book, including Judith Byfield, Courtney Cogburn, Brett Gadsden, Lily Geismer, Cheryl Greenberg, Tikia Hamilton, Jeannette Hopkins, Rob Karl, Annelise Orleck, Laurence Ralph, and Bruce Schulman. Uri McMillan was always an email away and was often the calm, rational voice in the middle of crises. Our daily group chats are always the highlight of my day. Michael Ralph has always had so much confidence in this project—and in me. By this point, I think he's provided feedback on every single draft of the manuscript. Though I've only known Al Tillery for a few years, I feel like I've known him forever. He's been so warm and genuine—to both my family and me. His insights helped me develop the strength necessary to bring this project to a close.

Chuck Myers at Princeton University Press believed in this project in its earliest stages and continues to support the book from afar. I am also appreciative of the patience, persistence, and advice of Eric Crahan and Eric Henney at the Press, along with the Politics and Society in Twentieth Century America series editors and the production team who have turned this manuscript into a tangible book.

Excerpts of this book appeared in different forms in three articles published by the author: "Conscience of a Black Conservative: The 1964 Election and the Rise of the National Negro Republican Assembly," *Federal History Journal* 1 (January 2009): 32–45; "Making a 'New Majority': Black Republicans and the Nixon Administration," in *Painting Dixie Red: When, Where, Why, and How the South Became Republican*, edited by Glenn Feldman (Gainesville: University of Florida Press, 2011), 240–290; and "'The Challenge of Change': Edward Brooke, the Republican Party, and the Struggle for Redemption," *Souls* 13, no. 1 (Winter–Spring 2011): 91–118. Thank you to the University of Florida Press, Taylor & Francis/*Souls*, and *Federal History* for granting permission to reprint these materials.

Funding helped make my dream of writing a book become real. As such, I am grateful for the support of the Andrew W. Mellon Foundation, the Meigs Fund at Wesleyan University, the Oberlin College Archives, the Social Science Research Council, and the presidential libraries of Lyndon B. Johnson, Gerald R. Ford, and George H. W. Bush. Recognizing the value of a sabbatical, Wesleyan University allowed me to take a semester's leave, coupled with another leave sponsored by the Woodson Wilson-MMUF Junior Faculty Career Enhancement Fellowship. Several prominent political leaders graciously permitted me to interview them on multiple occasions, particularly Senator Edward W. Brooke III, Secretary of Transportation William T. Coleman Jr., former Republican National Committee official Clarence L. Townes Jr., and Secretary of Labor and Senator William E. Brock III. Their first-person accounts truly brought this story to life.

By the time I submitted the final manuscript, I'm sure that dozens of archivists and librarians had grown tired of my incessant badgering. For that, I apologize! Without the help of archivists and librarians, this project would be nothing. Many of these men and women exposed me to thousands of untouched historical documents, which were an integral component of this book. In 2006, for example, Betty Culpepper of the Library of Congress, introduced me to more than one thousand pages worth of primary and secondary sources on modern black conservatism.

In particular, I'd like to thank the staff at the following locations: the National Archives; the presidential libraries of Dwight D. Eisenhower, Lyndon B. Johnson, Richard Nixon, Ronald Reagan, and George H. W. Bush; the Library of Congress; the Rockefeller Archive Center; the Dole Archives and Special Collections; the Howard Gotlieb Archival Research Center at Boston University; the James Branch Cabell Library at Virginia Commonwealth University; the Hoskins Library at the University of Tennessee; the Cushing Library at Texas A&M University; the Hoover Institution Archives; the Charles E. Young Research Library at the University of California, Los Angeles; the Oberlin College Archives; the Iowa Women's Archives, The University of Iowa; the Arizona Historical Foundation; Arizona State University, Archives and Special Collections; Syracuse University Libraries; the Wilcox Collection of Contemporary Political Movements at the Kenneth Spencer Research Library at the University of Kansas; the Moorland-Spingarn Research Center at Howard University; and the Burton Historical Collection at the Detroit Public Library.

As most authors know, writing can be an isolating experience. Good friends alleviated much of my "writer's loneliness"; in particular, I would like to thank Adrian Bell, Gary Brifil, Lemu Coker, Hillary Crosley, Crystal Gist, Stacy Harper, Aquilla Raiford, and Kimberly Thurman-Rivera. Though we are no longer Princeton neighbors, Diana Hill regularly lent a sympathetic ear and urged me to enjoy my social life and family. Thank you for always checking in on me. Eva Haldane is such a sweet and sensitive soul (and has been for as long as I can remember). Thank you for dragging me to the UConn Law Library in the middle of winter to kickstart the manuscript revision process and for being one of my scholarly accountability buddies. Your faith in my ability to finish was far more important than you realize; I also appreciate your willingness to join me in my couch-potato shenanigans and love that you're just a phone call away. Megan Ming Francis is my intellectual fashionista soulmate—a sister-friend from another mother and father. Watching you go through the manuscript writing-revision process (and doing it with your signature flair and brilliance) was inspiring; and having you stand next to me while I was going through the process a few months later (with you shouting in my ear "You will finish!") was deeply moving in a way I cannot express. Thank you for always being there and for making me tougher and, really, just for caring so much.

My family, both immediate and extended, is boisterous, feisty, hilarious, and fiercely loyal. Family functions always involve at least twenty minutes of conversation about "the book" followed by another forty minutes worth of heated debate over race, politics, and social issues, followed by a mean game of Taboo. It's amazing, and I wouldn't have it any other way. So to the Edmeads, Grangers, Magubanes, McCabes, Mjis, Rigueurs, and Wrights—thank you. My only lament is that my grandfather Rodman Edmead, who passed away in 2004, can't be here to engage in the festivities. I also like to think that maybe he would have liked "the book" (though he surely would have instigated all kinds of arguments with the rest of the family). I'm comforted by the fact that my wonderful grandmothers, Una Edmead and Lyda Wright, have more than enough wisdom to go around. Although it's subtle, I think some of their sharp wit made it into the manuscript. To my sister, Tia Benjamin Silas, thank you for being my best friend, my confidant, my shoulder to cry on (as dramatic as that sounds), and one of my biggest cheerleaders. Your friendship continues to help me overcome any major hurdle that I come up against. You know I've always admired your drive, determination, and intelligence; I'd like to think that I channeled a bit of that in finishing up this book. I hope you like it. I am also grateful for the omnipotent insights of Jason Wright, Thulani LeGrier, Zine Magubane, and Sibongile Magubane. Their contribution to this project has been immeasurable. Reading drafts, providing provocative critiques, engaging me in tireless debates, providing career advice, listening to my writing woes, and then proposing a plan of attack—the list goes on and on.

Dana Wright, Elease Wright, and Kyle Wright—my family—are incredible. They are generous of mind, spirit, energy, and resources. My brother may be the most absent-minded person I know, next to myself; he's also one of the smartest and most confident men I know. He's such a joy to be around and I'm so proud of the man he has grown up to be. My father is the calmest (yet fiercest) man I know. He's also the most confident. While I was finishing this book, he would visit me in my office, take his shoes off, tell me to chill out, and start humming a tune. It always worked (or at least it made me laugh). He was also notorious for dropping in and giving me a rallying talk that usually ended with him telling me to get my act together and "go kick some ass." Again, it was a pretty effective motivating tool. Finally, my mother is superwoman, as anyone who knows her will attest. The nights that I stayed up until sunrise writing, my mother was right there next to me, reading drafts, asking questions, and disagreeing with my logic. She read draft after draft and consistently pushed me to finish the project. If writing the book was akin to running a marathon, my mother was cheering me on from the sidelines and was the first person to hug me at the finish line. Though it may sound redundant by this point, there's no way to express how grateful I am for everything she, and my entire family, has done.

To Philip Rigueur and Austin Vladimir Rigueur—my biggest supporters —thank you and I love you. We did it. I hope I make you proud.

A Brief Note on Sources

WHEN I STARTED THIS BOOK, I ASSUMED THAT FINDING ARCHIVAL SOURCES and documents would be nearly impossible, since black Republicans were, and still are, a political minority within their racial communities and a racial minority within their political party. Discussions with other historians confirmed my assumptions, as did a review of the secondary source material.

I could not have been more wrong.

The sheer amount of primary source material on black Republicans is remarkable and rich. I started with the Barry Goldwater Archives at the Arizona Historical Foundation and moved on to the Library of Congress and the Presidential Libraries accessible through the National Archives and Records Administration. These starting points held a treasure trove of information, leading me to more collections that I ever could have imagined. There are hundreds of collections that contain information on African Americans within the Republican Party from 1936 through the present day, but these records are disparate, scattered in various libraries and institutions across the country. Assembling a comprehensive list of the papers of self-identified black Republicans is a challenge in and of itself, especially since many of these collections are private, classified, restricted, still being processed, or sitting in someone's basement, all but forgotten.

Many of these smaller archives featured the stories of figures who were "proudly Republican," while others offered glimpses into the worlds of "quiet" party members—black men and women who kept their political preferences hidden from their public lives, or dabbled in GOP politics, moving in and out of the party depending on the broader political context. By the time my research came to a close, I had close to twenty thousand primary source documents, with the prospect of collecting even more. These sources range from the local to the national level, and from the grass roots to the state; they contained memos, agendas, letters, manifestos, policy papers, paraphernalia and propaganda, oral history interviews, print media, radio and television, private letters and public declarations, speeches, and much more.

Given the sheer volume of this information, it was necessary to limit the scope of my research and carve out a representative and clear guide for you, the reader. In this respect, and it pains me to say this, there are many figures, groups, and institutions that simply are not discussed within these pages, all of which are deserving of further study. I focused on the ideas and events that held widespread collective meaning to those black Republican leaders tied to a national movement; this does not mean that there are not local stories that offer critical insight into race, civil rights, conservatism, and the GOP.

Abbreviations

AA	*Afro-American*
ABC	Abyssinian Baptist Church
ACME	Advisory Council for Minority Enterprise
ADW	*Atlanta Daily World*
APP, UCSB	*American Presidency Project*, University of California, Santa Barbara
BAA	*Baltimore Afro-American*
BANA	Black Americans for Nixon Agnew
BCRP	Black Council of Republican Politics, Inc.
BD	Black Desk
BE	*Black Enterprise*
BERO	Black Elected Republican Officials
BERO Papers	Black Elected Republicans 1970 folder, Manuscript Division, Library of Congress
BEU	Black Economic Union
BG	*Boston Globe*
Black Desk Files	People for Ford Office, Black Desk Files
BMG Papers	Barry M. Goldwater Collection
BPC	Black Power Conference
BRAC	Black Republican Appointees Council
Brock Papers	William H. Brock III Papers
BSMC	Black Silent Majority Committee
C100	Council of 100
CBA	Council of Black Appointees
CBC	Congressional Black Caucus
CCRC	Capitol City Republican Club
CD	*Chicago Defender*
CFOA	confidential oversized attachment
CFR	Citizens for Reagan
Clements Papers	Rita Crocker Clements Personal Papers
CLT Papers	Clarence L. Townes Jr. Papers
CORE	Congress of Racial Equality
CP	*Cleveland Call and Post*
CQ	*Congressional Quarterly*
CR	*Congressional Record*
CREEP	Committee to Re-Elect the President

CRO	Council of Republican Organizations
CSM	*Christian Science Monitor*
CT	*Chicago Tribune*
DDE Library	Dwight D. Eisenhower Presidential Library
DeBolt Files	Edward DeBolt Subject Files
DNC	Democratic National Committee
DNC Papers	DNC Records
EEOC	Equal Employment Opportunity Committee
EFM Papers	E. Frederic Morrow Records
EWB Papers	Edward W. Brooke III Papers
FEPC	Fair Employment Practices Committee
FERA	Federal Emergency Relief Administration
Finch Files	Robert Finch Files
Fletcher Files	Arthur A. Fletcher Files
GAA Files	Gwen A. Anderson Files
Garment Files	Leonard Garment Papers
GHWB Library	George H.W. Bush Presidential Library
GOP	Grand Old Party
GRF Library	Gerald R. Ford Presidential Library
GSA	General Services Administration
HBCU	Historically Black Colleges and Universities
HC	*Hartford Courant*
HCC	Harlem Citizens Committee
HE	*Human Events*
HEW	Health, Education and Welfare
HJH Papers	Senator H. John Heinz III Archives
HUD	Housing and Urban Development
Hugel Files	Max Hugel Files
IA	*Issues and Answers*
JCPES	Joint Center for Political and Economic Studies
JCPS	Joint Center for Political Studies
JR	Jackie Robinson
Keyes Files	Robert Keyes Files
LAS	*Los Angeles Sentinel*
LAT	*Los Angeles Times*
LBJ Library	Lyndon Baines Johnson Presidential Library
LDF	NAACP Legal Defense and Education Fund
LIRE	Lincoln Institute for Research and Education
MLS Papers	Mary Louise Smith Papers
NAACP	National Association for the Advancement of Colored People
NAC	Negro Advisory Committee

NACW	National Association of Colored Women's Clubs
NANB	National Association of Negro Business
NBL	National Business League
NBPC	National Black Political Convention
NBRC	National Black Republican Council
NBRN	*National Black Republican News*
NBVRB	National Black Voters for Reagan-Bush
NCAAR	National Council of Afro-American Republicans
NCCAAR	National Council of Concerned Afro American Republicans
NCCBR	National Coordinating Council of Black Republicans
NCNW	National Council of Negro Women
NFRW	National Federation of Republican Women
NNRA	National Negro Republican Assembly
NPC	National Press Club
NR	*National Review*
NRO	Negro Republican Organization
NUL	National Urban League
NYA	National Youth Administration
NYAN	*New York Amsterdam News*
NYC	*New York Courier*
NYT	*New York Times*
OFCC	Office of Federal Contract Compliance
OIC	Opportunities Industrialization Centers
OMB	Office of Management and Budget
OMBE	Office of Minority Business Enterprise
OP	*Oakland Post*
ORC	Ohio Republican Council
Panzer Files	Office Files of Fred Panzer
Patterson Files	Bradley H. Patterson Files
PC	*Pittsburgh Courier*
PFC	President Ford Campaign
PFC Records	President Ford Committee Records
POIC	Philadelphia Opportunities Industrialization Center
POQ	*Public Opinion Quarterly*
PS	*PS: Political Science and Politics*
PSQ	*Political Science Quarterly*
PWA	Public Works Administration
RCC	Republican Congressional Committee
RCV	Richmond Crusade for Voters

RF	*Ripon Forum*
RFI	Reagan Focused Impact
RGA	Republican Governors Association
RJB Papers	Ralph J. Bunche Papers
RJD	Robert J. Dole Archives and Special Collections
RN Library	Richard Nixon Presidential Library
RNC	Republican National Committee
RPC Report	Republican Program Committee Report
RR Library	Ronald Reagan Presidential Library
RRPC Papers	Ronald Reagan 1980 Presidential Campaign Papers
RTH Papers	Robert T. Hartmann Papers
SBA	Small Business Administration
SCLC	Southern Christian Leadership Conference
Shadegg Papers	Stephen Shadegg Collection
SN	*Star-News*
SNCC	Student Nonviolent Coordinating Committee
SPT	*St. Petersburg Times*
SR	*Sun Reporter*
SSCPCA	Senate Select Committee on Presidential Campaign Activities
SSS Papers	Stanley S. Scott Papers
SW Papers	Sheila Weidenfeld Files
TAP	Training and Advancement Program
TM	*Tuesday Magazine*
UWB Papers	Ulysses W. Boykin Papers
VIDN	*Virgin Island Daily News*
WAA	*Washington Afro-American*
Watergate Hearings	Select Committee on Presidential Campaign Activities, Executive Session Hearings
WE	*Wichita Eagle*
WHCF SMOF	White House Central Files, White House Staff Member Office Files
WMA	Wright-McNeill and Associates
WP	*Washington Post*
WPA	Works Progress Administration
WSJ	*Wall Street Journal*
YAF	Young Americans for Freedom
YRNF	Young Republican National Federation

The Loneliness of the Black Republican

The Paradox of the Black Republican

THERE IS A FASCINATING *SATURDAY NIGHT LIVE* SKETCH FROM 1980, A piece almost entirely forgotten by most viewers of the NBC comedy show. The sketch survives in the pop culture arena only because it features the *SNL* debut of comedian Eddie Murphy. Airing about a month after the country elected an ex-actor to the presidency (ousting a former Georgia peanut farmer in the process), the skit is a spoof of *Mutual of Omaha's Wild Kingdom*, that unconventional animal wildlife series sponsored by an insurance company. In the *SNL* piece, a Jim Fowler–type zoologist braves the "savage" landscape of a tony Manhattan cocktail party in search of an elusive subject: the Negro Republican. Tracking the "migratory patterns" of African Americans "fleeing the liberal lake wastelands" for the "fertile promised land of the GOP," the scientist stumbles badly—a hilarious case of mistaken identity—when he assumes that a black funeral parlor direc-tor *must* be a member of the GOP. Undeterred, he spots another black man nearby—a thorough examination of speech patterns, clothing, musi-cal tastes, and economic interests confirms that the subject is indeed the evasive Negro Republican. With great care, the zoologist sedates the "ex-otic creature," attaching a blinking transmitter disguised as an American flag pin to the man's lapel. As the disoriented man awakens, the scientist quickly hides, emerging to take notes on his subject from afar once the Negro Republican has wandered back into the "wild."[1]

"In Search of the Negro Republican" is a riveting political satire, inter-esting not for the writing or the cast's performance but for the ideas con-veyed by the sketch—ideas about popular perceptions of African Ameri-can members of the GOP. A black Republican, it would seem, was a rare fellow in 1980—a political opportunist and an economic conservative who, seduced by the promise of a Reagan Revolution, had disavowed his longtime home in the Democratic Party. By that same token, a black Re-publican was a racial turncoat—a Benedict Arnold in blackface who had appropriated clichéd notions of middle-class whiteness: a stuffy voice, a preference for the Carpenters over the Isley Brothers, the choice of a drab, unsophisticated suit, and a degree of comfort with the quintessen-tial symbol of American patriotism, Old Glory. A black Republican was a curiosity—a creature to be observed, sedated, and studied.

The *SNL* sketch, as with any satire, is a primer in exaggeration, entertaining precisely because it taps into stereotypes of black Republicans—caricatures that we know logically are absurd, yet nevertheless still make some kind of intuitive sense. The uneasy racialized undertones of the sketch are rendered practically invisible because something about the parody *resonates*. Stripped of nuance, the stereotype works because it exposes the fundamental question that so many of us ask: Why would an African American join the Republican Party? The question is an old one, an ubiquitous inquiry that many people, Democrats and Republicans alike, have posed consistently since the 1930s—the decade when black voters first began to flee the Republican Party, then known as the "Party of Lincoln," an ideological home so very different from what "Republican" means today. Since then, the link between blacks and Democrats has become a knee-jerk one, a relationship that is taken for granted by all sides. Over the decades, the concept of a "black Republican" has come to seem a contradiction in terms, invested with an odd kind of alienness. "Since President Franklin and the New Deal," wrote the editors at the *Chicago Defender* in 1976, "being black and Republican was about as compatible as being black and aspiring to leadership in the Ku Klux Klan."[2]

Beneath the stereotypes and the made-for-TV satire, our notions of black Republicans rest on two basic truths. First, without question, blacks are the most partisan of any racial group in the United States.[3] Since 1948, a substantial majority of African Americans has identified as Democrat; since 1964, that lopsided figure has only increased, as more than 80 percent of black voters have cast their ballots for the Democratic Party nominee in every presidential election. By 1980, more than 90 percent of the nation's five thousand black elected officials were Democrats, including all of the members of the Congressional Black Caucus. And in 2012, African Americans played a vital role in helping reelect Barack Obama to the White House, offering the president 94 percent of their votes. This partisanship, as Michael Dawson, Nancy Weiss, and others have suggested, "was never blind or random but was based on a realistic assessment of which party would best further black political and economic interests." And as the extensive histories of civil rights and black politics make clear, African Americans made critical and significant advances for racial equality and social justice by way of the New Deal and the Great Society programs, thereby "anchoring" African Americans in Democratic liberalism.[4]

Second, the GOP of today bears little resemblance to the "Party of Lincoln" to which black voters had been fiercely loyal since the era of Reconstruction. Instead, the modern Republican Party is indelibly associated with Herbert Hoover's "lily-white" movement, "Operation Dixie" of the 1950s, and Richard Nixon's "southern strategy." It is a party whose 1964 presidential candidate voted against the landmark Civil Rights Act passed in that year, and whose 1980 nominee launched his official presidential campaign with a now-infamous "states' rights" speech in Philadelphia, Mississippi—the town in which three civil rights workers were murdered sixteen years earlier.[5] As politicians shaped the GOP from the "top down," ordinary white city dwellers and suburbanites from all backgrounds and income levels along with an "army" of conservative activists, influenced the direction of the GOP from the grass roots, *reacting* to changing social and cultural norms, the liberalism of the civil rights movement and the radicalism of Black Power. In short, the GOP is a party whose conservatism, to quote Robert Smith and Hanes Walton, seems to make it "virtually impossible for blacks, given their history and condition," to accept.[6]

These two strands of thought are mutually reinforcing, confirmed through our everyday experiences: individual encounters, media reports, fictional depictions in television and film, and scholarly studies all work in concert to produce a pervasive vision of the past century that leaves little room for the coexistence of African Americans, conservatism, and the Republican Party. All of our instincts, scholarly and otherwise, tell us that *African Americans should not be Republicans, nor should they be conservatives.* Yet black Republicans do exist—and their inevitable existence, of course, complicates our assumptions. Some black families never left the Republican fold, while other individuals have found their way back to the GOP. The past three decades alone have witnessed the rise of a number of prominent African American members of the Republican Party: Samuel Pierce, Clarence Thomas, Colin Powell, J. C. Watts, Condoleezza Rice, Michael Steele, Constance Berry Newman, Alan Keyes, Robert A. George, Herman Cain, Michael Powell, Lynn Swann, Allen West, and Tim Scott, to name a few. But rather than erasing public curiosity, the appearance of black Republicans merely intensifies it, often infusing a new urgency into the original underlying question of *why.*

That curiosity is often suffused with a measure of frustration: the question of *why* quickly becomes a more loaded inquiry: *How could they?* For some, anger with black Republicans is an implicit rejection of a larger accommodationist tradition. To their critics, black Republicans are Booker T. Washington's successors, racial apologists whose affiliations and beliefs mark them as traitorous individuals, complicit in an age-old crusade to "delegitimize the black quest for racial and social justice."[7] A black Republican, the *Pittsburgh Courier* spat in 1992, "is a kind of bogeyman dressed in a Black tailored suit or immaculate silk dress, to cajole Blacks into believing the Republican Party and its brand of conservatism is a trumpet-tongued angel playing the jazz of economic salvation and racial harmony." Such music, the black newspaper criticized, "is nothing more than bubbles of gas emanating from the butt of reptiles." However, as we shall see, the "songs" of black Republicans are far more complicated and multivocal.[8]

In contrast, white Republicans often heap gratuitous public praise on African American members of the GOP, applauding them for having the gumption to leave the "plantation politics of the Democratic Party," as Pat Buchanan did on CNN in 2011, while defending Herman Cain. This line of thinking stems from the flawed and simplistic belief that African Americans have been brainwashed into voting for the Democratic Party and, as a result, ignore the benefits of belonging to the GOP. The trope of the Democratic Party as a slave plantation has been a recurring feature of GOP rhetoric since at least 1968, when Richard Nixon mentioned it in an interview with *Jet* magazine; predating even this, black Republicans have used the phrase regularly since 1964. Such thinking is problematic—often condescending and occasionally even bigoted, insinuating that Democrats have "bought" the black vote with "government handouts," and that African Americans are therefore unable to make their own rational political choices, thereby sidestepping the GOP's role in repelling black voters.[9]

More broadly, however, both of these perspectives, like much of our understanding of black Republicans, are deeply unsatisfying. They tell us little about who black Republicans are, why they join the GOP, and what they really believe and why. Our assumptions about blacks in the Republican Party are teleological and ahistorical, informed by the Republican Party as it exists in the present; thus our views are often flat, lacking historical depth. Surely this understanding denies us the messiness that is at the heart of our beliefs and at the core of our personal politics: the ongoing debate that each one of us has with ourselves and with others about which politicians and policies we should support and about what ideologies we should embrace.

Our implicit views of black Republicans—either as strange alien creatures or as noble exceptions among their duped Democratic brethren—reject the notion of political choice; too often we assume that blacks in America are Democrats by default; though not intentional, that assumption denies agency to an entire group of citizens. In this scenario, black Republicans are simultaneously invisible and hypervisible: isolated political misfits who provoke extreme reactions. These views, whether voiced by liberals or conservatives, of any race, are troublesome, muting reality and history and ignoring the complex ways that race and politics intersect in the United States. Simply put: our views obscure the fascinating diversity that exists within this "strange" group known as black Republicans, obscuring their historical significance over the past three-quarters of a century; this, in turn, conceals a richer understanding not only of black politics but of American politics more generally.

My aim in this project is to offer a new understanding of the interaction between African Americans and the Republican Party and provide insights into the seemingly incongruous intersection of civil rights and American conservatism. Exploring black politics over nearly half a century, as we will see, disrupts many of our perceptions about African Americans who support the GOP; at times we find not a peculiar group of blacks, desperate for white acceptance or out of touch with American realities but rather a movement of African Americans working for an alternative economic and civil rights movement. At other moments, we see a cadre of figures who make cynical concessions in order to maintain a modicum of power. I argue that the complex nature of this story reveals the links between the black freedom struggle and the American conservative movement, uncovering the forgotten efforts by African Americans, some of whom attempted to forge new pathways to equality, even as many within the GOP appeared hostile to that very idea. This study illustrates that black Republicans occupied an ostensibly irreconcilable position in that they were simultaneously shunned by African American communities and subordinated by the Republican Party. In response, black Republicans vocally, and at times viciously, critiqued members of their race and their party, attempting to regulate and influence the attitudes, behaviors, and public images of both black citizens and the GOP.

Over the past two decades, there has been an explosion of first-rate scholarship that explores the intersections of race, ideology, and American politics through local histories and studies of the lives of "ordinary" American citizens.[10] My study, by contrast, is by necessity national in emphasis, with a focus not on a particular local community but on African American involvement with the Republican Party on every level—local, state, and national. The most crucial figures in this narrative were a relatively small group of black men and women—activists, leaders, officials, politicians, and occasionally intellectuals—who helped steer the machinations of the GOP on a national level; still, from time to time, I also take into account the efforts of a much larger group of African Americans who were solely active in local and state-level politics. This is an expansive endeavor, covering forty-four years of American social and political history, tracing black involvement in the Republican Party from the political realignment of the New Deal to the beginning of the so-called Reagan Revolution. And though the importance of local studies on social and political history cannot be overstated, adopting a wide yet targeted framework is crucial to this book, allowing me to examine the ways in which members of a group who have long been both a political minority in their racial community *and* a racial minority in their political party interacted with each other, with the Republican Party, and with other African Americans. Moreover, employing a national focus also allowed me to tell a subtle but important story about the evolution in the opinions and behaviors of rank-and-file blacks who voted for Republicans in local, state, and national elections between 1936 and 1980.

By no means have scholars ignored the political ideologies of African Americans; the sheer amount of work on black political thought and action is tremendous, offering critical and nuanced readings of African Americans' embrace and rejection of philosophies, including liberalism, radicalism, feminism, and nationalism, and nearly any combination and variation thereof. Because so much of the "action" has taken place on the left, most of the scholarship has concentrated on this political history. More recently, however, a rapidly growing body of literature has started to address the dearth of scholarship on African American "conservatives," focusing exclusively on black conservatism in the nineteenth and twentieth centuries, offering interpretive readings of the black tradition, and highlighting the existence of an "everyday" form of conservatism among almost a third of African Americans (which rarely translates into votes for the Republican Party). In addition, many of these texts illustrate the development of a form of "black neoconservatism" in the 1980s and 1990s, wherein some black men and women became vigorous spokesmen for contemporary right-wing Republican policies and programs, placing the "onus of responsibility" on African Americans for their social and economic woes and urging black voters to join the GOP.[11] Similarly, a small group of historians has turned its attention to expanding the scholarship on race and the Republican Party, revealing the existence of a moderate and liberal tradition within the GOP, one that consistently clashed with the party's more reactionary elements over the course of the twentieth century and pushed Republicans to address equality in a way that spoke to the needs of all American citizens.[12]

While the perspectives on black conservatism and liberal and moderate Republican politics are unequivocally important to this project, readers will notice that my project differs from this scholarship, as my focus is on the *intersection* of race, civil rights, conservatism, and party politics and addresses both the "nuts and bolts" of black Republican activism and the ideas that motivated these actions. My choice of historical period is also distinct, for most studies of black conservatism focus on either the late nineteenth or late twentieth century, while most works on the Republican Party view African Americans as only *adjacent* to Republican politics, focusing instead on the actions of white members of the GOP.

This "middle period" between 1936 and 1980 is devoid of scholarship, in part, for two reasons: we focus on the most evident and productive centers of action—the liberal coalitions between blacks and the Democratic Party; and we assume that no African American would want to be associated with the Republican Party after the rise of Barry Goldwater in 1964.

I revise this broader narrative by pointing to a long history of black Republican activists, a cadre of figures who were middle-class professionals—lawyers, doctors, entrepreneurs, and businessmen and women—who hailed primarily from California, Michigan, New York, Ohio, Virginia, and Washington, D.C. They were mostly men—at least until the 1960s, when black women, despite being the least likely of any racial demographic to vote for the Republican Party, increasingly played an important public role in party affairs. Many were members of local chapters of civil rights organizations like the National Association for the Advancement of Colored People (NAACP), National Urban League (NUL), and Congress of Racial Equality (CORE)—and some were even leaders and officials in local and state chapters of these groups. At the same time, many black Republicans actively distanced themselves from the direct-action and civil disobedience protests that characterized the classical civil rights movement of the 1950s and 1960s and publicly repudiated the Black Power cries that exploded in the late 1960s and early 1970s.

Most of these black party members joined the Republican Party (or never left it) out of a belief in what they called "traditional" conservatism: anticommunism, free market enterprise and capitalism, self-help and personal responsibility, limited government intervention, and a respect for authority, history, and precedent, along with Western institutions and traditions. In this sense, their beliefs were aligned with those of their white counterparts; and like their white counterparts, black Republicans' traditional conservatism also reflected their dissatisfaction with the Democratic liberalism of the New Deal and the Great Society. Reflecting the political diversity of the Republican Party more generally, there were three broad wings of black Republican thought, a great ideological gamut that encompassed liberal, moderate, and conservative factions. Equally important—and especially baffling to critics—most black Republicans, regardless of their ideological differences, believed that racial egalitarianism was in keeping with the Republican Party's principles. Indeed, the majority believed that in times of crisis, the government had a right to intervene on behalf of the nation's citizens; consequently, African American party members' traditional conservatism often included a belief in federal intervention in specific matters of civil rights and racial equality.

Black Republicans' faith in traditional conservatism was not their sole motivator for working with and within the Republican Party; they also did so for pragmatic purposes, viewing two-party competition as the most efficient and practical way to achieve sociopolitical power. Sharing their Democratic Party counterparts' mistrust of third-party political systems, black Republicans were committed to working within a two-party system. Still, they differed from their Democrat peers in seeking to push an agenda of equality through conservative networks and institutions of power. This allegiance to two-party competition was, and still is, central to black Republican thought and action. Since 1936, when more than 70 percent of African Americans first cast votes for Franklin Roosevelt, African American Republicans have consistently argued that large black constituencies could mean substantial black influence if applied to both political parties, insisting that the black vote should be "flexible enough to swing between the two parties according to the momentary interests of Blacks."[13] In theory, this strategy would allow African Americans to institute major social and economic changes from within *both* political parties. Neither were black Republicans alone in advancing this thesis: prominent black Democrats made similar arguments throughout the twentieth century with the hopes of forcing concessions and instituting reform within their own political party.[14] As we shall see, however, the notion of two-party competition was, and still is, deeply flawed, causing black Republicans endless frustration.

A central problem that this study bumps up against, again and again, is exactly what—or better yet *who*—a conservative is. What did it mean to be "conservative" and black during the twentieth century, and what did it mean to affiliate with the Republican Party? Some may argue that the black Republicans at the heart of this story were not "authentic" conservatives. Such a notion of authenticity assumes that conservatism is a rigid ideology, fixed over time and space, when in fact the reality is far more complicated and interesting.[15] I have identified various black individuals and groups as "conservative" because they identified as such or were so labeled by political observers of the period.[16] Furthermore, the more we look across the decades in question, the more we see how intellectual and political *ideas* of conservatism changed for black Republicans between 1936 and 1980. Their definition of "conservative" and "conservatism" was not constant; they used the terms in a myriad of contradictory and confounding ways, as we shall soon see.

In an attempt to provide the reader with clarity, I have outlined four of the most common manifestations of conservatism among black Republicans between 1936 and 1980, keeping in mind the advice of Peter Eisenstadt, who has suggested that the dilemma for those studying black conservatism is that the ideology "will not be true of all black conservatives" and "may be true for many who are not black conservatives."[17]

To put it another way, the boundaries between these manifestations of black conservatism are messy at best and at times fragile. First, black Republicans' brand of conservatism was an ideology rooted in nineteenth-century middle-class mores of respectability, built upon a faith in the Protestant work ethic and the lodestones of self-help, personal responsibility, morality, and political involvement. This was a model propagated by the black elite, as many scholars have convincingly argued, and was an imperfect challenge to white supremacy in an era of second-class citizenship; it was reflected in the economic and business ethos embodied by Booker T. Washington and the class privilege inherent in W.E.B. Du Bois's theory of a talented tenth uplifting the "best" of the race.[18]

The second manifestation of conservatism was as a traditional set of broad principles, as we have already seen, historically connected to the Republican Party. Likewise, the third manifestation was a wing of black Republican thought; these were the conservative African Americans who held a more rigid interpretation of traditional party principles, despite their racially egalitarian beliefs. The final manifestation of conservatism among black Republicans is perhaps the most complicated to outline, since it includes those who affiliated with the reactionary wing of the mainstream Republican Party. None of the four manifestations are static categories, of course, but arguably, this is the display that changed the most dramatically throughout the latter half of the twentieth century. At first, these figures sat at the margins of black Republican thought, including those who opposed the civil rights legislation of the 1950s and 1960s; yet as the GOP's right wing adjusted the language of its conservatism—polishing it into a seemingly race-neutral ideology of individual rights, freedom of choice, and free market enterprise—more and more African American party members came to support it, despite regular opposition from their more liberal black counterparts.

Moreover, in spite of conservatism's association with the right wing of the modern GOP, black Republicans have long seen the ideology as a legitimate solution, one that should be considered seriously in the struggle for racial equality. Thus, African Americans attempted to influence the direction of conservatism—not to destroy it but rather to expand the boundaries of the ideology in order to include black needs and interests. This interpretation of conservatism has been flexible, by both definition and necessity, since issues of race, representation, and power guided black Republicans' actions. Perhaps even more remarkable, in the half century between 1936 and 1980 this pragmatic definition of conservatism was broad and elastic enough to encompass black citizens from across the political spectrum, including African American leaders *outside* of the Republican Party. As civil rights leader Jesse Jackson argued in 1978, African Americans "must pursue a strategy that prohibits one party from taking us for granted and another party from writing us off. The only protection we have against political genocide is to remain necessary."[19] And as we shall see, even President Barack Obama, the scourge of Republicans everywhere, has sounded a lot like the black Republicans of the 1960s and 1970s since taking office in 2008.

This book covers three different waves of national black Republican thought and activity, a period that begins in 1936—significant not only for the major political realignment of African American voters but also for the remarkable voting fluidity of the black electorate (see tables 1–3 in the appendix); in fact, through 1962, nearly a third of black voters pulled the lever for Republican candidates in midterm and presidential elections. The decision to nominate Barry Goldwater as the GOP presidential nominee in 1964 marks the beginning of the next wave of black party activity, as the Arizona senator's right-wing agenda sent shockwaves through black Republicans' ranks, motivating them to organize on a national scale in pursuit of intraparty reform. Many began to look to state and local politics, hoping to duplicate the electoral success of Massachusetts's Edward W. Brooke; and, as we will see, the black senator reinvigorated the idea of pragmatic politics for black Republicans, or, rather, the pursuit of power through party hierarchies in a way that could reconcile conservatism with African American needs. Likewise, they also looked to the Republican-led White House in the late 1960s, where a small band of black appointees was able to introduce an economic civil rights agenda.

The third and final wave reflects the confusion and chaos of the 1970s, a period in which black Republicans, ousted from the White House, turned to the Republican National Committee (RNC) to push party reform, still invested in a pragmatic approach to achieving power. Though their solidarity movement found moments of success, black Republicans also experienced colossal failures. Just as significant, the second and third wave of activity coincided with the passage of the major federal civil rights laws of the 1960s and a society-wide shift from explicit forms of racism to implicit and institutional forms of discrimination.[20] The enactment and the enforcement of this legislation gave black Republicans a kind of freedom, or the leeway, to become more conservative, and adhere to mainstream party ideas about racial equality, *if they so chose*. This distinct outlook enabled black party members to concurrently embrace new types of nonpartisan strategies for wooing black voters *and* partisan techniques for nullifying the black vote. Our story ends in 1980, with black Republicans placing their hopes in the ascent of Ronald Reagan—a man many of them had once rejected.

The year 1936 is an obvious point at which to begin this book; less clear are my reasons for ending in 1980. No one, least of all black Republicans, could have predicted the fundamental way that Ronald Reagan's victory would alter the American political landscape; nor could they have anticipated the way in which some of their ideas—a nuanced and often conflicting set of beliefs articulated over forty-four years—would suddenly gain widespread traction in both the mainstream GOP and broader American political culture. This brings us to one of the many paradoxes posed by the disjuncture between historical and contemporary black Republican politics: it is difficult, if not impossible, to categorize African American members of the GOP, because they do not square neatly with any existing narrative nor do they fit within our modern understanding of the state of American politics. In other words, *we do not have an adequate name for the black Republicans described in this book*, nor do we differentiate between the types of black Republicanism. Thus, I end the narrative in 1980 to demonstrate just how *different* the pre-1980 period was for our reality, in order to bring a better sense of understanding to contemporary American politics; indeed, the preceding period represented intense variety, possibility, and flexibility, whereas the following period witnessed the hardening of the ideological boundaries that divided liberal, moderate, and conservative black Republicans.

• • •

Having spent much of this introduction defining the scope and nature of this study, I think it is reasonable for me to provide the reader with some boundaries by devoting a few words to what this project is not. This book is not a comprehensive study of all black ideologies or politics, nor is it focused on Democratic Party politics or liberalism. It is not an expansive guide to the black freedom struggle; and it is not a primer on the twentieth-century American conservative movement. I do not offer a study of *white* Republicans, whether conservative or moderate or liberal. Neither is this book an investigation of famous black Republicans or conservatives, although some do make appearances in the narrative. I intentionally chose not to focus on figures like George Schuyler and Clarence Thomas because there is a strong body of scholarship on both of these men; furthermore, one of the reasons that we have such a limited impression of black Republicans is that our understanding of this slice of the political sphere is dominated by the individual stories of a few notorious yet significant individuals. By looking past these few men (and, to date, nearly all have been men), it is my aim to reveal a much larger national community of black Republicans.

Throughout this book, I employ polls, statistics, and studies from the period, analyzing them as primary source documents. While such figures are important, they are also flawed. In fact, public opinion data and voting statistics on African Americans are terribly inconsistent, offering contradictory information through the 1980s—a problem often bemoaned by political scientists and historians alike. I have attempted to cobble these facts and figures together in a way that makes sense, pointing out patently obvious issues whenever necessary. But more important than these data, I believe, is the content of black Republican activity; at the center of this story stand the discussions and arguments that black members of the GOP had with themselves and with others, in their perpetual attempts to make conservatism a beneficial option for African Americans.[21]

• • •

This study introduces readers to key figures across a spectrum of black Republican politics and examines their ongoing struggles to effect meaningful change both for African Americans and within the Republican Party over the course of nearly half a century. This project illustrates the ways in which black Republicans were conservative *and* not conservative, and how their ideas overlapped and clashed with even the most reactionary wing of the Republican Party. Most important, this project demonstrates how they tried to reshape and expand the boundaries of conservatism to incorporate a racially egalitarian perspective. In no uncertain terms, black Republicans offer a dilemma of sorts; they were far more conservative than their Democratic counterparts but far less conservative than white reactionary Republicans. They identified with a traditional conservative ideology, to be sure, but they also identified with the various wings of the Republican Party. Above all else, most held fast to a pragmatic ideology that was informed by their day-to-day racial experience rather than by an abstract, dogmatic interpretation of American politics.

CHAPTER ONE

Running with Hares and Hunting with Hounds

"THE REPUBLICAN PARTY," MUSED AN AFRICAN AMERICAN VOTER IN THE early 1930s, "is the party for all, regardless of race, color, or creed." Added another: "It was good enough for my father and it's good enough for me." "My politics is like my religion," insisted a black Chicago resident. "I never change. I am careful about serving my Lord and voting the Republican ticket." "The Democratic party is controlled by devils from below the Mason-Dixon line," offered yet another.[1]

For almost seventy years, such declarations accurately captured the political sentiments of nearly all African Americans. After emancipation, black voters firmly aligned with the Republican Party, supporting the GOP out of a sense of loyalty to the "great emancipator" Abraham Lincoln; even in the aftermath of Reconstruction, as the political rights of African Americans were constrained with a renewed intensity, black voters continued to see the Republican Party as the defender of civil rights. The Democratic Party, in contrast, was an intolerable political alternative, the antithesis of progressive racial reform, instituting racist policies and laws, violently suppressing black voting below the Mason-Dixon Line, and turning a blind eye to black repression.[2] Such was the inextricable link between African Americans and the GOP that continued through the early twentieth century. As journalist Marc Sullivan observed in 1936, "Any Negro who voted Democratic was threatened with social ostracism if not bodily harm . . . no respectable Negro would dream" of affiliating with a regime that celebrated white supremacy; or, as one black skeptic facetiously asked, "How can a Negro be a Democrat?"[3]

Most black voters endorsed Republican incumbent Herbert Hoover as their presidential choice in 1932.[4] "Hoover is like Booker T. Washington," one African American loyalist explained, "a man of God who has borne the sorrows of the world."[5] Just four years after African Americans had rallied around the slogan "Who But Hoover?" and after more than half a century of staunch Republican support, however, something remarkable occurred. On November 3, 1936, 71 percent of black voters cast their ballots for the Democratic incumbent Franklin Delano Roosevelt.[6] That choice would mark the beginning of a radical realignment in American politics, a change so deep and lasting that in the present era, most find it hard to believe that a majority of the black electorate ever voted for Republican presidents. But on that historical day, the visceral frustration of a still-stagnant economy was far more influential than any loyalty considerations. Disappointed with the Republican Party's failure to offer tangible solutions to their economic woes, black voters turned to the recovery and relief programs of Roosevelt's New Deal. Economics, however, was not the sole reason for African Americans departure from the "Party of Lincoln"—many also appreciated the humanitarian efforts of First Lady Eleanor Roosevelt, an active and public advocate for racial equality.[7]

While no one predicted the permanence of this shift toward a Democratic president, the decision of so many voters reflected a gradually mounting frustration. A growing number of African Americans argued that since the demise of Reconstruction, Republican presidents had failed, as historian Nancy Weiss describes, to "measure up to the Legacy of Lincoln." As if the despair and suffering ushered in by the Depression was not enough to question the economic conservatism of Herbert Hoover, the president also displayed a record of "disregard and disrespect" toward African Americans in his attempts to cultivate "lily-white Republicanism" within the South.[8] In 1930 Walter White, then executive secretary for the National Association for the Advancement of Colored People (NAACP), decried Hoover's attitude, labeling the president as "the man in the lily-White House," clearly uninterested in the problems of African Americans and unwilling to consider legislation and "government action."[9] Black leaders debated whether Hoover and the party's decisions came out of complacency, indifference, or a more insidious racism, but the result was clear: Republican leaders neglected both the economic and civil rights needs of black citizens; the progress of African Americans was as stagnant as the economy, with few victories in the struggle against segregation, discrimination, racial violence, and disenfranchisement. The defeat of black Republican stalwart Oscar S. De Priest at the hands of black Republican-turned-Democrat Arthur W. Mitchell in 1934 perhaps best embodied African Americans' growing disenchantment with the GOP; black voters in Chicago ousted the sole African American member of Congress after he rejected federal emergency relief and opposed tax increases for the wealthy.[10] *Time* would later capture the essence of this frustrated relationship, writing, "Political gratitude is paying the GOP steadily diminished returns . . . Lincoln's name . . . no longer works its oldtime magic."[11]

Thus, while the realignment of the black electorate between 1932 and 1936 was remarkable, it was not a surprise. Many African Americans were "ripe for courting" from a shrewd Democratic presidential incumbent;

they also had nothing to lose by leaving the Republican Party, whereas political coalitions with northern Democrats hinted at the possibility of racial and economic progress. Moreover, the Roosevelt administration was the first administration since Lincoln's to actively minister to the needs of blacks, though many of the programs were not deliberately targeted at African Americans.[12] Black citizens benefited from relief payments, public housing assistance, Public Works Administration (PWA) job quotas, and the initiatives of the National Youth Administration (NYA). In 1933, for instance, 35.8 percent of African Americans in urban areas in the Northeast received funds through the Federal Emergency Relief Administration (FERA); just two years later the figure reached 53.7 percent. In 1937, 35,000 African Americans were enrolled in school with NYA assistance. That same year, 390,000 blacks were employed in Works Progress Administration (WPA) projects, and the PWA invested $7 million in black school construction projects in the South. In Cleveland, 92 percent of black residents received payments via either the WPA or the FERA. And as their economic fortunes rose, so too did the black vote for Franklin Roosevelt. In 1932 black voters in Cleveland gave Roosevelt 17 percent of their vote; by 1936 they offered him 61 percent. In Philadelphia, 27 percent of black voters supported the president's first bid; four years later, he earned 69 percent of their support.[13] This increased political support was also aided by a savvy racial symbolism inherent to the Roosevelt White House; for example, the president's publicly naming of a "Black Cabinet," a group of African American advisers who consulted with various administration agency and program directors, suggested to black constituents that they would be included at the highest level of politics; in this and other actions, the administration appeared to signal that no longer would African American voices be excluded.[14]

However, the growing frustrations and shifting votes of African Americans were not representative of a larger ideological realignment. Over the next three decades, the black electorate would be "substantially divided" as African Americans were in no way a "monolithic Democratic voting bloc."[15] Despite Roosevelt's Black Cabinet, the Democratic Party during and immediately after the New Deal offered few bold civil rights initiatives. The programs and agencies of the New Deal were rife with discrimination; in this sense, the Republican and Democratic parties of this era did not display clear-cut differences in their civil rights policies. The result, then, was a surge in Democratic support among the black electorate but "not the total liquidation of Republican backing."[16] The declared affiliation of black voters demonstrates the murkiness of these years; despite the sharp jump in electoral support for the Democratic Party in 1936, African Americans continued to identify as Republicans.

That same year, 44 percent of black voters registered as Democrats, 37 percent registered as Republicans, and 19 percent characterized themselves as independents. By 1940, black voters claimed equal affiliation with both Republicans and Democrats with 42 percent; and in 1944, each of the major parties maintained equivalent shares, at 40 percent.

Which party you affiliated with varied widely depending on age and region. For older black voters, or individuals recently migrated from the South, it was nearly impossible to identify with the Democratic Party. As one Chicago man observed, "The colored voter cannot help but feel that in voting the Democratic ticket in national elections they will be voting to give their . . . approval to every wrong of which they are victims, every right of which they are deprived, and every injustice of which they suffer." But for younger African Americans, especially those who came of "political maturity" during the economic crises of the 1920s and 1930s and were a generation removed from the first wave of the Great Migration, support for the Democratic Party was just as viable as backing the Republican Party, if not more so.[17]

Black voters also demonstrated a strong sense of political independence, along with a growing awareness of the power of their vote; thus, for most, political allegiance was fluid. In a December 1936 article on black voters' "leaning away" from party affiliations, the *New York Amsterdam News* proposed that "independent voting will guarantee voters recognition: candidates will be compelled satisfactorily to solicit their votes, and the voters will hold the key to elections instead of the party figureheads, as it has been in the past. . . . It means that split-ticket voting will be a feature of future elections."[18] A calculating black politician also ruminated on this idea a few years later: "The Negro should divide his voting strength between the major parties," he declared. "Political solidarity is a myth."[19] After the shift of 1936, many within the GOP sensed that African Americans would no longer be swayed by sentimental appeals or past political loyalties. In some GOP circles, this spurred new efforts to reach out to African Americans and reintegrate them into the "Party of Lincoln." For the next three decades, the Republican Party attempted a balancing act between appealing to black voters and ignoring them, depending on whether these efforts would alienate white voters. In turn, African Americans tried to decipher the most useful electoral options for achieving racial and economic equality. To better understand the great shifts across these three decades, we will focus on three figures in particular—Ralph Bunche, E. Frederic Morrow, and Barry Goldwater— whose actions offer insight into the larger trajectories of black Republican politics in modern America.

ADAMANT AND INDIFFERENT: WOOING THE BLACK VOTE

As the dust from the presidential election of 1936 settled, mainstream Republican leaders were disheartened to discover that the party's nominee, Alf Landon, had received only 28 percent of the black vote; in just four years, the party had lost more than 50 percent of its black supporters—losses that became the Democratic Party's gain.[20] Democrats successfully attracted African Americans with economic relief programs and important demonstrations of racial egalitarianism, which trumped many black voters' long-standing dismay over the southern segregationist wing of the party.[21] Publicly, enthusiasm for Franklin Roosevelt was readily visible. Speaking with the *Pittsburgh Courier* a few days after the election, Martha Carpenter of Nashville, Tennessee—born before the Civil War—proudly announced that she had voted for the first time in the election: "I voted for the best man," she stated. "Mr. Roosevelt." A Chicago preacher shared his excitement, declaring to his congregation, "Let Jesus lead you and Roosevelt feed you!"[22] Republicans found themselves outmatched in their attempts to woo black voters in 1936, despite the best efforts of black party members and a few astute white party officials. The Democratic Party seated thirty-two black representatives at its national convention, picked African Americans as campaign managers, and invested nearly $500,000 into northern black outreach efforts. The returns went further than the White House—black voters also helped elect twenty African American Democrats to state legislature positions in nine northern states; attempting to explain this shift, the *New York Amsterdam News* accused the Republican Party of political apathy, suggesting that the party "based its hopes for Negro support on the traditional Republicanism of the race" instead of building "efficient political organizations." Perhaps most damaging of all, when pressed by black constituents to provide an economic alternative to the New Deal programs, Alf Landon delivered "feeble answers," such as his suggestion that the Roosevelt administration "takes from those who have and gives to those who have not. There is no brotherhood in the present relief set up."[23] Talk of "brotherhood" seemed hypocritical and insincere, given that the GOP had offered no firm solutions to African Americans' plight. Moreover, as sociologist St. Clair Drake concluded, "Who was looking for brotherhood when he could get a good WPA job?"[24]

But the 1936 campaign also highlighted tensions within the Democratic Party, namely, between the southern and northern wings of the party. Though it had attempted to "swallow" black outreach as "political expediency," the segregationist faction struggled with the national party's decision to court black voters. Tensions flared most notably during the Democratic National Convention in June 1936. Irate over the recognition of black representatives, Senator E. D. "Cotton Ed" Smith of South Carolina threatened to "boycott" the events so long as African Americans participated. The ornery delegate walked out in the middle of an invocation given by a black minister; just two years later, he resurrected what one reporter described as Smith's "traditional campaign plank: White Supremacy." In 1938 news that fifteen hundred African Americans had been allowed to vote in Texas sparked an ugly intraparty battle over the "legal right" to disenfranchise black voters.[25]

Many white southern politicians feared that the programs of the New Deal would improve the economic and social position of African Americans, numbering the days of "lily-white" southern rule; consequently, President Roosevelt found himself tightly constrained by the southern wing of his party. Antilynching legislation was of special concern—in 1938, for instance, southern legislators launched a six-week filibuster against the Wagner–Van Nuys antilynching bill. Dismayed by the president's apparent indifference to the needs of black constituents, black newspapers railed against Roosevelt; in one article, the *Chicago Defender* argued that a "word" from the chief executive would have guaranteed the antilynching bill's passage. African Americans "widely interpreted" the president's silence on the matter as "opposition to the measure which was offensive to the south." Roosevelt would never pass, let alone enforce, an antilynching provision, reasoned *Time*, for if he did, "all the money in the Federal Treasury could not hold the already troubled South in line for him."[26]

In these tensions and others, Republicans saw an opportunity to regain lost political ground by capitalizing on the unstable coalition politics forged by the New Deal. Black Republicans in Chicago railed against the president's failure to "dislodge southern Democrats" from matters of importance to black constituents. "If Roosevelt was such a good friend of the Negro," they scoffed, "why were southern [politicians] allowed to block antilynching legislation?" The eager politicos pledged that if African Americans supported Republican candidates and officials, the party would end "southern domination in Congress." Their criticisms were also targeted at white Republicans whose actions they construed as antiblack. For instance, they publicly berated New York congressman James Wadsworth for voting against antilynching measures; likewise, black Republican leader Robert Church of Memphis denounced local party officials as "incompetent" and "thoughtless spokesmen," for attempting to explore outreach to white southerners.

For black Republicans, ridding the party of those who would undermine civil rights efforts was a significant goal, but so too was convincing their white peers that black needs were in line with traditional Republican principles. Moreover, they recognized that in order to win new voters, including African Americans, the party had to provide reasonable economic alternatives to the New Deal. However, their focus was narrow and elitist, as it failed to understand the magnitude of black poverty. "The Negro is not satisfied with the enforced pauperism of the New Deal and hopes for an industrial revival which will give us an opportunity for honest employment," argued one New York black Republican, "rather than a place in the breadline, or as a recipient of a hand-out on some 'boondoggling project.'" In this regard, African American party members shared their white counterparts' faith in private industry and economic uplift, sneering at the idea of federal relief and condemning it as dishonorable.[27]

While most mainstream party leaders were dismayed over the black exodus in 1936, others were long aware of the growing political dissonance. During the election, Massachusetts congressman Joseph Martin Jr. worked to salvage the crumbling relationship between black voters and the GOP. Using the Republican National Committee (RNC) as a vehicle, Martin collaborated with Francis Rivers—a young Harlem civil rights activist and member of a group of black Republicans dubbed the "Negro brain trust" by *Time*—in an attempt to make the party relevant to the needs and goals of African Americans.[28] Their "Republican Negro Drive" learned from and adapted to the programs and policies of the New Deal, fusing genuine concern for racial equality with alternative economic incentives. Seizing on black dissatisfaction with the New Deal and attempting to "steal the Democrats' thunder," for instance, one black loyalist declared: "Fifty per cent of Negroes are out of work. We are the last to get jobs, and we have inadequate relief. Some Negroes who get on WPA are removed for white men . . . My platform is: jobs, security, better housing, higher wages, cash relief, old-age assistance—thirty dollars or more per month."[29]

In lobbying black voters to support Republican candidates, Rivers and Martin adopted a platform calling for equal opportunity, increased employment, and antilynching legislation. In their cross-country travels, Rivers and Martin reached out to influential black leaders, including local politicians and clergymen; they also enlisted the support of popular black figures to better convey their ideas to African American constituents. During the 1936 election campaign, for example, Olympic gold medalist Jesse Owens toured thirty eastern cities on behalf of Alf Landon, addressing more than thirty thousand potential black voters. The track star maintained that Landon would protect the economic rights of African Americans, create more jobs than the New Deal, and instill confidence in private enterprise and American businesses.[30] "This country was built on the sweat and blood of the Negro race and this fact hasn't yet been recognized," Owens stated during a September 1936 press conference in Manhattan. "I believe . . . Landon will recognize it. His election will be good for America and for the people of the colored race."[31] Four years later, boxer Joe Louis—the "Brown Bomber"—would also tour the country on behalf of the GOP, criticizing the Democratic Party's platform and promising racial and economic reform on behalf of the GOP.[32] As historian James Kenneally illustrates, from 1936 onward, such thrusts were the centerpiece of Martin's and Rivers's black recruitment strategy. The two Republicans also developed a theme whereby they argued that the New Deal and the Democratic Party had failed black citizens by "consciously and effectively seeking to make all Negroes relief recipients rather than provide employment." Such a solution provided only temporary respite, they reasoned, and would serve only to perpetuate economic and racial inequality, since the Democrats had made little effort to fully integrate black constituents into the public life of the nation. "The Republican Party will not stand by and allow any American citizen to want for the necessities of life," Martin once told a group of black party leaders in New York City, "but will not ask him to deposit his soul and self-respect as security for a mere loaf of bread."[33] The GOP, Rivers and Martin insisted, would offer African Americans "re-employment" rather than handouts; they promised that the party would integrate the workplace and offer black voters tangible solutions to their economic and racial uncertainties.[34]

The Negro Drive had some impact on African American voters in midterm elections, though it did not stop the growing wave of defections in presidential contests. In the 1938 senatorial and gubernatorial races in Ohio, more than 50 percent of black voters in Cleveland cast ballots for Republican nominees; the same was true of the 1939 mayoral election. Likewise, between 1938 and 1940, the Chicago black electorate consistently split its vote in various local, state, and national races.[35] Certainly, some of these shifts were particular to the nuances and peculiarities of local politics; still, by 1940, Martin had earned a reputation as being a "champion" for issues of black concern, such as antilynching legislation, and for appointing "young, vigorous, and self-assured" black men and women to positions of power and influence within the Republican Party.[36]

Hoping to institutionalize its Negro Drive, the party took further steps to resolve its black voting problem. In 1940, for instance, black Republicans held a conference to determine the impact of the New Deal on Republicans' "most tried and true friends—our nation's Negro citizen." Among the list of speakers was Howard University political scientist Ralph Bunche, whose lecture, "New Deal Social Planning as It Affects Negroes," offered a critique of the policies and programs of Franklin Roosevelt.[37] The speech capped more than a year of collaboration with the Republican Program Committee (RPC), a two-hundred-member group formed in 1937 to review the policies of the New Deal, assess Republican principles in light of the political realignment of the American electorate, and create a list of policy recommendations for party revival. In February 1939, Thomas Reed, director of studies for the RPC, approached Bunche about commissioning a report on the "peculiar relationship between the Negro and the Republican Party." The committee asked Bunche to create a "work plan on the Negro," addressing social security, relief, health and medical care, finance, agriculture, and labor, urging him to be candid in his assessment, since his report would inform the party's 1940 platform.[38] Bunche applauded the party's ambition as "sound" and "constructive; in his words, as a "Negro and a member of a disadvantaged minority group," he was concerned with "any measure or policies leading toward an amelioration of the problems" of his race.[39]

Nevertheless, Bunche took precautions by insisting that the RPC "formally declare" the objective nature of his task, lest his work be mistaken for partisanship.[40] He revealed to Reed that he considered himself an independent, unaffiliated with any political party.[41] As a graduate student at Harvard in 1928, he had worked extensively on the nuances of black political thought and independence, calling for a radical overthrow of blind loyalty to political parties in favor of a "more pragmatic local politics." In that same year, he published "Negro Political Laboratories," an essay criticizing both the Republican and Democratic parties for "scorning" and "repudiating" black citizens. The two-party system, he argued, was for "majorities—let the Negro bargain with them, use them, by coalition with their rivals, defeat them, and then *forget* them!" Racially enlightened ideas were more important than party affiliations; consequently Bunche suggested that opportunism on behalf of the entire race was a necessary component of black political behavior. As he concluded, the "Negro must ever be on the alert to make the best of any and every opportunity which presents itself to send a Negro representative or a friendly white one to city, state, or national legislative chambers."[42] Though the radicalism of his graduate school years gave way to a more "mainstream" liberalism by 1939, Bunche nevertheless considered himself outside the spectrum of political partisanship, offering criticism to all political parties and ideologies on the basis of their racial shortcomings. In this sense, Bunche was uniquely suited to serve as a consultant to the RPC as he demonstrated a willingness to objectively critique the programs of the New Deal.

Over the course of four months, Bunche traveled the nation collecting data, interviewing African Americans, and meeting regularly with Republican officials to discuss his preliminary findings.[43] When news of the report leaked in the black press, African Americans besieged the political scientist with letters and phone calls, demanding to know more about the project and Bunche's relationship to the GOP.[44] Bunche delivered the three-part report to the RPC on June 12, 1939: it contained a general survey on the status of African Americans, an analysis of the effect of New Deal policies on the "position of the Negro," and Bunche's recommendations to the Republican Party.[45] To be black and American, he wrote in the introduction to the 137-page report, was to be the "forgotten man": tormented by racial hostility, disenfranchisement, inequality, and economic despair.[46]

Bunche's analysis offered a significant critique not only of the Democratic Party and the New Deal but also of the GOP. He chastised Republicans for their failure to guarantee equal rights for African Americans, an accusation that extended to black Republicans. In fact, Bunche found that African Americans believed that black party loyalists—the small but important group of black Republican politicians, officials, and strategists—were unwilling to risk their "precarious position" in the party to aggressively represent the best interests of the race. In order to recruit voters, the party needed to move beyond stagnancy: African Americans, Bunche reasoned, were eager for a "new Negro Republican leadership to arise, assert itself vigorously, and pitch its appeal to the Negro voters on an entirely different level."[47]

Yet neither party had offered substantive progress on issues of racial equality, Bunche also maintained. Though it provided African Americans with a desperately needed economic boost, the New Deal fell short of meeting the needs of blacks. The Roosevelt administration, Bunche concluded, "has often run afoul of racial prejudice," missteps that meant it was possible for African Americans to make a significant and swift return to the Republican Party. Since 1936, black voters had a clearer understanding of their political power, recognizing that they could trade ballots for "social improvements."[48] Thus, in order to regain its former level of support, the GOP would need to formulate an effective economic and political program for African American advancement:

> What this report boils down to is that the Negro is in need of everything that a constructive humane, American political program can give him—employment, land, housing, relief, health protection, unemployment and old-age insurance, enjoyment of civil rights—all that a twentieth century American citizen is entitled to.[49]

Simply put, party leaders needed to produce a platform that offered *more* than that of the Roosevelt administration, and African Americans needed to experience concrete progress under Republican leadership. Bunche urged the party to offer "concrete evidence" of economic and social solutions; his specific recommendations included enacting antilynching and civil rights legislation, pledging universal health care for black citizens, and creating a racial quota system in labor and employment to help speed African American integration into the work force. If the GOP truly wanted to win black voters, it could not sacrifice their needs for the white southern vote; in other words, as Bunche stated, "one cannot successfully run with both hare and hound, and the Republican Party will need to decide whether it prefers to court the dissident white vote of the Democratic South, through continuance of its lily-white program and an absence of Negro policy, or really desires the Negro vote. It cannot seduce both."[50]

A flurry of correspondence between Bunche and Republican officials indicated that the RPC was initially excited over the "tone and content" of the report; as Thomas Reed declared, "It seems to me to represent a very complete statement of the Negro's relation to the principal economic and social problems of the day and in this respect it is just what we wanted."[51] Reed requested that copies of the report be sent to members of the RNC, party legislators, and dozens of other figures—Bunche was also invited to meet with black Republican leaders and to present his findings to at a July 1939 meeting of the RPC in Chicago.[52] Amid the excitement surrounding the report, party leaders still found fault with Bunche's conclusions. "No political group could include the whole of such a program in its platform," Reed argued in a June 1939 letter to the black political scientist. "To do so would be to invite defeat and actually do harm to the cause of the Negro." Officials quickly rejected some suggestions, deeming them too "explosive"—in particular, they recoiled over Bunche's recommendation for "universally compensatory and publicly subsidized health insurance." Instead, Reed suggested that given the "controversial nature" of the report, it made more sense for the committee to address targeted inequalities rather than attacking the entire spectrum of discrimination. For example, providing a new form of "government aid" through the establishment of hospitals, clinics, and "facilities for training black doctors and nurses," stated Reed, was a far safer way of tackling racial inequality and health care. Apparently Bunche agreed with some of the RPC's revisions, as he ultimately redrafted the report by the end of June, dropping the recommendation for national health care.[53]

Despite wrestling with Bunche's progressive recommendations, the RPC appeared to take the suggestions seriously, passing a resolution in favor of the critical document.[54] Still, despite arriving at a consensus over the controversial contents of the report, the RPC never published the findings. Bunche and the RPC ultimately disagreed over which portions to publicize—party officials wanted to publish only Bunche's criticisms of the New Deal, whereas he insisted that the report be published in full.[55]

Bunche's work raised tensions within the broader GOP, as officials argued that his suggestions were "too 'impractical,' too 'revolutionary,' and too reflective of the temper of the New Deal."[56] The struggle was not so much over the content as it was with the subjects; that is, racial progressives within the party pushed to incorporate civil rights and social reform into the Republican platform, whereas racial conservatives advocated for a "lily-white" agenda at the expense of black citizens. Neither segment of the party, at least in 1940, was strong enough to outpace the other. The result was either an indecisive continuity of the status quo or a cagey effort to placate both factions of the Republican Party. The schism played out in the party's confusing treatment of the "Negro" issue; in February 1940 the RPC's final report contained both a resolution acknowledging racial discrimination and bigotry, and a plank urging continued appeals to southern Democrats.[57] As long as the GOP could slowly woo black voters through local outreach efforts without alienating potential "lily-white" constituents, the party would continue to pursue both "hare and hound."

By 1940, the GOP had increased its share of the black vote but only by four percentage points. Republicans again suffered defeat in the national contest, with 32 percent of African Americans supporting the party's presidential nominee Wendell Willkie.[58] On a regional level, Wilkie received nearly 50 percent of the black vote in western and midwestern states; even in the Northeast, where support for Roosevelt remained firmly entrenched, the Republican nominee managed to earn 49 percent of the black vote in NJ. Nationally, the party drew most of its support from wealthy and middle-class African Americans; these voters cited a myriad of reasons for endorsing the candidate: support for lower taxes, integration into the economic mainstream, opposition to federal relief, distaste for the racial politics of the Democratic Party, the GOP's position on civil rights, and enthusiasm over the outreach efforts of the national committee and the Willkie campaign.[59]

In 1944 the party would win support again from a third of black voters; for African American party members, this was not enough, as they believed the GOP's progress since 1936 was too modest. In fact, in the midst of the 1944 campaign, three hundred black Republicans from thirty-six states had gathered in Washington, D.C., to create what would become a seven-point agenda designed to help the party recruit black voters in future elections. They called for an end to discrimination in the military, African American appointments to federal policy-making positions, and federal protections in collective bargaining, equal employment and education opportunities, and voting rights; likewise, black Republicans reiterated their support for antilynching legislation. The list was exceptional, except for its refusal to endorse a permanent Fair Employment Practices Commission (FEPC), the result of a divide between older and younger African American party members. The elder group labeled support for the FEPC "militant," insisting that it be omitted from the conference's agenda, a point that the younger delegates attempted to "howl down"; in truth, the former group feared that such a proposal would alienate white Republicans, the majority of whom rejected a permanent FEPC as an unnecessary intrusion by government.[60] These generational differences were a reflection of evolving approaches to addressing race-related issues; in particular, the younger group, many of whom had experienced segregation at home and abroad in the military, saw the federal government as having a duty to address racial and economic inequality. A few months later, many of them would form the Republican American Committee (RAC), a lobbyist group of two hundred African Americans who pushed Republican politicians to endorse federal legislation for the FEPC. Without support for a federal law, committee chair Robert Church argued, explicitly pointing to Ralph Bunche's recommendations, the party would never attract black voters.[61]

The GOP's multiplicity did not last, for within the decade—as Bunche rightly warned–the continued pursuit of both the "lily-white" vote and the black vote alienated the majority of the black electorate, a division exacerbated by the civil rights activism of the presidential administration of Harry S. Truman. In December 1946, Truman established the President's Commission on Civil Rights—the committee's subsequent report, released ten months later, shocked the nation.[62] "To Secure These Rights" documented lynchings, racial violence, poverty, segregation, and discrimination, broadcasting the "special problems of the Negro in America" and the desperate need for government intervention. In a critical federal policy shift, the committee suggested a legislative solution for solving racial inequality. In February 1948, Truman delivered a daring speech on civil rights—a decision that *Ebony* later declared one of the "biggest political gambles of any president in history."[63] The president called for a ten-point program to secure the civil rights of the nation's citizens, including support for a permanent FEPC; and, in a move that boosted his popularity among African Americans and enraged southern Democrats, he issued Executive Order 9981, mandating the desegregation of the Armed Forces. The president's efforts provoked outright rebellion from Deep South segregationists, prompting politicians, officials, and legislators to break with the party and form the "States' Rights Democratic Party." Advancing "Segregation Forever" as its platform, the nascent party nominated South Carolina governor Strom Thurmond as its 1948 presidential nominee.[64]

Truman's civil rights initiatives and the temporary departure of the seg-regationist wing of the Democratic Party solidified black support for the president, as did the GOP's equivocation over racial issues, including the party's refusal to support a permanent FEPC. Truman received more than 75 percent of the black vote in the 1948 election. Countless black citizens, recalled journalist Carl Rowan, hailed Harry Truman as a "better friend of the Negro than Roosevelt—or even Lincoln."[65] As evidence of a deeper kind of voter loyalty, 1948 also marked the first year that a majority of black voters—56 percent—identified as Democrats, while only 25 percent registered as Republicans.[66] As one Truman supporter recounted, "The freeing of the slaves was as much a gift of fate, or history, as of any belief Lincoln had in racial equality. . . . Roosevelt's New Deal started the Negro toward economic security to the extent that he could stop thinking about his stomach and begin agitating for the basic rights that gave other Americans a sense of dignity and pride. . . . [But Truman] . . . was seen as something deeper . . . throwing the weight of the Presidency against segregation." For the Republican Party, the election of 1948 was problematic in various ways, but especially in that party strategists determined that had 15 percent more African Americans voted for the GOP, Thomas Dewey would have been president.[67]

Black Republicans were "strangely silent" in the months and years following the 1948 election. The *Pittsburgh Courier* pondered whether they were "moping and mourning" or hiding and "licking their wounds" after their defeat; still, the newspaper urged black Republicans not to "stand by apathetically" because their party needed them more, now than ever.[68] Yet apathy did not accurately describe black Republicans during the period—a better characterization was "shaken," as the 1948 election unraveled most of their work from the previous twelve years. Those few black Republican leaders that emerged from the shadows of the election accused the party of everything from mismanagement and negativism to "lethargy and apathy" in its failure to woo African American voters.[69] The GOP, black Republicans further argued, had relied on a stale strategy of attacking the programs of the New Deal and criticizing the Democratic Party's civil rights failures to entice the black electorate; instead, much like Bunche had done nearly a decade earlier, African American party members maintained that the GOP should have offered new and constructive solutions to address the economic and social problems of African Americans. But perhaps the most serious of the charges levied was that of a burgeoning "unholy alliance" between Republicans and southern Democrats in Congress. "For the past five years," Robert Church bitterly charged in a series of 1949 letters to the RNC and GOP officials, "it seemed that the leaders of our party were determined not to bring the colored electorate back into the Republican Party, but to demonstrate, both in Congress and in state legislatures, that the colored electorate had nothing to hope for from the Republican Party. . . . This illegitimate intimacy between a majority of Republican Senators with Southern Poll Tax Dixiecrats is a national scandal and a disgrace to the party of Abraham Lincoln." Such a union, black Republicans argued, had strangled civil rights legislation and would continue to do so, thereby impeding progress with African American voters.[70] Black Republicans and African Americans alike insisted that unless the party repudiated such sinister alliances and embraced positive and "progressive ideas," the GOP would be "definitely on the way out."[71]

Certainly black Republicans' accusations were on target. As historian Timothy Thurber points out, the Republican Party "downplayed" civil rights between 1947 and 1950. Leaders ignored most of Ralph Bunche's recommendations, took no positive legislative action on racial equality measures, allied with southern Democrats to filibuster civil rights legislation, and omitted civil rights from strategies for constituent recruitment.[72] In April 1949, for instance, black Republican William O. Walker's initial excitement over the Ohio state committee's efforts to restructure the party quickly soured when he realized that white Republicans had omitted any mention of civil rights or African American: "Mere formulation of a new policy will not be sufficient," he complained in an editorial. "The Republican party . . . will have to take the pig out of the bag if they expect the Negro voters to even be interested in buying it."[73] Less than a year later, House Republicans released a "tepid" statement endorsing civil rights; unsurprisingly, the weak response disappointed the GOP's racially progressive members. As Thurber further suggests, white Republicans' behavior on the matter of civil rights and black voter recruitment was complex and somewhat fluid: while there were many within the party that spurned civil rights and African American recruitment for explicitly racist reasons, others—including so-called racially progressive politicians—avoided racialized talk, instead arguing on "practical" terms that the GOP should look to the South because the northern black vote was "irrevocably lost." Critical to this philosophy was the belief that African Americans had a negligible impact on elections; in short, some party strategists, rationalized that they did not *need* black voters to win national elections, so long as they could attract a large enough constituency of white southerners.[74]

Proponents of the southern outreach approach appeared vindicated by the subsequent presidential election results. In 1952, nearly a quarter of a century since the nation last elected a Republican president, Dwight Eisenhower bested Adlai Stevenson, winning 55 percent of the popular vote. Among the black electorate, 21 percent supported the Republican nominee—a figure significant insomuch as it reflected minimal change from 1948. While the black vote remained static, party affiliation did not, instead decreasing to 18 percent, a drop of seven percentage points in a four-year span. As with every presidential election since 1936, the bulk of the Republican Party's supporters in 1952 were "northern middle-class Negroes." The demographics highlighted the continuing significance of class divisions among African Americans and implied that the party's national efforts had found little support among poor and working-class black voters. Still, even without sizable black support, Eisenhower won all but nine states, including four southern states—Florida, Tennessee, Texas, and Virginia.[75]

Reflecting on the 1952 election a few years later, Carl Rowan suggested that the fundamental difference between Truman and Eisenhower was the manner in which the two men understood "the race problem."[76] Eisenhower's "moderate conservatism" appealed to the American electorate, including white southerners; the well-liked military hero walked a fine line between endorsing popular New Deal programs and supporting states' rights.[77] Racial issues, Eisenhower argued, were matters best resolved through a policy of gradualism—he encouraged African Americans to be patient and "place their ultimate faith in time," a position that most blacks rejected.[78] In addition to rejecting the president's racial gradualism, the majority of black voters also rejected the party's policy of "fiscal responsibility" or self-help. A 1963 study found that "underprivileged" Americans did not find such policies appealing; this was especially true of racial minorities, since their struggles were compounded by racism and discrimination.[79]

In Ohio, days after the election, African Americans interviewed by the *Call and Post* displayed mixed emotions over an Eisenhower presidency, with most admitting that they had not voted for the Republican nominee, though no one gave any indication that they viewed his win as cause for alarm. A black woman from Cleveland summed up the surprisingly mundane reaction to the new president: "I wanted the Democrats to win but Eisenhower deserves a chance."[80] On the one hand, the party's attitude toward civil rights felt less volatile under Eisenhower than the "lily-white" segregationist alternative—indeed, in private meetings with the NAACP during the 1952 campaign, Eisenhower had promised to advance the cause of civil rights through legislation and enforcement—a stance that was incorporated into the GOP platform. On the other hand, the president resolutely opposed civil rights measures like the FEPC, while his gradualist approach reinforced African Americans' growing belief that Republicans were disinterested in civil rights.[81]

Nevertheless, in spite of their suspicions of a Republican-led White House, African Americans did celebrate the president's appointment of E. Frederic Morrow as the White House officer for Special Projects in July 1955.[82] *Ebony* magazine deemed him the sole "triple threat" of the administration: White House official, presidential race adviser, and "Negro spokesman."[83] More important, his tenure in the White House illustrated the nature of the Republican Party's constant equivocation over issues of racial equality and civil rights. In fact, the party's approach to the struggles of black citizens proved to be Morrow's "deepest conflict"—an internal battle he described in a February 1956 diary entry:

> I am an appointee . . . with loyalty to [the] Administration, the party and the President, but I am also a Negro who feels very keenly the ills that afflict my race in its efforts to secure . . . all the privileges and responsibilities of citizenship that have been denied . . . for three centuries . . . It is my responsibility to explain to white people how Negroes feel on this matter, and by the same token, explain to Negroes the Administration's attitude.[84]

As if the struggle between being a "Negro and an American" was not enough, Morrow gradually recognized that his "devotion" to the Republican Party and Dwight Eisenhower exacerbated these "dueling personalities"; as he wrote in May 1958, his loyalties to his race and to his party remained in "never ending conflict."[85]

Still, such dilemmas did not prevent the White House aide from continuously presenting the party with clear strategies for reintegrating African Americans into the Republican apparatus. As he bluntly explained to officials in March 1956, "For the majority of Negroes, it is all or nothing." In the face of rising racial tensions, the president could no longer employ "platitudes and give lip service to Democratic ideals"—African Americans demanded a direct program of action. To be sure, white southerners were "equally adamant" about defending segregation; still, Morrow reasoned that this group was a "lost cause," hopelessly aligned with the Democratic Party. By the 1950s, Morrow argued, the black community had moved beyond the "bread and butter" concerns that propelled them initially into the Democratic Party; thus, in order to return to the Party of Lincoln, black voters required solid evidence of an authentic commitment to progressive economic *and* racial initiatives.[86] "Negroes today are voting for men and measures that are in sympathy with their determination to become first-class citizens in this generation," Morrow maintained in October 1958. To offer anything else—even gradualism—was "high treason."[87]

E. Frederic Morrow worked behind the scenes on many issues related to civil rights between 1955 and 1960. For example, throughout the fall of 1955, the "racial trouble shooter" urgently called for the president to issue a strong statement denouncing the horrific murder of fourteen-year-old Emmett Till in Mississippi.[88] As he wrote in a tense memo issued in November 1955, "we are on the verge of a dangerous racial conflagration in the Southern section of this country. . . . My mail has been heavy and angry, and wherever I go, people have expressed disappointment that no word has come from the White House deploring this situation." Such a statement, he added, would "be a demonstration for the whole country to see that the responsible leaders, white and Negro, have a deep concern about this situation and wish to sit down and talk about it intelligently and dispassionately."[89] If the party neglected Till's death, Morrow argued, it would suffer enormous repercussions from African Americans, especially during the 1956 presidential election.[90]

Certainly then, the party's ensuing silence was symbolic of the type of equivocation that contributed to the widespread belief that the "Republican Party deserts [the Negro] in times of crises." On more than one occasion, Morrow struggled to comprehend his administration's policy of leaving black southerners to the "mercy of state governments that have manifested their intention to violate all laws human and Divine."[91] As the black official pointed out, Eisenhower's ideological views on law, order, and government compelled a firm public stance; however, any such progressive stance on the festering tensions between the races had the potential to alienate white southerners, a constituency the GOP continued to pursue.[92] Thus racial gradualism remained the administration's master outlook. As Morrow summarized in August 1956, "there is a great reluctance . . . to talk about civil rights legislation. . . . It is one of the most disturbing notes in the whole situation here, and I am greatly pained when the matter comes up and there is an immediate effort to squelch all discussion."[93]

Morrow was particularly disturbed when in 1956 Secretary of the Cabinet Max Rabb complained bitterly that "Negroes had not demonstrated any kind of gratitude" for the civil rights policies of the administration, thereby alienating "most of the responsible officials in the White House." African Americans were "too aggressive in their demands," Rabb angrily stated; he claimed their "ugliness and surliness in manner was beginning to show," and that their demands far exceeded any "reasonable" concessions that white officials might otherwise allow. Despite professing to "always stand for what was right," the cabinet official sharply warned Morrow that he could no longer argue that it would be in the administration's best political interest to support African Americans. "It is difficult to make any white person understand that you cannot tell intelligent, loyal, battle-tested, young Negro Americans to accept gradualism," Morrow offered, reflecting on Rabb's outburst. "Each Negro today wants first class citizenship in his own time, and is not appeased by the observation that some future generation will benefit by his sacrifices."[94]

This is not to suggest that Morrow's efforts were for naught; in fact, at times, the black official's attempts to push Republicans to campaign seriously among black communities worked well, as with the 1956 presidential campaign. After months of lobbying, Morrow convinced party officials to engage African Americans through publicity initiatives—for instance, Helen Edmonds, a black history professor at North Carolina College was selected to deliver Dwight Eisenhower's seconding speech at the Republican National Convention. Encouraged by the decision, Morrow, along with Val Washington of the Negro Division of the RNC, traveled across the country, campaigning for the president. Despite internal Republican sabotage, Morrow witnessed a "ground swell" of black support for Eisenhower in Tennessee, North Carolina, New York, and New Jersey. In November 1956, the enthused White House aide cheered that a "great many Negroes are eager to be convinced that Eisenhower is the man they should support." His persistence was worth the effort, for, as Morrow described, "thousands of Negroes across the country broke their ties to the Democratic party," and offered Republicans 39 percent of their vote in 1956, helping the president claim reelection.[95]

As the *Washington Post* noted with surprise, black returns from the election showed dramatic but complicated gains for the Republican Party. For example, 85 percent of black voters in Atlanta supported Eisenhower, whereas four years earlier, only 31 percent had done so.[96] Detailing the findings of an NAACP postelection survey in the summer of 1957, Henry Lee Moon observed that during the election, twenty-three southern cities boosted their vote for the president by nearly 40 percentage points. In 1952 Eisenhower carried only two black areas—Leavenworth, Kansas, and Zanesville, Ohio; in 1956, in contrast, majorities of black voters in twelve southern cities and ten northern cities cast their ballots for the Republican incumbent. In Louisville, Eisenhower won 58 percent of the black vote—the exact figure garnered by Adlai Stevenson four years prior.[97] Even in Harlem, which remained a Democratic stronghold, Congressman Adam Clayton Powell threw support behind the president for strategic purposes; consequently, 34 percent of the Harlem electorate cast ballots for Eisenhower in the presidential contest, doubling his 1952 tally. "Negro voters in 1956, like other citizens," Moon stated, explaining the reason behind the electoral shift, "were concerned about peace and prosperity, taxes and the atom bomb. School desegregation and other civil rights issues were also vital issues with them as they were with white Southerners." More than that, however, Moon also suggested that some civil rights decisions—especially the Supreme Court's landmark 1954 decision in *Brown v. Board of Education*—brought "to the surface the ancient sectional split within the Democratic party," loosening the uneasy political alliances launched by the New Deal. "It is noteworthy," wrote Moon, "that in the South where this issue was sharp and inescapable," black voters' "switch was most pronounced," whereas in the North, black voters registered their displeasure by staying home on election day. In the tense atmosphere of racial equality in the mid-1950s, the NAACP argued, black voters saw no real difference between Adlai Stevenson and Dwight Eisenhower; as such, they "punished" the Democratic Party for its inability to control segregationists within its midst.[98]

Attempting to explain this perspective in his diary, Morrow wrote: "It would have been the same old story: a Democratic President, able to give eloquent lip service to human ideals, but unable to translate this into action because the southern wing of his party controlled the committees and refused to get these ideals into bills and out on the floor for votes."[99] Herein lay the significance of the 1956 shift: black voters "returned" to the GOP fold because of the Democratic Party's failure to deal with its segregationist wing. Some black voters undoubtedly supported the party in 1956 for other reasons—including increased campaigning in black areas, relatively high employment levels, and the continued existence of a "stable and substantial middle class with Republican leanings." However, as the NAACP's report suggested, these voters most likely would have voted Republican anyway, as they represented the traditional constituency of black GOP supporters.[100] Still for the African American party faithful, the jump in party fortunes in 1956 also left them hopeful, especially when they considered that 24 percent of black voters identified as Republicans—an increase of six percentage points in four years. As the *Call and Post* mused, perhaps Eisenhower's campaign promise of "Modern Republicanism," or an ideology that served citizens regardless of "birth, race, or color," would be the impetus to "bring Negro voters back to the Republican Party" and keep them there.[101]

In the months immediately following the 1956 presidential race, there were those who genuinely attempted to incorporate a concentrated black outreach initiative into the agenda of the Eisenhower administration. Morrow in particular was buoyed by the efforts of Max Rabb to arrange a series of presidential meetings with influential and prominent black civil rights leaders. Morrow also grew increasingly concerned over the passage of Eisenhower's proposed civil rights legislation; though the potential bill passed in the House by June 1957, southern legislators quickly engaged in "delaying tactics" once it reached the Senate.[102] "Any visit with the President by Negro leaders at this time," Morrow fretted, "could be interpreted by the Senators as pressure to make them act." Morrow was equally troubled by his image within black communities; he complained that African Americans bombarded him with phone calls, holding him personally responsible for the administration's "equivocating" attitude over the legislation.[103] Upon hearing that a diluted version of the bill might make its way to the president, Morrow irately insisted that an "emasculated civil rights bill" was "worse than none at all." Given that the original version had been "completely riddled by amendments," the black official argued that it would be weak and ineffectual. "I sincerely hope the president will veto it," he wrote on August 7.[104] September brought a barrage of racial problems, none more controversial than the Little Rock desegregation crisis in Arkansas.[105] After years of lukewarm support for school desegregation, Eisenhower was forced to address the concrete reality of what had long been an abstract concept. In a dramatic gesture, the president sent national troops to protect black students as they entered Little Rock High School; nevertheless, despite the president's enforcement of equality rights and desegregation orders, Morrow insisted that Eisenhower's reaction was that of a man who was ambivalent on matters of racial equality. African American leaders agreed, insisting that the president had failed to speak and act forcefully on civil rights; even in the case of Little Rock, NAACP leaders argued that such dramatic gestures "would have been unnecessary if positive measures had been taken earlier," and Eisenhower had used the "moral suasion" of the presidency.[106] The president never fully understood the scope of the problem, Morrow lamented in a 1968 interview; while the president believed that "people were entitled to equal treatment and equal opportunity," he also believed that these were issues that could not "be legislated"—this, despite the fact that the black aide regularly urged Eisenhower to consider that "sometimes we needed legislation to give the person opportunity."[107]

Questions of "race and color" tormented Morrow during his tenure in the White House.[108] Besieged with letters and phone calls from angry black citizens and disillusioned with the president's "moderate stand on civil rights," Morrow ultimately concluded that the administration's position was both indefensible and ridiculous. It was impossible to adequately address simmering situations without a "strong, clarion, commanding voice from the White House, righteously indignant" over the plight of African Americans who were simply "fighting for their God-given rights of human dignity and self determination." The sole barrier that prevented Morrow from leaving was his own conscience, as he rationalized that without his presence, the administration would be bereft of a "Negro presence" and would grow even more aloof toward African Americans. "As long as I am [in the White House]," he reasoned, "there will always be a pipeline to the President and the top members of Congress."[109]

After more than a year of lobbying, Morrow's "pipeline" resulted in a meeting between Dwight Eisenhower and the men he and the black press had taken to calling the "Negro Big Four": Roy Wilkins, executive secretary of the NAACP; Lester Granger, executive secretary of the National Urban League (NUL); A. Philip Randolph, head of the Brotherhood of Sleeping Car Porters and vice-president of the AFL-CIO; and Martin Luther King Jr., president of the Southern Christian Leadership Conference (SCLC). The White House aide declared the June 1958 meeting a success, applauding the black leaders for doing a "masterful job" and celebrating Eisenhower's "reassuring" approach. "It was a creditable performance," Morrow breathed with relief, "I feel that both the President and the group benefited from the meeting."[110] In theory the meeting should have had some kind of an impact on the administration and its policy toward African Americans, but in truth Eisenhower's approach toward the black community and civil rights shifted little. In the weeks following, officials grumbled that the Eisenhower meeting had produced few tangible increases in popular support among African Americans. An October 1958 *New York Times* survey seemed to corroborate this perspective—the report found that black voters increasingly believed that nationally "neither party is worth a damn" when it came to civil rights. The survey had jarring implications for those Republicans invested in black recruitment: poor and working-class African Americans vowed to continue voting for the Democratic Party *or* to abstain altogether, while black middle-class northerners threatened to leave both parties and adopt independent political maneuvers.[111] Inwardly, Morrow raged, frustrated that his white colleagues would never understand such racial attitudes, nor did they care to understand the desperation of racial inequality in America. African Americans, he rationalized, were well aware of Eisenhower's positive efforts at racial progress; yet they were also conscious that their social and economic status in the nation was at all times "terribly insecure."[112] For Morrow, the blueprint to the party's success was simple: provide unwavering and resolute support for racial and economic uplift for African Americans, as the black community would always reject equivocation from the Party of Lincoln.[113]

Morrow's lament over the lack of strong black GOP leaders matched his frustrations over white Republicans; he wondered about the potential impact of black Republican mobilization as a counterbalance to the party's ineptitude:

It distresses me that there is no Negro Republican politician with stature enough to fight this thing. . . . If there is a weakness in this Administration as far as Negroes are concerned, I feel it is because there is no strong political group to do battle with any degree of effectiveness in a crisis such as this.

Morrow concluded that the GOP needed a strong black group and leader—someone who could "stand up and bellow any place in the country and get results from the leadership of the party."[114] For all their efforts, by 1958 there were only four black members of Congress: William Dawson, Adam Clayton Powell, Charles Diggs, and Robert Nixon. All were members of the Democratic Party.

In the wake of the November 1958 midterm elections, Morrow privately rejoiced over the GOP's "crushing defeat" in the hopes that the loss would "indicate, even to the most obtuse, that something must be done organically from top to bottom if Republicans are to survive." In truth, the opposite would occur—in a later interview with *Ebony*, a dejected Morrow claimed that the party's attitude changed for the worse after the midterm election, since the president began to feel as though "Negroes didn't appreciate his effort."[115] Tired of working for party success and being ignored, in April 1959 Morrow finally snapped in public, after an impatient party official demanded to know how Republicans could "make friends with the Negro and get his vote." In separate speeches to the Wayne Country Republican Club in Detroit and the Republican Women's Convention in Washington, D.C., the Eisenhower aide accused the party of forcing African Americans to the fringes. "Until he is taken in, given a full-fledged part, and permitted to have a voice in party councils and aspire to office, it will be a long time before the party can count on his allegiance," Morrow stated sharply. "The Negro," he added, "never sees the top leaders; his desires and wants must be made known through some straw boss who offer[s] stupid solutions." Concluding each speech with restrained ferocity, to standing ovations from both audiences, Morrow ripped the party's sense of entitlement and demands of black gratitude: "Republicans could not expect Negroes to be extremely grateful for what Lincoln did, since in effect he had merely returned to them their God-given rights of freedom and personal dignity."[116]

While African Americans across the country celebrated Morrow's speech, most of his Republican associates labeled him a traitor and an "ingrate" for his actions. The aide's brazenness roused the interest of Richard Nixon, who soon approached Morrow about assisting with race and civil rights issues during the 1960 presidential campaign. Not only did Morrow join Richard Nixon's team, but he worked resolutely for the man who gradually convinced him to remain a member of the GOP. Morrow's commitment to Nixon was the result of a long-standing friendship and working relationship; for example, the White House aide had accompanied the vice president on a three-week tour of several African countries in March 1957.[117] Moreover, Morrow *believed* in Nixon, seeing him as a figure who could affect major changes in the GOP's attitude toward African Americans and civil rights. By the late 1950s, the vice president had emerged as somewhat of a "racial liberal" in the Eisenhower administration: endorsing the *Brown* decision; helping to push through Congress the Civil Rights Act of 1957; and chairing the President's Committee on Government Contracts, which, among other duties, investigated racial discrimination charges in federal employment. As historian James Meriwether argues, Nixon's "biggest political liability" with black voters in 1960 came from his affiliation with the White House, as most African Americans believed the administration had "failed to lead a strong enough charge for civil rights."[118] Still, among black Republicans surveyed by *Jet* in August 1959, Nixon was by far the most popular of candidates for the presidency, especially given his civil rights record.[119]

It was this outlook that informed Morrow's decision to assist Richard Nixon's 1960 presidential campaign; furthermore, in appointing the black aide, Nixon broadcast his intentions to compete with the Democratic Party for the black vote. But the vice president, much like the Democratic nominee, also worried about alienating potential white southerners. The result, Morrow would later argue, was a disappointing campaign steeped in racial symbolism.[120] In some ways, these criticisms overstated the GOP's failures, ignoring the substantive gestures that party officials took in their pursuit of the black vote. During the 1960 Republican National Convention in July, for example, Nixon successfully pushed delegates to adopt a far more aggressive civil rights plank into the party platform, one that expressed support for civil rights legislation and the *Brown* decision and promised the full eradication of discrimination.[121] Though weaker on a few points than what some progressive Republicans would have liked, the final plank met the approval of a number of black leaders, including Roy Wilkins. After reading the party's civil rights declaration, the NAACP official deemed it a significant improvement from years past; the GOP's plank, he argued, demonstrated the same concern for equal rights as the platform passed by the Democratic Party earlier in the month.[122]

Nixon also invited Morrow to weigh in on significant campaign matters—during the July convention, he invited the black Republican to join a "secret midnight caucus" to pick the vice presidential nominee. The only African American seated among powerful white officials, Morrow ultimately offered a vote for Henry Cabot Lodge, reasoning, "Not even the NAACP can be against his superb liberal record."[123] In another gesture that was both symbolic and meaningful, the campaign selected Jewel Rogers, a black Chicago attorney, to second Nixon's nomination for president. As one of eight "distinguished" Republicans, Rogers was the only African American to offer a seconding speech; her fervent words, noted the *Chicago Tribune*, conveyed excitement over the party's future. Offering praise for the nominee's "positive, progressive position on civil rights," Rogers declared that a Nixon presidency would realize the party's civil rights pledges, a point that was met with a "tempest of applause" from convention delegates. Two months later, vice presidential nominee Henry Cabot Lodge announced that the Chicago attorney would serve as his "special consultant on civil rights."[124]

Nevertheless, Morrow's later criticisms were also accurate, as the Nixon campaign floundered during the 1960 election season, regressing to "incredible ineptness"—neglecting to provide black Republican leaders with funding and ignoring hundreds of memos on wooing the black vote. Despite being brought into the campaign as a trusted adviser by Nixon, Morrow and other African Americans increasingly found that high-ranking officials blocked their access—and thereby their *influence*—to the Republican nominee. The role given to black Republicans was a maddening vacillation between vital and insulting, the result of the party pursuing both the black vote and the white southern vote—groups at odds with one another.[125] Dozens of other incidents highlighted this dilemma; for instance, while speaking at a rally in Harlem in October 1960, Henry Cabot Lodge promised that Nixon's presidential cabinet would "contain at least one Negro." His statement provoked fury among white southerners, who demanded that Nixon renounce such claims; in turn, black audiences urged him to stand firm on Lodge's promise. Nixon's response did not satisfy either group—the presidential nominee stated that the "best man should be appointed, regardless of color."[126]

Despite repeated missteps and equivocations, Morrow found one final decisive move for securing the black vote for Richard Nixon. In the final days of the presidential race, Martin Luther King Jr. was arrested and jailed in Atlanta. For Morrow, this was a pivotal moment, a time for "American leadership to speak." The black aide urged Republican aides to have Nixon call King, write a letter to the mayor of Atlanta, and issue a statement denouncing the SCLC head's imprisonment. Desperate, he reached out to Nixon's managers through repeated phone calls, memos, telegrams, and in-person visits; at one point, he even gave the vice president's press secretary a copy of a predrafted missive for the mayor. While waiting for a response, a devastated Morrow discovered that Kennedy had done exactly what Morrow had encouraged Nixon to do—calling the King family to offer comfort, contacting the city mayor, and arranging to have the civil rights leader released. Consequently, as *Time* observed, King publicly endorsed the Democratic nominee; in a particularly painful blow, the elder King announced that though he had originally planned to vote for Nixon, his political loyalty had shifted since "Jack Kennedy has the moral courage to stand up for what he knows is right."[127] Inconsolable, Morrow wrote, *This act won the election.* Kennedy's action electrified the entire Negro community and resulted in tens of thousands of Negro voters going over to the Democrats' banner." Indeed, while Nixon received a healthy 32 percent of the black vote, Kennedy's 68 percent tally gave him enough of an edge to claim victory on November 8, 1960.[128]

But the King incident, no matter how dramatic, was but one episode in the greater campaign—to attribute Nixon's loss to *one* incident ignored Republicans' consistent missteps throughout the 1960 election. Even before King's arrest, black voters indicated that they would support Kennedy—in an October piece in the *Wall Street Journal*, written days before the Atlanta incident, Robert Novak accurately predicted that the Democratic nominee would win a "surprisingly fat majority" of black voters, a conclusion based on the newspaper's survey of hundreds of African Americans.[129] For Morrow, the party's critical mistake lay in the decision to pursue the white southern voters and ignore the black electorate. "Negroes," he fumed in the days following the 1960 contest, "were determined to play a vital part in this election. They stood in the wings, just waiting to be wooed and won by the candidate who understood their mood and concern over the matter of first-class citizenship. . . . For the candidate who understood and listened, this was the easiest campaign of all." Morrow's closing assessment of the Republican Party, much like Bunche's in 1939, cautioned the GOP against alienating African Americans by equivocating over matters of racial equality, since there was no bargaining, he insisted, with the "Negro's unrelenting and courageous determination to get freedom *now!*"[130]

Furthermore, "bread-and-butter issues" also contributed to African Americans' decision to vote for Kennedy; a 1960 study suggested that for most poor and working-class black northerners, unemployment and the recession were two of the most critical issues of the election. This was significant, particularly for those voters who saw little difference between the two political parties on civil rights.[131] Lemon Hughes of Chicago, who voted for Eisenhower in 1956, explained that, though he believed that "Republicans are superior to the Democrats in the civil rights field," he planned to support Kennedy because "the Democrats could do much more in making sure that people have jobs." A black citizen from Pittsburgh stated that he was voting for Kennedy because he would do "something about unemployment" and that he had little faith in either party on matters of civil rights.[132] Even in the South, where pollsters found that African Americans universally abhorred southern segregationist Democrats, nearly 40 percent of black voters affirmed their support for the national Democratic Party, seeing it as the party of the "working man" and characterizing the GOP as the party of "depression, big-business, favoritism, and mistreatment of workers." While such attitudes resulted in a drop of only seven percentage points in the black presidential vote for the Republican Party in 1960, the shift was still important since it eroded many of the gains made by Eisenhower four years earlier. Though many of the reversals were small—a shift of a few thousand voters in the South, for example—they nevertheless provided Kennedy with enough of a boost to snatch electoral victory in states including South Carolina, North Carolina, Missouri, and New Jersey.[133]

Those black voters who supported the GOP in 1960 did so for various reasons, none more apparent than their opposition to southern Democrats on matters of civil rights. In fact, strategists and pundits from both parties were somewhat surprised that more African Americans did not reject the Democratic Party in 1960, given that Lyndon Johnson, a Texan, was on the ticket. But when asked, black voters were often either "totally unaware" of the vice presidential nominee or unbothered by his presence. As such, those African Americans that supported Nixon in 1960 largely consisted of two groups: black southerners who distrusted white southerners and the Democratic Party, and upper-middle-class northerners who could "afford" to overlook the bread-and-butter issues of African Americans.[134] Above all else, the returns from the 1960 election suggested that if the Republican Party was to make serious inroads among black voters of all demographics in the future, the party would need to offer not only aggressive civil rights measures but also bold economic and employment initiatives that resonated with African Americans.

The figures from the 1960 election appeared to indicate that little had changed for the GOP in the twenty-four years since African Americans had first left the party in droves; black leaders confidently declared as much in postelection analyses. On the surface, much of this was true— over the course of nearly a quarter of a century, the black vote for the GOP had experienced a net increase of only four percentage points, while party identification declined from 37 to 23 percent between 1936 and 1960. All signs seemed to point to a stagnant relationship between African Americans and the Republican Party, despite the best efforts of those invested in minority outreach. The political flexibility of black voters during this period, however, was much more nuanced than presented by this picture. In reality, African Americans moved in and out of the Democratic Party and the GOP, abstained from voting, and articulated a desire to remain politically independent. In perhaps the most illustrative expression of the latter, the number of black citizens identifying as independent remained consistent in this twenty-four-year period, peaking in 1960 at 23 percent.

Moreover, despite the national GOP embracing an economic policy at odds with the needs of the majority of African Americans, displaying erratic and uneven attitudes toward civil rights, and demonstrating a willingness to pursue the white southern vote, more than a quarter of the black electorate, on average, consistently voted for the GOP and identified as Republican during this period. Certainly, this provided evidence of class cleavages among African Americans, as well as a cautious understanding of the Democratic Party. However, it also proved that the Republican Party's black engagement efforts, though limited, were invaluable—but not in the way that party progressives had hoped. Instead of enticing African Americans back into the "Party of Lincoln," engagement measures helped prevent further party abandonment between 1936 and 1960. That the Republican Party did not lose *more* black voters in this period was a testament not only to the political flexibility and diversity of African Americans but also to the value of the GOP's limited black outreach measures.[135]

NEW INTERPRETATIONS OF REPUBLICANISM

As E. Frederic Morrow and others were lobbying the Republican Party for increased civil rights efforts, providing officials with blueprints for black outreach and warning the party against extremism, there were those within the party who were delving into new interpretations of Republican conservatism. In many ways, the emergence of new definitions was the result of a growing intellectual movement that coalesced in the mid-1950s.[136] But in other respects, this shift was also a result of the election of 1960—as party officials and leaders attempted to understand Richard Nixon's loss, they offered a multitude of agendas for increasing the strength of the GOP. During the next four years, Republicans would continue to struggle over the vision and identity of the Republican Party, with the party's treatment of black voters and civil rights remaining a significant part of the debate.

Although not the first to offer a new perspective of Republican conservatism and civil rights, Barry Goldwater provided the most controversial and arguably the most dominant interpretation. In March 1960, the Arizona senator released *Conscience of a Conservative*—a book that, according to the *New York Times* review, derived its ideological conservatism from an appreciation of God and morality but also contained "too many things that not enough voters like."[137] Segments of the American public did embrace *Conscience*, as the book sold over half a million copies in just six months despite an original print order of 10,000.[138] Arguably ghostwritten by L. Brent Bozell, *Conscience* took the lofty ideological arguments of lesser-known conservative intellectuals and made them relatable to the general public. Much of the book's appeal stemmed from Goldwater's reinterpretation of Republicanism—supporters agreed with the senator's complaints of "MeTooism," in which he accused the GOP of embracing the objectives of the New Deal and hiding them in a language of soft conservatism; at one point, the senator rejected Eisenhower's "Modern Republicanism," dubbing it a "dime store New Deal."[139] His followers, reporter George Sokolsky observed, admired him for this "loud and clear voice" and, as such, delighted in the thought that he had no obligation to the liberalism of the Democratic Party and would push a principled agenda of anticommunism, private enterprise, individual freedom, and states' rights.[140]

Goldwater's supporters also embraced the senator's "Statement of Republican Principles, Programs and Objects," drafted in January 1961. Known as the "Forgotten American Manifesto," the twenty-nine-page report was a less rigid version of *Conscience*, outlining a doctrine of "progressive conservatism" that appealed to the "dragooned and ignored individual." The United States, argued Goldwater, had become a society of competing interest groups: "self-seeking servitors" who formed powerful organizations geared to achieve material gains.[141] The senator blamed organized labor, civil rights organizations, and "so-called cultural and artistic" groups for destroying the rights of individuals, calling for the GOP to adopt measures designed to halt the "dehumanizing trend" of the expanding federal government. The irony of Goldwater's use of the term "progressive" to advance his argument was not lost on African Americans; indeed, "progressive" was an adjective that black Republicans had used for several decades to describe their efforts to reintegrate the party—and now the Arizona senator was using it for nearly opposite ends.

In pledging to meet the needs of the "Forgotten American," the senator—whether inadvertently or deliberately—advocated for restricting the rights of African Americans, angering nearly the entire black community.[142] The problem, as the *Wall Street Journal* explained, was that the senator employed both rhetoric and strategy that placed black citizens on the fringes of the American political system. Goldwater also appeared to have no interest in wooing black voters, reasoning that the party would gain little by pursuing black voters, suggesting that they as a bloc were irreversibly lost to the Democratic Party; although not the first Republican to make this argument, the senator was among the first to do so in such a public and aggressive fashion.[143] As he expounded during a March 1961 meeting, the party should "quit trying to win Negro votes" since the African American electorate had no sense of loyalty or gratitude. "Party leaders should face up to the fact that although Republicans have done more for the Negro," Goldwater complained, "Democrats are getting more and more of their votes."[144] A speech to Atlanta residents delivered later that same year was blunter: "We're not going to get the Negro vote as a bloc in 1964 . . . so we ought to go hunting where the ducks are." Though he later tried to clarify the quote—arguing that he meant that the party should campaign broadly to all Americans, irrespective of special group "minority interests"—his rhetoric nevertheless ostracized black citizens by positioning their needs as inferior to those of the American "majority."[145]

While Nixon's 1960 defeat provided the Arizona senator with an avenue through which to advance "Goldwater conservatism," it also boosted the resolve of liberal and moderate Republicans interested in attracting black voters. Among the Arizona politician's critics was Thruston Morton, chair of the RNC. The moderate official publicly censured Goldwater for his rhetoric, arguing that it retained "too strong a flavor of conservatism for many a Republican to swallow." Rejecting black voters on the basis of the 1960 election returns was a foolhardy strategy, Morton contended; if anything, Kennedy's majority share demonstrated that party leaders needed to redouble their efforts to recruit black citizens by "battling zealously for civil rights."[146] Morton was not alone in his opinions; in a 1962 interview with *Ebony* magazine, Richard Nixon grimly confessed, "I could have become President. I needed only five per cent more votes in the Negro areas. I could have gotten them if I had campaigned harder." For more than two hours, the former vice president discussed the ways that the future of the Republican Party dovetailed with the future of African Americans:

> We can't say to Negroes "Come to us," we've got to go after them. We've got to change the image of the GOP among Negroes. The Democrats are well organized and well financed—but we've got to get into the Negro areas if we expect to mould a party for all people. We've got to convince Negroes they're better off economically under a GOP president.[147]

If the party was to survive, Nixon urged, it had to tackle such problems in new and innovative ways. However, it would be a mistake for the GOP to "accept the beliefs of . . . Barry Goldwater and write off the Negro vote," he asserted. "If Goldwater wins his fight, our party would eventually become the first major all-white political party. And that isn't good. That would be a violation of GOP principles." Morton's and Nixon's attitudes were all the more significant given that both officials had bitterly dismissed black voters in the weeks immediately following the 1960 election.[148]

The findings of the national committee's special task force on "Big Cities" certainly found evidence to support claims like those of Morton and Nixon. In March 1961, the fourteen-member subcommittee issued a preliminary six-page memo that attributed the politician's defeat in 1960 to the GOP's failure to identify aggressively with the "interests of African Americans." Significant decline occurred in many of the nation's major metropolitan areas—particularly those which were heavily populated by black constituents. For instance, the black electorate in Chicago voted against Nixon by a margin of 20 to 1, evaporating his Illinois lead. Nixon's 91,000-vote advantage dissolved in Missouri when African Americans cast their ballots against him by a 12 to 1 rate; this in turn provided Kennedy with a 100,000 vote surge in St. Louis—just enough to win the entire state.[149] Much of the fault lay with the inaction of local party machines. As task force chair Ray Bliss deciphered, local and state outreach to "predominately Negro wards" was "woefully weak and just as frequently nonexistent." Jackie Robinson, the first black man to integrate professional baseball and a recent convert to the GOP, pointed out that party officials—even those with the most laudable civil rights records—often failed to connect with African Americans. The trouble, he stated, was that politicians rarely visited predominately black localities—perhaps out of fear of alienating white southerners—and therefore had no idea of *who* African Americans were and *what* they wanted. Ultimately, the report emphasized that if the party hoped to carry states with large cities in future elections, then it could not ignore the Negro vote. It was critical, argued committee member L. Judson Morhouse of New York, that the Republican Party "go all out in organization efforts and become 'soundly progressive' to attract greater Negro support." As such, the task force representatives contended that Goldwater's "non-approach" to black outreach was the surest way to guarantee permanent political minority status. "It is impossible to reconcile the arbitrary and impractical view of a prominent party leader," Morhouse criticized, "who says 'The Republican Party has not attracted Negro voters . . . we cannot get them . . . so let's quit trying.'" Summarizing the frustrations of the subcommittee, Morhouse glumly concluded that Goldwater envisioned a "requiem for the cities" when in reality, the times demanded a "Republican reveille."[150]

Alongside Goldwater's brazen vision of the party's future, liberal and moderate Republicans at the other end of the ideological spectrum were also searching for new interpretations. They adopted strategies aimed at attracting black voters, including sponsoring voter registration drives, holding community meetings, speaking with local black officials, meeting publicly with prominent national leaders, and championing civil rights issues. For example, a twelve-member committee composed of "established Negro and white members" traveled throughout the New York City area in an effort to persuade African Americans to join the GOP and to "cultivate the Negro vote with vigor."[151] In February 1962, New York governor Nelson Rockefeller attempted to put Jackie Robinson's recommendation into action by paying a visit to Harlem and delivering a lecture at Abyssinian Baptist Church. Preaching from the pulpit, Rockefeller railed against racial discrimination, disenfranchisement, and segregation. Equality, he argued, was the "burning issue before America" and required an immediate resolution through federal legislation and enforcement.[152] He broadcast that the "doors to the Republican Party are always open to all Americans"; accordingly, in the early 1960s, the New York official opened his home to the Westchester County chapter of the Urban League, hosting a $50,000 fundraising luncheon. The keynote speaker, Martin Luther King Jr., offered a passionate speech repudiating Goldwater and the notion of states' rights. Not surprisingly, he made sure to applaud the governor and the Rockefeller family for their support of "human rights and human dignity."[153]

Still, for many African Americans, such outreach efforts were not enough, for the party still relied heavily on the historical loyalty of black voters, rather than concrete policies and plans. As attorney George Russell, a black member of the party from Baltimore stated, "Republicans have to learn that the image of Abraham Lincoln is dead. They'll have to find something new to attract colored voters."[154] Similarly, David Scull, a white Republican official from Silver Spring, Maryland, suggested that party leaders should find a way to merge conservative principles with racially liberal values and convey these solutions to the public in a sensitive and appealing manner. He argued that the GOP had to

> demonstrate that they believe in states' responsibilities, as well as states' rights. . . . We must see to it that problems such as aid to education, civil rights . . . and urban affairs are actually acted upon by the Republican Party, at the state or local level. Let it never be said that the party of Lincoln failed our colored citizens in their struggle for social justice. Let us remember that more than just property rights are at issue . . . and that to close the door on a man because of his color . . . is to deny him the right to be respected and the ability to retain his self-respect.[155]

In advocating such arguments and approaches, moderate and liberal Republicans constantly found their efforts undermined by those within the party who continued to insist that the rights of the "universal" individual trumped civil rights protection from the federal government, insisting that the GOP had to make it clear that it was the party of conservatives. Goldwater, in particular, argued for an aggressive distancing from the "big government, big labor, and big business" of the Democratic Party—as he later recalled, he believed that the nation needed a "choice, not an echo."[156] But for African Americans, Goldwater's conservatism denied them not only equal citizenship but also much-needed economic relief *and* equal employment. To put it simply, Goldwater's notion of individualism worked so long as citizens had the benefit of equal treatment under the law. As second-class citizens, blacks were systemically denied equal rights and thus could not accept—or even consider—the senator's principles, lacking the necessary federal protections to be treated as individuals.

Central to this dilemma was the Arizona senator's stance on states' rights and civil rights. The GOP leader suggested the solution to racial inequality lay not with the federal government but instead with citizens, suggesting that local problems were best handled by local people. Such logic provoked fury within black communities, because, as Goldwater ruefully admitted on more than one occasion, such an argument undoubtedly affected the "integration issue." The South's embrace of states' rights as a mode of segregation was the "most conspicuous expression of the principle," he acknowledged in *Conscience.* "So much so that the country is now in the grips of a spirited and sometimes ugly controversy."[157]

Goldwater did maintain that there were some rights that clearly were protected under the law and superseded the states' rights principle—for example, the right to vote, which, he reasoned, was protected under the Fifteenth Amendment. The Fourteenth Amendment also offered similar protections in that African Americans were entitled to "full and equal benefit of all laws and proceedings for the security of persons and property." The problem, Goldwater proposed, was that the Constitution did not provide protection for things like education—as a result, he insisted that schools should not be forced to integrate and the federal government did not have the right to make them do so. And though he claimed to agree with the objectives of *Brown v. Board of Education*, the senator ultimately disagreed with Eisenhower's decision to use federal power to compel schools to obey the Supreme Court ruling. As he declared in *Conscience*, he was not prepared to impose his personal judgment on the people of the South, or tell them "what methods should be adopted and what pace should be kept in striving toward that goal."[158]

Goldwater's interpretation of states' rights and civil rights—though he vehemently and consistently denied it—offered white segregationists a meaty rationale for defending the racial code of the South.[159] A December 1961 party strategy meeting held in Atlanta highlighted this development;

in a move that the *Pittsburgh Courier* said would "virtually file divorce papers" from the black community, Goldwater and 670 Republicans from fourteen states, gathered to discuss the political promise of the South.[160] The senator's keynote speech generated thunderous applause among the delegates, no more so than when he questioned, "Why is the South turning . . . is it because liberalism has stifled . . . the Southern conservative voice of the Democratic Party?" In what the *New York Times* described as a bid for "support among Southern segregationists," Goldwater promised attendees that he "would bend every muscle to see that the South has a voice on everything that affects the life of the South," at future Republican National Conventions. The promise of white southerners, the *Courier* noted disapprovingly, had again trumped the appeal of a growing black electorate. Goldwater's announcement that he was in favor of diluting the party's stance on civil rights had a "jarring effect" on southern black Republicans, fifty of whom had attended the meeting, envisioning blacks as an integral part of the GOP's future outreach efforts in the South; thus, they were stunned when white Republicans dismissed African American voters as irrelevant. As George W. Lee, a black party official from Tennessee mourned, this was a "time for tears." The GOP, he dejectedly stated, "will never regain the White House if it listens to Mr. Goldwater's council to let the Negro vote go by default to the Democrats."[161] In a confirmation of the relationship between Goldwater conservatism and the South's interpretation of states' rights, the meeting ended with the election of Wirt A. Yerger Jr., an avowed segregationist, as state chairman of Mississippi. "All we're asking the national Republican Party is not to try to out-promise the Democrats on civil rights."[162]

As Goldwater's appeal and support steadily increased, so did the hostility of African Americans toward the politician.[163] Voicing the frustration and confusion of many black citizens, P. L. Prattis scornfully considered the motivations behind Goldwater attempting to make "Republicans out of Southern Democrats":

> Is it because he believes in states' rights? If so, does he believe that when he talks about states' rights and when [Democrat governor] Ross Barnett of Mississippi talks about states' rights, they are talking about the same thing? Ross Barnett means he wants to reserve the right to keep his foot on my neck. Does Goldwater want Barnett to move over and give him a share of my neck?

The journalist insisted that the problem was simple: "Are Negroes to be first class citizens or not? Are you in favor of that—or are you in favor of the Southern Manifesto?"[164] Joseph Alsop of the *Washington Post* cautioned that even the most innocent endorsement of states' rights could imply only one thing—"support for southern opposition to extended civil rights." Though he could see the abstract appeal of such a southern strategy, the reporter bluntly surmised that adopting Goldwater's principles would mean "farewell forever to the Negro."[165] Likewise, in a 1962 editorial column, Jackie Robinson frostily declared that the senator's position was "political suicide"; but more than that, it sabotaged genuine Republican outreach efforts. "Many of us reluctant Republicans have been forced into the Democratic camp almost by the default of our own party," despaired Gertrude Wilson of the *New York Amsterdam News*. The "last straw" for those who clung to liberal and moderate Republicanism was the "mere idea of Barry Goldwater being anywhere on the scene."[166]

In the early 1960s, the Republican Party was moving toward an explosive conflict, divided between those who championed a strategy of black engagement as the "Party of Lincoln" and others who advanced a platform that blatantly alienated the black electorate. African Americans were clear on where they stood: a March 1963 editorial in the *Chicago Defender*, for example, championed Nelson Rockefeller as the symbol of "new Republicanism" that was "morally committed to the concept of first class citizenship for all Americans." To support Goldwater was inconceivable, wrote the editors, since the senator would merely "ignore the Negroes."[167] Political journalists Rowland Evans and Robert Novak offered a glimpse into the party's crisis in a June 1963 article, arguing that an influential group of party leaders was working privately to establish the GOP as the "white man's party" on the basis of three assumptions: black voters—especially the poor and working-class—were inextricably linked to the Democratic Party; President Kennedy was losing the South because of his pro–civil rights stance; and the growing civil rights movement was stirring fear among white Democrats, even in the North. Equally important, Evans and Novak maintained, this group was using Goldwater's political philosophy to advance its ideas. Using "Goldwaterism" to create "lily-white Republicanism," they argued, was a foolhardy strategy. With the inevitable end of segregation, African Americans would "break through the bonds" of discrimination; consequently, the GOP's approach, they foreshadowed, would alienate black voters that might otherwise "be naturally attracted to the Republican Party along with millions of other middle-income Americans."[168]

• • •

In May 1964, eighteen thousand Goldwater supporters, hailing from New York, Pennsylvania, Connecticut, and Massachusetts, packed Madison Square Garden for a rally supporting Barry Goldwater's presidential bid. As "Goldwater Girls" dressed in red cowboy hats, blue skirts and white blouses led supporters to their seats, the crowd thundered "We Want Barry" over and over, drowning out the voices of the thirty-member black choir singing "Battle Hymn of the Republic." The frenzied audience howled and roared with approval, interrupting the senator's speech 108 times, as he blasted the Democratic Party and contended that civil rights was a problem of the "heart and of the mind" unable to be legislated through federal law; his supporters also made sure to boo loudly whenever Goldwater mentioned Nelson Rockefeller and other party liberals. The *New York Times* spotted three black Goldwater Republicans in the crowd; wearing buttons that bore the politician's face, their presence was a sharp contrast to that of the choir, which had to overcome "rebellion in the ranks" when a baritone quit in disgust midway through the rally. As Goldwater closed his political sermon, his flock erupted into a ten-minute standing ovation. The choir watched the entire spectacle in stony silence, with director Paul McKnight grimly vowing never to perform for another Republican again, likening the experience to "singing for the Ku Klux Klan." It appeared that for multiple audiences, Goldwater conservatism had made its mark.[169]

African Americans' aversion to Goldwater stemmed from his refusal to acknowledge the successes of the civil rights movement by virtue of his public stand on states' rights. And despite repeated claims of his moral embrace of civil rights philosophy, the senator had not endeared himself to black Republicans. Thus when Goldwater proposed that he had done "more in Arizona for the Negro than any other man," pointing to his local desegregation efforts, his lifetime membership in the NAACP and NUL, and his support for the 1957 and 1960 Civil Rights Acts, black party leaders quickly rebutted this by pointing to his tendency to vote with the southern political bloc 67 percent of the time, his popularity with southern segregationists, and his vote against the 1964 Civil Rights Act. Indeed, the politician joined five Republicans and 21 southern Democrats in voting against the act, a position roundly criticized by the twenty-seven Republican and forty-six Democratic senators who voted in favor of it.[170] What genuine consistency, the editors of the *New York Times* asked, could be gleaned from declaring "'this is the time to attend to the liberties of all' when it is the 'freedom for all' and the 'liberties of all' that the bill is intended to secure?"[171] It was exactly this basic denial of civil rights, even on principled constitutional grounds, that created new levels of tension between African Americans and the GOP, especially as black voters increasingly came to see the senator as the new face of the party.

Though Goldwater was not singularly responsible for African Americans' rejection of the GOP, his rise exacerbated underlying problems, forcing the party's racial issues onto a national stage. One study, for instance, found that by 1963, the majority of black southerners believed that the Democratic Party was the better party for economics *and* civil rights, despite the continued presence of white segregationists in the party's ranks. A mere two years earlier, more than half of the black group had argued that the GOP was the better party for racial equality.[172] Adding to this, in 1963 President John F. Kennedy pledged to move an aggressive civil rights bill through Congress, an action that overshadowed southern Democrats' rejection of the measure. To be sure, African Americans juxtaposed Kennedy's bold decision with Goldwater's lukewarm reaction to the proposal. That same year, a *Congressional Quarterly* (*CQ*) audit of RNC and House and Senate campaign activities found that Goldwater's supporters largely controlled the party's major political decisions, holding "numerous key posts" in the upper echelons of GOP hierarchy and pouring money into "Operation Dixie," an RNC subcommittee launched in 1957 to target white voters in the South. In contrast, divisions on racial minorities, cities, and labor were "strapped for funds" despite just one year earlier being identified as key areas of revitalization, necessary for party victory.[173]

But even within this context, there were those within the party who consistently made overtures toward African Americans and campaigned in black areas, as we have seen. Moreover, such interest was not limited to liberal and moderate party members, as some self-identified Goldwater Republicans also pushed the party to pursue the black vote. Among them was George H. W. Bush in Texas, who collaborated with civil rights advocate and black Republican Grant Reynolds on local black outreach. Soon after taking over as chairman of the Harris County GOP in 1963, Bush penned a private letter wherein he argued that his goal was to better "communicate with the Negro community here in Houston," noting that Republicans had done "miserably" among black voters. "I am determined," he wrote, "that we work diligently toward finding an answer," unwilling to accept that his conservatism would alienate African Americans. With Reynolds help, Bush opened up headquarters in black neighborhoods, spending nearly double on black appeals as he did on women's outreach. Likewise, black Republican Albertine Bowie, also of Texas, joined Reynolds as an adviser to the RNC; she attempted to recruit black women to embrace the Republican Party, traveling around the country on behalf of the Women's Division, through 1964.[174]

However, as Reynolds and Bowie traveled throughout the country, their work was undercut by the RNC; as early as May 1963, the RNC was giving black Republicans the cold shoulder, excluding them from strategy meetings and blocking them from having any meaningful input. This was just another example of Republican "stupidity," declared one black political observer, accusing the national committees of attempting to transform the GOP into the "Dixiecrat Party." Moreover, critics also blamed party liberals and moderates for allowing Goldwater Republicans to take over the party; among African Americans, criticism was sharply directed at black Republicans, as well. The "Negro conservative," wrote columnist Nat Williams in March 1963, had been the last to "take the handkerchief off his head"—a cowardly "play-it-safe man" who had stood silently on the sidelines, passively watching as extremists commandeered the GOP.[175]

This was hardly an accurate assessment; as scholars have indicated, party moderates and liberals conceded nothing, battling vigorously with the party's right wing throughout the 1960s; likewise, polls from the spring of 1964 showed that nearly half of rank-and-file Republicans preferred Henry Cabot Lodge as the presidential nomination, whereas 14 percent chose Goldwater, and 13 percent identified Nelson Rockefeller.[176] Certainly black Republicans played a role in party affairs at the state, local, and even national level in the early 1960s, as was the case with Reynolds and Bowie. These were scattered and disparate efforts, though, as there was no national black Republican mobilization effort—a point dramatized by Goldwater's ascent and the concurrent explosion in grassroots civil rights activism.

Over the course of twenty-eight years, black Republicans had worked within the GOP on behalf of African Americans—efforts that had helped keep about a quarter to a third of black voters ensconced in the Republican Party since 1936. But as black party leaders' work, along with the efforts of white Republican liberals and moderates, was undermined and overshadowed, African Americans truly began to say farewell to the party of Lincoln. As we shall see in the next chapter, the final straw for black voters was the party's decision to nominate Goldwater for president; his selection—and what it symbolized—obscured the racially progressive actions of Republicans; to that point, the *Chicago Defender* declared that the senator's nomination represented the death toll for the Republican Party, at least among African Americans.[177]

Goldwater's rise unsettled even the most loyal of black Republicans, initially generating a sense of helplessness among them, recognizing what his nomination would mean for African Americans and the GOP. As one distressed Georgia black Republican explained, he felt as though he had "no choice" but to cast a ballot against his party and Barry Goldwater and insisted that most of his black GOP peers would do the same, or abstain from voting.[178] Ultimately, the Arizona senator would provoke an ideological war within the party; but beyond that conflagration, his nomination would serve as a necessary impetus for a national mobilization of black Republicans, introducing the "new" and defiant leadership that both Bunche and Morrow had so strongly championed.

CHAPTER TWO

A Thorn in the Flesh of the GOP

ON NOVEMBER 3, 1964, MORE THAN 60 PERCENT OF AMERICANS CAST ballots for Lyndon B. Johnson in the presidential election, a decision that was as much a referendum against his Republican challenger, Barry Goldwater, as it was a victory for the Democratic incumbent. No group was more visibly alienated by the candidacy of Goldwater than the black electorate. Abandoning the Republican Party en masse, only 6 percent of African American voters pulled the lever for the GOP nominee in the national election. The percentage was a stunning drop—even considering the vacillation of the black vote over the past three decades—from the 32 percent Richard Nixon received in his 1960 loss to John F. Kennedy, and the 39 percent that Dwight Eisenhower amassed during his 1956 reelection over Democratic candidate Adlai Stevenson.[1]

A report produced by the *Chicago Defender* illustrated the severity of the black rejection of Goldwater on a local level: in Washington, D.C., Johnson outperformed Goldwater by a 99 to 1 ratio in black districts; in Tennessee, Johnson received 99.5 percent of the black vote. Six million black voters registered for the election, nearly two million of them in the South—an increase of more than 500,000 from 1960. That more than 43 percent of black southerners, despite political repression and violence, registered to vote in 1964 was remarkable; also impressive was their near unanimous support for the Democrat Lyndon Johnson, considering that just four years earlier, a sizable contingency of black southerners had supported the Republican Party. Speaking with the *Defender* about the staggering figures, Edward Brooke—black Republican attorney general of Massachusetts—joined the chorus of Goldwater naysayers, remarking, "Negroes simply could not accept his marriage to Southern reactionaries."[2]

Black voters rejected Goldwater's brand of politics for many reasons, most notably the Arizona senator's outspoken support for states' rights and opposition to the Civil Rights Act of 1964. The two positions were intimately connected, inasmuch as the federal government was the linchpin of civil rights enforcement. For many, Goldwater's disapproval of the legislation on constitutional grounds was an explicit endorsement of segregation and racial inequality. It mattered not that Goldwater had declared that he was "unalterably opposed to discrimination of any sort," because his political platform opened the door for segregationists' public embrace of the GOP. Roy Wilkins, executive director for the National Association for the Advancement of Colored People (NAACP), attempted to explain the rationale behind African Americans' anti-Goldwater sentiment, noting that the senator's stance was akin to leaving civil rights in the hands of Alabama governor George Wallace or Mississippi governor Ross Barnett.[3] For many, the party's "open-armed welcome" of South Carolina senator and 1948 Dixiecrat presidential candidate Strom Thurmond was the final unpardonable offense.[4] Reflecting on the campaign in a November 1964 letter to the *Wichita Eagle*, reader Paul McBride noted that there was terrible incongruity in allowing "the candidate of the party of Lincoln to trample the right of the Negro."[5]

The irony of the situation was not lost on the party's most precarious faction—black Republicans. With the exception of a select few, the party's black members had watched the rise of Goldwater Republicans with anger and dismay. African American loyalists were disheartened by the party's apparent inability to support civil rights, a position that reinforced black Republicans' already marginal role within the GOP. In a September 1964 *New York Times* survey, for example, only three out of thirty-five black Republicans indicated that they supported the Republican nominee, while the rest relayed their plans to support Lyndon Johnson or abstain from voting completely. Likewise, by that point, all but one of the black consultants to the Republican National Committee had resigned in protest, including Albertine Bowie and Grant Reynolds, who had spent the better part of three years trying to convince black voters to support the "party of Lincoln." One man from Cleveland, who voted for Richard Nixon in 1960, simply shook his head at the mention of Goldwater, stating "the man isn't for us . . . and I'd be a damn fool if I voted for a man who's against me."[6] In Connecticut, black Republican and attorney general of Hartford William Graham also refused to vote for Goldwater in the general election, arguing that the senator's nomination was not indicative of the majority feeling on civil rights in the party. Frustrated, Graham argued that he could not vote for Lyndon Johnson either, given the president's "liberal economic and foreign policy views." Meanwhile, in Harlem, black Republican Charles Hill banned all Goldwater paraphernalia from the borough, doing so even though it undermined his own political advancement, as the New York State Committee had selected him to join the Goldwater-Miller election slate. "It would be an insult to the people if we support him," rationalized Hill. Nonetheless, the seventy-year-old leader grudgingly admitted that he "would have a mandate from the people" to cast his vote for the national ticket, in the event that Goldwater received the state's electoral support.[7]

For many black Republicans, endorsing Goldwater was tantamount to betraying their race. Athlete-turned-activist Jackie Robinson aggressively promoted New York governor Nelson Rockefeller as a respected alternative to Goldwater; he asserted that any black leader who demonstrated support for the nominee would lose power and influence since "the Negro is not going to tolerate any Uncle Toms in 1964."[8] Likewise, in an August 1964 editorial letter to the *New York Amsterdam News*, Jackson R. Champion, a black party member from New Rochelle, announced he would not join the ranks of Goldwater supporters. "Any Negro who helps the cause of Goldwater, should be declared anything but a Negro, because they will be a traitor to the Negro people." Despite his ties to the GOP, Champion said he would resist the national "slap in the face" by working for the election of Johnson as if he was "being paid by the Democratic Party."[9] The United Republican Club of Harlem echoed Champion's threats, as did the New Central Ward Young Republicans Club of Newark, New Jersey. Speaking on behalf of the Newark organization, Mary Edmonds insisted, "It was time that someone in our party convinced us that the GOP is really interested in Negroes."[10]

For black voters, boycotting Goldwater represented more than a rejection of the presidential candidate—it also meant repudiating any affiliation with the GOP. By 1964, only 8 percent of African Americans identified as Republican, a drop of 15 percentage points from 1960; in contrast, identification with the Democratic Party soared during the period, increasing from 54 to 82 percent. "I . . . no longer wish to be counted as a member of a decadent, lifeless political group," wrote one former black Republican in an August letter to the *New York Amsterdam News*. "A Negro would have to be stupid, naïve, stubborn or hopelessly subservient to help make Barry Goldwater President of the United States."[11] Implicit in this accusation was censure not only of the Arizona senator but also of the entire party for allowing Goldwater to become the party's nominee; in short, African Americans saw *all* Republicans as complicit in the conservative politician's ascent.

For those African Americans who remained affiliated with the party, the 1964 election placed them in an unstable position. Such a situation forced black Republicans to assert a voice and define an independent identity that addressed these seemingly irreconcilable loyalties. The *Los Angeles Sentinel* ruthlessly pointed out this bizarre relationship in December 1964, arguing that the election made "wishy washy Negro Republicans take open stands on topics they had skirted or about which they had double-talked for years."[12] Goldwater, the authors declared, "Will be remembered by the American Negro as the man who not only jolted him further awake, but made him fighting mad as well." Scornful tone aside, the *Sentinel*'s words reveal the urgency that informed black Republican politics in the 1960s. The 1964 moment—in essence, the public nadir of the GOP—served as a catalyst for black party members. Galvanized into action, they fought for greater voice and recognition within the party; the hallmark of their efforts was a unique agenda of racial equality and black advancement. Once reconciled with civil rights, black Republicans claimed that the "Party of Lincoln" would be uniquely suited to meet the needs of African Americans.

But mere claims were not enough as African American party loyalists were confronted with doubt from both sides, struggling to persuade black voters that the GOP had something to offer and fighting to convince the Republican Party that it would not succeed without the support of African Americans. Highlighting the contradictions inherent to this relationship between black Republicans and their party, the *New York Amsterdam News* observed that in order to survive, the mainstream party needed to collaborate with a group it consistently scorned:

> The irony lies in the fact that these same Negroes were virtually read out of the Party . . . at the last Republican National Convention. But as the Grand Old Party begins its search for building material with which to construct a new party it cannot escape the fact that the very cornerstone of that new building must be the levelheaded Negro Republicans who were not stampeded by Barry Goldwater and who held to the ideals of the Party at a time when the Party deserted them.[13]

This ironic relationship also presented an invaluable opportunity for black party members. The widespread alienation of the majority of the American electorate forced Republican leaders to confront the immensity of their institutional problem and to consider alternate strategies for rebuilding the party. Thus, while the rise of Goldwater clearly exacerbated the tumultuous relationship between the Republican Party and black America, it also prompted efforts to unify, as part of a desperate attempt to neutralize the widespread failures of the party.

Goldwater's nomination simultaneously provoked turmoil and opportunity. At least sixteen splinter groups formed among the party, divided along ideological lines; black Republicans launched one of these organizations, united by their shared racial philosophy and heritage and their opposition to Barry Goldwater.[14] While many African American party members became Democrats, a small but vocal contingency remained, determined to revitalize and transform the character of the party. Roused into action, they created the National Negro Republican Assembly (NNRA), which proclaimed itself the official channel for party reconstruction and African American outreach; in fact, the organization's presence was made all the more notable, because it was the only black Republican group active on a national level. Adopting an increasingly aggressive approach to American politics, the NNRA demanded that the GOP recognize and address racial equality, integrate the mainstream party machine, promote black advancement, and champion liberal and moderate Republican philosophies.

Historian William Chafe has suggested that, within the context of 1960s Democratic liberalism, the vehicle for civil rights achievement was grass-roots community organizations—a "base of operations independent of control of influence." Surely this theory is applicable to a Republican framework as well, as the NNRA also tried to establish an independent grass-roots foundation to strike at the "cultural and economic heart of white racism." Hence, parallel to liberal and radical black activists, the members of the NNRA "aspired to accomplish what Booker T. Washington had attempted eight decades earlier—to organize blacks for their own self-development and definition," albeit through an alternate Republican framework.[15]

The NNRA and the 1964 Republican National Convention

Speaking to an audience of prominent black Republicans at an August 1964 luncheon in Philadelphia, Pennsylvania, George Fleming, a black party member from New Jersey, issued a robust call-to-arms to all African American party loyalists. "We are here to support our friends in the Republican Party," he declared, "and, within the framework of the Party, to defeat those who have infiltrated the party and are seeking to drive us out."[16] Fleming continued his address, stating:

> We are met . . . to accept a "Challenge to Greatness" and "To issue a call to Statesmanship." We are here to let it be known throughout this land that we have looked upon the face of the enemy . . . and understood his danger to the party of Abraham Lincoln and to the ideas and institutions of this country. . . . We are here to declare a war for the votes of every man, woman and youth, in every registry and at every polling place. . . . We are here to raise an army led by Negroes whose unique contributions through the history of this party and this nation has been to provide a catalyst for the conscience of America and a touchstone for her dreams.[17]

Fleming's words were the highlight of a passionate meeting of self-proclaimed Republican "outsiders" who had answered an emergency summons issued in the aftermath of the Goldwater nomination. The

group, christened the National Negro Republican Assembly, first assembled as a loose coalition during the Republican National Convention in
July 1964. Its subsequent call-to-arms stemmed directly from its belief
that Goldwater conservatism was a threat to black Republican survival,
and that party extremism would lead to the "separation of the Negro
from the Republican Party."[18] Assessing this development, reporter John
Averill reasoned that the situation seemed to transcend conservatism,
since by definition most black Republicans were "strongly conservative
themselves."[19] To be sure, black Republican leaders of the GOP held
views that placed them firmly to the right of their Democratic Party peers,
especially in their embrace of capitalism and their belief in limited government; at the same time, their conservatism was different from that of
their white Republican counterparts because it was informed by their
racial experience as second-class citizens; consequently, many black party
members argued in favor of a strong federal legislation on matters of
racial equality.

The bitterness between black party members and Goldwater Republicans reached a breaking point during the July convention. Arriving at
the Cow Palace in San Francisco, black Republicans were unsettled by
the chants of fifty thousand anti-Goldwater protesters gathered outside,
including local CORE demonstrators who held a coffin with signs that
read: "Republican Party—Born 1860, Died 1964." Inside the convention
hall, the forty-three black Republicans were also outnumbered, composing little more than 1 percent of total convention representatives. The
shift represented the loss of seven black delegates, turning the 1964 convention, in the words of black Republican William O. Walker, into "lily-
Whiteism's greatest triumph." Some of the delegates, like George W. Lee
of Tennessee, were barred from attending by their state party's bureaucracy, solely because of their race; in fact, 1964 marked the first time
in fifty years that none of the southern delegations had seated a black
representative.[20] After expressing anti-Goldwater sentiments to the press,
several black delegates were detained by Republican National Convention security, while others were threatened with violence and verbally
assaulted by Goldwater supporters. Clarence Townes, a "Rockefeller,
Scranton, Romney kind of guy," later claimed that "being black and from
Virginia made me a target," recalling among other incidents, a physical altercation with Goldwater supporters who "messed my clothes up."
Pennsylvania delegate William Young received perhaps the worst attack
of the convention when his suit was set on fire during another Goldwater
protest: "Keep in your own place," shouted his attacker.[21] For George
Fleming, the harassment was simply too much; one evening, the black
delegate ran sobbing from the convention floor, crying that he was sick of

being abused by Goldwater supporters. "They call you 'nigger,' push you and step on your feet," he muttered to reporters, wiping tears from his eyes. "I had to leave to keep my self-respect."[22] In spite of these indignities and others, there were a handful of black Goldwater supporters who still continued to insist, as Edward Banks of Arizona did, that the senator was a "friend to the Negro" and was "no Ku Kluxer." Consequently, he found himself "snubbed, assailed" and "ignored" throughout the convention—one furious black delegate even refused to pose for a picture with Banks, snapping, "You're crazy. . . . You need to have your head examined."[23]

The relationship between Goldwater conservatives and black Republicans was already a combustible one, and the convention's verbal and physical attacks incited an explosive shift. Black representatives aggressively denounced Goldwater and accused his supporters of organizing a calculated "hate-vote" effort to disenfranchise African Americans at the convention; white Republicans protested this characterization, despite shouting down a convention rule change that would have banned discrimination among delegations.[24] In the words of the black delegates, this moment was a "whirlpool of controversy" that sparked a "refreshing unity of action and political maturity in direct contrast with previous appearances."[25] Indeed, over much of the previous three decades, black Republicans had agonized over the return of African Americans to the party fold; and as the reality of Goldwater's nomination settled and spurred by the attendant insults of the 1964 convention, a vanguard of black party members forcefully insisted that the problem lay not with their departing African American brethren but rather with the party itself.

In an effort to seize momentum, on the first night of the convention, William Young issued a call for solidarity to all black Republicans. Gathering in a "war room" at the Fairmont Hotel, the forty-three delegates developed an action plan to counteract their silencing. Calling themselves the Negro Republican Organization (NRO), the black party members asked three pivotal questions: Should black representatives walk out of the convention? Should black delegates and alternatives leave the Republican Party? If they chose not to leave, how could black loyalists effectively express their deep anger and resentment over their treatment? After an intense debate, most of the coalition agreed to remain and fight for their beliefs, declaring, "Under no condition, would Negroes walk out of the Republican Party. They [will] stay in, to support their friends and attempt to reshape the party, in the image which led to its birth!"[26]

Key to the members' resolve was their determination not to defect to the Democratic Party but to stay and enact change from within the organization; many believed that a defection to the Democratic Party would be an act of self-silencing, compounding the efforts of extremist Republicans.

This decision undoubtedly arose from black party members' unwavering belief in two-party competition. Arguing against black bloc voting, Clarence Townes maintained, "Two-party government is good. . . . You have choices in close races. You have competition. And with minorities, competition is good, particularly in the South. . . . When you don't have two-party competition, you have a one-party domination."[27] This modified theory of two-party competition did not mean that African Americans should join the Democratic Party; instead, black Republicans' "pragmatic" definition meant that *more* African Americans should join the Republican Party, while those already within the GOP should force the party to address civil rights and racial equality.

By the end of that first meeting, the NRO had produced a manifesto stating its desire to "maintain a strong two-party system," campaign on behalf of local and state Republican candidates who were civil rights advocates, "oppose any attempt to give the public any impression that Negro Republicans can unite behind Goldwater," and "make every effort to defeat that minority segment which appears determined to establish a lily-white Republican Party."[28] Over the four days of the convention, NRO members distributed copies of their "Negro Position Paper," embarking on a carefully orchestrated campaign to expose the systemic discrimination of "Negroes, Jews, and Catholics" by Goldwater Republicans and to overthrow "those who are attempting to make the party of Lincoln a machine for dispensing discord and racial conflict." The NRO took other measures to oppose the Goldwater nomination, including distributing anti-Goldwater paraphernalia and advocating for the nomination of Pennsylvania governor William Scranton as part of the interracial "Draft Scranton" coalition of liberal and moderate Republicans. Importantly, the delegates also took pains to distance themselves from mainstream civil rights groups, including the NAACP, CORE, and SCLC, rationalizing their aloofness by maintaining that they were not a part of the civil rights establishment but rather a firmly independent Republican group concerned with racial equality and civil rights.[29]

When Goldwater received the party's nomination, it predictably inspired the resentment of both the NRO and the party's interracial liberal and moderate base. Addressing an audience during the convention, while being booed and pelted with garbage, Nelson Rockefeller railed against the nomination, alleging that the GOP was in "real danger of subversion by a radical, well financed, highly organized" minority bloc. In his autobiography, Goldwater later acknowledged the gloom that surrounded his nomination, bitterly lamenting postconvention reports that provided the country with a bleak, frightening picture of a "ruthless Goldwater machine, crushing opponents, denying anyone who disagreed with us the right to speak, and dishonoring the process by which parties select their presidential nominee."[30] In the wake of the nomination, the NRO seized on such themes, announcing that its members would abstain from voting in the presidential election and instead concentrate on campaigning in state and local elections for Republicans supportive of civil rights initiatives. A few days after the national convention, however, Jackie Robinson offered a belligerent dissent to the group's resolution, launching a chapter of "Republicans for Johnson." Explaining this decision in a September editorial, he argued that abstaining was a passive move, one that "aided and abetted" the Goldwater campaign; "splitting the ticket" by casting ballots for Lyndon Johnson and New York Republican Senator Kenneth Keating, concluded Robinson, was a far more powerful political statement.[31]

In truth, remaining loyal to the Republican Party in 1964 was far harder than NRO ever imagined. After the convention, five black Washington, D.C., delegates and alternates quit their delegation rather than "enthusiastically" campaign for Goldwater; adding insult to injury, their delegation chair, Carl Shipley, had publicly ranted against "well-dressed, responsible Negroes running wild like in the Congo," belittled the black representatives as elitist "Cadillac Negroes," and promised to replace them with young blue-collar African Americans who would campaign vigorously for Goldwater.[32] Where Shipley planned to recruit these blue-collar workers was a mystery, since most newly registered African American voters characterized themselves as Democrats. Nevertheless, the Washington, D.C., representatives insisted that they still believed in the principles of the NRO; as George Parker asserted, the black Republican leaders were determined to "reshape the party into a coalition that provided equal opportunities to all."[33]

Given these and other difficulties, NRO members agreed that it was crucial that they harness their newfound momentum and solidarity. On July 27, Pennsylvania's John Clay issued a summons to attend an August convention dedicated to establishing a permanent organization within the framework of the Republican Party, increasing the number of future delegates to the national convention, encouraging more black Republicans to run for public office, and developing other programs "to insure that our voice be heard in the party."[34] Fifty black Republicans from sixteen states and the District of Columbia accepted the invitation, arriving at the Sheraton Hotel in Philadelphia on August 22 for the two-day workshop.[35] Welcoming the participants and reminding them of their common bonds in the face of turmoil, George Fleming opened the conference by stressing the seriousness of the occasion and declaring that for years, the GOP "has been counting the Negro out, because he has lacked the spirit, drive and the muscle to count himself in." Placing equal accountability on the GOP and black Republicans was a troublesome assessment; but it was merely Fleming's flawed attempt to motivate black party members, by imbuing them with a sense of urgency and agency. He underscored these points by pointing to the lack of black Republican communication and solidarity, political representation, and grass-roots voter registration; with conditions like these, Fleming asked, "How can we expect to survive, let alone develop positions of strength?"

The fiery speaker bemoaned the financial naïveté of black party members, criticizing them for failing to pool resources on behalf of African American political candidates and jockey for influence in mainstream party circles. Evaluating black Republican longevity, Fleming berated his audience for neglecting to incorporate black youth into the party structure. Moving beyond the problems with the GOP, Fleming begged his audience to recognize the magnitude of American inequality by offering a stark picture of an unstable nation divided over civil rights. "Mississippi is Hell!" Fleming thundered from the podium. Pointing to black poverty, urban and rural alike, as well as poor living conditions and high unemployment, he warned black Republicans not to delude themselves into thinking that "Kingdom has come for minorities in the United States." Fleming's appraisal of African Americans captured a distinct truth: most black Republicans were elites—middle-class and wealthy African Americans, disconnected from the devastating intersection of race and class inequality. Even those born into southern segregation existed in worlds far removed from the day-to-day experience of the black poor and working class; consequently, African American party members' class privilege often insulated them from the full reality of racial inequality.

Fleming closed by asserting that the chaos and instability of the 1960s called for a concrete plan for advancing equality, voice, and recognition within the GOP. "We know our progress toward human dignity cannot be maintained or advanced if we permit any one party to put the Negro vote in its pocket, because it has no where else to go," he insisted, referring to African Americans overwhelming support for the Democratic Party. "It would be equally disastrous," he reasoned, for the "Negro to succumb to those [Republicans] who propose a retreat from the 20th Century. Thus, we are here to change this picture."[36] In short, Fleming and the other conference attendees argued that a vibrant two-party political system was necessary in order to ensure racial equality, for without political competition, African Americans risked losing their opportunity for substantive and long-term legal and social change.

The delegates eventually voted to concentrate on several areas including developing a grass-roots operation; increasing the influence of black Republicans; creating a youth group, women's subdivision, and fraternal subdepartment; and drafting a program to "explain to Negroes why they must join and support the Republican Party."[37] The group enacted a mandatory five-dollar membership fee, with the hope that the money would allow the coalition to remain financially independent from the mainstream party and enable the distribution of information, and assistance to local subgroups and political campaigns. After some debate, members also voted to rename the group the National Negro Republican Assembly and unanimously endorsed a slate of executives that included President George Fleming of New Jersey, Secretary Jeannette Weiss of Michigan, Treasurer Clarence Townes of Virginia, and Executive Director John Clay of Pennsylvania. Finally, the delegates adopted a detailed constitution that outlined the organization's purpose and strategic vision:

1. To create a new atmosphere within the framework of the Republican Party that will make it unmistakably clear that the Negro is needed, wanted, and welcome;
2. To encourage and support republican [sic] candidates whose concepts can be approved as compatible with traditional Republican concepts;
3. To pursue such objectives as will give Negro citizens representation within the Republican Party at all policy making levels;
4. To develop an education program . . . to increase delegate . . . representation at all future republican [sic] conventions;
5. To implement the Republican Party's historic principle[s] of Free Enterprise, Justice, Individual Freedom and respect for human dignity;
6. To initiate conferences and programs in cooperation with labor and industry to create jobs for all without discriminatory distinction;
7. To urge Negroes to join forces to maintain and preserve the two party system vital to the future of the United States.[38]

The NNRA's fundamental mission was to promote racial equality and black advancement through the integration of African Americans into the Republican Party. Hence, the group pledged to mount an "untiring effort" to serve as "the liaison between the Republican Party and the Negro voter" in the quest for equal opportunity for success, satisfaction, and security, envisioning itself as a watchdog organization and the conscience of the GOP. Employing a language of black populism, the NNRA also claimed to offer a unique vision for addressing the needs of black unskilled laborers, unemployed youth and adults, forced retirees, and impoverished families. The group insisted that its adherence to a mix of private and public enterprise would stimulate economic growth, create new jobs, and reinvigorate the black community, and it also made clear that without enforcement and protection, such successes were unrealistic for most—a stance that explicitly separated the NNRA from the GOP's reactionary faction. The organization closed its statement of purpose by declaring that the "Civil Rights Law of 1964, and all previous civil rights laws, must be unequivocally and vigorously enforced—that law and order must prevail—that the lives and property of all must be protected. We reaffirm our belief in God, Country, and the dignity of man throughout the world."[39]

With mission and purpose defined, the NNRA moved forward with its strategic plan, determined to grow both membership and activity. Tapping into this determination in a September letter to the organization's members, John Clay wrote, "It appears that Senator Goldwater will be greatly defeated, and we must meet and be organized to rebuild the Republican Party image." Anti-Goldwater sentiment was a motivational tool and a call for empowerment: after reminding members that there was a drastic need for "Negro Republicans to stand up and be counted," the executive director declared that no sacrifice was too great since the "future of the Republican Party rests in our hands."[40]

Along with its standard declarations of support, the NNRA also stressed the dangers posed by the increasing number of southern Democrats joining the ranks of the GOP. Discussing the matter during a press conference, newly elected Political Action chair Grant Reynolds argued that "an era of blackest despair would develop and doom the Party of Lincoln to oblivion . . . if cast-off Democrats, repudiated Dixiecrats, segregationists, racists and exponents of hate and bias" were permitted to gain power within the party. "It is deplorable," he complained, "to even think that the racist elements now entering the Republican Party should even presume to believe they could be comfortable."[41] To combat the "infiltration" of the party, the NNRA emphasized support for campaigns of pro–civil rights Republicans and new recruitment initiatives designed to woo black voters. Black Republicans, Reynolds proposed, should use social, educational, and voter registration programs as an alternative method for disseminating political information on civil rights, two-party competition, and the Republican Party. Importantly, Reynolds relied on his experience working not only within the RNC but also with A. Philip Randolph; in 1947 the two men had cofounded and cochaired the Committee Against Jim Crow in Military Service and Training, an organization that had played an instrumental role in desegregating the Armed Forces.[42]

In particular, voter registration was seen as a crucial means of recruitment—it not only was a powerful display against segregation and disenfranchisement but also provided direct access to new voters. Drawing inspiration from the registration efforts of civil rights organizations, the NNRA collaborated with church groups, such as the Richmond Crusade for Voters (RCV). Speaking on a dinner panel in late September, RCV president George Pannell lauded the grass-roots registration efforts of the NNRA, claiming that in one Virginia district registered black voters had risen from four thousand in 1956 to eighteen thousand in 1964. Pannell speculated that with continued effort the NNRA could register thousands more in Virginia before Election Day.[43] These numbers resonated with the members of the assembly, since they provided tangible evidence of the power and potential of an independent grass-roots black Republican movement.

Another significant aspect of this grass-roots technique was a mass-mailing campaign to potential members and donors. In an October 1964 mailing, for example, Grant Reynolds described the NNRA's commitment to remain steadfast in its fight against those who would destroy the Republican Party, riling his readers' sense of outrage by mentioning the "indignities" suffered at the "hands of the Goldwater mob." He referred to the assembly as an independent agent of change, whose members sought to "salvage their Republican Heritage and yours."[44] The mass mailings were both a political rallying cry for solidarity and an alternate way of collecting untapped capital through nationwide donations.

By the time of the presidential election, the NNRA estimated that it had 250 members with chapters in more than twenty-five states, with most hailing from Memphis, Atlanta, New York City, Philadelphia, and Los Angeles. Although small in comparison to groups like Young Americans for Freedom (which enlisted more than five thousand new members alone in the summer of 1964), the NNRA was still notable because it contained an "aggressive concentration" of blacks invested in the progress of both African Americans and the Republican Party.[45] The group's growth—an increase of more than two hundred black Republicans in a three-month period—instilled confidence in its membership, which inspired bolder actions. In one such display, the organization publicly endorsed forty-one "Negro Friendly" Republican candidates from nineteen states, two days before the national election. Among those celebrated were New York congressman John Lindsay, Pennsylvania senator Hugh Scott, Michigan governor George Romney, and Rhode Island governor John Chaffee; nearly all of those selected were white; the exception was Edward Brooke, the black attorney general of Massachusetts. Endorsements for the presidential candidates, Democratic Party politicians, and

Republicans from the Deep South were noticeably absent. "Candidates who are being endorsed," the NNRA declared, "are true and tried friends who have and will continue to work for all Americans that believe in civil rights. They have prodded the Administration to make sure that legislation will be enforced fully and fairly. . . . These Republican candidates are men that were alert to civil rights needs before the great crisis arose and are certainly alert now. They have not been fair weather friends who needed Birmingham to jolt them into action."[46] Establishing political alliances with liberal and moderate Republicans was critical to the black group's agenda, especially since racially progressive legislation was the cornerstone of the NNRA's vision for equality, as members placed their faith in legislative influence via the voting booth, eschewing the public protests and civil disobedience of the grass-roots civil rights movement.

Though the NNRA had both a vision and a vehicle to challenge the extremist elements of the GOP, the organization had no direct and effective way to penetrate the upper echelons of the mainstream party and command attention, so long as Goldwater Republicans dominated the national hierarchy. The senator's historic loss in the November contest, however, amended these restrictions, providing the NNRA with the opening it needed. To be sure, the presidential election was an unforgettable political massacre for the Republican Party. In defeat, Barry Goldwater earned only 38.5 percent of the popular vote, winning the five Deep South states and Arizona—figures that did not fully convey the enormity of his loss. The senator amassed 27 million ballots to Johnson's 43 million; of these voters, only 6 million were "hard-core, down-the-line" Goldwater supporters, a group mostly comprised of white, southern, wealthy men—many of whom identified as Democrats. Three million of the senator's backers were motivated by racism and opposition to the Civil Rights Act of 1964; another 18 million supported Goldwater "out of party loyalty," expressing concerns over his foreign policy and civil rights views. Even self-identified conservative voters labeled the Republican nominee a "radical," articulating their opposition to a "right-wing takeover" of the GOP.[47]

Moreover, according to a postelection Gallup poll, only 15 percent of Republican voters considered Goldwater the party's "most representative" candidate; yet another survey found that more than 60 percent of registered Republicans wanted the Arizona politician replaced as a party leader. Reflecting on the election, New York State chair Fred Young stated that "the Republican Party has paid a shattering price for the erratic deviation from our soundly moderate 20th century course."[48] In truth, Goldwater's defeat revealed the American public's distain for the politician's dogmatic interpretation of conservatism; consequently, in the days and weeks following the electoral disaster the GOP was a party in political crisis, searching for a new "identity." Just as important, the party's failure was the NNRA's fortune, granting the black assembly a valuable opportunity to negotiate for a return to the "traditional" principles of the so-called Party of Lincoln.

ELECTORAL AFTERMATH: IN FAILURE, AN OPPORTUNITY

In the days immediately following the November election, the mood of most Republicans was one of despair and frustration—disunity reigned. The contest badly fractured the party and "washed away every traditional stronghold."[49] The damage inflicted was widespread, reverberating far beyond the presidential race; by the time the political dust had settled, the party had lost two seats in the Senate and thirty-eight in the House, the lowest level of Republican representation in twenty-eight years. By the end of 1964, stated GOP leader Leonard Hall, the party had lost "75 percent of the Roman Catholic vote, 80 percent of the Jewish vote, and from 75 to 96 percent of the Negro vote." The severity of the party's loss led Republican official Ray Bliss to solemnly observe, "We are excluding from our party the Americans we need most."[50]

For the NNRA, this was a moment of opportunity, one that triggered an explosion of activity. Two days after the election, Vice-President-Secretary C. L. Townes Sr. wrote to the assembly's leadership, warning that decisive action was needed:

> I hope you fellows with "proper contacts" will lose no time in influencing the liberal wing of the GOP to take immediate steps to change the image of the leadership to what it should be. The Conservative element has just about wrecked the party and I don't see how we can make much headway in the next four years if the present National Committee with its Goldwater influence does not voluntarily resign; or is removed by those who have the know how to do it.[51]

Within days of receiving the letter, NNRA officials held several press conferences calling for the ejection of Goldwater Republicans from the party's national bureaucracy. Grant Reynolds reserved some of his harshest criticisms for Dean Burch, the chair of the RNC and a Goldwater supporter; the black Republican demanded that the national committee official be replaced with a moderate or liberal party leader—a move, Reynolds asserted, that would help convince black voters to rejoin a reformed party. Following the advice of the NNRA was the first crucial step in transforming the party's national image from "a party of big business and of the lily white forces" to one that supported the "aspirations of the people."[52] Reynolds speech offered more than dramatic rhetoric—it also signified a new sense of class consciousness on the part of black Republicans. Previous generations of African American party members certainly had been interested in the intersection of race and class; however, their efforts were scattered, divided, and largely confined to state and local activities. Moreover, as leaders in the NNRA became more and more aware of their middle-class privileges, they increasingly tried to move away from their exclusionary identities in the hopes of reaching more African American voters.

In an attempt to capitalize on anti-Goldwater momentum, the NNRA added a national speaking tour to its campaign. The assembly's grass-roots canvassing provoked many reactions, none more forceful than that of the Pennsylvania chapter of the NNRA in December 1964. While delivering a speech on new types of black Republican politics, Reynolds apparently sparked thoughts of a "political revolution." When his talk ended, a skirmish erupted as nearly forty members attempted to unseat state chair William Young on the grounds that the black leader was "negligent and not vigorous enough" to ensure positive change for the future.[53] The incident exposed the heightened intensity of the NNRA and its members; and while the group's activities prior to the November election reflected a certain level of forcefulness, Goldwater's defeat elevated the emotions and actions of black party members, producing a far more urgent approach to party politics. The shift signaled the emergence of a "New Republican Negro," a proactive political figure embodying an increased determination to transform the party and advance the cause of African Americans. For the time being, the "New Republican Negro" did not identify as a member of the "Party of Lincoln," Eisenhower, or Rockefeller; nor did he or she identity with the politics of the Democratic Party. "I have no national affiliation," Grant Reynolds bluntly told *Jet* in the fall of 1964. "I'm an independent Republican."[54] NNRA leaders professed an allegiance to racial egalitarianism, two-party competition, and black uplift, while maintaining a faith in free market enterprise; likewise, their philosophy reflected a turn toward independence within the boundaries of traditional conservatism because, in the eyes of black citizens, the situation—specifically the civil rights movement and the fractured Republican Party—demanded it. The time had come, black Republican Bill Robinson proclaimed, for the party and America to heed the "rise of the New Negro and the goals of [the] social revolution" of the twentieth century, and to do so through the Republican Party; though highly critical of the GOP, Robinson nevertheless insisted that it was a better choice for African Americans than the Democratic Party, which he described as hypocritical and insincere. In essence, the New Republican Negro rejected Goldwater conservatism and Democratic liberalism alike, opting instead for an "alternative" way to insert civil rights into the two-party political system.[55]

Acting as the vehicle and voice of the New Republican Negro, the NNRA continued to exist both as an autonomous group—separate from civil rights organizations and independent of the mainstream party—and as an integrated part of party decision making. The group's stance did not always find favor within black communities; for example, in a scathing editorial, the *Chicago Defender* denounced the NNRA for "self-segregated" and "antebellum" practices. "To come out," wrote the *Defender*, "with a self-imposed Jim Crow organization in the midst of a social revolution . . . is the surest means of keeping the great mass of equality-minded Negroes away from the Republican Party." Calling for the NNRA to disband, the newspaper insisted that to do otherwise would be an "impediment to the assimilation of the Negro people into the main politic of a rejuvenated Republican Party." However, in deeming the NNRA an antiquated segregationist group, the *Defender* failed to recognize the philosophical implications of autonomy for black Republicans. A radical concept, the NNRA's separatism was a crucial part of its strategy. Separation guarded against a marginal position within the mainstream party and gave the NNRA the freedom to make assertive demands of the GOP. In spite of its criticisms, the *Defender* acknowledged that it found no fault with the NNRA's guiding principles, ultimately accepting the organization's mission as analogous to the goals of mainstream civil rights groups.[56]

Some white Republican leaders expressed support for the concept of black autonomy, including Illinois state official William Howell, who reasoned that independent splinter groups like the NNRA were needed since minority involvement in party affairs "has been and still is an uphill fight." Distancing himself from Barry Goldwater's version of the GOP, the politician asserted, "I want to be active in the Republican party not because of the days of Lincoln . . . I want to be active because of what the party stands for today."[57] Similarly, three weeks after the election, Pennsylvania Republican Committee chair Craig Truax defended the actions of black Republicans while speaking to an interracial audience at an event hosted by the Pennsylvania State Council of Republican Women and the Pennsylvania Negro Republican Council:

> Stop the ridiculing of Republican Negroes. Recognize their right to Republican beliefs. Recognize that he or she may well be your best hope for gaining a position of enduring influence and stability without

our two-party system. Realize that the growth of leadership by Republican Negroes will rightfully earn a new measure of respect for you in both parties. The Negro, 20 million strong, is having a profound effect upon our destiny as a nation. Twenty million American citizens . . . regardless of who they are . . . are important to us personally, and to our nation's life. What a community of 20 million Americans decide on Election Day, and how and why they decide, is of utmost importance to each of us."[58]

Organizational separatism did not exclude collaborative efforts with white or interracial Republican groups; in fact, the NNRA was invested in building interracial coalitions and seeking partnerships with other autonomous GOP groups, including the Committee to Support Forward-Looking Republicans, Republicans for Progress, the National Conference of Republican Workshops, the Committee of '68, the Ripon Society, and the Republican Governors' Association.[59] In late November, the organizations formed a liberal and moderate umbrella group, the Council of Republican Organizations (CRO). Soon thereafter, council representatives convened at the Republican Governors Association (RGA) conference in Denver to devise a plan for revitalizing the party by reaching across the party's ideological divides—a "desperate task of heroic proportions," remarked Idaho governor Robert Smylie.

The statement that emerged from that conference spoke to the shared frustrations of an interracial alliance of liberal and moderate Republicans, as the delegates called for party inclusiveness, denounced racial discrimination, and urged the party to use the power of the local, state, and federal government to address the pressing social and economic needs of Americans. The attendees also reiterated the NNRA's stance on RNC head Dean Burch, insisting that it was "inevitable" that the national committee chair would be forced out of power. Yet, where most of the conference participants shied away from demanding Burch's resignation publicly, the NNRA continued to voice its condemnation of the RNC official. Such were the boundaries of the CRO; member organizations repeatedly stressed that they were not splinter groups and had no intention of going to "war with the Republican Party." The black assembly, in contrast, envisioned its struggle in the party as a vital political battle.[60] Despite the differences of approach, these collaborative efforts nevertheless were crucial, providing another method for the NNRA to generate publicity and gain access to the upper echelons of the GOP.

As the NNRA continued to gather momentum, the hierarchy of the Republican Party showed serious signs of strain. Analyzing the situation, NAACP chair Roy Wilkins declared that the party was in shambles, observing that it had lost upwards of 500 seats in state legislatures and that House Republicans "were down to 140 out of 435" while those in the Senate "numbered 32 out of 100." Such figures were significant not only because of their lopsided nature but also because they gave President Johnson and the Democratic Party a mandate to enact their specific policy agenda.[61] Failed North Carolina gubernatorial candidate Robert Gavin insisted that black voters had played a crucial role in the party's state and local disasters, divulging that he had received only 3 percent of the ballots cast by African Americans in the November contest, despite having a better record on civil rights than his Democratic opponent, an avowed segregationist. The reason for the party's loss, Gavin maintained, was the "determination of the Negro race to defeat our national ticket. No one man in North Carolina can spot his opponent 200,000 votes right from the start and expect to win. In my election, it was decisive. . . . It was equally decisive in Tennessee . . . in Texas with George Bush, in Ohio with Bob Taft, Jr., and in Illinois with Chuck Percy." Warning his fellow Republicans to evaluate the "Negro problem" with care, Gavin noted that dismissing black frustrations in the future could have severe repercussions in his state, since in his estimation, registered black voters would number approximately 300,000 by 1966.[62]

Moderate and liberal leaders initially proved willing to explore new strategies for reconstructing the Republican Party. Pennsylvania governor William Scranton, for instance, emphasized the possibilities in an interview held three days after the election, declaring his eagerness to "make it clear that the party of Lincoln is a great national party, eager to return to its heritage and welcome all Americans to our ranks." Reflecting on the party's woes, he lamented that "many Americans" now believed that the GOP was "opposed or indifferent" to racial and ethnic minorities. "This is completely contrary to the true tradition of the Republican Party," he asserted, "It concerns me deeply."[63] An RNC postelection report issued two months later also touched on these themes, concluding that in order for the party to return to prominence, it needed to rely heavily on the "elements of victory from the diverse groups which comprise the American electorate," including African Americans.[64] The liberal Ripon Society articulated a parallel thesis in its 124-page election analysis but also emphasized the need for Republican solidarity on issues like racial equality, urging the party to disassociate from "far-right extremist groups" and reverse the white southern appeals of the Goldwater coalition. "Only by championing the cause of civil rights," wrote the authors, "can the party make real and permanent gains in the South and retain strength in the North." The report closed by challenging the GOP to earn at least 20 percent of the black vote in the 1968 election—proof of how far Republicans had fallen since 1960, when more than 30 percent of the African American electorate supported the party. Ripon suggested that party leaders start this effort by conducting voter registration drives, nurturing positive relationships with black media outlets, publicly apologizing to civil rights leaders and seeking their counsel on issues of black concern, exerting national pressure on state organizations to enforce existing civil rights legislation, and appointing a black Republican as an associate chair of the RNC.[65]

Addressing the overall situation in a January 1965 letter to Dean Burch, Republican Congressional Committee (RCC) chair Bob Wilson suggested that the national committee speak directly to members of the NNRA to identify areas of concern and proposed that the RNC head appoint a special committee of party leaders to generate an "effective and cooperative link with eminent Negro members of the party." Burch may not have read Wilson's missive, however, because by the time the letter reached the RNC official he had resigned—to be sure, this was a moment of celebration for the NNRA, as was the subsequent appointment of Burch's successor, Ohio moderate Ray Bliss. Members embraced the new RNC official, encouraged by his pronouncements that he intended to operate pragmatically and from the political center and be open to projects that would produce substantial results at the polls.[66]

That same month, four NNRA leaders traveled to Chicago to attend a meeting of the RNC, presenting a three-page list of recommendations to the 132-member executive committee. The black delegation proposed that the RNC install a "qualified Negro" as a deputy chairman, appoint a minimum of four black members to the RNC, and provide funding for programs aimed at African Americans; likewise, the assembly officials reiterated their support of progressive Republican candidates, commitment to two-party competition and voter registration, and belief in the principles of traditional conservatism. Their presentation was met with mixed success. On the one hand, many of the white attendees kept the black delegates at "arm's length" throughout the three-day conference and forced them to omit negative references to Goldwater and racism from their statement in the name of "party unity." On the other hand, the white delegates took the NNRA's suggestions seriously, voting to explore the black group's proposals, endorse a resolution that called for abandoning "racist-segregationist attitudes," and recruit at least 20 percent of the black vote in the 1968 presidential contest. Bliss closed the conference, in part, by promising to meet with the NNRA in order to create a detailed plan for wooing black voters in the 1966 midterm elections. These reactions led some of the assembly's leaders to disregard white Republicans' ambivalent behavior during the meeting: "I would like to say that the committee received our recommendations soberly," New York NNRA chair George Fowler mused, following the Republican gathering "and that it was an effective move."[67] The notion that the assembly would have faith in the RNC, despite the party's slothlike pace of change, was peculiar, especially given the NNRA's intense sense of urgency. But in truth, after being shunned from party decision making at the hands of Goldwater Republicans, some black party members were satisfied, believing that their voices were finally being heard in the upper echelons of the party.

Despite the national committee's interest, there were some within the party that would have preferred that the RNC disregard the NNRA's ideas. In February 1965 Georgia state senator Joseph Tribble offered a mathematical counterargument to calls for African American voter registration efforts, reasoning:

> Suppose you register three whites and are reasonably sure two of them will vote for you; then register three Negroes believing that only one of them will vote for you, where should you spend your time and money? As Barry Goldwater said, "You'll go hunting where the ducks are."

Black voters, Tribble argued, would never act as a controlling factor in American politics. Echoing this sentiment, South Carolina GOP chair Drake Edens suggested that the party "play the odds" and conduct recruitment and registration efforts among white southerners.[68] The historical record is rife with reiterations of this argument; for some Republicans, the election results merely reinforced the belief that African Americans were irrelevant to the GOP's electoral success and that white southerners were far more important for future wins.

Other party officials, especially liberal and moderate Republicans, challenged antiblack hostility, dismissing the logic of said arguments. Senator Thruston Morton of Kentucky insisted that such rationales incorrectly considered the black electorate as a monolithic group, incapable of participating in a two-party voting system. In reality, he argued, many African Americans viewed their participation as a fluid, ever-changing act. Roy Wilkins also acknowledged the fluctuating votes of black voters, stating, "I'm sure they will be split up again" and noting that many had crossed "over to the Democratic line because they didn't like the nominee." Those voters, he predicted, "will go back."[69]

Interestingly enough, a group of southern GOP politicians also rejected antiblack logic but for different reasons than Wilkins; in the Georgia state legislature, all but one of Tribble's eight Republican colleagues disavowed his beliefs, insisting that if the party wanted to attract white voters, it would also need to appeal to African Americans—but only in a race-neutral way. This was a reflection of changing social attitudes in the nation, as white constituents—even in the South—were increasingly uncomfortable with lending their support to a "political movement that smacks of racism." At the same time, the party shied away from race-specific outreach, fearing that "black issues" would alienate these same white voters. The compromise was "colorblind" appeals aimed at a broad audience that included African Americans. To be sure, this was a deeply contentious issue, one that divided Republicans along lines that transcended ideologies and geographic boundaries; but even as many party officials maintained ambivalent personal attitudes about race, they nevertheless insisted that the GOP could not win elections "on a racist foundation."[70]

Meanwhile, the NNRA continued to argue that the Republican Party offered a desirable political choice for black voters, one that was better than voting for the Democratic Party or not voting at all; in turn, mainstream party leaders offered black Republicans an opportunity for voice and recognition. In fact, by 1965 party officials were actively searching for African Americans to run for local and state offices. In Michigan, for example, Governor George Romney recruited real estate broker Joseph Bell to run for vice-chair of the party's state committee in the hopes of making "a showing at the Republican State convention."[71] In New York, Republican leaders sought African Americans to run for city council president or comptroller, considering, among others, Judge Samuel Pierce, former National Urban League executive director Dr. Lester Grange, and NNRA New York chair George Fowler. The move was enough to impress the *New York Amsterdam News*: reporter James Booker praised the Republican Party for its recognition of the "major importance of the growing Negro vote."[72]

The implications in considering a black nominee, although not decisive by any means, were unpredictable, especially since GOP officials still had doubts about attaching an African American to a major ticket. Nevertheless, in March 1965 New York Republicans placed Fowler's name on the public list of seven potential mayoral candidates—a significant inclusion given that it was the first mainstream party endorsement of a black candidate for a major city office.[73] Both the NNRA and white officials praised the preliminary resolution, hailing it as an important move that would boost the party's image among the American public, create symbolic intraparty unity, and generate interracial collaboration among New York Republicans.

Two weeks before being identified as a potential mayoral candidate, Fowler had joined two thousand protestors in the second march on Selma, organized by the SCLC and Martin Luther King Jr. He later described the fifty-four-mile trek as a necessary demonstration of support for equal voting rights for African Americans in the face of inequality.

Characterizing his journey as "heartening" to a black audience at the Baptist Ministers Conference in April 1965, Fowler recalled watching "typical Negroes," in full view of their "white masters," run toward the marchers, "with hope and happiness on their faces while they clapped their hands with joy." Never again, he promised his listeners, would these black southerners "be afraid," for they had learned that "freedom is theirs if they will but seize it, and the only thing that have to fear is fear coupled with inaction." In spite of the NNRA's talk of "black populism" and class awareness, members still struggled with their middle-class biases, as Fowler's paternalistic rhetoric illustrates. And while he understood himself to be part of a broader black community, Fowler implicitly believed himself to be *different*—perhaps even superior—to the "typical Negroes" of the South. Not only did he cast himself as an enlightened savior for poor and working-class black southerners, he also held them accountable for their own disenfranchisement, scolding them for their political inaction. Still, the NNRA leader was eager to participate in the grass-roots civil rights struggle, which distinguished him from previous generations of black Republicans, many of whom had been content to remain on the sidelines.

Furthermore, in spite of his classism, Fowler's concern for racial uplift was no less genuine. He closed his speech by urging audience members to be strategic in their political efforts, since calculated use of the two-party system would spur interest and competition between political parties over black voters. Success, he urged, ultimately hinged on disabusing the black community of the conviction that political parties were akin to religious institutions or "something to be loved." This was an attempt to disrupt black Democratic partisanship—a move designed to subvert one-party rule by warning African Americans that dogmatic allegiance to any one political party was dangerous and to encourage black voters to be loyal solely to the needs of their race. His words were born out of the NNRA's belief that a political party was not an immutable institution but "a medium through which the electorate achieves its goals."[74] The irony behind Fowler's argument was that black Republicans had refused to leave the GOP when dissatisfied with their own party.

Nevertheless, the NNRA believed that the mayoral race was an emblematic vehicle through which to reenergize the black electorate, redefine widespread perceptions about black Republicans, establish an equal power dynamic with mainstream party leadership, and make a bold statement about black equality. Thus, when city officials—nervous over Fowler's chances of winning—pushed the lifelong Republican to pursue city council or comptroller positions instead of a mayoral bid, he refused, stating, "It's the number one position, or nothing."[75] As the relationship remained at an impasse, the NNRA voted to endorse Fowler's mayoral candidacy and threatened to launch an independent campaign—a move intended to broadcast black Republican autonomy and voice the group's dissatisfaction with the slow pace of change within the party.[76] The group's strategy was also designed to attract new types of black voters: individuals unhappy with the Democratic Party, intrigued by a black organization using the Republican Party to its advantage, and inspired by the NNRA's vocal criticisms of its own party. In fact, the assembly skewered the Republican theme of party unity as hypocritical, angered by the lack of mainstream support. Reynolds went so far as to denounce the chair of the RNC at a convention luncheon, shouting, "I'm not so sure that Ray Bliss is the doctor with the right medicine to cure what ails the Republican Party!"[77]

NNRA members' faith in Fowler was not theirs alone—quite the opposite. An April 1965 *New York Courier* poll found that Fowler overwhelmingly was the black respondents' first choice.[78] Nevertheless, in private, members of the NNRA, including Jackie Robinson, despaired that Republican officials had no real interest in developing a thriving two-party system for black voters.[79] Adding to this anguish was Adam Clayton Powell Jr. who mocked Fowler's candidacy as an "uncle Tom ticket." The influential Harlem congressman's comment was made all the more significant given that the NNRA's goal in running a mayoral campaign was partly to dispel underlying race-traitor stereotypes about black Republicans. A few days after Powell's insult, the weary members' fears were finally confirmed when GOP leaders released their shortened mayoral list, which no longer included any reference to Fowler.[80]

Instead of launching its threatened independent bid, the NNRA shifted tactics and placed its support behind the campaign of Republican John Lindsay, who was running for mayor on a fusion ticket with the Liberal Party of New York.[81] A year earlier, the group had named Lindsay as a civil rights ally; consequently, assembly members later pledged their "full and enthusiastic support," labeling him a progressive Republican and citing his legislative record on civil rights and dedication to revitalizing the two-party system. In general, Lindsay motivated a "large number" of disaffected black Republicans, many of whom had retreated from party politics by 1965. Equally important were Lindsay's actions—he spurned existing party structures and mechanisms and appealed to minority voters by opening headquarters in black areas including Harlem and Brooklyn.[82] He even gained the backing of the Harlem Citizens Committee (HCC), a prominent group of African American elites who assembled with the sole purpose of providing the Lindsay campaign with advice on black voters. Though the committee claimed to be bipartisan, most of those involved were black Republicans; members included, among others, James Farmer of the Congress of Racial Equality (CORE), jazz musician Lionel Hampton, entertainer Sammy Davis Jr., former Eisenhower aide E. Frederic Morrow, boxer "Sugar" Ray Robinson, and Reverend Wyatt Walker, former chief of staff to Martin Luther King Jr. and former assistant pastor at Abyssinian Baptist Church. "[Lindsay] has demonstrated the vigor and honesty that the leadership of our nation's largest city demands," stated Walker. "He possesses the deep social sensitivity to grapple with the severe problems of the inner city that have been neglected so long."[83]

In spite of the NNRA's relationship with John Lindsay, the assembly's general broader campaign struggles highlight the difficulties in navigating a turbulent party landscape and the rancor that persisted between black Republicans and the mainstream GOP. The mayoral battle was but one of many of the NNRA's larger complaints of party insincerity. National issues, such as an April 1965 incident with Alabama congressman William Dickinson, buttressed the NNRA's cynicism over party unity. In the weeks following the Selma marches, Dickinson delivered a series of public speeches denouncing the protests as displays of "sexual misconduct," angering African Americans across the country. The NNRA and CRO crafted a sharp rebuttal to the congressman, providing eyewitness testimony from marchers to contradict the politician's claims, delivering copies to four liberal Republican congressmen who promised to read the statement to the House. Expecting to hear their proposal come from the mouths of Republicans, the NNRA and CRO were shocked when they instead heard a Democrat articulating their statement. "The attack on the Montgomery march was made by a Republican and answered by Democrats," an NNRA member grumbled. "That fact will be in every Negro newspaper in the Country." African American party members were livid at the notion that the black press would likely overlook the irony that an interracial Republican coalition had created the proposal; just as important, the NNRA was furious that RNC chair Ray Bliss had failed to intervene.[84]

The NNRA's disillusionment with the Republican Party marked an important shift in the organization's perspective on civil rights. When asked about this shift from aloofness to involvement, Clarence Townes theorized that it was impossible to be black and unaffected by the civil rights movement. "I lived it and felt all of the pain," insisted Townes. "I was involved."[85] For many black Republicans, the attacks on nonviolent civil rights activists compelled a personal response that went beyond simply promoting racial equality. After witnessing and participating in protests like "Bloody Sunday," where Alabama police brutally beat and assaulted more than six hundred nonviolent voting-rights marchers, it was inconceivable to NNRA members to maintain a quiet, behind-the-scenes approach to civil rights or remain withdrawn from civil rights organizations, regardless of philosophical differences. It was here that the 1965 voting rights bill emerged as a crucial component to the NNRA's investment in both the civil rights movement and the Republican Party. A legislative response to the constant pressure of civil rights activists and the devastation of the Selma marches, it struck down restrictions to electoral voting on the federal, state, and local levels, established a streamlined voter registration process, prohibited the use of poll and literacy tests, and provided the federal government with the power to facilitate and enforce the voting process.[86] The bill was an attempt to dismantle a notoriously virulent and violent system of black disenfranchisement; on average, in the six southern states explicitly targeted in the legislation—Alabama, Georgia, Louisiana, Mississippi, South Carolina, and Virginia—only 30 percent of African Americans were registered to vote; in the worst of these areas, like Mississippi, fewer than 7 percent of blacks had registered to vote in 1964.

The NNRA unequivocally supported the bill as voting rights stood at the heart of its campaign. Aside from their personal investment in the civil rights movement, members also believed that enfranchisement was the first step to political empowerment. This concept permeated the assembly's philosophy of the importance of two-party competition, the success of which rested on the NNRA's ability to register and recruit black voters. Succinctly illustrating this idea, reporter J. A. Rogers declared, "Negroes have been growing more and still powerfully politically since World War I. It is even more so now. Negroes are going to vote for the candidate who puts American citizenship entirely before color of skin."[87]

The NNRA urged Republicans to aggressively support the voting rights bill, insisting that it was an opportunity to demonstrate to African Americans that the party was committed to racial equality and thereby increase the likelihood of future support from the black electorate. And to some extent, white Republicans agreed. In February, thirty-one elected Republican officials issued a statement calling for Johnson to pass voting legislation. The politicians boasted of a voting rights bill introduced by Illinois congressman Donald Rumsfeld earlier in the month, contrasting it with the president's inaction during that same period. Indeed, many saw support for the legislation as an opportunity to wrest the civil rights mantle away from the Democratic Party and cast off the anti–civil rights legacy of Goldwater.[88]

Yet, in spite of this general agreement, the process was marred with tension, a fight that played out in public and attracted the ire of civil rights organizations and the NNRA. Within the House, Republicans objected to various provisions of Johnson's proposed version of the voting rights bill, arguing that it failed to combat discrimination and was arbitrary in its focus. Throughout the spring and summer of 1965, Republicans introduced alternative amendments, including one that would have broadened the scope of the administration's measure to include the entire nation. The GOP's protections including assigning federal voting registrants to areas where a minimum of twenty-five black voters had issued complaints and had evidence to support these claims. But its proposals also sanctioned literacy tests, so long as they were applied fairly to all races. Democrats, with the exception of the southern bloc, quickly denounced these alternative measures. "By sanctioning literacy tests in states that have plainly abused them in the past," they accused. "Republicans would be perpetuating the exclusion of unschooled Negroes while allowing illiterate whites to stay on the voting rolls." Republican leaders were aware of their proposal's shortcomings; as one congressman noted, "We knew we'd left a hole, but the only way to close it was to require re-registration of all voters in order to weed out white illiterates . . . our Southerners couldn't live with that sort of provision. . . . And they'd stretched so far to go along with the rest of the bill that we just couldn't run over them on this."[89]

The party's drawn-out negotiations over voting rights provoked swift and harsh responses from black leaders and officials alike and prompted new disagreements with RNC chair Ray Bliss. In June 1965, civil rights activists in Ohio picketed several local events honoring the national chairman, proclaiming their general impression of "Republican hostility to civil rights legislation."[90] The NNRA wrote to Bliss during the summer of 1965, again urging the chairman to vocalize his support for black constituents and to reject right-wing and southern pandering. Bliss did not respond, nor did he keep his January promise to meet with the leadership of the NNRA This prompted Jackie Robinson to use his syndicated newspaper column to question Bliss's commitment to rebuilding the GOP; he warned that no black voter would sacrifice his dignity to work for a party unable to decide what and whom it stood for:

> We are truly fed up with the brand of Republican which wants Negro loyalty and, at the same time, hopes to avoid offending the South . . . the Negro is no longer ignorantly and blindly voting for Mr. Lincoln or for Franklin Roosevelt. He is aware that both of these gentlemen are no longer with us—and in many instances neither are some of the principles for which they stood.[91]

The *New York Amsterdam News* agreed with Robinson and offered its own scathing indictment of recent events two weeks later. "We think that this is the height of stupidity," the self-proclaimed bipartisan editors wrote, "And we don't blame the Negro Republicans for being disgusted." Perplexed by the party's constant equivocation on issues of black concern, the writers stated, "It seems that it has always been hard for Republicans to look upon qualified Negro Republicans as an integral part of the Party. They have, instead attempted to treat Negro Republicans as some kind of dependent 'colony' from which they could 'take much and give little return.'" Bemoaning the party's stubbornness, the authors concluded by warning their readers that Republican officials had neither the will nor the way to call upon the members of the NNRA to help lead the party "out of the darkness."[92]

Members of the NNRA were incensed; despite assertions that black Republicans were the nuclei of party rebuilding efforts, Republican leaders continued to sidestep issues of black concern. And while many influential Republicans did emerge as allies in the battle for racial equality, black party members maintained that the image of the GOP as the "party of Goldwater" persisted, owing to the party's inability to comprehensively address racial issues. The assembly's response to the party's inconsistency was forceful: members increased their civil rights efforts and adopted a message of black Republican militancy. "Although there has been a great talk from so-called liberal Republicans," Jackie Robinson observed, "There seems to have been very little action." Members of the NNRA, he maintained, "intend to do more than just talk."[93]

THE MARCH TOWARD MILITANCY

On August 6, 1965, as Americans throughout the country watched on television and listened on their radios, Lyndon Johnson signed the Voting Rights Act into law. Seated in the Capitol Rotunda, flanked by statues of Abraham Lincoln and surrounded by an audience of eight hundred civil rights activists, politicians, and lawmakers, the president declared, "Today what is perhaps the last of the legal barriers is tumbling." For millions of citizens, this was a hard-earned accomplishment, a triumphant moment in the battle for equal rights. And for the NNRA, it was a resounding victory for black advancement as well as for the organization's philosophy of two-party competition.[94] For black Republicans generally, the GOP's role in the bipartisan passage of the act was certainly a relief—most Republicans in Congress had overcome their grievances with Lyndon Johnson and supported the president's version of the bill.[95]

Just five days later, on the opposite side of the country in the Watts section of Los Angeles, a white police officer arrested a young black man for driving under the influence, exacerbating long-simmering community issues over police brutality, inequality, and discrimination, triggering six days of horrific violence in the black neighborhood and beyond. By the time the rioting ended, the district had sustained more than $40 million in property damage. More than fifteen thousand National Guardsmen had been deployed; at least one thousand residents were hurt; and, most sobering of all, thirty-four people were dead, including twenty-five African Americans.[96] The devastation was a searing reminder that despite the utopian pronouncements that came with the passage of the Voting Rights Act, the fight for civil rights and equality was far from complete.

It was within this broad and nuanced context that the members of the NNRA added a new dimension to their already complex relationship with the Republican Party. Soon thereafter, assembly members intensified their party watchdog role, dedicating themselves to the promotion of racial equality, the resistance of white southern appeasement, and the ouster of Goldwater Republicans. In fact, just one day after Lyndon Johnson signed the Voting Rights Act into law, Jackie Robinson warned African Americans that the "conservative troops which marched behind Barry Goldwater" were still on "active duty." The Voting Rights Act was a political and social coup but only to the extent that African Americans mobilized and used their vote as a "potent weapon" in the two-party political system. The Watts riots added a new layer to Robinson's concerns; although highly critical of the violence in Los Angeles, he understood why it erupted. In an editorial written a week after Watts, he suggested that denying African Americans equal citizenship for so long had produced a generation "unafraid to die" and "intolerant of the virtues of patience"—black men and women who "don't slap first, nor will they turn the other cheek." As Robinson concluded, "the power structures . . . better get the message which burns in the hearts of this new Negro."[97] Taken together, his message was one of vigilance and power, one that was directed not only at his black readers but also at white politicians and officials—especially those within the GOP.

Moreover, the NNRA knew that some party leaders still hoped to win black votes, despite continued Republican missteps and various civil rights apprehensions. And with good reason—within a year of the Voting Rights Act, black registration in the targeted southern states surged by sixteen percentage points, hitting 46 percent. Mississippi offered the most dramatic results; though only 33 percent of African Americans were registered in the state, it was a massive increase from the 6.7 percent in 1964. These voters, however, were not registering as Republicans since, as a 1965 study discovered, "practically no Republican effort has been made." In Louisiana, for example, only 1,155 of 49,000 newly registered black voters identified as Republicans; certainly this was a "smack across the face" for the party, but it was a much needed one.[98] The NNRA therefore provided a timely means and strategy for recruiting from this new constituency; in turn, the party's need for voters provided the NNRA with the bargaining power it had desired since black Republicans had first gathered in their "war room" at the Fairmont Hotel in 1964. Ray Bliss certainly recognized this—in September 1965, in what was a remarkable step for the ordinarily sluggish RNC, Bliss agreed to institute one of the NNRA's long-standing recommendations: appointing a "prominent Negro GOP official" to the national committee. In a meeting with a group of black Republicans that included two NNRA members, Bliss promised that the black assistant would be "responsible only to the chairman" and would be assisted by an RNC-affiliated advisory council.[99]

The November 1965 election of John Lindsay as mayor of New York City reinforced this understanding. The congressman garnered 43 percent of the black vote, demonstrating that despite the Goldwater backlash, African Americans were not lost to the GOP. Those black voters who supported the politician did so because in Lindsay they saw someone who supported civil rights in both theory and practice, campaigned in black communities, and listened to African American concerns. They viewed him as an individual candidate, rather than a dogmatic torchbearer for the GOP. Here, Lindsay's election emerged as a critical part of the NNRA's narrative, demonstrating that Republicanism and civil rights were far from incompatible. His mayoral success also validated the group's belief in the importance of competing for and wooing black voters, since black voters had helped carry Lindsay to victory in 1965. The impact of black voters in New York City carried an important message: *neither* party could afford to ignore African Americans.[100] The "youthful" and "aggressive" leaders of the NNRA had pushed this theory for over a year, Jackie Robinson noted in a December column; what's more, the black assembly was right: Lindsay's win proved that black voters could be an effective part of a multiracial Republican coalition.[101]

Not surprisingly, party officials who once declined to meet with black Republicans soon showed a willingness to meet with NNRA delegates. In California, three gubernatorial candidates arranged for a special session with the state's NNRA chapter in March 1966. Gathering at the Miramar Hotel in Santa Monica, Republicans George Christopher, William Patrick, and Ronald Reagan addressed an audience of one hundred black party members and attempted to position themselves as supporters of issues of black concern. The conversation began smoothly enough with the three candidates criticizing the "unwanted federal paternalism" of the Democratic Party, insisting that African Americans be involved in GOP affairs, and apologizing for white Republicans' lapses in leadership.

Perhaps no candidate was more aware of this last point than Ronald Reagan, recognizing that black voters viewed him with suspicion because of his support of Barry Goldwater in 1964. His public opposition to the 1964 Civil Rights Act only added to this mistrust: had he been in Congress at the time, Reagan once declared, he "would not have voted for the civil rights bill." Consequently, he incorporated black outreach into his 1966 campaign, meeting with black political leaders, both Democrats and Republicans, throughout California.[102] Speaking with the California NNRA was but one way to assuage African American fears over his position on civil rights and race; moreover, it also provided a means for him to reassure white voters that he was not racist. During the meeting, he proclaimed his support for the equality premise of the Civil Rights Act but admitted that he viewed the actual law as unconstitutional. Qualifying his support for the 1964 party nominee, Reagan told the audience, "If I didn't know that Barry Goldwater was the opposite of a racist, I could not have supported him." Riled by such responses, George Smith, a NNRA member from San Diego, took a targeted jab at Reagan; while questioning the three candidates about equality, Smith criticized Reagan's ability to serve as governor, given his reference to the Civil Rights Act as a "bad piece of legislation." Seizing on the comment, Patrick tried to paint Reagan as a conservative extremist, calling the former actor's civil rights platform "indefensible." Joining the assault, Christopher declared that Reagan was dangerous because of his affiliation with the Goldwater campaign. "We're still paying the bill for that defeat," he blasted. "His situation still plagues the Republican Party. Unless we can cast out this image, we're going to suffer defeat now and in the future."

The heated accusations provoked a visceral reaction from the already-sensitive Reagan. As his face flushed, the angry conservative threw his note-cards to the floor, rocketing to his feet. In a voice "cracking with emotion," Reagan shouted that he resented the accusations of bigotry and the attack on his integrity. "I will not stand silent and let anyone imply that—in this or any other group," he bellowed to the stunned audience. Then, in a "display of temper"—or perhaps acting finesse—a teary-eyed Reagan stormed out of the room, clenching his fists and muttering inaudibly. He was so angry that he left the hotel and drove back to his Simi Valley estate; upon discovering the abrupt exit, event organizer and NNRA member James Flournoy—a Reagan supporter—drove the hour's ride to the candidate's home, and convinced the politician to return to Santa Monica for the evening session.

Attempting a cheerful demeanor at the NNRA's reception, but unable to mask his irritation, Reagan insisted that his anger was not directed at the members of the NNRA but rather at "demagogic inferences that I was a racist or a bigot." The politician attempted to alleviate the damage of his outburst by repeatedly vocalizing his support of civil rights on moral grounds, but as the other Republican gubernatorial candidates quickly noticed and criticized, Reagan also stood firm in his rejection of the constitutionality of the Civil Rights Act of 1964. The candidates' infighting was so intense that California GOP chair Gaylord Parkinson feared a repeat of the 1964 disaster, which led him to issue the "11th Commandment": "Thou Shall Not Speak Ill of a Fellow Republican."[103] Later in the campaign season, the GOP chairman attempted to downplay the discrimination charges against Reagan, telling *Time* magazine that if Reagan was elected, "you'll see Negroes and Mexican-Americans on [his] staff."[104]

The GOP chairman's official order may have silenced the intraparty fighting of the Republican gubernatorial candidates, but it did not prevent the NNRA from voicing its complaints. Lamenting the public spectacle, Reverend Laurence Thomas, an NNRA member from Oakland, revealed that he was "afraid the Republican Party in California—the power structure—actually does not understand the problems facing Negroes." Given the situation, Thomas concluded that he had no plans to leave the party; rather, it was necessary that he remain a "thorn in the flesh" of the GOP. James Flournoy also encouraged black Republicans to use the incident as motivation for increased political activity. "We want recognition on the national level, the state level—every level that we live in," he announced. "Just let us have something to say."[105]

Two months later, during their May 1966 convention, the California assembly members refused to endorse any of the Republican gubernatorial candidates, despite impassioned speeches delivered by Patrick and by Christopher's surrogate. Still recovering from his previous encounter with the NNRA, Reagan declined to attend the convention. Christopher was the clear favorite, as thirty-seven of the assembly delegates voted to support his candidacy. However, twenty NNRA members elected to endorse Reagan, attracted by his private-sector approach to solving economic problems; moreover, his outreach efforts convinced them that he was no "racist or bigot." Unable to come to a two-thirds majority consensus, the California assembly members decided not to endorse any of the candidates. Their silence was a political act of solidarity, designed to broadcast their apparent strength to the mainstream party despite the delegates' differing perspectives.

By contrast, assembly members agreed to endorse several politicians campaigning for local, state, and national office, including NNRA member James Flournoy, who was running for a Los Angeles congressional seat. They also passed two resolutions with little debate: the first declared their support for a California fair housing law, to prevent discrimination in the sale or rental of housing; the second called on the Republican Party to "adopt a platform plank specifically against discrimination by money-lending agencies." The convention was a significant event, demonstrating the power of the "largest Negro Republican organization of recent years," chapter vice-president Virgil Brown proudly announced. This was no exaggeration—the organization was the first and largest national black Republican group; by the spring of 1966, it had roughly one thousand members across the country, connecting groups of like-minded black GOP leaders with similar experiences, which in turn, made them feel less like party outsiders. Certainly, the NNRA also struggled to move beyond party bureaucracy in 1966; despite holding meetings, advancing strategy proposals, and offering progressive resolutions on civil rights, the organization was unable to generate substantial financial contributions or guarantee appointed positions in Republican-led state and local governments.[106] Nevertheless, the assembly's growing ranks had translated into a measure of political influence—party officials, politicians, and groups regularly consulted with the black organization on issues concerning African Americans and civil rights. In February 1966, for example, the Council of Republican Organizations elected Grant Reynolds as its chairman—in fact, NNRA members made up nearly half of the liberal and moderate interracial umbrella group's executive board. Likewise, that same month, Nelson Rockefeller appointed Jackie Robinson as special assistant on community affairs.[107]

But while the NNRA declared its California convention a success, in reality, the event actually exposed the ideological fractures that divided assembly members—the split over the gubernatorial candidates illustrated this tension. Moreover, even as Jackie Robinson publicly berated the actor-turned-politician on behalf of the NNRA, some black Republicans privately applauded Reagan's positions on limited federal government, private industry, business, and unemployment. "Every time we begin to talk Republicanism, we get emotional," complained one black Republican detailing his support for Reagan. "We think the Republicans won't do anything for Negroes, and this is a farce."[108] NNRA members' public displays of unity were purely symbolic, obscuring very real ideological disagreements; thus, as the NNRA marched steadily to the left of the political spectrum, it forced its more conservative and moderate members of the assembly to question the feasibility of black Republican solidarity.

In truth, party unity, regardless of ideology, was a theme heavily touted by the national committee, although the NNRA's relationship with the

RNC was anything but unified. It was so unstable and contentious that one reporter described it as a "hornet's nest."[109] The thorny situation was exacerbated further in the spring of 1966, when the RNC appointed former NNRA treasurer Clarence Townes as a high-ranking special assistant. The appointment was a political milestone of sorts: though African Americans had served as consultants to the RNC for decades, never before had an adviser been elevated to such a prominent position or given so much support. Townes's appointment appeared, at the very least, to be the type of insider access for which black Republicans had fought; but their victory was overshadowed amid the assembly's infighting, as his selection infuriated the more militant members of the group. Critics accused him of being too conservative, worrying that he would fail to promote a "vigorous program to regain Negro votes." Perhaps no one was angrier than Grant Reynolds; he had, after all, served as legal counsel to the RNC in the early 1960s, lobbied aggressively for a black RNC appointee, and represented the outspoken liberal wing of the NNRA since the group's founding. The editors at the *New York Herald Tribune* puzzled over the selection of Townes, as they had assumed Reynolds was the logical choice for the RNC position.[110] When asked by a reporter why he was not appointed, Reynolds brusquely retorted, "Bliss is used to telling Negroes what to do and not to do . . . and I refuse." Several political observers concurred, noting that the RNC rejected several prominent black Republican leaders for being "too aggressive and outspoken," characterizations that aptly described many of the more liberal NNRA leaders. Revealingly, an RNC press release detailing Townes's appointment made no mention of his involvement with the NNRA.[111]

Adding insult to injury, following Townes's appointment, Reynolds was accused of political corruption. His anonymous accusers (the Ripon Society fingered Townes and Bliss) charged Reynolds with using his NNRA office for "his own political purposes" and called his association with the NNRA "undesirable." Whether accurate or unfounded, the claims found fertile ground with some mainstream Republican groups, including state party chairmen from the Midwest, who discussed the topic at a regional meeting, and the Organization of Republican Women and the Michigan Organization of Republicans, whose members displayed a "noticeable coolness" toward Reynolds. The accusations also took root among the more moderate and conservative members of the NNRA, like Michigan delegate George Washington, who broached his complaints during an early May chapter meeting in 1966. The claims had a significant impact on other chapter members, particularly since the Michigan branch was sponsoring the NNRA's national convention at the end of May. Members feared that the controversy would affect participation; their concerns were confirmed when several prominent black leaders "returned unexpected word that they could not attend" after hearing the accusations against Reynolds.[112] Robust conference participation was critical in boosting the morale and financial success of the assembly and in providing valuable resources in the members' uphill battle to reintegrate and reform the GOP. In a May letter to Nelson Rockefeller, written days before the convention, Jackie Robinson articulated this concern, agonizing over the "tremendously difficult campaign among Negroes" that the Republican Party would face in the midterm elections. The anxious Robinson, however, did have a familiar solution: dismiss the accusations and instead bear down on the assembly's primary purpose, pressuring Republican officials to demonstrate sincerity and seriousness toward black voters and their issues.[113] The RNC also seemed to be of similar mind—accusations and rumors notwithstanding—showing an early interest in the NNRA convention, writing cheerful letters of support to assembly members, and donating party literature for distribution at the conference.[114]

On May 20, 70 delegates and 100 guests traveled to the Sheraton Cadillac Hotel in Detroit, Michigan, for the opening of the three-day national convention of the NNRA. One of the first events was a cocktail party, hosted by Clarence Townes as a way of introducing him, in his new RNC role, to the 170 conference participants. The lively gathering eventually gave way to a smaller private meeting in Townes's hotel room; there, he and a group of Michigan black Republicans conspired to bar Grant Reynolds from assuming control over the NNRA. The assembly was no more than a "paper organization" argued Townes; it was potentially useful to the RNC but only under the direction of new leadership. "He was there to save the convention," delegate Myron Wahls later recalled. "Grant Reynolds would bring about its destruction."

At first, the secretive backroom dealings of the black Republicans seemed overblown, as Reynolds was selected as president of the NNRA in a bloodless election on the third day of the conference; in fact, the entire slate of candidates was elected effortlessly, including Jackie Robinson as chair of the board of directors. Yet immediately following the victory, dozens of assembly dissenters—many from the Michigan delegation—launched a "Stop Reynolds" movement.[115] Aided by the members of the nominating committee, the anti-Reynolds faction reopened the election and challenged the presidency, nominating a thunderstruck Jackie Robinson. The showdown was a heated battle, wrote the Ripon Society, a "test of strength between Bliss-aligned forces and the independent, militant, Negro Republican leadership," devised by the RNC to throw the assembly into chaos and ultimately dismantle it.[116] Robinson viewed the onslaught in much the same way, forcibly declining the nomination and declaring, in an emotional statement, that Grant Reynolds was the only Republican "who could keep the organization together and give it the necessary political leadership." Still, there was little doubt that the political tug-of-war had an adverse impact on the assembly. Internally, it exacerbated the existing ideological differences between members; externally, it worsened the enmity that existed between the NNRA and the RNC. As one baffled white observer questioned, after watching the convention melee unfold, "how [can] these Negroes still be Republican, after Goldwater . . . and after the attack on their own leadership?"[117]

Though the political skirmish was still fresh in their minds, the NNRA delegates nevertheless managed to unite to produce a comprehensive national platform, consisting of twenty-three resolutions. The agenda reaffirmed the assembly's commitment to civil rights and racial equality and reflected the increasingly militant tone of the organization's leadership. Indeed, on the final day of the convention, the NNRA issued a statement declaring that it was "militantly dedicated to resolving" the problems of African Americans *and* the Republican Party, through nonviolent means.

Chief among the group's concerns was the challenge of the "Urban Ghetto." Condemning the Watts uprisings, the NNRA maintained that the conditions that led to the California riots—racism, segregation, discrimination, and police brutality used to "degrade and brutalize the Negro and the poor"—could be found in urban areas across the nation. Lest another city erupt, the NNRA urged party officials to strengthen federal civil rights legislation; to do so would mean advocating for "full integration" and enforcing fair practices in housing, education, and employment. On a local level, the organization called on cities and states to institute aggressive public and private economic measures that addressed chronic underemployment and unemployment. Likewise, the black group proposed rehabilitating relationships between African Americans and the police through local law enforcement training programs in "civil and human rights.

Other resolutions stressed the NNRA's continued interest in the power of the black ballot, as the assembly aligned itself with "other Negro and white organizations" in condemning persistent voter repression in the South. The group also proclaimed its support for the efforts of Illinois congressman Donald Rumsfeld, who had recently called for public hearings on black voter suppression in Mississippi. Such declarations highlighted the group's continued commitment to forging alliances with those mainstream party officials who advocated for civil rights. The collaborations were needed as they allowed for a wider range of interracial appeals to varying constituencies, an argument that convention delegates underscored when they boasted that both "Negro and white Americans look to the NNRA for civil rights leadership." Thus another plank in the agenda tackled the assembly's intention to become the first Republican organiza- tion to join the National Civil Rights Leadership Clearing House with the goal of sharing ideas and generating support from a new audience. Yet another resolution called for strategic coalition building with religious groups dedicated to promoting racial equality, such as the Episcopal So- ciety for Cultural and Racial Unity; as they had done in 1964, members speculated that an alliance with groups of the "Roman Catholic, Protes- tant, and Jewish faiths" would strengthen the NNRA's attempt to assume power within the hierarchy of the Republican machine.[118]

In forcefully repudiating the discriminatory practices of Republicans opposed to racial equality measures, the NNRA also attempted to brand the GOP as a viable political alternative for black voters. The assembly's militancy thereby mandated its aggressive opposition to all forms of in- traparty inequality. As such, after stressing the importance of primary elections in setting the tone and direction of the party, the NNRA voted to censure the gubernatorial candidacy of Ronald Reagan. In doing so, the national delegates sidestepped the recommendation of their Califor- nia peers, who had tussled over the issue just two weeks earlier. And while the organization also condemned southern Democrats, it reserved its harshest criticisms for those Republicans who advocated discrimina- tory ideology. As the delegates wrote in their final resolution:

> NNRA categorically, clearly, and without reservation, disavows and pledges its continued attack on the John Birch Society, the Ku Klux Klan, the National States Rights Party, the Communist Party and other . . . extremist organizations that abhor the fundamental processes of our form of government. . . . The NNRA further resolves that mem- bership in such organizations is absolutely inconsistent with member- ship and activity inside the Republican Party.

Amid their adamant proclamations, however, NNRA leaders admitted that the GOP faced a daunting task in increasing the size and strength of the party; nevertheless, black Republicans recoiled at the idea that the situation necessitated the open-arm welcome of fringe elements, in- cluding southern segregationists, whose interpretation of conservatism was the antithesis of that espoused by the NNRA. Instead, the assembly demanded that the party fill its political void by mobilizing individuals throughout the country "who are attracted to the traditional Republican principle of equal rights for all American citizens," lest the GOP be de- feated in the 1968 election.[119]

The ideas espoused by the NNRA were not unlike those of civil rights groups like the NAACP or the NUL; in truth, some aspects of the

NNRA's platform were actually more conservative than the agendas advanced by the moderate civil rights organizations. Though the NNRA did not explicitly demand welfare reform, for example, it *hinted* at doing so, denouncing the "inadequate, self-perpetuating and humanly destructive policies, programs and practices" of federal relief. Such language evoked a long history of antiwelfare rhetoric employed by black Republicans since the days of the New Deal and, in some respects, even called to mind conservative Republican denunciations of federal relief. However, the NNRA softened its stance by deploring the "man-in-the-house rule of welfare" as racist, echoing the complaints of prominent civil rights and social welfare groups including the NAACP Legal Defense and Education Fund (LDF).[120]

When compared against the rising radicalism of civil rights groups like the Student Non-Violent Coordinating Committee (SNCC), the NNRA's "militancy" actually appeared to be a traditional form of moderate black politics. Soon after being elected SNCC chair in the spring of 1966, Stokely Carmichael criticized two ideas advanced by the NNRA: he described integration as an "insidious subterfuge for white supremacy" and insisted "third parties were necessary because neither major party adequately provides representation for Negroes."[121] But where the assembly and Carmichael disagreed vehemently on philosophy and approach, they overlapped in their basic understandings of unity and power. Carmichael's August 1966 ruminations that African Americans should politically "organize themselves so they can speak from a position of power and strength rather than a position of weakness" sounded remarkably similar to Jackie Robinson's declaration, uttered nearly a year earlier, that African Americans needed a "riot of black unity" to "let the white power structure know that we can create a black power structure and that we do not intend to fight this battle as individuals or small groups, but as one people."[122]

Thus, when viewed within the context of the Republican Party, the NNRA's platform was indeed militant. The organization's vocal support for civil rights and racial equality, combative posturing on its demands, unwillingness to let white Republicans influence assembly affairs, rigid intolerance for the Goldwater faction of the party, and impatience with the slow pace of change within the GOP—all of these characteristics identified the NNRA as a militant black Republican organization. At the same time, the assembly constantly qualified its interpretation of militancy, insisting that "militant" also meant the pursuit of racial uplift and intraparty reform, through nonviolent means. Still, though *all* of the members of the NNRA rallied around racial equality and civil rights, only the liberal faction of the group embraced its pugnacious attitude. In other words, the organization's shift toward militancy alienated its more moderate and conservative members.

The May 1966 convention was a clarion call for black Republican militancy—one that insisted on the embrace of a philosophy that demanded change through aggressive action but left little room for a conservative or moderate black Republican approach, or even for those interested in partnering with the RNC. Nonetheless, in a revealing press conference held in the days following the NNRA's convention, Grant Reynolds and Jackie Robinson boasted that the gathering had improved solidarity among members, strengthened the resolve of the "militant wing of Negro Republicans," and proved that the assembly could be a "powerful force in building the Republican Party and the two-party system." Going forward, Reynolds speculated that the assembly would become stronger and more powerful, developing the "big muscle which the Negro vote can become."[123]

When probed about the RNC, the duo suggested that the NNRA neither welcomed nor desired the help of the national committee, instead preferring to focus on collaborations with the CRO and other, smaller liberal Republican organizations. "Ray Bliss and no one else is going to dictate to us," Robinson remarked. "I think we have made that clear."[124] He took a different but no less forceful approach in a May letter to Bliss; describing the assembly members' enthusiasm for an "all-out-effort" to bolster the Republican Party, Robinson championed the idea of working for the triumph of *principled* conservatism and the expansion of two-party politics but also declared that he was unwilling to absolve Bliss of wrongdoing, berating the RNC chair for interfering in the affairs of the black assembly. "We do not intend to be dictated to or taken over," wrote Robinson, with resentment. "We would not, could not, and should not seek to [help African Americans and the GOP] wearing the collar of an outside force."[125] This rigid stance, Robinson later explained in a June editorial, came from the NNRA being "born out of protest." Given these roots, assembly leaders believed that the organization should remain an "alert and militant instrument to be used for the good of the people." Independence was key to the NNRA's tricky position and its ability to act as both a vehicle and voice for both the black community and the Republican Party; members of the NNRA therefore argued that, as loyal members of the GOP, they had the right *and* responsibility to voice their concerns, rather than uniting under a false banner of party unity. Considering the value the organization placed on autonomy and voice, the NNRA had no choice but to forcefully resist any outside influence that might seek to dominate or corrupt it, thereby derailing its goals. Ironically, this decision weakened the organization at the very moment the

NNRA claimed to be at its strongest. Self-determination may have indicated autonomy, but it also meant no financial or moral assistance from the RNC; likewise, the group's militant position alienated members from across the country, leading to a loss of funding and support.

Throughout the summer of 1966, NNRA leaders grew increasingly vocal about the candidates they would and would not support. Nearly all of their ire was directed at Ronald Reagan, labeling him a less honest version of Goldwater. For assembly militants, the California politician embodied the "lunatic fringe right" of the GOP, despite his polished and friendly Hollywood veneer; consequently, members of the NNRA viewed his boilerplate responses and efforts to campaign among black voters as fraudulent.[126] Among NNRA leaders, Robinson's zealous opposition to Reagan was unique, compelling the sports legend to violate a key assembly principle when he joined the reelection campaign of California governor Pat Brown, a Democrat. As with Republicans for Johnson in 1964, Robinson had no qualms in 1966 about urging black voters to reject two-party competition—at least as it applied to Ronald Reagan in California. To the NNRA leader, campaigning against the party's nominee was a logical extension of the assembly's militant work, since a victory for Reagan was a victory for Goldwater Republicanism. Moreover, Robinson's endorsement, although extreme, demonstrated the NNRA's belief that Republicans had to embrace civil rights measures, lest they lose black voters to the Democratic Party.[127]

If Ronald Reagan represented the consistent threat of right-wing conservatism in 1966, then, for Jackie Robinson, Nelson Rockefeller certainly symbolized a "return to 'progressive Republicanism.'" While campaigning against the California Republican, Robinson simultaneously worked for the reelection of the New York governor, calling the effort "one of the most rewarding experiences of my life"—a sentiment shared by the New York chapter of the NNRA.[128] Members invested time and finances into aiding the Rockefeller camp, viewing the governor as a significant ally in the fight for racial equality. Attorney Joseph Williams, for example, arranged community meetings in Harlem and Brooklyn, with the aid of Jackie Robinson and local black ministers; the sessions informed black voters about Rockefeller's record of civil rights philanthropy and his "gubernatorial programs that "favored poor persons in need of education, medical insurance, and housing rights." Branching out into previously untapped areas, New York NNRA members created an antipoverty task force in 1966; held several fundraisers, including a yacht cruise down the Hudson River for "hundreds of influential brothers"; and ran pro-Rockefeller advertisements in the *New York Amsterdam News* and *Jet*. But although they wrestled with economic and racial inequality in their campaign appeals, members' efforts were still informed by their middle-class biases—the New York chapter's slogan, for example, was "Rockefeller . . . We Need Him More Than He Needs the Job" a catchphrase that surely rankled those black voters who had complained of the governor's paternalistic attitude toward African Americans.[129] Still, many African Americans responded to the NNRA's overtures: "For the first time in my life, I felt we could win the Negro vote with an even greater margin than Mayor Lindsay," Jackie Robinson wrote to Rockefeller, after attending several black outreach events. "Without bragging, I feel I have made great gains for you. The door is open . . . you have a chance to move in and grab this vote. Let's move to solidify it."[130]

A day before the November midterm election, the NNRA distributed its annual press release outlining its concern for the problems faced by the nation and its black citizens, voicing its disapproval of the "extremist" faction of the GOP and suggesting that the party was ripe for gains from black voters; the assembly argued that Republicans on the state and local level had "far outshone the Democrats in civil rights and in genuine progress in the field of human dignity." The assembly offered eighty-two endorsements for liberal and moderate Republican candidates, including incumbents Governor Nelson Rockefeller and Congressman Donald Rumsfeld of Illinois, in addition to Maryland gubernatorial challenger Spiro T. Agnew and Massachusetts senatorial candidate Edward Brooke.[131] The midterm elections proved to be a success for the black assembly; dozens of NNRA-endorsed Republicans won their campaigns; Rockefeller, for instance, won reelection in New York with the support of 35 percent of the black vote. And while some of the party's gains disheartened the militant leaders of the group (particularly South Carolina senator Strom Thurmond's first win as a Republican and Ronald Reagan's California gubernatorial victory), they were still exuberant over the victories of liberal and moderate party officials, especially the triumph of Brooke, the first black senator elected since Reconstruction. "We've got a two-party system going again," Grant Reynolds declared to *Jet* two weeks after the November election. "For the next two years, we'll have a new ball game."[132]

• • •

Between 1964 and 1966, the NNRA—a small splinter group born out of protest—had established itself as an important organization in a revitalized Republican Party, playing a crucial, yet understated role in the spread of liberal party philosophy and promoting a vision of uplift that paralleled the goals of moderate civil rights organizations. The assembly's urgency also contributed toward a broader shift in party attitudes toward black voters, as party officials, irrespective of ideology, increasingly considered the merits of including African Americans in party outreach efforts.

This suggested there was space in the mainstream party for groups like the NNRA and that the organization would thrive, as its leaders predicted in the spring of 1966; at one point, Grant Reynolds insisted that as an "out-of-favor irritant," he could provoke the GOP into "doing what is essential to the party's salvation."[133] But nothing was further from the truth. After the midterm elections, the assembly all but disappeared, with the exception of the New York division—not coincidently, the chapter of Grant Reynolds and Jackie Robinson. Six months after the midterm election, aided by funds from Nelson Rockefeller, forty delegates from New York state met in Albany to discuss the future of the GOP. Though excited about the party's liberal and moderate gains, the representatives nevertheless declared that little about the GOP had changed. The group issued a five-hundred-word position paper warning of a brewing "major revolt among Afro-American Republicans." The statements contained within were indistinguishable from the manifesto issued by black delegates at the 1964 Republican National Convention. For the remaining active members of the NNRA, it was as if nothing had changed over the course of three years; for them, the party remained tainted by Goldwater's legacy—its direction driven by his reactionary successors, despite the presence of the party's liberal and moderate factions. Believing that the GOP was ever on the cusp of a nightmarish return to 1964, the NNRA asserted that its members refused to "sell out their principles" and "become the creatures of either great white fathers or black uncle toms."[134] The assembly's position paper took a pessimistic view of party affairs, condemning the RNC for its failure to support, both morally and financially, the outreach initiatives of the NNRA and "responsible and effective" black leaders; this was a baffling argument, coming from a group that prided itself on its autonomy and had resisted ties to the national committee. In truth, however, this was a reflection of the difficulties faced by the organization: without institutional support from the national GOP, the group struggled to enact its grass-roots political agenda.[135]

A little over a year later, Grant Reynolds, Jackie Robinson, and five other NNRA officials joined more than 150 "concerned" black Republicans to discuss African Americans' participation in the GOP and the party's resistance to change. From this meeting, the delegates would form the National Council of Concerned Afro American Republicans (NCCAAR). Though the group appeared identical to the NNRA, it was not: where the NNRA had argued that the policies and philosophies of conservative

Republicans were discriminatory, NCCAAR insisted that the *structure* of the party apparatus was discriminatory. In other words, the NNRA uniformly rejected Barry Goldwater, Ronald Reagan, and eventually even Richard Nixon, whereas the NCCAAR solely railed against black exclusion from the party hierarchy. Illustrating this point: as Jackie Robinson denounced Nixon as a covert racist in the fall of 1968, NCCAAR's Michigan chapter issued a press release endorsing the crafty politician.[136] This was the NNRA's central dilemma; though its members anointed themselves the authentic and unified voice of black Republicanism, they articulated only a liberal perspective. And while members' initially believed that their shared racial experience and concern for civil rights was enough to unite them, their approaches were too divergent to last.

The enactment of the civil rights acts of the mid-1960s, coupled with white Republicans' rejection of segregationist appeals and embrace of "colorblind" outreach, gave some black Republicans the latitude to support candidates and leaders that they would not support earlier. Yet for others, including the militant leaders of the NNRA, this evolution was impossible, particularly since many white Republicans continued to equivocate over race, even as they championed the significance of the black vote. Jackie Robinson, for example, changed his affiliation to independent in August 1968 and disavowed the Republican Party, arguing that a few gestures and overtures did not demonstrate a genuine concern for African American needs. "I'm a black man first," he calmly stated while appearing in a 1968 television interview, "an American second and then I will support a political party—third."[137]

In this respect, the rise and fall of the NNRA tells a significant story; as the organization began to achieve some of its civil rights objectives, standing on the cusp of *real* power, it disintegrated. In fact, the group's successes indirectly allowed the ideological differences of the group members to rise to the surface. The organization's militant tone left little room for a moderate or conservative black Republican approach, a pragmatic approach that would come to influence party politics for decades to come.

CHAPTER THREE

The Challenge of Change

IN NOVEMBER 1966, IN ONE OF THE COUNTRY'S MOST INTENSE SENATO-rial races, Massachusetts attorney general Edward W. Brooke stunned the nation when he soundly defeated his Democratic challenger, Endicott Peabody. Earning the support of more than 60 percent of the Massachusetts electorate, Brooke skirted the political bureaucracy of a volatile Republican Party to become the first black senator since Reconstruction. His triumph occurred in the midst of a nationwide white backlash, an onslaught of the "worst displays of anti-Negro feelings which [lay] in the souls of whites."[1] Brooke's victory was a tremendous statewide upset; but more than that, his success represented a transformative moment in the rapidly changing arena of racial politics in America. Newspapers and magazines cheered the "progressive" nature of the Massachusetts electorate, while political commentators described the black official as the "hope of the nation," the "hope of his party," and the "future of American politics." As California representative W. E. Barnett proclaimed at Brooke's senatorial swearing-in ceremony, this was the type of landmark event that had the potential to renew the "confidence and faith" of the American public; one noted magazine even gushed that the senator was the "change that America . . . needs." Brooke's rapid rise, another political observer concluded, would soon "shatter the myth that the country wasn't ready for a black president."[2]

In truth, Edward Brooke's election was also a moment of profound achievement for both black Republicans and the larger GOP apparatus. Viewed as a political phenomenon, he not only represented the abstract goals of the National Negro Republican Assembly but also captured an image that moderate and liberal Republican leaders had struggled to harness since Barry Goldwater's unnerving rise in 1964; for a party traumatized in the aftermath of defeat, Brooke provided much needed proof that moderate Republican candidates could appeal to an interracial cross section of the American public. Drawing on a broader black middle-class tradition of respectability politics, he won his elections by running a campaign that was simultaneously race neutral and race conscious—a paradox, to be sure, but one that allowed an interracial audience to embrace him and his politics. His role in American political life reflected the convergence of civil rights and American conservatism, anointing him a "winner" in party circles during a period when the GOP was struggling to define its philosophy and its identity. Consequently, his intraparty influence was at its peak in the four years following the 1964 election. Using his prominence as a platform, he successfully lobbied the mainstream GOP to adopt centrist policies rooted in ideas of racial egalitarianism, insisting that it was possible for the party to merge liberal ideas about race with traditionally conservative principles, so as to create solutions that addressed the needs of the American electorate.

For black Republican leaders, mired in the sludge of party bureaucracy and equivocation, Brooke was a prototype for action; even as they argued among themselves over ideology and strategy, they rallied around the black official. In particular, those who worked for the Minorities Division of the Republican National Committee charted a moderate course modeled on Brooke's centrist approach to politics, electing to work with rather than independent of the national committee, instituting a series of important—if flawed—plans for repairing the broken relationship between African Americans and the Republican Party.

To be sure, Brooke was an enigma to both the nation and his party. As a black Protestant Republican in a predominately white Catholic Democratic state, he confused even the most seasoned politicians, including Richard Nixon.[3] He offered paradoxical ideas and engaged in contradictory behaviors—so much so that it is difficult to classify him; thus any understanding of him needs to embrace the paradox that he—and other black Republicans—represented. In many ways, he was attempting to do something that had never before been done in the postwar era: be a black Republican on a national stage. And while there were many black Republicans working on the state and local level and within national organizations, Brooke became a pivotal figure who moved beyond this to an elected position in the Senate that had nationwide implications.

Toward a Theory of Progressive Conservatism

"Ed Brooke," wrote *Time* magazine, "runs hard—'like a Democrat.'"[4] The editors were referencing the Massachusetts politician's 1962 campaign for the state attorney general position—running on a hearty law-and-order platform, the young Republican used his easy manner and quick intelligence to capture a decisive political victory.[5] Cheering Brooke's win as a turning point in American race relations, the *Pittsburgh Courier* declared that the election meant that "qualified Negro candidates would be supported on the basis of merit rather than racial ancestry" and that black voters "would support candidates on the basis of their commitment to issues instead of party politics."[6] To be sure, Brooke fought fiercely to convince African Americans to join the Republican Party, urging black voters to make the most of their political power. Eager to reintegrate the party, the ambitious official proclaimed that he was part of a new generation of Republican politicians, ready for change.[7]

This new cadre of leadership to which Brooke referred, however, was distinct from that of autonomous black Republican groups like the NNRA. Outside of the GOP, both he and the members of the black assembly embraced the moderate black politics approach to civil rights struggles. Brooke, for instance, once served as the president of the Boston chapter of the NAACP and vice-president of the local Urban League. Within the GOP, he molded himself after the state's elected Republican politicians, like Congressman Joseph W. Martin Jr., Senator Leverett Saltonstall, and Herbert L. Jackson—a black party official repeatedly elected to municipal office in the 1940s and 1950s by a predominately white constituency in Malden.

This embrace of civil rights and the Republican Party was, to some extent, a reflection of Brooke's upbringing. Born into a middle-class black family in Washington, D.C., in 1919, he was raised in an environment that was racially segregated but insulated from the harsh realities of the Deep South. As Brooke understood it, his segregation was subtler but was no less real: he rarely interacted with the white community and was protected from most, if not all, of the blunt realities of racial discrimination and violence. Still, upon graduating from Howard University, Brooke was quickly indoctrinated into racism's very tangible reality. Soon thereafter, he enlisted in the army, fighting as part of a segregated combat unit during World War II, an experience that took him to North Africa and Italy over the course of five years; his time in the military was instrumental in forcing him to reconsider his "veneration" of Franklin Roosevelt, given the president's unwillingness to desegregate the military.[8]

He returned from the war intent on pursuing a career in social justice and politics, an ambition he shared with thousands of returning black soldiers. Moreover, as was the case with scores of black Republicans, his political interests were informed by the "principles of traditional conservatism," or a belief in self-help, personal responsibility and accountability, free market enterprise and capitalism, limited government, and a "conservative regard for history and precedent." As he later explained in his memoirs, he was inspired by the legacy of Abraham Lincoln and Theodore Roosevelt, declaring the "government should do for the people only that which they cannot do for themselves." Yet this understanding of traditional conservatism was flexible enough to take into account the economic and social realities of modern society; hence, Brooke reasoned that there were times when "government must do for the people—most notably in the area of American civil rights." Coming of political age in Massachusetts during the Eisenhower era, he witnessed Massachusetts Republicans enacting antidiscrimination measures, while Democrats resisted them; thus, as he perceived it, the GOP was the party of the future while the Democratic Party was "devoid of ideas."[9]

He was adamant that the GOP was truly the party of the American people and the "common man," announcing, for example, to an audience at the Massachusetts Republican Convention in 1960: "We are a united party and will destroy the myths of class, race, creed, wealth, antilabor, suburbia, which the Democratic Party attempted to shackle us with." Like many black Republicans, Brooke viewed civil rights as inherent to the Republican code, as the Constitution guaranteed freedom of equality for all citizens. Support for equal rights, he declared, was "merely a reaffirmation of our principle 'with liberty and justice for all.'"[10] Such rhetoric leaned heavily on the "Party of Lincoln" trope, casting Republicans as the civil rights protectors not only of the individual but also of the collective nation, irrespective of race; though mostly bombastic political rhetoric, his allusion to slavery was somewhat fitting, since he characterized Democrats as historical and contemporary oppressors.

Given such impassioned sentiments, it was unsurprising that Brooke considered Barry Goldwater's presidential nomination offensive. He found the candidate's repeated public opposition to civil rights legislation painful, considering his interpretation of the party's core values. Brooke publicly broke with the GOP's nomination after the 1964 convention, imploring Republicans not to invest in the "pseudoconservatism of zealots." To do so, he argued, would be a devastating rejection of the better part of Republican ideals and tradition; conservatism with blatant ties to segregation and racism would be an "insult to the origins and history of the party.[11] He took little comfort from the presence of other black delegates to the national convention; he did not huddle in the black Republican war room at the Fairmont Hotel, nor did he help draft the "Negro Position Paper." He did, however, adopt a similar philosophy to the African American delegates when he chose "not to walk out" of the party but rather to stay and "fight it out," and he authorized the use of his name in support of their manifesto.

Likewise, throughout the fall of 1964, he consistently refused to endorse Goldwater, a public and vehement repudiation of the Arizona senator that ultimately helped the attorney general win a landslide reelection in 1964.[12] In a year when voters, of all races and backgrounds, ran from the national party in droves, Brooke won by a plurality of nearly 800,000 votes—the highest margin of victory of any Republican candidate in the nation. His rejection of Goldwater, of course, was not the only reason for his win: after all, Brooke was a popular state attorney general, well-liked among nearly all of his Massachusetts constituents, who declared that he had done an "outstanding" job in getting rid of crime.[13]

With the sharp contrast between his decisive victory and the nation-wide electoral woes of the Republican Party, Brooke instantly became a voice of authority in the quest to understand the devastation of the 1964 contest and how the party could recover from its massive failure. Less than a week after the November 3 election, Brooke and Republican politician John Lindsay appeared on NBC's *Meet the Press*; in this interview, as well as with subsequent appearances, the black official called the election the "worst he'd ever seen." Goldwater's candidacy deprived voters of choice and "backed Negroes into a corner," leaving them no option other than voting for the Democratic nominee or abstaining altogether.[14] President Johnson, Brooke railed, "had *not* been challenged; he did *not* have to defend the policies and programs he had set before the nation and was proposing for the future. What did he have to defend them against?" In short, the Republican Party had failed by allowing Lyndon Johnson to secure the White House "by default."[15]

Much like the members of the NNRA, Brooke suggested that African Americans shared a common bond over issues of racial equality. This community loyalty was "something they are born with, that they have to live with," he explained. A vote for Goldwater then, was akin to being a traitor to the race and to the cause of civil rights. Yet one's blackness did not guarantee a blanket acceptance of the programs and policies of the Johnson administration; to the contrary, Brooke insisted, for many it simply represented an "anti-Goldwater vote." For Brooke then, as with other black Republicans, the real damage of the 1964 election was the public's "measurable" distrust in the Republican Party. Devoid of tangible assets, ideas, programs, and solutions, the GOP appeared to lack both purpose and direction. "You can't say that the Negro left the Republican Party," Brooke reasoned, "I'm convinced that the Negro feels like he was evicted."[16]

Encouraged by an outpouring of positive responses, the spirited attorney general continued to offer blunt criticisms of his party in the months following the election. But even more important, he began to soften his rhetoric and spend more time proposing strategies for Republican revival.[17] Chief among these was his suggestion that the party hold an off-year national convention; he even urged Goldwater and his supporters to attend, so that party members of all ideological leanings could "hammer out an agreement for the future of the party" and draft a responsible platform to address economic and social issues of importance to African Americans, women, the elderly, and the poor—the "very groups that had rejected the party in droves."[18] In February 1965, while speaking to an audience of two thousand at a Lincoln-Douglass dinner hosted by Cleveland's Eighteenth Ward Republican Club, he proposed that "true" Republicans should seize control of the national organization and start presenting positive programs of action to subvert the party's image as "do-nothing reactionaries."[19] Accomplishing such a task would never be simple, Brooke admitted; nonetheless, the party could begin to make inroads to the "Negro problem" by demonstrating clear support for the enforcement of the Civil Rights Act of 1964 and reintegrating the party by welcoming the "sons, the grandsons, and the great grandsons of slaves."[20]

Brooke's emergence as a Republican spokesman for racial equality was notable, for, as *Time* observed, the attorney general "never rallied his race to challenge segregation barriers with the inspirational fervor of a Martin Luther King" and had "triggered none of the frustrated fury of a Stokely Carmichael."[21] Writer Chuck Stone, in his 1968 assessment of black political leadership, would later label Brooke the archetype of "non-Negro politics," or a politician who "happened to be black."[22] Although Stone used the phrase with scorn, "non-Negro politics" is still a useful term, for it contextualizes Brooke's often-contradictory approach to state and national politics. His race, as the *Call and Post* assessed in a July 1964 editorial, forced the politician to walk a political tightrope. As an elected official from a predominately white state, he could not push too hard for civil rights lest he alienate his constituents. At the same time, his race *required* that he vigorously support and work for equal citizenship—to ignore this community mandate would mean earning the title of a self-hating "Uncle Tom" from black voters.[23]

Brooke addressed this dilemma by modifying his rhetoric to reflect his audience and environment; for instance, while speaking in front of a predominately black crowd of seventy-five hundred in Boston in the spring of 1963, the attorney general expressed support for the African American men, women, and children who had been viciously assaulted by white segregationists in Birmingham in April and May of that year. "The pressure is mounting," he told his audience, "It has been smoldering for some time—many, many years. And it is a justifiable impatience." Three months later, as the keynote speaker for the annual National Urban League convention, Brooke reiterated his support for the civil rights movement, declaring that demonstrations were "useful" for "dramatizing the discrimination problem." He closed his speech by calling for the organization to "redouble its efforts" to desegregate business and labor and to continue its push for equal rights—even in places like Massachusetts, where prejudice, he argued, persisted, albeit on a far subtler level than in the South.[24]

Less than a year later, Brooke offered a very different perspective on the civil rights movement to the audience of *Harper's Magazine*, stating that he was solely concerned with political results. "Boycotts, sit-ins, and demonstrations don't achieve the desired consequences in the Commonwealth," he argued. "On the contrary, they merely intensify the resentment of the population at large and undermine the best interests of the Negro community. I believe the Negro must win allies, not conquer adversaries."[25] This rhetoric also corroborated with his strict enforcement of the law—in 1963, he had angered a group of black citizens when he ruled that a proposed boycott of Boston's segregated schools was illegal, reasoning that his decision was fair since the law prohibited children from being kept out of schools.[26] In truth, though his shift in language appeared contradictory, Brooke had long believed that legislation, produced through interracial coalition building, was the best approach to achieve civil rights gains. In this respect, law and order did not simply mean the strict enforcement of the law; it also represented Brooke's belief that changing the laws themselves was the most efficient way to enact societal change. Thus, while Brooke felt *empathy* for protestors and demonstrators, and agreed with their goals, he could still find fault with their methods and approaches.

Furthermore, the black attorney general's interpretation of the law was just as much about conflicting ideas about approaches to racial uplift as it was about assuaging white fears. While articulating his commitment to ending racial inequality for African Americans as a collective group, Brooke simultaneously reassured white voters that he respected their individual rights. Here, Brooke employed both race-neutral and race-conscious strategies when dealing with black and white communities. "I see myself as Attorney General of *all* the people," he declared in 1964. "The moment I become a specifically *Negro* Attorney General I cease to do justice to my office and in fact I squander whatever effectiveness I might have in advancing civil rights."[27] In his 1972 biography of the black politician, historian John Henry Cutler explored this balancing act, arguing that Brooke recognized the "difference between theory and practice." He was as "anxious as black militants" to enrich the lives of African Americans, but he also understood that he could make gains for civil rights by engaging in "pragmatic" identity politics.[28]

These tactics, Brooke further asserted, effectively nullified the persistent stereotype among white constituents that black politicians could not govern intelligently.[29] More important, perhaps, was his belief that, as an elected official, he could influence his party's philosophy and push racially egalitarian policies rooted in social justice. This embrace of a civil rights agenda and "non-Negro politics" is made all the more important given his conservative views. Certainly, a number of Brooke's philosophies came as a "shock" to many—for instance, in 1965 he lobbied forcefully for increased accountability among African Americans: "In this respect, I'm purely Republican. I believe very strongly in self-help. Otherwise, you make parasites out of people. Sometimes, if you have too many crutches, you will never learn to walk. . . . Hand in hand with the legal battles and demonstrations, there must go self-help. There must go with this quest for equal opportunity an awareness of equal responsibility."[30] Such views earned the black official his share of black and white critics, including Chuck Stone, who once referred to Brooke as a "Colored Honkie." Along similar lines, the editor of the *Harvard Crimson* coolly dismissed Brooke as an "Uncle Tom," who "plays the role well," citing, among other things, the fact that the politician was president of the Boston Opera House: "A softvoiced [sic] and articulate speaker, he only vaguely looks like a Negro."[31]

Most voters in Massachusetts in 1965, of all races, found such opinions irrelevant. A 1965 statewide poll found that voters, irrespective of partisan identification, simply *liked* the attorney general, with fewer than 3 percent of constituents defining him as either "too conservative" or "too liberal." His middle-class image—a reflection of both his upbringing and his Republican affiliation—was the one area of concern for voters; fewer than twenty of respondents believed that the black politician was interested in the poor and unemployed, or was on the "side of the Workingman." Yet even here, only 2 percent of voters believed that Brooke was "biased in favor of the rich."[32]

With his calculated approach to American politics, as well as his emergence as a "ballot box sensation," Brooke generated intense national interest. His crushing success amid the party's electoral disaster in 1964 elevated his status to that of a Republican leader who, as the *Washington Post* theorized, could "potentially do more than any other to win back Negro votes." Quite a few prominent officials pushed the attorney general as the centerpiece of a GOP revival, including Dean Burch; while speaking with a group of young and disgruntled Goldwater supporters in February 1965, the former RNC chair begged his audience to "pay attention" to the black politician, insisting that Brooke had the ability to solve the party's "Negro vote" problem. Burch also argued that the party should work to retain Goldwater's gains in the South, doing so without relying on "racist appeals, overt or covert." Instead, the GOP should emphasize economic change, irrespective of race. That same month, Bill

Brock of Tennessee, one of the few Republican congressmen to vote against the 1964 Civil Rights Act, told a group of white GOP officials that conservatism and segregation were "incompatible philosophies." It is "impossible to believe in the worth and dignity of the individual," he stated, critiquing his own vote against the civil rights legislation, "while denying some individuals their full rights." Importantly, one of Brock's proposals for reviving the GOP involved Brooke; the politician urged southern Republican legislators to meet with the black official in order to find common philosophical ground on civil rights and conservatism.[33]

In March 1965 Richard Nixon led a strategy session in Washington, D.C., that identified Brooke as a logical choice to serve as a liaison between African Americans and the Republican Party, whose responsibility would also include analyzing issues of black concern. Attempting to assess the former vice president's interest in black voters, the *New York Times* highlighted that the ever-shrewd Nixon believed that contributing to racial advancement would boost the party's future prospects with African Americans, especially since the black electorate was poised to swell with the passage of voting rights legislation. To these ends, the party launched initiatives like the "Republican sponsored public service announcements" on civil rights, distributed to black radio stations throughout the country in 1965. During the radio programs, Brooke discussed race-related issues, interweaving them with his recommendations on urban disorder, housing, and health care. Prominent party officials also appeared on the show, offering commentary and offering GOP-related solutions.

The *Pittsburgh Courier* speculated that such approval indicated that GOP leaders were grooming Brooke to be the vice presidential nominee in 1968. Such a nomination would strengthen the Republican machine, the editors reasoned, since it would destroy the "honeymoon relationship" between the Democratic Party and black voters.[34] The attorney general's early collaborative relationship with the upper echelons of the party, however, spoke more to his interest in changing the party's philosophy rather than any calculated designs on the vice presidency. For Brooke, solutions to the party's deep-seated woes had to begin with a substantial overhaul of Republican ideology. Survival rested on "constructive innovation," an idea he and an aide from the Ripon Society fleshed out in a draft of an April 1965 speech to the National Press Club.[35] In a tightly worded four-page outline, Brooke suggested that the GOP needed to invest in domestic issues in a completely different manner; rather than reacting to the initiatives of the Democratic Party, Republicans should propose their own creative measures to address the civil rights and equality issues facing the American population. Brooke and his aide specifically focused on domestic housing policies, arguing that Republicans could "seize the

initiative," for example, by calling for the creation of rehabilitation programs in low-income neighborhoods, to foster "pride and self respect" in
local residents.

It is worth noting that these ideas were far from groundbreaking; instead, they were rough and incomplete thoughts, often vague, as Brooke
had no experience writing policy. Nevertheless, constructive innovation
appeared novel within the context of a party desperate to shed the image
of Barry Goldwater. The concept had political implications—policies
rooted in constructive innovation could easily attract voters, of all races
that were interested in moderate approaches to urban issues.[36] Here then,
constructive innovation was Brooke's way of placing concern for equal
rights squarely within a Republican framework; in no uncertain terms,
he insisted that the party advance "forward-thinking" ideas or risk being
on the wrong side of history. Moreover, his line of thinking suggested that
by building equality measures into the fabric of the party, and excluding
racists and extremists, civil rights would no longer be a deciding factor
in American politics. Voters—especially African Americans—could then
choose to embrace "authentic" conservatism if they so desired, as it no
longer conflicted with their reality.

Brooke's faith that African Americans would choose the Republican
Party mirrored the insistence of the NNRA and other black Republicans
as they gradually recovered from the Goldwater disaster. In April 1965,
NNRA member Clarence Townes offered an interpretation suggesting
that the full appeal of the party lay in its history, principles, and traditions: "If conservatism means the preservation of our traditional doctrine
of equality, liberty, freedom and constitutional guarantees of the pursuit
of happiness," he proclaimed, "then the American Negro citizen is a most
dedicated conservative."[37] That same month, journalist Lillian Calhoun
also tapped into this sentiment, levying a warning to the GOP at the same
time. The black Chicagoan implored the party to correct its ideology or
"keep losing elections." African Americans may have voted in droves for
Lyndon Johnson, she argued, but some black voters were open and receptive to the GOP, but only if the party was genuinely committed to racial
equality and civil rights. If the party refused to challenge its reactionary
wing, Calhoun warned, "Even Jesus running on the Republican ticket
might not get a respectable vote."[38]

Brooke characterized his approach at length in his book *The Challenge
of Change: Crisis in Our Two-Party System*, released in March 1966. In
it he elaborated on his growing number of policy proposals, expanding
those suggestions into an ideological commitment to "progressive conservatism," a philosophy markedly different from the theory advanced by
Barry Goldwater in 1961.[39] In their intellectual treatises on conservatism,

both party leaders cast themselves as "progressive" reformers, intent on reshaping the Republican Party; but where the Arizona senator argued that civil rights legislation was outside the scope of conservatism, Brooke insisted on the opposite. In his review of *Challenge*, Jackie Robinson referred to it as a "brilliant" work that offered a "sound and eloquent analysis" of the Republican Party. Other critics delivered equally effusive praise, with one calling the book a brilliant manifesto for the two-party system that pointed the way to a "renaissance and reestablishment" of the GOP.[40]

Much of the significance of *Challenge* rested in its demand for Republican-initiated policies and programs that addressed the needs of all the nation's citizens. "We are not merely the minority party," Brooke wrote, "we are the *perennial* minority party." Republicans would continue in this state, he argued, so long as they resisted genuine appeals to minorities: "Democrats have not won them so much as we have lost them. In fact, we all but exiled them." The party's biggest weakness was its failure to produce authentic solutions, he argued, whereas the Democratic Party, since the days of the New Deal, had sought new answers and proposed and implemented new legislation. As such, the GOP had assumed a public identity characterized by its "dogged determination to speak out *against* the proposals of others."[41] Insisting the party look to its history, Brooke claimed that Lincoln and subsequent Republican leaders had once embraced "daring and radical measures" when the times demanded it, some even going so far as to use government as an instrument of social betterment; thus, an "eagerness to meet the challenge of change, to innovate, to channel new social and economic forces within new political institutions . . . was entirely in harmony with . . . the spirit that made the party great."[42] Though Brooke indicated that he shared Barry Goldwater's belief that the GOP should stand firmly for conservatism, he ultimately pegged the Arizona senator's interpretation as distorted as it denied the responsibility of government to *every* American. Here then, one of the most important contributions offered by *Challenge* comes when we contrast the text to *Conscience of a Conservative*: Brooke's interpretation of liberty and freedom was inclusive, whereas Goldwater's perspective, whether deliberate or unintentional, conveyed an alienating message, one in which concern for racial equality or poverty was "un-American."[43]

For Brooke, conservatives had a duty to create permanent solutions, engineering change in order to prevent the destruction of American ideals; or, as he described it, an "all-out effort to help the disadvantaged . . . join the mainstream of American life." His blueprint lobbied for a negative income tax (a proposition supported by both conservative economist Milton Friedman and the liberal Ripon Society), a guaranteed minimum income for the nation's poor, job training for the unemployed and under-employed, an economic industry corps for entrepreneurs and business-men, and a vast increase in federal funding for education. It was these suggestions that provoked the stormiest of reactions from Brooke's crit-ics. In the spring of 1966, a group of Goldwater supporters in Massachu-setts attacked *Challenge*, questioning Brooke's definition of conservatism and labeling the politician an "ultra-liberal." Another local detractor ac-cused the official of being a "reverse racist" who promoted discrimina-tion in favor of African Americans. The most blistering criticism came from within the ivory tower: scholar Robert Schuettinger spurned *Chal-lenge* as the "half-hearted" effort of a centrist milquetoast politician, who had concealed Democratic solutions under the cloak of Republicanism. "There certainly is a need for a coherent statement on progressive Repub-lican principles," Schuettinger wrote. "But this book is not it."[44]

Schuettinger was right to complain that the book was a centrist po-litical tome; in fact, centrism was the hallmark of Brooke's progressive conservatism. Contrary to the scholar's critique, however, the black poli-tician took great pains to clarify that this centrism was not an embrace of Great Society liberalism but learned from it and proposed alternatives. As he declared:

> If the [D]emocrats call themselves the party of the people, then we are the party of the individual, concerned with the place and dignity of man; his rights and his welfare, his future in a free society. A party demonstrating this concern *will deserve* the support of the American people. A party demonstrating this concern *will win* the support of the American people.

Though he accepted the humanitarian aspect of the Great Society, Brooke rejected the approach as fundamentally inadequate. Of particular con-sternation to the black official was the mélange of antipoverty programs, assembled in a "slapdash" manner; such programs, Brooke insisted, kept people on welfare in "perpetuity," providing them with little incentive to become a productive member of society. Johnson's "War on Poverty," the black official contended, had provided a "steady increasing dosage of aspirin" to society's ills instead of "eliminating the source of the pain."[45] In this respect, *Challenge* was Brooke's attempt to reconcile traditional Republican principles with the realities of the 1960s; thus, the solution to the party's woes lay in its ability to develop *useful* social and economic programs within the framework of traditional conservatism.

There are numerous early instances of Brooke testing his theory of pro-gressive conservatism and offering Republican solutions to the nation's problems. Soon after publishing *Challenge*, he distributed ten thousand copies of "Negroes and the Open Society," a white paper containing twenty-three pages of detailed criticism of the Johnson administration. Rejecting the Great Society, as he had in *Challenge*, Brooke called for an "Open Society" or a nation that extended to its citizens access to equal treatment under the law, quality education, decent housing and health, and the "economic benefits" of free market enterprise. Rather than relying on the federal government or transferring responsibility exclusively to the states, Brooke proposed a collaborative effort between the two branches and expanded the relationship to include a heavy emphasis on private partnerships. The persistence of racial discrimination necessitated such an approach, he argued, given the widespread and interconnected system of racism and inequality. Housing segregation was linked to de facto segregation in schools; poor education was related to high unemployment and underemployment; and limitations on work restricted "income and economic mobility." All of these issues, Brooke accused, were exacerbated by the Johnson administration's uneven enforcement of civil rights laws.

In addition to criticizing the Great Society programs, "Negroes and the Open Society" provided dozens of specific policy recommendations, addressing discrimination and inequality. In education, Brooke suggested that the federal government cut off funding from all public schools engaged in legal and informal segregation, *including* institutions in the North; state governments and private industries collaborate to build new schools and establish training opportunities for black teachers; and local and state school boards incorporate minority history into education curricula. In housing, Brooke reiterated a stronger version of the ideas proposed in his National Press Club outline in April 1965, insisting on the enforcement of federal and state fair housing laws, and calling for public and private coordination in the production of low- and moderate-income housing. Highlighting the high unemployment rate for African Americans, the attorney general proposed that cities enact systems to bar labor unions from excluding black workers and that the private sector create "Metropolitan Job Councils" composed of industry leaders who would assist with integrating African Americans into the private work force. He closed the white paper by urging greater federal protection of civil rights workers, of all races; moreover, he proposed a federal "Indemnification Board" to provide monetary restitution to those individuals whose "federally protected rights" had been trampled by segregationists and racists. "Negroes and the Open Society" was far more precise in its solutions than Brooke's previous scholarship, adding a layer of concreteness to his theories of constructive innovation and progressive conservatism. In focusing on abolishing discrimination, Brooke articulated a Republican vision of race in which blacks were individual citizens *and* Americans, thereby casting opposition to civil rights legislation as unconstitutional and undemocratic. As he wrote in the conclusion to the white paper, all citizens should have the "right to achieve their individuality" and "participate in the American dream."[46]

Many within the party latched on to such concepts, including RNC officials. Precinct returns from the November 1965 election showed strong black support for Republican candidates at the local and state level in areas including Philadelphia, Louisville, and New York. Eager to better understand the context in which these candidates won, the RNC commissioned a report in mid-November 1965 that focused on John Lindsay's New York City mayoral win, with the hopes of identifying the driving force behind the politician's success among black voters and replicating his strategy on a larger scale in different cities. Ultimately the RNC report, along with analysis from other liberal and moderate organizations including the Ripon Society, came to the same conclusion that black Republicans had advanced for years: the election findings proved that the party had a significant opportunity to make inroads with African Americans, so long as the GOP abandoned a racist "southern strategy" and invited African Americans to play an important role in party affairs. There is "ample evidence," remarked Ray Bliss in a February 1966 interview "that Negro voters will support Republican candidates when they offer attractive and constructive programs dealing with the important issues of the day."[47]

In the months surrounding the launch of *Challenge*, the national committee officially introduced its Negro Advisory Committee (NAC), a working group of a dozen prominent black Republicans, assembled to aid the GOP in creating a black outreach campaign. The committee, RNC officials proudly announced, represented a "solid cross section of the Negro community," a declaration that was clearly false, since all the appointees came from middle-class backgrounds and all but one were men. What the members of the NAC *did* reflect was a spectrum of black Republican personalities. At least three members of the NNRA, each representing a different ideological wing of the black assembly, sat on NAC. Likewise, all of the committee members had experience with party affairs on a state and local level. Elaine Jenkins, for instance, was vice chair of the District of Columbia Republican Committee and had enthusiastically supported Barry Goldwater's presidential bid.[48] The chair of NAC, William Walker, was publisher of the *Call and Post*, and ran the Ohio Republican Council, a statewide organization for African American members of the GOP, founded in 1958. Two committee members had served as state legislators—one in Kansas and the other in Illinois; a third, Q. V. Williamson of Georgia, was a city alderman in Atlanta, known for bailing dozens of black student protestors out of jail in the early 1960s.[49]

Despite their ideological differences, all of the committee members shared a belief in integration, two-party competition, and economic uplift through free market enterprise. They also all agreed on the necessity and constitutionality of civil rights legislation. In some ways, NAC was not dissimilar from the NNRA, as both groups shared comparable philosophies and identical goals—evidently a reflection of overlapping memberships. One critical difference separated the two groups: the advisory committee was far less militant than the black assembly's leadership, instead sharing the moderate political approach of Edward Brooke. NAC believed in working with and within the national GOP, explicitly disavowing any interest in developing into an autonomous splinter group.[50] As one of the group's first actions, members demanded the ouster and replacement of Clay Claiborne, a charlatan in the eyes of many African American party members. Two years earlier, the black RNC staffer had been indicted (and later acquitted) on charges of election fraud, after distributing 1.4 million pamphlets urging African Americans to vote for Martin Luther King Jr. for president—a move, one black Democrat official accused, that was a "last-minute effort by Goldwater supporters to nullify the black vote." Consequently, firing Claiborne was a vital step in rebuilding African American's trust in the RNC.[51]

Regaining the confidence of blacks was but one part of the party's problems, a point that NAC member Clarence Townes consistently vocalized during the committee's early meetings. While the NNRA official (who would soon split with the black assembly) was not nearly as militant as Jackie Robinson or Grant Reynolds, his private complaints still shared some of the liberal black Republicans' forcefulness in both tone and conviction. In a March 1966 session with members of NAC, he argued that the GOP's issues went far beyond the party's "Goldwater problem," afflicting most white Republicans, many of whom did not *understand* black voters. Townes's argument offers a significant detail, one that spoke to Republicans' inability to fully comprehend the devastating nature of racial oppression and inequality. Unable to grasp the experiences of those unlike them, in both race and class, GOP leaders, officials, and members continued to perpetuate an image of insincerity and hostility through their rhetoric and behavior. Even among Republicans who declared their interest in black voters, their first instinct was to lean heavily on the memory of the "Party of Lincoln," an image no longer germane to the day-to-day experiences of blacks in the 1960s. Townes articulated a succinct version of Ralph Bunche's thesis offered twenty-five years earlier: black hopes were tied not only to civil rights but also to economic equality; the party's failure to address both of these issues comprehensively had created an entrenched political image of a party against racial and economic progress.

Black outreach, Townes somberly predicted, would yield few immediate gains on the national level, warning the NAC and RNC to expect slow progress with multiple failures. His gloomy tone was a far cry from his public optimism—he once boasted to a crowd that the GOP expected to win 40 percent or more of the black vote in the 1968 election. In private, however, this bravado disappeared as he darkly speculated that even a popular "Eisenhower" figure with liberal leanings could not compel black voters to support the GOP in a national election. Out of all the Republican predictions on the black vote, this grim private assessment was perhaps the most accurate, taking into account the nuances of the class and racial problems that persisted within the GOP and capturing the gulf that existed between black voters and national GOP leaders.

Townes thus proposed that the party needed compassionate Republicans who empathized with the experience of African Americans and would introduce economic and social policies that spoke to black needs—officials appealing enough to win over white voters as well. Channeling Brooke's centrist stance, Townes urged the national committee to adopt a pragmatic approach, one that would permit Republican leaders to understand the aspirations of the "New Negro who has evolved since the 1930s" and provide viable solutions based on traditional conservatism; in short, the black Republican insisted that the GOP "learn how to successfully sell our product" to modern African Americans.[52] The similarities between Brooke's policy proposals and Townes's statements embodied the divide that would grow within black Republican communities as the 1960s progressed; while Townes's former colleagues in the NNRA grew more militant, the NAC official embraced centrism not only as an ideological choice but also as a practical way to influence the party on equal rights without alienating white power brokers.

One of Townes's more interesting ideas also seemed inspired by Brooke's ascendance. In the spring of 1966, the advisory board member proposed that the RNC cultivate a "Negro Goodwill Ambassador," a high-ranking African American official that would develop a positive appreciation for party policies on civil rights and economics and draw cogent links between traditional conservatism and black issues and ambitions—a situation that could be of benefit to the entire party, as goodwill representatives had the potential to open doors in the black community otherwise inaccessible to white Republicans. This hypothetical ambassador, Townes deliberated, should be a "fresh name," a figure of moderate and pragmatic ideology, able to advance nuanced party philosophies and innovative ideas, while appealing to both black and white voters. "We must do it this way," he insisted, "because it will send a message to the public that we are serious about a new and real program . . . and we are in tune with the 'new day.' . . . We need a bold new dramatic program to get black support."[53] One month later, in April 1966—in what *surely* was not a coincidence—NAC unanimously voted to appoint Townes as the RNC's Negro goodwill ambassador, elevating his rank to that of special assistant to RNC chair Ray Bliss.[54] At the same time, the national committee reactivated its Minorities Division—a unit that had been dormant from the day Barry Goldwater received the GOP's presidential nomination. In its first year, Bliss would invest $75,000 into the unit—a notable amount given the party's history of spending "peanuts on trying to win Negro votes."[55]

Clearly, black Republicans also saw Ed Brooke as an unofficial goodwill ambassador who could navigate the treacherous relationships that existed among blacks, whites, and the Republican Party. So dogmatic was their faith in the black official that they willingly sidestepped their ideological differences in their support of the attorney general. In May 1965, for example, Grant Reynolds announced his endorsement of Brooke for vice president in the 1968 election. Almost two years later, in January 1967, George Schuyler of the John Birch Society did the same. Despite the vast philosophical gulf that separated the two men, they both argued that the Massachusetts official represented the solution to some of the party's more acute issues. In many ways, their pragmatic rationales were similar, as both the liberal NNRA leader and the black conservative writer envisioned Brooke as an "established vote-getter," equally appealing to black and white audiences. Yet where Reynolds saw a liberal black leader outspoken on civil rights and economic equality, Schuyler saw a moderate figure who avoided speaking on racial issues and who was a "Negro leader" only insofar as he was born black; equally significant, Reynolds's endorsement came at a point in time when Brooke was at his most conservative, while Schuyler's support arrived as the Massachusetts official was becoming increasingly liberal. That these two figures— one associated with a "militant" black Republican group and the other associated with a white reactionary organization—could both endorse Brooke was important but not astonishing: the black politician's "non-Negro" approach was centrist enough as to be palatable to multiple audiences. For black Republicans, this also meant envisioning Brooke the way *they* wanted to see him, and overlooking those attributes that did not align with their personal philosophies.[56]

DRIVING A REPUBLICAN RESURGENCE

Brooke's vision of progressive conservatism was more than a theory; it also had a practical component, which largely explained his decision to run for senator in 1966. In an astute assessment of the official's political jockeying, a *Washington Post* reporter observed that a senatorial position offered the Massachusetts leader a greater opportunity to "exploit what the Republican Party has to offer Negroes."[57] Brooke hoped that his candidacy would demonstrate that African Americans could be successful within the framework of the Republican Party, as he believed that serving in a more prominent elected role would provide practical counter-evidence to the assumption that only the Democratic Party cared about racial and economic equality. As the *Milwaukee Sentinel* stated, Brooke's bid had the potential to "erase the distasteful image the party won in the Goldwater debacle."[58] Moreover, as someone interested in political reform and the law, securing a role in the Senate was perhaps the most efficient way to assume such power.

Brooke's decision to run for a position in the U.S. Senate was also part of a general surge of black Republican activity during the period.[59] In Virginia, for instance, Clarence Townes ran for a seat in the House of Delegates in 1965. Inspired by Brooke's landslide reelection as Massachusetts attorney general, galvanized by the Goldwater fiasco, and provoked by segregationists within the local Democratic Party, Townes proclaimed, "In this time and at this stage of our history, our efforts . . . must provide the Negro's answer to the call for statesmanship. We must—and we will accept the challenge to greatness as Republicans."[60] The *New York Times* agreed, concluding that the black Republican's candidacy was a symbol of the "growth of the two-party and two-color politics in Virginia." Applauding the Republican Party for taking a "militant stand" against the "racist policies" of the state's Democrats, the editors argued that the GOP's progressive actions clearly demonstrated that Republicans could still embarrass "Democratic-segregationist regimes" and ultimately win southern black votes.[61]

Brooke's appeal, however, was distinct: as a twice-elected high-ranking party official, he already had a mandate that compelled access to upper-echelon circles in the party. For moderate and liberal voters alike, he appeared to have a special aptitude for attracting frustrated voters regardless of race or political affiliation. Even Barry Goldwater was moved to donate to Brooke's senatorial campaign, writing in a short February letter, "I believe your election to the U.S. Senate would be good for the country and for the party." Likewise, Carl Shipley, who had derided black Republicans as elitist "Cadillac Negroes" when they refused to campaign for Goldwater in 1964, threw his support behind Brooke in 1966, co-establishing a district fundraiser for the senatorial hopeful. The black official received hundreds of verbal and financial endorsements over the course of his campaign, not only from Republican figures like Nelson Rockefeller, John Lindsay, George Romney, and Thruston Morton but also from newspapers, magazines, celebrities, and various partisan and nonpartisan groups. Back in Massachusetts, Republicans at the state convention delivered their rousing support for Brooke, providing him with nearly thirteen hundred more votes than the nearest contender.[62] "If Brooke wins," the *Newark Sunday News* announced, "He will be pioneering the way for other Negroes who are moving up in elective [positions] all across the nation." Brooke's crossover pull was broad, as both white and black citizens found him appealing, as did Republicans, Democrats, and independents. In fact, the only group that appeared indifferent to him was organized labor: during the campaign, union leaders contributed $32,000 to Democrat Endicott Peabody's campaign chest and donated nothing to Brooke.[63]

It seems odd then, that race would become such an issue in Brooke's senatorial contest, a storm cloud that hovered over the politician's campaign, growing in intensity as violence and rioting broke out in cities across the country.[64] Despite running on a platform of law and order, Brooke quickly fell victim to the threat of white backlash. It began in earnest when his strong poll numbers suddenly dropped in the fall of 1966, a low point that coincided with the release of a series of surveys that asserted that white backlash was "gaining momentum" nationwide. Fears of racial retaliation were stoked by gloomy reports of the growing unease and resentment among white voters, attributed to the "course of the Negro revolution," demands for integrated housing, and the "menacing rhetoric of the 'black power' movement." Brooke would surely lose because of this ominous pattern of white resentment, media and political observers concluded. "Nowhere outside the Deep South," wrote reporter Marianne Means, "are the tense and tangled relationships of white men and black men more volatile this campaign season than in Massachusetts." The "mere color of Brooke's skin," predicted the *Washington Post*, would be the candidate's downfall. If not for his race, the paper lamented, Brooke would be a "sure winner."[65]

Public sentiment in Massachusetts appeared unpredictable as well; in Boston, a devout Republican angrily declared that he would not vote for Brooke because he was "fed up with riots and with Negroes pushing too fast." Stated another voter: "The only reasons I'm for Peabody is I don't want Brooke. I'm angry at his people . . . his people don't work like we did. They want everything handed to them." An editorial cartoon from the fall of 1966 provides a jarring illustration of the media's frenzied response to the possibility of backlash affecting the black official's campaign; the image depicts a grim-faced shirtless Ed Brooke, hunched over with the word "Backlash" whipped into his back, with the phrase "INNOCENT VICTIM?" floating over his head—to his right, a small sign reads: "It Can Happen Here." In its use of slave imagery, the cartoon conveyed a profound message, suggesting that race was an insurmountable and inescapable problem, even for a popular and a "safe," middle-class Republican, who happened to be black; the image offered an indictment of the Massachusetts public, challenging the notion of the northern "progressive" mystique.[66] Unintentionally illustrating the complex nature of the local attitudes on race, civil rights, and Brooke, Louise Day Hicks of the Boston School Board warned that the "backlash is definitely growing. We are feeling the impact from disturbances around the whole country. The backlash will adversely affect Brooke and that's undeserved. If anything, he is less liberal on civil rights than [Endicott] Peabody." A notorious busing opponent and a staunch Democrat, Hicks insisted that she had more in common with Brooke's "law and order" approach to civil rights than with Peabody's liberal philosophy; there's a measure of irony in her decision, to be sure—she endorsed a "colorblind" approach to politics, reassured by Brooke's so-called conservatism on racial issues.[67]

Throughout the campaign, Brooke was bombarded with questions about white backlash and race. During a radio interview, he defensively dismissed such talk, snapping, "I don't think anyone in Massachusetts is going to vote against me because of a riot that took place in Chicago or in Atlanta."[68] And despite persistent fears of white backlash, it seems as though Brooke was right—throughout the fall, his numbers recovered as he campaigned in earnest; by the end of September, he was leading Peabody by 25 points in the polls. By October, 100 percent of the state's electorate knew that Brooke was black—an awareness that had little negative impact on his approval ratings. A public opinion research firm tracking racial attitudes for the campaign found that nearly 80 percent of voters liked the black official. Moreover, while 7 percent of the electorate disapproved of Brooke, 19 percent viewed Peabody in an unfavorable light, characterizing the former governor as an indecisive, ineffective, and blindly partisan politician.

The opinion group's studies also revealed that, in spite of threats of white resentment, the state's voters did not disapprove of the "federal government's involvement in civil rights." Still, their tolerance stopped short in two areas: 60 percent rejected a state law that withheld funding from schools practicing de facto segregation; likewise, 68 percent believed that an individual should be allowed to "refuse to sell his house to a Negro." Brooke had consistently rejected both of these positions, addressing his opposition to such perspectives in *The Challenge of Change* and "Negroes and the Open Society"; in fact, his support for ending discrimination in housing and education were core principles of his 1966 campaign. Nevertheless, by September 1966, only 4 percent of the Massachusetts public felt as though Brooke had done "too much" to help African Americans gain equal rights, whereas 20 percent actually believed he had done "too little" and 50 percent suggested he had done "just the right amount." Even when the research firm split voters into groups on the basis of racial prejudices, Brooke still tallied uniformly positive ratings. Endicott Peabody, on the other hand, failed to achieve high marks from any group.[69]

Brooke's popularity increased even further after he made a decision to address the issue of race "head on" in a series of widely publicized speeches and appearances repudiating Black Power advocates. During a talk at Harvard University in October, he told thirteen hundred rapt college students that the civil rights movement had "taken a turn in the wrong direction":

> After the chant of 'black power' . . . fear swept the across the nation . . . and the percentage of American people believing in equality for all dropped . . . and the 1966 civil rights act was defeated. I trust there will be a rejection of both 'black power' and the echoing cry of 'white power.'[70]

Black Power, like white supremacy, he warned, would "multiply racial woes" instead of solving them. "I intend to raise my voice at every opportunity against extremists of both the right and the left," he declared, "to look for them, seek them out and expose them." Brooke relayed a message to multiple audiences over the course of the campaign that he was a "law and order guy" by trade; thus, equality was a battle best fought through "non-violent, peaceful, lawful procedures." Rioting and violence, he insisted, would only lead to "bloodshed, deeper fears, and a greater gulf among peoples." Such rhetoric was designed to soothe the anxieties of white voters and stem the threat, however big or small, of white backlash. And by putting distance between himself and black militants, Brooke conveyed a message to voters that he was a benign figure and that his blackness did not prevent him from being an average, law-abiding American citizen. Black rioters, he told a group of college students in the fall of 1966, were "just as bitter against the successful Negro businessman as the white man. They are people sitting on the side of the road rebelling against society." As he closed at one press conference: "A vote for me is a vote against Stokely Carmichael."[71]

This language of reassurance and safety highlighted the widening philosophical gulf that existed between Brooke and the militant members of the NNRA. A few months before Brooke's speech, Jackie Robinson had announced to an interracial audience of Ohio party members, "I am certainly not a safe Republican. . . . I am weary of the black man going hat in hand shoulders hunched and knee pads worn, to 'Uncle Tom' to the enemies of our progress." Such obvious and sharp differences in approach, however, did not stop the NNRA from championing Brooke's campaign—the organization's leaders merely ignored that aspect of the politician's rhetoric. The NNRA could easily point to the attorney general's advocacy of civil rights to soothe its own anxieties; what's more, Brooke's "qualified" definition of Black Power was similar to its own. Appearing on a television talk show in the midst of the fall campaign, Brooke argued that Black Power would be an acceptable concept if it indicated nonviolent "economic and political power of the Negro in order that it might improve their lot."[72] His language was virtually indistinguishable from Robinson's malleable concept of power, as we have already seen; once combined with the symbolic value that the NNRA leaders placed on a victory, the group's continued reverence for the Massachusetts official makes far more sense.

In many ways, Brooke's repudiation of Black Power was an extension of a campaign fixated on treating the candidate's racial background in a neutral manner. At one point during the senatorial contest, Brooke's campaign manager tossed away twenty thousand political buttons and bumper stickers because they bore the slogan "Proudly for Brooke." The phrase, his adviser contended, would trigger negative thoughts of race pride in the minds of voters; consequently, the slogan was changed to "Brooke: A Creative Republican."[73] Brooke's managers were unquestionably sensitive to issues of race, but so was everyone surrounding the campaign—even national political commentators and observers. Hundreds of media outlets profiled the attorney general, fascinated not only by his race but also by his appearance, his Italian-born wife, and his middle-class segregated upbringing.[74] He was, writer John Skow proclaimed in a seven-page piece for a September issue of the *Saturday Evening Post*, a "Negro Brahmin." Like most profiles of the Republican candidate, Skow's article placed race as central to the campaign; however, unlike most profiles, the journalist deconstructed Brooke's so-called race-neutral approach, suggesting that the black official was not as colorblind as most assumed, at least in his treatment of major social and economic issues, including racial equality and Black Power.[75]

Skow, of course, was correct—Brooke was not colorblind, at least not in the way that most of the public imagined him to be. In fact, in decrying black and white extremists, Brooke echoed the position of middle-class, "legislatively oriented" moderate civil rights leaders. Two months before Brooke delivered his race speeches, Roy Wilkins of the NAACP wrote a caustic editorial in the *Crisis* denouncing Black Power:

> The term "black power" means anti–white power. . . . It is a reverse Mississippi, a reverse Hitler, a reverse Ku Klux Klan. . . . It is the ranging of race against race on their relevant basis of skin color. It is the father of hatred and the mother of violence.[76]

Wilkins also blamed Black Power advocates for the failure of the 1966 open housing bill, just as Brooke would later do. Similarly, in October 1966, eight prominent civil rights leaders issued a three-quarter-page advertisement in the *New York Times* broadcasting their commitment to racial justice and integration and their rejection of Black Power. Like Brooke, they distinguished between militant groups and civil rights organizations, condemning "rioting and the demagoguery that feeds it."[77] And like the editorial's authors, Brooke often referred to the desperate need to address the frustrations of African Americans and to look to the economic and social triggers of the anarchic outbursts engulfing the nation's cities. Though he rebuked both Black Power advocates and white extremists, Brooke also demanded that black and white constituents alike be progressive in their concern for civil rights and conservative in their respect for law and order.

Moreover, black citizens, as a collective, were neither excluded nor denounced in Brooke's speeches; instead, he created a division between "good" group behavior and "bad" individual actions, a position that sounded almost identical to the stance outlined by the eight civil rights leaders in their October manifesto. "It is a cruel and bitter abuse," they wrote, "to judge . . . the overwhelming preponderance of the Negro population, by the misdeeds of a few."[78] This was respectability politics at work, an unmistakably moderate and middle-class approach to racial uplift that suggested that equal citizenship rested on an established moral code of acceptable black behaviors that fit within societal norms.[79] Brooke's ideas were at home in the mainstream of black political thought; even within this context, though, some of his beliefs sat to the right of moderate civil rights leaders. In several of his speeches on Black Power, for instance, he urged the civil rights movement to tackle welfare reform, asserting that government "handouts" destroyed personal dignity and ambition; far preferable, according to Brooke, was a system that provided incentives for the poor to work and be "productive members of society," so that "75 percent of the Nation will not be supporting 25 percent of the Nation."[80] It was this kind of classist thinking, rooted in notions of self-help and capitalism that Brooke's black critics rejected; in fact, his perspective inspired Stokely Carmichael to deride Brooke as an "Uncle Tom" in the final days of the 1966 campaign.[81]

Despite the fact that Brooke had placed considerable distance between himself and Black Power advocates, political observers continued to make bleak predictions; the night before the election, the *Chicago Defender* despaired that Brooke's defeat was inevitable since the state's white residents would never tolerate a "Negro political takeover."[82] Given such dire expectations, the nation was shocked when Brooke trounced Endicott Peabody by a plurality of nearly half a million votes. A varied coalition of voters cast ballots for Brooke: Republicans, Democrats, and independents; Catholic, Protestant, and Jewish voters; men and women from cities, suburbs, and rural and small towns; scholars and academics; and constituents from every economic background. The only groups that rejected Brooke were working-class Irish and Italian voters. African Americans of all backgrounds, by contrast, provided the black politician with 86 percent of their votes. Though they composed fewer than 3 percent of the state's electorate, blacks nevertheless demonstrated significant support for Brooke, taking great pains to locate his name on the ticket and vote for him, often leaving the rest of the ballot blank. There was a strong element of pride in pulling the lever for Brooke, though postelection studies also found that half of registered black voters in the state identified as either independents or Republicans, and those who were Democrats felt little connection to Peabody. This was perhaps one of the most unexpected outcomes of the race, illustrating that black voters were partisan—just not in the way that political analysts expected. When the dust from the election had settled, Brooke was the second highest vote winner in Massachusetts in sixty-six years, second only to his Republican predecessor Leverett Saltonstall, outperforming two of the state's most famous senators: John F. Kennedy and Edward M. Kennedy.[83]

Brooke's election, Martin Luther King Jr. proclaimed, demonstrated that backlash had been defeated and that "millions of white voters remained unshaken in their commitment to decency." The editors at the *Crisis* declared that his win "heralds the dawn of a new day in which candidates will be judged on the basis of their political stance and their individual merit, regardless of race, religion or national origin." Likewise, black Republicans celebrated Brooke's win as a massive victory, a concrete victory in the struggle for equal rights. It was "significant," wrote Jackie Robinson in a December 1966 column for the *Chicago Defender*, "because it was the most resounding reply which could have been given to those who predicted that white backlash would triumph."[84]

Yet the assertion that Brooke had defeated backlash was a questionable one at best, since racial "backlash" never truly existed in Massachusetts, at least for Brooke. As we have seen, by the time Brooke delivered his Black Power speeches in October, he had a comfortable lead over Peabody, and while the two men shared similar views on civil rights, Brooke went to great pains to cast himself as a moderate candidate, invested in law, order, and equal rights. Peabody on the other hand, was still dealing with the very public fallout stemming from his mother's 1964 arrest in Florida, after she and an interracial group of protestors tried to desegregate the lunch counters at the Ponce de León Motor Lodge in St. Augustine.[85] In other words, even if voters wanted to participate in some kind of "racial backlash," they had no idea which candidate to protest. Nationally, however, backlash did help some candidates in the 1966 elections. In Georgia, Democrat Lester Maddox, the "South's symbol of resistance to civil rights for Negroes," won his gubernatorial contest easily.[86] Backlash was also a bipartisan affair—in California, Republican Ronald Reagan benefited from calls for law and order, in a race that was, one black columnist complained, broadly indicative of a white public that marked racial prejudices and anti-integrationist attitudes behind colorblind support for "freedom of choice." Still, white resentment was not an "overriding issue" in the way that analysts expected it to be: according to *Congressional Quarterly*, about 70 percent of candidates threatened by backlash ended up winning their races. Still, this did not imply that white resentment over civil rights, racial progress, urban outbursts, or Black Power did not exist, but rather that it simply failed to show up in many white citizens' candidate voting decisions in 1966.[87]

Countless news sources rushed to document Brooke's historic win, including *Time*, which placed Brooke—along with Reagan, George Romney, Charles Percy, Mark Hatfield, and Nelson Rockefeller—on the cover of the November 18, 1966, issue under the headline "Republican Resurgence." Just three months later, the news journal would devote an entire cover to Brooke, championing him as a "new style and a new hope" for the Republican Party.[88] The black statesman's success inspired an outpouring of support from African Americans around the country, evidenced in the thousands of letters, telegrams, and speaking requests the politician received. Arriving at the Senate in January 1967 for his swearing-in-ceremony, he was greeted by a cheering crowd of five thousand black well-wishers. Such reactions were not unusual since the senator generated a distinct brand of reverence and pride among African Americans. Underscoring this point, some black voters went so far as to change their political affiliation to Republican in a show of support, claiming they were inspired by Brooke's genuine loyalty to "certain goals and ideals, not to the party." Probing such reactions, *Time* suggested that Brooke was the embodiment of the "Negro's deeper vision of equality with white Americans in terms of individual intellect, ability and dignity."[89]

But for some African Americans, it was not this simple; though they understood Brooke as one of their own, they still worried that his middle-class background, appearance, conservatism, and assimilations ideology would put him at odds with the urgent needs of poor and working-class black communities. In the early part of 1967, a Bronx woman grumbled that Brooke was "more white than colored," while a Detroit man complained that the official "does not even want to be our champion." A better title for the senator, he mocked, would be "NUT: Negro Uncle Tom." Both critics pilloried Brooke's middle-class respectability politics and integrationist philosophies, echoing broader militant critiques of the politician. At the other end of the spectrum, there were African Americans like Elizabeth Williams of Memphis who argued that Brooke "expresses the sentiments many of us feel. . . . With men like Brooke, [Whitney] Young, and [Roy] Wilkins, Negroes have the leadership they deserve." Many African Americans viewed Brooke as *their* senator—implicit was the understanding that he would represent their desires. As Simeon Booker of *Ebony* mused, Brooke now had "five million white constituents in Massachusetts and . . . 20 million black ones across the country."[90]

Brooke's success was but one notable example of several (see tables 4 and 5 in the appendix); indeed, GOP resurgence was evident all over the country in 1966. The editors at *Time* argued that the election had pulled the Republican Party back from the brink, erasing the "Goldwater image of a narrow, negative clique, replacing it with the vision of a cohesive, inclusive party."[91] The party gained four seats in the Senate, forty-seven in the House, and seven hundred in state legislatures; likewise, half the nation's governors were now Republicans—an increase of eight positions. Taking note of the party's revival, Lyndon Johnson wryly remarked that it was nice to "see a healthy and competent existence of the two-party system."[92] While not earth-shattering increases by any means (Democrats still held majorities in Congress), they were powerfully symbolic gains for a party just beginning to recover from the trauma of 1964. The election was also a triumphant moment for moderate Republicanism, as historian Geoffrey Kabaservice has argued; centrist party members seemed poised to push the GOP past the ghost of Goldwater. It was no coincidence that five out of the six Republican politicians featured on the November 1966 *Time* cover were moderates or liberals. In fact, as we have seen, Reagan, the new "darling" of the Goldwater wing of the party, was showing signs of tempering his political dogma in an effort to attract followers of all ideological leanings.[93] Though African Americans remained skeptical of the ex-actor, some—like writer Almena Lomax—argued that his victory was mitigated by the electoral success of moderate figures including Ed Brooke. "Just in the nick of time," she gushed in a glowing op-ed for the *Los Angeles Times*, "the Republicans came to life with flesh-and-blood men of the 20th century." In November 1964, this type of response would have been unimaginable; that African Americans would celebrate the success of the GOP, just two years later, speaks to the importance of the 1966 midterm elections. "It looks to me," RNC chairman Ray Bliss announced, "as if we have a very live elephant."[94]

The real impact of Republican efforts to woo black voters can be measured in electoral returns, and at first glance it appears as though the party made significant strides in rehabilitating its image among African Americans. Nationally, 19 percent of the black electorate supported the GOP in 1966—a stark contrast to the meager 6 percent tallied by Barry Goldwater two years prior.[95] "The Negro, it would seem," crowed one party strategist, "was little interested in party labels [and] immensely interested in the candidates themselves."[96] In Arkansas, for instance, gubernatorial candidate Winthrop Rockefeller, brother of Nelson, racked up 96 percent of the black vote, overpowering his segregationist opponent. Running as a party moderate, Spiro T. Agnew, a politician who just two years later would come to personify the "silent majority" of backlash politics, received 79 percent of the African American vote in the Maryland governor's contest; his political adversary, Democrat George Mahoney, had run on an anti–fair housing platform and attempted to rally white backlash voters around the slogan, "Your Home is Your Castle—Protect It!"[97] Michigan governor George Romney received a respectable 35 percent of the black vote in his successful reelection effort; and in Houston, Texas, nearly a third of the black electorate helped George H. W. Bush claim victory in his congressional contest.[98] In a five-page spread, *Ebony* magazine celebrated the party's "triumph," claiming that the GOP had established a bold new style, attractive enough to convince African Americans to "return to the party of Lincoln in surprising numbers."[99]

On closer scrutiny, however, the midterm numbers are not as shocking as they first appear to be, though they are still significant. Some of the figures are remarkable—even vibrant—especially when juxtaposed with the 1964 results; but the 1964 returns were so odious that any increase, however small, was a dramatic victory. Likewise, the midterm elections demonstrated that liberal and moderate candidates performed well within their historical range; thus, when GOP officials and political commentators argued that the 1966 contests proved that blacks would support a Republican if the candidate demonstrated a genuine interest in

African Americans, this was a fact that had been true for decades. Nelson Rockefeller, for instance, sliced off more than a third of the black vote in 1966, 1962, and 1958; the only thing astonishing about the governor's support among black New Yorkers was how consistent it was.[100]

A look at the party's longer electoral history hints at a slightly more nuanced story, one wherein the party's state and local outreach problems were different from its national presidential woes—perhaps an obvious point, but one that the party had wrestled with in the past and would continue to grapple with in the future. The intimate nature of local politics made it easier for African Americans to support Republican candidates as individuals, most notably, those liberal and moderate party officials who offered policies and programs that intersected with African American needs. Coupled with the lingering presence of racist southern Democrats, this allowed some black voters to support specific party officials, although it made it no less difficult for them to identify as a Republican.

Furthermore, many of the results from the midterm contests were far more complicated than party officials initially acknowledged, as was the case in Ohio. Governor James Rhodes, well known in communities for his interest in African American issues, received 47 percent of the black vote in Cincinnati and about 26 percent in Cleveland. His "genuine interest" in black issues remained constant; however, in the latter city, his precinct team exhibited a "cool, if not actively hostile" treatment of black voters. Cincinnati, in comparison, had a liberal Republican organization that aggressively campaigned among African Americans.[101] Here then, the collective behavior of state and local Republican officials also influenced the decision of black voters; thus it was not enough for an individual candidate to demonstrate genuine concern: the nominee's entire campaign staff also needed to demonstrate sincere interest. Such discrepancies did not prevent black Republicans from relishing in the victory of 1966. In fact, the results soon inspired Clarence Townes to declare to a private meeting of national committee officials that the GOP would win more than 30 percent of the black vote in the 1968 presidential election.[102] This was an ambitious but naïve prediction, given that it obscured the complex nature of black support for Republicans. Townes's optimistic forecast also seemed to mark a shift in his outlook from a few months earlier when he had privately offered a bleaker, far more realistic perspective.[103]

After the election, the Minorities Division initially embraced symbolic gestures as a means of recruiting black voters—viewing, for instance, the January 1967 appointment of Junius Griffin, Martin Luther King Jr.'s former press secretary, as one of its biggest accomplishments. Here was a civil rights figure whose ties to the movement lent the GOP a level of credibility, or so Republicans believed. He began his tenure with a bold declaration: the Republican Party, he announced in a press conference, had "never separated from the aspirations and the demands of the Negro."[104] Such statements contributed a revisionist interpretation of the party's history, one in which Republican racial antagonisms had never occurred. On the one hand, such language felt like hackneyed rhetoric, made all the more insincere because it intentionally sidestepped the party's still-active reactionary wing; it also deliberately ignored the fact that this wing had separated from African American needs and interests. On the other hand, Griffin's words conveyed black Republicans' earnest faith in liberal and moderate party leaders as the standard-bearers for Republicanism. This was a logic that even *Ebony* embraced in the months following the 1966 election: so long as the GOP continued to demonstrate a commitment to racial progress, the writers argued, all signs pointed to a "glowing reconciliation between the Republican Party and the Negro."[105] Such optimism seemed endemic to a certain strand of political pronouncements, a language of perpetual possibility shared by Democrats and Republicans of all ideological stripes. But for black members of the GOP in particular, such optimism held particular consequences.

This urgency eventually compelled Townes to move beyond symbolic gestures and incorporate significant changes within state and local Republican Party organizations. Throughout 1967, he launched minority division branches in nineteen states in an effort to show white Republicans how to garner support from the black electorate. In the summer of 1967, for example, representatives from the Missouri GOP wrote that state Republicans were "most anxious" to develop an "aggressive program" to win the black vote in the 1968 election. The white officials sounded all of the right notes, stating that a "sincere, honest, effort" was necessary in order to build rapport with local black communities. Working with Townes, they enacted a plan to address local black issues, such as discrimination in housing and employment; the most significant of these solutions was the development of community centers in African American neighborhoods in St. Louis and Kansas City. The physical spaces, Townes declared in a confidential memo, would create community areas where African Americans could find assistance for the basic problems of day-to-day living. And in truth, the Missouri centers did address such needs: private businesses offered job training and employment opportunities geared toward the unemployed and underemployed; likewise, black locals found programs that helped with everything from the mundane to the essential: free breakfast, tax adjustment, pest control, household budgeting and repair, legal advice, and childcare. The programs appeared remarkably similar to Great Society measures; yet the Republican-led initiatives differed from those of the Johnson administration because they were self-help programs that relied heavily on voluntary partnerships with the private sector.

At the same time, the underlying motivation of these initiatives was political. Every center in Missouri had a voter registration program and was considered a training space for local black leaders with "political potential." And while all programs were open to all African Americans, regardless of party affiliation, it was "vital," Townes asserted, that these black constituents understand that Republicans were helping them, so that the party "may benefit from it on election day." Adopting a nonpartisan language to convey interest in African American affairs did not mean becoming politically neutral, for as Townes reasoned in a July 1967 outline, a "display of genuine concern . . . will reap a better return." Neither were these political rewards limited to black voters; to the contrary, as a Minnesota Republican leader explained to Townes, showing interest in African Americans would also "appeal to civil rights conscious whites."[106]

Between March and November 1967, similar initiatives cropped up in cities across the country. In Watts, party officials used funds from private industries to help local residents launch black-owned and operated companies, while in Houston, Congressman Bush and local black Republican businessmen initiated a minority bank deposit program and established a summer job program for black youth. In Detroit, the Metropolitan Action Center provided job training, offered a summer camp for black children, served as a housing advocate for black homeowners and renters, and hosted seminars and workshops on redefining Black Power in America. That some white Republicans were now adopting some of the tenants of a militant ideology they once condemned was one of the noteworthy by-products of Townes's efforts; certainly party officials embraced the more malleable, "safer" principles of Black Power, like black pride, political self-determination, and economic uplift; nevertheless, they still embraced these tenets in an attempt to find common ground with African Americans. Across the country, local and state party officials joined the Minorities Division's efforts, pumping money into civil rights commissions, appointing African Americans to high-level state government positions, and sponsoring equal rights legislation. The open housing, fair employment, and injunctive relief bills promoted by Pennsylvania governor Ray Shafer, for example, put him at the "forefront of 'progressive' administrations."[107]

As he was working with white Republicans in 1967, Townes also attempted to convince African Americans of the GOP's sincerity, traveling to twenty states in a ten-month period, speaking with black audiences. During these talks, often aimed at nonpartisan civic and professional groups, Townes tried to place black Republicans' efforts within a broader civil rights genealogy, ultimately connecting it to recent trends in black politics. Instead of waiting to get political power, he told one audience full of NAACP members, black Republicans—like black Democrats—were "going out actively seeking it" by campaigning for positions at every rank of the GOP. Black Republicans, he continued, were "full of young ideas and racial pride," advocating for civil rights on a state and local level; moreover, white Republicans were responding, he suggested, thus proving that Republicans were committed in "equality for all."[108]

Outwardly, these programs appeared to be just the type of initiatives that would help local and state party organizations establish fruitful relationships with African American voters, a third of whom, according to an October 1967 Gallup poll, were unhappy with President Johnson, blaming him for the war in Vietnam and continuing racial and economic inequality.[109] That same month, Michigan congressman John Conyers, a lifelong Democrat, told a meeting of black elected officials that unless his party confronted issues affecting the black poor and working class, African Americans would either vote Republican or stay home in 1968; either way, he warned, the Democratic Party would lose the presidential election.[110] Conyers threat was a provocative power play, designed to get the president and the Democratic Party to further "liberalize" its position on unemployment, poverty, and housing.[111] Such rhetoric, when combined with poll numbers, encouraged the *Christian Science Monitor* to assert that if the GOP nominated the "right" liberal or moderate Republican for president, the party would win between 20 to 30 percent of the black vote. The Minorities Division echoed this argument, but also continued to sidestep the party's tense history with African Americans, spending considerable time trying to rehabilitate the image of right-wing Republicans; for instance, they cast Ronald Reagan as a civil rights advocate, championing the governor's positive record of black appointments and ignoring his repeated attempts to repeal or veto California's equal rights laws.[112]

Equally problematic was the Minorities Division's inability to address African Americans' problems comprehensively. While some of the state and local Republican-led measures began to address some of the needs of African Americans, they did so in a case-by-case manner, tailored to the individual problems of African Americans, rather than those of the collective group. The realities of 1967, however, warranted more than piecemeal efforts; pervasive segregation in housing, education, and employment; police brutality; unequal treatment under the law; poverty; and political alienation were systemic issues that required serious intervention not only from private industries but also from every level of government. Republican self-help initiatives simply could not provide this kind of aid. GOP centers in Detroit, for example, crumbled when riots tore through the city in July 1967. By the time the uproar subsided, more than forty people were dead, twelve hundred were injured, seven thousand had been arrested, and the "war-torn" city had suffered more than $50 million in property damage. Center staffers worked with local churches and civil rights groups in a sincere effort to distribute much-needed supplies to thousands of area residents in the aftermath of the riot; and yet, as the GOP staffers bitterly complained, they received no publicity for their efforts. This was a difficult reality for the Minorities Division; as violent upheavals broke out in more than forty cities in the summer and fall of 1967, they overshadowed the small-scale black outreach efforts that party officials had made throughout the years.[113]

LAW AND ORDER WITH SOCIAL JUSTICE

If the riots obscured the Minorities Division's community initiatives, then surely the rhetoric of national party leaders on urban uprisings completely erased those outreach measures from the minds of the African American public. Party leaders bandied about the phrase "law and order" as if it were the panacea for the nation's ills: "We've got to make it very clear to potential rioters that in the event that something starts," Richard Nixon once warned, "the law will move in with adequate force to put down rioting and looting at the first indication of it."[114] The notion of "law and order" was an alienating concept for most African Americans; though "colorblind," it carried a coded message that domestic peace could be maintained only through repressive means devoid of justice and equal treatment. By the mid-1960s, as Ed Brooke later observed, the phrase had "racist undertones" that implied oppressive "police-state attitudes" toward African Americans and served as a reminder to "keep Negroes in their place."[115]

The party's law and order demands clearly undermined the Minorities Division's attempts to rehabilitate the party's image among African Americans, destroying its revisionist interpretation of the GOP as a vanguard for black equality. Likewise, measured Republican responses to the riots were often upstaged by the reactionary politics of conservative party officials; in Congress, for example, Charles Percy's plan to introduce a $1.1 billion emergency fund to "ease tensions" in urban areas by creating housing and jobs was overshadowed by Florida congressman William Cramer's "Stokely Carmichael" legislation—a bill that promised to punish citizens that traveled across state lines to "incite" riots. The proposal, Cramer admitted, was not designed to address the root inequalities that caused rioting but rather to punish and police the incendiary rhetoric of Black Power advocates.[116]

In the middle of this debate sat Edward Brooke. He denounced the lawlessness of rioters, blaming black militants for escalating racial tensions in the cities, but also condemned the "reactionary vigilantes" in his party for seeking scapegoats rather than solutions to urban violence. "Black Power," he told the NUL in a July 1967 lecture, was merely a reaction to "white irresponsibility." Answers lay not in blanket demands for law and order, but rather in "law, order, and justice." He maintained that any legislative approach that focused solely on the rioters instead of on the conditions of inequality that sparked the riots was a pointless endeavor, since lawmakers needed to examine causes, instead of symptoms so as to solve the problems of the country's cities.[117] Brooke was still a centrist at his core, committed to his "non-Negro" approach of engaging both black and white constituents; however, his rhetoric here hinted at a subtle ideological shift. More specifically, his willingness to hold whites accountable for persistent inequality demonstrated that the senator was becoming more liberal. That same month, in a speech to the NAACP, the politician offered a forceful lecture on solutions to urban turmoil, much to the satisfaction of the five thousand audience members. The conditions of the cities, he boomed, warranted creative solutions utilizing the federal government. The animated crowd interrupted the senator's speech more than forty times with spontaneous applause, delivering a standing ovation when he announced plans to introduce a fair housing bill in Congress in the upcoming months. The most important solution, he closed, was for African Americans—especially the black poor—to organize into a grass-roots political movement to demand power in society. "Power has the ability to change conditions so that opportunities are open, rights respected and enforced, and a man's future made secure, [and it] is the essence of the democratic process." In essence, this was Brooke's answer to urban despair: to turn black rage into a respectable and productive effort to bring about social and economic change.[118]

Brooke's actions offered a meaningful public counter to some of the more draconian measures launched by his congressional counterparts. In July 1967, while House Republicans were championing the anti-riot bill and opposing increases in rent-supplement programs, the black politician became the first senator of either party to introduce a resolution calling for a formal investigation into civil disorders. Two days later, President Johnson issued an executive order creating the National Advisory Commission on Civil Disorders (Kerner Commission), appointing Brooke and ten others to the bipartisan committee.[119]

One month after Brooke's appointment to the Kerner Commission, Minnesota senator Walter Mondale crossed party lines to discuss cosponsoring a fair housing bill with the black official. Backed by a coalition of fifteen civil rights organizations, the politicians introduced the proposal into the Senate in February 1968, attaching it to a pending civil rights workers protection bill. Segregation was fundamentally undemocratic, Brooke and the bill's proponents argued, since it was the "rejection of one human being by another without any justification but superior power." As one legal observer later explained, "No matter a man's university degrees, his income level, his profession, he could suffer the degradation and humiliation of being told he was not good enough to live in a white neighborhood." In this way, Brooke envisioned fair housing as one way to ensure a racially egalitarian society, with equal access for all. Moreover, failure to live by a democratic code of ideals and to end racial discrimination in housing, he maintained, would only lead to black frustration, which in turn would transform into resentment, thereby provoking violence in the nation's cities. In a series of congressional hearings in February, Brooke testified that fair housing was the first step in transforming the country into an "Open Society," one in which African Americans could access the same opportunity that "generations" of whites had enjoyed. An important part of this argument was rooted in the notion of individualism: the bill's supporters argued that while fair housing addressed discrimination against African Americans as a collective, it posed no threat to individual freedom or rights because no one could be forced to sell or not to sell a house; instead, the measure merely leveled the playing field, creating an "open and fair access situation where every seller or landlord must by law treat his customers equally," regardless of race. In short, as black Republicans had argued for years, racial discrimination was the antithesis of individualism.[120]

As the debate over civil rights and open housing roared in Congress, the Kerner Commission issued its final report, a four-hundred-plus-page document charging that the nation was moving toward "two societies, one black, one white—separate and unequal." The report offered an indictment of white racism, arguing that systemic discrimination was the root cause of the 1967 riots. While black agitators had contributed to a tense racial atmosphere, white institutions had produced the conditions that gave rise to urban disorder—producing, sustaining, and condoning racial and economic inequality through a seemingly endless list of offenses, most of which African Americans had decried for generations. The report proposed a long detailed list of several dozen recommendations for addressing inequality, the most conspicuous of which, given pending congressional legislation, was a demand for Congress to pass a "comprehensive and enforceable federal open housing law" to address discrimination in the sale or rental of housing.[121]

Brooke's and the Kerner Commission's warning that the nation would be "torn apart" without the passage of civil rights legislation struck a nerve in several Republican politicians. Senate minority leader Everett Dirksen of Illinois—described by the *Los Angeles Times* as a "consummate flip-flop artist" on civil rights legislation—had helped guide the 1964 Civil Rights Act and 1965 Voting Rights Act through Congress but had opposed the passage of the open housing bill in 1966, which arguably led to the measure's failure. Two years later, he reversed his stand, playing a critical role in shepherding the bill through the Senate. His about-face, one commentator observed, was due in part to pressure from liberal and moderate Republican senators, including Charles Percy and Ed Brooke; their presence in the Senate, one party official noted, made it difficult for "Republicans to stick by their conservative stance." Party leaders also observed that support for open housing could help rehabilitate the GOP's record among black voters—privately, one conservative senator even demanded that Republicans not align with southern Democrats in defeating the bill, out of fear that such an alliance would "harm the party's image among Negroes in an election year." Thus, for some party politicians, including Dirksen, voting for fair housing was a strategic move, designed to keep the GOP from appearing hostile to "Negroes' aspirations."[122]

On March 11, 1968, after weeks of debate and negotiations, the Senate passed the civil rights bill by a vote of 71 to 20. Only four of the Senate's thirty-six Republicans voted against the bill, breaking with the GOP to align with southern Democrats. It was a tremendous achievement, one that inspired NAACP official Clarence Mitchell to share his exhilaration with Brooke: "You have helped to make it possible for me to face [blacks] with new vindication of my belief in the power of the US Constitution to right wrongs and promote progress," he wrote.[123] In the House, the bill faced stiff resistance, languishing in Congress until April 4, 1968, when Martin Luther King Jr. was assassinated in Memphis, Tennessee. "There are moments in the life of a nation when grief and outrage strike its people dumb," a somber Brooke wrote to his constituents, "when words will not come because no words can express the agony in the nation's soul. . . . The murder of Martin Luther King, like the murder of John Fitzgerald Kennedy, tears from us a noble and irreplaceable leader. No nation can sustain such a loss without feeling abrupt shock and lasting pain."[124] Within a week of King's death, the House passed the 1968 Civil Rights Act; and, as the nation mourned and as citizens rioted out of grief, Lyndon Johnson signed the bill into law. To be sure, the final act was a compromise, as it contained the Cramer anti-riot provision and did little to address suburban discrimination; but it also included Mondale and Brooke's fair housing measure, thereby banning discrimination in the sale or rental of housing on the basis of race, color, religion, or national origin. Over the course of the next three years, the Massachusetts senator would add three additional provisions dubbed the "Brooke Amendments," which added protections for poor and low-income renters. To be sure, this was a critical point for black politicians, one that demonstrated the influence of Edward Brooke during a tumultuous period in American politics; in integrating the upper echelons of the Republican Party and facilitating civil rights change through legislative action, he forced the GOP to acknowledge the significance of race in a way that other black Republican leaders had struggled to do.[125]

• • •

When probed about his longtime commitment to the Republican Party, Edward Brooke commented, "I've had my problems with the party, but I believe in the vitality of a two-party system of government. I think I can do more inside the party than outside. I can do more to bring it closer to the center. You might call me a centrist. I've tried to bring the Republican Party back."[126] In truth, Brooke and other party moderates and liberals did bring the party closer to the center, if but for a moment; the passage of the Fair Housing Act suggests as much.[127] The efforts of the Minorities Division also pushed state and local party organizations in new directions, despite being overshadowed by the turmoil in the nation's cities and the inflammatory rhetoric of some members of the GOP. Between 1966 and 1969, Townes's staff of black ambassadors would grow from eight to more than thirty, as they began the gradual work of integrating African Americans into state and local party organization hierarchies.[128]

The mid-1960s was a period of possibility for party moderates, including black Republicans—a moment where red, white and blue bumper stickers reading "The New Look—Romney and Brooke '68" appeared on the cars of American citizens, both black and white.[129] Such was the hope of this moment that in the months and days preceding the nominating convention, Brooke could confidently tell reporters that he had not been ruled out for the second spot on the presidential ticket.[130] As *Ebony* reasoned,

> Republicans could well make their greatest showing among Negroes since Reconstruction. . . . Party strategists now seem convinced that, with growing Negro registration in the South, a great interest in the North, and a ground swell of enlightenment among younger whites,

no truly reactionary candidate can win an important office in mid-20th century America.[131]

However, this was an overly optimistic prediction—the reality was far more complicated. As one reporter shrewdly explained, despite the "Republican Jubilee," party members were ever aware of the "rumbling of right wing thunder" in the background. The fate of the Republican Party was contested territory during this period; Brooke and fellow moderates were ascendant, but their victory was by no means assured.[132] More than that, by 1968 most conservative party leaders had disavowed explicit racism, embracing an apparently race-neutral approach to politics; nevertheless, many of these appeals continued to alienate black voters, who saw such overtures as implicitly racist or exclusionary in tone.

Although the GOP was plagued by factional skirmishes, liberal and moderate Republicanism still played a crucial role in party affairs, especially in the buildup to the presidential nomination. In the spring of 1968, Brooke, like many other black Republicans, endorsed Nelson Rockefeller for president, pinning his hopes to the candidacy of the New York governor.[133] In August, the RNC named the black senator temporary chairman of the Republican National Convention—a symbolic position, but a high-profile one nonetheless, as the temporary chair presided over the first two days of the convention, organizing the seating of delegates. Four years earlier, it would have been inconceivable to have a black Republican serve as the opening chair of the Republican National Convention.[134] "Order must prevail but it will prevail only when there is a will to obey," Brooke declared to the thirteen hundred Republican delegates, "And the will to obey will only exist when every citizen is assured the benefits of equal opportunity and equal justice."[135] This was an important moment; in a party that had toed the line of racism with harsh accusations of "law and order," here was a black senator declaring to thousands of *white* Republicans that racial equality and equal justice under the law were the solution to the nation's turmoil. It was a bittersweet moment, wherein Brooke articulated black Republicans' concerns at a gathering where they were marginally represented; only twenty-six black delegates—1.9 percent of the convention total, a marginal increase from 1964—sat in the crowd as Brooke spoke.[136]

It was a convention full of contradictions. Richard Nixon received the party's presidential nomination, marketing himself as the "moderate" choice. He considered, among others, John Lindsay, George Romney, and Ed Brooke for his running mate, and eventually settled on Maryland governor Spiro T. Agnew. African Americans had a visceral reaction not only to this selection but also, more generally, to Nixon's nomination as the party's presidential choice. Though a third of black voters had supported the crafty politician in 1960, eight years later, they recoiled at his attacks on the Kerner Report, his use of the racially charged language of "law and order," and his backroom dealings with white southerners, including Strom Thurmond. Arriving at Martin Luther King Jr.'s funeral in April 1968, for example, Nixon found himself barred from entering by outraged African Americans; he gained access only after his friend (and political supporter) Wilt Chamberlain brokered his admittance.[137]

Nixon's selection of Agnew for the second spot on the ticket simply further fanned these flames. African Americans had given Agnew overwhelming support in 1966, but much had changed in two years; by 1968, the relationship between the governor and his black constituents had soured over disagreements about fiscal budgets and racially insensitive rhetoric. Agnew's obnoxious rhetoric on "Cadillac" civil rights leaders and "savage" black looters quickly anointed him the new spokesman for law and order.[138] The choice of Agnew, the *Chicago Defender* wrote, was indefensible, sending a clear message that the party "does not need the black vote to capture the White House." The "moderate" ticket, the newspaper warned, was in actuality a "reaffirmation of a racial mood which would employ brute force to smother black voices crying out for social justice and economic opportunity." A *New York Amsterdam News* survey of black New Yorkers came to a similar conclusion; respondents argued Nixon and Agnew were racists and predicted that the president would dismantle much-needed federal antipoverty programs and undo civil rights progress.[139]

In reality, Nixon's approach was more of a "suburban strategy," marketed to middle-class southern suburbanites; he positioning himself as a respectable centrist alternative to the "reactionary racial platform" of third-party candidate George Wallace and the Democratic liberalism of Hubert Humphrey. His 1968 Republican National Convention speech, as historian Matt Lassiter argues, embraced "racially inclusive imagery," identifying white *and* black citizens as the "forgotten Americans, the non-shouters, the non-demonstrators," the "good," hard-working people who "give lift to the American dream."[140] This was the kind of rhetoric that Brooke had employed in his 1966 senatorial campaign, a "colorblind" appropriation of the black politician's "non-Negro" politics; consequently, despite disagreeing with Nixon on civil rights legislation, busing, and racial gradualism, Brooke agreed to campaign on behalf of the party's nominee and serve as an informal adviser, in the name of party unity.

It was this association that would weaken Brooke's standing among black audiences. Brooke argued that he could influence Nixon, believing that the presidential nominee was "fundamentally moderate." The *New*

York Times followed Brooke as he traveled on Nixon's campaign jet in September and October 1968, concluding that the senator was, in fact, influencing Nixon; the candidate had tempered his language in response to Brooke's council, for example, adopting the phrase "law and order with justice."[141] Yet for some black audiences, this was not enough. At a campaign event in Houston, Brooke was caught off guard when a young woman in the audience calmly asked him, "How does it feel to be a house nigger?"[142] Jackie Robinson, who had once argued that Brooke was the party's best hope for redemption, labeled him a "white folk's Negro," stating: "One cannot honestly claim to be working for the best interests of black people and climb into bed with a Nixon who has prostituted himself for the Strom Thurmonds of the Old South."[143] The irony here was that as the NNRA official was condemning Brooke, the black politician was actually moving closer to the assembly's liberal position. The *Chicago Defender* summarized these views after Nixon simultaneously applauded desegregation and labeled federal intervention on desegregation dangerous: Senator Brooke, they wrote, "should understand by now that he is helping neither the Negro cause nor himself by this muddy relationship with Nixon. Any prolongation of that association would rightly come within the purview of the saying that birds of the same feather flock together."[144]

This was but one aspect of the contradictions presented by Brooke; indeed, midway through the campaign, he quit after disagreeing with Nixon's position on desegregation, only to rejoin a few days later. And though his image suffered because of his association with the party's nominee, he still maintained a level of respect from the black electorate —a level that no other black Republican was able to replicate. "We of the Minorities Division [of the RNC] submit that at no time has the black voter been more aware that he is a captive of one-party politics, and that his only chance of liberation is meaningful involvement in a true two-party system," wrote Clarence Townes in a 1968 report. "Negroes are waiting, virtually on the edge of a social disaster, for Republican candidates to offer them viable alternatives—methods by which they might personally achieve their political liberation."[145] Yet despite such bold proclamations and the Minorities Division's outreach efforts, the group still struggled, both in attracting black voters nationally and in getting black Republican candidates elected in 1968. That year, eighty-four black Republicans ran for public office; only five were elected; at the time, more than one thousand black Democrats sat in office, compared to forty black Republicans. Likewise, only 10 percent of African Americans would vote for Nixon in 1968.[146] The Minorities Division's refusal to address the party's troubled legacy undermined its earnest outreach efforts, contributing to the GOP's mythmaking and damaging its credibility among black audiences. It was constrained by its association with Nixon and Agnew; in shunning the militancy of the NNRA, the division made significant inroads among white Republicans, but underestimated the damage that came from being associated with a presidential ticket that offended many African Americans.

Part of what makes Brooke's political rise so distinct is that he accomplished what other black Republicans, including the NNRA and the Minorities Division, were unable to do—commanding the respect of the party on racial issues, which in turn allowed him to steward civil rights legislation through Congress. But even Brooke was unable to shape the GOP presidential nominee. The Massachusetts politician's individual story illustrates some of the difficulties faced by black Republicans writ large, as they struggled to be not only relevant locally but influential nationally.

Despite his challenges, many believed that Brooke transcended the divisiveness of the Republican Party, ushering in a new era of politics. As Clarence Mitchell wrote in an emotional letter to Brooke in 1973, "In all honesty, I must say that ten years ago, the thought of a black man becoming President would be dismissed as day-dreaming. [But] your impressive victories . . . and the whole manner in which you served in the Senate have helped to change the picture immeasurably. No matter what you may decide to do, I feel greatly comforted by the knowledge that the country is moving toward recognition of ability in candidates for public office rather than consideration based on race or national origin."[147]

This influence extended beyond the partisan boundaries of the GOP, crossing into black Democratic politics. In Brooke, some black Democrats saw an opportunity for coalition and black political independence. During his years in Congress, he formed a strong working relationship with the Congressional Black Caucus (CBC), although not a formal member; likewise his keynote for a caucus event in 1973 would publicly inspire civil rights activist Jesse Jackson to declare, "There is no more qualified candidate in the Republican Party than Ed Brooke." Shirley Chisholm and Charlie Rangel would echo this statement urging, as both did, politicians to forgo partisanship and support Brooke for vice president, applauding his "measured but forceful approach to domestic needs."[148]

Chisholm and Rangel supported him even though his positions on issues such as social welfare and foreign policy often differed from their own. Their goal was to push an agenda through both parties; thus they saw Brooke as an ally who could work through the Republican Party. As political scientist Ronald Walters has noted, Brooke's presence in the Senate was "extraordinarily invaluable" for both Republicans and Dem-

ocrats, as he could easily act as a liaison between both groups.[149] Ultimately, Brooke as well as other black Republicans would influence party
politics and policies—albeit in a painfully protracted way—especially as
Richard Nixon assumed a new degree of executive power through the
1970s.

Figure 1. E. Frederic Morrow meets with President Dwight D. Eisenhower. In July 1955, Eisenhower appointed Morrow as the White House Officer for Special Projects. (Source: The National Park Service, Dwight D. Eisenhower Presidential Library)

Figure 2. Civil Rights leaders, including Martin Luther King Jr. and A. Philip Randolph, meet with President Dwight D. Eisenhower and E. Frederic Morrow at the White House. The black Republican and former NAACP organizer played a key role in arranging this meeting and others, throughout his tenure in the White House. (Source: The National Park Service, Dwight D. Eisenhower Presidential Library)

Figure 3. Jewel Lafontant, a prominent Chicago attorney and civil rights advocate, delivers the seconding speech for Richard Nixon as the GOP's vice-presidential nominee at the 1960 Republican National Convention. (Copyright © Oberlin College Archives)

Figure 4. Richard Nixon shakes hands with a young African American supporter while campaigning in Memphis, Tennessee, in 1960. (Copyright © Bettman/Corbis/Associated Press)

Figure 5. Exuberant supporters greet Barry Goldwater at a presidential campaign stop in Indiana in 1964. His followers celebrated the Arizona senator's "loud and clear" brand of conservatism, which pushed an agenda of anticommunism, states' rights, free market enterprise, and individual freedom. (Copyright © Associated Press)

Figure 6. Jackie Robinson denounces Barry Goldwater to journalists outside the Cow Palace at the 1964 Republican National Convention. Arguably the most prominent of Goldwater's detractors, Robinson—like millions of other black voters who rejected the senator's presidential bid—criticized the Republican politician for his outspoken support for states' rights and opposition to the Civil Rights Act of 1964. (Copyright ©Bettman/Corbis/Associated Press)

Figure 7. Senator Hugh Scott and a GOP official present Senator Edward W. Brooke with a gavel to commemorate his selection as Temporary Chairman of the 1968 Republican National Convention in Miami, Florida. Brooke was the first African American to hold the position. (Source: Richard Nixon Presidential Library)

Figure 8. Supporters of New York governor Nelson Rockefeller and Senator Edward Brooke greet the black politician in Miami during the 1968 Republican National Convention. During Brooke's twelve years in Congress, the "Brooke for VP" movement gained traction among a bipartisan and racially diverse cross section of advocates, including voters, politicians, and activists. (Copyright © Associated Press)

NEW DIRECTIONS '68

Published By The Minorities Division, Republican National Committee, 1625 Eye Street, N.W., Washington, D. C. 20006

Volume 1   Number 3

CLARENCE L. TOWNES, JR., and National Chairman, Ray C. Bliss, discussing "Big City Push for '68."

Bliss & Townes: GOP Push For '68

As of today, Republican prospects for 1968 look better and better—but with seven years out of the White House, no one, especially at the National Committee level, is taking any chances on wishing their way back into full political power.

All areas and sections of the country will continue to see a stepped up drive by the Party with particular emphasis being placed upon urban and suburban voters. National Committee Chairman Ray C. Bliss will be heading up this "big push for '68" assisted by his Special Assistant Clarence L. Townes, Jr.

Townes, who also serves as Director of the Minorities Division, works with a staff of seven, coordinating various minority voter activities in cooperation

Continued on Page 3

GEORGE BUSH—
Action In Houston

Freshman Congressman, George Bush, from the newly created 7th Congressional District in Houston, Texas, is probably one of the busiest and most effective new GOP members on the Hill.

As part of the "bumper crop" of new Congressmen and Senators the GOP sent to Washington after the 1966 elections, Bush has concerned himself with most of the major problems facing Americans in the 60's and has offered many constructive proposals for their solution.

None of this, however, surprises his constituents back home, because Bush was functioning as a Congressman even before he was elected.

During the Spring and Summer of '66, for instance, Bush in his capacity

Continued on Page 2

CONGRESSMAN GEORGE BUSH with Bush All-Stars, a softball team which he sponsored in the spring of 1966.

Figure 9. *New Directions '68* was published by the Minorities Division of the Republican National Committee (RNC). The brainchild of RNC special assistant Clarence L. Townes Jr. and RNC Chair Ray C. Bliss—both pictured in the top photo—the newsletter was part of the national committee's broader attempt to appeal to African American voters. Also pictured is Congressman George H. W. Bush. (Copyright © Special Collections and Archives, Virginia Commonwealth University Libraries)

Figure 10. President Richard Nixon meets with the Council of Black Appointees in 1970. Incensed by the president's reactionary actions toward African Americans, black appointees increasingly voiced their concerns as a collective, as they did during this frank meeting with the president. Although the administration attempted to use the session as a public relations display of diversity, the appointees continued to call for Nixon to abandon his "southern strategy." (Source: Richard Nixon Presidential Library)

Figure 11. Richard Nixon, Jim Brown, and two members of the president's "black cabinet"—Stanley S. Scott and John Wilks—discuss black economic empowerment circa 1971. The football player-turned-actor regularly met with White House officials to discuss federal funding for his "black-owned" business ventures, as part of the black capitalism initiative, which fell under the umbrella of the Office of Minority Business Enterprise. (Source: Richard Nixon Presidential Library)

Figure 12. Gerald Ford meets with black Republican leaders at the White House in 1974. Black Republicans initially viewed Gerald Ford's ascent to the presidency as a symbol of much-needed Republican rebirth; the new president's welcoming attitude seemed to encourage as much, as he reassured black party members that he wanted their input on federal policy—a promise that turned out to be largely rhetorical. (Source: Gerald R. Ford Presidential Library)

Figure 13. Supreme Court Justice Thurgood Marshall and William T. Coleman share stories as they prepare for Coleman's swearing-in ceremony as secretary of transportation in 1975. Coleman was the second African American member of a presidential cabinet and first for the Republican Party. (Source: Gerald R. Ford Presidential Library)

Figure 14. After endorsing the Republican ticket in 1980, Ralph Abernathy raises the hand
of presidential candidate Ronald Reagan aloft while vice presidential nominee George
H. W. Bush applauds. The famed civil rights activist was not alone in his endorsement;
others, including Hosea Williams, of the Southern Christian Leadership Conference, also
endorsed the Reagan-Bush campaign. (Copyright © Associated Press)

Figure 15. President Ronald Reagan discusses African American issues with black
Republican leaders in 1981 including Gloria Toote, Jim Cummings, John McNeill, Henry
Lucas, and Ed Sexton. This was a significant moment for black Republicans, as they
professed their loyalty to a politician many of them had once shunned, suppressing their
doubts about his right-wing conservatism while celebrating his interests in capitalism and
business. (Source: Ronald Reagan Presidential Library)

CHAPTER FOUR

Richard Nixon's Black Cabinet

WHEN READERS OPENED THE NOVEMBER 1968 SPECIAL ELECTION ISSUE
of *Jet* magazine, they were inundated with slick political advertisements
from three of the four presidential candidates. The black weekly offered
no-nonsense messages from Freedom and Peace Party representative
Dick Gregory and Democratic contender Hubert Humphrey; not to be
outdone, the Republican Party also tried its hand at wooing the magazine's African American audience.[1] Richard Nixon's two-page glossy insert opened with a close-up of a young, well-dressed black man clutching
a thick stack of books. "This Time," the headline solemnly advised, "Vote
Like Homer Pitts' Whole World Depended On It." On the next page, the
party explicitly linked the fate of "Homer Pitts" with that of the black
electorate:

> He'll get his degree. Then what? . . . laborer, factory job . . . or his own
> business? A vote for Richard Nixon for President is a vote for a man
> who wants Homer to have the chance to own his own business. Rich-
> ard Nixon believes strongly in black capitalism. Because black capital-
> ism is black power in the best sense of the word. It's the road that leads
> to black economic influence and black pride. It's the key to the black
> man's fight for equality—for a piece of the action. And that's what the
> free enterprise system is all about. This time . . . Nixon.[2]

Mr. Pitts, it would seem, was a budding entrepreneur—an African American who embraced the racial liberalism of the 1960s while accepting the
respectability politics traditionally heralded by the black elite. The ad adopted the language of Black Power, but softened it, much in the way that
black Republicans like Ed Brooke had done a few years earlier. Through the
advertisement, the campaign implied that Nixon had practical solutions
to address the ailments and aspirations of African Americans—that the
GOP would succeed where the Democratic Party had "failed" and that
the Republican nominee could help black citizens "help themselves."

Implicit in this message was the understanding that Nixon's solution was not a universal approach but rather was aimed at middle-class,
college-educated African Americans, and those who aspired to someday
be a part of this group. The Republican Party, *Time* observed, was trying

to develop a new "Negro managerial class to lead, hire, and inspire."[3] To be sure, the campaign's black outreach strategy was premised on making gestures toward black respectability, one that emphasized self-help and personal accountability—an elastic tradition embraced by various black communities, ranging from the wealthy, to the militant, to the religious.[4] Expounding on these ideas in a lengthy *Jet* questionnaire, Nixon wrote: "I am the only candidate who truly believes that black people, on their own steam and with 'remedial' help from the government are going to make it." African Americans like Ed Brooke, he continued, were "symptomatic of what I hope will be an increasing political phenomenon in this country; the realization by black people and their leaders that their best hope lies not in the Democratic plantation politics of the past, but in the kinds of programs as I have put forward."[5]

Richard Nixon's classist appeals for minority enterprise mirrored a theme central to black Republican thought and action; as we have seen, African American party members consistently proposed variations on a single core agenda, wedding liberal appeals for racial equality with a belief in traditional Republican principles. In particular, they had long called for the creation and implementation of a movement for economic civil rights, as an alternative means of reaching full equality.[6] A June 1968 article in *Time* highlighted the prominent position of this centerpiece of black Republican thought, noting that all three Republican presidential primary candidates had incorporated the concept into their campaign rhetoric.[7] New York governor Nelson Rockefeller proposed "multibillion-dollar schemes for urban redevelopment," while his conservative counterpart in California, Ronald Reagan, promoted solutions aimed at the "economic salvation of the ghettoes."[8] Most notably, in "Bridges to Human Dignity," broadcast on CBS radio in April 1968, Richard Nixon outlined a sweeping program of black capitalism, emphasizing black pride and self-help. "For too long, white America has sought to buy off the Negro—and to buy off its own sense of guilt—with ever more programs of welfare," he stated. What African Americans needed was "the bridge of black success —a bridge that can only be built by those Negroes who themselves have overcome, and who by their help or their example can show that the way to the American dream is not barred by a sign that reads, 'Whites Only.'"[9]

Nixon's rhetoric of black capitalism was at once problematic and intriguing; on the one hand, he offered an unsophisticated and at times insulting view of black poverty; on the other hand, he used the same language employed by black critics of Democratic liberalism, most conspicuously, black Republicans *and* black militants. Consequently, after he received the GOP's presidential nomination, some African Americans eagerly endorsed the president, citing their interest in black capitalism. *Call and Post* publisher W. O. Walker was so impressed by the initiative that he confidently declared, "Nixon will do more for [African Americans] than has been accomplished in the last hundred years. Sound economic gains and restoration of pride and dignity are in store for minority groups."[10]

Even as prominent white politicians echoed black Republicans' ideas, blacks themselves were divided about those same politicians. "I agree with Richard Nixon's ideas of black capitalism, but I cannot support his candidacy," Harlem resident James Greene stated. "He will have too many debts to pay for the conservative, reactionary southerners that won the nomination for him."[11] To many, these actions and others undermined Nixon's endorsement of black capitalism, universal human dignity, and party unity and instead implied a willingness to spurn the black electorate.[12] Jackie Robinson best expressed liberal black Republican frustrations with the Nixon-Agnew team in a September 5, 1968, letter to Arizona's Barry Goldwater:

> Picture yourself a black man, standing before your television set hearing Strom Thurmond . . . telling the country of his veto powers. . . . I have yet to hear a denial of these allegations. . . . I condemn riots and violence as vigorously as does Nixon. . . . But my emphasis is on law and justice. For without the presence of justice, order is placed in jeopardy. . . . Mr. Nixon . . . impressed me in 1960, but in 1968 his dealing with Thurmond made a kingmaker out of the former Democrat.

"Because I am proud of my blackness and the progress we have made," he concluded, "I refuse to support this ticket."[13]

The November election was a close one, with Nixon barely scraping out a victory. Though he won 301 electoral votes and 43.4 percent of the popular vote, to Hubert Humphrey's 42.7 percent, the president-elect was nearly undone by Alabama politician and third party candidate George Wallace, who received more than 13 percent of the vote and won the five Deep South states. Nixon received only 10 percent of the black vote, a poor return compared to his 1960 showing, but still better than the 6 percent garnered by Barry Goldwater four years earlier—a point Clarence Townes emphasized in a postelection Minorities Division report.[14] Nevertheless, 10 percent was still an abysmal number when compared to the party's initial projection of 30 percent, reflecting the party's electoral woes with African Americans.[15]

Despite the misgivings of African Americans, most black party members viewed Nixon's presidential win as a cautious victory of their own, believing that a Republican administration had the potential to be a powerful venue for advancing, developing, and implementing their solutions and policies. Floyd McKissick, the former executive director of the Congress of Racial Equality (CORE), underscored this thinking when he announced that Nixon would do "one Hell of a job" in the White House. Echoing these sentiments, John Silvera, a deputy aide to Nelson Rockefeller stated:

> While the majority of black citizens "may" be disappointed in the results, I'm not. I feel that if the necessary changes are to come . . . there needed to be a change in the administration. We should all now pool our collective resources and talents to assist this new administration to go in the direction we want it to go. That is my idea of black power.[16]

Black Republicans had a clear goal: influence and inform the policies, programs, and direction of the Nixon administration on African American issues. In the White House, and with access to the power of the federal government, they finally saw an opportunity to showcase their solutions on a national scale.

Central to this effort was Richard Nixon's "Black Cabinet," a small loose-knit group of black Republican appointees who pushed an agenda aimed at the needs and aspirations of middle-class African Americans. Economics was their strongest priority; consequently, their notion of black capitalism would come to mean more to them than the program first proposed during the 1968 campaign, ultimately evolving into what they called an "alternative" civil rights movement. As we have seen, this economic focus was not new, as African Americans of all ideologies had long looked to the intersection of race and class to motivate a black uplift movement. But where many civil rights and Black Power organizations believed that capitalism had failed African Americans, black Republican believed that access to the "free market" was the best option for solving racial equality and introducing economic parity. Though not a formal collective group until 1970, they shared a common concern for minority enterprise and two-party competition; likewise, they were united by their desire for moral support as they navigated the treacherous landscape of a protean White House.

The black appointees successfully enacted a broad economic initiative that encompassed minority business enterprise, education, and affirmative action, an agenda that was both ambitious and classist, privileging the perspective of the black middle class over the needs of the black working class and the poor. Nevertheless, the success of the "Black Cabinet" is significant in the wider spectrum of black GOP politics, for it was the first time that black Republicans used a presidential administration to enact their specific agenda. Ultimately, the members of the Black Cabinet viewed economic uplift, coupled with political shrewdness as the final, critical step in the struggle for racial equality and black independence. "Earning Power," Arthur Fletcher explained, "is the name of the Game. The black man's future, his rights to equality, his freedom of choice. . . . What matters for us blacks is economic liberation."[17]

CONSTRUCTING THE BLACK CABINET

Within days of the Republican Party's November presidential victory, black party members publicly called for the president to appoint qualified African American Republicans to the new administration. According to the National Council of Concerned Afro-American Republicans, black loyalists had "worn the battle cry in the heat of the day" and demonstrated their steadfast allegiance to the Republican Party. This unwavering commitment, the organization argued, compelled recognition for "those who have worked for and supported the party in season and out of season since the great exodus of 1932."[18] Echoing a similar, albeit less partisan refrain, *Ebony* magazine speculated on the prospects of a Nixon-appointed "black brain trust," consisting of prominent Republican figures such as Clarence Townes, Arthur Fletcher, former Equal Employment Opportunity Commissioner (EEOC) Samuel C. Jackson, Michigan GOP vice chair Earl Kennedy, Black Power Conference secretary Nathan Wright, and, of course, the ubiquitous Edward Brooke.[19]

As an enigmatic adviser to Nixon throughout the fall 1968 campaign, Brooke and the president-elect had discussed, on a number of occasions, the possibility of a cabinet appointment. After the November election, Nixon offered the Massachusetts senator his choice of positions, including secretary of Housing and Urban Development (HUD) or Health, Education and Welfare (HEW), or ambassador to the United Nations (UN). Black newspapers also reported that the president had offered Brooke the position of U.S. attorney general—a rumor that the senator refused to confirm or deny.[20] In a press conference, Brooke explained that he had declined Nixon's offers because he felt he could "best serve the country" and the president-elect in the Senate. In truth, it was far more likely that the black politician believed that serving as a cabinet member would restrict his freedom and his voice, since he would be obligated to offer support for the Nixon administration or risk losing his appointment.[21] Despite Brooke's statement that he planned to work with the administration in "other capacities," many were disappointed by his decision; giving voice to this anguish was the *Chicago Defender*, which had imagined Brooke as the nation's first black attorney general. In a biting op-ed criticizing the senator's decision not to accept a cabinet position, the editors wrote:

> [Brooke] made a misjudgment of his services to the country and to Nixon. . . . [As] Attorney General he would do more for civil rights in a manner that would inspire confidence in the communities where racial tensions are high. . . . His counsel to the black masses . . . would calm passions, quiet anxieties and restore order and peace. . . . In these days of turbulence, violence and uncertainty, the role of the Department of Justice becomes increasingly more significant and powerful. Here lies the responsibility for enforcing those legal injunctions which are meant to preserve the dignity and rights of all Americans.

That Brooke had possibly rejected this role, in addition to declining other cabinet positions, was astonishing to the *Defender* precisely because each appointment carried so much symbolic and meaningful weight for African Americans. The staff's diatribe concluded with a grim warning for the senator to accept Nixon's offers: placing the "wrong men" in the "wrong Cabinet posts" would bring "irreparable discredit" to the Nixon administration's fragile relationship with black communities.[22]

The White House, however, did manage to appoint black Republicans to high-ranking positions in the new administration, many of whom would become part of the Black Cabinet.[23] Among the first was Robert J. Brown, designated by the press as the "White House ambassador to American Negroes." Dubbed a "true black capitalist" by reporters, the thirty-three-year-old bespectacled North Carolinian was a self-made entrepreneur who carried a "switchblade knife in his White House attaché case as a reminder" of his impoverished upbringing in the South. He was uniquely suited for his position as Nixon's only black special assistant; as a former police officer and federal narcotics agent, he had a demonstrated respect for law and order, and as the founder and operator of a successful black public relations firm, he held fast to self-help mantra that characterized black respectability politics. Brown was also a civil rights advocate, active within both the NAACP and the SCLC, forming a friendship with Martin Luther King Jr. while working with the SCLC in the early 1960s. As a registered Democrat, he had worked on the presidential campaign of Robert F. Kennedy; and in the wake of the candidate's horrific June 1968 assassination, Brown quietly joined the GOP at the urging of Clarence Townes, working with the Minorities Division throughout the rest of the summer. In interview after interview, Brown declared that he had joined the party because he was impressed by Nixon's promise to reform government and make it more responsible to the people, believing that the politician could "accomplish more for black people." In truth, with the death of Robert Kennedy, Brown also lost his enthusiasm for the Democratic Party, unable to envision Hubert Humphrey as a viable presidential contender; likewise, joining the Republican Party also gave him the opportunity to rapidly climb through the party ranks and assume a role in national party affairs.

As the president's special assistant, Brown was charged with developing a comprehensive black capitalism campaign to serve as a viable replacement to the Great Society programs of the Johnson administration. "There's a great challenge in this job," Brown shrewdly observed. "We're not making any grandiose promises, but we want action." Brown equated this "action" with black economic enterprise, prompted through self-help and self-determination.[24] He sought inspiration from local models that had joined these principles successfully—like Reverend Leon Sullivan's Philadelphia Opportunities Industrialization Center (POIC), whose guiding principle was "Helping People Help Themselves."[25] For Brown, the solution to racial equality lay not in violent struggle but rather in economic strength. "You've got to keep pressing," he maintained. "I mean politically and economically, not with firebombs. . . . We have to work with the framework of the system to change it and make it more responsive to the people."[26]

Brown was fully aware of the onerous battle facing him as a black Republican, a struggle that became clear one cold evening in December 1968. During a televised broadcast from his New York City office—as Brown watched quietly from behind the cameras—the president angered black Republicans when he brought out Walter Washington and announced the black Democrat's reappointment as mayor of Washington, D.C. Nixon simultaneously managed to offend African Americans from across the political spectrum when he closed the broadcast by cheerfully introducing the new members of his "lily-white" presidential cabinet.[27] Although a few of the cabinet members, including HUD Secretary George Romney, were seen as liberals and moderates, civil groups and black media outlets still reacted harshly to Nixon's political address, levying accusations of racism. Decrying the president's cabinet, the *Chicago Defender*, *Jet*, and the *Pittsburgh Courier* argued that it represented a significant civil rights setback. The charge was difficult to ignore, given that Lyndon Johnson had appointed the first African American presidential cabinet member, HUD secretary Robert C. Weaver, in 1966. "Johnson, a President from Texas, desegregated the Cabinet, while Nixon, a President from California, resegregated the Cabinet," NAACP official Clarence Mitchell sardonically commented.[28]

The countless accusations provoked an angry rejoinder from Robert Finch. In an embarrassingly candid interview, the HEW chief insisted that black leaders' fear of being labeled "Uncle Toms" was the sole reason for the lack of racial diversity in the presidential cabinet—a description that obscured the real problem faced by the administration: the president's behavior in the period leading up to the 1968 election alienated many African Americans. Thus, black officials feared that by accepting positions, they would appear to be condoning the Nixon administration's racial equivocations. This was not an illogical fear—Ed Brooke lost a measure of credibility among some black audiences for his association with the Nixon-Agnew ticket in 1968.[29]

In an attempt to address this, the administration created a task force on black federal appointees in December 1968. Bob Brown and Len Garment, Nixon's former law partner and a liberal Jewish Democrat, led the search committee, with a goal of integrating African Americans into the upper echelons of the federal government. Harry S. Dent, who designed many of Nixon's southern suburban appeals during the 1968 campaign, also played a role in the task force, working with Garment and Brown to recruit black leaders into policy-making positions in the administration. The former aide to South Carolina senator Strom Thurmond explained this apparent paradox in his 1978 memoirs, writing:

> Bob and I worked together closely. We were both southern boys, albeit black and white. But we understood our Southland and the practical problems associated with the race question. . . . While President Nixon was pursuing a southern strategy he was also putting more blacks in key government positions than ever before. Orders were issued to . . . concentrate on minority appointments.[30]

Brown's relationship, with both Garment and Dent, was important, particularly when viewed within the context of African American fears of a racist presidential administration. Their work created a conduit through which members of the African American community could access the White House and introduced a system through which black federal appointees could make their "input" heard in a Republican administration.

Throughout the selection process, Whitney Young, executive director of the National Urban League (NUL), also assumed an important but discreet position. For Young, adopting a flexible stance toward Richard Nixon was crucial in pushing an agenda of black uplift. He had adopted a similar attitude with the presidential administrations of John F. Kennedy and Lyndon Johnson throughout the 1960s. Soon after the 1968 election, Nixon privately offered the black official a cabinet position, as secretary of HUD, but like Brooke, Young declined; in fact, in public, he repeatedly denied that Nixon had ever offered him such a role.[31] His neutral public profile offered him a certain amount of political leeway in black communities and in both the Republican Party and the Democratic Party; and, as he later argued, his nonpartisan approach allowed him to make significant gains with both parties for African American progress.

In the case of the Nixon White House, Young's prominence drew the attention of Len Garment, who enlisted the help of the moderate civil rights leader in identifying African Americans for government appointments. In a December 1968 letter to Garment, Young pledged to help "squelch" the rumors that surrounded the administration and festered in black communities. In his response, a frustrated Len Garment railed against the "aggressive black press," blaming it for souring the White House's progress. "We have been working very hard to find and suggest . . . the names of highly qualified Negroes," wrote Garment. "As we move along, these rumors will end—that has to be our common objective." Within a day of receiving Garment's note, Young produced dozens of names, many of whom were appointed. Still, the administration ignored several of Young's recommendations, including his suggestion that Nixon find a place in the White House for National Negro Republican Assembly leader Grant Reynolds. He "is a highly qualified individual, known as 'Mr. Republican' among Negroes," argued Young. "It would be a smart move to find a spot for Mr. Reynolds' capabilities." Those within the administration apparently disagreed, as Reynolds's résumé languished in the personnel files until 1970, when he was finally appointed to a regional HUD position.[32] His private support of the task force, however, did not prevent Young from criticizing the White House in the early days of the administration; however, he espoused a cautious optimism over the role of Nixon's black appointees, as he did in an early 1969 interview, suggesting that African Americans should trust that the black men and women in the White House would "faithfully" represent black interests. "After all," he stated, "I don't think the President will respond to demands wrapped around a brick and thrown through the White House window."[33]

The behind-the-scenes machinations of the task force quickly helped the administration achieve its "first real breakthrough," with the appointment of James Farmer. Already a highly recognizable public figure for his leadership of CORE and for his role in orchestrating the 1961 Freedom Rides, Farmer had drawn further attention by running for a congressional seat in Brooklyn, with the backing of the Liberal and Republican parties, during the 1968 election.[34] In spite of his loss to Democrat dynamo Shirley Chisholm, Farmer still managed to command the interest of the White House. Just weeks after his defeat, he found himself being recruited by Nixon officials, who offered him his choice of three subcabinet positions, despite campaigning against Nixon *twice* in 1968: first, while aiding Nelson Rockefeller during the Republican primaries and, second, while supporting Hubert Humphrey in the general presidential election. While dining with Robert Finch in New York City, early in 1969, Farmer admitted to the HEW secretary that he was hesitant to accept a role given that he had publicly repudiated Nixon during the 1968 campaign. "I will not reject it out of hand," he stated, "But it will be a very difficult decision for me. . . . Nixon is very unpopular among blacks." Like others, Farmer was genuinely concerned that an association with the president would be political suicide among black audiences. "I would be painting a bull's-eye on my chest, my back, and both of my sides," he complained to Finch.

But Farmer also reasoned that an appointed position offered a valuable chance to play a significant role in federal policy making and demonstrate that African Americans could achieve "maximum political leverage" by "not being 'in the bag'" for the Democratic Party. Seeking guidance, the activist spoke with former colleagues from CORE, civil rights leaders including Whitney Young and Roy Wilkins of the NAACP, and hundreds of students during a two-week tour of black colleges. Almost everyone urged Farmer to accept the position. As one black militant argued, "We have to have somebody who knows where the bodies are buried—somebody who knows where the pots of money are that the organizations can go to, to get funding for community projects. We have to have somebody we can trust there."[35] Farmer eventually accepted the administration's offer, taking a job as an assistant secretary in HEW, believing that it commanded "considerable power and influence." In addition to working on matters of urban affairs, he was tasked with creating a line of communication between the White House and "strident young blacks interested in government . . . particularly a Republican government." The Nixon administration surely "got mileage" out of the presence of a high-profile civil rights activist—a point that provided Farmer with a certain amount of leverage, he recalled, some years later.[36] Moreover, such appointments carried multiple meanings for African American audiences. For some, Nixon's attention to black positions in the administration was symbolic yet significant in that it seemed to represent a genuine interest in black communities. It held similar meaning for black Republicans, who also believed that it was an illustration of their potential power and an opportunity to broadcast their distinct blueprint for racial uplift.

Richard Nixon's January 1969 inauguration gave black loyalists a platform to broadcast their vision of racial equality, integration, and economic uplift. After years of existing on the margins, black Republicans finally had the chance to be included in both party and community politics.

The three-day celebration offered black party members a brief glimpse of a nation that consisted of a responsible and responsive Republican institution and a receptive black population. Though difficult to imagine in the present, given Richard Nixon's tarnished legacy, in the historical context of 1969 the optimism of black Republicans was high, their euphoria tangible. Beyond the carefully cultivated lawn of the White House, the scene was quite different, as thousands of protestors stormed the nation's capital. The contrast was notable; as black party members prepared to usher in the new administration, "counter-inaugural" activists—many of whom were white—marched down Pennsylvania Avenue, gripping five-foot-tall posters of Martin Luther King Jr. and signs that read "Down with Racist Brass!" and "Non-Violence . . . Our Most Potent Weapon!" Adding to the irony, the dissenters were flanked by Nixon's massive security force—30 percent of which was black. The tension highlighted the inauguration's unusual social dynamics: white protestors on one side of the political uproar, and black Republicans and police officers on the other.[37]

In truth, the "surprisingly integrated" inauguration crowd shocked many African Americans. As one reporter noted, "Democratic Negroes experienced difficulties in telling the story of the GOP inaugural that was supposed to be lily white." Black members of the inauguration committee made an aggressive effort to incorporate a minority presence into every aspect of the event, beginning with the arrival of fifteen hundred black VIPs. Edward Brooke hosted one of the largest GOP events, a glitzy affair that hundreds attempted to crash. Watching white dignitaries "awed" at the sight of a powerful black politician was a "refreshing turnabout in roles," acknowledged one writer. The senator's reception was a showcase for black party members, who flaunted their sense of racial equality and progress. Cleveland councilman John Kellogg mingled effortlessly with Secretary of Transportation John Volpe, while Nathan Wright—secretary of the Black Power Conference (BPC)—made a bold entrance, arriving in a colorful African robe, and spent the entire night chatting with white attendees about black militancy. Black newspaper editors, some of whom had once berated Brooke for associating with Nixon, now reserved their highest praise for the Massachusetts senator, lauding the "pulling power of his name."[38]

Black Republicans found other ways to highlight their vision as well; Berkeley Burrell, the party's first black chair of the concession committee, arranged for African American businessmen to oversee most of the vital services of the inauguration, including souvenirs, tourism, and photography. Maurice Moore, a soul food entrepreneur, handled meals for more than seven thousand guests, while Autoways executive Ernest Matthews supplied them with chartered buses and limousines from his company.

The spirit of black capitalism flourished during the festivities, netting the proprietors more than $1 million in profits in just three days.[39] African Americans also contributed a unique musical element to the presidential affair; Nixon supporters and jazz legends Lionel Hampton and Duke Ellington dazzled guests, as did Dinah Shore who belted a heartfelt rendition of "God Bless America." But the highlight of the celebration was the performance of "Soul Brother No. 1," James Brown—sliding out onto the stage in a tuxedo, the singer hollered "Say It Loud, I'm Black and I'm Proud!" Black audience members shouted along and soon, "even a few whites . . . found themselves caught up . . . and they, too, were saying they were black and they were proud." Brown's closing number, "Maybe the Last Time," apparently stirred deep emotions in quite a few black Republicans. After the concert, Earl Kennedy, head of Black Americans for Nixon Agnew (BANA), declared that the GOP finally had a chance to help African Americans. "If it does not do this job, this could be the last time," he warned. "There are people around who have become very tired of waiting for this thing called equality—equality in everything."[40]

The presidential swearing-in ceremony also motivated the confidence of black Republicans for both symbolic and literal reasons. Staunch Nixon supporter Bishop Charles Ewbank Tucker of the African Methodist Episcopal Zion Church opened the ceremony; surrounded by a group of prominent religious figures, including southern Baptist preacher Billy Graham, Tucker delivered the invocation in front of an audience of thousands. As the president took the stage to deliver his speech, African Americans watched him from "spots of honor" reserved for figures of prominence from both sides of the political aisle; among them sat Supreme Court Justice Thurgood Marshall and Senator Edward Brooke.[41] The president delivered a purposefully veiled speech, urging Americans to "go forward together" and "give freedom new reach." His carefully crafted words resonated with black party members, as it deftly joined elements of conservatism with African American aspirations, values, and concerns:

> America has suffered . . . from inflated rhetoric that promises more than it can deliver; from angry rhetoric that fans discontents into hatreds; from bombastic rhetoric that postures instead of persuading. . . . For its part, government will listen . . . to the voices of quiet anguish . . . the voices that have despaired of being heard. Those who have been left out we will try to bring in. Those left behind, we will help to catch up. . . . Our greatest need now is to reach beyond government, to enlist the legions of the concerned and the committed. [This] has to be done by government and people together or it will not be done at

all . . . the essence of freedom is that each of us shares in the shaping of his own destiny.

In a moment that simultaneously evoked and rebuked Goldwater conservatism, the president declared that the laws of the nation had "caught up with [its] conscience." All that remained, he asserted, was to abide by the law—ensuring that "as all are born equal in dignity before God, all are born equal in dignity before man." Here then, Nixon's remarks seemed to echo black Republicans' arguments about civil rights and equality, locating both principles within a GOP tradition and suggesting, at least rhetorically, that the law provided necessary protections for individual rights—and with those protections in place, all Americans should look to alternative solutions in their pursuit of individual freedom. Nixon closed his inaugural statement thoughtfully, offering a vision that black party members eagerly embraced: "Our destiny offers not the cup of despair, but the chalice of opportunity. So let us seize it not in fear . . . let us go forward, firm in our faith, steadfast in our purpose . . . [with] sustained confidence in the will of God and the promise of man."[42]

The overt symbolism and promise of the inauguration, coupled with the concrete appointments of blacks to the White House, spurred not only activity from black party members but also a cautious truce from African Americans of varied political backgrounds, many of whom adopted a "wait and see" approach of indifference. In the spring of 1969, for example, 43 percent of African Americans indicated that they were "withholding judgment" on Richard Nixon, while 40 percent approved of the president and 17 percent disapproved of him.[43] Significantly, Republicans saw these figures as positive harbingers, given how badly black voters had rejected Nixon in the 1968 election.

By April 1969, the administration's black task force had appointed ten African Americans to subcabinet positions in the departments of HUD, HEW, and Labor.[44] Relieved, *Ebony* mused that perhaps African Americans had been too hasty in their initial assessment of the Nixon administration and black Republicans. "The black man has been handicapped in the past because he did not have men 'on the inside' in government," reasoned the editors, reiterating James Farmer's logic. "Now that he does have the opportunity, he should take every advantage of it. The very presence of a black man in an office . . . helps keep the white majority from forgetting us."[45] Reader Sandra Lee of Berea, Ohio, agreed, writing:

> Negroes can accomplish a lot more by working within the system than by standing outside and criticizing it. . . . If Nixon is re-elected . . . are the black "leaders" in American simply going to sit back and criticize for four more years? I feel that we should work with Nixon for needed

improvements in the black community, if only because we have no other logical choice."[46]

Lee's pragmatism was similar to the political motivations of the black appointees; establishing a positive rapport and an influential relationship with the White House was crucial to their pursuit of a broader racial agenda. As one black party member had suggested earlier in the year during a Minorities Division gathering, "black Republicans, black Democrats, Black Panthers and black students" needed to unite, work together, and lobby the administration for help in advancing African American–focused initiatives.[47]

Theirs was a "quiet" approach to civil rights, a method that was understandable, sympathized reporter James Naughton, since Richard Nixon's open dealings with southern politicians appeared incompatible with an "open and avowed civil rights crusade." However, the appointees were not necessarily concerned with pragmatic politics for the sake of southern white voters. Instead, they hoped to use the administration's resources to advance an economic campaign, believing that their strategy for racial equality would offer concrete results rather than idealistic rhetoric. "This Administration is not going out promising more than it can deliver," one black appointee boasted. "[It] is not going to spread itself thin over the whole range of civil rights activities . . . it's going to concentrate on economic opportunities. We got so hung up on the idea that civil rights was a social problem that we failed to see the connecting links. We've got to talk economics." It was this philosophy, along with the appointees' distinct racial experience, that made their role in the administration vital. They insisted that they could offer both the Nixon administration and the black community a "viable alternative" to Democratic liberalism through economic solutions for racial advancement. "Civil rights is not on the back burner in this Administration," stressed one African American appointee. "We may be quiet, but we intend to get results."[48]

GETTING RESULTS THROUGH FEDERAL POLICIES

On March 5, 1969, surrounded by representatives from more than thirty African American, Latino, and Native American groups, Richard Nixon announced that first wave of black capitalism would fall under the broad auspices of minority affairs. Signing Executive Order 11458 "with a smile," the president established the Office of Minority Business Enterprise (OMBE), a federal coordinating agency designed to promote the "establishment, preservation and strengthening of minority business."[49] Though

OMBE was housed within the Commerce Department, it was designed as a central clearinghouse where minority entrepreneurs could access information, specialized resources and training, and most important, project funding from more than twenty federal agencies. In all, OMBE handled more than one hundred funding programs; it also had an outreach arm in the form of the Advisory Council for Minority Enterprise (ACME), composed of business leaders from communities of color. "Encouraging increased minority-group business activity is one of the priorities of this Administration," Nixon declared during the press conference, committing the federal government to providing "expanded opportunity to participate in the free enterprise system at all levels." The ultimate goal, the president confidently stated, was to share economic benefits and "encourage pride, dignity and a sense of independence" among communities of color. In reality, however, OMBE was a targeted outreach effort, designed to increase the number of middle-class racial minorities—or, as a White House official put it, to help move minorities from "the ghetto" into the "mainstream."[50]

Within the context of black Republican politics, the launch of OMBE was a tremendous achievement; for all of the programs flaws, it nevertheless represented the concrete realization of black Republicans' proposed ideas. As the business leaders and White House officials drifted from the press conference into a reception for minority entrepreneurs, they chatted about the future of OMBE and its potential for racial progress, declaring, as Robert Brown did, that the administration intended to put "words into action—and within the next few weeks." But despite the optimistic demeanor of the black Republican appointees, many African Americans still questioned just how effective the program could be at instituting meaningful economic change within black communities, especially since OMBE did not have its own budget. Nixon's announcement was met with a lackluster response from African Americans, illustrating their general wariness not only of the president but also of his efforts. Likewise, while the affair was significant for the black leaders who attended—like Margaret Belcher of the National Association of Negro Business (NANB), Berkeley Burrell of the NBL, Dorothy Height of the National Council of Negro Women, and Roy Innis of CORE—it was just as remarkable for those who declined to attend, like Roy Wilkins of the NAACP. As one prominent civil rights activist coldly explained, "I can think of nothing more harmful to black people than the substitution of the delusion of black capitalism for the absolute necessity for Federal programs to provide all Negroes with dignified employment, decent housing and superior schools." Rooting black uplift in self-help, capitalism, and the growth of the black middle class, he accused, was analogous to "forsaking the ultimate goal of economic liberation."[51] Still, such criticisms did not prevent

some African Americans from taking Nixon's minority enterprise promises seriously—or so it appeared, judging by the thousands of business
proposals that soon swamped Brown's office.[52]

Black middle-class constituents were the "bread-and-butter" of black
Republicans' outreach efforts; for years, as we have seen, African American party members had pushed an aggressive sales effort that attempted to
capitalize on black dissatisfaction with the Democratic Party, with much
of their attention going to the black middle class—a group that would
more than double in size between 1960 and 1974, increasing from 13
to 30 percent of the black community.[53] Republicans consistently pulled
their slice of the black vote from this demographic in presidential races,
including the 1968 contest. In Los Angeles, for instance, about a third
of voters in Baldwin Hills—one of the wealthiest black enclaves in the
nation—supported Nixon; similarly, in Crenshaw—then a middle-class
black district, more than 20 percent of African Americans endorsed the
Republican presidential nominee. In comparison, black voters from poor
and working-class neighborhoods spurned Nixon—he received 6.6 percent of the vote in Watts and 2.4 percent in Compton. Moreover, nearly
half of the voters in Baldwin Hills and Crenshaw supported James R.
Dunn, the Republican candidate for the U.S. House of Representatives;
they attributed their support to the candidate's aggressive black outreach
campaign, seeing Dunn as a liberal Republican in the tradition of New
York mayor John Lindsay. But while he won tremendous support from
wealthy and middle-class blacks, Dunn's "inability" to separate his image
from conservative party members—like Ronald Reagan—had damaged his
chances of winning support among a wider swath of African Americans.[54]

Republicans' campaign appeals, on both a local and a national level,
thus resonated among some wealthy and middle-class African Americans;
as Clarence Townes concluded in a January 1969 Minorities Division report, however, this group simply was not big enough to get a healthy block
of the black vote in presidential elections. The GOP could no longer spend
millions on attracting white voters and pennies on black constituents, he
argued; likewise, it needed to move beyond the black middle class, specifically by creating tangible party initiatives and federal policies that were
relevant to the needs of blue-collar and poor African Americans.[55]

The RNC acknowledged Townes's diligence, raising the Minorities Division's budget to $175,000 in 1969—an increase of $51,000 from 1967.[56]
But within the White House, black Republican appointees disregarded
Townes's advice, choosing to focus on an economic agenda aimed at the
expansion of the black middle class, reasoning that this "increasingly
sophisticated audience" was more likely to embrace a movement grounded
in traditional Republican principles. Thus, when Richard Nixon called for

the "imaginative enlistment of private funds, private energies, and private talents" to solve the nation's racial crises through black private ownership and economic inclusion, he was appealing explicitly to a "segment of the black population that would be more apt to come aboard."[57] Or, as Edward Brooke later reflected, the Republican Party "wasn't reaching down to poor blacks. . . . [It] was reaching out to educated businessmen, the small businessman. People who could comprehend and be thankful for and benefit from this, if you know what I mean."[58]

The senator explored the intersection of capitalism and politics as the keynote speaker for the National Insurance Association's annual conference in New Orleans in July 1967, telling the predominately black audience that he wanted to see the same "energy and imagination that had developed the nation's system of free enterprise" injected into the development of African American economic opportunities. "We must act on this because it threatens the ultimate success of the civil rights movement," he urged. He argued that Great Society liberalism had perpetuated race-based economic inequality, suggesting that the initiatives were discriminatory, as they assumed that African Americans could only be laborers, workers, and "potential employees" rather than managers, owners, and entrepreneurs. The "development of a new Negro business class," he argued, would facilitate equal citizenship for African Americans—a task accomplished through the encouragement and training of talented African Americans whose "abilities and inclinations" qualified them for "more sophisticated position[s] on the economic ladder." Brooke closed his spirited address by offering his listeners a few words of warning. "These problems will not be solved solely by government," he cautioned. African Americans "must retain their sense of responsibility for their own . . . success. . . . [They] must be creative and develop their own solutions . . . and guard against mediocrity."[59]

By structuring their outreach to the black middle class around economic uplift, black party members held fast to their ideas about respectability, an idea that cut across partisan lines, and a philosophy that Nixon had appropriated during his presidential campaign and would use throughout his first term in office. But while black capitalism was the president's general effort to tap into a black middle-class tradition, it also signified something much deeper for the black Republican appointees, many of whom viewed their work as an attempt to reconcile the enlarged role of the federal government with the "inherent conservatism" of African Americans and traditional Republicanism.

Of particular interest were those everyday middle-class black citizens, disillusioned with Democratic liberalism and dissatisfied with the anarchy of urban disorder. The African American appointees looked for communities where self-help ideology thrived and where black frustration had manifested not in violence but in a redoubled dedication to self-reliance, self-preservation, and economic growth. Or, as *Time* crassly observed, "Instead of incinerating their neighborhoods, many [African Americans] have begun concentrating on building them up."[60] Although a minority of the black population, both black and white Republican strategists reasoned that the size of the group would increase with economic incentives and targeted assistance; more important, the administration initially believed this segment could be a reliable source of votes. "Middle-class Americans didn't riot. They had something to lose, homes and families to protect. Valuing good schools and law and order," Nixon once calculated, "middle class blacks like suburban whites should rally to Republican virtues." This was the essence of an argument consistently offered by Bob Brown, as he urged the president to cultivate goodwill among blacks who shared the same hopes as whites.[61]

Although they supported the president's calculating outlook on the political benefits of growing the black middle class, black Republicans' rationales for focusing on this demographic differed from those of Nixon, as they also believed that individual success was important inasmuch as it ameliorated conditions for the *entire* black community. In many ways, their views were similar to those expressed in Ellen Boneparth's 1971 study of black business owners. Respondents argued that the achievements of the African American middle class facilitated uplift for their "less fortunate" brethren, thereby linking "black business" to class uplift for everyone within the community, including the poor. Such attitudes, Boneparth concluded, not only reflected an acute awareness of their individual privilege but also revealed an overwhelming belief in the notion of a collective fate of all African Americans; still, there was a layer of classism inherent to these perspectives—a kind of talented-tenth mind-set or benevolent paternalism that reinforced hierarchies of power and privilege within African American communities.[62]

Like Boneparth's black businessmen, the members of the Black Cabinet viewed individual success and the achievements of the middle class as vital to the progress of the entire community. "Getting a piece of the action" was more than a catchy campaign slogan; for the appointees, black capitalism implied a complicated set of beliefs based on shared racial history, commitment to racial progress, and an embrace of traditional conservatism. Accordingly, as liaisons for the Nixon administration, they sought African Americans who embraced community and minority enterprise initiatives, like the collaborative efforts between Harlem's Freedom National Bank (FNB) and the NAACP. Assessing the project, the *Cleveland Call and Post* captured black Republican attitudes, writing,

"The community goals are not to get something for nothing . . . but to get their own without having to ask someone else for it."[63]

More broadly, OMBE was a starting point for a much wider agenda built on equal employment, minority enterprise, and economic uplift. Ten days after the March OMBE announcement, the president appointed Arthur Fletcher as an assistant secretary of labor, making him, as *Ebony* proclaimed, "one of the highest ranking Negroes in the Republican administration."[64] The president had long viewed Fletcher as the embodiment of black capitalism. An overview of the black official's records confirms the president's perspective; between 1965 and 1967, the lifelong Republican had launched the East Pasco Cooperation Association, a self-help program in Washington State. Describing the project as a "sweat equity" alternative to urban renewal (or as Fletcher called it, "black removal"), he insisted that purchasing shares of their own neighborhood instilled a sense of pride in local residents, empowering them to feel self-reliant. A year later, his bid for lieutenant governor of Washington propelled him to the national spotlight—the *Los Angeles Times* speculated that the nation was watching the "next Ed Brooke." Throughout his campaign, he championed economic philosophies of self-help, deriding federal antipoverty programs as "handouts" and spoke of his desire to "build a bridge" between African Americans and the GOP.[65] The black politician did not disappoint when he appeared before the Republican Platform Committee in July 1968; in fact, Republicans ended up incorporating his economic proposals into the party's national civil rights plank—ideas that Nixon would use during the campaign to enrich the scope of black capitalism. Such was Fletcher's involvement that many within the black press soon christened him the "Godfather" of black capitalism.[66]

By the time Fletcher arrived at the White House in April 1969, he had already determined his agenda: create a bold economic civil rights movement within the aegis of black capitalism.[67] Economic inequality was the fundamental problem faced by African Americans, he argued, both scandalizing and intriguing audiences when he repeatedly proposed that new civil rights laws were no longer "relevant to the needs" of blacks.

"I feel we have achieved all we are going to through legislation," he once reasoned. Instead, for Fletcher, wealth and capitalism were the most important components in the movement for racial equality:

> If you have money you can send your children to the best public and private schools, you can exercise your voting rights intelligently. . . .
> We have open housing now, but I can't afford a decent home unless I have some money in my pockets. I can walk into the finest hotel . . .
> but I can't stay unless I can pay the bill. . . . We are now entering

the most difficult period of the civil rights struggle, the struggle for economic freedom. . . . Gradually more blacks will buy more homes among white people; it means more white people will end up working under black supervisors. Sharing in the wealth also means that more black parents will be able to afford a better break in education.[68]

He equated Democratic liberalism with ineffectual government policies, "empty promises" that ignored the economic plight of black citizens. Yet much like Ed Brooke, Fletcher did not dismiss all of the principles of liberalism; rather, his criticism stemmed from his belief that the Johnson administration had created "demeaning" programs that encouraged government dependency and intensified economic disparities between races. African Americans, he argued, needed policies that would help them get "their fair share" of the nation's wealth.[69]

Fletcher's solution to African Americans' intertwined race and class dilemma came via the Labor Department, in the form of the Philadelphia Plan, a policy that reframed the concept of "preferential treatment." At its most basic level, the Philadelphia Plan was simple: its aim was to end discrimination by increasing the number of highly paid minority construction workers employed on federally funded projects. The White House initially plucked the idea from the Johnson administration. Executive Order 11246, issued in 1965, required government contractors to take "affirmative action" toward underrepresented minority employees. Employers were forced to document these measures, lest they risk contract termination—a threat enforceable through the Office of Federal Contract Compliance (OFCC).[70] During 1966 and 1967, the labor department instituted a series of solutions designed to test the new policy within the union-controlled construction industries in St. Louis, San Francisco, Cleveland, and Philadelphia, where discrimination was rampant. Clusters of unions thrived on nepotism, rewarding family members and friends with lucrative jobs and "incidentally" preventing equal access to nonwhites.[71] In the rare event that black workers did make it through the complicated system, they were forced to wait for the union to admit them; as the NAACP once bitterly complained, that was akin to "letting George Wallace decide who is qualified to vote in Alabama." Unions aggressively resisted the implementation of the policy, ironically accusing the government of violating the Civil Rights Act of 1964. And while civil rights legislation did offer protection against discrimination, the process was *reactive*—thus claims were filed only *after* discrimination had occurred and could take weeks, months, and even years to resolve. Nevertheless, the comptroller general agreed with the unions, prematurely killing the Johnson administration's initiatives.[72]

Just two years later, the Nixon administration announced the revival of the plans, under the direction of Labor Secretary George Shultz and Arthur Fletcher. The Philadelphia Plan, they maintained, provided an opportunity to force the "hiring halls" of construction and labor to include minorities. In 1969, roughly 9 percent of the nation's 1.3 million construction workers were African American; of that black group, almost all were laborers, the lowest paid in the industry. The federal plans, however, applied only to the "worst offenders" in the industry, in an attempt to provide racial minorities with "their fair share" of high-paying jobs. In Philadelphia, the numbers were atrocious; for example, among the most lucrative unions, fewer than 2 percent of skilled electricians, plumbers, and carpenters were black. For the first year, the administration encouraged unions to aim for 4 to 5 percent minority representation, with a goal of reaching 25 to 26 percent by 1974.[73]

Schultz and Fletcher sold Nixon on the Philadelphia Plan by asserting that it created equal opportunity without racial quotas and was "consistent with a spirit of self-reliance." To be sure, the president's reasons for endorsing the plan were complex and myriad; as many scholars have suggested, he initially supported it out of a genuine interest in equal opportunity. At the same time, he also recognized that the policy was a political goldmine. Aside from opening high-wage positions to minorities, the Philadelphia Plan had the potential to enlarge and diversify the nation's work force, lower overall construction costs, alleviate racial tensions in urban centers, and destroy one of the Democratic Party's most tenuous coalitions—that between organized labor and the civil rights establishment.[74]

On June 27, 1969, the administration launched its reinvigorated Philadelphia Plan. Fletcher unveiled the labor policy to the "City of Brotherly Love" with a forceful yet measured set of remarks, designed to convey the significance of the moment:

> A vital freedom guaranteed by our Constitution is the right to equal participation in the economic processes of our society. This freedom has been denied to groups within our country. This denial of fundamental participation in the advantages of capitalism has never been institutionalized in our society. . . . Segregation didn't occur naturally —it was imposed. In that process quotas, limits, boundaries were set. Sometimes written—sometimes unpublished. . . . The effect was total, decisive, and . . . contrary to the American sense of fair play.

Fletcher's speech paralleled Lyndon Johnson's Howard University address delivered four years earlier, with both men drawing connections among freedom, opportunity, equality, and results, spurring their audiences to recognize the challenge of institutional racism. "The Federal government has an obligation to see that every citizen has an equal chance at the most basic freedom of all—*the right to succeed*," Fletcher demanded.[75] In issuing the mandate, the Department of Labor bypassed any mention of colorblindness in racial equality, implying that preferential treatment was, in fact, constitutional. While a necessary component of civil rights legislation (as it banned discrimination on the basis of race), "colorblindness" was also an incomplete solution, one that had no method for addressing implicit and persistent racism; thus the Philadelphia Plan offered an approach that recognized race as a means of rectifying past wrongs and creating equal access to American institutions. The policy was in keeping with black Republicans' notions of equality; specifically, the plan offered protection from a racially biased system, a necessity in order for African Americans to realize their individual rights. While simple in concept, the Philadelphia Plan was both complicated and controversial in its principles; in seeking to eradicate institutionalized racism—generations of discrimination ingrained in the fabric of the nation—Fletcher promoted a solution that prevented discrimination *before* it happened, by recognizing underrepresented minority groups and facilitating access to the economic mainstream.[76]

Predictably, the same angry foes that opposed the plan in 1967 quickly revived their opposition in 1969. For Fletcher, this meant facing more than legal challenges—it also signaled violent resistance, which he soon encountered in September 1969. During a visit to Chicago for a series of OFCC hearings, Fletcher was forced to spend the day hiding in his hotel room as two thousand "hard-hat" unionists crowded the courthouse—blocking all entrances, swigging beer, singing "God Bless America," and occasionally yelling "no coalitions!" with their clenched fists raised high. As witnesses and lawyers approached the doorways, they were "grabbed, punched and shoved" by the angry crowd, including one man who was badly beaten in a case of mistaken identity when his attackers confused him for Fletcher. A full-blown riot erupted when a group of black men attempted to force its way into the building. Not only did the mob seize and beat these witnesses; they also attacked Chicago police officers, smashed cars, and defaced the surrounding public property.[77]

By 1970, labor officials revised the Philadelphia Plan yet again, drastically expanding it to apply to federal contractors across all industries receiving contracts in excess of $50,000, and broadening the definition of "underrepresented minorities" to include women. That same year, the labor department introduced voluntary "Hometown Plans" that encouraged private industry to introduce its own plans for racial and gender integration; mandatory federal plans also persisted, as was the case with the Washington Plan, aimed at making the District of Columbia's construction

work force 45 percent African American by 1975.[78] To be sure, Fletcher
played an important role in the administration, reflecting the impact of
the black Republican appointees—he had, after all, assumed a major
policy-making role that helped shift how the nation understood equality.
"I have access to life at the White House," Fletcher boasted in April 1970,
"and to the decision makers there."[79] Such access, he insisted, would facilitate a transformative goal: complete economic equality for African
Americans by 1980. In a May speech to the St. Louis Urban League,
Fletcher revealed that he had already met with the president to discuss
a ten-year plan for economic liberation, a proposal that had the strong
backing of Shultz, as well. While such an optimistic projection appears
shocking, given the contentious nature of the Philadelphia Plan, it was
nevertheless a claim wholeheartedly embraced by Fletcher's audience in
1970. With deafening roars and cheers from the enthusiastic crowd encouraging him, the labor official closed with a booming proclamation: "If
we can put a man on the moon, then both parties should be able to end
economic discrimination in the next decade!"[80]

The Philadelphia Plan fell well within the boundaries of black capitalism, complementing the economic empowerment vision of OMBE, and
providing another avenue for African Americans to advance economically.[81] "This is the chance to give the black worker [an opportunity]
to put decent clothing instead of burdens on the backs of his family,"
Fletcher once explained. "This gives him a chance to put food into their
mouths and books into the hands of his kids. This is the golden opportunity for black workers to retrieve their manliness and family tradition."[82]
Here was an attempt to merge liberal ideas of redistributive wealth with
conservative ideas of the free market; moreover, within the construct of
black capitalism, black Republicans envisioned the Philadelphia Plan as
an initiative that would provide an economic base for working-class African Americans to advance into the middle class, while OMBE, with a
parallel agenda, would strengthen and expand the existing black middle
class. As Commerce Secretary Maurice Stans proudly told *Jet* in April
1970, OMBE awarded more than $16 million to black businessmen in its
first year of operation, and planned to hand out more than $100 million
in contracts in 1971. Coordinating for all of the agencies and departments, OMBE delivered a total of $200 million in assistance to minority
businessmen in 1969 and $315 million in 1970.[83] "We are seeking to
encourage minority manufacturers to participate in the annual federal
procurement program," Stan eagerly remarked. "The government . . .
provides a readily accessible market for newly organized businesses."[84]

In some ways, black capitalism did have a measurable impact on the
economic success of the black middle class; as Boneparth's 1971 study

on black businessmen illustrated, for example, nearly 75 percent of participants declared an increase in economic opportunities, attributing the shift to various factors including government intervention, assistance from white-dominated private industry, greater availability of capital, educational and training advancements, and protests from civil rights groups. Progress had been achieved in a number of areas, the black entrepreneurs argued, including an increased availability of credit for African Americans, stronger enforcement of equal employment opportunity laws, and access to government contracts.[85] Nevertheless, despite setting the groundwork for an alternative economic and political uplift movement, black Republican officials continued to struggle enormously with the twinned demands of their party and their community. Many of the appointees were unnerved by criticisms of black capitalism; Angela Davis, for instance, described black capitalism as a "myth" created by Richard Nixon as a means of disrupting black unity; Boneparth's black businessmen offered a similar observation, remarking that they could never really trust the program since anything with the president's name attached "must be a political trick." Other African Americans, like Federal Reserve Board governor Andrew Brimmer, argued vehemently against the initiative, calling it a form of racial separatism that would only serve to marginalize the black community. As one disgruntled entrepreneur complained in 1970, "No one ever stuck 'white' in front of the word 'capitalism.'" Likewise, some black men and women criticized black capitalism as a form of public assistance and rejected the initiative on the ground that federal aid implied government dependency and was therefore dangerous, believing that "the government starts out helping people and ends up supporting them forever."[86]

Along these lines, even self-proclaimed conservative African Americans viewed black capitalism with some hesitancy, stressing that though the government should play a role in African American economic uplift, that role should be limited and indirect. Instead, the Nixon administration, they argued, should pressure the private sector to facilitate the assimilation of black businesses. As one New York businessman rationalized:

> This is . . . a capitalistic country which means the most of the wealth is owned by private sources . . . . blacks should look to an alliance with private industry. . . . If black business has a government-based foundation, it will always be more socialistically oriented than traditional business, and . . . wouldn't be business . . . Private enterprise should do it—not Uncle Sam.[87]

Such disagreements revealed an important diversity of African American opinions on economic modes of uplift; equally important, the debates exemplify the slowly growing ideological divide that existed among black Republicans, some of whom believed that Nixon's Black Cabinet was not conservative enough.

For those black Republicans who advocated an economic civil rights movement, such accusations were deeply unsettling. "Black capitalism has not failed," Floyd McKissick angrily complained, "It was never given a chance."[88] But for African Americans and political observers alike, the problem was intrinsic to the shortsightedness of the initiative itself; *Time*, for example, suggested that black capitalism was just another "catchy and promising phase" as it had failed to produce substantive results, while the *New York Times* called the concept a "deeply disappointing" program that served as a "façade to hide governmental inactivity in areas vital to Negro welfare." Meanwhile, black congressman John Conyers of Detroit railed against the administration for the better part of three years, demanding required initiatives that would institute substantive changes in corporate racism and discrimination and create employment and man-power training programs. By April 1970, African Americans owned only 2.5 percent of the nation's 5.4 million businesses; and while the size of the black middle class had increased since the early 1960s, African Americans still generally found it nearly impossible to obtain loans, contracts, and insurance as entrepreneurs.[89]

The flaws of black capitalism are well documented in the historical re-cord; from day one, for example, OMBE was plagued by in-fighting and mismanagement, a situation that was exacerbated by public and private agencies' unwillingness to cooperate with the minority clearinghouse. To make matters worse, the Small Business Administration (SBA), which provided much of OMBE's funding, was marred by scandals, most of which could be traced back to the agency's inept leadership.[90] Further-more, black capitalism appeared to have little impact on the lives of most African Americans, offering, in the words of an Equity Research Associ-ates study, "no answer to the riots, poverty, crime and human degrada-tion" of black communities.[91] It was, to be sure, an initiative that reflected the middle-class bias of black Republicans; unsurprisingly then, many of the program's advocates overlooked or underestimated the very devastat-ing issue of African American poverty and unemployment. "The fallacy of black capitalism is that it's talking about an economic ceiling for a few entrepreneuring black people," Jesse Jackson once criticized, "what we need is an economic base for all black people."[92]

Removed from the vehemence of this debate, however, we can now see that while black capitalism had a significantly mixed record, it was more expansive and influential—*for the black middle class*—than most real-ized. Critics of the program rarely linked the administration's involvement with higher education with the notion of black capitalism; but, as Bob Brown observed during an interview, "promoting colleges was a priority," one inextricably linked to black progress and economic liberation. The Nixon aide devoted a significant amount of time fusing the notion of black economic independence with higher education; throughout the 1970s, he steadily lobbied for increased federal funding to historically black institutions. In doing so, he forced the administration to examine a serious financial disparity between black and white universities and, as *Jet* observed, "generated new official interest in black education."[93] In the fall of 1969, after discovering that black colleges received only 3 percent of the $4 billion allocated annually to higher education, Brown convinced the president to take an active interest in the situation, arranging a meeting between Nixon and more than a dozen black college presidents. The session ultimately produced a promise of more than $100 million in funds.[94] During a July 1970 press conference on campus unrest and violence, Robert Finch and Bob Brown announced that black colleges would receive an additional $30 million in federal funding annually, to address their unique needs.[95] In private, Brown also negotiated millions in future earmarks for scholarships and salaries, campus programs and resources, and overall building construction.[96] In total, the Nixon administration increased federal funding to black colleges by more than 230 percent ($129 million to $400 million), between 1969 and 1973.[97]

Brown succeeded in creating an access channel for African Americans in higher education to gain expanded access to federal funds. The White House also established a new kind of relationship with dozens of black colleges, using the schools to directly recruit talented African American students. Black appointees saw this as an opportunity to mix education with employment and economic opportunity; in this sense, many within the administration believed that they were facilitating the growth of the black middle class by providing black students with access to education, resources, and future high-level employment opportunities. James Farmer, for instance, instituted a policy at HEW that reserved 50 percent of management intern spots for underrepresented minority students, many of whom hailed from black colleges. This allowed Farmer to place these students in federal policy-making positions, since management interns were eligible after graduation for midlevel appointments at HEW.[98] Along similar lines, African American administration officials established a Black Minority Recruitment program, traveling to schools like Clark College in Georgia and California State College and encouraging students to work for the federal government; consequently, by 1971 African Americans made up 18 percent of the college trainee pool at the General Services Administration (GSA) and 52 percent of the Training and Advancement

Program (TAP), an initiative designed to facilitate "upward mobility" within the federal government.[99] By brokering a mutually beneficial working relationship with predominately black schools, Brown created an institutional channel for minority advancement, paralleling the other black capitalism initiatives, including the Philadelphia Plan and OMBE.

Black capitalism, for all of its many failings, began to reap "rewards" as early as 1970.[100] Although it experienced a difficult start, Arthur Fletcher's "baby"—the Philadelphia Plan—managed to boost minority manpower in the construction industry by more than 12 percent in a two-year period. *Ebony* was elated over the employment and economic developments of the policy; singing his praises, the magazine anointed Fletcher the "Watchdog of Labor," triumphantly declaring him "one of the most powerful men in the Nixon administration, irrespective of color."[101] Likewise, between 1970 and 1973, OMBE's umbrella widened considerably, especially when it finally received its own budget of $40 million in 1972 and $60 million for 1973. During that same period, the SBA increased its loan volume by more than 30 percent; in 1971 alone, the agency provided $217 million in minority enterprise loans, while 710 black firms received government contracts worth $58 million. Under OMBE, black citizens also received training opportunities—for example, the residents of Roosevelt City, Alabama, received law enforcement materials, resources, and funding for skill development purposes in 1971. Within a year, the federal government had created more than 1.25 million minority-training opportunities in the public sector, along with 700,000 jobs for black teenagers.[102]

African Americans also received greater access to credit and loans through the September 1970 launch of the Minority Bank Deposit initiative, a program wherein the government placed federal funds in black repositories; the deposits strengthened the lending power of black banks, which in turn, boosted access for black entrepreneurs. Between 1969 and 1970, the number of black-owned banks nearly doubled, increasing total lending power by more than 33 percent; moreover, between 1970 and 1973, public and private deposits in these banks increased from $400 million to $1 billion.[103] Finally, under the federal procurement program, the government purchased $200 million worth of minority services by 1973; for example, Garland Foods, Inc., a black-owned company from Dallas, Texas, earned a $5.2 million contract to supply the military with canned and smoked meat; likewise, that same year, SBA supplied Wood Oldsmobile Company of Washington, D.C., with a contract worth $200,000 to repair and maintain seventeen hundred government vehicles. In all, as *Jet* would later note with some surprise, the black Republican appointees were responsible for pumping more than $1 billion into black colleges, businesses, and communities during the 1970s.[104]

Without question, many of these opportunities were beyond the reach of most African Americans. As economist Timothy Bates later proved in a 1973 study, these initiatives largely benefited the black middle class: a group that represented no more than a third of African Americans.[105] But Bates's results should come as no surprise, because the black middle class was the group targeted by black Republican appointees from the start. And for some within that specific group, the administration's economic outreach did, in fact, work well. For example, the Reverend Leon Sullivan received $10.7 million through OMBE to expand his POIC program into forty cities over an eighteen-month period.[106] Former college and professional athletes were also among the prime beneficiaries of black economic outreach. In 1969 alone, more than one thousand new "black athlete-entrepreneurs" opened businesses with the help of the Nixon administration. Jim Brown, the actor and former Cleveland Browns football star, met regularly with White House officials to discuss OMBE funding for his Black Economic Union (BEU), an organization that provided its own stream of financing for potential black entrepreneurs. Basketball star and Nixon pal Wilt Chamberlain received federal funds to support his franchise of Los Angeles diners, as did former Pittsburgh Steeler Brady Keys. In fact, the football player's "All-Pro Chicken" was popular enough to merit 150 franchises in eleven cities by 1970—many of which were opened by other black athletes with the help of federal financing. For black athlete-entrepreneurs, their degrees, reputation, and personal finances afforded them certain privileges that, combined with government support, created favorable conditions for *individual* entrepreneurial success.[107]

On a community level, the idea of an economic civil rights movement rooted in free market enterprise seemed to penetrate the political consciousness of black elites. Although they regularly berated the administration, African American periodicals also argued that Nixon's black appointees exerted an important level of influence in federal policy-making. *Ebony* would consistently make this argument over the course of the president's first term in office, including Nixon's "Black Cabinet" along with Ed Brooke in its annual list of the "100 Most Influential Black Americans."[108] Although dozens of black business-oriented groups, like the NBL, had celebrated capitalism for generations, scores of new organizations and journals materialized during the early 1970s, hinting at the possibilities of a "post–civil rights" moment, one in which African Americans had finally started to integrate the free market.[109] *Black Enterprise (BE)*, launched in August 1970, was among the most notable of this new crop, holding fast to the notion that racial uplift could be achieved through inclusion in the "economic mainstream." The inaugural issue opened with a two-page feature of *BE*'s founder, Earl Graves, and its twelve-member advisory board, which included Edward Brooke, Shirley Chisholm, FNB president William Hudgins, and SNCC activists-turned-politicians Julian Bond and John Lewis. Despite their partisan differences, the board members spoke of their shared interest in building black wealth and helping African Americans become full participants in the "American marketplace"; the launch of *BE,* aimed at an "upwardly mobile" black audience, signaled a willingness to engage ideas of private industry and free market enterprise in a new way—surely a reflection of the success of the civil rights movement but also an indication of elites' interest in the alternative economic solutions introduced by black Republicans.[110]

THE CONSTRAINTS OF COMMUNITY AND POLITICAL AFFILIATION

As Nixon's black Republican appointees worked within the federal government to impact the policies and program of the Nixon administration, they also wrestled with the weighty pressure of irreconcilable loyalties, caught between their community and their party. By 1970, the euphoria of the 1969 inauguration had vanished; in its place: frustration. During his first term in office, Nixon vacillated between support for racial equality and outright hostility toward civil rights. In many ways, he charted a liberal and moderate course of action; at times, though, he embraced the very worst of reactionary politics. Likewise, he occasionally made aggressive efforts to publicize his civil rights efforts in an attempt to woo minority voters; but then, in other moments, he deliberately concealed or downplayed his progressive actions lest he offend white constituents. As he poured millions into minority enterprise and introduced a progressive "Family Assistance Plan," for instance, he also cut nearly $3 billion from federal antipoverty programs, demonstrated a "go slow" approach to southern desegregation, opposed a five-year extension of the Voting Rights Act, and nominated Clement F. Haynsworth—a South Carolina judge with an offensive record on civil rights—for a position on the Supreme Court. Three months after that nomination failed in the Senate, Nixon nominated *another* white southerner, G. Harrold Carswell of Florida, a judge who was perhaps best known to the public for actively opposing desegregation efforts and who had signed an "allegiance to white supremacy" treaty in 1948. Though the Senate rejected Carswell in the spring of 1970 (at the vocal urgings of Ed Brooke, no less), the nomination confirmed African Americans' worst fears of Nixon as a president controlled by the interests of white southerners, with little regard for equal justice under the law.[111]

Between the spring of 1969 and the fall of 1970, the president's unfavorable rating among African Americans skyrocketed from 17 to 72 percent. Ironically, the relationship between Nixon and blacks deteriorated at precisely the moment that the black appointees' programs were beginning to achieve discernible results.[112] For those working for the administration, the mercurial attitude of the White House was maddening, for it not only lessened the impact of the appointees' policy success but also often obscured their actual presence in the White House. Nixon's black Republican appointees, Milton Viorst of the *New York Times* would later write, were but "mere window-dressing—with large titles but little influence—in an Administration bent on a 'Southern strategy.'" And while black newspapers presented a far more nuanced reading of the efforts of the African American appointees, they too often discounted the appointees as "powerless," given the president's misdeeds.[113]

At the root of the black appointees' woes was Richard Nixon's pursuit of a "silent majority" of voters, a group crowned "Man and Woman of the Year" by *Time*. These were the men and women, the magazine's editors remarked, who prayed in schools, scorned campus dissent and protest, and were readily patriotic—plastering American-flag bumper stickers on their cars, supporting the president's Vietnam policies unequivocally, and declaring their support for the "law and order" rabble-rousing of Spiro T. Agnew. They were the hard-working citizens who blamed activists, radicals, and protestors for the nation's problems and who spoke nostalgically of an imagined "older world of Norman Rockwell icons." Many were Democrats, articulating a fierce loyalty to John F. Kennedy and Robert F. Kennedy; most important: these citizens were *white*— working-class and middle-class suburbanites, some of whom were liberal enough to have rejected explicit racism, but conservative enough to oppose the idea of court-mandated busing for racial integration.[114] It was this group that articulated a language that *appeared* colorblind, increasingly depicting its members' success, as historian Matt Lassiter asserts, as the "class-based outcome of meritocratic individualism rather than the unconstitutional product of structural racism."[115]

Theirs was a race-neutral language that was simultaneously race conscious in its exclusion and entitlement; it was this perspective that Nixon would attempt to harness during his first term in office, employing rhetoric "designed to conceal class divisions among white voters while taking advantage of the convergence of southern and national politics." Strategists and officials alike conceptualized the silent majority as the "virtuous middle" of the nation: blue-collar and middle-class whites were depicted as orderly, law-abiding citizens, while blacks were generally identified as disorderly, criminal, and dangerous.[116] Nixon and his appointees would wrestle with the idea of incorporating African Americans into the silent majority; indeed, many of the black appointees argued that their economic initiatives could be used to cultivate political support among a "great" silent majority of African Americans, *who were just like whites.*[117]

However, most African Americans were not like their white peers, for their racial experience as second-class citizens informed their political perspectives; neither had civil rights legislation afforded them the entitlements long afforded to whites. Thus, the concept of individualism, meritocracy, and freedom of choice was painfully shortsighted for African Americans—even the black middle class—because they lacked the racial privilege and access of the nation's white citizens. As we have seen, black Republicans' initiatives were designed to erase this racial barricade for the black middle class and help the country someday reach a place where genuine meritocracy existed, while tapping into a respectability ethos among African Americans frustrated with the turmoil in the nation's cities.

But where Nixon's black appointees saw opportunity, instead there was only an impasse. White members of the "silent majority" may have embraced the colorblind "principle of equal opportunity under the law," but they also rejected the race-conscious programs designed to dismantle inequality—the same initiatives that African Americans applauded. Richard Nixon would attempt to harness these race and class resentments, advancing a race-baiting "southern strategy" in 1970 and a colorblind "suburban strategy" in 1972; many African Americans would interpret *both* campaigns as racist, on the basis of three "code" words used by the president—busing, quotas, and welfare: the first, *Ebony* would later explain, hinted at hordes of blacks intent on violating the sanctity of white neighborhoods; the second identified African Americans who wanted to "steal" the jobs of white men; and the third characterized blacks as lazy citizens who wanted to "do nothing but multiply" at the expense of taxpayers' money. At different points in time, depending on the mood of the administration, the White House would attempt to incorporate African Americans into its silent majority outreach; as *Ebony* asserted, though, by 1970 most blacks still believed that the administration's implicit slogan was "Vote for me and I'll set you free—from niggers."[118]

Such was the dilemma faced by those African Americans in an administration regularly engaged in antiblack antagonisms. "By remaining in Nixon's service," a black militant group declared in October 1969, "Black appointees lend credence to the hypocritical posture of [the] Administration, with the added danger of becoming spokesmen for it." If the appointees refused to resign in protest, the organization warned, the "Black community," would "expose them as co-conspirators of Mr. Nixon's ever increasing anti-Black policies." The group's stance, though extreme, sheds some light on the public's reaction to the "Black Cabinet"; to work *within* the White House was comparable to condoning the president's actions. Between 1969 and 1972, as the black press was highlighting the "influence" of the appointees, critics of all races accused the appointees of being powerless Nixon flunkies, apologists, race traitors, and even "house niggers." This was, in the words of Clarence Townes, a community "morality play"—working quietly behind the scenes was no longer enough.[119]

In truth, black Republican appointees initially said little about the administration's erratic behavior. In media appearances, they cheered the White House's civil rights efforts and remained silent when questioned about Nixon's antiblack decisions. In private, they railed against the president; in some extreme cases, even working to sabotage the White House, as James Farmer did in February 1970, when he leaked a copy of Daniel Patrick Moynihan's "benign neglect" memo to the *New York Times*.[120] That year marked a turning point of sorts for the black appointees as a collective; increasingly aggravated by the president's reactionary behaviors, they began voicing their complaints as a collective, as nearly forty of them did during a frank and sharp discussion with Nixon during a March 1970 meeting.[121]

A week after the session, the black Republican appointees collaborated with thirty-seven delegates from the Black Elected Republican Officials group (BERO), holding a two-day conference at the White House to discuss the administration's civil rights record and its policies affecting African Americans. They were joined by Nixon and most of the members of his cabinet, along with representatives from more than a dozen federal departments and agencies, both houses of Congress and the RNC. That the administration and the national committee would attempt to use the session for publicity to nullify charges of racism mattered little to most of the attendees, who saw the conference as a cathartic opportunity to air their collective frustrations. As the keynote speaker, Edward Brooke chided the administration for spurning black voters in a calculated effort to woo white southern suburbanites. "I have seen very little for black people to applaud during this Administration," he challenged—a serious accusation given the senator's involvement in publicizing many of the ideas surrounding minority enterprise and black capitalism. Turning his attention to the audience of black "brothers and sisters," Brooke declared that they were the "representatives of 23 million" African Americans. "Black Republicans must carry the ball," he argued, for the duration of Nixon's tenure in the White House, shouldering the responsibility of black uplift.

Many of the participants spoke of the embarrassment they faced within their communities because of the administration's apparent hostility to African Americans; they also expressed their anger that some of the White House's more conservative white staffers and strategists were making decisions on issues related to blacks. "The day is over," one attendee insisted, "when white men stand on the sole authority" on African Americans. Likewise, the delegates passed a resolution declaring their opposition to Nixon's Supreme Court nominations and presented a lengthy catalog of recommendations—most of which reaffirmed support for the economic initiatives of the "Black Cabinet." Black Republicans, wrote journalist Audrey Weaver, "weren't mildly irked, they were fighting mad" over the White House's posturing on racial issues; in particular, she took great delight in one participant's statement that he would "tar and feather" Richard Nixon "out of the Presidency if [the] procedure were still in fashion." But although furious over the president's repeated attempts to placate reactionary whites, the conference attendees nevertheless left the conference hopeful that they had gotten through to Nixon, helping the president to understand the frustrations of black citizens. "We plan [to] use our power to improve conditions and bridge this gap between our party and blacks," John Kellogg stated in a press conference. "We are not pleased with the party's actions, but we're also not disillusioned. There is hope."[122]

After the conference, the president made a few meaningful overtures, some small, some large; for example, he acted on several of BERO's recommendations, including expanding Bob Brown's status in the White House. As previously discussed, the administration's black economic programs continued to swell; likewise, in the spring of 1970, Nixon twice called for Congress to enact a $1.5 billion plan to help speed desegregation, over the course of two years.[123] Yet at the same time, the president undercut these efforts by pursuing a "racially polarizing Southern Strategy," that used the language of resentment to create a coalition of white southerners and midwesterners; more specifically, throughout 1970, the White House aligned itself with reactionary southern candidates—some Republican, others Democrat or independent—who openly defied federal desegregation mandates, while simultaneously stoking the flames of "racial resentment" among working-class whites.[124]

It was this racially charged reality that led Nixon's black appointees to form the Council of Black Appointees (CBA) during the summer of 1970. Members of the forty-person council saw the group as a way of voicing their collective frustrations with the direction of the administration. Not only did the CBA lobby the White House on issues of black concern; it also acted as a support network for the small group of mostly Republican appointees that worked within the upper echelons of the federal government. Some black officials, including several appointees from the Johnson administration, ridiculed the CBA as a kitchen cabinet—a powerless group of black Republicans who "meet at one another's homes on a Saturday night and, over Scotch-on-the-rocks and potato chips, agonize over the Administration's relations with . . . black Americans, and collectively search their souls to justify their own participation in it." Though mean-spirited, the assessment was not entirely incorrect: as individuals, the appointees certainly held a measure of influence within the administration, but as a collective, the group spent the better part of a year talking, holding meetings, and issuing statements, rather than influencing the White House's political strategy.[125]

In a way, appointees founded the CBA to help them survive in an administration driven by a president bent on displays of constituent loyalty and winning at any cost. Likewise, while Nixon toyed with the idea of wooing black voters in 1970, he also reasoned that the administration could not "win over our enemies—youth, black, Jew."[126] To those ends, the president downplayed and concealed many of his administration's civil rights accomplishments in 1970 and disbanded the Minorities Division of the RNC. "We don't want the black vote," a visibly dejected Clarence Townes told reporters in June 1970:

> There's a total fear of what's called the Southern strategy. Blacks understand that their well-being is being sacrificed to political gain. There has to be some moral leadership from the President on the race question—and there just hasn't been any. To the blacks the President has placed the name of the Republican [P]arty in greater darkness than it was in under Goldwater. . . . Sure there are some blacks with nice titles working for the Administration. Some of them are doing a lot for their people. But they've got no power. Politically, they ain't scratching nothing.[127]

A month later, Townes quit the RNC. Black appointees also began to trickle out of the administration, including James Farmer, who resigned in December 1970. Their departures highlighted black Republicans' general feelings of disillusionment and disappointment—the group that had seemed so optimistic in 1969 was miserable and demoralized by the end of 1970.

Black Republicans' predictions of a poor showing in the 1970 midterm elections proved true, and the returns also offered an indictment of the southern strategy. Though the GOP gained two seats in the Senate, it lost nine positions in the House, 11 governorships and more than 200 seats in state legislatures. The party won 10 percent of the black vote—a substantial drop from the 19 percent it had received four years earlier. As defeated Florida governor Claude R. Kirk noted during a television interview, his "racially oriented, anti-school busing campaign" had hurt him in the polls. "A lot of black voters came out against me," he lamented, observing that his "use of the issue" had not led to a massive increase in white support.[128]

In an attempt to repair the damage of the 1970 midterm elections—not only among black voters but also among white moderate constituents who had also rejected the naked discrimination of the party's midterm appeals—the president *again* changed tactics, at one point, advocating an "Open Door" policy toward African Americans, and even contemplating nominating Ed Brooke to the Supreme Court.[129] One of the most vivid examples of this shift came when the president met with Whitney Young in December 1970 to discuss the "unique capabilities of private, non-profit local organizations like the Urban League." Nixon and the NUL formed a working partnership through which the black group would operate a variety of social service programs for African Americans with funds from federal agencies and departments.[130] The collaboration was ultimately more than just a partnership for racial progress—it was an endeavor that allowed both the administration and the NUL to broker influence in their respective domains. For the administration—particularly black Republicans and liberal and moderate staffers—this was an opportunity to appeal directly to the middle-class membership of the urban league and gain publicity, whereas for the NUL, the relationship provided a means of obtaining valuable federal funds and influencing the administration to support an equal rights agenda. Young recognized the inherent value in negotiating and working pragmatically with a Republican federal government; thus, when the *New York Times* offered a spread exploring whether Young should be called an "Oreo Cookie," "Whitey Young," "Uncle Whitney," or a genuine civil rights leader, on the basis of his work with the Nixon administrations and previous presidents, the NUL head dismissed the chatter as foolish, arguing "Nobody's who's working for black people is a moderate. . . . We're *all* militants in different ways. I can't afford the luxury of a completely dogmatic position that says, 'I won't make any compromises,' because I'm dealing with the real world."[131]

Within weeks of the December meeting, the Nixon administration offered the urban league more than $21 million in federal contracts harnessed from eight government departments. "Judging by the tabs that the federal government picks up," *Ebony* slyly observed, "the marriage is mutually beneficial." Many of the programs, in fact, did serve a dual purpose, introducing Republican ideas into hard-to-reach black enclaves; proposals, like the one received in the spring of 1971 from the NUL's southern office, were highly desirable, primarily for this reason.[132] The organization's suggestion for a yearlong series of economic education workshops in black localities in twelve southern states was well received—as Bob Brown commented in his evaluation, "The Administration has a strong interest in efforts of this nature." The seminars, approved with funding from the Departments of Labor and Education, outlined and promoted Nixon's revenue-sharing plan; moreover, administration officials participated in the session, studying black opinions and offering insights on policy misconceptions.[133]

The relationship between the White House and the NUL suffered a devastating blow when Whitney Young drowned while swimming at Lighthouse Beach in Lagos, Nigeria, in March 1971. For all of the president's faults, Nixon had genuinely come to appreciate the civil rights leaders' moderate approach to racial uplift; consequently, the president arranged to have a military plane bring Young's body's back to the United States. He also delivered the eulogy at the NUL head's Kentucky funeral, rooting his remarks in ideas of personal responsibility. "[Young] was not a moderate man in terms of his goals, but he knew the uses of moderation in achieving those goals," Nixon stated. "At a time when it is so often the custom whenever we have a problem to throw up our hands and say, 'What is the government going to do?' This man said, 'What can I do . . . to help the American dream come true?" A year later, President Nixon announced the creation of an occupational skills training center in Young's honor—an initiative funded with $1.9 million from HEW and the department of labor.[134]

Despite Nixon's promise that the "effort launched so ably by Whitney Young will go forward," both sides slowly began to chip away at the partnership, without the diplomatic presence of the civil rights leader. As early as May, NUL officials accused the White House of discrimination and demanded that the administration prove its loyalty in the wake of Young's death.[135] The NUL's accusations were not unfounded—though many of the programs proceeded smoothly for the most part, some agencies refused to cooperate; and given the White House's lax attitude toward intragovernment enforcement, the federal divisions could easily get away with such actions.[136] After a few tense months, and with pressure from Bob Brown, Nixon officials finally cracked down on the delinquent agencies. Likewise, at the urging of the black Republican appointees, George Shultz, now the director of the Office of Management and Budget (OMB), gave the keynote address for the NUL's annual national conference in July 1971. Invoking the memory of Arthur Fletcher's urban league keynote, delivered one year earlier, Shultz declared that free market enterprise was vital to racial uplift. "For the most part, we have the civil rights legislation that we require," he reasoned. "The need is not for new programs or prohibitions but to make the ones we have work." Black independence, Schulz continued, would occur by returning "power and responsibilities to states, localities, and individuals." By suggesting that black economic liberation was in tune with Republican principles, the Nixon official could thereby easily finesse antibusing approaches into an appreciation for black neighborhood schools, propose welfare reform as a black empowerment initiative, and rationalize ineffective voluntary "hometown plans" as black-controlled "hometown solutions." The administration's peacemaking efforts appeared to mollify the NUL, as the organization's national leadership showed renewed but cautious enthusiasm for future collaborations. "There is no question we are getting heard," NUL chair Vernon Jordan later declared. "We have been able to disagree with them on basic issues and continue a creative partnership."[137]

That same month, the NAACP offered arguably the most surprising about-face on the Nixon administration. In July 1971, in front of an audience of nearly three thousand delegates, Bishop Steven Spottswood—who one year earlier denounced the White House as the "most anti-Negro" administration since Woodrow Wilson—asserted that the White House had earned "cautious and limited approval among Black Americans." It was a purposefully vague statement, with no real details, but it was one shared by NAACP leader Roy Wilkins, who privately stated that the administration had made some strides in civil rights, particularly in economic advancement. "The situation is better than it was a year ago," Wilkins grudgingly told Stan Scott, a black Republican appointee. "But it's often not fast or far enough for me as head of the NAACP." The black leader bemoaned Nixon's abrasive political approach arguing that the president could "double or triple his vote in the black community," without sacrificing white voters. As Wilkins wearily pointed out, by recruiting black voters, Nixon would "gain some of the so-called white liberal votes." This is not to suggest that the NAACP suddenly embraced the White House uncritically; to the contrary, the organization clearly still believed the agenda of the Nixon administration was flawed and therefore adopted a prudent approach, much as the NUL had done. As Wilkins argued, it was "pure folly" for blacks to "sit back and just criticize rather than try to develop a dialogue and working relationship" with the executive office.[138]

Indeed, the NAACP still levied heavy criticisms at the administration, attacking, for instance, the failures of the Philadelphia Plan to curb discrimination in unions. By 1971, as we have seen, Fletcher had pushed through a few federally mandated plans, while the labor department also introduced voluntary hometown plans aimed at private industries; nevertheless, the black official often found his attempts to enforce the provisions of the plans stonewalled as federal agencies and departments, unions, and private businesses often ignored the government's nondiscrimination mandates.[139] Fletcher's problems reflected an administration-wide shift away from the Philadelphia Plan, as Nixon feared that the initiative would alienate white constituents; he also believed that nothing he did would be enough to win over a sizable cadre of black followers—ignoring the fact that his overtly hostile rhetoric undercut any goodwill gestures made toward African American voters. "We got less than 10% of the black vote [in 1968]," wrote Charles Colson, the president's liaison on unions and labor organizations. "We had close to 40% of the labor vote . . . and we could do better, except that we appear to be trying not to." Colson urged the president to make subtle political gestures to "loyal" labor groups by quietly transferring Fletcher to a "powerless advisory committee"—someplace where he would have little influence over domestic policy. By September 1971, Fletcher—once dubbed the most "powerful" African American in the White House—had been transferred out of the labor department and appointed as an alternative delegate to the United Nations, a position he would quit within three months.[140]

Throughout the ordeal, Fletcher steadfastly professed his loyalty to the Nixon administration, defending the administration's civil rights record, as did many of the other black Republican appointees. Fletcher, Bob Brown, Stan Scott, and HUD assistant secretary Samuel C. Jackson, for example, called a two-hour press conference in July 1971 to discuss Nixon's accomplishments in civil rights, in what turned out to be a distinctly uncomfortable meeting, for both the appointees and the attending reporters. The black Republicans' boasts quickly turned into defensive arguments once the press asked the appointees to reconcile their civil rights initiatives with the president's political appeals to whites. "I am not even going to try," Sam Jackson stated, with annoyance.[141]

In truth, there was no satisfactory answer to the question; consequently, the appointees' silence on the issue captures their constraints, as they struggled between community and partisan loyalties. In a sense, black Republican officials were trapped. They sincerely believed that working through a Republican-led White House was the best means of achieving racial equality, yet there was no way for them to reconcile the administration's overt *and* covert appeals to white citizens at the expense of African Americans.

• • •

In March 1972, Richard Nixon asked Congress for a temporary moratorium on busing, a move that was uniformly condemned by civil rights leaders *and* antibusing advocates. From the president's perspective, the proposed initiative was a compromise, for it avoided the political extreme of a constitutional amendment banning busing.[142] In response to Nixon's request, CBA—chaired by Sam Jackson—issued a six-page report challenging the president's busing stance. Instead of keeping the assessment under wraps, as members had done with their complaints in the past, the CBA publicly blasted the administration, holding press conferences detailing the report and criticizing the administration's approach to desegregation. The White House's actions, the council declared, "has already had a chilling effect on black people and others, insomuch as it is made to appear that the resources of the federal government under your leadership, are coming down on the side of those who stand in opposition to the constitutional rights of minority schoolchildren."

The statement was a forceful one, especially coming from a group of appointees known for their "silent" approach; yet at the same time, the CBA's report was carefully crafted, making it clear that black Republicans were loyal not only to their race but also to their party. In an attempt to soften the harshness of the group's statement, Jackson attributed the president's behavior not to racism or discrimination but rather to an inadvertent "lack of perspective."[143]

This "quiet" approach to politics was the trademark of black Republicans appointed to positions in the White House; theirs was a quiet dissent, as they understood that they had limited freedom to express dissatisfaction given the temperamental nature of Richard Nixon. For many political observers, quiet gestures were not enough; for many, real, tangible political power meant influencing not only the president's policies but also his political strategies. Black Republicans, suggested a black Democrat in the early 1970s, paled in comparison to Lyndon Johnson's "Black Mafia," a tight-knit group of black appointees that regularly advised the president and vice president on racial issues. "These men recognized that they represented a major force—the black vote," he continued, nostalgically. "As a result, the 'Black Mafia' did make an impact."[144] While an overly simplistic reading of the Johnson years that ignored the very real struggles faced by black Democrats within that administration, the statement nevertheless highlights the many paradoxes faced by black Republicans seeking power within the Nixon White House.

Nixon's Black Cabinet erroneously assumed that an economic civil rights movement would translate into political rewards, underestimating the size of the so-called black silent majority of African American conservatives and moderates. To be sure, the appointees actually had an audience: moderate civil rights organizations, such as the NUL, consistently engaged the economic policies and programs of the administration.

Likewise, ideas of capitalism were readily accepted in many black communities; in other words, there was an opportunity to make inroads among some African American voters, or at least maintain the levels the party had achieved in the 1966 election, were it not for the party's aggressive dalliance with the politics of racial resentment.

The administration's actions stymied black Republicans; as they launched their economic civil rights initiatives, their efforts were undercut by Nixon's behavior. Moreover, the appointees were constrained by their conflicting loyalties. If militantly outspoken, they ran the risk of being ostracized, fired, or replaced; yet their commitment to racial uplift also demanded displays of righteous outrage on behalf of their community. Like the Minorities Division before them, the Black Cabinet's work was hampered by an affiliation with the Nixon administration, a dilemma to be sure, given that the White House supported and funded many of black Republicans' projects.

Black appointees constantly grappled with their position in the White House, questioning if the end goals justified the means. For many, their emotional response to the administration was superseded by their pragmatic calculations on the nature of power and racial uplift; as writer Carlos Russell explained in 1972 the Black Cabinet's balancing act was both understandable and mind-boggling. But it was also a miscalculation, as the restrictions placed upon its members by the White House muted their overall impact—at least among African Americans, who expected black Republican appointees to influence not only Nixon's economic policies but his racial politics as well. In a sense, black voters felt betrayed by their "inside men," accusing them of failing and being passive at their jobs. Articulating this sentiment, the *Afro-American* argued that the black appointees had lost their "credibility in their own community."[145]

This was a viewpoint made all the more salient by the rapid changes transforming the landscape of black politics. In particular, black voters began to use the upper echelons of the Democratic Party to translate "protest into politics" during the 1960s. By 1970, for example, thirty-six African Americans ran for senatorial, congressional, or gubernatorial seats, whereas only seven of these candidates ran as Republicans. Likewise, in 1971, the thirteen black members of the House of Representatives launched the Congressional Black Caucus (CBC). Seen as righteous combatants in the next wave of equality struggles, the CBC members, many of whom were young black political stars in their communities, presented a stark contrast to the quiet Council of Black Appointees, whom the *New York Amsterdam News* derided as no more than "propaganda machinery designed to sell the President's civil rights record during the 1972 Presidential campaign." Moreover, the CBC not only had the support of a black voter base but also had its own money: in its first fundraiser, the organization raised more than $250,000 in a display of a "new and potent political thrust."[146] In effect, the CBC appeared to be thumbing its nose at political bureaucracy in a show of black political independence in a way that Nixon's black appointees simply could not do.

Going forward, black Republicans would try to redefine the boundaries of the administration's constraints, through a complex demonstration of partisan loyalty in the 1972 presidential election. But that contest would not bring the results they so desired; instead, it would exacerbate the chaos and confusion that existed among black Republicans both inside and outside of the Nixon White House.

CHAPTER FIVE

Exorcising the Ghost of Richard Nixon

BY THE EARLY 1970S, BLACK REPUBLICANS UNDERSTOOD THAT THE GOP
was on the cusp of a major transformation—a political crisis that appeared to motivate even the most cynical within their ranks. At a moment
when black appointees inside the White House were fighting to retain
some semblance of influence on President Nixon's policies and political
strategies, black Republicans in the rest of the country were in the midst
of a revolt. Refusing to abide by the GOP's "eleventh commandment"
and remain silent, black Republican "outsiders," or those who worked
outside of the Nixon administration, aired their frustrations publicly in
a noisy and urgent fashion. In its earliest stages, this black intraparty
dissent was characterized by public disavowals of antiblack attitudes
and strategies, as newly formed splinter organizations pushed the GOP
to reject discriminatory practices and bring African Americans into the
"economic mainstream" of society.

The appearance of grass-roots black Republican groups was far from
novel; a spirit of self-determination had buttressed the formation of the
National Negro Republican Assembly (NNRA) in 1964. But autonomy,
political influence, and growth—the objective goals for most, if not all,
black Republican groups—simply was not the reality, as most splinter
organizations deteriorated just as quickly as they had risen. The NNRA
was reduced to a passing biographical reference by 1969, as most members shifted their political energies elsewhere, while the group's successor, the National Council of Concerned Afro-American Republicans
(NCCAAR), disbanded a year after its launch, as a result of infighting
and lack of funds.

As black Republican splinter organizations launched and dissolved,
members continued to hold on to their frustrations, unhappy with their
treatment in party circles, and with the GOP's erratic interest in black
voters. In her 1970 study of black party leaders in New York, political scientist Joyce Gelb found that the party hierarchy—on every level—
was "unable to provide more than symbolic recognition for those blacks
who identify with it." Despite the advancements of the NNRA, Edward
Brooke, the Minorities Division, and Richard Nixon's Black Cabinet,
blacks in the GOP reported seeing little change in the party from the

late 1950s. Gelb's subjects viewed reform efforts as incomplete, stunted by the party's inability to fully share power with its black members and make consistent and genuine appeals to African American communities.[1]

It was this kind of dissatisfaction with the GOP that united black Republicans throughout the country in the early 1970s, triggered by long-festering party ailments over race, integration, and equal rights. Blacks in the GOP publicly and privately berated their party with an exhaustive list of complaints, covering everything from the Nixon administration's "southern strategy" to the lack of racial diversity in state and local party organizations. "It is a lily-white structure—not that much different from Mississippi," one black party member lamented, referring to New York's state GOP organization. "Negroes are shut out." Though his criticisms contained an element of hyperbole (New York was not nearly as racist as Mississippi in 1970), they were also telling: even in the bastion of liberal Republicanism, white party officials continued to omit African Americans from influential roles and positions in spite of the constant prodding from black party members.[2]

Nationally, the situation was dire enough to inspire 100 black party leaders to reactivate NCCAAR in 1971, under a new moniker: the National Council of Afro-American Republicans (NCAAR).[3] Importantly, they and other black Republican leaders were angered not by the economic initiatives of the White House but by the party's behavior and attitude, especially its failure to integrate and publicize the civil rights advancements of the Nixon administration, alongside its repeated excursions into racist political strategies—covert or otherwise—at the expense of black voters. This made for an interesting dynamic, as a March 1972 survey of African American party elites illustrates. In the study, the black leaders declared support for an "independent Black Republican Organization" that would "espouse Mr. Nixon's domestic programs . . . help elect more Black Republicans to the Congress," and "beat the drums of Republicanism loud enough to attract" black voters. Later in the survey, respondents unanimously complained that the party was neglecting African Americans and accused unnamed "bigoted White Republican leadership" of employing divisive tactics to keep black party members "fighting among ourselves so that our effectiveness and claims for political rewards are totally negated."[4] Black Republicans saw no contradiction in applauding Nixon's economic policies while attacking the party and the president for employing discriminatory strategies. They insisted that they were still loyal to the party, having no desire to desert the ranks of Republicanism; instead, as many others had done before them, they suggested that it was their job to remain within the GOP and reform the party. As one black member put it in 1971, "Black Republicans must remain independent and with the right to fight within the Party for our people and to maintain the right to offer constructive criticism."[5]

The fractured life cycle of black Republican organizations in the 1970s, moreover, necessitated reevaluation as African Americans struggled to reposition their role within the GOP. "I am the first to admit that success has eluded [black Republicans]," conceded NCAAR official Curtis Perkins in March 1971. "[We] are too fragmented and too prone to suicide in terms of 'togetherness' to be effective."[6] True efficacy, for Perkins—just as for the past three decades of black Republicans—required racial integration at every level of the party, aggressive minority outreach, and an increase in black Republican appointees and elected officials in policy-making positions.[7] Though meaningful developments in these three areas had emerged over the previous five years (particularly with the rise of the president's Black Cabinet), African Americans of *all* political backgrounds nevertheless argued that any power accrued by black Republicans was meaningless, since the administration's coded racial appeals to white suburbanites and working-class ethnics continued, often at the expense of black needs. This was the dilemma that black Republicans faced in the early years of the 1970s; they agonized over their inability to turn positive economic accomplishments into political influence among white Republican leaders and black voters.

It was within this context that the tenor and texture of black Republican calls for autonomy shifted. Instead of assembling in isolated splinter groups, African Americans attempted to unite under the mantle of a single umbrella organization—one that would promise national consensus from the nation's black Republican leaders and serve as an effective coordinating vehicle for voicing black Republicanism. In theory, a black national council meant not only the bolstering of African American solidarity and strength but also the realization of political autonomy. While such an objective appeared to conflict with their demand for party integration, black Republicans saw the two concepts as complimentary, believing that freedom from the yoke of white control would allow African Americans to integrate every facet of the party structure, from the national to the local. Intraparty sovereignty, black Republicans insisted, could be used to gather support for the mainstream GOP *and* implied a myriad of rights: the right to critique the party and its leadership, ideologies, and policies; the right to guard against "cynical and selfish" black Republicans who would "sabotage black unity" within the party; and, finally, the right to advance and implement policies and initiatives without the omnipresent gaze of white party officials.[8] Consequently, in spite of their professed loyalty to the broad values of the Republican Party, black party leaders understood that many within the GOP, including the president, had adopted strategies and policies that were hostile to African American needs.

For hundreds of black GOP leaders, the creation of an autonomous consensus organization was crucial to turning effort into measurable and tangible political results. Yet autonomy did not preclude financial support or recognition from the GOP—quite the opposite. Black Republicans insisted that in order to thrive, an umbrella group needed to be sanctioned and funded by either the administration or the Republican National Committee, or both, and supported by Republicans of all races. In 1971 NCAAR proposed that the RNC contribute nearly half of the black group's $310,000 operating budget, insisting that the party was obligated to do so, given its historical and ongoing poor treatment of African Americans. "We need the money—not begging, mind you—from where it is and which has been spent for decades on an almost lily white Party," asserted the group's leaders.[9] During that same year, Nixon's black Republican appointees requested more than $800,000 to fund an independent black outreach campaign.[10] Generating interest and reforming the party, African Americans argued, required a stronger commitment from not only black party members but the mainstream Republican Party as well. These types of demands for financial and moral support indicated a new kind of forcefulness among African American party members and reflected not only changes wrought by the civil rights movement but also black Republicans' soft embrace of *some* of the tenets of Black Power.

Furthermore, African Americans' intraparty dissent was both complex and reactionary. At first, black Republicans were split between "insiders" who worked within or closely with the administration and "outsiders" unaffiliated with the White House. As we have seen, the former group advocated for a quiet, often silent kind of dissent, understanding that it had limited freedom to express discontent given the temperamental and vindictive nature of Richard Nixon; the latter camp, in contrast, had few ties to the administration, rejected subversive protest as ineffective, and aired its complaints in stormy public displays of defiance. Yet by 1972 the lines between the two groups had eroded and blurred, as African Americans began to switch tactics and approaches in a labyrinthine manner—loudly denouncing the party in one breath, for instance, and counseling patience with the next. Black Republicans initially reacted solely to the administration's and the party's creeping extremism; later, they would eventually react, as a collective, to their exclusion from positions of influence during Richard Nixon's second term in the White House.

Black intraparty dissent, likewise, was an attempt at proactive reform, as African American party loyalists tried to capitalize on their accomplishments, while responding to the RNC's rhetoric of broadening the GOP's voting base. All the while, they held fast to their notions of solidarity. From these calls for unity materialized a plethora of coordinating organizations, many of which were markedly different from one another and from the splinter groups of the past. Of these organizations, the National Black Republican Council (NBRC) and the Council of 100 would emerge as the most significant, often working in tandem, despite striking dissimilarities: the former was the national consensus organization for which black Republicans had been clamoring, while the latter was a small exclusive lobbyist group with a liberal agenda. The Black Silent Majority Committee (BSMC) would also become one of the more important groups of the period; however, unlike the NBRC and the Council of 100, the BSMC developed not from intraparty protest but from a reactionary impulse to the changing social landscape of the United States. These three groups illustrate the chaos and ideological diversity that raged within the GOP throughout the 1970s, highlighting the turmoil and contradictions faced by black Republicans as they sought to increase their status and influence in a rapidly transforming Republican Party.

QUIET DISSENT AND CONCESSIONS OF POWER

That black Republicans were still invested in wooing black voters in the early 1970s was impressive, given that more than two-thirds of African Americans viewed the president and the party in a negative light. As White House strategists highlighted in a 1971 memo, the administration's southern strategy had "nullified" any positive effects from initiatives like black capitalism.[11] Nevertheless, black Republicans, both inside and outside of the administration, pursued outreach on behalf of Richard Nixon and the GOP, fundamentally believing in the economic civil rights approach of the Republican Party. Black Republicans also justified their campaign efforts by pointing to studies of African American political attitudes, including one from 1971 that suggested that black citizens believed that their lives had improved since 1968. Despite strongly believing that the Nixon administration and Republicans were hostile to black interests, nearly a quarter of African Americans also reported that they had become "more conservative" over the prior three years. This shift even applied to black voting-age youth, about 20 percent of whom identified as conservative, while 40 percent characterized themselves as moderate. Black strategists also took a small measure of comfort in the fact that while almost a quarter of young black men and women identified as liberal, only 5 percent saw themselves as militant.

Moreover, the studies, based on data mined from black voters between 1968 and 1971, challenged the notion of a monolithic black population, disrupting what had passed for conventional wisdom for several years: that African Americans were loyal *only* to the Democratic Party. Harris polls, for instance, indicated that the number of blacks identifying as Republican had jumped from 7 to 17 percent during Nixon's first term in office; polls from Gallup and the Michigan Survey Research Center were far less dramatic, but recorded notable increases, just the same. In no way did these findings guarantee black support for Richard Nixon or the Republican Party—after all, the majority of African Americans still disapproved of the president's performance in office and remained partisan Democrats.[12] Still, the studies did have important implications for strategy; assessing the studies as a collective, party strategists concluded that many blacks found the Democratic Party "inadequate for their . . . goals," pointing to the roughly 20 percent of African Americans who identified as independent. To put it simply, dissatisfaction with the Democratic Party, coupled with a black cadre of conservative voters, suggested that black Republicans had a reasonable opportunity to sway some black voters.[13]

Armed with this information, black Republicans pushed the administration to repair its image and launch a public outreach campaign. Their aim: winning 20 percent of the black vote—in other words, doubling the president's 1968 tally. Had Nixon garnered 18 percent of the black vote in 1968, strategists noted, he would have won the states of Maryland and Texas, and solidified narrow margins of victory in Missouri, New Jersey, and Ohio. Consolidating their ideas, Nixon's black appointees proposed what amounted to an orchestrated public relations campaign for the president. "The program plan is based on the premise that the current Black political posture is pragmatic—the feeling being that the Black voters should be practical and selfish on behalf of Black people—that they should not be taken for granted—that they must take whatever they can from whomever they can—and that they should support, with less regard to Party, whoever offers the best response to a developing Black agenda."[14] These were targeted interests; as Bob Brown proposed in a 1971 memo, black outreach should concentrate exclusively on the African American demographic "most likely" to respond to the administration's outreach gestures. A "low-key voter education" program at black colleges could help the campaign win 20 to 30 percent of young African American voters, Brown speculated, while specific appeals to black groups like the National Baptist Convention, the National Business League, the National Association of Colored Women's Clubs, and the Links, Inc.— whose presidents were all vocal Nixon supporters—would garner increased support, as would fielding and financing strong African American candidates in predominately black districts.[15] "Responsive" black constituents also included those African Americans who had financially benefited from the economic thrust of the administration; in fact, black Republican insiders regularly scoured federal agencies and departments for additional sources of grant and loan money to distribute to African Americans willing to be publicly "supportive" of the president's reelection campaign.[16] All of these efforts were in keeping with the black appointees' focus on the black middle class. Underscoring this classism was a cynical belief that the party could never win the votes of the black poor or working class; as one strategist wrote in the early 1970s, the goal was to "neutralize a portion of Black voters which cannot be won over" by aggressively publicizing the actions of those who could.[17]

Of special interest were southern black voters, 42 percent of whom continued to view the president favorably in 1971, in stark contrast to the political opinions of the rest of the nation's black citizens. Beginning in 1971, the administration sent white officials and a "Black Blitz Team" to woo black southerners, assuring them that they were "wanted and needed as active partners" in the GOP and promising them that they would be included in the White House's campaign efforts. In October, for example, Bob Brown and Harry Dent held an "emotional" meeting with eighty black Republicans in Atlanta. Although they emphasized their faith in two-party competition, the group also "sharply criticized" the White House's refusal to support court-ordered busing to achieve desegregation, accusing the president of deliberately stoking white racial resentment to shore up votes. Ultimately the group proclaimed its loyalty to Nixon but demanded more "black patronage jobs," increased southern judicial appointments, and rehabilitation of the administration and the party's image to boost black membership in the GOP.[18] Though such meetings were small, they were noteworthy, journalist Ethel Payne explained in a November 1971 column, assessing black Republicans' solidarity efforts and their push for increased clout in party affairs. "While publicity has been centered on black Democrats demanding changes in the party structure to give them a greater voice in policy," she wrote, "little attention is being paid to a significant move among black Republicans to make their party more responsive."[19] The *Chicago Tribune* made similar observations, commenting on the spike in black Republican unity activity across the country; in an interview with the newspaper, a black Republican observed that these sessions were about assuming power within the party on behalf of African Americans, and they intersected with Nixon's reelection campaign to encourage black voters to "participate in both parties, so that they can't be ignored by the Republicans and taken for granted by the Democrats." Here then, black Republicans still held fast to their belief that two-party competition only meant that more African Americans should join the Republican Party rather than the Democratic Party.[20]

A one-day conference at the White House, held in December 1971, illustrated black Republicans' complex shift toward unity—African American party elites rallied with Harry Dent to mobilize black Republicans into a "political propaganda network" for Richard Nixon. They declined to talk to reporters: as one black attendee coldly stated, "We'll fight over our grievances among ourselves and not in the newspapers. . . . We're not going to be dissatisfied. If we don't agree with everything that Agnew and Nixon are doing, we'll let the proper people know." Behind closed doors, the conveners revealed that they envisioned two-party competition as a "two-way proposition" with the GOP. They would support the administration and urge black voters to do the same, so long as the party acted on black Republicans' suggestions.[21] Though the end goals were the same, this strategy was a far cry from the disruptive protests that had previously characterized black Republican protest. In truth, by the end of 1971, many black Republicans had abandoned their combative tactics and adopted the quiet approach of Nixon's black appointees, a shift that was symbolic of African Americans' hunger for political influence. They hoped that aligning with the White House would bring them a measure of clout, while others—some of whom had received grants and funds from the administration—saw this as a means of clinging to the power they already had. Thus, while their private words contained a heightened sense of forcefulness—a not-so-veiled threat against party inaction—their public behavior also revealed both the paradoxical boundaries faced by African Americans in the GOP and the concessions blacks made as they attempted to gain and retain influence.

By the start of the 1972 primary season, black Republicans collectively came to believe that a display of political loyalty was the best way to ensure party reform. They insisted that improving the president's outreach efforts among black voters would satisfy multiple goals: first, it would create leverage for organizational efforts by creating a sizable base of black party members; second, black Republicans' hard work on the campaign trail would ensure Nixon's reelection victory; and third, their contribution to the president's success would ensure a reward of increased influence within party circles. Though naïve, given the president's mercurial attitude toward African Americans, black Republicans' faith in patronage politics was, in many ways, in keeping with the times. Moreover, as a practical matter, African American party elites understood the potentially negative consequences of opposing Richard Nixon's reelection effort. A July 1971 survey by Political Associates illustrates this understanding: more than 90 percent of black Republican leaders and officials polled indicated the inevitability of Richard Nixon becoming the party's 1972 presidential nominee.[22] Most also believed that Nixon would be reelected, so to oppose the president would be akin to political suicide, ostracizing African Americans party members from both the administration and the mainstream party.

Organizational efforts coalesced in the months leading up to the 1972 election as black Republicans channeled their frustrations into small-scale movements, all of which centered on increasing their influence on GOP affairs. Spurning the "outsider" move toward calculated silence, NCAAR offered the most "militant" approach, demanding that blacks constitute at least 10 percent of the delegation to the 1972 Republican National Convention and threatening a class-action lawsuit against the "white party hierarchy" for discriminating against African Americans by failing to provide them with "grass-roots representation" on the RNC's executive committee.[23] That same month in Memphis, black Republicans turned out in "record numbers" to a state convention to defeat an anti-busing resolution and elect three African Americans to the "powerful" Tennessee Republican Steering Committee. African Americans attributed their "unusual display of political ability and hidden black Republican strength" to a network of two hundred members in forty locations across the state. Their goal, a spokesman for the political cohort argued, was to mobilize African Americans in the party, bring them into the "real action" of GOP affairs and have an impact on "politics and economics."[24]

Such assertiveness was but one part of a broader movement among African Americans for increased political relevancy. As black Republicans were fighting to change the party structure and gain a bigger voice, so too were black Democrats.[25] Similarly, the National Black Political Convention embodied this broader movement for increased power: in March 1972, more than eight thousand African Americans met in Gary, Indiana, to discuss and debate the concept of an independent black political movement and building strength within the two-party political system. It was remarkable, the *New York Times* noted with some amusement, to see Nixon appointee Samuel C. Jackson playing an "active role" in the same physical space as Black Panther Party founder Bobby Seale, Amiri Baraka, and members of the Congressional Black Caucus; to witness such a diverse assembly of black political figures and groups, Jesse Jackson concurred, was a "light-weight miracle."[26]

Such was the nature of the Gary convention: the delegates pushed for mass black solidarity and the creation of alliances across partisan and ideological lines. As the delegates' opening declaration stated: "Both parties have betrayed us whenever their interests conflicted with ours (which was most of the time) and whenever our forces were unorganized and dependent, quiescent and compliant."[27] These assertions voiced African Americans' dissatisfaction with the two-party political system, warning of being taken for granted by one party and being ignored by the other—the same rhetoric of two-party competition and independence that black Republicans had employed for decades. Though not the first time that blacks unaffiliated with the party had used such language, it marked the first time that so many had incorporated the language of two-party competition into a consensus document meant to speak for all African Americans. Here then, the Gary convention seemed to validate black Republicans' basic premise of two-party competition; and even as the delegates debated over the merits of a third-party movement, it nevertheless signaled the possibility of future black support for a "progressive" GOP.

To those ends, black Republicans took an active role in convention affairs, including Sam Jackson, who chaired the platform committee, which drafted the final black political agenda. Though he did not attend the black summit, Ed Brooke watched the proceedings on television with interest; to him, they proved that African Americans "are heterogeneous rather than homogeneous, and it is difficult, if not impossible, to get one clear voice." The difficulty of drafting a consensus agenda spoke to the senator's point, exposing the heterogeneity of black America; nationalists from CORE, for example, joined with delegates from South Carolina, Florida, and Maryland to endorse community control of schools and lobby against busing. Thus, while they denounced Richard Nixon as a racist, black-busing opponents found themselves supporting the president's position, much to the horror of thousands of convention participants.[28]

Even though the Gary convention illustrated the difficulty in forging a representative agenda that spoke for all African Americans, it nevertheless highlighted the weighty potential of political solidarity. Black Republicans left Indiana interested in the idea of bipartisanship, but only if it would aid in their insistence on two-party competition as a way of enticing black voters into the party to leverage increased influence. The convention also reinforced a belief that unity was crucial to black Republican success, even within the boundaries of the GOP. Calls for reconfiguring black party organizations were a common refrain by 1972, as black Republicans argued that consolidation would improve effectiveness in the face of party hostility. A national coordinating council, many argued, would benefit black outreach by "minimizing competitiveness" among African American party members, while providing for maximum involvement.[29]

Three months after the Gary convention, an "impressive array" of nearly twenty-five hundred African Americans met in Washington, D.C., for a two-day political conference in June 1972, under the banner "Getting Ourselves Together." Sponsored by the Black Vote Division of the Committee to Re-Elect the President (CREEP), the attendees represented a diverse cross section of public life. Politicians, administration appointees, educators, entrepreneurs, religious leaders, and celebrities mingled with hundreds of rank-and-file men and women, about one hundred of whom would journey to the neighboring hotel to participate in NCAAR's parallel convention. It was a "weekend of political wonders," Paul Delaney of the *New York Times* sarcastically noted, describing the two conferences, where Nixon was compared to "Christ, Churchill, Bismarck and the prophets Isaiah and Amos" and where South Carolina Senator Strom Thurmond, "long a foe of civil rights," was celebrated for "changing the state party, integrating his staff, and encouraging more black participation in state party affairs."[30] Conference participants were motivated mainly by a pragmatic support of the administration's black economic programs, rather than dogmatic interest in the presidential candidate. Privately, only 42 percent of black Republican leaders supported Nixon's candidacy—the rest preferred Nelson Rockefeller or Edward Brooke.[31]

Anticipating a Nixon victory in the November election, African Americans suggested that a practical endorsement of the president was useful, as they believed patronage to be a powerful leveraging tool. And on the final evening of the CREEP conference, black Republicans raised $250,000 for Nixon's campaign in a bid for exactly that. The star-studded event exuded symbolism as black Republicans delivered a riveting performance of political loyalty: chartering airplanes and limousines to ferry black supporters from around the country to the fundraiser; seating members of the Black Cabinet onstage with celebrities and civil rights notables including Jim Brown and Betty Shabazz; and performing a rousing round of Lionel Hampton's original song, "We Need Nixon," as the black "Nixonettes" showed African American and white Republicans how to do the accompanying dance in a cheerful display of camaraderie.[32]

As the gala attendees pulled out their wallets, black Republicans testified their devotion to Richard Nixon. Ethel Allen, a Philadelphia city councilwoman declared that "black women [will] rally behind the President," while Floyd McKissick, formerly of CORE and now the director of Soul City (a black capitalism-inspired town in North Carolina), declared that African Americans would "no longer be satisfied with the sugar tit handed [to] them by the Democrats."[33] The best speech, the *Pittsburgh Courier* argued, came from Jerome Green, a Malcolm X College student who had received a Purple Heart for his service in Vietnam and who swore that there were seventeen thousand angry Vietnam veterans in Chicago "ready to go all out for Mr. Nixon" and local Republicans in the November election. Underneath the speakers' bold but questionable claims was a simplistic *quid pro quo* understanding: help the president and receive power in return. Green, for instance, later remarked that he had looked "where the power was going to lie in the next four years" and had decided that "loyalty to Nixon" would give his local veteran rehabilitation programs a "better chance" at survival.[34]

Surely, black Republicans' "handsome contribution," argued the *Chicago Defender*, mandated an important role for African Americans in Republican decision making; no longer would they be "relegated to the role of 'kitchen cabinet' with only backdoor entrance to the White House."[35] Just as black Republicans had done, the *Defender* assumed that money was the key to black political influence—a point the periodical had also asserted a year earlier while discussing the Congressional Black Caucus's successful fundraising venture. But the *Defender*'s argument, much like black Republicans' naïve strategy, was an oversimplified assessment that neglected to consider the president's calculating attitude on race. To be sure, political contributions were important, but they were not as significant as African Americans and the black press made them out to be, especially when they represented a fraction of the president's $40 million campaign chest.[36] Equally important, donations offered no guarantee of patronage or power *because the contributors were black*. This point, emphasized ad nauseam at the Gary convention three months earlier, should have been one of the takeaway lessons from that conference; instead, black Republicans and the *Defender* assumed that an organized demonstration of loyalty would be enough to win major concessions from Richard Nixon. A political donation from African Americans, no matter how large, was not enough to mandate a prolonged and thorough commitment to racial egalitarianism from the administration and the entire party.

The June events marked strategic attempts to define African Americans' role in the GOP, increase their influence within the party, and coordinate a "new surge of black GOP election year activity" into a measure of organizational solidarity and consensus. "We are proceeding to implement the spirit of Gary's Black Political Convention," asserted Curtis Perkins, without a trace of irony, "by making our party responsible to black needs and goals."[37] Black Republicans would get a chance to test the bonds of their solidarity two months later during the 1972 Republican National Convention in Miami Beach, an event that would prove to be a showcase for white male "members of the old guard." Black delegates composed a mere 4 percent of the representatives, a paltry sum when juxtaposed with black representation to July's Democratic National Convention, which totaled 15 percent. Black journalists joked about playing "spot the black

Republican" throughout the August Republican convention; in fact, the *Miami News* questioned whether African American party members were even present, given the "racism, implied or intended," and "negative anti-black buzz words" that marked the most reactionary of the convention speeches.[38]

The Republican delegate tally for 1972, however, was somewhat mis-leading—it actually represented a 115 percent increase from 1968 and constituted the highest concentration of black representation since 1936. Furthermore, despite their small numbers, black Republicans infiltrated the hierarchy of convention politics; twelve African Americans, for in-stance, sat on committees, including two black women on the platform committee. "Black Republican Power," crowed Jackson R. Champion, publisher of *Grass Roots News*, was evident throughout the partisan gathering—from the presence of Nixon's black appointees, to the key-note speeches of Senator Edward Brooke. Black Republican power could be found within the ritual of the political convention, in orchestrated and spontaneous demonstrations, calculated scripted speeches, backroom ne-gotiations, and attempts to organize as a collective.[39]

Intrigued by black Republicans' efforts at solidarity and clout, Vernon Jarrett of the *Chicago Tribune* observed that African American partici-pants "sincerely wanted to get together and make significant demands on the conservative power structure," despite their public relations push to "sell" Nixon and the party to black voters. Such efforts, he concluded, were insignificant since black Republicans "don't really want to offend the sources of funds and power."[40] Yet, while he correctly identified the tension underlying black Republicans mobilization efforts in Miami Beach, Jarrett was mistaken in suggesting that African American party members were unwilling to voice their dissent. To the contrary, during the convention black Republicans' praise for the administration's economic programs bled into "sharp criticisms of party shortcomings," as divisions among African American party members that had receded months earlier reappeared as a result of the intense atmosphere of the national conven-tion.[41] The partisan gathering was a tightly scripted affair for everyone *but* the black delegates, who abandoned the quiet approach of admin-istration insiders, noisily voicing their complaints. While meeting with black delegates, for instance, Julie Nixon Eisenhower was greeted by po-lite applause that quickly turned into jeers and "audible groans" from the audience (much to the horror of the president's black appointees), when she refused to address incisive questions about her father's antibusing statements. "[Our] backs are against the wall when we try to sell this party to the black community," one African American representative as-serted during a meeting with black appointees. As White House outsiders, the delegates suggested that they had no choice but to vent their griev-ances, as they had been "either ignored or left out" of party affairs.[42]

The delegates revived frustration was a response to the reactionary elements of the convention, arguing that the party had dismissed civil rights in favor of "far right" catchphrases and positions. "I did not come here to whine and cry," stated Charles Hurst, president of Malcolm X College in Chicago," but I really don't think the Republican Party wants black people in it. We are here to demand participation in every facet of this country's political life."[43] In truth, black Republicans' gripes were not so much about policies as they were about the GOP's structure and the party's failure to integrate African Americans into that fold. A dispute over a "positive action" resolution illustrated black Republicans' woes. The motion was paramount to African Americans' future success, for it would have mandated that state parties increase minority representations on state delegations to the national convention. In fact, a similar rule change was behind the record number of black delegates attending the Democratic Party's 1972 national convention. And by all means, a *massive* increase in black delegate representation could have helped black party members establish a stronger, more meaningful role in the process that determined the party's presidential nominee and ideological plank.[44] The positive action issue was of the utmost importance, Carole Ann Tay-lor of New York City and Ethel Allen of Philadelphia told an audience of black Republicans. White conservative party members, they warned, were attempting to "dilute black power in the Republican Party" by opposing the resolution. Thus when white delegates succeeded in weakening the proposed rule, deadening the aggressive intent of delegate reform, black Republicans seethed over the GOP's reactionary obtuseness.[45]

The hostility of the convention initially sent black Republicans' or-ganizational efforts into a tailspin, as the African American participants berated white Republicans and trashed the "quiet "approach of the black appointees. From here on out, spat an irate Charles Kenyatta of New York, "any black who allows himself to be called a participant . . . is a traitor to blacks."[46] Likewise, intraracial conflicts erupted along genera-tional lines, as younger participants—many of whom were recent converts to the GOP—acted as a "thorn in the side" of their older black Republican counterparts, prodding them to mix "black activism" into their critiques of the party.[47] This would prove to be quite the quandary for young black Republicans who worked within the administration but identified with the soft militancy espoused by liberal African American party members. Sam Jackson, for example, at one point tried to downplay the delegates' complaints, minimizing the nature of their demands in interviews with the press. He also lost his composure during his testimony to the platform committee, delivering a stinging criticism of the party in what the *Washington Afro-American* labeled the only genuine display of "black power" at the convention.[48]

These contradictions and tensions were made all the more significant because of what was at stake. A sense of crisis undergirded black Republicans' behavior in Miami Beach, in some ways reminiscent of the urgency that informed the actions of the delegates to the 1964 convention, who later launched the NNRA. Eight years later, Michigan delegate Edward Bivens Jr. attempted to do the same, rushing to mobilize a "maverick black caucus," independent of the influence of White House officials, party leaders, and black Republican appointees. But unlike the 1964 convention, most black delegates in 1972 spurned the idea of an unofficial splinter organization: despite their quarrels and complaints, black Republicans at the convention still maintained that a national consensus organization was the most efficient path to political power.

It was this shared belief that ultimately convinced black Republicans to cooperate with one another and collectively lobby for the successful passage of different but no less important amendment, a resolution that provided for the future creation of a national black consensus organization as an auxiliary group to the RNC. The chair of the yet-unnamed association would be appointed by the chair of the national committee and sit on the executive council of the RNC.[49] This was an important shift, for it was the first time in the party's history that the GOP had officially recognized a racial auxiliary group, distinct from the Minorities Division of the national committee. The recognition placed the group on the same rank as other RNC-sanctioned organizations like the Young Republican National Federation (YRNF) and the National Federation of Republican Women (NFRW).[50] A figurative coup d'état, the passage of the resolution seemed to validate the existence of black party members. Surely black Republicans believed as much, for they abruptly switched tactics; by the time the national convention was coming to a close, the same group of delegates that offered frenzied objections to the actions of the president and the party joined members of Nixon's cabinet, the black appointees, Leonard Garment, Donald Rumsfeld, and about one hundred other black Republicans in "toast[ing] each other" and the president aboard two luxurious yachts docked outside Miami's famed Fontainebleau Hotel.[51]

At first glance, the actions of black Republicans seem inconsistent and perplexing, but a closer look reveals that most black Republicans never truly abandoned their pragmatic "loyalty" to the president. The convention was a tremendous hiccup, to be sure; but at the same time, African Americans still wanted to be a recognized part of whatever coalition of supporters put Nixon in office. By the time Richard Nixon delivered his

presidential nominee acceptance speech to party delegates, calling on
Democrats, Republicans, and independents to "join our new majority—
not on the basis of the party label you wear on your lapel, but what you
believe in your hearts," black Republicans desperately wanted to believe
such rhetoric but remained "quietly" aware that the party had treated
them poorly.[52] Charles Kenyatta, who in a heated moment had accused the
convention participants of being race traitors, carefully backtracked his comments in a September editorial: "The Black Republican at this moment in
history has the greatest opportunity as a minority to ask for the power
to fulfill the American Dream."[53] With the close of the convention, black
Republicans returned to their quiet dissent because the impending election
compelled them to do so. By the fall of 1972, African American insiders and
outsiders shared a similar burden, as aggressively critiquing the party and the
president could result in losing everything for which they had fought.

During this period, black Republicans' strategy was both cynical and
idealistic. They believed that full-blown opposition would result in loss
of power, while a demonstration of loyalty would endear them to the
president and the party. In New York, for example, a group of African
American women campaigning for Nixon in October argued as much.
Wearing buttons with the slogan "Don't Be Taken for Granted," the
women parroted the public-relations lines of the campaign on matters
of economic civil rights and two-party competition but quietly peppered
their conversations with accusations that the party continued to ignore
the black electorate. One woman, a self-described "renegade Republican," offhandedly remarked that she had quit the party in 1971, feeling
alienated by the president. She had reregistered a year later, for pragmatic
reasons, citing the inevitability of Nixon's reelection. "The Negro has got
to be on the winning team," she told her fellow campaigners, "And when
you bring something to the team then you have a seat on the team."[54]

Arthur Fletcher offered a far more comprehensive version of this rationale in a fall 1972 editorial for the Wall Street Journal. African Americans
had practiced "poor politics" over the previous four years, he argued;
though they had rightly condemned the negative initiatives of the administration, they had also stubbornly rejected the White House's positive
efforts, as well—a decision that meant that African Americans had seen
their "interests either jeopardized or completely ignored." He urged black
voters to become "political pragmatists," pointing to white union and
labor leaders who had rallied around Nixon—in spite of their intense dis-
like of his administration—in order to push their pro-labor agenda. To do
otherwise, Fletcher warned, would mean that African Americans would
be "left sitting on the sidelines or up in the bleachers watching the game"
during Nixon's second term in office.[55]

Fletcher's thesis undoubtedly stemmed from the woes of the Nixon's black appointees; though angry with the White House and organized labor's attempts to undermine his antidiscrimination measures, he also blamed African Americans for the president's actions, arguing that the lack of black support had left black appointees "powerless" by the end of Nixon's first term. This interpretation of black accountability was a strategic plea—a brusque way for Fletcher to encourage support for the president's possible second term in office. The best way for African Americans to ensure racial uplift, he concluded, was to work with the administration, placing political partisanship aside and aligning with Richard Nixon's proposed "New Majority" coalition of voters. To be sure, Fletcher offered a fair reading of the president's fickle loyalty system of political reward and punishment; yet by that same measure, the black official's interpretation still relied on the same problematic understanding of patronage articulated by his fellow black Republicans—a system wherein race rendered displays of political loyalty null and void.

When One Door Closes, Another One Opens

On November 8, 1972, Richard Nixon won reelection to the presidency in a landslide victory over his challenger, George McGovern. In fact, calling the president's win a "victory" is an understatement. Nixon clobbered the South Dakota politician, amassing more than 60 percent of the popular vote and winning all but one state and Washington, D.C. Election returns showed that the president's "New Majority" was indeed real, as Nixon received dramatic support from various constituent groups including suburbanites, blue-collar workers, organized labor, Catholics, and white ethnic voters. His "suburban strategy" of coded colorblind appeals also enticed former George Wallace supporters, more than half of whom voted for Nixon in 1972.

But while the election was a massive success for the president, it presented more of a lackluster performance for the Republican Party. "Despite the Nixon landslide," Lou Cannon wrote in the *Washington Post* a day after the election, "the Republican Party perpetuated its minority status" in politics. "After you take the President's personal landslide," RNC chair Bob Dole commented, "there wasn't any landslide at all." Offering perhaps the most astute postelection assessment, a GOP official stated, "For all the good he did us, Nixon may as well have been running as a Democrat."[56]

The Ripon Society would later observe that 1972 was a record year for ticket splitting, as Nixon's victory did not translate into a "New Majority" realignment of voters for the rest of the GOP. Republicans, for instance, fell far short of their "landslide" predictions in politics, winning a dozen or so seats in the House and losing two spots in the Senate; moreover, both houses of Congress remained Democrat-controlled. The election also reaffirmed the GOP's intraparty struggle over ideology. Though most liberal and moderate incumbents, including Ed Brooke, were reelected to office, the party nevertheless moved to the right as conservative officials, like Jesse Helms of North Carolina, entered the ranks of the GOP and liberal politicians, such as Floyd Haskell of Colorado, switched to the Democratic Party.[57]

For black Republicans, the 1972 contest appeared to be a major disappointment. In spite of their public relations driven outreach efforts, Nixon received about 13 percent of the black vote, an increase of four percentage points from 1968. Many African Americans abstained from voting altogether: the Joint Center for Political Studies estimated that only 40 percent of voting-age blacks cast their ballots in 1972, a drop of six percentage points from four years earlier. Dissatisfaction with Nixon and political alienation were certainly important factors in the presidential contest, but there were other issues for black Republicans; for example, the Black Vote Division of CREEP was beset by problems. While working as a field coordinator in 1972, John Wilks was horrified by the financial woes of the group. In his postcampaign assessment, he recounted that the "inadequate budget" provoked threats of violence from rank-and-file black Republicans in cities across the Northeast. On the rare occasion when financial support arrived, it was ineffective, materializing in one instance three days before the 1972 presidential election.[58] Such campaign mishaps led Wilks to a significant conclusion, one in keeping with what black Republicans had been arguing for several years: rather than blaming the calculated indifference of Richard Nixon and CREEP, Wilks suggested that the *party* desperately needed a structural plan for black solidarity and organization, along with a program for African American recruitment. Not only should the GOP fund the initiative, he wrote; it should also "provide the staff, leadership, and continuity to achieve this goal."[59] Offering similar sentiments in yet another postelection analysis, Ed Sexton called for a "well organized structural group" situated within the upper echelons of the national party apparatus; the national committee's consultant on black affairs argued that such an organization could access the muddled landscape of local black GOP clubs and groups and identify strategies for "creating interest among articulate and promising young Blacks, to involve them more in the programs of the Republican Party," and to groom them for elected office and community leadership roles.[60]

The need to organize in an official capacity was all the more pressing, Wilks and Sexton argued, because the election had reaffirmed the existence of a "silent black majority" of African Americans willing to vote for Richard Nixon. While the president's share of the black vote fell short of strategists' predictions of 18 percent, black Republicans nevertheless believed that "significant gains were made in terms of attitude change and achieving an open-mindedness."[61] As black Republicans looked at specific data from the election, they uncovered a more nuanced picture: in small cities and rural counties, 31 percent of black voters supported President Nixon; likewise, in suburban areas, 34 percent of the black electorate endorsed the Republican incumbent.[62] Wilks and Sexton clearly sidestepped the fact that the majority of black voters in 1972 either rejected the president or abstained from voting. The two strategists' work did highlight something that had been obvious for more than two decades: demographically, the Republican nominee pulled most of his black support from suburban and rural middle-class voters; the majority of these voters was concentrated in the South—an important shift from previous decades. In Louisville, Kentucky, for example, 30 percent of black voters endorsed Nixon, whereas four years earlier, only 15 percent had supported the president.[63] Thus it turned out that a particular cadre of African Americans was, in fact, a part of Richard Nixon's "New Majority" coalition of voters.

For those African Americans that backed the president in 1972, most cited their faith in black capitalism, patronage, and two-party competition. But some rank-and-file black supporters also adopted the language of individualism, placing their self-interest ahead of their concern for a black collective. For instance, despite expressing an extreme disdain for Nixon and the GOP, Cleo Jackson, a black hairdresser from Los Angeles, nevertheless declared, "I'm a Republican (this year)—a "capitalistic pragmatist" out to get her fair share of the economic pie. Likewise, members of "Black Democrats for Nixon," one of the campaign groups organized for the Black Vote Division of CREEP, offered similar rhetoric, steeped in the language of economic individualism.[64] Such support was not fully partisan for many of these voters still identified as Democrats; in other words, their vote for the president stemmed from economic self-interest rather than a broader ideological commitment to Nixon or the GOP. In fact, it was this kind of support that had motivated Julian Bond's brutal "political prostitutes" comment in August 1972: "Their political allegiances are not tied to party or principle but to pennies," the Georgia civil rights activist had argued in front of the National Urban League, "not to devotion to race and pride in self but to devotion to dollars and the race for power."[65] To be sure, some African Americans found that their individual economic beliefs aligned squarely with those of the

Nixon administration; in this sense, although their racial politics were at odds with those of Richard Nixon, a new cadre of black voters embraced the economic politics of the right, despite continuing to self-identify as Democrats.

Furthermore, state and local returns for black voters reaffirmed a long-standing reality, seen in many election cycles since 1936: African Americans across the country demonstrated a willingness to vote for the GOP on a state and local level in 1972, but only for those liberal and moderate candidates who had campaigned in black areas. The more racially liberal the Republican, the Ripon Society also observed, and the more racially conservative the Democrat, the more likely African Americans were to support the GOP candidate. In Illinois, for instance, more than 90 percent of the black electorate voted for George McGovern; these same voters, however, overwhelmingly cast their ballots for Charles Percy in his successful senatorial reelection bid, condemning the antagonistic "backlash campaign" of his Democratic opponent. But the contest also demonstrated that class was still a salient predictor of political support; though Percy garnered 80 percent of the black middle-class vote, he received less than a third of the black working-class and poor vote.[66] In short, economic self-interest influenced African Americans' votes on the state and local level, even as the needs of the black collective informed their votes in the presidential election.

In the wake of the 1972 election, black Republican elites rushed to capitalize on such findings, with the hopes of transforming such support into long-term political gains for African Americans within the GOP. At the same time, acting on the resolution from the 1972 convention, the RNC appointed San Francisco black Republican Henry Lucas to a seat on the executive council of the national committee.[67] The convention resolution had also provided for the creation of a national black consensus organization; despite sharing *the same goal*, black Republicans debated over who would control this group, what it would represent, and how it would operate. This was black Republican politics at its messiest—more than half a dozen organizations erupted by January 1973—all calling themselves coordinating councils or umbrella groups.[68]

Adding to the confusion, the RNC worked closely with many of these organizations throughout the year. Given their negative experiences with white party officials and their demands for autonomy since at least 1964, black Republicans' interest in working with the national party organization seemed puzzling, to say the least. But African Americans dismissed most of these concerns, reasoning that their objectives closely aligned with those of the RNC and its newly elected chair, George H. W. Bush. Although the Texas politician was a Goldwater Republican—campaigning for the Arizona senator during the 1964 presidential election—black party members viewed Bush as a political moderate, largely on the basis of his record of black outreach in his adopted state.[69] In 1963, for example, he had insisted that the Harris County Republican Party should not abandon thousands of black voters; instead, he argued, "We should make an honorable appeal to the [N]egro vote, realizing we are working against very difficult odds. . . . As long as we maintain our principles and do not try to out promise anybody I think the effort is worthwhile."[70]

Bush's black outreach during the 1970s reflected the efforts of party moderates and liberals to become the "Open Door" party and diversify GOP ranks by increasing the presence of women, racial and ethnic minorities, youth, and the elderly. In fact, the Rule 29 Committee, established through a resolution adopted during the 1972 national convention, was created for precisely this purpose.[71] Beginning in the spring of 1973, the committee and the RNC held a series of "New Majority Workshops," geared toward those whom the committee dubbed "special" constituents. During discussions, Republicans polled members about party-building activities; in turn, citizens shared their communities' respective concerns and issues.[72] The RNC's "Open Door" policy, it would seem, appeared to provide ample room for black Republicans' reform agenda. In particular, the RNC's emphasis on state and local activities was attractive to African American party members, as they believed this focus would be more effective than a top-down bureaucratic strategy. Thus, for black party members, aligning with the RNC was a strategic and savvy move, one that could transform local black solidarity into real political influence.

Several of the 1973 New Majority workshops focused on strengthening black Republican unity, as rank-and-file African American members of the GOP stressed the need for a cohesive black Republican voice. Among their concerns, black Republicans expressed a commitment to five broad ideas: "(1) making the Political System Responsible to Blacks (2) Voter Registration and Education (3) Black Candidacy and Recruitm[ent] (4) Minority Political Participation—Statewide (5) The Roles Black Women Play in Determining Community Destinies."[73] The self-evident importance of these tenets, however, belied the often-tense atmosphere at these meetings, during which black Republicans' frustration and anger were palpable. Bob Brown—the Nixon "loyalist with unchallenged credentials" who initially cautioned patience in the first weeks of the president's second term—perhaps best articulated the tenor of these grievances. "Blacks," he decried in September 1973, "have been made to feel unwelcome in the Republican party." Not only had the GOP neglected black Republican causes and candidates, he asserted, but the president had also started to oust African Americans from influential positions in the White House.[74]

Brown accurately characterized what was the culmination of a long and gradual shift in administration policy, a predicament that the black press routinely characterized as a tragic satire of black Republican life.[75] During his first term in office, Nixon had appointed more African Americans to federal posts than any other president, attempted to appoint an African American to a cabinet position, and even considered nominating Ed Brooke to the Supreme Court. At the same time, over the course of those four years, the president often went to great lengths to sabotage his black appointees, even going so far as to force several to resign.[76] By the start of his second term in office, Nixon had decided to once again turn a cold shoulder to African Americans, appointing very few to meaningful policy-making positions.

For black loyalists, the White House's icy treatment was insulting, angering even the most devout of African American appointees, many of whom had mistakenly assumed that efforts on the campaign trail would yield at least a modicum of political patronage during Nixon's second term. In spite of his public pleas for patience, Brown had sensed the administration's change in attitude as early as January 1973. "I am deeply concerned," he wrote in a confidential White House note, "because it seems that another kind of criteria is being developed for some key jobs in the Administration."[77] Political observers were far less cryptic in their assessment: "Black Republicans," mocked the editors of one black newspaper, "must be harboring dark thoughts while wringing their hands in contrition. Thus far, their efforts, time and money have yielded no commensurate rewards. There is nothing left but crumbs, and even the crumbs are being scooped up by second rate white Southerners and the hardhats who cast their ballots last November for Nixon, although some of them can hardly read."[78] Within a month of sending his memo, Brown resigned, returning to his public relations job in North Carolina; with his departure, nearly all of the African American appointees responsible for Nixon's economic civil rights programs, including James Farmer, Art Fletcher, and Sam Jackson, had resigned or been forced out of the administration. African Americans still held appointments in the White House after 1973, but such positions were few and far between and were often deliberately limited in their influence and scope.[79]

African Americans' anger, especially among Richard Nixon's former black appointees, was critical to the development of a realistic form of black Republican solidarity; their experiences reinforced their desire for a unified national consensus organization, while cementing their decision to seek asylum through the RNC rather than the White House. They largely united around one national black consensus group, the National Black Republican Council (NBRC), founded, in part, by Arthur Fletcher in December 1973. Of the more than half a dozen national coordinating and umbrella councils that existed during this period, the NBRC was the only group to gain traction, as it was the sole organization with the financial and moral backing of the RNC. With that kind of prominent mainstream support, the NBRC had few problems overshadowing competing black Republican groups; in fact, over the course of the 1970s, it eventually subsumed or outlasted many of these splinter councils.[80]

As an umbrella council, the NBRC was distinct from previous black Republican organizations and absorbed existing local and state clubs and groups. Over the years it would also help rank-and-file black Republicans start affiliate organizations in their respective towns and counties, all under the national banner of the NBRC. The organization provided black Republicans with a centralized and institutionalized communication network for the first time—a method whereby black Republicans across the country could share information, learn about candidates, issues, and events, and even gain assistance with local campaigns; the umbrella structure of the organization created a pathway through which rank-and-file black Republicans and African American party elites could formally establish their voice in mainstream party affairs.[81] In many ways, the launch of the NBRC took some of the loneliness out of being a black Republican, connecting African American party members to something bigger, in a way that previous organizations had been unable to do.

For the leaders of the NBRC, the organization embodied independent solidarity in an official capacity. Sanctioning the group as an official auxiliary organization, the national committee provided the NBRC with a permanent position on the RNC executive council, a small yearly operating budget of $40,000, logistical support, and rent-free office space in the party's Washington, D.C., headquarters.[82] As we have seen, this kind of consolidated support was necessary for black Republican groups to survive and flourish, but it also presented a host of contradictions. Though they finally had their own recognized vehicle, black Republicans were now subject to the whims of RNC officials. The black organization's chair, for instance, was selected and appointed by the head of the RNC. "We overlook the fact," one black Republican leader would later grouse, "that we have not been allowed—or have failed to advance our support sufficiently—to select our representation in most posts of high consequence."[83] Whether black Republicans acknowledged it or not, white influence still played a key role in their decision-making abilities.

From day one, the NBRC agenda was dedicated to reform—no surprise, since the organization was borne out of dissatisfaction with the status quo of Republican politics. The group never envisioned a militant revolution for the party, imagining instead an intraparty renaissance for racial liberalism and equality. Within its constitution and bylaws, the organization declared its faith in America's "ethnic mosaic" and the GOP, describing the national institution as "epitomizing" the values in which NBRC members' believed. African Americans that joined the NBRC were proud to be Republicans—a pride that differentiated their critiques from the many attacks on the GOP that came from outside the party. Although NBRC members maintained that the GOP had the "finest principles with its strong belief in freedom, and the integrity of the individual," they also acknowledged the "unfortunate but well known" truth of Republican hostility to "Americans of African descent."[84]

Combating that hostility was the NBRC's overriding goal, as was increasing the "stature and the effectiveness of Black Republicans throughout the Republican Party." Members desired nothing less than to influence the scope, identity, and direction of the GOP, from the local to the national level. Through state coordinating councils and affiliated local clubs, the NBRC labored to simultaneously cultivate black solidarity and greater involvement in the party. Black outreach, needless to say, was integral to the organization's strategy since establishing power within the GOP would be impossible sans the active involvement of black voters. At the same time, black Republicans emphasized their loyalty to the Grand Old Party, stressing their commitment to persuading African Americans of the relevance of specific party candidates, principles, and policies.[85]

Like the NNRA, the NBRC envisioned itself as a watchdog organization, invested in racial equality and uplift. But in terms of strategy, the two organizations were entirely different, as the NNRA was far more militant than NBRC. The former organization had pushed for intraparty reform aggressively, battling publicly with both the RNC and the reactionary wing of the Republican Party. Nearly a decade later, the NBRC also expressed dissatisfaction with the state of party politics; nevertheless, it elected to align with the RNC and was willing to work with every ideological wing of the party, and pushed a consensus agenda that reflected the varied beliefs of the black groups and members that fell under its wide umbrella. The black council's inaugural leadership, for instance, represented a range of ideologies. A February 1974 meeting of the NBRC steering committee highlights this: included among the thirty-two attendees was a black militant, a self-identified Goldwater Republican, a professed Reagan Republican, a few men and women who had campaigned for Nelson Rockefeller, and a former Democrat that had worked on Shirley Chisholm's 1972 presidential campaign.[86]

Aside from their dissatisfaction with party politics, members and leaders in the NBRC shared a common faith in free market enterprise. "Minorities hear a different drumbeat: economics," asserted an NBRC member in August 1974. "Capitalism is a word shared and respected on Wall Street or in Harlem."[87] But theirs was not a traditional embrace of free market enterprise; like Nixon's black appointees, the NBRC advocated for an increase in government spending, despite black Republicans' professed fiscal conservatism and bootstrap mind-set; this was true not only for the NBRC but for most black Republican groups more generally during the period.

Such demands were a product of black Republicans' pragmatism; they saw financial support as imperative given the reality of persistent racial and economic inequality. In a 1974 survey of 750 black Republican leaders, the bulk of the respondents argued that lasting solutions must be centered on the economy: everything and anything from pumping government aid into black colleges, equal opportunity programs, job training initiatives, minority set-asides, black banks, and public works projects for the underemployed and unemployed. African American party leaders were particularly interested in black entrepreneurship, urging the federal government to create five million jobs through OMBE and the SBA. The leaders were also invested in eradicating institutional racism, calling for the dismantling of private-sector companies that engaged in any form of discrimination.[88] Jackson R. Champion, a member of the NBRC steering committee, expanded on the organization's economic philosophy, declaring, "Power lies in free enterprise. . . . Social reforms can take you only so far in our system." The organization's emphasis on two-party politics signified more than political astuteness; for Champion and others, it also represented a means for African Americans to create meaningful economic change. The NBRC leader argued that politics itself was a form of free market enterprise, reasoning that it was far more pragmatic for black citizens to "use this system than to fight to change it." African Americans, Champion concluded, "must learn that only when they have political control will they have economic control."[89] In espousing a faith in economic uplift, these black Republicans, like their predecessors in Nixon's Black Cabinet, argued that for African Americans politics and policies were inextricably linked.

The implications of political control extended beyond economics and into broader domestic policies; the NBRC proposed a varied set of solutions that often were amalgamations of conservatism and racial liberalism, a concept that Elaine Jenkins wrestled with during a 1974 interview. "We've tried to be more sophisticated in developing a program for the seventies with a pragmatic rather than an idealistic approach," she explained.[90] Reflecting this overarching paradox, black GOP leaders enthusiastically endorsed an ambiguous notion of "welfare reform," declaring themselves moral authorities on African American social welfare concerns.[91] Black Republicans had been fixated on welfare since the era of the New Deal, often rationalizing their demands for reform in both conservative and liberal terms. Furthermore, their concerns were rooted in a paternalistic view of the poor, as they believed that their economic status and experience afforded them the right to criticize members within their community. In the 1970s, their calls for welfare reform appeared all the more paradoxical because black Republicans endorsed an economic civil rights agenda—or what was essentially a form of economic welfare for the black middle class. As contradictory as these welfare ideas seemed, black Republicans nevertheless viewed them as harmonious. Their moral outlook celebrated "work," disdaining welfare as "handouts" that destroyed ambition and promoted indolence. Hence, black Republicans viewed federal economic civil rights initiatives as programs that empowered African Americans to become *producers*, whereas welfare turned the poor into powerless *takers* who capitulated to the federal government.[92]

In 1974, turning these ideas into an agenda, especially for the NBRC, was still a difficult proposition, as many of the organization's ideas were vague and still in their infancy. During its first year of operation, the black group focused almost exclusively on the "nuts and bolts" of grassroots organizing in black communities. The difficulty of wooing black voters encouraged the NBRC to emphasize local politics, as the organization believed that building alliances and solidarity neighborhood by neighborhood would be far easier than amassing national support. More important, members also viewed local power as a more authentic form of influence. "In a democracy," NBRC leaders wrote in 1974, "the ultimate ruling power resides in the people. People give power and people take it away." The organization reasoned that as people joined local black Republican clubs, the potential for African American influence, at every level of the GOP, would multiply. The group declared that clubs would become mediums for ordinary citizens to engage in bloc voting, elect desirable Republican candidates, and in turn shape public policy. "The sure way to win a friend in your state legislature, in the Governor's office, in the U.S. Congress, or even the White House," stated the NBRC, was to play an instrumental role in winning local elections.[93] In the abstract, this was a smart and savvy rationale, but in practice, as time would soon show, it was ultimately unsound, blunting the overall effectiveness of the black consensus organization.

Despite its bravado, the NBRC clearly approached black communities with care; this implied a delicate handling of African Americans, while touting the positive achievements of black Republicans.[94] Successfully engaging black communities, the NBRC recognized, meant emphasizing individual Republicans, rather than the collective party. In fact, the organization intentionally downplayed its relationship with the mainstream party, understanding that the GOP's collective image and message alienated African Americans. As a means of stimulating black engagement in partisan activities, the NBRC employed a *nonpartisan* strategy, organizing African Americans into "Candidate Clubs" that emphasized individual politicians rather than the party as a whole. The organization stressed that such clubs should be open to all African Americans, irrespective of political affiliation; no one, not even avowed black Democrats, was to be spurned from membership. Clubs should "be careful to take no action by which it could lose its appeal" in black communities; the NBRC even specified that groups adopt monikers that were "definitive and appealing" to potential members, bypassing the use of "Republican" in club names. The organization encouraged black Republicans to take a personal, direct, and inclusive approach to wooing African Americans: hosting public rallies and casual coffee caucuses, holding "grass-roots" meetings in the comfortable private homes of black leaders and supporters, and urging clubs to waive or charge no more than a nominal membership fee lest black Republicans appear unwelcoming or exclusive. Here then, the NBRC tried to create a nonpartisan sense of political belonging among African Americans; in turn, the organization speculated that black voters would invest in Republican candidates, an interest that might just expand into a personal partisan attachment to the success of the greater GOP.

Still, expanding nonpartisan individual attachment into partisan political investment in the GOP was by far, the hardest of the NBRC's goals, because most African Americans viewed the mainstream party as anti-black. Transcending the legacy and history of the Republican Party thus rested squarely on the behavior of white party leaders. Compelling black citizens to join the GOP necessitated an investment on the part of white Republicans: "lip service" and public relations ploys were not sufficient. The NBRC urged white leaders to engage black communities, through "visits to churches, Sunday schools, Black gatherings . . . parties for children, [and] ladies teas" so as to show African Americans that "Republicans do care."[95]

As the NBRC promoted the development of nonpartisan candidate clubs, it simultaneously encouraged the launch of distinct local partisan organizations. Not only would such groups make black Republicans feel "at home" in the party, the NBRC suggested, but they would also provide invaluable access to white Republicans. Local black Republicans should explicitly reference the GOP and either race or location (or both) when choosing a title for the partisan club, urged the NBRC, pointing to sample names like the "Frederick Douglass Republican Club" and "Black Republicans of Cleveland." The national group also warned that all local club activities should supplement rather than replace the efforts of the mainstream party, since ultimately the goal of the partisan clubs, the NBRC suggested, was threefold: prevent splinter groups from developing, "secure workers" for the GOP, and "assimilate" black Republicans into the mainstream party. Instead of registering any and all African Americans, as the local nonpartisan candidate clubs did, the NBRC therefore directed all of the partisan groups to focus solely on black Republicans and independents, to the exclusion of black Democrats.[96] Given that most black citizens at the time were Democrats, this partisan approach was troubling, especially as one of the NBRC's goals was increasing black participation and interest in Republican politics.

FROM THE FRINGE TO THE MAINSTREAM

While appearing on ABC's *Issues and Answers* on Sunday November 4, 1973, Edward Brooke became the first Republican in Congress to call for Richard Nixon's resignation. The black politician "reluctantly" suggested that the president had been involved somehow in the Watergate scandal and as a result had lost both his "effectiveness as the leader" of the country and the trust of the American public. Ten days later, as the president's favorability rating plummeted, Brooke would *again* urge the president to resign, this time much more forcefully during a face-to-face meeting with Nixon at the White House. Over the course of the next nine months, party officials and leaders from every wing of the party would come to echo Brooke's demand; by the time Nixon announced his resignation on August 8, 1974, the president was practically a political pariah, shunned by the American people and distrusted by many within his own party.[97]

Over the span of two years, Watergate—initially a bizarre political debacle that began with a June 1972 break-in of the Democratic National Committee (DNC) headquarters—had evolved into a bloated, nightmarish fiasco for the Republican Party and Richard Nixon. Surveys from November 1973 indicated that more than two-thirds of Americans believed that the president was involved in some aspect of the Watergate break-in or subsequent cover-up, while a Harris poll from that same month indicated that the scandal had erased any gains made by Nixon among voters in the 1972 election. Gone was his dream of realignment, as more than half of the nation's voting electorate remained firmly ensconced in the Democratic Party fold.[98]

A low point for the modern Republican Party, the administration's widespread involvement in political malfeasance bolstered African Americans' already negative perceptions of the president and the party. "There

was little sadness in America's Black communities" over Nixon's departure, wrote the editors of *Jet* about two weeks after the president resigned, especially since the White House's dogged attempt to placate the
country's white voters had undermined the few "bright" accomplishments
of the administration. Black Republicans made similar observations, arguing that Watergate was irrelevant to their agenda, since the relationship between African Americans and the president was already so grim. "A black
Republican campaigning in a predominately black district is campaigning before people who are not surprised at all by . . . Watergate," mused
Arthur Fletcher in March 1974. "They have been the victims of all kinds
of political shenanigans . . . on the other hand, the white candidate is confronted with it because Watergate seems to have embarrassed the kind of
idealism that much of white America has allowed itself to believe existed
in our political system." Elaine Jenkins offered a far more brusque assessment: "Watergate," she stated a month before the president's resignation,
"is a white man's fight."[99]

These claims were an acknowledgment not only of the rancor that
persisted between Nixon and African Americans but also of the estrange-
ment that existed between black Republicans, the administration, and
white party officials. Thus blacks in the GOP viewed Watergate as significant only insomuch as it would allow them to cultivate autonomy by way
of moral righteousness in the face of their white peers' lapsed integrity.
"Blacks in our Party," declared a group of black Republican leaders in a
1974 position paper on Watergate, "can serve as a moral force from the
Country level on up to the State Committee and the National Committee
to help rebuild the great Republican Party. There is no doubt that it must
be rebuilt."[100]

Ironically, however, black Republicans were not exempt from the moral
lapses of Watergate. In 1974 the Senate Select Committee on Presidential
Campaign Activities provided compelling evidence that many of Nixon's
black Republican appointees had engaged in campaign misconduct, favoritism, and bribery; but even these misdeeds were presented by black
Republicans in a way that underscored this notion of moral righteousness. When asked by investigators if he had coerced federal agencies into
providing contracts for black businessmen, Bob Brown replied: "Damn
right, I did. I fought for more Black involvement, and I'm proud of it. I
wish I had done 10 times more."[101] Even as the administration was crumbling around them, the black appointees continued to argue that their actions were ethical because their motives were "pure," rooted in notions of
black uplift; the charges, diabolical and corrupt as they might be, inadvertently exposed just how much "power" Nixon's "Black Cabinet" actually
had.

African American party leaders reacted to the administration's moral lapses in different ways; NCAAR, for example, demanded that Nixon return African Americans' $250,000 campaign contribution, with the intention of repurposing the money to fund the political aspirations of ten black Republican candidates for the U.S. House of Representatives.[102] A far more realistic proposal came from Sam Jackson in August 1974. As Richard Nixon left the White House, his former appointee launched the Council of 100, a group dedicated to advising party politicians and officials on African American issues. Working with more than a dozen black party leaders, Jackson founded the organization with the intention of creating a small, invitation-only group of influential black liberal Republican elites. Members adopted a calculating attitude toward politics, stating that they were willing, if necessary, to work with anyone regardless of political affiliation or ideology, so long as it contributed to the success of black Republican politics. Reflecting this, the council's board of trustees was interracial in composition and diverse in Republican ideology, composed of prominent party leaders including Bob Brown, Ed Brooke, Jacob Javits, Bob Dole, and even Barry Goldwater.[103]

Boasting of its "outside independent" status in party affairs and the financial self-sustainability of its membership, the Council of 100 likened itself to a "citizens' lobby," preferring to advocate discreetly for changes within the GOP. Like the NBRC, the council's objective was to influence party affairs and institutions, especially in securing prominent appointed and elected positions for African Americans. The two groups also shared a faith in the power of local politics; while the NBRC worked on establishing grass-roots political networks in black communities, the Council of 100 focused on raising $250,000 to help finance the campaigns of future black Republican congressional aspirants. Moreover, the two groups were not in competition: as the council would later clarify and the NBRC would confirm, the Council of 100 was not a splinter organization. Although a separate organization, it tried to work jointly with the NBRC to "broaden the base of the Republican Party."[104]

Still, in spite of these similarities, the two groups differed in significant ways. Unlike the NBRC, whose political agenda privileged the black middle class, the Council of 100 declared that it intended to use its clout to influence the creation of "progressive programs" to aid the "poor and promote entrepreneurship for minorities and women." The smaller group's agenda was far more liberal than that of the NBRC—in 1974, the council promised to lobby aggressively for an extension of the Voting Rights Act and continued federal support for unemployment and poverty.[105] At the same time, the council was nowhere near as militant as the NNRA; the assembly would have balked at the notion of working with Barry Goldwater in any capacity, let alone putting him on the board of trustees. The Council of 100 was no less exclusive than the NBRC—the smaller organization was, after all, an elitist group that deliberately limited its membership to those who could finance the rebirth of black Republican politics. Though the council demonstrated a genuine concern for the poor and unemployed (perhaps more than any other black Republican group of the 1970s), this interest was still paternalistic, falling within the boundaries of respectability politics and resting on a "talented tenth" tradition of black uplift, dating back to the late nineteenth century.

The Council of 100's exclusivity was a key component of its political strategy: by restricting membership, group leaders could *control* the direction of the organization and craft an agenda that reflected a progressive Republican outlook. A wealthy and middle-class constituency would help ensure that the council remained financially self-sufficient. In fact, the council characterized itself as a "self-help organization"—an identity that came from members' belief that they should rely on themselves, rather than predominately white Republican institutions, to achieve power within the GOP ranks, a rationale undoubtedly informed by Sam Jackson's struggles as an appointee in the Nixon White House. This is not to argue that the Council of 100 was opposed to working with Republican-led institutions; to the contrary, the group simply believed that African Americans should not be financially dependent on the party apparatus. Importantly, this was an approach that *initially* gave the council more political leeway than both the NNRA and the NBRC. Simply put: the Council of 100 had money *and* independence, something that black Republican groups had lacked in abundance in the past.

For all of these dissimilarities, the Council of 100 and the NBRC still followed a similar path, rooted in dissatisfaction with the status quo of the mainstream Republican Party. By the tail end of 1974, it appeared that many black party leaders had aligned themselves and their respective organizations with either the NBRC or the council, by either choice or necessity; in truth, though both organizations may have pushed unity as a mode of strengthening black Republican power, they may have just as easily done so as a means of holding on to the reigns of political power. Despite this "consensus," though, a few splinter organizations persisted throughout the 1970s; most notable among them was the National Black Silent Majority Committee (BSMC), a group founded by a small coterie of black Republicans on the Fourth of July, 1970, in Gary, Indiana.

Like the NBRC and the Council of 100, the BSMC professed a faith in free market enterprise and two-party competition. Unlike these other black Republican groups, the BSMC offered neither public nor private complaints about the state of GOP politics; instead, though the group espoused solidarity with a black collective, it also celebrated the increasing conservatism of the Republican Party. The brainchild of former RNC consultant Clay Claiborne, the BSMC was headquartered in Washington, D.C., directly across the street from the national committee. A visit to the group's office in 1970 would have provided viewers with visual testaments to the BSMC's party loyalty: poster-sized autographed letters from Richard Nixon decorated the walls, as did enlarged photographs of Nixon's black appointees.[106]

In embracing the name "National Black Silent Majority Committee" the group borrowed from Richard Nixon's rhetoric of a forgotten class of Americans, expanding the definition to include black citizens. Like most black party members during the 1970s, the BSMC held fast to the flawed notion of a vast majority of silent African Americans, committed to Republican values. The conservative group, however, was distinct: it included middle-class *and* working-class African Americans in its definition of a "forgotten" black constituency, an idea that was very much in line with white Republicans' inclusion of middle-class and blue-collar whites in their characterization of the silent majority. In its founding creed, the BSMC spoke of "millions of black Americans who work every day, keep their kids in schools, have never been in jail, pay their taxes, shop for bargains," and "have never participated in a riot." These "legions" included black factory workers, teachers, police officers, farmers, laborers, lawyers, veterans, and businesspeople. All were "hard-working, responsible men, women and students," individuals who were "sick and tired of the agitation, shouting, burning and subversion carried out in their name by self-styled militant groups." Groups like the Black Panthers, the BSMC would declare over and over again throughout the 1970s, "don't speak for us, and they never could."[107]

The group was dogmatic in its embrace of conservatism, adhering to an anticommunist, antiwelfare, antibusing, anticrime agenda and embracing the rhetoric of law and order to police African American behavior.[108] In addition to attacking black militancy and radicalism as the root causes of the nation's racial tensions, the BSMC also asserted that Great Society liberalism had condemned African Americans to a "hopeless cycle of poverty and welfare and despair." Likewise, as BSMC members understood it, crime was a function of individual behavior and the breakdown of law and order, rather than systemic inequality, poverty, and discrimination. In employing such conservative rhetoric, the BSMC attempted to change the public's image of African Americans; as one BSMC member put it, ordinary hard-working black citizens were "afraid to walk the streets at night," locked their car doors, and feared that their homes might be burglarized—just like white Americans.[109]

The BSMC based its claims in reactionary conservatism and deliberately avoided criticizing Republican-led government, bypassing the problems of racial discrimination. Instead, the BSMC established Democrats and black militants as "straw men," responsible for the problems of African American communities. Here, the BSMC was unique among black Republican organizations during the 1970s as it placed accountability exclusively on the backs of African Americans, absolving white citizens of any guilt or wrongdoing. Such an approach was not without critics—in 1970, Julian Bond called the BSMC a "trick by the authors of 'benign neglect' to subvert black political hopes on the altar of white supremacy and political expediency." The real "tragedy," Bond asserted, was that African Americans had colluded in a "conspiracy" against black political power.[110]

Bond's criticisms were not without merit. As we have discussed, Clay Claiborne was indicted and acquitted on electoral fraud and voter suppression in the mid-1960s. Nevertheless, the BSMC inspired public loyalty from dozens of prominent African Americans, many of whom were active in state and local GOP politics. In spite of the organization's right-wing inclinations, members initially represented the continuum of black Republican thought. Cofounder Eloise Banks, for instance, had supported Goldwater's 1964 presidential bid, whereas executive board member C. A. Scott (publisher of the *Atlanta Daily World,* the South's oldest black newspaper) was a self-identified moderate Eisenhower Republican. Likewise, during a meeting of fifteen thousand "Negro Elks" in 1971, the organization's national president offered a "100 per cent endorsement" of the BSMC, maintaining that the fraternal group's membership "typifies the black silent majority"—a declaration that was met with cheers and roars of approval from the crowd.[111] Support in individual letters, like those of Phillip Willis of Jersey City, New Jersey, were no less riveting: "I am black, 42 years old . . . fought in two wars . . . My wife works as a nurse and I send my two children to school. I have never been in jail. I pay taxes and shop for bargains. I am also a Democrat. I would like to join your organization."[112]

Although far from the mainstream of black political thought, such responses indicate that the BSMC's message resonated with a particular subset of African Americans, irrespective of partisan affiliation; indeed, within two years of launching, the BSMC claimed to have eighty-five hundred card-carrying members in more than thirty states. For all of its reactionary rhetoric and in spite of its clear partisan bent, the BSMC marketed itself as a nonpartisan organization, open to Republicans, Democrats, and independents. The group used a language that was *inclusive,* identifying blacks as hard-working Americans and incorporating them into a broader vision of the "American Dream." Members were attracted to the organization's attempts to distinguish between ordinary and radicalized African Americans and to signal that black and white Americans shared similar aspirations and motivations. The organization's message was premised on the notion that the United States, at its core, was a fair nation, a country that belonged to all Americans, including African Americans. Supporters were also drawn to the BSMC's celebration of patriotism and racial harmony; members proudly wore the organization's logo, believing that the image of clasped black and white hands on an American flag symbolized that they, too, were peaceful citizens. The group's rhetoric tapped into idealistic ideas of merit, rooted in a black Protestant work ethic; in other words, America was a land where African Americans could get ahead simply by working hard enough. This argument was far from new; in fact, the BSMC employed similar arguments to those offered by Ed Brooke during his 1966 senatorial campaign, albeit without the senator's critique of systemic discrimination and inequality. As one reporter observed, BSMC supporters embraced the organization because "a youth with a petition in one hand and a gun in the other does not speak for a majority of any race."[113]

On a local level, the Atlanta chapter, founded in 1971, offered the most representative illustration of the national character and priorities of the BSMC. The group launched an anticrime committee, a youth group, and a neighborhood watch and spent most of its time policing black neighborhoods for violent crimes and "repudiat[ing] radical agitation." At one point, the chapter even held an award ceremony for a white police officer who had apprehended an armed bank robber. It was a "fine gesture from the black community," wrote the *Atlanta Daily World*, and a "good signal to black organizations to get involved [and] bring people closer together in an orderly world." Members rallied to assemble a coalition of "law abiding blacks" as a means of demonstrating that African Americans were "neither apathetic toward nor tolerant of violent acts." Such a coalition, the Atlanta chapter reasoned, would have a "tremendous psychological impact" on lawmakers, rooted in "meaningful, rather than rhetorical black community pride."[114] There is a certain kind of dissonance here, between local and national rhetoric of law and order. The phrase held a racially charged meaning when used on the national stage, but among the bipartisan Atlanta chapter of the BSMC, "law and order" held different meaning because it emanated from within black communities.

Black ministers offered some of the most vocal support for the Atlanta chapter of the BSMC, partnering with the organization for "Anti-Crime Sundays," during which they warned their congregations about the impact of crime on black communities. More broadly, on a national level some black ministers declared that they were "sick and tired of radical groups like the Black Panthers" and joined the BSMC's seventy-eight-city "Black Crusade for Patriotism" tour in 1970. Similarly, black women were among the most dedicated of the BSMC's backers. Half of the speakers for the 1970 tour were African American women, all of whom urged African Americans to "work within the system" and cooperate with local police in order to maintain safety in black neighborhoods. Likewise, as part of the BSMC's fifty-two-city "Black Youth Voter Crusade" in 1972, Mary Parrish encouraged groups of young black men and women to support the GOP, in the name of supporting black politics and civil rights. The former Democrat, who had started her political career working for Shirley Chisholm in the late 1960s, promised that a vote for the Republican Party was akin to a vote "cast for the advancement of black people."[115] The emergence of black women as figureheads for the BSMC was significant, particularly since they were the least likely demographic to support the GOP; here, they assumed key roles in a black conservative organization. Arguably, this was a reflection of what scholar Angela K. Lewis has called an "everyday" form of black conservatism that sometimes translated into partisan support for the Republican Party.[116]

The BSMC's conservative message was not entirely dissimilar from the respectability politics of moderate civil rights elites, who also denounced riots, Black Power, and militancy; nevertheless, civil rights leaders couched their grievances in critiques of structural inequality and white supremacy— conditions that the BSMC resolutely ignored. The absence of white culpability and accountability actually helped the organization raise its profile among white Republicans, some of whom became vocal champions of the black organization. As early as November 1970, the BSMC admitted that its "greatest response" had come from whites; similarly, the Republican Congressional Committee (RCC) heavily endorsed the black group, providing start-up funding for the BSMC, financing the organization's cross-country "crusades," arranging meetings with prominent white officials, and routinely highlighting the organization in the RCC newsletter.[117]

Thousands of ordinary white citizens also expressed an interest in the BSMC, cheering the values and actions of the group in a manner that held fast to the racialized guidelines of respectability politics. "This is the thing we've been waiting for! Now you're talking like the black people I know. Good, responsible citizens," declared a woman from Ohio. "You are to be congratulated for your efforts in enlightening the black people about constitutional government, law, order and justice," wrote Milton Wells of Illinois. "This is—and should be—the prime objective toward enlightening all good loyal Americans." Peter Diamandis of New York, publisher of *Mademoiselle* magazine, summarized white support for the BSMC most succinctly: "Thank God for Mr. Clay Claiborne! Thank God for logic! Tha[n]k God for guts!"[118]

Among white GOP leaders, Strom Thurmond was among the most vocal of the BSMC's advocates. In July 1970, the South Carolina senator devoted his congressional remarks to celebrating the black group and its principles:

> Black revolutionaries and militants do not speak for the vast majority of black people. Further, [the BSMC] said the vast majority of blacks disapprove of current disorders and are working for a living, trying to keep their children in school, and are law abiding. . . . It is encouraging to hear such words spoken about blacks by blacks. . . . Frankly, whites might well follow this good example, for there are plenty of white radicals on both sides of the political spectrum who try to speak for groups which they do not actually represent.[119]

The BSMC also found a powerful ally in Richard Nixon, who took an interest in the black group's development, regularly praising the organization's ideas. Three months after Thurmond's speech, Nixon applauded the group for highlighting the ways in which African Americans had contributed to the prosperity and success of the nation. The BSMC, he declared, had advanced "true social justice."[120] To be sure, white party officials—specifically those invested in winning the white "silent majority" vote in the 1970s—could safely endorse the BSMC without fear of alienating white voters, given that the black organization uncritically reiterated white Republicans ideas. In turn, this support allowed the BSMC to disseminate its ideas as authentic black Republicanism, despite the fact that by 1974, the group's beliefs were vastly different from those espoused by the NBRC or the Council of 100.

By 1974, all three groups would look to Gerald Ford to help advance their respective causes, although the NBRC and the Council of 100 were most outspoken about this new endorsement. Many black Republicans viewed the Michigan politician's August 1974 ascension to the White House as a symbol of Republican rebirth, suggesting that his presidency represented a "new freshness" for the GOP. "The despair and frustration of Watergate has receded into clear waters that have a glitter of hope under the new administration," declared NBRC Far West Director Ted Short following Ford's confirmation as president.[121] The black consensus organization's leadership was particularly enthusiastic about the new president's "Open Door" policy, believing that Ford's willingness to meet with almost any and all constituent groups, including race-based organizations, illustrated the administration's commitment to broadening the party tent. NBRC officials argued that Ford's first actions in office, including appointing Nelson Rockefeller as vice president, indicated that the administration would adopt a "moderate posture," signaling a "new day for Black Americans and our country as a whole."[122] Indeed, Ford's informal policy was a significant shift in approach from the cold shoulder of the Nixon administration and led to a series of domestic policy meetings in September 1974 with African Americans, including black Republican leaders. *Jet* called it a "whirlwind effort to 'touch base' with Black America." The "Open Door" policy, wrote Simeon Booker in *Jet*, "has broadened the base of GOP Blacks."[123]

The sessions were held at the urging of Gerald Ford's special assistant, black Republican Stan Scott; the former journalist argued that such meetings would "erase the unwarranted gap" that had existed between African Americans and the Nixon administration and "personally assure" black leaders that Ford wanted and needed "their support in building an America for all Americans."[124] For black Republicans, at least, the meetings did, in fact, signal that the White House was receptive to their agenda; after all, Ford opened the black Republican summit by announcing, "You have a friend in the White House!" Presenting position papers on domestic policy issues relating to African Americans, the black Republican leaders also espoused core NBRC objectives and values: as council chair Henry Lucas wrote, "Our job of organizing grassroots campaign help will be made possible only to the extent that people see [that] the Administration recognizes the existence of Blacks and is doing something about the problems. Thus the more the White House is on top of the agencies and the appointees who head them, the more favorable impact it will have on the entire political process."[125] Although the president reassured black party members that he wanted their input "at the highest levels" of government—promising to hold future sessions on black economics, business development and growth, civil rights, education, and employment—the promise was largely rhetorical. As RNC chair Mary Louise Smith wrote in her notes from the September session, the GOP questioned: "Can we deliver?"[126]

Nevertheless, black Republicans earnestly assumed that the White House was no longer impenetrable and believed that the administration would enlist African American party members' input on "policies and programs of significance to Blacks." Within the pages of its newsletter, the NBRC boasted that the administration would call upon black Republicans to decide "what programs Blacks want, which ones they don't want," and that the full resources of both the RNC and the White House would be "used to get the job done." In their eagerness to embrace the new president, black Republicans again displayed a remarkable sense of political naïveté; yet they were not alone, as black journalists and specific members of the CBC also expressed a similar idealism. During congressional hearings on Ford's confirmation to the presidency, for example, Georgia congressman Andrew Young spoke positively on behalf of the Michigan official; likewise, *Jet* profiled the new president in a lengthy August 1974 spread questioning if Ford would do a "political flip-flop" from conservative politician to an "equal opportunity champion" in the White House, "At the moment," the editors wrote, "the prospects look good."[127]

As Ford assumed the presidency, black party members found themselves consumed with the upcoming midterm elections and devoted as much time to publicizing black Republican campaigns as they did to reviving their relationship with the White House. In particular, the NBRC leaders spent time identifying and grooming electable contenders for public office and political appointments who shared beliefs similar or identical to those of the organization, confident that such candidates and appointees would create meaningful policies once elected. The group also employed "political expediency" as a rationale, promising "great opportunities" within the GOP in an attempt to entice young black men and women to run for office as Republicans. In short, the NBRC encouraged African Americans to join the GOP because there were fewer blacks in the party and thus fewer obstacles in the assuming political power. In some ways, this was a fair assessment—one based entirely on the fact that there were far more African Americans vying for political positions in the Democratic Party. Yet the NBRC's argument that blacks who chose the Republican Party would have a "greater ability to influence" American politics was overly idealistic at best and spurious at worst, given that over the previous decade, black Republicans (including the most successful among this group) had struggled to translate their efforts into tangible wide-reaching influence within the party.[128]

Focusing on the midterm election, the NBRC devoted most of 1974 to publicizing the "refreshing" campaigns of thirty young black Republican candidates, taking great care to highlight the fact that 20 percent of those running were black women. The NBRC profiled the would-be-politicians as exciting and forward-thinking newcomers, committed to the principles of free market enterprise and to the needs of African Americans.[129] Going into the November contests, the black organization was publicly confident, only to be shaken by the results of the midterm elections, which were disastrous for the party. An ongoing economic recession and public outrage over Gerald Ford's pardon of Richard Nixon dashed the party's hopes of success. The GOP lost four governorships, forty-nine seats in the House, and five positions in the Senate. Moreover, only 8 percent of the black electorate voted for Republicans; and among the NBRC's chosen black candidates, all but three lost.[130]

Immediately following the midterm contests, the NBRC gathered feedback from the candidates, most of whom relayed their enthusiasm for the general political process, pointing out that even in failed races, black Democrats had "crossed party lines" to support black Republicans, as was the case for Thaddeus Garrett Jr. of Ohio, who lost by 2 percent of the popular vote. The twenty-six-year-old political prodigy's affiliation with Congresswoman Shirley Chisholm certainly aided his campaign; the black Republican was well known in African American communities for being the liberal Brooklyn Democrat's chief legislative aide.[131] The same was true for Jesse Woods of Philadelphia, Pennsylvania, whose campaign received a boost when local African American ministers launched a statewide crusade promoting black "ticket splitting." Nevertheless, many candidates voiced frustrations over weak support from "established" party leaders and institutions, accusing them of neglecting black campaigns. Washington, D.C.'s Capitol City Republican Club acknowledged this problem early on, admitting, "Our candidates can expect little help financially."[132] Mildred Morries of Milwaukee complained that the state party ignored her campaign, instead electing to promote white candidates. In that same vein, black candidates complained of lack of support from rank-and-file registered white Republican voters, many of whom abstained from voting in their local midterm elections. In Woods's election, for instance, only 37 percent voted—a dismal figure, considering that normally, 80 to 90 percent of this group turned out for midterm and general elections.[133] The most serious of allegations came from James "Buddy" Brannen of Colchester, Connecticut, who attracted national attention when he charged the GOP with racism for failing to support his bid for a seat in the U.S. Senate.[134]

Almost all of the black candidates complained that the GOP was guilty of "talking out of both sides of its mouth about supporting strong, viable candidates."[135] Their accusations suggested a return to outspokenness, reminiscent of the forcefulness of the NNRA—a willingness not only to criticize the party in general (which black Republicans had been doing for years, in varying degrees) but also to make specific and pointed charges of illegal and unethical behavior. Certainly this was part of the "Watergate" effect, as black party members increasingly asserted their moral authority over what they perceived as party corruption and unfairness. In addition, the election results proved that financial and moral support from mainstream party leaders was critical to black Republican success; without it, African Americans candidates struggled not only with black constituencies but with white voters as well. Even the normally buoyant editors of *Black Republican News* felt compelled to end their postelection newsletter on an accusatory note; they published an op-ed that complained about the limited funding and staff provided by the RNC, implicitly drawing comparisons between the national committee's treatment of the NBRC and its two other auxiliary groups, the YRNF and NFRW.[136]

Black Republicans' criticisms, however, did not prevent them from finding a measure of hope from the midterm returns. A month after the election, the NBRC proudly announced that almost a third of black local and state candidates for public office had run as Republicans: ten in the House, one for the Senate, and seventy in state legislatures. Rather than seeing the 1974 election as a failure, the black organization viewed it as a success, insisting that the races had set the groundwork for future elections.[137] Importantly, black party members were excited that African Americans were running as Republicans despite continuing public suspicion about the integrity of the GOP—so much so that they willingly glossed over the midterm losses. Consequently, while blacks in the party had an entirely new host of problems and complaints, they still were hopeful in the days and weeks leading to 1975.

• • •

In an effort to alleviate the NBRC's financial woes, the Council of 100 quietly incorporated a fundraising arm in 1975, holding its first fundraiser in November of that year. The gala was a splashy affair, designed to help underwrite the campaigns of "worthy" black Republican candidates for Congress; twelve hundred black and white leaders, journalists, and party officials joined event cochairs Senator Ed Brooke and Presidential First Lady Betty Ford, as the council raised more than $250,000. Applauding black Republicans' effort, the editors at the *New York Amsterdam News* declared their support for two-party competition, writing: "We think the idea is sound and we wish them well in their venture. . . . Let's keep all of our Black Democratic congressmen in office—and let's add some Black Republicans." Similarly, Julian Bond—who had berated some black Nixon supporters as "political prostitutes" three years earlier—applauded the Council of 100's initiative in a positive op-ed, arguing, "We ought to wish them success. . . . If an undemocratic Dixiecrat can be dumped by a race conscious brother in a Republican cloth coat, we'll be all the better for it."[138]

Nelson Rockefeller delivered the evening's keynote address, employing rhetoric saturated in black Republican values, denouncing racial discrimination, and applauding the economic policy initiatives of African

Americans. In a display that seemed to come straight from the NBRC's organizing manual, the vice president ended his speech with a flourish, asserting that the "way to work towards one's legitimate goals in our system is to make the political system work for the best interests."[139] He also urged the party to correct its disparities through black outreach and through the creation of creative socioeconomic solutions rooted in both the private and public sectors. His speech spoke to black Republican's frustrations, aspirations, and strategies; it was a powerful statement for African American GOP leaders: here was the nation's vice president—a longtime supporter of black Republicans' efforts—publicly acknowledging and forcefully criticizing the party's neglect of blacks and discussing approaches to wooing them back into the GOP. Symbolizing the uncanny optimism of black Republicans, one African American party member declared that there would be "a resurgence of participation in the Republican party in '76."[140]

Certainly, the event represented a moment of possibility and hopefulness for black party members, as they seemed to have the moral and financial support of both the RNC and the moderate Ford administration. They achieved a number of goals in 1974 and 1975; for example, Stan Scott, Gerald Ford's special assistant, was instrumental in reestablishing a genuine "Open Door" policy for African Americans, irrespective of partisan affiliation, at the White House. Ford also endorsed a seven-year extension of the Voting Rights Act, a concrete victory for both the NBRC and the Council of 100. Both groups experienced some success with helping the party integrate state and local GOP organizations; at one point, the Council of 100 even helped in the "refashioning" of Strom Thurmond's racist image by getting the senator to pledge publicly to "strengthen the role of minorities in federally funded agencies."[141]

Yet in truth, black Republicans' optimism masked the full extent of their troubles. The early- to mid-1970s was a period of growing pains for them, reflecting inconsistent moral and financial support from the GOP. The creation of the NBRC generated a sense of power among black party leaders, but that sense was tempered by the organization's struggles to make an institutional long-term impact on American politics and the party apparatus. Elections provided a cruel reminder of their problems; by 1975, fewer than 4 percent of the nation's thirty-eight hundred black elected officials were members of the GOP.[142]

Many of black Republicans' woes were connected to the party's broader shift to the right in the mid-1970s, as more and more Republicans embraced an agenda that, among other points, strongly opposed busing and affirmative action and articulated a colorblind vision of outreach that often alienated black constituents.[143] Interest in African Americans persisted throughout this transition, despite often being at odds with actual black outreach. In other words, many party officials were interested in reform but shied away from the explicitly race-conscious solutions that were necessary for that reform. Consequently, as the GOP shifted to the right, the agendas of groups like the NBRC and the Council of 100 began to fall by the wayside.

In particular, as an auxiliary of the RNC, the NBRC could pursue only what the national committee countenanced; equally significant, as a consensus organization, the NBRC represented the full ideological diversity of black Republicans, including members who were liberal and those who were conservative. It embraced an agenda that was a moderate amalgamation of those philosophies. Nevertheless, in attempting to forge a moderate path, the organization found itself restricted; and while the Council of 100 attempted to alleviate those restrictions, both groups' influence was eclipsed by the BSMC, whose conservative agenda was identical to that of the mainstream party.

The NBRC and the Council of 100 offered little commentary on the BSMC during the early and mid-1970s; their silence is striking given black Republicans' declarations of unity, the NBRC's dedication to eradicating splinter organizations, and the Council of 100's self-identified liberal outlook. The two groups simply may have viewed the BSMC as an irrelevant organization at the margins of black Republican thought; but a far more likely and complex explanation is that *some* African American party leaders, from both the Council of 100 and the NBRC, may have actually supported the BSMC's agenda—individuals like Mary Parrish, who, after joining the BSMC's "Black Youth Voter Crusade" in 1972, became an inaugural member of the NBRC Steering Committee in 1974; or figures like Bob Brown of the Council of 100, who had insisted on the existence of a "hard-working" black silent majority since 1969. In essence, in espousing unity politics the centrist NBRC and the liberal Council of 100 welcomed some of the same black conservative Republicans embraced by the BSMC.

In fact, leaders in all three organizations overestimated the existence of a silent black majority of Republican-leaning African Americans, while underestimating the depth of hostility between black communities and the GOP. In particular, the NBRC's "partisan approach" alienated African Americans; rather than allowing black Republicans to transcend the party's history, it reinforced the very legacy the NBRC was trying to reinvent, conveying an image of an organization loyal to Republican mandates, rather than a group invested in independent Republicanism. Instead, the NBRC focused on the so-called advantage of a shared black cultural identity and history; members believed that their blackness would facilitate

African American interests in clubs and make citizens "more willing to identify themselves with the Republican [P]arty."[144] Likewise, the BSMC received some support within African American communities; however, that support did not necessarily translate into an endorsement for the GOP; indeed, African Americans' "everyday" conservatism did not mean that they would support the Republican Party.

Here, once again, was the ongoing dilemma of black Republican politics; that African American party members neglected this problem in their quest for influence was all the more troublesome. Only the Council of 100 seemed to be able to transcend this issue, prompting accolades from black leaders for its commitment to civil rights; despite the group's pragmatic approach, though, its liberal philosophy was often at odds with mainstream party views. All of these paradoxes and contradictions bring into focus the breadth of ideological variance that existed among black Republicans—a heterogeneity of thought that lay underneath African American party members' shared racial heritage and experiences and that would increasingly divide them over time.

CHAPTER SIX

More Shadow than Substance

WHEN GERALD FORD ANNOUNCED HIS NOMINATION FOR SECRETARY OF transportation in January 1975, no one—not even black Republicans—was prepared to hear William T. Coleman's name. Though black leaders and political elites had bandied about his résumé for years, they could not have predicted that a Republican president would appoint a black man to a cabinet position. The National Newspaper Publishers Association, representing a conglomerate of more than one hundred black publishers, congratulated Ford for his "tangible demonstration" of equality—a "commendable first step," the group noted, that illustrated the new president's commitment to appointing African Americans to influential decision-making roles. Expressing more cautious praise in the pages of the *Chicago Defender*, Louis Martin wrote, "I share the hope of most black Americans, regardless of party, that President Ford's nomination of Coleman to his cabinet will mark a turning point in the traditional Republican attitude toward us . . . the Coleman appointment is an excellent beginning."[1]

Spring brought a swift and painless confirmation process for Coleman, with the Senate unanimously endorsing Ford's selection. Days later, in the grandiose East Room of the White House, the president and an interracial audience of three hundred cheered as the first black Supreme Court justice, Thurgood Marshall, inducted Coleman into the annals of modern American history. Robert Weaver, the first black member of a presidential cabinet, was among those "beaming with joy" as the second took his oath. The moment signaled, as the *Chicago Defender* stated, a "refreshingly new day for Washingtonians of the darker hue, a new and hopeful outlook for a democratic society."[2]

The Philadelphia corporate lawyer was widely known and respected for his civil rights work as president of the NAACP Legal Defense Fund and one of the legal advisers on *Brown v. Board of Education*.[3] The joy surrounding his appointment came with the understanding of the gravitas of an African American assuming such a position of influence. As secretary of transportation, Coleman was responsible for overseeing one of the largest federal departments, managing a budget of more than $12 billion and directing a staff of more than 100,000. "Coleman's appointment," the *Call and Post* hailed, "represents a long climb for blacks from the back of the bus to the directorship of the total transportation system of our country."[4] Coleman's placement resonated with African Americans, in part, because the black freedom struggle was so intertwined with the ability to move freely from one part of the country to another.

Although the second black member of a presidential cabinet, Coleman's appointment still presented a first of sorts—at least for the modern GOP. Not only was the Philadelphia lawyer the first African American to be appointed to a cabinet position by a Republican; Coleman was also the first black Republican to accept such a prominent role. Active in local and national party affairs for three decades, his presence illustrated the possibility of reconciling racial and political loyalties and still being a national success. Coleman, along with Edward Brooke, embodied the policy-making potential of black Republican politics in the 1970s, beyond the state and local level where most black Republicans continued to struggle. For African American members of the GOP, Coleman's appointment was of tremendous consequence, holding dual meaning: not only did it mean addressing civil rights and African American issues with the force of the federal government; it also signified the integration of black Republican voices into the upper echelons of the GOP in a manner that was different from previous attempts. The latter was a point that John Wilks contemplated while attending the transportation secretary's induction ceremony. "It's a very historic occasion," the NBRC executive director stated solemnly. "We've waited so long to see one of our people getting the proper recognition."[5]

But as black Republicans publicly cheered the success of one of their own, they also despaired over their unchanging status within the party. Coleman's ascent to the upper echelons of the GOP was a clear victory for black Republicans; yet his appointment, much like Brooke's isolated presence in the Senate, did not realize the full objectives of black members of the GOP. By 1975, in spite of the "united" front presented by black Republican groups, African Americans had not experienced a substantial increase in their ability to affect change within the GOP, nor had they witnessed a meaningful expansion in the number of black elected officials or policy-making appointments. Despite Gerald Ford's "Open Door" promises, Coleman's appointment was one of only a few made by the administration. And while they did see a boost in the number of appointments to federal advisory boards and commissions, black Republicans protested that all but a handful of these roles were meaningless, and that the Ford administration was only marginally better than the "cold shoulder" of the Nixon administration. Though such complaints were somewhat overstated (underestimating the power of an appointment to the U.S. Civil Rights Commission, for example), they nevertheless accurately assessed the lack of black appointees within the White House.[6] In the rare event that African Americans were appointed to high-ranking government positions, Jackson R. Champion accused, they were confined to "Equal Employment Opportunity type" roles—nominally necessary posts that "clearly have no real power."[7] Black Republican Helen Edmonds launched similar complaints against the Ford administration in 1975, after receiving multiple invitations from the White House to sit on national boards. "I am not interested in serving on any more advisory councils," the irate stateswoman wrote. "I have served on enough. . . . [It] is an unbearable pill to swallow. . . . I have borne the Republican label unchangingly from 1954 to the present. . . . But the people who carry the message are not awarded with the full-time positions."[8] Nor were such problems confined to national politics. At the local level, black Republicans accused white officials of obstructionism, as when African Americans claimed that Senator Charles Percy sabotaged Jewel Lafontant's nomination to the Seventh U.S. Circuit Court of Appeals in Chicago.[9]

Certainly, Gerald Ford's commitment to inclusivity was more pronounced than that of Richard Nixon, in both language and behavior; in his first eight months in office, the "accidental president" met with more black leaders and groups than any previous White House resident and was a regular speaker and fixture at African American civic, religious, and political events. His outspoken support for a five-year extension of the Voting Rights Act earned him African American supporters from both political parties. "With the support of the President," stated black presidential aide Stan Scott in April 1975, "we have been able to open up the doors of the White House."[10] Ford's "Open Door" policy was an outward reversal of the Nixon administration's icy attitude toward African American groups; yet within months, the contradictory and divisive actions of the GOP, coupled with the lumbering behaviors of the White House, would ultimately render Ford's platitudes of inclusion untrustworthy.[11]

As the 1970s progressed, black Republicans could claim clear victories in their march toward equality: the expansion of the NBRC; the incorporation of African Americans into the RNC hierarchy; scores of black Republicans integrating state and local party hierarchies; and individual examples of black Republican success. African American party leaders could even point to their ability to forge a consensus voice among the disparate political ideas of black Republicans. Despite their ideological differences, they collectively rejected white hierarchies of power, demanding change for blacks both within the GOP and throughout the country. Nevertheless, black Republicans quickly realized that their strategy did not reform the party institution; despite the GOP's rhetoric of broadening the party base, the party's identity moved even further to the right. As black Republicans realized the crisis they faced and as their fortunes rapidly declined, they not only fought viciously among themselves but also made concessions about black outreach in order to maintain a semblance of influence and power within the GOP.

CRACKS IN THE FOUNDATION

While William Coleman was desegregating the "lily-white" presidential cabinet in the spring of 1975, across town at a Washington, D.C., hotel, the NBRC was integrating the Republican National Committee's leadership conference. Hundreds of black Republicans, at the request of RNC chair Mary Louise Smith, joined thousands of fellow party leaders at the two-day March summit as they worked to rehabilitate the party's philosophy and image. "Republicans Are People Too," read the bright sunshine-yellow buttons passed out to attendees; and, in truth, much of the purpose of the televised conference was to convince the nation that Republicans were "ordinary" people, erasing the image of a corrupt, privileged political machine. The participants' cheerful façade, however, concealed their anxiety over the outcome of the convention. As the *Los Angeles Times* observed, the meeting offered a preview of the "escalating struggle" that would "decide the future of the sorely troubled Republican Party."[12] Would the GOP become an inclusive, "big tent" party? Would moderates and conservatives compromise on outreach? Did minorities, women, and youth deserve a genuine place in the party structure? All of these were troubling questions that Republicans sought to resolve under the banner of their leadership conference.

The GOP's African American members not only sat in the middle of this brewing squall—they also anticipated it. Alongside the leadership conference, the NBRC held a parallel symposium to insist on its "continued input into party affairs." Its specific focus was to ensure that the recommendations of the Rule 29 Committee would glide through the party approval process without being diluted by right-wing conservatives.[13] Of special concern to both the NBRC and the RNC conferences were two suggestions: the first proposed extending national committee voting privileges to auxiliary groups, including the NBRC; the second called for state parties to adopt "positive action programs" and was, by far, the most controversial of all of the proposed resolutions. As part of the party's broader reform initiative, which included holding "outreach workshops," voter education events, and public speaking engagements, the positive action programs required state parties to submit inclusion dossiers, documenting their efforts to coax underrepresented groups into the GOP apparatus. In turn, the RNC could, if it so chose, "review and comment" on the state reports. Though not nearly as aggressive as the affirmative action plans instituted by the Democratic National Committee in the early 1970s, the positive action plans were radical within the context of the GOP—a party that had long struggled with the idea of *positively* recognizing difference and with the notion of regulating the behavior and attitudes of its members. Aggressive measures such as these were needed, argued John Wilks, given the increasing significance of the black vote on the American political system. "Moving into 1976," he warned, the party "will have to take a cold, pragmatic view towards the inclusion of blacks and other special interest groups in all party business."[14] Gerald Ford arrived at much the same conclusion in his evening speech to the RNC leadership participants. "We must discard the exclusiveness that has kept the Republican Party's doors closed too often while we give speeches about keeping it open," the president stressed. As his enthusiastic audience clapped and nodded in appreciation, he bellowed the winning line again for emphasis: "We must discard the exclusiveness that has kept the Republican Party's doors closed too often while we give speeches about keeping it open!"[15]

But as the conference progressed, discussions of broadening the tent devolved into nasty and emotional debates over the merits of the positive action programs. Black Republicans, as well as other party reformers, must have been keenly aware of the irony of Ford's dinner speech as they listened to critics attack the reform committee's signature initiative as a ploy to pad the ranks of the GOP with liberal subversives. Conservative members' shrill accusations highlighted their implicit fears over what they believed racial and ethnic minorities, women and youth embodied. Positive action programs, they argued, constituted a violation of states' rights; a "monitoring program" that contained the "seed of mischief"; and an immoral and perilous quota system, nearly identical to that which had recently "destroyed" the Democratic Party. Offering a hyperbolic analysis of the positive action programs to conference attendees, Ronald Reagan suggested that broadening the GOP base via targeted outreach was akin to rejecting conservative principles. "No one can quarrel with the idea that a political party hopes it can attract a wide following, but does it do this by forsaking its basic beliefs? By blurring its image so as to be the indistinguishable from the opposing party?" he questioned, as audience members murmured in agreement. "More serious still," M. Stanton Evans wrote in the conservative journal *Human Events*, "is the spectacle of a political party founded on voluntarism and respect for the individual gravitating toward the quota mind-set, and a party whose major opportunity lies in the rise of national conservative sentiment fixated on the question of securing liberal votes. The labors of the Rule 29 Committee, indeed, are a masterful proof of Republican confusion."[16]

Such references lent credence to the notion that white conservatives wanted a party, as the *Chicago Defender* suggested, where there was little room for "the poor, the blacks or the common man."[17] For critics of the plans, an unspoken assumption was that the groups targeted by the initiative would *weaken* and ultimately destroy the GOP, rather than strengthen the party—ignoring the fact that those attracted to the Republican Party, even among underrepresented groups, tended to be conservative. The notion that renegade blacks suddenly would join the "establishment" GOP and dismantle conservatism was specious at best. Moreover, even as they advocated for race-conscious approaches to address the structural inequalities of party hierarchy, black Republicans still firmly believed in individualism: thus, the positive action plans were merely a way for African Americans to ensure equal access so that they could guarantee their rights as individuals.

After two bruising days of debate, Republicans agreed to dilute the language and, implicitly, the spirit of the positive action programs. Plans were no longer mandatory, nor could the RNC punish state parties for failing to submit—or even create—outreach programs. The compromise was a halfhearted and uneven one, as an incredulous *New York Times* reporter noted: it conveyed a message that Republicans should "seek more members among women, minorities, youth and the elderly—but that [the RNC] would not interfere if they decided not to." To be sure, the amended resolution was a victory for right-wing conservatives, whose intraparty movement, political commentators noted, was slowly growing in strength—a bitter pill for party moderates, reformers, and black Republicans to swallow, as they had lost their battle by only one vote.[18]

In the days immediately following the conference, the NBRC, which had gloated over the positive action programs before the event, was conspicuously silent about the resolution failure. Instead, it chose to publicize the RNC's commitment to extend voting rights to auxiliary groups. Ultimately, however, even this was an inconsequential victory; after mild protests from conservative party members, the leadership delegates had simply tabled the auxiliary voting debate for discussion at the 1976 Republican National Convention.[19] This decision—to celebrate a hollow victory, rather than to criticize the GOP's larger failure—was but one of a growing number of example's of the NBRC's increasingly fragile position.

Rank-and-file black Republicans, once again, carried the burden of the party's cognitive dissonance between its language of inclusion and actions of exclusion. Within days of the conference, African Americans wrote to the RNC, relaying their confusion over the incongruity between the national party and local organizations.[20] Phill Trevillion proudly described being elected to a GOP committeeman position in Chicago, employing the party's "Open Door" philosophy to encourage African Americans and "welfare recipients" to support Republicans. Yet the young official complained of being excluded from local and state party activities and being hampered by the GOP's refusal to financially endorse him. Most distressing of all was the "open or covert opposition" by white Republicans to Trevillion's message of inclusion.[21] Charles Hurst of Chicago also offered lavish praise for the RNC's inclusive philosophy; but like other black Republicans, he questioned the "deceased corpse" that passed for state Republican organizations. State parties and African Americans could easily "use each other in mutually selfish ways to improve their relative positions," Hurst noted, but the state parties refused to do anything substantive. "For some strange reason," Hurts argued, the state GOP "rejects the notion of strong black involvement. Just as so many top Republicans at the national level say, 'damn the niggers, full speed ahead,' many top [state] Republicans say by their actions that they would rather be mandated out of existence than to court the black electorate."[22]

The dilution of the GOP's positive action program turned the concept of inclusion into a public relations banality, designed to make the nation feel at ease with an emotionally fragile party. Black journalists, who months earlier had offered cagey optimism for the Ford administration, were especially brutal in their criticisms of the White House, attacking, for example, the "mass exodus" of black appointees, many of whom were ejected from their positions by Ford, just two or three years after Richard Nixon had conducted his own round of ousters. "Gerald Ford, who should be setting a national example," wrote journalist Chuck Stone, "is slowly evolving into an unequal opportunity . . . employer, disregarding the cornucopia of black talent readily available at the executive level."[23]

Gloria Toote, an assistant secretary at Housing and Urban Development (HUD) in charge of equal opportunity and fair housing, was among the "talented" black personnel ousted within Ford's first eight months in office. During her two-year stint in the White House, Toote had established herself as a "vigorous" advocate for racial minorities and the poor, arguing, as she often did in her NNPA syndicated column, that the "thrust of our nation must be to improve the economic plight of the minority American." As an executive member of the NBRC, she held fast to the organization's faith in free market enterprise, suggesting that discrimination was harmful not only for moral reasons but also because it limited competition and innovation in the marketplace. Likewise, her view of the federal government was consistent with that of many other black

Republicans, who advocated for an interventionist approach in matters of equal opportunity while concurrently championing partnerships with private industry. Equality could be reached only through a "series of sustained reallocation of society's resources," she once declared. Moreover, the ultimate goal of equality, she insisted, was to make "individual rights" a reality for *all* Americans by offering African Americans and the poor "choice" and "freedom" in housing and employment.[24]

Yet despite wrangling more than $130 million in contracts for minorities in 1974 alone, the Harlem lawyer was unceremoniously fired by newly appointed HUD secretary Carla Hills in the spring of 1975. Though the exact circumstances of her removal are muddy, Ford's critics insisted that Toote, like others before her, was dropped for her aggressive enforcement of equal opportunity policies; moreover, the administration's detractors noted the irony of a white Republican woman, who had publicly struggled against sexism, firing the highest-ranking black Republican in the federal government. Where was "Women's Lib?" demanded reporter Simon Anekwe. "Gloria Toote has served her nation, her party, and the cause of equal opportunity well," the National Newspaper Publishers Association declared in a damning editorial. "If the Republican Party allows a highly capable woman to depart from an effective role of service in the federal establishment," then there was "no hope for Blacks in the GOP."[25] The news of the black official's departure sent the NBRC into a panic, as the organization contemplated the impact that her absence would have on the economic and social mobility of African Americans. Certainly, their frustrations were contradictory: black Republicans had criticized African American appointees as powerless, yet their panic over Toote's dismissal demonstrated that they viewed these "token" appointments as significant. Thus, the black official's dismissal was a double blow to black Republicans' objectives, for it affected both their push for power within the party and their agenda of black uplift. Likewise, Toote's ejection reinforced the notion that autonomy was still beyond reach for black Republicans, as white officials continued to exert control over black Republicans' decision-making abilities.

The lopsided nature of power dynamics between black and white Republicans also hinted at a far subtler intraracial struggle among black Republicans—namely, that the tremendous implications of power and influence practically mandated that African Americans within the party impose authenticity tests. "Who genuinely represents the voice of black Republicans?" was a constant challenge hurled by African American members of the GOP, as they contested agendas and approaches that differed from their own. Writing in the spring of 1975, for example, Maurice Dawkins of Philadelphia criticized the Ford administration's handling of high-ranking government appointments. The Opportunities Industrial-ization Center (OIC) executive demanded that the president and party consult "trusted" black Republican leaders about significant positions that affected black life. Choosing the wrong appointee, he warned, had ramifications that affected not only black livelihood but also the GOP's potential gains among African American voters. Dawkins pointed to the example of Equal Employment Opportunity Commission (EEOC) chair-man John H. Powell, who had resigned recently amid charges of misman-agement and a staggering backlog of 120,000 discrimination cases. The EEOC head's spectacular failure, Dawkins argued, stemmed from the fact that white party leaders, rather than black Republicans, had chosen Pow-ell; the disgraced African American's approach and perspective, Dawkins therefore concluded, were not representative of so-called authentic black Republican politics.[26]

If Powell was the antithesis to authentic black Republican politics, then William Coleman was the exemplar, espousing an economic uplift agenda identical to that of groups like the NBRC. Coleman, like Edward Brooke or the members of Nixon's Black Cabinet, thrust the views of black Republicans into the national spotlight. In doing so, he provided black Republican elites with a figure on which to focus their attention, lest the party's ideological battles distract them from their pragmatic po-litical agenda. Within days of taking office, Coleman announced that he planned to use the Department of Transportation to address the eco-nomic and mobility woes of the nation's African Americans. To those ends, as one of his first acts in office he met with the Congressional Black Caucus (CBC) to discuss eradicating discrimination in hiring and promo-tion within his own department.[27] He also envisioned transportation as a massive civil rights project, telling *Black Enterprise* in June 1975, for ex-ample, that he was interested in revitalizing urban mass transit systems, in part because poor people and minorities relied on them. Detailing a partnership with the city government of Cincinnati, the secretary noted that funding from his department had permitted transit authorities to decrease fares; consequently, he claimed, ridership had increased by more than 50 percent. "If you look at those buses—and the people who ride them—you will see that the poor or the minorities . . . have a much better life as a result of this activity. And that's what we're trying to do."[28]

Arguably, Coleman was most proud of his work with Atlanta mayor Maynard Jackson. Within weeks of assuming control of the Transporta-tion Department, the secretary provided Jackson with more than $10 million in federal funds for the revitalization and expansion of Atlanta's Hartsfield International Airport.[29] Over the summer, while appearing with Coleman at a National Urban League luncheon, Jackson gushed over the black official's actions, stressing the importance of the federal boost. Not only had Coleman secured funding for the airport project; he had also rallied for an affirmative action component of the project, thereby ensuring employment for more than five thousand minority contractors and construction workers; in other words, political influence had translated into economic power, thereby benefiting black progress. African Americans, Coleman declared, as Jackson stood next to him, grinning with appreciation, were finally "winning some political power" and learning "how the system works." The "power play" of Atlanta's first black mayor—a Democrat—negotiating with Gerald Ford's lone black cabinet member—a Republican—was not lost on African Americans. The *Chicago Defender* insisted that the bipartisan alliance provided ample evidence of the power of two-party competition and the necessity of African Americans learning how to "manipulate the system" for maximum economic and social gains. "Whatever the goal . . . Airport funds for Atlanta or public service jobs for the jobless," concluded the *Defender*, "it requires political clout. Political power does not come out of the barrel of a gun. It comes out of the ballot box."[30] Coleman's actions turned the NBRC's theories into a reality, underscoring black Republicans' claims about using their influence within the GOP to dictate positive results for African Americans, and demonstrated that African Americans *could* assert themselves within a two-party political system, using their integration into Republican and Democratic hierarchies to effect policy.

Speaking to the same audience as Coleman and Jackson, Ed Brooke offered an even stronger argument for the Atlanta mayor's thesis that politics was the "civil rights movement of the seventies" by connecting it to specific economic policies. This was merely another version of what Brooke had been insisting upon a decade earlier: that legislative change, rather than demonstrations and protests, was going to be what made the real difference in African Americans' lives. Economic booms, he argued, were not enough since African Americans were still crowded around the margins of the market. Brooke pushed a multitiered vision for reform similar to that which the Council of 100 had articulated nearly a year earlier and that which the NBRC would adopt in the coming months. First, he called for a family assistance program, akin to Richard Nixon's stalled 1969 plan, to replace the existing welfare system, and for a guaranteed minimum income for the unemployed. He also announced his support for a full employment bill, one in which the government and the private sector would guarantee work for every willing American. Such legislation, he argued, would "attack the root cause of many of our social and economic difficulties," and would be "far more effective than continuing to apply band-aids in the form of unmanageable, overlapping government programs in welfare, health, education, and housing." Second, power was rooted in property, he insisted. Thus homeownership, he reasoned, was a "ticket to the economic mainstream," and as such, he pushed for congressional legislation to assist poor and working-class families in becoming homeowners. Third, Brooke endorsed financial education and counseling to support the "American Dream," the goal of which, he relayed to his audience, was to build an economically viable community with safer streets—a community where African Americans owned not only homes but also shops and stores.

It is worth noting that Brooke and Coleman agreed on almost everything *except* their understanding of full employment; the senator suggested that the government should guarantee jobs when private industry was unable to do so; the cabinet official, in contrast, argued that full employment should come solely through the private sector. This was a disagreement, as the *Atlanta Daily World* observed, of "means, not the end," reflecting the subtle but significant ideological divides that existed among black Republicans; equally important, Brooke's ideas here highlight his shift to the left. Moreover, like Coleman and Jackson, the black senator reminded his NUL audience that a black political agenda was meaningless without action. "We must talk about how we get that agenda translated into public policy. We must talk politics," he argued. The solution then was to form political coalitions to best serve their interests and split the ticket when necessary. "We have no permanent friends, no permanent enemies, just permanent interests. Without question these interests are economic."[31]

It was within this landscape that the NBRC plugged away, attempting to build its status as an organization and resolving to strengthen the organization's thirty state councils by providing local, hands-on support. Widening communication among black Republican networks and cementing political bonds among the national organization and regional and local groups were the NBRC's focus, but so too was the organization's original goal: to provide both rank-and-file and black Republicans elites with an official vehicle through which they could effectively voice party grievances.[32] The organization spent much of the spring and summer of 1975 quietly reorganizing its national structure and launching state and local councils. In Georgia, for example, Robert Wright, director of the southeastern region of the NBRC, assisted black Republicans with "developing a mechanism to provide input into the decision-making body of the National Republican Party." In Florida, 150 black Republicans did the same; and in New York, Gloria Toote initiated a chapter that promised to examine the quality of education, housing, and employment in Harlem.[33] This commitment to organizational strength also gave way to a revival of the Black Republican Appointees Council (BRAC). First created as the Council of Black Appointees (CBA) in 1970, this group of Ford's African American appointees met regularly to discuss and debate the administration's policies and programs and advise the White House on government programs from an African American perspective. Despite their small numbers, and perhaps *because* of their precarious standing in the White House, these appointees declared that they intended to serve as a conduit for "input from the Black community to the administration"—a statement that was both a sincere and a calculated effort to demonstrate their worth to the administration and to the Republican Party.[34]

However, as African Americans concentrated on strengthening the bonds of partisan solidarity, the fissures among them became more apparent. Individuals and organizations continued to battle over the contested concept of an authentic black Republican voice. African American officials within the White House were often at the center of these conflicts, a fact that Stan Scott bitterly noted in private correspondence from August 1975. Responding to a litany of complaints from Helen Edmonds, Scott wrote, "I respond . . . with a degree of sadness, knowing that much of your criticism of the Republican Party is valid . . . I continue to enjoy the support of the President despite vicious efforts by some of our Blacks to kick me out and . . . destroy each other. And people wonder why our gains are so few. . . . Unfortunately, our opportunities are not as frequent as they should be. . . . Helen, we all despair at times. Don't give up . . . the options are even worse on the other side of the political fence."[35] Black Republicans, as we have seen, had consistently fought with one another, jockeying for power and control; Scott's case was no different, as his critics demanded his resignation, charging that he failed to deliver "contracts, appointments and programs for the benefit of the black community." Still, in a broader context wherein black Republicans were publicly championing solidarity and unity, the quarrels between critical black party members and Scott suggested not only that power was still up for grabs but also that black party members understood that the stakes were rising.[36]

Intraracial tensions were but a symptom of problems within the larger Republican Party. Crucial divisions were growing between dogmatic conservative purists and flexible moderates over appeals to poor and minority voters, warned the alarmed editors of the *Pittsburgh Courier*. Would the GOP choose to "goose-step" behind right-wing conservatism, worried the black periodical, or embrace the "semi-liberalism" of black Republicans and the party's reformer wing?[37] In August 1975, Howard "Bo" Callaway, head of the President Ford Campaign (PFC), noticed this correlation; reflecting on his meetings with the NBRC and other black

Republican leaders, he observed that it was "obvious" that African Americans were "going to push pretty hard" for their agendas, despite the "power struggle" going on within their ranks.[38]

Blacks quickly realized that Callaway was part of their problem. A familiar face during the Nixon administration, the PFC head was part of a new cohort of southern Republican politicians who concealed segregationist-inclined sensibilities beneath the exterior of respectable colorblind conservative politics—in fact, the Georgia Republican had advised the Nixon White House on silent majority appeals designed to woo white southern suburbanites with racially coded rhetoric in 1968.[39] As black Republicans watched their efforts to maneuver the president stall, they witnessed, with frustration, the ascent of a Goldwater conservative. Despite Callaway's protests that he had no intention of launching an exclusionary campaign, his appointment as the head of Ford's reelection effort delivered the unmistakable message that the president was interested in pursuing a strategy similar to that of Richard Nixon in 1972—an approach that had netted minimal gains for the party among black voters. The *Call and Post* accused Callaway of orchestrating the ousting of the administration's black appointees as part of this strategy. He and his "southern projects," the editors condemned, "don't want Negroes in visible jobs at the White House."[40]

That Ford would appoint a "southern strategist" to lead his presidential campaign understandably alienated many African Americans. For those at the *Chicago Defender*, the conclusion was simple: Gerald Ford was the "same old sour wine in a new bottle," relying mainly on antibusing myths to attract white voters. The president's repeated use of the phrase "forced busing," for example, was a loaded political slogan employed by Richard Nixon, conveying the faulty belief that busing was "less than legal" and "anti-white."[41] Moreover, antibusing rhetoric distanced African Americans because it was an "invitation to disorder, to violence in contravention to public order," as the *Defender* maintained. Ford's repeated decisions not to send federal troops to quell white violence against bused African Americans, while black children suffered, the *Defender* further argued, was hypocritical and proved "without a shadow of a doubt" that the president had embraced the philosophy of his predecessor.[42]

However, though the White House employed Callaway to launch the president's campaign, the administration was not uninterested in black outreach. In truth, Ford was interested in the potential of wooing black voters—as long as it fit within a burgeoning conservative narrative and required minimal Republican effort.

Soon after taking over PFC, for instance, even Bo Callaway met with the Georgia chapter of the NBRC, reassuring members that the campaign planned to appeal to black voters, despite the fact that "nothing" had been done yet to "rally the support" of ethnic and racial groups.[43] Moreover, while white Republicans expressed surface interest in exploring outreach possibilities with groups like the NBRC, they appeared just as interested—if not more so—with more conservative black groups like the Black Silent Majority Committee, an organization that echoed the language and supported the policies of both the Ford administration and white conservative Republicans, particularly on matters of busing.

As Ed Brooke battled the passage of antibusing amendments in the Senate in 1975, the BSMC launched its "Black Brigade Against Busing," with the goal of establishing the organization as an "important, powerful and listened-to Public Voice" in the broader legislative debate.[44] Touring the country in a "National Crusade Against Busing" and engaging more than one hundred black communities, the BSMC cataloged the grievances of African Americans, likening their complaints to those of white antibusing protestors. Gerald Ford lauded the group's actions in an April 1975 personal letter, writing that he had "followed with great interest the growth" of the BSMC and the "various projects which it had undertaken to focus attention on the activities of the many black citizens of this country who desire to build rather than destroy our national traditions and heritage." The president's remarks—widely reprinted and criticized in black newspapers—also noted his special interest in the black group's busing crusade: "I shall be interested in learning the results of your tour as well as your impressions and the opinions which you absorbed along the way," he wrote, subsequently urging the group to meet with him in the White House to discuss its findings.[45]

Certainly, the group found antibusing sentiment within black communities—Gallup and Harris polls from the 1970s found that more than 45 percent of surveyed African Americans expressed opposition to busing.[46] Among them were individuals like Bill Moss, who the BSMC profiled in 1975 after he was elected to the Columbus, Ohio, school board on an antibusing platform.[47] The organization's rejection of busing was rooted in a critique of modern liberalism; in its antibusing pamphlet, for instance, the group attacked Democratic liberalism as a paternalistic and bigoted ideology that implied that black schools were "inherently inferior" and unworthy of investment. In making such arguments, the BSMC employed the same language used by disenchanted African Americans of disparate political backgrounds, later appropriated by white conservative politicians of both political parties.[48]

Unlike most mainstream African American busing opponents, however, the BSMC offered no such criticism of conservatism, conflating black antibusing sentiment with support for a constitutional ban on busing. While a few common antibusing complaints crossed racial lines, the texture and tone of black and white opposition to busing was largely different. In addition to their anger over the implied inferiority of black educational institutions, African Americans were frustrated at the unequal state of neighborhood schools and the unequal treatment of black students. Many also feared for African American children's safety, given white citizens' propensity for violence and disregard for "law and order" in the face of court-mandated busing. And though the BSMC also saw violence as the central issue in the nation's busing crises, the group's "colorblind" pleas to respect law and order were far from race neutral, as they were directed at African Americans; white citizens, often the instigators of busing violence, were not held accountable. Rather than analyze the systemic inequalities or the sociological implications of busing-related violence, the BSMC misinterpreted black sentiment, declaring that the policy should be banned. Reacting to the organization's visit to Ohio, the *Call and Post* dismissed the group as a bunch of political opportunists and racial sellouts, whose "sales pitch" would allow BSMC members to "write [their] own assignment order" in the White House.[49] The conservative group's visit to California provoked similar sniping from *Los Angeles Sentinel* columnist Lin Hilburn: "By what authority does [the BSMC] come to California and presume to tell us how to act. . . . The nerve of these people . . . coming out here as if we were likely to follow a person who (by his hair process) does not want to be black."[50]

That the BSMC misrepresented African Americans perspectives was irrelevant to antibusing advocates within the Republican Party, as the organization's perspective coalesced with the new, far more refined—possibly even inclusive—veneer of the GOP's conservative wing. Republicans used the BSMC to elicit broader political support by arguing that the organization's footwork proved that hundreds of thousands of African Americans supported antibusing legislation. In October 1975, Congressman Bob Wilson of California offered the House of Representatives excerpts from the BSMC's antibusing handbook as proof that a "large segment" of the country's black voting population opposed the practice. The "untold story," Wilson continued, was one of "black families who resent the shameful waste of tax dollars . . . who are grossly inconvenienced by busing, whose children's safety is imperiled, and who stoutly cling to their right to freedom of choice and quality education. . . . Courage to speak the sentiments of legions of silent black Americans on this issue deserves our attentive notice and should create within our hearts the desire to face the schoolbusing [*sic*] issue forthrightly. Let us move on the proposals for a constitutional anti-busing amendment and return all American school children to a sane and sound educational environment."[51] White Republicans championed the cause of groups like the BSMC, or even individual antibusing perspectives, recognizing the possibility not only of a plethora of silent black conservatives but also of African American support, even of the imaginary variety, that could insulate the GOP against accusations of racism or antiblack hostility. Moreover, for Gerald Ford, the BSMC's agenda was safer than that of black Republican consensus groups like the NBRC, because it did not risk alienating white constituencies or force the president to reconsider his unyielding stance on busing.

For African Americans within the GOP, the BSMC's antibusing crusade was significant inasmuch as the organization's opinions were being used as a proxy not only for genuine African American sentiments but for "authentic" black Republican politics as well. Black Republicans certainly held multiple, often conflicting views on busing; nevertheless, as with mainstream black communities, these disparate perspectives did not prevent most black Republican elites from seeing the party's antibusing rhetoric as counterproductive, hypocritical, and discriminatory. While not the best solution, argued Edward Brooke, busing was the only reasonable existing prescription. More important, he argued, *it was the law*. A constitutional amendment barring busing, he warned, would "bring back racial separatism" and "completely undo 20 years of desegregation progress."[52] Even the conservative *Atlanta Daily World* shied away from the BSMC's rigid stance. The black newspaper, a longtime cheerleader for the organization, declared that it shared the BSMC's preference for the "neighborhood school," as did many black Republicans. Adopting the language of "freedom of choice" advocates, the editorial staff asserted that busing should be on a strictly voluntary basis. But from there, the black conservative gazette broke with the BSMC, a critical decision given that the paper's editor in chief, C. A. Scott, was on the executive board of the BSMC and helped launch the local Atlanta chapter, and that the *Atlanta Daily World* echoed the black group's stance on nearly every issue, from crime to black militancy. Like Brooke, the editors stated their emphatic opposition to a constitutional ban on busing, cautioning that such amendments could easily be "construed to check integration."[53] That the *Atlanta Daily World* could reject both busing and a constitutional amendment barring the practice highlighted the complex beliefs of African American members of the GOP; their understanding of racial inequality and persistent discrimination mitigated their conservatism, rendering them unable to endorse the party's rigid antibusing language and position.

Despite the major conflicts between black Republicans and the GOP —on everything from the "southern strategy," to reducing black appointees, to the constitutional ban on busing—and in spite of the fact that black

Republicans were already hovering on the outskirts of party politics, Gerald Ford did not stop wooing African Americans. Moreover, despite the growing right-wing shift of both Ford and the party more generally, the president actually *increased* his rhetoric of inclusion, ignoring the blatant incongruity of calling for black outreach while engaging in behaviors that alienated African Americans. Among black audiences, he simply avoided the busing issue, concentrating instead on topics like the link between economics and politics. Appearing at the National Baptist Convention in St. Louis, Missouri in October 1975, Ford touted his "Open Door" philosophy and professed an appreciation for quality education for all. As "roaring black applause" and hearty "Amens" punctured his address, he delivered a winding soliloquy on modern black history, tracing the black church's involvement in the civil rights movement, praising the political gains made by African Americans, and reminding the ten thousand black delegates that a Republican president had been at the "forefront" of extending the Voting Rights Act. As John H. Jackson, president of the six-million-member religious convention and a Ford enthusiast watched approvingly, the president assured the crowd that he favored quality education for all.[54]

A month later, however, in a seething *Crisis* editorial, the NAACP shredded Ford's interpretation of quality education, accusing the president of sowing the seeds of racial discord across the country. "He abdicates his role as the nation's leader when he articulates personal positions contrary to the ruling of the courts," the civil rights institution charged, arguing that Ford's public and repeated disagreements with court-ordered busing encouraged the perilous anarchy and violence of white protestors. "He becomes a divisive force when he urges obeying the law on one hand, and on the other declares that the law is all but wrong."[55] Such accusations captured black Republicans' dilemma. The issue was not so much busing as it was the president's dogmatic appeals to contradictory principles because it implied a degree of insincerity, undermining Ford's discussions of "inclusion." To be sure, the disjuncture between his administration's rhetoric and its behavior was disconcerting and would only grow more so over the course of the 1976 campaign.

THE BALANCE OF POWER

The president's Janus-like behavior and intentional obtuseness on issues affecting African Americans certainly emerged at an inopportune moment for black Republicans, who were trumpeting the NBRC and the

Council of 100 as a "potent new force on the American political scene."[56] The same month that black Republicans extracted thousands of dollars from black and white donors at the council's "Foundation to Elect Black Republicans to Congress" soirée, their keynote speaker and moderate icon, Nelson Rockefeller, announced that he would not seek the vice presidential nomination in 1976. Although the vice president insisted that the decision was his and his alone, critics and black Republicans alike declared that this was a move orchestrated by Ford to "divest himself of any remnant of a liberal image" so as to defeat Ronald Reagan, the "darling of the right-wing Republicans" in a bitter primary fight.[57] For black party members, many of whom were moderate Republicans and saw the vice president as a centrist fulcrum in GOP politics, Rockefeller's departure was a monumental setback. Dozens of similar missteps peppered the period, highlighting the contradictions faced by black Republicans during the 1970s. The NBRC, for instance, along with the Council of 100 and BRAC, lauded the December 1975 appointment of John Calhoun, who replaced Stan Scott as the presidential assistant for minority affairs; its celebrations indicated its renewed faith in the White House position as a pipeline for influencing the president on African American issues.[58]

Yet behind the closed doors of the executive office, Calhoun, like Scott, struggled to influence Ford. Within days of being honored by black Republican organizations, a shocked Calhoun pleaded with the administration not to cut funding for OMBE, frantically stating that the $3.2 million in proposed budgetary slashes would have a "disastrous political impact on the communities of Blacks, Hispanics, and other minorities." As the most "popular and visible program started by a Republican Administration geared specifically to minorities," Calhoun cautioned, OMBE was "viewed as the single domestic program positively identified within minority communities as a Republican brainchild." Scuttling the initiative, he told the White House, would be "tantamount to an [admission] of lack of concern and sensitivity and would offset previously made gains in this area among minorities." The administration, he insisted, was viewing the program in the wrong manner: OMBE was not a "handout program but rather an initiative toward self-help and greater participation in the economic system of our Nation."[59]

NCAAR offered identical sentiments in a February 1976 telegram, declaring that OMBE was "urgently needed to foster self-help" among African American businessmen and entrepreneurs. "We intend to fight for an effective OMBE," Curtis Perkins warned, detailing African Americans' contributions to Ford's electoral efforts. "We have tried to keep this in the Republican Family. . . . We are prepared to document" and "bring this into the open."[60] Though OMBE was but one of many black Republican-endorsed programs and policies, it exemplified black Republicans' arguments about the crucial link between politics and economics. The end of OMBE would represent a blow not only to black Republican's economic philosophy but also to their political strategy.

Such was the tenor of the Council of 100's complaints after a campaign strategy briefing session with the White House in December 1975. The organization's harsh denouncement conveyed black Republicans' frustrations over the administration's inconsistent approach to black outreach; African American party members were antagonistic not to Ford's reelection desires but rather to the president's reelection campaign's "gross underinvolvement of black Republican leadership." Political strategy "often necessitates a major focus on winning," the council stated, with controlled anger, but "we reject the view that we can be overlooked at this stage . . . and then be brought in the campaign after the convention largely for window-dressing campaign activities." The council, in no uncertain terms, believed that leaving strategy decisions to white officials would surely result in blacks being ignored.[61]

Eventually, the Council of 100 was successful in proposing an African American outreach program and convincing the administration that "black involvement in the campaign" was a "significant matter."[62] The prospect of retrieving more than 18 percent of the black vote, as North Carolina governor Jim Holshouser had done in 1972, intrigued Ford officials, subsequently encouraging them to launch the "Black Citizens Program" in December 1975. A voluntary initiative, limited in scope, the outreach program relied on the local campaign efforts of black Republican leaders, who in turn, served as "advisors on issues pertinent to [the] black community."[63] The White House also viewed black Republicans' organizational networks as an added boost, believing, as Bo Callaway explained in a confidential memo, that they would ensure that Ford had "good Blacks" on his side during the president's anticipated bitter primary battle with Ronald Reagan.[64] But with a staff of two unpaid black Republicans, a restricted nine-month budget of $60,000, and an emphasis on "public relations" displays instead of meaningful ideas, the Black Citizens Program was limited in impact, at best.[65] Although it secured financial and moral support from prominent black party members like Bill Coleman, the outreach initiative nevertheless struggled to become viable.[66] In one instance, two months after launching, the program coordinator reported registering three thousand new black Republicans, despite being hampered by severe financial constraints, "Expenses were less," Larnie Horton wrote, explaining his political survival, solely because "Black Republicans housed and fed us in their homes."[67]

In spite of their frustrations with the party, rank-and-file black party members offered PFC a steady stream of such support. They also swamped the campaign with suggestions on black outreach between 1975 and into 1976. Some, like John Keenan of Washington, D.C., even sent sample speeches for Gerald Ford's use, drawing heavily on the words and concerns of moderate black Republicans.[68] Imploring the president to accept their offers of help, African Americans proposed that Ford speak to black churches, businesses, neighborhood groups, fraternal councils, youth organizations, and labor unions.[69] Lowell Perry urged PFC to stress black family values, arguing for the "importance of the family" as a means of promoting Ford's candidacy among African American communities; the newly minted EEOC chair also prodded the administration to woo black women aggressively, erroneously believing that they would "come out front as Republicans before Black men" and would provide "substantially more support for the President."[70]

PFC ignored most, if not all of these suggestions, consistently fumbling black outreach, despite steady interest from African American constituents, employing a campaign philosophy of indifference—a strategy that most reporters would later categorize as a new form of "benign neglect."[71] Documenting the activities of "special voter groups" in an early spring 1976 memo, Bob Marik offered few specifics on black voter outreach, omitting the efforts of the Black Citizens Program. Still, he reassured officials that something "should be in place within two weeks."[72] A few weeks later, campaign officials complained about repeated inquiries from black Republican groups and leaders, including the president of the California chapter of the NBRC. "Obviously he feels we should have a Black Program in the works," one woman grumbled in a memo to PFC leaders. "I have not told him we do not."[73]

This kind of treatment clearly had an effect on African American constituents, some of whom were "turned off because of the lack of overt efforts to get their vote," as a dejected John Calhoun explained after returning from a spring recruiting trip in Kentucky. In Michigan, his efforts to motivate black Republicans were met with mixed success. After one session, for instance, a black businessman was inspired to rent several vans, decorate them for Gerald Ford, and take "groups of mini-skirted Black girls and music into Black neighborhoods to pass out literature to generate support for the President." Far more common was the "great deal of ambivalence" that Calhoun discovered among the state's black Republicans "who felt that they were being ignored by the PFC."[74]

To be sure, Republicans sought African American voters, but they wanted to secure this support without exerting meaningful effort or enacting any significant policy changes.[75] Nathan Wright said as much in a February 1976 editorial for the *Call and Post*. The party would never concede influence voluntarily, the black Republican argued, nor would it allow African Americans to assume a "powerful place overnight." The "sad fact has been," Wright mused, that the Republican Party, "for nearly several generations now, has been largely more shadow than substance." Yet black Republicans' cause was not without hope, Wright concluded. To the contrary, the presence of an "understandably angry" NBRC was a move in the right direction, one that could force the party to incorporate African American demands. Anger and frustration, therefore, were positive emotions here, as they had the potential to help launch meaningful intraparty reform as opposed to despair and despondency, which would only weaken black Republicans' offensive.[76]

NBRC leaders' lukewarm response to Ford during the primary season offers a particularly illustrative example of the "benefits" of anger. Some initially offered mild to lukewarm enthusiasm for the president, incensed by his erratic behavior, while others elected to support Ronald Reagan's presidential ambitions. The western regional branch of the organization declined to endorse any candidate, stating its members' preference for dealing with the "issues." Likewise, after a "heated discussion" in February 1976, nearly a quarter of the executive board of the Florida NBRC chapter voted to endorse the California politician.[77] Although many of the more conservative members of the black umbrella organization preferred Reagan to Ford, their liberal and moderate black peers rejected the official's extremist following and claimed to abhor his right-wing philosophy; nevertheless, they occasionally endorsed the governor as a strategic measure, designed to publicize their dissatisfaction with Gerald Ford and his public relations approach to African Americans. In a manner of speaking, this was a warning—a political threat to compel the president to listen to black Republicans, lest they cast their lot with his aggressive and unyielding primary opponent.

Black coverage of Republican politics adopted an increasingly "gloomy" tone in 1976, lamenting the unlikelihood of African American members of the GOP gaining greater influence. Writers at the *Pittsburgh Courier* sneered in April 1976 at the "unwanted morsels" tossed to African American party members in the "spirit of benign charity." Black "voices in the high council of the party," the *Courier* coldly asserted, "are unimportant and if heard, they bear no useful repercussion." That Ford would pay only token attention to black outreach was to be expected, the president's critics argued, since the administration had pledged to avoid making "special" promises to racial interest groups.[78] Still, black Republicans publicly disputed such accounts, insisting with false bravado that they were "more spirited, more rejuvenated and more in numbers than ever before." Although they constituted fewer than 4 percent of the nation's black elected officials, NBRC officials dismissed such statistics as "superficial," reasoning that "you can't measure spirit by a computer."[79]

But in closed and private meetings, black Republicans often expressed the same emotions as those captured in black newspapers' pained accounts of GOP affairs—a not always successful struggle to balance optimism for the future with the reality of the present. Corresponding with John Calhoun, one black PFC volunteer expressed "grave concerns" about the impact of the campaign's attitude of indifference. "I have sincerely tried to do what I could to aid my party with black" voters, the black Republican despaired. "But it gets frustrating for we do not get any help from [the] TOP. . . . We have many blacks [who] would enlist in [the] party now, but they cannot see . . . anything being done for blacks already involved in the party."[80]

Such was the topic broached by Ed Brooke during a spring speech to the western region of the NBRC. The Massachusetts senator revived 250 melancholy black Republicans with a much-needed "shot in the arm," reminding the group of the significance of African Americans to national politics. A boisterous cheer erupted when Brooke mentioned a spring 1976 poll by the Joint Center for Political Studies that documented an uptick in the number of African Americans identifying as Republicans and independents. "Go out there and get that 35 percent uncommitted to join our party," he shouted to the excited NBRC members. "We have a golden opportunity. . . . But we must insist that our party speak to the needs of Black people. They want results." Brooke likely knew that the statistical increase was misleading, since even those African Americans who identified as Republican were just as likely to vote for a Democrat or abstain from voting altogether; nevertheless, the idea that black independents could swing to the Republican Party was enough to bring a measure of hope to black Republicans in these gloomy days. Closing out the session, NBRC chair Henry Lucas offered perhaps a more genuine feeling of cynicism toward party politics, charging members to go forth and make their "presence felt in the political arena in 1976. We either participate in the government or we become victims of government."[81]

The western symposium was but one of several NBRC regional events held over the spring and summer of 1976, as the organization attempted to soothe black Republicans' apprehensions and bolster African American intraparty solidarity in the months leading to the group's first national convention. "Until this time Black Republicans didn't have leverage, on all party levels, to make the impact that would attract more Blacks into the party fold," NBRC executive director John Wilks declared, in a press conference in the days preceding the organization's convention. "This is no longer true."[82] Indeed, leverage was the strategy of the hour at the national conference, a "grueling" two-day session, held immediately prior to the August 1976 Republican National Convention. "From Douglass to Brooke," was the theme of the black parlay, with the NBRC envisioning the Massachusetts senator as the faithful political descendant of the nineteenth-century icon. Attendees participated in workshops on coalition politics, economic development, and employment; they also met with RNC chair Mary Louise Smith and other mainstream party officials to discuss their role in party hierarchies.[83] The conference was of tremendous importance to black Republicans, hundreds of whom traveled from twenty-five states to Kansas City, Missouri, to "solidify black Republican power" and strategize about how best to influence the GOP platform.[84]

Yet the NBRC conference made headlines not for its power-grabbing unity strategies but rather for the "knock-down, drag out" fights that peppered the political sessions. Reporting on the confab, writers for *Jet* and the *New York Times* were scandalized by "shouting matches" and the regular appearance of security guards, summoned to maintain order among the 350 rowdy delegates.[85] The "quiet-surfaced ranks of black Republicanism have shown a few noisy spots of late," one reporter remarked, "suggesting a possibly deeply ingrained unhappiness inside."[86] Although the participants reached a consensus on the importance of economic uplift, all other topics were up for vigorous debate.[87] The organization's first national election was particularly contentious as six African Americans lobbied ferociously for the chairmanship. Members discarded the NBRC's mantra of power through solidarity, as conference delegates demanded the ousting of the "old guard," calling for new leaders that were "creative" and "aggressive." Delegates from the Council of 100 also jumped into the fray, forming an alliance to ensure the victory of James Cummings of Indiana. The organization's battle was reminiscent of the NNRA's political brawl from a decade earlier, and like that skirmish, this was rooted in demands for power; yet unlike the 1966 moment, the NBRC's melee transcended ideological differences as each side drew support from various conservative, liberal, and moderate factions.

African American party members were rightfully frustrated about their political struggles, but during the elections they hurled accusations at everyone but white Republicans, even blaming professional athletes and celebrities for institutional failures.[88] Underneath their scattershot accusations, black Republicans feared a loss of control over their own organization, as they believed that African American party elites were susceptible to white Republican influence. In spite of their willingness to work with mainstream party institutions, many African Americans still resented the input of white Republicans, seeing it as a form of inappropriate authority.

Furthermore, it constrained autonomy; thus, white influence over black Republican matters was the antithesis of African American party members' objectives because it created boundaries over black political influence and power. This was especially true of the NBRC, as several of its executive positions were appointed by the RNC. "It is deeply disturbing that we cannot . . . elect our own leaders; they too often are chosen by whites," Jackson Champion observed. "This represents at this point in our time the very thing we seek to overcome, for it reflects that we are still captive of the white power structure, and 'awarded' recognition not by our own criteria but the criteria of this power structure."[89]

That delegates were able to forge a position paper from the divided remnants of the conference was a testament to the NBRC's stubborn commitment to advancing a unified voice, despite the utter lack of unity at the conference. The organization's platform was significant, for it was the first time that the organization produced a consensus document advancing the social and economic positions of African Americans in the Republican Party. The resolutions attended to the compelling needs of African Americans, albeit from a distinctly Republican perspective, declaring, for example, that the nation was "built not by government but by the people, not [by] welfare but by work, not by shrinking responsibility but by seeking responsibility." Yet while the NBRC argued that welfare exploited "human dignity" by subjecting citizens to the "demeaning effects of public handouts," the black organization still emphasized the GOP's duty to protect Americans from the "degradation of poverty" via work incentives, income maintenance, and wage supplementation. The goal, the NBRC argued, was to make self-help possible by way of "people power." As was the case with nearly every black Republican initiative, economic issues composed the substance of this revised social safety net; or, as the NBRC insisted, every citizen should have the chance to "achieve independence, respect . . . and personal dignity through the ability to get a job irrespective of race." Likewise, although black Republicans pressured private companies to address minority employment, they also concurrently advocated for a federal policy of full employment—in effect, a compromise between the opposing positions articulated by Edward Brooke and Bill Coleman in July 1975.

According to the NBRC, economic opportunity was also connected to health and housing policies; thus the organization urged support for a comprehensive national health care plan, pushed support for stronger federal enforcement of fair and open housing laws, called for federal rent and housing subsidies for the working poor, and proposed tax breaks to stimulate private development to revitalize low-income urban areas. When coupled with the enforcement of affirmative action in public and private industries, the NBRC asserted, such solutions would enable the realization of a truly "equitable society."[90] Black Republicans drew connections between health and housing and economic opportunity, believing that in order for African Americans to work and participate as *producers* in a free market economy, the playing field needed to be leveled, which meant preventing sickness, ensuring affordable homes, and eradicating institutional bias through the enforcement of existing federal and state laws.

As a consensus document, the NBRC's position paper concisely summarized the beliefs of its members but also highlighted the dilemma in balancing the conflicting perspectives of all black Republicans. For example, Henry Lucas, the group's chairman, articulated a forceful opposition to social welfare, minimum wage laws, full employment, and government intervention in housing and education. "Yes, I am conservative," Lucas once remarked, "probably more conservative than most white conservatives." Other officials, like Jackson R. Champion, adopted a more moderate stance; assisting African Americans through targeted federal intervention, he argued, should be the objectives of "liberal and conservative alike"; at the same time, he also concluded that aid was a temporary "springboard" for racial uplift, likening social welfare to a dangerous "control device" employed by the government to smother black ambition. The NBRC had to square these perspectives with the far more liberal positions of figures like Sam Jackson and Ed Brooke, who supported federal intervention in areas *beyond* economic enterprise.[91]

This tension was glaringly evident in the NBRC's education plank. Rather than denouncing a constitutional antibusing amendment, the organization adopted a weaker approach, affirming its support for the principles of desegregation and carving out a middle-of-the-road position between liberal and conservative arguments on busing. Behind closed doors, some black Republicans even attempted to solve the busing crisis by exploring alternate desegregation methods, without relying on the alienating rhetoric of white leaders. In the spring of 1976, for instance, NBRC executive and RNC consultant Arthur Fletcher suggested a "low profile project" to investigate the "thinking of black leaders on the matter of goals in secondary education" and the "means for achieving them without the emotional reliance on the technique of busing."[92] The NBRC's position paper offered a similar prescriptive, calling on the GOP to deemphasize busing and focus on original solutions that supported equal educational opportunity and freedom of choice. A "national program of open enrollment" by way of a reorganization of the nation's "tax allocation" was the fairest way to assure a constitutional right to equal education, the group argued. Taking pains to emphasize that the GOP had a moral responsibility to aid minorities, especially the poorest and most vulnerable of African Americans, the NBRC consequently called for a federal increase in early childhood education programs, vocational training opportunities, and compensatory programs and an increase in financial assistance for minority students from poor and working-class families.[93]

As delegates and alternates of all races gathered for the 1976 Republican National Convention, held three days after the NBRC conference, black Republicans struggled with how best to leverage their vote. In an August 1976 editorial, Eddie Williams of the Joint Center for Political Studies suggested that, despite their small cohort, black Republicans had a rare political opportunity to act on a "balance of power" theory and affect genuine change at the convention. Though the percentage of African American representatives to the 1976 gathering had declined from four years prior, the actual number of black delegates and alternates increased by ten, bringing African American participants to 150—the highest tally the party had seen in more than sixty years. More than half of these representatives were uncommitted to a presidential nominee, meaning that black Republicans could engage in political maneuvering, withholding their votes in order to compel the candidates and the party to address black concerns.[94] Oregon delegate Brenda Plummer suggested exactly that during a convention meeting with black Republicans, as did Henry Lucas in a controversial NBRC letter. "Those blacks who do not serve black folks' interests must be 'excused' from party appointments," the NBRC chair declared "and those candidates who do not address themselves to our needs must not receive the black Republicans' support."[95] But the decision to leverage their vote was not an easy one. On the one hand, threatening to support Ronald Reagan could be used to demand concessions from the party on major issues like affirmative action, equal employment, and busing; on the other hand, black delegates viewed Gerald Ford as the more moderate candidate on racial issues and therefore the more logical choice, despite their frustrations with the president.

Interestingly, both Ronald Reagan and Gerald Ford were aware of the power of black delegates, recognizing that a small number of uncommitted representatives could swing the presidential nomination to either candidate. Here, Reagan was far more persistent than Ford, according to some black delegates and alternates. Before the GOP convention, the California governor phoned a number of black representatives to discuss their concerns; likewise, during the convention, in a closed session with black Republicans, he vowed to "uphold civil rights programs even at the 'point of a bayonet.'"[96] In yet another meeting, Reagan's vice presidential running mate, Richard Schweiker, discussed his liberal positions with black delegates, promising to "look after black needs." As the Pennsylvania senator nervously flipped through dozens of note cards, he remarked on the powerful role African Americans could play at the convention in determining the future direction of the GOP.[97] At least one black delegate found the politician's presence on the Reagan ticket reassuring: Gloria Toote argued that Reagan's vice presidential selection was a "bold effort to assure the poor and minorities that the Reagan administration would have sensitive leadership on issues with impact upon minorities, and the poor."[98]

Gerald Ford also met with black delegates, but in contrast to Reagan, he evaded discussion about the actions of his administration, insisting that no civil rights questions be posed—a demand that black Republicans angrily condemned as the administration's "muzzling" policy. Calls for the president to incorporate the NBRC's resolutions into the party's 1976 platform were ignored, as were efforts to press Ford to select Edward Brooke as his vice presidential running mate (though the president had considered it privately on more than one occasion).[99] Miffed, black delegates announced that Ford was placating them with meaningless platitudes, lest he offend white conservative delegates. While their suspicions were accurate, the president also avoided serious engagement with the black delegates and alternates because he believed that they had no choice but to vote for him, given Ronald Reagan's conservative reputation and record on matters of civil rights.

Pondering their position, African American delegates wondered if they had enough power to force Ford to incorporate their demands and agendas. They contemplated walking out of the convention, disappearing during delegate roll call—anything to "wreak havoc" on the voting process and make "black votes . . . the deciding or decisive votes for the Republican presidential nominee."[100] However, as Eddie Williams of the JCPS cautioned, engaging in such political games could have disastrous outcomes for the would-be group of black political strategists. Williams predicted a convention meltdown of black participants, all of whom were unaccustomed to "finding themselves in a position where they could, in fact, hold the balance of power"; because of their novice status, he concluded, black delegates were arguably not ready to "seize" their opportunity.[101]

In truth, black delegates' attempts at leveraging their votes to demand concessions from Gerald Ford and the Republican Party were scattered and bitterly divided. After receiving a copy of the Lucas note urging delegates to support Reagan as a strategic move to force concessions from Ford, some black party members strenuously objected. "Everyone's playing games here," complained one. "Black folks are being led up and down these aisles without knowing why, by whom and what for." Negotiations took their toll on black delegates, exposing their "uneasiness" at leveraging their vote.[102] In a moment of confusion, for example, a Chicago delegate falsely accused a black Reagan supporter of bribing her to switch her vote to the California politician.[103] Moreover, many of the delegates were paralyzed by their fear—should Ford get the presidential nomination without their assistance, for instance, black Republicans feared that the president would dismiss their concerns altogether. A Reagan nomination, meanwhile, might bring concessions but would place the GOP in the "hands of the crazies" from the extremist wing of the party.[104] Undoubtedly, many black Republicans simply could not bring themselves to support Reagan as the party's nominee, likening his chances to the 1964 Goldwater. "Sell Reagan to other black folk? Hell, man, I haven't been able to sell him to me yet," one black delegate laughed when questioned by the *Chicago Tribune*. For some black Republicans, their disagreement was slightly more complex; for example, in a letter to Reagan, Maurice Dawkins argued that the party needed to develop a strategy that merged economic conservatism with a "positive policy on equal opportunities for minorities. Noting that he agreed with Reagan's distaste for the "left-wing thrust" of the Democratic Party, Dawkins nevertheless concluded that he could not support the California governor. "I agree with your diagnosis of the problems and disagree with your prescription for a cure," he wrote.[105] Thus, a meaningful mutiny among African Americans at the 1976 GOP convention never materialized, as black delegates largely resigned themselves to voting for Gerald Ford, despite his weak support of African American issues. "President Ford," one weary delegate explained, "is the least of the two evils."[106]

A few bucked the trend, casting votes for Ronald Reagan. Among them was Gloria Toote, who notably offered the seconding speech for Reagan's nomination, at the California governor's request, making a very unlikely pair alongside North Carolina Senator Jesse Helms. "Without the influence and prestige of the White House," Toote stated in her nationally televised speech, Reagan "was capable of fashioning a philosophy and scope of appeal the Republican party has never known before. . . . Of all our national political figures, only one—Ronald Reagan—dealt with issues and action rather than rhetoric."[107] As one of the more liberal delegates, Toote's support of Reagan came as somewhat of a shock to black political observers, including editors at the *New York Amsterdam News*, who struggled to reconcile the well-known Harlem lawyer's support for court-ordered busing with her endorsement of a candidate whose antibusing position was even more extreme than that of the president. After all, this was the same politician who, as the conservative *National Review* put it, espoused a more polished version of Goldwater conservatism: "strong defense, resistance to Communism abroad, limited government at home, and rejection of moral permissiveness." Nevertheless, in an interview with the *New York Amsterdam News*, Toote explained that she had voted for a Reagan nomination because she "abhorred President Ford taking my vote for granted." In short, Reagan had demonstrated an interest in black Republicans' ideas, whereas Ford had merely ignored them.[108]

Unable to leverage concessions from the president, black Republicans were devastated when they viewed the party's final platform, which omitted nearly all of their suggestions, starkly clarifying the limitations of African Americans' intraparty influence. "I disagree with all of it," Ed Brooke seethed. "I hope President Ford does not run on this platform with such stands on every issue." While many of the planks in the final platform were of concern, black Republicans were especially perturbed by the busing resolution; Republicans not only declared their opposition to "forced busing to achieve racial balances" in schools but also maintained support for a constitutional amendment "forbidding the assignment of children to schools on the basis of race."[109] In spite of her endorsement of Ronald Reagan—whose supporters had a heavy hand in drafting the party platform—Gloria Toote also condemned the education resolution, deploring it as "unnecessary and bound to hurt the party among Blacks in November."

In fact, the only black Republicans that appeared satisfied with the busing plank were the national leaders of the BSMC, who echoed the GOP's call for a constitutional amendment. Busing, declared Clay Claiborne, was the "most open and obvious cause of black-white tension that the nation has seen since the urban riots of the 1960s." Support for busing was both dangerous and misguided, stated BSMC official Walter Robinson, because advocates of the policy "mistakenly equate quality education for blacks with forced busing."[110] In contrast, the Council of 100 vowed to fight the prevention of an antibusing amendment, while other black Republicans simply despaired, as was the case with Sinita Walker of New York, who glumly stated that she was "uncomfortable and a little disturbed" by her party's positions.[111] The harshest criticism came from W. O. Walker, the publisher of the *Call and Post*, in the form of a fire-and-brimstone editorial denouncing the GOP platform and those who supported it. "They wrap themselves (klan like) in the United States flag to hide their disdain for the freedom our government supposedly stands for," he bemoaned. And though he berated Gerald Ford for failing to speak out on racial issues, Walker's fiercest attack was reserved for those white conservative delegates pursued by Ford throughout the convention: they "are either Republicans who still live in the nineteenth century, or are potential fascists who embody all the racism of Hitler."[112]

Black Republicans left the national convention, as *Jet* noted, in a daze, "still trying to figure out how Black delegates, with the greatest strength on the floor in history, couldn't even get President Ford to issue one civil rights statement."[113] Black delegates had worked to the best of their abilities, argued John Wilks of the NBRC, while others insisted that by standing behind Ford, they had demonstrated their loyalty by helping the president win a bitter convention battle. "[If] we are going to have our presence felt and get our piece of the pie," one black delegate suggested, justifying his support for Ford, "some of us must be wherever power is being distributed."[114] Yet the pained faces and voices of black Republicans in 1976 left little question as to how they felt about the outcome of the convention, as African American party leaders conceded that both the president and the GOP appeared to be moving to the right—a weighty observation, given that many of the black delegates were shifting rightward as well. Likewise, several black party members complained that the black delegates could have "stood up" and "damn near deadlocked the convention." In 1976, "as in 1865," one representative bitterly remarked, "the Black delegates this year bowed their heads and begged the Lord to help Massa' Ford get back in the big house."[115]

To put it simply, accused Vernon Jarrett in a postconvention column for the *Chicago Tribune*, black Republicans had blown their opportunity to "make political history."[116] But from the start, *there was no opportunity to make political history.* The "balance of power" theory was deeply flawed: in order for black delegates to seize power, white Republicans first had to be willing to acknowledge and act on African Americans' demands. When they presented their agenda, only Reagan had entertained their ideas, since Ford considered the group an already-captured faction. Similarly, the president feared that by seriously engaging black delegates on racial issues, he would lose support from white delegates. For the balance-of-power theory to work in practice, black Republicans would not only have needed to support Ronald Reagan en masse (a bold but risky move), but also both he and Gerald Ford would have needed to be willing to act on what were largely rhetorical promises.

FORGOTTEN BLACK REPUBLICANS

Maintaining their organizational base in the face of failure was not impossible for black Republican groups—if anything, it strengthened their outward resolve. However, as the national convention fiasco faded, black Republican solidarity was tested from within as black Republicans sued each other for control of their organizations. In the fall of 1976, NBRC treasurer Ed Bivens, alongside three other black Republican officials, sued the umbrella group and the national committee in *Bivens v. Republican National Committee*, in an attempt to dethrone the organization's newly elected leaders.[117] The Michigan Republican, along with three other NBRC officials, accused the black organization and the RNC of violating their civil rights. "Unless restrained and enjoined" through legal means, the disgruntled Republicans warned, the RNC would "continue to control NBRC, its officers and programs."

In court affidavits, NBRC and RNC executives testified that such charges were baseless, describing the consensus group as an "independent political association" over which the national committee had no control. In spite of these claims, clearly the RNC did have some measure of influence over the NBRC, since the national committee controlled the black organization's budget, staffing, office space, and other operating logistics—in fact, two years earlier, NBRC officials had complained about the tight purse strings of the RNC limiting their organizational effectiveness. Likewise, because of its relationship with the national committee, the group was constrained in its actions: in other words, the organization could do only as much as the RNC chair was willing to allow.[118] Though the courts quickly dismissed the lawsuit, Bivens's accusations illustrate the seriousness with which black Republicans viewed the NBRC, competing viciously over their organization because the stakes were so high: controlling the eight-thousand-member organization and serving as the official mouthpiece for black Republican power. The intensity of the fight over the leadership of the NBRC also indicates that black Republicans understood that they were failing to achieve their objectives.

By the summer and fall of 1976, the black organization had not seen any increase in meaningful African American outreach, nor had it witnessed an increase in black elected officials, despite the growing coffers of the Council of 100. Just as important, while the mainstream GOP and the president had shifted their rhetoric to become more inclusive, their actions demonstrated that the party was not fully committed to racial inclusivity, at least not in any meaningful way.[119] Along similar lines, black PFC volunteers were devastated by the campaign's lack of interest in black outreach and local black Republican candidates, recognizing that financial and moral support from the national GOP was critical to the success of local black Republican campaigns. In a private memo from July 1976, California NBRC official Bob Keyes lobbied PFC on behalf of black candidates in Chicago, urging the national campaign to donate maximum financial and moral assistance as part of a "larger strategy to give Blacks an alternative." It was important that the candidates be progressive, Keyes argued, so as to attract black voters; they should also be well financed by white Republicans, so as to attract maximum publicity for the GOP. Even if the candidates lost, he continued, their presence would be a boon to the party, playing a "key role in neutralizing some of the Black votes that would go Democratic without any GOP effort." Ford needed black Republicans, Keyes calculated, because their existence conveyed the belief—whether real or imagined—that the president cared about the black vote. "It is not that the Democrats are invincible," he insisted. "It is that the Republicans are seemingly unwilling to challenge the Democrats with an effective Black campaign."[120]

As we have seen, this "neutralizing" strategy was not a new approach; in their efforts to gain and retain power and influence in party circles, black Republicans sometimes made troublesome political concessions to advance their respective causes. In 1964 Clay Claiborne focused on neutralizing as many black voters as possible, while working as a consultant for Barry Goldwater's presidential campaign; likewise, in the early 1970s Richard Nixon's black campaign strategists concentrated their public relations effort on the black middle class, seeing this as a means of nullifying the impact of poor and working-class African American voters, almost all of whom were Democrats. Keyes's strategy in 1976, however, was distinct from both of these approaches, as he counted on the mutual self-serving interests of black and white party leaders. In short, African Americans wanted financial support and publicity to help their chosen black candidates win, whereas white officials wanted to win converts *and* neutralize the black vote, without appealing to racism.

It was this kind of strategy that informed black Republicans' maneuverings throughout the fall campaign season. To these ends, both the Council of 100 and the NBRC resolved to influence the direction of PFC, lobbying for aggressive involvement in Ford's presidential campaign. "The small efforts that have been made to gain Black votes have lacked planning, organization, and finance," observed the NBRC in one of its many proposals. "Such efforts have been made through selected individuals—often lacking even adequate contact with, and support in, the Black community—who were capable of implementing little more than a token program with the funds, personnel and facilities made available to them."[121] The organization requested more than $250,000 to fund a black recruitment campaign on behalf of the president, which would have included the "Winning Edge '76," a fundraising weekend designed to link the president to a dozen NBRC-approved black candidates for elected office.[122] Arguably the most controversial of the NBRC's proposals was a series of debates on African American issues, scheduled for the fall of 1976. Aimed at black audiences, the contests would have pitted NBRC officials against members of the Congressional Black Caucus, squaring off on the civil rights records of the presidential nominees. Reiterating Bob Keyes's black outreach strategy, the NBRC argued that such events would convince African Americans of Ford's "sensitivity and concern" or "at least neutralize their political activity."[123]

Notwithstanding an interest in neutralizing black voters, PFC largely rejected the support of the NBRC. It appears that only one of the organization's programs took place: a meeting between party legislators and eight black congressional hopefuls, supported by a donation of $1,500 by the Republican Congressional Committee.[124] Publicly, PFC lamented that it was "virtually impossible for us to do anything" about the NBRC's proposals; privately, both the campaign and the White House colluded to ignore the black organization, electing to work with disparate state and local black Republican affiliates.[125] Members of the NBRC still found avenues through which to participate in the Ford campaign, including serving on the voluntary black outreach steering committee. In the months leading to the presidential election, an influx of NBRC officials joined the Black Citizens Program, which eventually became PFC's "Black Desk." Loosely imitating, perhaps purposefully, the structure of the NBRC, the Black Desk was composed of five regional chairmen and a twenty-two-member steering committee, nearly all of whom were members of the NBRC or the Council of 100.[126]

Bob Keyes ran the desk—a former professional football player and special assistant in Reagan's gubernatorial administration, the NBRC executive had supported Ford since the early days of the campaign. The Black Desk, or as Keyes called it, the "affirmative action arm of People for Ford," shared identical objectives to the NBRC and estimated that, with black Republicans' cooperation, Ford had the potential to win from 16 to 50 percent of the black vote, a startling estimate.[127] Black Desk volunteers justified these figures by alluding to private conversations with black Democrats, who pointed to the "erosion and disenchantment" of black voters with the Democratic Party. Black Republican officials also highlighted the presence of the ever-expanding black middle class who, although registered Democrats, were increasingly identifying as independents. "They are employed and concerned about the high cost of living, the manner in which their tax dollars are being used, the eroding conditions of the inner cities, neighborhood crime, the ineffectiveness of our local schools to adequately prepare their children to compete," mused Black Desk operative Martin Dinkins in September 1976. "In essence they are fed up of reams of promises and very little performances." Still, in spite of his overly optimistic projections, Dinkins conceded that the GOP would not get black votes "by default." Instead, he worried, "without resorting to ethnic designation, Blacks must be invited to participate in all areas and aspects" of Republican political life. Dinkins's words highlighted a crucial paradox for black Republican strategists in the mid-1970s: how could the GOP make explicit appeals to African Americans *without* emphasizing race? Black party leaders wrestled with adopting a "race-neutral" or colorblind approach to outreach, particularly since racial equality was an ideal that still did not exist. They decided to emphasize class-based economic solutions. Undoubtedly, this was an ironic decision: the desk called itself the affirmative action arm, when in fact it tried to find ways to remove race from the campaign.[128]

Working with a limited three-month budget of $70,000, the Black Desk brought the creativity of the NBRC into Ford campaign headquarters, forming an auxiliary "blue ribbon" committee of celebrities, businesspeople, athletes, and prominent black party leaders, holding a White House conference on black concerns, and launching a minority voter information initiative and a black Republican advocate program.[129] Yet, as with its immediate campaign predecessor, the Black Desk was plagued by an abundance of financial, logistical, and organizational problems. Within weeks of assuming control of the desk, Keyes complained of "serious staffing problems" and financial woes, a problem that PFC campaign leaders acknowledged, writing, "We cannot give them any big sum of money although it might be possible to raise some outside money—and create a better climate."[130] In local and state sessions, black Republican volunteers were eager to show their loyalty but were also emphatic about their need to receive "appropriate literature, sample ballots and money, money, money." But as with the NBRC, the Ford campaign ignored many of the Black Desk's proposals. When PFC did approve black-related events for the president, the functions were slapdash affairs, chiefly designed to publicize Ford's alleged interest in issues of concern to African Americans. In Missouri, for example, four young, prominent black ministers, all newly converted Republicans, repeatedly expressed an interest in campaigning for Ford in black communities—a request that was ignored despite the pleas of the Black Desk. The extent of Ford's involvement with the ministers was a brief photo-op during a short campaign stopover in St. Louis. Likewise, as presidential challenger Jimmy Carter was campaigning in Harlem and the Bronx, frustrated Black Desk volunteers were begging the president to "at least drive through selected Black areas" in various states. One of the more embarrassing moments came in October 1976, when PFC bungled a Michigan advocate event with Bill Coleman. As a high-ranking official, popular among African American party members, his presence should have been a rallying call for the state's black Republicans; in fact, Michigan was home to one of the largest NBRC chapters, with more than two hundred members. But only four people came to the event—all of them staunch Democrats. Mortified, the Black Desk attributed the disaster to a "miscommunication" with the state's PFC volunteers: in their haste to assemble the program, the white organizers astonishingly failed to advertise the event to the state's black Republicans.[131]

Rank-and-file black Republicans swamped the Black Desk with complaints, accusing the black volunteers of incompetence. The problem, William Seawright of Cleveland wrote, was that the black Republicans heading the campaign were "unknown" and thus untrustworthy to African Americans.[132] Though Seawright's claims had a degree of merit, the Black Desk's problems were bigger than authenticity challenges. Reports from the desk offered a picture of a group in disarray, with city and state affiliates lacking in funding and organization, segregated from the mainstream campaign's activities. In a fall 1976 memo, for instance, Marty Dinkins complained that in several regions, ranking PFC officials had forgotten to notify black state managers of significant appointments.[133] In other areas, Black Desk affiliates were "treated coolly and turned off" by PFC officials. When questioned, one of the white coordinators offered a troubling explanation for his actions: he had assumed that the volunteers were seeking payment and would eventually move on to the Democratic Party fold *because they were black*. All of the African American state and regional groups complained of nonexistent resources, as was the case in Chicago when black Republicans concluded that their financial woes would render outreach ineffective. Instead of campaigning, they adopted a strategy of doing "nothing to increase Carter's Black Vote support," in the hopes of harnessing black voter apathy.[134]

By October 1976, Ford was no longer a refreshing presence in the GOP, as his supporters had once described him; instead, his critics charged, he was an "anti-Black, anti-people" president. Nevertheless, black Republican elites continued to champion Ford's cause, despite their frustrations and private beliefs. For example, appearing on an October *PBS* panel on African Americans and the 1976 election, alongside former Nixon aide Bob Brown and Reagan supporter Stephanie Lee-Miller of California, presidential assistant John Calhoun defended the party's rhetoric on busing, arguing that the policy of busing was "ridiculous," akin to saying "Black [is] bad" by insinuating that African Americans were "incapable of doing or learning by ourselves." Though he stopped short of advocating for a constitutional ban on busing, Calhoun sounded not unlike the national leaders of the BSMC; and while far from militant, he also used rhetoric that was similar to the language espoused by Black Nationalist groups opposed to busing.[135]

In contrast, speaking as advocates for the administration at separate events in October, both the NBRC and Arthur Fletcher consistently repeated black Republicans' mantra of pragmatic politics and two-party competition. The black organization and the prominent official both placed the onus on African Americans, insisting, as NBRC official Willie Williams did, that "blacks must begin to vote for people who can best serve their needs rather than voting emotionally." In his speeches Fletcher also adopted an additional tactic: urging African Americans to support the president and black GOP congressional candidates, he exclusively emphasized black Republicans' support for *progressive* federal legislation, including the Voting Rights Act and Equal Employment rights. "If there is any one priority we Blacks have," Fletcher told multiple audiences in 1976, it "is to prepare to take and play our rightful role in the political arena."[136]

Such perspectives captured the contradictions faced by black Republican leaders, who had few choices in the 1976 election. "Black Republicans going to the Ford-Dole cupboard find it bare of even bone chips insofar as their interests are concerned," argued journalist Ethel Payne, who noted incredulously that there was still a sizable "amount of loyalty among this small . . . band." In a sense, some black party leaders felt trapped; to vote for the Democratic nominee was out of the question, as they viewed Jimmy Carter as a racist snake-oil salesman. Thus they remained loyal to the president with the hopes that he would incorporate African American concerns into his agenda if he retained the White House in November. Moreover, there were some black Republicans, as Payne also observed, "who pride themselves on their conservatism, and are therefore, quite comfortable in the Republican Party." They too were bound by the GOP, sharing the same outlook as the mainstream party; and yet, to African American party members' frustration, the party's conservatism no longer seemed to have room for them.[137]

On November 2, 1976, just four years after Richard Nixon's "New Majority" landslide, Jimmy Carter bested Gerald Ford in the presidential contest, a loss that was keenly felt by Republican leaders. Slightly more than half of the nation's voters cast ballots for the Georgia Democrat—a tight race to be sure, but not close enough to secure a victory for the presidential incumbent. "Gone is the dream of 'realignment,'" wrote reporter Jack Bass, as he surveyed the casualties of the 1976 elections. Nearly 30 percent of voters who had endorsed Nixon in 1972 voted for Carter four years later; similarly, the president-elect edged out Ford among nearly every constituency, reestablishing the New Deal political coalitions of years past: liberals and moderates; labor and blue-collar workers; Catholic and Jewish voters; urban and suburban constituents; and racial and ethnic minorities. The election also erased Nixon's gains in the South; although 55 percent of white southern voters supported Ford in 1976, he nevertheless won only one southern state—Virginia. In fact, the Michigan Republican tallied clear majorities from only a narrow section of the national electorate: conservatives, wealthy citizens, elderly constituents, and voters from rural areas.[138]

Ford's defeat was not his alone. Between 1974 and 1976, the GOP collectively lost more than 40 percent of its representatives in state legislatures and more than 20 percent of its southern seats in the House and Senate. The press attributed the GOP's poor performance in the November elections to a handful of weighty problems that had gnawed away at the party since Nixon first uttered the words, "I am not a crook." Gerald Ford's decision to pardon the disgraced former president; the public's disillusionment with the executive office and Congress; a lingering economic recession coupled with high unemployment; dissatisfaction with the "extremist conservative elements" within the Republican Party—all of these issues contributed to the party's collapse in 1976.[139]

Many of these points resonated with African American voters; consequently, Gerald Ford received a mere 8 percent of the black vote in 1976.[140] One black grievance stood out from among the rest, differentiating African American complaints from those of their fellow citizens; when explaining why they had decided to support Carter at the polls, black voters consistently cited the party's indifference to African Americans, especially on economic issues. Three days before the election, the editors of the *New York Amsterdam News* had outlined this rationale in a pithy editorial endorsing Jimmy Carter. "The selection of Mr. Carter over his rival, President Ford, was not a difficult choice for us," they wrote. "Throughout his campaign, President Ford has shown little or no interest in offering and developing a program to deal with the most crucial issue facing Black people in America today. . . . Jimmy Carter, on the other hand, has walked the streets of Harlem and made it plain that as President, one of his greatest concerns would be to put Black people back to work again."[141]

Black Republicans also seemed to reject Gerald Ford; longtime black Republican leader William O. Walker refused to use his newspaper, the *Call and Post*, to endorse the president, accusing the party of appealing to a southern strategy, a blunder that had cost the GOP the election. Blasting Ford for spurning black Republicans' campaign strategies, Walker warned that neither an ideological campaign nor a "colorblind" effort focused on middle-class and wealthy white suburbanites would win elections. Likewise, Walker's fellow columnist A. S. Doc Young lashed out at both Republicans *and* African Americans, belittling the "plantation politics of blacks and the Democratic Party," while criticizing the exclusionary tactics of the Ford campaign. PFC's outreach, he argued, should have been rooted in empathy toward the entire country, *including* African Americans, grappling with the plight of the underprivileged, rather than focusing on negativism. In a "nation as rich as ours," Young argued, "EVERY citizen should be free from the shackles of bigotry, poverty, and joblessness."[142]

Offering a similar view, Jackson Champion criticized Ford for having had no economic program geared toward minority voters, unlike Nixon, who for all his failings had at least offered black capitalism. Most disappointing for Champion was the president's "turn to the extreme right." It was a sharp accusation, all the more so since Champion was conservative himself, especially on matters of social welfare. Moreover, PFC actually adopted a variation of the colorblind suburban strategy that had worked for Richard Nixon in 1972; and, much like Nixon's, Ford's rightward shift was somewhat rhetorical, especially since his moderate philosophies on other issues tempered his conservatism. Central to black Republicans' anger, however, was Ford's "colorblind" approach; the president's so-called race-neutral appeals seemed hypocritical when racial minorities were deliberately excluded for fear of marginalizing white voters. And though the Black Desk had tried to use economics as a way of subverting the constrictions of race-neutral appeals, its impact was scant, as it had little funding or support.[143]

A review of campaign documents better illustrates these claims. In postelection assessments, white PFC staffers admitted that the Black Desk effort had been a disaster from the start. Confirming their indifference to African American outreach appeals, the officials wrote that blacks had been neglected throughout the campaign: "Not enough care was given to the [members of the Black Desk]," one functionary wrote. "They worked under very difficult conditions. The desk was not funded adequately."[144] But this was something that Robert Keyes already knew, and that black Republicans had suspected; perhaps best articulating black Republicans' anger and despondency in the aftermath of the 1976 contest, the Black Desk executive issued a lengthy postelection memo that characterized the PFC effort as a "traditional white-oriented campaign, with virtually no minority or female input in the phantom decision making process" that downplayed its relationship with African Americans out of fear that "overt actions or appeals by President Ford would stop the trend of southern white rednecks and right wingers who were allegedly coming on the Ford bandwagon in sufficient numbers which would justify our continuing the exclusionary-type of campaign we were waging."[145] The Black Desk had been charged with an unworkable assignment: convincing black

voters to support a president who had done little during the campaign—
"verbally or otherwise"—to demonstrate that he cared about African
Americans. Black voters, Keyes mourned, "felt that the Black [D]esk was
a showpiece with absolutely no muscle, no ability to deliver the President
or key administration people for appearances in the Black community or
secure messages that would show concern for their interests."

Keyes outlined the sins of white Republicans in meticulous detail,
stressing that nearly every recommendation supplied by the Black Desk
had been rejected "with no explanation, ignored, or put off until" the
final days of the campaign. Ford had represented himself as someone
who was oblivious to African Americans' "peculiar problems" and thus
could not address those problems. Significantly, black Republicans were
not asking Ford to change his policies dramatically. For example, the
NBRC's busing platform called for the party to deemphasize busing as a
solution and offer instead creative alternatives that took into consideration rank-and-file African Americans' perspectives, rather than just the
party's heavy-handed support for a constitutional ban. Likewise, when
Republican officials complained that antibusing sentiment was bipartisan
in nature, black party members argued that the GOP had more to prove.
Here then, empathy *again* emerged as a crucial concern for black Republicans; white party members, it would seem, viewed African Americans as
irrelevant to the dance of American politics.[146]

"Quite frankly, as a Black Republican, it's getting lonelier and lonelier," wrote a heavy-hearted Keyes, concluding his memo, "and I wonder
how much longer I will be able to make excuses and avoid the issues of
the ineptness of our Republican Party leadership." And yet, in spite of
his frustrations and his cynicism, the black official ended his assessment
with equal parts defiance and idealism that spoke to African American
party members' blind faith in their ability to change the hearts and minds
of the GOP and blacks: "I think it's time we get on with the business of
revitalizing the Republican Party and making the slogan 'The Party of the
People' truly a reality."[147]

• • •

"After years of soul searching," mocked the *Pittsburgh Courier* in a blistering 1976 editorial, "bedraggled" black Republicans "have come to the
realization that the GOP is no longer the party of Abe Lincoln." At this
stage, the editors scoffed, "It is rather late in the night for black Republicans to show their teeth against a party that has slammed its door on them
for these many years."[148] Contrary to the newspaper's claims, 1976 did
not represent the year that black Republicans finally realized the party of

Lincoln was no more; instead, that year documented black Republicans' slow and gradual awareness that GOP officials still believed that African Americans were politically irrelevant—a moment that was all the more distressing for black GOP leaders given that the party's *potential* to transform into an inclusive "big tent" was clear in the mid-1970s.

Even as black Republicans became more conservative, the rest of the party outpaced them; at a time when many black Republicans' philosophies seemed set to align with the mainstream GOP, party officials again moved away from a reformist agenda that could have started the difficult process of reintegrating Republican bureaucracies and the party's ranks. Though officials continued to make overtures to blacks, many of these gestures were symbolic, lacking money and support. In many ways, the Ford campaign's actions felt regressive: after all, nearly ten years earlier, Clarence Townes and the Minorities Division had pushed an empathetic approach and had warned Republicans about shallow, disorganized, and poorly funded outreach to African Americans.

Initially, the NBRC was launched to help overcome Republican inertia; yet despite building a network of clubs and organizations at the state and local level, the group found itself ignored by the mainstream party during the campaign. In fact, the RNC practically dismantled the group, canceling the NBRC's newsletter, revoking the organizations headquarters, downsizing its staff, and doling out a budget that was a fraction of what the Minorities Division had received at its peak in 1969.[149] When the NBRC first mobilized, black Republicans had expected autonomy—a naïve assumption to be sure, but one that represented their hopeful outlook. Instead, they found themselves tightly bound, limited in what they could do and say. The organization was hard hit by its woes; immediately following the 1976 election, membership dropped to a low of five thousand, and while it would surge eventually in 1978—reaching ten thousand members—that two-year stretch was a calamitous period for the group. The NBRC found its agenda stymied by party officials who, in the cryptic words of James Cummings, "consider a strong, cohesive, Black political organization to be a threat to their benign neglect of Black citizens." Though the black group managed to hold a few programs, GOP leaders consistently blocked the NBRC from pursuing its original agenda. As a frustrated Cummings argued during a meeting of the Arizona Black Republican Council, "Unless we . . . change the Republican Party . . . blacks will not be able to gain power within the party."[150]

Likewise, marginalized by their party, black Republicans bitterly fought with each other—infighting that cut across ideological lines, centering instead on *control* and vision. Political observers oftentimes reduced their arguments to ideological factionalism—conservatives versus liberal Republicans, for example—but in truth, by 1976, many black Republicans were becoming *more* conservative, despite the resolutely liberal presence of political mainstays like Ed Brooke and Sam Jackson. In some respects, black party members' conservatism began to look much more like that of white Republicans; likewise, more and more black party members started to espouse a rhetoric that reflected the party's broader mainstream shift to the right. Glimpses of a right-wing slant had long been visible in black Republicans' ideas about social welfare. Yet by 1976 black GOP leaders began to articulate an antistatist position that was much more rigid; they also started to dabble in the language of colorblindness, even as they remained committed to race-conscious strategies. For some, this was a natural reflection of their personal dogma; for others, this was a compromise—a concession necessary to obtain power and influence within the belly of the GOP. "It takes power to meet with power" in order to command "ears and actions," mused NBRC executive John Wilks in 1976. "Power never has to be equal . . . but just sufficient to be unquestionably advantageous."[151]

Two former NBRC executives, Robert Wright and John McNeill, recognized the prerequisite of conservative and savvy compromise for black Republican power early on, forming a Georgia-based Republican firm in the mid-1970s that focused on building grass-roots support for the GOP in local black communities. Where the NBRC and Council of 100 had failed, Wright and McNeill would succeed, a success that allowed them to assert a greater amount of influence within the GOP as the party struggled to recover from the loss of the 1976 presidential election. As the next chapter discusses, theirs was an approach that straddled the racial gulf between black and white Republicans—a strategy that most black Republicans eventually embraced and one that required them to place their faith in a conservative politician they had once denounced.

CHAPTER SEVEN

The Time of the Black Elephant

ON A BRISK JANUARY MORNING IN 1978, REPUBLICANS FROM ACROSS THE nation traveled to Washington, D.C., for a special meeting of the Republican National Committee. Upon their arrival at the Mayflower Hotel's Aviation Club, more than a few of the delegates were "visibly shocked" to see Jesse Jackson standing behind the main podium, dressed in a colorful three-piece suit and sporting a large Afro. The RNC members puzzled over his presence on the conference agenda, as they were well aware of his outspoken criticisms of the GOP. But minutes after the session was called to order, the "spellbinding country preacher" dazzled his audience with nearly an hour of "political gospel rock," enticing the delegates with the notion of an "influx of millions of black voters" in future political elections. "Black people need the Republican Party to compete for us so that we have real alternatives for meeting our needs," Jackson asserted, sounding not unlike a black Republican. "I am not just speaking theoretically when I say blacks will vote for the Republicans who appeal to their vested interests and engage in reciprocity."

Moving rapidly through dozens of complex issues, the civil rights leader captivated the delegates by deftly linking African American interests with traditional conservative principles. At one point, Jackson chastised the party for failing to select Massachusetts senator Edward Brooke as the 1976 vice presidential nominee. Had Republicans taken that approach, Jackson argued, Gerald Ford would still be in the White House. One of the best methods of wooing black voters, he continued, was to encourage visible black Republican leadership. Summarizing his political sermon with flourish, the spirited Jackson declared, "An all-white Republican national, state and country leadership apparatus designing a strategy to win black voters will not work!" The fiery rhetoric brought party leaders to their feet for an astonishing five-minute standing ovation; watching the scene, RNC chair Bill Brock offered an interesting and provocative criticism: "I wish we had Republicans who could talk like that."[1]

Jesse Jackson's speech to the Republican National Committee was a monumental event, receiving significant coverage in the national press, unsettling Democratic politicians and officials, and disputing persistent assumptions of a monolithic black electorate. As Charles Hucker of *Congressional*

Quarterly wrote, Jackson's appearance seemed to indicate a "glimmering of black interest in . . . Republican overtures."[2] The public declarations also underscored arguments that black Republicans had promoted for decades; in fact, the RNC meeting represented but one part of a larger program designed to engage these black Republican suggestions and reintegrate the GOP. Though the concept of a black outreach campaign was not unusual given the previous efforts of the party's African American members, it was certainly unique for the mainstream GOP to lobby aggressively in public for such measures.

The period demanded drastic action as a means of repairing the national damage inflicted by Watergate and exacerbated by an economic recession. Polls from the mid-1970s broadcasted a cynical American public that had little faith in politics or government. In 1976, respondents for one such survey labeled politicians as "dishonest and crooked," while another study found that more than half of Americans felt alienated from Congress and the White House; the average voter, pollsters wrote, believed that "people with power are out to take advantage of [them]." The Grand Old Party bore the brunt of the public's alienation: internal party polls showed that 18 percent of voters identified as Republicans, a figure that was vastly outnumbered by the 42 percent who identified as Democrats and the 40 percent who identified as independents.[3]

For African Americans, the events of the mid-1970s only served to reinforce an already contentious relationship with the GOP—frustrations that were born out of the party's years of equivocation over issues of black concern. As we have seen, Ford stumbled badly among the black electorate, earning only 8 percent of African Americans' votes. Postelection analysis suggested that blacks provided Carter with his margin of victory in more than half a dozen states, including Ohio, where an increase of just four percentage points among African Americans would have resulted in Ford winning the state; in Mississippi, a shift of ten percentage points would have provided the ousted president with a desperately needed electoral boost. Had Ford won *both* those states, he would have remained comfortably ensconced at 1600 Pennsylvania Avenue (see table 6 in the appendix). As Jesse Jackson so bluntly remarked, "Hands that picked cotton in 1966 did pick the President in 1976, and could very well be the difference in 1980."[4]

Jackson's was a bold and important claim, one that spoke to the significance of the black vote, not just to the Democratic Party, but to the GOP as well; yet Ohio and Mississippi were the only states where slight changes among black voters would have produced a Ford victory. In those areas, Carter's winning margin was small enough that subtle shifts in the black vote would have had a dramatic impact on the entire election. In other states, Ford would have needed to more than quadruple his share of the black vote in order to overcome the Georgia Democrat's hefty margin—not a preposterous task for a Republican in a state or local election, as we have seen, but a highly unlikely scenario for a conservative-leaning GOP presidential nominee.

This is not to suggest that black voters were unimportant in the 1976 presidential contest or that Ford's lukewarm approach to African American outreach was justified; in fact, the opposite is true: slight increases in the black vote combined with stronger support from unionists, women, Latinos, and Jewish voters would have allowed Ford to retain the presidency in 1976. In other words, he could have created a diverse coalition that included African Americans. Lyn Nofziger, an adviser to Richard Nixon and Ronald Reagan, came to a near-identical conclusion after the election, suggesting that had Ford devoted more time to black outreach, he probably would have held on to the White House. Likewise, African American leaders offered similar assessments: "Gerald Ford might still be in the White House had he just gone down to some black churches," commented National Urban League official Daniel Davis.[5] Benjamin Hooks of the National Association for the Advancement of Colored People was a bit more insightful, maintaining that while black voters were not particularly impressed with Jimmy Carter, they had "edged him into office because they felt they had no meaningful alternative."[6]

The GOP's extreme electoral woes with African Americans were rooted in Goldwater's enduring legacy; more than a decade later, black voters still held an image of a national party driven by states' rights advocates, white southern conservatives, anti-civil rights politicians, and wealthy elites who distained the "common man."[7] The *Washington Post* observed that the Republican Party appeared to be a political machine engaged in constant antagonisms and reactionary battles and had done very little to dispel its negative identity with black communities. The party at times, though, seemed to be guided by liberal and moderate perspectives; this ideological schism, black voters argued, indicated that the party was confused about its brand, identity, and—most important—its principles.[8]

The plight of the party deeply troubled black Republicans; for decades they had warned of the risks associated with ignoring the black vote. In a heated March 1977 letter to the national committee, black Republican Joseph Sanders demanded that the party enlist the aid of its African American members to engage the black community. Arthur Fletcher's expertise, connections, and "political acumen," he argued, would be enormous assets in obtaining black support to repair decades of damage. "As a 'Minority, Middleclass, Midwesterner,' I feel qualified to make such a recommendation," Sanders wrote, "I know whereof I speak!"[9] As the volume of these irate black voters grew, party officials finally began to acknowledge that the party needed to get a "chunk, if not a majority of the black vote to prevent Democrats from carrying close elections."[10] Six months after the November 1976 election, House minority leader John Rhodes candidly admitted that his party had neglected black voters for years; going forward, he eagerly promised, the party was ready to change its ways and was committed to a "serious effort to convince black Americans that they can have a home in our party and that we want them to have a home in our party."[11] This was a familiar phrase, one that the Republicans had repeatedly uttered and undermined since 1936. The GOP's promise, however, held a slightly different edge in 1977, because party officials believed that black voters could influence a presidential election, whereas in the past their significance was the subject of much debate.

Among white Republicans, no one was more vocal about this issue than Tennessee Republican Bill Brock. A casualty of the 1976 elections, Brock lost his senatorial seat by nearly 78,000 votes. African Americans played a tremendous role in Brock's upset, contributing 130,000 ballots, or 93 percent of the black vote, to his Democratic challenger Jim Sasser.[12] The loss was a wake-up call for Brock, forcing him to conclude that a post-Watergate party revival required aggressive public outreach to African Americans. Needless to say, this was an argument that black Republicans had been advancing for years. But Brock's experience was unique: as a prominent and powerful white Republican, he had a greater degree of flexibility in pushing a black outreach agenda as a national initiative in a manner that previous white officials were unwilling to do.

As Ed Brooke later explained, Brock made "more of an effort to integrate the party than any other chairman. . . . He really had the desire, had the interest, and did something to bring about integration and to bring blacks into the Republican Party."[13] However, while Brock provided critical funding and institutional support for black outreach, as we will see, a black Republican owned-and-operated consulting firm—Wright-McNeill & Associates—conceptualized, orchestrated, and spearheaded the initiatives. In 1977, the Georgia-based organization optimistically declared, "the Black vote *can* be obtained by many Republican[s], *if* more than a token effort is aimed at the black community."[14] Together, Wright-McNeill and Brock created an ambitious and distinct black outreach campaign, one that sought to reintegrate, reinvigorate, and reinvent the Republican Party, in a way never before attempted.

BILL BROCK, WRIGHT-MCNEILL, AND THE INTEGRATION OF THE GOP

"The Republican Party," Bill Brock declared on January 14, 1977, "has the makings of the greatest new majority the country has ever seen." As he assumed control of the RNC, the party leader announced his intentions to reinvent the nature of party recruitment, though Brock's strategy was not so much a reinvention as it was a revision, as his "big tent" philosophy channeled the reform efforts of former RNC chairs, including Joseph Martin, Ray Bliss, George H. W. Bush, and Mary Louise Smith. Unlike his predecessors, however, the Tennessee politician took a dramatic step forward by insisting that *all* Republicans would recruit African American voters aggressively. "We had no rules by which to play the game," he later explained, the party "had lost its pride and its arrogance, and to a degree its direction." Thus, broadening the GOP base, Brock argued, was more than just an opportunity—it was the "most awesome responsibility" the party had faced "in the last 50 years."[15] At first glance, Brock's words can be read with a healthy degree of skepticism, since he was affiliated with the southern conservative wing of the party and, as a congressman, had voted against the Civil Rights Act of 1964. With Brock in charge, the *New York Times* argued in January 1977, the party would be under "firm conservative control," with its moderate and liberal wing "cut off from any position of real influence." In reality, a closer review indicates that Brock's rhetoric was genuine, as he viewed no incongruity between his conservatism and his interest in black voters; by 1977, his ideological outlook did not neatly align with that of the party's right wing; for instance, he once stated, "the worst vote I ever cast was against the 1964 Civil Rights Act," calling Goldwater Republicans' constitutional opposition to the law "garbage . . . a patina we put on to justify our actions."[16]

Some political observers picked up on the nuances of Brock's shifting ideology, expressing cautious optimism about the RNC's declarations. The *Christian Science Monitor*, for instance, outlined and analyzed the national committee's preliminary plans and suggested that the party chair was actually serious about black outreach.[17] As Brock revealed to the public in January 1977, his approach was part of a long-term effort to rebuild the "eroded base" of Republican support around the country. The GOP had no choice, for as Brock explained, after suffering defeats in the 1974 *and* 1976 elections, the party had what was essentially a "white, Anglo-Saxon, Protestant, Buick-driving, middle income, and male" constituency. "There sure aren't enough ducks in this party to elect anyone as it is, we've proven that," the national committee chairman once offered. Consequently, the party's full endeavor necessarily encompassed other alienated groups such as Latinos, organized labor, women, and white ethnic voters, with the core of the effort focusing on improving communications with black communities. In fact, Brock announced that the RNC planned to invest more than $2 million into black outreach; when questioned, Republican state chairman vigorously agreed that this was a wise strategy. "We just want to cut into the black vote now going to the Democrats," explained one midwestern official. "If we could get 3 out of 10 blacks to vote Republican, that would give us a big boost." When compared to Brock's interest in attracting black voters, the language of the state party chairmen offers a very different picture of Republicans' interest in outreach. Whereas Brock insisted that Republicans needed to "grow up" and woo African Americans by providing viable solutions that addressed African American interests, some party officials had no such concerns; instead, they merely wanted to prevent blacks from voting for Democrats.[18]

The RNC initially focused on its auxiliary organizations, more than tripling the National Black Republican Council's budget to an impressive $140,000 in 1977, funds to be used to mount a multiyear national membership drive and create "progressive" Republican solutions to African American issues. Though the organization's budget would drop to $126,000 in 1978, the national committee's support of the NBRC is still striking, given that the RNC deliberately neglected the group in 1976. Moreover, the same year that he dramatically increased the NBRC's funding, Brock signed a two-year $800,000 contract with Wright-McNeill & Associates, with the goal of introducing the "Grand Old Party to the descendants of the . . . people Abraham Lincoln emancipated."[19] In some ways, the actions of the national committee suggest that the fate of the NBRC and Wright-McNeill were intertwined; and certainly the two organizations had identical goals and occasionally worked together on their agendas. The consulting firm, however, had a measure of freedom not afforded to the black council; indeed, leaders of the NBRC privately railed against Wright-McNeill, occasionally going so far as to accuse the firm's leaders of sabotage, in their pursuit of intraparty power.[20]

A 1977 memo between Wright-McNeill cofounder Bob Wright and Bill Brock spelled out the nature of the party's "black" problem in stark terms: overwhelming black support for Carter; the number of Republican candidates "who continued to lose by a few percentage points in predominately Black areas"; and the poor quality of previous black outreach efforts. As Brock explained to Wright, the RNC was interested in pursuing black votes on a more "effective and technical level" than it had in the past.[21] The reason the national committee turned to Wright-McNeill & Associates instead of the NBRC for outreach assistance was because the consulting firm had something the party desperately wanted: the knowledge and ability to convince African Americans to support Republican candidates.

Founded in 1974, Wright-McNeill had a reputation for helping Republican candidates in Georgia garner major support from black communities. In 1976, when Gerald Ford could "barely grasp the black vote," the consultants helped their white clients earn the support of 54 percent of the state's black electorate, while the firm's African American clients garnered 93 percent of the black vote. Both consultants relied on their own extensive backgrounds in politics, race relations, and civil rights: Richard Wright was a three-term city councilman in Columbus, Georgia, with strong ties to the state Republican committee, the Department of Health, Education and Welfare (HEW), and the Small Business Administration (SBA). Likewise, John McNeill was known for his work on black voter registration drives, as well as his experience as an adviser to the RNC, the Republican Congressional Committee (RCC), and local and state party organizations.

Both men had close ties to the NBRC, helping to launch the Georgia chapter and serving the national group in various leadership capacities through 1976. In that year, the relationship soured—or at least it did for John McNeill, who was one of the coplaintiffs who sued the party and the NBRC in *Bivens v. RNC*. As we have seen, the case offered a significant critique of the NBRC as a powerless organization, one that had struggled to translate rhetoric into tangible political results on a local, state, and national level. And while both groups had financial ties to the national committee, Wright-McNeill's history of electoral success in areas where the NBRC had failed (and where the party now desperately needed assistance) meant that the firm could actually influence the RNC's black outreach agenda.

Wright and McNeill's experiences had taught them how to bridge the formidable divide between the Republican Party and African Americans on a state and local level; now the party hoped to use the consultants' skills on a much broader scale.[22] As a May 1977 memo detailed, the firm's core responsibilities included:

1. The recruitment of Black candidates to seek public office on all levels as Republicans.
2. To recruit other Republican candidates, who can articulate a sensitivity to the needs of the black community and all people problems in general.
3. To assist . . . candidates in developing campaign strategies geared toward the Black community, but strategies that are an integral part of the overall campaign plan.

4. To develop permanent campaign mechanisms or organizations within the Black community for Republican candidates.[23]

Wright-McNeill's primary focus was not black voter registration and partisan education but candidate recruitment. The consultants' job then was not so much about permanently enrolling African Americans in the party's ranks as it was about getting African Americans to vote for individual candidates. In a sense, the firm employed an "improved" version of the NBRC's nonpartisan approach to partisan politics. Consultants handpicked candidates, demanding that potential officeholders demonstrate a willingness to make aggressive appeals to African Americans: visiting black neighborhoods, churches, and social events, and "shaking hands" with black constituents—a modest test, Wright once sighed, "that most white Republicans can't pass." The firm's entire approach was premised on *trust*: Republican candidates needed to demonstrate genuine sincerity in order to woo black voters. To do so, Wright argued, meant that the party could slowly "chip away" at the black vote and "get our share up to 10%, then up to what it used to be, 15% to 20%, and then keep going from there."[24]

Wright-McNeill's approach was distinct from previous outreach efforts as the black consultants blended liberal and conservative ideas in a way that was attractive to even the party's right wing. "What is striking about this effort," wrote conservative periodical *Human Events* in December 1977, "is the theme: wooing the black vote with a distinctly conservative approach that matches mainstream Republican [philosophy]." Party officials, Wright-McNeill insisted, could make inroads in local and state politics without dramatically changing their conservative outlook, so long as their solutions somehow addressed African Americans' issues and needs. For example, the same month as the *Human Events* article, a Wright-McNeill consultant declared that there was "nothing wrong with calling for educational tax credits so blacks can send their children outside the public school system that in many cases is failing them." This was a dramatic about-face. In 1976, the NBRC had denounced tax credits as a racist scheme used by whites to avoid integration; now, a little over a year later, Wright-McNeill was suggesting that the initiative was harmless, so long as it included African American parents, as well.[25] In many ways, Wright-McNeill attempted to temper the discriminatory aspects of conservatism, not by changing the ideology but rather by explicitly showing white conservative Republicans how their ideas could be used to solve African Americans' pressing issues.[26]

Many white Republicans found this premise attractive, for within months of signing their RNC contract, Wright and McNeill were inundated with hundreds of requests from GOP officials. Bob Dole was among those interested; in a 1977 letter, he applauded the black consultants' role within the party and suggested that field agents explore Birmingham, Alabama, as a viable testing ground. The city, Dole wrote, showed a "considerable growth pattern . . . indicating wider support in the black community for the Republican Party." Even more promising, the Kansas senator concluded, the consulting firm could rely on a "strong" cadre of local black Republicans as a sincere gateway into local community politics. Similarly, the Republican Congressional Committee gave the national committee and Wright-McNeill $50,000 in 1978, with the express purpose of wooing black voters.[27]

Between 1977 and 1978, Wright-McNeill helped dozens of local and state politicians increase their share of the black vote by an average of thirty percentage points.[28] In August 1977, for example, the consultants guided Louisiana official Robert Livingston through his successful congressional campaign, helping him win support from about a third of the black electorate in the special offyear election; in his failed congressional bid a year earlier, he had received just 3 percent of the black vote.[29] The firm's most effective piece of campaign propaganda was negative: a brochure highlighting that Livingston's Democratic predecessor had voted against the Congressional Black Caucus's high-priority issues more than 80 percent of the time. The firm also received an unexpected boost when a local segregationist group endorsed Livingston's opponent, Ron Faucheux; ultimately many black voters did not support the young Democrat —a point that Livingston used to his advantage as he and his family canvassed black neighborhoods, getting to know the African Americans of the district. One year later, he would receive more than 70 percent of the black vote in his successful reelection bid.[30] In total, only one of Wright-McNeill's protégées—Jackson, Mississippi, mayoral candidate Doug Shanks—lost in 1977, and even then, more than 40 percent of black voters cast their ballots for the young moderate Republican. But Shanks's loss also exposed an undercurrent of tension working its way through the GOP: many of his white campaign advisers attributed his loss to weak support among white working-class voters. As one strategist theorized, the balance between "appealing to the blacks and preserving the white vote is pretty exquisite, especially here in the South. I guess we leaned too far to the blacks and scared off the whites."[31]

Others within the GOP suggested that the concept of "party branding" was the real issue; once solved, strategists reasoned, problems of race and class would recede. Wright-McNeill embraced this theory as well, suggesting that the greatest barrier to making an "indelible impact on the Black electorate's voting pattern" was the party's negative image. But the consultants also understood that this negative image was more than a simple "branding" issue—it was rooted in the party's very real, and very lengthy, history of antiblack actions. To dispel this poor image among black voters, Wright-McNeill proposed a multifaceted strategy aimed at advancing a positive black agenda from *within* the Republican Party. Supported by an additional $500,000 in funds in 1978, the consulting firm reached out to black leaders including Jesse Jackson, Vernon Jordan, and Benjamin Hooks.[32] The consultants also helped to expand internal initiatives like the Black Advisory Committee (BAC), a program established in April 1978 as a joint partnership between the NBRC and Republicans in the House and Senate. Black Republicans collaborated with the politicians, helping them craft legislation that better addressed minority issues in employment, economics, education, and housing; likewise, the research arm of BAC monitored new legislation introduced into Congress, determined its impact on black citizens, and examined the civil rights voting records of officials. Reacting to these developments and others, the *Chicago Tribune* speculated that perhaps the Republican Party was ready to "step off the country club porch and into the ghetto"; offering his agreement, Ben Hooks mused, "I really think Brock may be halfway sincere."[33]

However, though the RNC embraced most of the black consultants' plan, the national committee also rejected Wright-McNeill's "image building" program, a crucial component of the firm's GOP rebranding efforts. Nevertheless, the consulting firm wove "image building" into its strategy, finding ways to address the party's antiblack history and reputation and forcing many Republicans to reconcile their ideological positions with their attitudes toward African Americans. In a 1978 memo on "responsibilities," sent to party officials and politicians, the consultants insisted that GOP leaders merge their conservative ideas with social programs directed at African Americans. Reconciling balanced budgets, tax cuts, and "laissez faire market attitudes" with "large expenditures of government money" was not an impossible feat, the black consultants concluded, particularly since Republicans had little problem squaring such issues when it came to white voters.[34] As expected, the black consultants refused to work with candidates who failed to meet the firm's requirements about race and ideology. In Houston, they rejected a request from congressional candidate Ron Paul, characterizing his efforts to win black support as pointless. "He is against 'everything' but offers no viable alternates," field analyst Thelma Duggin wrote in an April 1978 progress report. "His positions on the welfare system, minimum wage, and health care were too far to the right to offer the type of sensitivity Black voters were looking for." His perspective on most issues concerning African Americans was so extreme, Duggin observed, that it bordered on being racist. African Americans in Houston agreed; all of those polled by Wright-McNeill were viscerally opposed to Paul, with some even going so far as to berate the consultants for even talking to the white official.[35]

In contrast, in that same year, Wright-McNeill eagerly embraced black Republican Maurice Holman, a candidate for the Kansas state legislature. The firm viewed him as part of a preferred "new breed" of black and white GOP politicians: moderate, college-educated, and charismatic enough to break the electorate of "ingrained voting habits." This new cadre was crucial to the party's success, Bob Wright asserted on several occasions, highlighting the firm's budding relationship with more than half a dozen congressional hopefuls, including Newt Gingrich of Georgia and Melvin Evans of the U.S. Virgin Islands, and incumbent politicians such as Clarence "Bud" Brown of Ohio and Howard Baker of Tennessee. The GOP, Wright-McNeill reasoned, could alter its image through this group of Republicans since they were eager to speak publicly on issues affecting African Americans and committed to working with the black consulting firm.[36]

At first glance, Holman's district appeared to be hostile territory: black voters, nearly all of whom were registered Democrats, composed 66 percent of the electorate; the remaining white constituents were almost all blue-collar Democrats and independents. Thus with virtually no GOP base from which to draw, Holman's greatest challenge, as Wright-McNeill defined it, was convincing blacks to see *beyond* partisan affiliation and make it "socially acceptable to vote for a Republican" in 1978. Still, the election held some measure of promise, the black consulting firm stated, since the Democratic incumbent, Norman Justice, appeared to inspire little enthusiasm among constituents. Significant emphasis was placed on aggressive door-to-door grass-roots efforts, regular meetings with black voters, and consistent attendance at local political and social events in black neighborhoods; the firm also delivered thousands of brochures featuring an article by Jesse Jackson on the "legitimacy of blacks being Republican."[37] At Wright-McNeill's urging, Holman attempted to address concerns over black unemployment and underemployment aggressively; to these ends, the would-be-politician's campaign theme was "Let's Talk Money":

> You and I work until May each year to support the promises made by people like Norman Justice. . . . They deliver a lot of noise but take our money. My campaign is about one thing: With every vote I cast, I will work to restore our money to us. Justice is part of the problem, not the solution.[38]

In attempting to reconcile black needs with conservative economics—specifically extensive tax relief and "restrained" government—Holman and

Wright-McNeill shifted the political dialogue, employing a language that was familiar to both African Americans and white conservatives by denouncing government representatives as ineffective and insisting that tax breaks would bring money and employment back into the community. Likewise, that same year, another one of Wright-McNeill's chosen black candidates, Ben Andrews of Connecticut, declared that the federal government was inefficient and wasteful and argued that the Kemp-Roth bill (which proposed a 30 percent federal income tax cut over three years) offered a useful means of stimulating the economy. In short, Wright-McNeill urged both men to grapple with issues that were of critical concern to black and white constituents, though rarely imagined through the lens of the Republican Party.[39]

On occasion, Wright-McNeill's hands-on approach to party politics extended beyond rhetorical campaign promises and into substantive economic policy recommendations. This was a selective strategy, as the consultants' initiatives deliberately avoided any kind of sweeping, detailed discussions on policy—especially on social issues. As Bill Brock later explained, Republicans believed that focusing on "contentious" legislative issues would have detracted from the party's broader outreach initiative by "making people run away." Trying to convey a sense of "optimism," the RNC and Wright-McNeill instead concentrated on abstract ideas tied to jobs, economic growth, and employment.[40] During such discussions, GOP politicians continued to use the private sector as a model for alleviating black underemployment and unemployment. "Too often, Republican orators latch on to the glories of private enterprise, extolling its virtues before starry-eyed audiences," Edward Brooke criticized during a speech to Operation PUSH in Chicago in 1978. "For some of them, private enterprise seems almost like a religion, with an emphasis on ritual instead of service." Though the senator, at this point, was far more liberal than Wright-McNeill & Associates, both he and the consultants could still agree that private enterprise solutions needed to be infused with a sense of "community-mindedness" or "sensitivity" toward African Americans.[41]

In a report to Democratic congresswoman Shirley Chisholm, Wright-McNeill tried to highlight this so-called commitment to merging free enterprise with black aspirations, by listing several pages of initiatives sponsored by legislators including Brooke, Howard Baker, Jacob Javits, and John Chafee. The firm emphasized Republican senators' support for the $240 million expansion of the Urban Homesteading Program, an initiative that allowed poor and working-class families to purchase abandoned urban properties for "nominal expenses" and renovate them; politicians' endorsement of legislation for tax incentives for black homeownership;

and officials' backing of resolutions to protect federally deposited funds in minority-owned banks.[42] Party leaders also tried to showcase their "new attitudes" through the introduction of a "comprehensive economic package" designed to expand private-sector jobs, create youth employment initiatives, offer business incentives for urban investments, and provide tax cuts to stimulate the economy. One particular initiative was modeled after Jesse Jackson's EXCEL program, which drew praise from GOP politicians for actively encouraging conservative "special virtues," including "hard work, study, self-discipline and 'take-off-your-hat-in-the-house' respectability." The Republican Party's parallel initiative offered educational tax credits, which party politicians theorized would enable "hard-working" black parents to send their children to private schools.[43] One *Chicago Tribune* journalist wryly observed that "under [Jackson's] Afro, as under the bald pates and tinted tresses of the [GOP], was the same respect for old-fashioned virtues." This was common ground, a shared philosophical space where Republicans could comfortably embrace black ideas of self-help and personal responsibility; even former Nixon speechwriter Patrick Buchanan admitted that African Americans' "economic issues" and "traditional ethical and moral values" appeared to mirror the principles of the Republican Party.[44] Here then, Wright-McNeill's interest was not in dismantling conservatism but in reframing the boundaries of the ideology in order to incorporate black interests by creating common ground between African Americans and the GOP, one wherein liberal ideas about race could be merged with conservative economic policies.

Still, Jesse Jackson's "conservatism" differed from that of the Republican Party in important ways. The black leader's brand of politics, for instance, reflected an "everyday" kind of African American conservatism, steeped in respectability traditions and broad ideas of two-party competition. In truth, however, Jackson ultimately held liberal views of government, calling for billions in federal aid to urban areas in 1978 and repudiating the Kemp-Roth tax cuts as a dangerous proposal. Though outside the mainstream of black Republican thought, his views nevertheless overlapped with those of liberal black Republicans, including Ed Brooke, who blasted tax relief advocates as political swindlers, humming a "siren song" of "selfishness" that lured American citizens with the "prospects of impossible tax cuts and the fallacy of cheap government."[45] In contrast, as we have seen, Wright-McNeill endorsed an approach that condemned government as a constraint on black economic opportunity and emphasized tax relief as the solution to African Americans' problems. In fact, this was a central component of Wright-McNeill's strategy; the consultants and the RNC stressed the "American Dream," positioning black citizens as ordinary people with the same desire to obtain "good education, and decent housing" as the rest of the nation. Rhetorically, this sounded *identical* to the language employed by the Nixon administration's black appointees in the late 1960s; the fundamental difference was that a decade later Bill Brock and Wright-McNeill argued that government policies were *not* the most effective solution. Black voters, Brock rationalized, were "being squeezed by the high cost of living, by rising taxes and by the intrusions of big government. . . . There are millions of them and most have never voted Republican."[46]

In an effort to capitalize on Wright-McNeill's approach, the RNC head implemented a parallel public relations campaign, purchasing advertising airtime on syndicated black public affairs television shows, speaking at the NAACP national conference in May 1978, and holding weekly lunch meetings and press conferences with black publishers, editors, and journalists.[47] The initiative focused on locations that the party had once ignored, like metropolitan cities in the northeast, and areas where they had long recruited, such as rural and suburban southern locales. In one instance, RNC leaders toured southern cities and were shocked to receive a "surprisingly warm reception" from African Americans. During Mississippi Republican Charles Pickering's speech to the Mississippi NAACP convention, he lamented his status as the "first live Republican . . . to speak" to the organization in decades. "Just the novelty of it," he remarked with astonishment, "was enough to make them sit up and take notice of what I was saying."[48] Whereas outreach efforts were strategically downplayed in previous decades, by the late 1970s, party officials were instructed to "canvass black communities as never before."[49]

Of course, there were those who staunchly opposed the RNC's outreach initiative. Despite admitting that African Americans and the Republican Party shared some common interests, Pat Buchanan publicly maintained that the GOP needed to "write off the black vote as hopelessly locked into the Democrats" and instead aggressively target "untapped" white ethnic voters.[50] Insisting that the black vote was the GOP's "weakest link," Republican consultant John Deardourff indicated that the party's new efforts were premature. "I'm not sure we should be concentrating so much effort on it now," he told the *Wall Street Journal*. "We've gotten a third of the Jewish votes, better than 40% of the blue-collar vote. It would seem to me you should go where you have some real prospects. . . . [Otherwise], we're ramming our heads against the wall." Another official pushed this rationale one step further, insisting that the party's black outreach effort was sabotaging the GOP's chance of attracting white blue-collar voters. Instead of avoiding discussions of racial quotas, for example, the party should have accused Jimmy Carter and Democrats of being "reverse racists" for their embrace of affirmative action policies, argued the anonymous Republican official.[51] The trouble with this approach was that it exploited racial hostility, assuming that the only way to entice white working-class voters was at the expense of African Americans, rather than adopting a strategy that touched on shared issues important to both groups, irrespective of race. Other Republicans were skeptical of the RNC's approach and struggled to reconcile it with the party's "colorblind" philosophy of individualism. "When you make a special effort it seems inconsistent to conservatives to separate out a group," offered Ray Barnhart, chair of the Texas Republican committee. "Sometimes this is construed as bigotry, but it isn't. It is an effort to be consistent . . . with our attitude about the equality of men."[52] Still, Barnhart mulled over the importance of the black outreach initiative, agreeing that the "problems of the black community must be addressed." And while such appeals had the potential to drive away the more extremist elements of the party, the Texas official proposed that ultimately it was vital for African Americans to be "integrated" into the Republican community.[53]

Even self-proclaimed conservative Republicans endorsed the black outreach initiative, including Lyn Nofziger, who suggested that "only the far right wing" would feel alienated by black outreach. Virtually no change would occur, Nofziger argued, since this constituency "had no place to go."[54] Ronald Reagan also appeared to embrace African American recruitment, a development that puzzled Edward Walsh of the *Washington Post*, who wrote that it was unthinkable that the "darling of the Republican Party's right-wing" would reach out to black voters. Speaking at a function in Atlanta in January 1978, Reagan did exactly that, citing the NAACP's opposition to the Carter administration's energy plan. The conservative politician accused the president of siding with those "bent on slowing economic development" and "denying low-income groups a chance for more prosperity."[55] Softening his usual approach, Reagan directed his rhetoric to a new target audience:

> I believe, black Americans want what every American wants: a crack at a decent job, a home, safety in the streets, and a good education for our children . . . And the best way to have those things is for government to get out of the way while the rest of us make a bigger pie so that everybody can have a bigger slice.[56]

Certainly there was a compelling reason for Reagan—or any other Republican politician—to appeal to African Americans during the late 1970s. Republicans recognized that they could take advantage of the rumblings of black discontent with the Democratic Party, hoping that African Americans would be "ripe" to abandon Jimmy Carter. A report by the Joint Center for Political Studies found that between 1976 and 1978 black partisan identification with the Democratic Party dropped from 80 to 66 percent; during that same period, the center also observed a "substantial increase in the proportion claiming independent status and in the number identifying themselves as Republicans." Specifically, blacks identifying as members of the GOP rose from 5 to 8 percent, while the number of black independents increased from 15 to 26 percent.[57]

An enthusiastic Robert Wright gleefully used such information to claim that black leaders were starting to challenge President Carter on his "all symbolism, but no substance" posture in February 1979, pointing to the NUL, NAACP, and Operation PUSH's harsh criticisms of the president. Exploring this theme in a 1979 *Ebony* article, Simeon Booker concluded that, though Jimmy Carter excelled in the symbolism of black appointments, he had disappointed blacks by failing to respond aggressively to problems of "inflation, energy, and a flagging economy." Of particular concern was the abysmal rate of black unemployment, which hit 14 percent in the mid-1970s. According to Urban League reports, the number jumped to 40 percent once underemployed workers were considered; and among black teenagers and young adults, the unemployment rate was 60 percent.[58] Black leaders argued that the president's decision to rescind his campaign promise of increased job opportunities for racial minorities further exacerbated African Americans economic woes; likewise, they maintained that Carter's approach to inflation threatened to destroy the gains of the black middle class and berated the president for cutting federal funding to historically black colleges. Some even went so far as to classify the president's black appointees as "inept" and "symbolic." An irate Jesse Jackson accused the administration of "gutting" domestic social programs, describing Carter's approach as an "all-out assault on labor, blacks, women and the poor," calling on African Americans to "fight back politically" through protests to force negotiations with the president.[59]

Disillusionment among African Americans was so high that some black Democrats began to echo Jesse Jackson's calls to consider political alternatives to the Democratic Party, "even in party affiliation." At one conference, held toward the end of the decade, a group of black Democratic officials debated over the merits of two-party competition and casting votes for the Republican Party, lamenting that the Democratic Party "can, and does, assume blacks have no place else to go." And yet, for many black Democrats, making a partisan switch to the GOP as a protest strategy would have been an impossibility because of their beliefs; as Detroit mayor Coleman Young argued, "There are a whole lot of bastards in the Democratic Party, but there are a whole lot more in the GOP." Yet he mused that *if* a viable alternative within the two-party system existed—one that sufficiently addressed African American needs in a substantive way—then leaving the Democratic Party would be a feasible option.[60]

Wright-McNeill & Associates quickly recognized that the Republican Party could take advantage of this fissure; for example, one consultant suggested that the GOP nominate the "right" kind of politician, so that black leaders—angry with President Carter—would be "hard pressed to again convince Black Americans that Jimmy Carter is 'one of them.'" Wright-McNeill also reasoned that pressing Carter on issues of black concern would force black Democratic politicians and officials into uncomfortable positions: defend the president, agree with the Republican Party, or remain silent—all of which would benefit the GOP. Nevertheless, even with Carter's missteps, wooing black voters into the Republican camp was far from a simple task. "Like Lazarus . . . Republicans are rising from their lowly estate. The curse of Watergate may almost be off the party," reflected Republican strategist David Gergen, acknowledging that the "party still has a tough road to go and needs to convert million of voters." Going forward, he proposed, the GOP needed to reconcile principles with the people; that is, Republicans "must show how a conservative philosophy can actually meet the needs of contemporary society."[61]

Party officials attempted to take advantage of Carter's political woes by targeting the black middle class; while not a new strategy, by the late 1970s, white Republicans were convinced that this constituency was becoming *more* conservative than their white counterparts. For example, a 1977 Quayle-Plesser poll seemed to indicate that the black middle class supported the conservative principle of "law and order" at a higher rate than its white counterpart; pollsters, consultants, and pundits thereby assumed that a sizable number of black Republicans lay in waiting. However, as we have seen, black voters drew a distinction between "law and order" and "law and order, with justice." Consequently, NUL head Vernon Jordan dismissed the idea of a "conservative black middle class partial to 'law-and-order' anticrime appeals." He concluded that black concern for crime was real and understandable, but so too was the reluctance of the black middle class to support law and order campaigns that translated into "sweeps of black communities and restrictions on their freedoms."[62]

The notion of a middle-class constituency, primed and ready for the Republican Party, was an appealing theory to many. The *New York Times* suggested that economic opportunity had replaced civil rights as the central issue of concern to the majority of black middle-class citizens; thus, "as they move up the ladder," reasoned the newspaper, "what is taken from them becomes more important than what is given to them, and conservative appeals make more sense." In some respect, the *New York Times* described what was a major development among the black middle class; likewise, black Republicans had endorsed such a shift from civil rights to economic rights for almost fifteen years. However, the *Times* assumed that civil rights and economics were mutually exclusive concepts. White politicians and political observers presumed that economics was race neutral, whereas African Americans leaders saw economics as intrinsically linked to race. So when the JCPS argued that "traditional civil rights questions have given way to economic issues" in 1978, the black center did not mean that race was irrelevant but rather than African Americans saw race and class as intertwined.[63]

Nevertheless, white Republicans were eager to read the shift from civil rights to economics through the lens of colorblindness, because it allowed them to focus on economics and the black middle class without explicitly talking about race. Some Republican politicians, like Bob Dole, formulated new ideas solely designed to appeal to African Americans "who identified themselves to pollsters as conservatives."[64] While the party would never attract the majority of the black electorate by adopting this approach, strategists observed that the party did not need a majority of black votes in order to win presidential elections; the *New York Times* assessed that the GOP needed support from only 15 to 25 percent of the black electorate. As Dole later concluded, "15 percent is a substantial number of Blacks, enough to swing a close election."[65]

In spite of his initial skepticism, Vernon Jordan eventually agreed that the Republican Party had a real "chance to slice enough black votes away from the Democrats," cautiously applauding Wright-McNeill's outreach strategy. Still, he warned that such support would not be obtained through a "continuation of malign neglect or courting . . . [the] black middle class." If the GOP was serious about its outreach, Jordan insisted:

> It will have to endorse programs and polices needed by the black community; it will have to nominate black candidates and admit blacks into prominent internal party positions of real authority, and it will have to take a more positive approach toward urban and poverty programs that affect blacks. . . . To date . . . the party has pursued policies perceived by blacks and whites alike as antiblack. Changing those policies holds the key to a Republican resurgence in American politics.

In short, Jordan argued that a colorblind approach to black outreach would not work. But abandoning such policies did not require a rejection of the party's "traditional position to the right of the Democrats," Jordan reasoned. On the contrary, there was "plenty of room for the party to move toward the center . . . [and] enunciate creative programs within its traditional philosophy." Jordan concluded by offering several recommendations on how the party might reconcile its traditional principles with a "black agenda." Several suggestions seemed to echo long-standing black Republican policy proposals; for example, Jordan pointed out that the "stress on private enterprise" necessitated federal policies that would "better enable the private sector to help solve serious urban, social and economic problems." The NUL chief also noted that the party's "long-standing suspicion of central government" did not have to indicate "support of bloc grants and community development laws . . . that take money from poor cities and give it to better-off suburbs."[66]

Though Jordan's perspectives clashed with some of the economic policies endorsed by both Bill Brock and Wright-McNeill & Associates, the RNC chair and the black consultants nevertheless welcomed such recommendations, as they believed that such perspectives reinforced the national committee's sincerity on African American outreach and generated a massive amount of publicity; and, by entertaining dissenting voices, it gave the appearance that Republicans were finally listening to African Americans. Moreover, as Wright-McNeill and Brock understood it, if the party developed genuine trust—by virtue of devising policies and strategies sensitive to the needs of black communities and convincing more African Americans to seek public office as Republicans—then perhaps black voters could be convinced to vote Republican. In the years after Ford's loss, the Republican Party was truly a party in transition, one that appeared to have the potential to become an inclusive space for at least some African Americans. Howard Baker succinctly summarized the GOP's new strategy during a June 1978 speech to the NRBC; in front of his Atlanta audience, the optimistic senator predicted that the party would claim at least 20 percent support from African Americans in the 1980 election. "Black voters are not the chattel property of the Democratic Party," he confidently proclaimed. "We want them more."[67]

PLACING FAITH IN REAGAN

By the end of 1978, African Americans had started the slow process of reintegrating the Republican Party—serving on the executive committee of the RNC, holding positions in state and local party organizations, and working as aides to dozens of Republican governors, congressmen, and senators. Likewise, in that same year, more than one hundred black Republican challengers ran for positions in state legislatures, attempting to join the one hundred existing incumbent officials; meanwhile, thirteen black Republicans ran for positions in the U.S. House of Representatives. Only one—Melvin Evans of the U.S. Virgin Islands—won his congressional race, making him the first black Republican to sit in the House in more than forty years.[68] For the RNC, such activity was proof that their outreach initiatives were beginning to take root—a 1978 memo cheered the emergence of black community spokesmen who were "carry[ing] the message of the Republican Party through black media, personal appearances, speaking engagements, as well as seeking office."[69] Moreover, the party had achieved crucial support among African American voters, Wright-McNeill research director Jerry Solomon noted in a November report; indeed, black voters had played an "instrumental" role in a number of Republican victories in the 1978 midterm elections. More than 15 percent of African Americans—double the amount from four years prior—cast ballots for party candidates in 1978, in some cases, they even provided the margin of victory for Republican nominees in five states. For example, Illinois senator Charles Percy was reelected with 32 percent of the black vote, while Pennsylvania governor Richard Thornburgh earned 52 percent; likewise, conservative Oklahoma congressman Mickey Edwards won reelection with a reported 80 percent of the black vote.[70]

The Republican Party's efforts, the *New York Amsterdam News* argued, appeared to be yielding slow dividends, noting with some fascination that black Democrats were beginning to trickle into Republican events. "I was getting nowhere with the Democrats," lamented Mary Walton of New York in 1978 "I decided to move over to the Republicans some time ago." Analyzing similar sentiments, reporter Andy Cooper determined that the "Republicans stand to reap" major gains "if they are serious about opening their ranks. There are enough Blacks . . . who are unhappy over either being taken for granted or completely ignored by the Democrats to begin the trickle Brock is looking for."[71]

In Massachusetts, however, the RNC's outreach efforts were unable to prevent Ed Brooke's defeat in the November midterm elections; the senator's loss was a blow to black Republicans' outreach efforts, as the black senator was one of the most widely respected black officials, irrespective of political affiliation, among African American audiences. Any discussions of the elections," wrote civil rights stalwart Bayard Rustin in November 1978, "must begin with the saddest news of all, the defeat of Senator Ed Brooke." Reflecting on the politician's twelve years in the Senate, Rustin declared:

> He was unusually effective. With his close links to the moderate wing of the Republican Party, Ed Brooke frequently acted as a bridge between the two parties constantly defending and articulating the pro-

gram of the civil rights movement. And, unlike some other contemporary political figures, Senator Brooke always understood the difference between compromise and selling out. In short, he was a marvelous Senator and we will miss him greatly.[72]

From the beginning, Brooke's campaign was plagued by problems. A primary challenge from conservative Avi Nelson hampered the senator early on. The young conservative opposed Brooke on nearly everything: abortion, affirmative action, federal protections for minorities and the poor, tax cuts, and gun control. And while the senator edged out his right-wing challenger with the assistance of a multiracial coalition of voters, the battle still left Brooke weary and strapped for campaign funds. In the general election, his liberal Democratic opponent, Paul Tsongas, received heavy support from both President Carter and Senator Ted Kennedy. The latter politician's endorsement was a shock, since he had remained neutral in the 1966 and 1972 contests in a gesture of political goodwill. Scandals also dogged Brooke throughout the year: an acrimonious public divorce, accusations of health insurance fraud, and charges of financial corruption sullied his political reputation. Despite endorsements from a diverse group of leaders—including feminist Gloria Steinem, civil rights leader Coretta Scott King, Jesse Jackson, and Henry Kissinger—Brooke lost to Paul Tsongas with less than 45 percent of the popular vote; the black official received more than 90 percent of the black vote and 70 percent of the Jewish vote, but was unable to pull support from Catholics, white ethnics, unionists, and white suburbanites. "Brooke didn't lose," one distraught black voter wept, after hearing the news, "the community lost."[73] With the liberal black Republican gone from the national stage, the lines between liberal, moderate, and conservative black party members became starker; to put it another way, by 1978, Brooke was the liberal counterbalance to black conservative Republicanism.

As African Americans mourned the political loss of Ed Brooke, a group of black Republicans was orchestrating the launch of what would become a major African American conservative organization. With the assistance of Republican senator Orrin Hatch of Utah, longtime Republican J. A. Parker established the Lincoln Institute for Research and Education (LIRE), a conservative black think-tank that examined public policy issues that "impacted the lives of black middle America," including minority enterprise, education, social justice, unemployment, welfare reform, and taxes.[74] LIRE claimed to "re-evaluate those theories and programs of the past decades" that had "failed to fulfill the claims" of Democrats and had been "harmful to the long-range interests of blacks." As Parker argued in 1978,

The very idea of black conservatism seems fanciful to some observers, both black and white. This reveals an almost total lack of understanding and awareness of black history and of the black intellectual tradition in the United States. . . . When we review . . . history . . . we see that today's black conservatives come out of a long and honorable tradition. Let us also not forget that the black community is a community of individuals, the vast majority of whom no longer seek a place for themselves on the liberal plantation.[75]

A year later, in addition to hosting a series of workshops, discussions, and seminars, the organization launched a scholarly arm, the *Lincoln Review,* a journal that provided a platform for "points of view that may fall outside conventionally defined 'black issues' and black perspectives but that are nevertheless of significant concern to black Americans."[76] The most innovative feature of the conservative quarterly, stated the *Wall Street Journal,* was that "it views black Americans as producers, actual and potential, whose interest lies in expanding opportunities rather than restricting ones. We hope the *Lincoln Review* will provide more of this perspective."[77]

Certainly, this was a vision shared by many black Republicans. LIRE's focus had far more in common with the party's right wing than with the philosophies of Ed Brooke. The group was similar to Clay Claiborne's Black Silent Majority Committee, sharing similar platforms and goals. Parker described LIRE as a black "neoconservative" organization, reasoning that the institute offered new kinds of conservative solutions to "old" problems, unrestrained by the boundaries of racism or racial inequality.[78] Many of the philosophies proposed by LIRE were ideas that black conservative Republicans had been suggesting for more than a decade; for example, the *Lincoln Review* was geared toward blacks who shared the same concerns as whites; the "only distinction between the two groups," Parker argued, sounding not unlike BSMC leaders eight years earlier, "is color." LIRE built on ideas of a black silent majority, reviving critiques of Democratic liberalism as "paternalistic, neoplantation thinking" that encouraged government dependency; the think tank admitted that it was targeting a specific cross section of African American voters, one that was middle class and "colorblind."[79] Likewise, the black institute was distinct in its informal mentorship of young African American men and women, assisting them in establishing prominent public careers; Clarence Thomas, Alan Keys, and Walter Williams were among those who would get their political start with the conservative organization. The organization also attracted the support of an interracial group of followers, including Roy Innis of CORE, Republican congressmen Mickey Edwards and Ron Paul, Black Power advocate Nathan Wright, and Chicago educator Marva Collins.[80]

By 1980, African Americans' frustrations with Carter, combined with the efforts of the RNC and black Republicans, meant that an increasing number of blacks were willing to consider voting for a Republican candidate in the 1980 presidential election. A survey conducted by *Trans Urban News* highlighted party awareness of this perceptible shift of attitude; of nine GOP presidential hopefuls, all suggested that winning a portion of the black vote was key to winning the 1980 election. When asked, "How important is the Black vote for 1980," responses ranged from "very important" to "absolutely vital."[81] Texas Republican John Connally was one of the standouts; in addition to enlisting the help of a black Chicago political consulting firm, he also hired seventy-nine African American campaign workers to conduct "black outreach." Likewise, the newspaper commended Illinois congressman John Anderson and Bob Dole for their outreach efforts; all three insisted that the black vote was of "higher priority now than in the past." The black electorate was a bigger constituency group now, reasoned another official. Many of the respondents went so far as to declare that the black vote had always been important to the party's success. Adopting a slightly different approach, Ronald Reagan asserted that his "appeal transcend[ed] color" since "Blacks understand leadership." In contrast, George H. W. Bush specifically listed nine states where black support was critical to the upcoming election; adding to this claim, Dole indicated that Massachusetts would be especially vital given the state's high number of registered black Republicans and independents. Tennessee senator Howard Baker mentioned that he was in the midst of assembling a "black issues team" for the election, while Minnesota congressman Harold Stassen hired a ten-state black advisory board and created a campaign group: "Concerned Blacks for Stassen." In what was surely the most provocative of the efforts, Anderson hired Dick Gregory—the black comedian who ran for president in 1968 on the Freedom and Peace Party ticket—as his chief adviser on black affairs.[82]

The Republican candidates' interest in black voters was genuine in some respects; but in other ways, it was just as calculated. Arthur Fletcher once lamented that even among liberal and moderate party candidates, there was an implicit fear that appealing to African Americans would cost them the votes of whites; yet all of the candidates interviewed by *Trans Urban News* also realized that appearing indifferent to black voters would hurt them among some of their target constituencies of white moderates, a desperately needed element to any winning Republican coalition. In March 1980, for example, Ronald Reagan's campaign strategists insisted that any presidential candidate that wanted to win the general election would need to earn support from a "substantial number of moderate ticket-splitters," which meant tempering the "arch conservative characterization of the Governor" by avoiding ideological discussions and creating an image of the politician as a "warm, compassionate, caring individual." Just as significant, while most of these campaign appeals would be aimed at white voters, the strategists noted that targeted outreach to African Americans and Latinos was also necessary, in order to win over white moderates. Consequently, Reagan's advisers argued in favor of appointing minorities to symbolic, high-ranking campaign positions in order to give the appearance of inclusiveness and urged the California politician to listen seriously to the suggestions of black Republican leaders.[83]

Following the advice of his strategists, Reagan met with black Republicans throughout the July 1980 Republican National Convention, urging them to support his presidential candidacy and promising to incorporate their ideas into his campaign. His actions quickly produced results: black Republicans cautiously endorsed him as their choice for the party's 1980 nominee, reasoning that he had demonstrated a sincere interest in African Americans. This was a stunning shift from 1976, a year when the majority of the black delegates had balked at supporting Ronald Reagan. Now, a mere four years later, most of the black delegates embraced the same conservative candidate that they had once feared. There were many reasons for this dramatic shift in attitude: some shared the governor's right-wing conservatism; others were comforted by his record of black appointments during his tenure in California and his faith in free market enterprise. A few, including Art Fletcher, remained skeptical but were relieved by Reagan's moderate choice of George H. W. Bush as the vice presidential running mate. All of the delegates were thrilled that the conservative official had helped incorporate their urban policy plank—"verbatim"—into the party's 1980 platform. In short, black Republicans finally felt *included*—enough so that many were willing to become "political bedfellows" with a man whose conservatism made many of them uneasy. As he held Reagan's hand aloft in a "symbol of victory" during a convention reception for black Republicans, NBRC head James Cummings captured African American party members' sentiments, telling the "wildly cheering" crowd that "Governor Reagan is the best hope for the future of Black America, and ALL America."[84]

Within days of becoming the Republican presidential nominee, Reagan launched National Black Voters for Reagan-Bush, helmed by Arthur Teele of Florida; appointed Gloria Toote, Henry Lucas, W. O. Walker, Art Fletcher, Bob Brown, and nearly three dozen additional prominent black Republican leaders to campaign positions; and enlisted Wright-

McNeill & Associates and the NBRC to help craft his black outreach strategy.[85] Reagan's campaign also poured an estimated $975,000 into African American outreach, devoting $70,000 solely for black media appeals with the aim of earning 12 percent of the black vote in the general election. "I would prefer to think we could expect to do better than former President Ford's 8% and less than President Nixon's 13%," wrote one strategist in an August memo.[86] Reagan's African American outreach efforts were selective—concentrated on eight states where he would need to win some portion of the black vote in order to win the presidency; likewise, recruitment solely focused on those black Republicans, Democrats, and independents who were "young, college educated, registered to vote," and interested in free market enterprise and business.[87]

For those black Republicans who campaigned for Reagan, the task was twofold. Their primary aim was to dispel any notion of Republican indifference or hostility toward African Americans. Throughout the fall contest, they arranged for the nominee to cosponsor Black College Day 1980, speak at the NUL annual convention, meet regularly with black ministers, reporters, and civil rights leaders, and declare his plans to enforce civil rights legislation if elected president.[88] This approach was designed not only to create a compassionate representation of Ronald Reagan but also to cultivate an image of his black supporters as ordinary, trusted, and caring members of the community, negating characterizations of them as conservative elitists, out of touch with the needs of African Americans. Wright-McNeill, for instance, proposed a series of advertisements that offered a balance of "liberal/conservative images" of down-to-earth black party members: a black woman wearing "blue jeans and discussing business with her colleagues at the National Committee"; a black doctor casually talking with his African American neighbors; a hard-hat-wearing black construction working trying to make a living; and a young black "activist-type" handing out information on Republican economic programs. Most important, Wright-McNeill noted, was that the advertisements not appear "patronizing" or "preachy"—and that they be geared toward all African Americans—even though the campaign was interested in only a highly specific subset of black voters.[89]

The second part of black Republicans' campaign duties was the enactment of a "proactive strategy" to use black voters to defeat Jimmy Carter. In a September 1980 memo, Bob Wright explained that this approach had two major aims: "Holding down the Black turnout," and "garnishing what vote we can." To put it another way, both black and white strategists believed that Reagan would never win substantial support from the majority of African Americans; thus, the campaign endeavored to *neutralize* the black vote. Wright continued, writing that the campaign's strategy "must be aimed at preventing [black] emotions from reaching a point where there is heavy turnout to defeat Reagan as opposed to low turnout to elect Carter." The point then was not to repress or disenfranchise black voters, but rather to exploit African Americans' political apathy toward Jimmy Carter by avoiding racial antagonisms, while emphasizing Reagan's "positive" attributes and launching negative attacks on the president as an *individual* rather than as a member of the Democratic Party.[90] Without question, black Republicans' dual objectives were contradictory: African American party members both encouraged blacks to participate in the GOP and advocated for black political apathy and voter abstention—an approach that was in keeping with a political tradition that had long privileged the black middle class.

Reagan's team attempted to address race tactically throughout the campaign, employing a strategy his advisers called "Reagan Focused Impact" (RFI), which relayed conservative messages to target constituent groups without appearing overtly conservative or hostile. RFI was not restricted to racial issues; indeed, Reagan used it to address thorny topics that cropped up throughout the campaign season, including military strength and global peace. Nevertheless, racial and economic issues provided the "first use" of RFI. The test case emerged on a sweltering summer day in 1980, within the decaying metropolis and "garbage-strewn streets" of the South Bronx—the same area that President Carter had visited in 1977, pledging to use the full power of the federal government to revitalize the blighted district. Now, almost three years later, on August 5, 1980, Ronald Reagan stood in an empty lot, surrounded by the "burned-out skeletons of vacant buildings" and told a boisterous crowd of five hundred African American and Latino residents that Jimmy Carter had "broken his promise." The Republican Party could fix the problems of urban decay and economic inequality, Reagan insisted, through tax breaks and public-private partnerships to revitalize the local economy. A day earlier, in Chicago, Reagan had given a similar speech to the annual convention of the National Urban League; that talk had ended with more than half of the black delegates on their feet, "heartily applauding" the California governor. But in the South Bronx, Reagan's urban sermon quickly deteriorated into a shouting match between the politician and about seventy demonstrators. As the protestors chanted "go home, go home," a flushed-faced Reagan bellowed, "I just want you to give me a chance!"[91]

In some ways, the South Bronx incident recalled Reagan's emotional blow-up during a 1966 meeting of the National Negro Republican Assembly. The 1980 episode, however, was different; as Reagan's staff privately claimed, the Chicago and New York events were victories, whereas the NNRA incident was a disaster. Both of the August 1980 appearances generated positive press, including accolades from black reporters, many of whom noted the candidate's willingness to campaign in black neighborhoods—something Gerald Ford had refused to do in 1976. Even at his angriest, during the South Bronx confrontation, Reagan had come across as empathetic. In fact, the *Washington Post* asserted that his frustration was commendable, since it seemed to stem not from hostility but rather from concern over urban decay and economic inequality. The *New York Amsterdam News* also found the NUL speech and the South Bronx shouting match somewhat reassuring, commenting that the events proved that Reagan was "no devil" and "has no horns." Despite the fact that this was a calculated approach, most political observers saw "no subliminal campaigning. . . . No euphemistically named 'Southern Strategy.' No big white Country Club members-only wink. No code."[92]

This was exactly the kind of reaction that Reagan's strategists anticipated; in a confidential August memo, they stated that both events had broadcast a conservative message to the American public without appearing racist, reactionary, or hostile; in turn, the appearances had generated massive amounts of positive publicity among Reagan's target constituency of "white, suburbanite ticket-splitters." The only major criticism offered by his staff was that the press had pegged the events as race-conscious appeals to minority voters instead of race-neutral outreach to urban voters. As a result, they argued, the campaign had missed a valuable opportunity to appeal to another key constituency: "Catholic urban ethnics." Importantly, in spite of Reagan's professed allegiance to colorblindness, his strategy was anything but race neutral, given that his efforts were explicitly aimed at white voters, including white ethnics. Furthermore, the RFI approach managed to "neutralize" African American criticisms of the California official; for example, the positive press from the Chicago and New York events overshadowed black leaders' negative reaction to Reagan's speech on states' rights, delivered on August 3 in Philadelphia, Mississippi—the same town where three civil rights workers had been murdered sixteen years earlier.[93]

As black Republicans campaigned with Reagan, they also worked on cultivating a new and vocal black leadership. In October 1980, John McNeill met with prominent black businessmen, including United Negro College Fund (UNCF) president Clyde Williams. The group quietly appealed to the RNC, proposing the development of a new national political base of "educators, Black professionals, and others of their constituency," centered on the "economic development of the Black community utilizing Republican economic policies." McNeill argued that this type of voter was crucial for the future:

> These guys are very turned off by the "Daddy" King's, Coretta Scott King's, Andy Young's, Jesse Jackson's and other self anointed spokespeople for Black America . . . they are quite concerned about the perception that the "New Right" movement is being attributed to the Republican Party.

The group's goal was to introduce alternative voices in the broader dialogue on black politics: African American leaders who were neither colorblind conservatives nor a part of the civil rights vanguard, but instead equated civil rights with economic rights and appreciated private enterprise, deregulation of the market, and tax cuts.

This economic thrust had been a mainstay in black Republican thought for decades, but in 1980 it incorporated a new appreciation for private industry. For example, campaign appeals blamed Jimmy Carter for forcing African Americans to "abandon" the "American Dream." Commercials aired on black radio stations and advertisements in black periodicals harped on high mortgage rates, inflation, and unemployment. One advertisement—"Jobs, Jobs, Jobs"—featured an image taken during the South Bronx incident, portraying Reagan shaking hands with a genial young black man, surrounded by a crowd of Latino and African American voters. Describing Reagan's economic platform as "refreshing," the advertisement explained how African Americans would benefit from the candidate's emphasis on business and employment. The ad explicitly stated that Reagan saw black voters as part of his "colorblind coalition," and that he was treating them equally, by speaking to them in the "same manner" that he spoke to "*all*" Americans."[94] Here again was the campaign's attempt to use "colorblindness" in a manner that was far from race neutral—this time by targeting middle-class African Americans and positioning them as part of a diverse coalition of constituents.

Reagan's appeals to African Americans are worth examining, especially when contrasted to his earlier attempts to "engage" race in presidential politics; for instance, though he still employed the coded language of states' rights, as he had done in the past, he also began to speak more of systemic inequality and discrimination to black audiences. This surely was a moderate black Republican vision of Ronald Reagan, crafted to make the black middle class feel comfortable with the California official and to project an air of inclusiveness, appealing enough to win over white moderates. By the time *Black Enterprise* sat down for a lengthy interview with the candidate in the fall of 1980, Reagan had modified his rhetoric to the point that he could argue that "much remains to be done" in "eradicating the cancer of racism." The same man who stubbornly argued that he would have voted against the civil rights acts of the 1960s had he been in Congress also told the black magazine that he understood and appreciated why African Americans had looked to the federal government to protect and enforce their rights, especially in an era where "states' rights" meant the aggressive denial of civil rights for blacks. He spent some time discussing urban uprisings, as well; expressing sympathy for rioters, he insisted that disorder had been triggered by inequality, lack of economic aid, and unequal treatment under the law. His remarks sounded astonishingly similar to those offered by Ed Brooke in the mid-1960s. Moreover, his comments allowed him to attack the Carter administration, by arguing that the federal government had failed to protect African Americans economic and civil rights in the 1970s. He closed by arguing that while the federal government was a necessary agent for preventing racial discrimination, it was ineffective at creating black wealth; he thus proposed that deregulating the market, establishing free enterprise zones in "inner cities," and offering tax incentives for private industries to develop businesses in urban areas with high unemployment would create new opportunities for prosperity that would affect not only the black middle class but also the black poor and working class, bolstering the entire community. While his policies were colorblind in focus—aimed at "urban" areas, rather than geared toward African Americans specifically—Reagan insisted that this was an unimportant distinction since African Americans were the majority demographic in urban locales and thus would be the prime beneficiaries of such programs.[95] Though a calculated approach, this was nevertheless an important rhetorical moment: Reagan not only managed to appropriate some of the language of the civil rights movement, Black Power, and black Republicans but also did so without dramatically changing his ideological outlook.

Though his proposals were untested, his words nevertheless rang true among a small but prominent group of civil rights leaders, who offered their support to the GOP presidential nominee. While preaching at a small brick church in Detroit on October 16, 1980, Ralph Abernathy offered a "surprise endorsement" of Ronald Reagan; daring other black leaders to question his decision, the civil rights official fiercely reminded the public, "I am the man in whose arms Martin Luther King died." Reagan, who was present during the announcement, was clearly unable to hide his glee from reporters, remarking, "I think it's magnificent. I think it's a great help. And something, uh, I could not have, I just didn't realize such a thing could happen. I'm overwhelmed." In private, Wright-McNeill had been working on securing such support for months; nevertheless, the endorsement was still shocking given that a mere two months prior,

Abernathy had declared that he would never vote for a "racist like Ronald Reagan."

Days after the Detroit announcement, SCLC head Hosea Williams seconded Abernathy's endorsement, stating "Jimmy Carter did not even do as much for the black people of Georgia as Lester Maddox did. . . . Ain't no way in the world brother Reagan can do worse." Likewise, Fayette, Mississippi, mayor Charles Evers—brother of iconic civil rights activist Medger Evers—joined the growing chorus, describing Reagan as the "best man for the job" because, applauding the conservative candidate's economic platform for turning "welfare into workfare."[96] Black leaders were shocked—many of them outraged and disappointed—by the endorsements. "My gut reaction when I saw [Abernathy] and heard what he had to say was that he was a traitor," angrily stated Michigan minister Darneau Stewart. If he were alive, Coretta Scott King coldly told reporters, her "late husband" would have opposed Ronald Reagan. Michigan preacher C. L. Anderson, however, applauded the announcements, declaring that it was only fitting that blacks have diverse political options and noting that he was impressed with Reagan's colorblind outlook.[97] Immediately following the Abernathy and Williams endorsements, Wright-McNeill was flooded with phone calls and letters from African Americans willing to declare their public support to the Reagan-Bush campaign; among them, as Bob Wright wrote in an October 22 memo, were leaders from CORE, including Al Starks, George Holmes, and the increasingly conservative Roy Innis, who relayed their interest in discussing an "official CORE endorsement of Ronald Reagan."[98]

Abernathy's, Williams's, and other black leaders' nods to Reagan both hinted at the success of black Republicans' campaign efforts and highlighted African Americans' dissatisfaction with the Carter administration. In truth, this was not so much a shocking moment as it was a pragmatic one. Some black leaders feared that they—and, by extension, African Americans—would be invisible if Reagan were to win the White House. In a sense, this was a balance-of-power move—an attempt to leverage their vote to gain concessions from both parties; in the past, African Americans had discussed using two-party competition, but few prominent leaders had been willing to take the risk. But in 1980, their concerns about influence, coupled with their hostility toward Carter, were enough to convince them to support Ronald Reagan and, in some cases, even switch their partisan affiliation, as Williams did in October; likewise, Reagan's "inclusive" conservatism provided a measure of reassurance to those, like Abernathy, who struggled with the candidate's "racist" reputation.

The November 4, 1980, presidential election proved to be a decisive victory for the Republican Party, with Ronald Reagan earning almost 51 percent of the popular vote to Jimmy Carter's 41 percent. The California politician won all but six states and Washington, D.C., including the entire South with the exception of the president's home state of Georgia.[99] A *New York Times* poll found that of those people that voted for Reagan, almost 40 percent believed that the nation "needed a change." As his strategists had predicted months earlier, he did not win the presidential election on the basis of ideology; indeed, only 11 percent of his backers cited conservatism as their reason for support. In the popular vote, "43 million people voted for Mr. Reagan, 35 million voted for Jimmy Carter," wrote the *Times*, explaining low voter turnout, "and 75 million voted for neither." To be sure, low turnout hurt the president but hardly affected Reagan, who won with the help of a broad coalition of voters. Reagan supporters included middle-class and wealthy voters from every region of the country, educated constituents, Catholics, and adults over the age of thirty; likewise, about 60 percent of white southerners, most of whom were moderate suburbanites, cast ballots for him. Though Carter scraped out majorities among unions and blue-collar voters, Reagan made serious inroads into these groups and others, including Latinos, who gave the president-elect more than 40 percent of their vote.[100]

As it turns out, African Americans were also a part of Reagan's winning coalition, providing the official with about 14 percent of their votes, the highest level of black support a Republican presidential candidate had seen in twenty years. Analysts also noted with some interest that this small cadre had played a key role in pushing at least two states into Reagan's column.[101] Despite the fact that this tally exceeded strategists' predictions, RNC chair Bill Brock stated that he was still disappointed that African Americans had largely "retained their loyalty to the Democratic Party." But this was not African Americans' problem, Brock mused; instead, it was the party's issue. The GOP "is not there yet," he admitted. "We have a long way to go in terms of building this party."[102]

African Americans offered mixed reactions to the Reagan election; for some, the election results were nightmarish: "What a majority of black Americans feared would happen has happened," Gilbert Caldwell ominously intoned. "An avowed conservative Republican will occupy the White House for the next four years." The Congressional Black Caucus, meanwhile, warned blacks to beware of the conservative revolution sweeping the nation and to apply "firm pressure" on conservative and progressive lawmakers. One survey found that 16 percent of African Americans believed Reagan would be a "great" president, while 31 percent thought he would shrink unemployment.[103] In contrast, Vernon Jordan adopted a neutral approach, suggesting that Reagan's election was symbolic of a national spurning of the Carter administration rather than a "massive swing to the radical right." African Americans, he posited, were now responsible for holding the president-elect to his campaign promises, forging links with the new administration to ensure black participation, and organizing effective coalitions to defend African American interests.[104]

Black Republicans publicly declared their excitement over Reagan's victory; Henry Lucas, for example, declared that blacks "must insist on having real inputs into the decisions made by whoever is in power." Asked by reporters if he took offense to being labeled a "right-wing lunatic" by outspoken black Democrats, Lucas declared, "Hell, no! I am happy that they introduced the subject of conservatism. It gives me an opportunity to present an alternative point of view." Gloria Toote, Reagan's longtime supporter, was "elated" with the GOP's win, insisting that the politician would keep his campaign promises to African Americans. Discussing Reagan's support for free enterprise zones in urban areas, the Harlem lawyer compared the proposal to Arthur Fletcher's plans from a decade earlier, maintaining that the president-elect's program was a much-needed step in helping racial minorities achieve economic opportunity.[105]

Toote was one of more than a dozen black Republicans, of varied ideologies, who quickly gained appointments to Ronald Reagan's presidential transition team, helping the incoming administration identify new personnel for various government agencies, departments, and commissions. For example, Reagan appointed liberal Republican Jewel Lafontant of Chicago head of the U.S. Civil Rights Commission transition team and appointed the conservative J. A. Parker as interim chair of the Equal Employment Opportunity Commission. The latter choice was provocative given the significance of the EEOC, the office responsible for enforcing federal antidiscrimination laws in employment; in Parker, Reagan selected a black conservative who shared his disdain for affirmative action policies and his faith in colorblind solutions and limited government. In spite of this, former Nixon and Ford aide Stan Scott dismissed black fears over Ronald Reagan. "I do not have a foreboding like . . . a lot of the Black leadership has," he remarked. "[Reagan] wants to be President of all the people. . . . I don't have fears about Blacks being forgotten." He reasoned that colorblindness would not prevent the president-elect from building a relationship with all constituencies, including African Americans; he concluded that the election provided both a mandate and an opportunity to recruit a "cadre of bright young people"—fresh faces who would bring "new thinking and new solutions for problems" plaguing the nation.[106]

Black Republicans, however, were *terrified* at being forgotten or rendered invisible in the GOP; that fear had been one of the defining features of their actions over the past twenty years. While many of them were conservative and moderate to begin with, this moment was distinct as they professed their loyalty to a politician they had once shunned, comforted by his economic programs—plans that they had helped build. That loyalty appeared to reap some rewards immediately: in addition to transitional roles, Reagan began appointing black Republicans to permanent positions within his administration. He appointed liberal black Republican Samuel Pierce as secretary of Housing and Urban Development, after considering Lafontant and conservative economist Thomas Sowell for presidential cabinet positions; likewise, Robert Wright and Thelma Duggin also received federal roles. It is worth noting, though, that Nixon and Ford had both made high-profile black appointments as well; thus, while a welcome sign by Reagan, it was nevertheless symbolic until proved otherwise.[107]

The election of 1980 also brought new African American faces into the Republican Party; the Maryland chapter of the NBRC, for example, experienced a surge in membership following the presidential race, going from a dormant to an active chapter with eighty members within a few months. Virginia Kellogg, a former Democrat who had worked on Marion Barry's 1978 mayoral campaign, had switched her party affiliation shortly before the 1980 election, campaigning vigorously for Ronald Reagan. "The time of the black elephant has come," she proudly declared in the wake of the party's November electoral success. Explaining his party switch, former Democrat Mel Williamson-Gray offered, "I never agreed with the liberal Democratic philosophy. I've always believed in self-help and hard work." Working with the Republican Party was a long and tedious process, another ex-Democrat acknowledged, but it was the "sure way" for African Americans to advance. Significantly, the Maryland NBRC members insisted that the "old kind of racism no longer exists" because of significant civil rights advancements.[108]

Such assertions were similar to those a dozen years earlier by Richard Nixon's black Republican appointees; and like the members of the "Black Cabinet," the Maryland party members maintained that African Americans needed to focus on developing new solutions to the problems that continued to pervade the system. Summarized an overly idealistic Winston Wilkinson, "I operate from the assumption that certain kinds of discrimination and racism that happened 20 years ago cannot happen again." And while the new NBRC members "flinched" at the mention of individual party members, including North Carolina senator Jesse Helms, they also introduced new perspectives on civil rights and equality; for example, the group eagerly explained its acceptance of states' rights as support for local power for black businesses, free market enterprise, and limited intervention on the part of the federal government. Where the phrase had once brought to mind an ugly history of inequality, violence, and repression, for most black Republicans a new cadre had emerged that attempted to redefine "states' rights" as a form of black self-determination.[109]

The Maryland Republicans represented but one part of black Republicans' most significant accomplishment: not only did they help integrate African Americans into the Reagan coalition; they also helped make Republican ideas palatable to black audiences in a way that the GOP had struggled to do in the past. When coupled with black dissatisfaction with Jimmy Carter, it created a context in which *some* African Americans publicly began to question their affiliation with the Democratic Party; and perhaps even more satisfying for longtime black Republicans, this "new" approach would validate, at least for the short term, strategies that black Republicans had advanced for decades.

BLACK ALTERNATIVES AND THE FAIRMONT CONFERENCE OF 1980

In December 1980, just one month after the presidential election, approximately 125 black professionals with an "air of prosperous self-assurance" met in the Fairmont Hotel in San Francisco, California, for a two-day conference to discuss new approaches to issues of African American concern. Arranged by black Republican Henry Lucas and conservative economist Thomas Sowell, and financed by the Reagan administration, the "Black Alternatives Conference" proposed that the "energy and creativity engendered by the old civil rights movement had run their course and spent themselves." Perhaps coincidentally, the hosts settled on the same location where the National Negro Republican Assembly had launched its alternative black politics movement some sixteen years prior.[110] "These are the voices that were drowned out in the rhetoric of revolution and protest in the 1960s and 1970s," journalist Herbert Denton described. "They point to evidence in national polls in claiming that their views are in many ways more in concert with masses of blacks than are the views of the civil rights organizations. They are bound to have an impact on national policy because of their close agreement with the views of the administration of Ronald Reagan."[111]

Participants cut a diverse swath through black America and included academics, economists, politicians, journalists, businessmen, and community activists. The gathering, as the *Washington Post* suggested, seemed to go beyond political partisanship, as the group's diversity showcased a full spectrum of political affiliation, with Republicans, Democrats and independents well represented.[112] For instance, panelists included Gloria Toote, journalists Chuck Stone and Tony Brown, political scientists Charles Hamilton and Martin L. Kilson, former Manhattan Borough president Percy Sutton, and J. A. Parker. Nevertheless, the ideological framework of the conference was conservative, although a group of black liberals and progressives attended: the underlying philosophy of the gathering was that liberal methods of government intervention had failed African Americans and the poor.[113] Although skeptical at first, reporters later admitted that black Republicans at the conference had "circulated refreshing ideas that challenged old assumptions about what is best for blacks."[114] Yet these were not new ideas; these were proposals that liberal, moderate, and conservative black party members had discussed since 1936. What was new here was the public's scrutiny of those ideas and a Republican president's willingness to publicize black party members' proposals as part of his platform; and, of course, it undoubtedly helped that these ideas wrestled with economics in a manner that Reagan could appreciate.

The objective of the conference, Henry Lucas declared on the first day, was to establish a black social policy agenda for the next four years; a secondary goal was to give voice to "alternative" black leaders, voices different from those within civil rights organizations. "There are people—black people—here who are competent, who are talented, who think differently, who want to examine the past; people who, if this is the case, are willing to say that some approaches have not worked and that we do need a change."[115] Acknowledging the necessity of the civil rights movement for contemporary black progress during one panel, Thomas Sowell nevertheless argued that it was no longer relevant to the needs of African Americans, suggesting that an overreliance on Democratic policies had impeded black advancement, thereby creating a dependent and paternalistic relationship "somewhat at odds with the spirit of the Thirteenth Amendment." This was a rather roundabout way of comparing blacks' relationship to the Democratic Party with "plantation politics." Consequently, Sowell asserted that if African Americans wanted true equality, they had to offer solutions rooted in "freedom of choice," allowing community members to decide their own fate, instead of relying on the decisions of bureaucrats and government officials.[116]

Dan J. Smith, a member of the California State Commission for Economic Development, echoed Sowell's remarks, offering a ten-year operating plan that used the Republican Party to advance black progress through wealth creation. The foundation for this advancement, moreover, rested on the middle class and the need to avoid "misconceptions about who black Americans really are." Smith proposed that solutions for racial equality had to consider the "average" African American: "83 percent work for a living, 77 percent are not on welfare, and 62 percent do not live in poverty." This method was not elitist, nor did it downplay the plight of the downtrodden, he argued; instead, he envisioned this approach as a way of upending stereotypes about African Americans as dependents, rather than producers, and broadcasting the socioeconomic diversity of the black community to policy makers and officials.[117]

Introducing a conflicting perspective, panelist Oscar Wright insisted that any meaningful exchange on African Americans must come from those most in need. As the founder of People Active for Community Education (PACE), Wright was a firm proponent of grass-roots activism, which included, at one point, mobilizing local community groups to oppose forced busing and support harsher sentencing laws on criminals. Though conservative, Wright blurred the lines between the ideology and Black Nationalism—aligning with the Reagan administration and lobbying for local control as a kind of black self-determination or "community control," seeing it as a method for "taking back" black neighborhoods, education, and economics.[118]

In another panel, Chuck Stone, an editor for the *Philadelphia Daily News*, adopted and expanded on Wright's theme. At the start of his talk, Stone—the same person who had derided Edward Brooke as a "colored honkie" a decade earlier—declared, "I see a great harmony between what I have long advocated and some of what I have heard in these sessions. And so would most blacks, if only they could get past the obstacle of current black 'leadership.'" Like the rest of the attendees, he staked his hopes in economic uplift, relaying a story about a July 1980 interview with Ronald Reagan to make his argument. The California politician had shocked the journalist when he appeared to endorse a "black-owned, black-operated philosophy," reasoning, "If you live in a ghetto and you need to buy a toothbrush, there's no reason why you shouldn't buy it from a black-owned drugstore." Astounded, Stone had commented, "Governor, you sound like a black nationalist!" Reagan, the consummate politician, had simply "smiled and . . . blushed." The economic self-determination themes of the story and the Fairmont conference were identical Stone proposed; likewise, they were the same themes offered at the Black Power Conference between 1966 and 1968. Of course, these were themes that black Republicans had emphasized throughout the 1960s and 1970s, especially during the Nixon years. Ultimately, economic self-reliance and independent black leadership, Stone concluded, would facilitate black progress: "These are the politics of change," he declared. "These are the economics of the new humanism."[119]

Departing from the conservative economic theme, liberal political scientist Martin Kilson tackled broad ideas of black political power. In order to achieve the goals of black uplift, new coalitions, officials, and leaders were needed:

We need . . . politicians who are increasingly expert at managing beyond and across ethnic and racial boundaries. Politicians of the kind
that Edward Brooke . . . [and] like the great Arthur Fletcher, who, in
many ways, is really the granddaddy of this occasion. . . . In short, we
need a new core of what I call trans-ethnic black political leaders, both
liberal and conservative, but especially the latter. And this conference
just might be one of the events that spark this group of trans-ethnic
black politicians.[120]

Years later, his remarks would spark a debate in liberal circles over the
merits of dialoguing with a group of black conservatives invested in dismantling social welfare programs and equal opportunity initiatives. But in
this moment, in December 1980, Kilson was preoccupied with the poten-
tiality of black politics, with the hopes of finding a new kind of politician
who could gain support from a multiracial coalition of voters; though
Kilson also mentioned several black Democrats who embodied "trans-
ethnic" leadership, his theory resembled Ed Brooke's "non-Negro" political approach. To put it another way, the political scientist was interested
in finding leaders who could use multiple political ideologies to advance
solutions and who could walk comfortably through disparate political
and cultural worlds. His emphasis on conservatism came from the same
rationale deployed by black Republicans for generations: "There is too
high a cost associated with black policy isolation from conservative initiatives in American political life."[121]

Such declarations were enough to coax Clarence Thomas, then a senatorial aide, into offering his remarks in front of the large audience; smiling
broadly, the black Republican praised his fellow conference attendees for
"having the courage to come together publicly and show the strength."[122]
Listening to Thomas's statement, reporter Juan Williams mused that perhaps "conservative blacks" had finally "found a home." As the black Republican continued, the *Washington Post* writer realized that Thomas's
conservatism was "born of the same personal anger at racism that fired
up the militants of the 1960s." Thomas, like most of the other speakers, did not deny that racism was still prevalent; nevertheless, he supported the consensus that it was no longer a significant barrier to black
achievement. For the aspiring politician, the "old-fashioned virtues" of
self-reliance, hard work, accountability, and "extra effort" provided more
than enough "alternative solutions."[123] But as we have seen, these were not
merely old-fashioned ideas; though rooted in a nineteenth-century black
middle-class tradition, these "virtues" were also part of the philosophies
of moderate civil rights organizations and black Republican groups. One
important difference emerged from Thomas's talk—instead of advocating

for complex race-conscious philosophies, as many black Republicans, of all ideologies, had done in the past, he endorsed a colorblind philosophy, one that aligned with the outlook of groups like the LIRE and the BSMC. In many ways, he pulled from an ideologically broad black Republican tradition, employing the "progressive" rhetoric of racial uplift, while framing it within the reactionary language of right-wing conservatism.

The Black Alternatives Conference was an ideological amalgamation, difficult to understand given the long legacy of hostility that existed between blacks and the Republican Party, that projected, albeit simplistically, the promise of a common political bond among African Americans.[124] Percy Sutton, a "card carrying NAACPer" and a black Democrat, called his presentation "A Skeptic Persuaded," noting that he had come to the conference to better understand the link between African Americans and conservatism; after two days of sessions, he announced that he finally grasped the concept. As a proud capitalist and a minority entrepreneur, he saw conservatism as "rational," even desirable. "I have become convinced—not yet converted, but convinced . . . that you have the potential here among you to exercise a real influence," Sutton declared, "so that four years from now those of us who are Democrats will say that the Republicans did better by blacks than did Democrats." Political conversion was contingent upon the impact of these alternative solutions; though economics was the common thread that appealed to both black liberals and conservatives, bipartisan black support necessitated that Republicans treat African American issues with care and attention.[125]

Closing out the conference, White House counselor Ed Meese, indicated that black issues would be treated with care by the Reagan administration, expressing strong enthusiasm for the new "thinking and new ideas" suggested in San Francisco. Recalling a recent session with a prominent group of black civil rights leaders, the Reagan official noted, "They were talking about the last ten years and the ideas of the last ten years. You are talking about the ideas of the next ten years or beyond."[126] Meese too thought the discussion was refreshing; but what made these ideas *feel* new was that the Reagan administration, in the words of Meese, was ready and eager to listen. A persistent conference demand, by both conservatives and liberals alike, was that African Americans be appointed to "substantive" White House positions on the basis of talents rather than race; Meese promised that the administration would do just that. Meese optimistically concluded that Ronald Reagan would address the problems of the nation in a manner that would benefit blacks as well as "Americans of all types"; drawing heavily on the recommendations of the conference, the white official pledged to "broaden the horizons"—as he declared in closing, "*We have an opportunity!*"[127]

The Black Alternatives Conference generated intense reactions from the black public. Critics were outraged over the solutions proposed at the symposium; for example, an NAACP official accused Thomas Sowell of preparing to play the "traditional role of 'house nigger' in the Reagan administration," for opposing Affirmative Action. Clarence Thomas took the brunt of the backlash—after being labeled a "race-traitor" by black politicians for criticizing the welfare system, the conservative black Republican angrily retorted that the "real mystery is how 90 percent of black Americans could support these policies and vote for Jimmy Carter." He further exclaimed that the protesting, marching, and seeking help from the federal government "hasn't worked. It isn't working. And someone needs to say that."[128] Criticism also came from within black Republican circles. J. Clay Smith, a self-described "Lincoln Republican," offered a lengthy critique of the conference in a 1983 *Howard Law Review* article. Though excited about the concept of alternative solutions, Smith scorned the eager kowtowing to conservative politicians; the attorney argued that this strain of conservatism would alienate African Americans and attract a "fringe element." Sowell's and Thomas's outlooks, he continued were classist and unworkable and would have "disastrous consequences in the long run." He specifically took issue with the notion of deregulation and colorblindness, noting that "regulation" had protected—and still protected—African Americans from racial and economic discrimination in both public and private industries. And while Smith agreed with black conservatives that stronger black entrepreneurship was desirable and necessary, he rejected the idea of an antistatist, private-industry-reliant, "self-help" approach. "Silence and blind allegiance by Black Republicans to the neo-conservative clamor," the liberal Republican closed, "will set the two-party system . . . back a century."[129] Even Juan Williams, who seemed to delight in announcing Clarence Thomas's arrival on the front page of the *Washington Post*, seemed conflicted about black conservatism; but unlike Smith or other critics, the journalist ultimately determined that the proponents could have a positive impact, so long as they remembered that "this country is not yet so sophisticated that blacks, even black Republicans, can say it makes no difference what color an American is."[130] This was an insightful observation; whether calculated or idealistic, the conference offered a naïve vision of a black political utopia, one that had both progressive and conservative elements. Indeed, the conference presumed that with the passage of civil rights legislation and policies, the legacy of racial inequality had been diminished to the point where federal involvement was no longer necessary.

Segments of the American public, including some black middle-class communities, responded positively to the conference; the gathering generated extensive coverage in the national media and spawned further conferences, documentaries, organizations, and public-policy debates.[131] Of greater significance, the conference—the culmination of Bill Brock and Wright-McNeill's outreach efforts—highlighted strategies and approaches historically vocalized by black Republicans and introduced new African American figures, intellectuals, and policy makers to and into the GOP. Since 1936, black Republicans had struggled to demonstrate their political relevance to both their race and their party, often conflicted by their irreconcilable loyalties. As they moved into the 1980s, the question was no longer are black Republicans relevant but what roles would they play in the party, and how would they influence American politics.

• • •

Throughout the late 1970s and into 1980, the RNC launched a vigorous outreach campaign to reintegrate the party and attract black voters, an effort that was built on the legacies and lessons, often painful, that black Republicans had learned over the course of nearly half a century. For Wright-McNeill & Associates, its mission was both straightforward and daunting: broaden the party tent, appeal to black constituents with proposals for realistic economic and social programs, and develop aggressive outreach efforts from the grass roots to the national level of the party.

The consultants and Brock succeeded in cultivating a new kind of interest among African Americans, especially in the South, Midwest, and Northeast; likewise, they also helped generate a widespread interest in black voters as part of a "winning" coalition of voters among *white* Republicans. During the 1980 campaign, for example, the black consulting group targeted five "highly contested" senatorial races, where the results "could have gone either way." Postelection reports, both from partisan and nonpartisan sources, demonstrated that Wright-McNeill's approach was instrumental in bolstering the Republican contenders' support among blacks, which in turn proved key to helping all five win. In Alabama 13 percent was all that Paula Hawkins needed to grab electoral victory, whereas in Oklahoma 41 percent of black voters backed Don Nickles, helping him best a Democratic incumbent.[132]

Black Republican strategies that had at one time seemed fringe now felt relevant to party officials as they began to actually *see* the effects of African Americans on local and state elections; even some of the party's most cynical strategists understood that outreach to African Americans (albeit through a race-neutral approach) was necessary, seeing it as crucial to wooing not black voters but white moderates. This is what made Wright and McNeill successful within party circles; their pragmatic, and at times, calculating approach to American politics allowed the GOP and middle-class African Americans to use each other for mutual gain. They straddled two very different communities, finding a language and a strategy necessary to bring parts of those worlds together, even if but for a moment. The consultants reinforced the idea, to the Republican Party, that black voters were *relevant*. Political scientist Pearl Robinson tapped into this idea in a 1982 report on blacks and the GOP; she also concluded that, while future shifts in presidential elections among black voters would be incremental, changes on the local and state level, in contrast, could be considerable, as a result of continued black outreach and Republican politicians' policy initiatives. These programs would likely be colorblind in nature, she argued (sounding not unlike Arthur Fletcher), thereby making it all the more important for African Americans to get involved with the GOP, so they could have a voice in crafting such policies. She pointed to Ed Brooke to illustrate her argument; and though Brooke's liberal outlook often put him at odds with an increasingly conservative Republican Party, the example is nevertheless relevant. Specifically, while in Congress, she maintained that the senator had adopted a colorblind approach that allowed him to create policies that addressed the "large social and economic groupings" and advanced the interests of the race; in other words, Brooke had employed, as we have seen, a "non-Negro approach" that blended colorblind rhetoric with race-conscious appeals.[133]

Blending race-neutral and race-conscious solutions was in some ways part of the topic of discussion at 1980's Fairmont Conference, a gathering that highlighted both the importance of long-standing black Republican ideas *and* the ideological differences that existed among African American party members—divides that would harden throughout the next decade. The ideas advanced throughout the Fairmont conference may not have been especially new, but black conservatives' modifications to these "old" ideas were important nonetheless. Where race and equality had once united black Republicans, it now divided them; those who favored a colorblind approach argued that race-conscious policies were an affront to individual rights, while those opposed to a purely race-neutral approach insisted that race awareness corrected inequality so that blacks *could* embrace individualism.

Black Republican men and women, old and young, newcomers and longtime party faithful sat on both sides of this debate, approaching the issue in ways that are still relevant in the contemporary period. Ultimately, the 1980s would usher in an era of new polices, new concerns, and a new, oftentimes antagonistic relationship between the Republican Party, African Americans, and those party members who straddled both worlds.

No Room at the Inn

THE DATE WAS JUNE 18, 1987. CLARENCE THOMAS, THE CHAIRMAN OF THE
Equal Employment Opportunity Commission, stood at the podium at the
Heritage Foundation in Washington, D.C., preparing to deliver a talk on
blacks, conservatism, and the Republican Party.[1] His audience, a group
of conservative Republicans, was mostly white, with the exception of
Thomas's mentor, J. A. Parker, of the Lincoln Institute for Research and
Education, who was nearly always in the crowd whenever the young
black conservative received some kind of public accolade.

Thomas was part of a rapidly growing group of African Americans
rising through the ranks of the American political system, jockeying for
a power long denied. Born in 1948 under the "totalitarianism of segregation" in Georgia, he and thousands of other African Americans embraced
the respectability tenets of self-sufficiency and personal responsibility,
and like so many of his peers, he was among the first generation to reap
the hard-won rewards of the civil rights battles of the twentieth century.
For Thomas, integrated schools, outbursts of collegiate Black Power, the
educational advantages bestowed by affirmative action policies, and a
remarkable mentorship with a powerful elected Republican official all
afforded him an equal opportunity version of the American Dream. Embracing conservatism in the 1970s, he became a dogmatic Ronald Reagan
adherent in 1980, and in 1991 President George H. W. Bush nominated
Thomas to the Supreme Court, touching off a firestorm of public debate
about the nature of racial inequality, sexual harassment, sexism, government intervention, and abortion rights. Today, he is a man who epito-
mizes the black neoconservatism with which we are all so familiar.[2]

But in 1987 Thomas was a man teeming with contradictions, whose
stance on issues like affirmative action had shifted wildly over the years,
teetering between the appreciative and the derogatory. "But for affirmative action laws, God only knows where I would be today," he had argued in 1983; four years later, he suggested that self-help was the best
approach to racial uplift, rather than "race-conscious policies" for which
black Republicans had fought since at least 1969.[3] And yet, on that June
day in 1987, the audience members at the Heritage Foundation received
no such polemic; instead, Thomas launched a diatribe against the behav-

iors of his own party. "Black Americans," he declared, "will move . . . toward conservatism when we stop discouraging them; when they are treated as a diverse group with differing interests; and when conservatives stand up for what they believe in rather than stand against blacks." He continued, arguing:

> Blacks are not stupid. And no matter how good an idea or proposal is, no one is going to give up the leftist status quo as long as they view conservatives as antagonistic to their interests, and conservatives do little or nothing to dispel the perception. If blacks hate or fear conservatives, nothing we say will be heard.

In the midst of cataloging his frustrations, he briefly and bitterly spoke of the hostility he had faced from many African Americans; nevertheless, Thomas still blamed *white* Republicans for such antagonisms and problems, blaming the GOP's indifference to African Americans and its apparent antiblack bent. Likewise, for those blacks already "convinced and converted" to the party, being a Republican was a torturous affair— acceptance often hinged on becoming, in Thomas's words, a "caricature of sorts, providing sideshows of antiblack quips and attacks." Republicans, he concluded, "must open the door and lay out the welcome mat" and demonstrate that they cared.[4]

There is a terrible irony, as Mary Frances Berry once suggested, in Thomas's criticisms of the GOP, given his subsequent years of marching in line with the party and several Republican presidential administrations.[5] No matter how peculiar Thomas may seem, though, he is far from alone. The irony of his perspective is one that we have seen before; indeed, that irony can be seen in every chapter of this book.[6]

Yet while Thomas's speech demonstrates how little had changed for black Republicans, his rhetoric also highlights something unique to the post-1980 period: the hardening of ideological divisions between liberal, moderate, conservative, and now neoconservative African American members of the GOP—a shift that distinguishes the forty-four years covered within this study. As Thomas momentarily acknowledged during his talk, his emphasis on neoconservative solutions had placed him at odds with "many black Republicans" with whom he had previously "enjoyed a working and amicable relationship."[7] In truth, it was one thing to discuss and theorize the merits of free market enterprise and an antistatist self-help approach to uplift; it was another matter entirely to see those theories put into action, with a detrimental impact on the black poor and working class.[8] Elaine Jenkins perhaps best captured the nuances of this widening ideological gulf; wrestling with black neoconservatives' approach to inequality in 1986, the "faithful black Goldwater Republican," who had worked with the NBRC, campaigned for Ronald Reagan, and served as chair of the Council of 100, argued that while she too believed in "colorblindness," ultimately a "race-neutral society cannot be achieved without affirmative action programs." Her philosophical embrace of conservative principles certainly kept Jenkins firmly rooted in the Republican Party, but her racial liberalism differentiated her beliefs from those of neoconservative black members of the GOP; their ideas, she insisted, were "out of step" with the beliefs of the vast majority of African Americans, including "those of decently conservative viewpoints who have tied their futures to the GOP."[9]

The fundamental ideological rift illustrated by Jenkins's and Thomas's philosophies spoke to an evolution of the thoughts and actions that black Republicans had advanced since 1936. In that year, about one hundred African American party members from New York gathered to discuss the party's responsibilities in times of crisis; for them, Republicanism symbolized government that was "by the people," that spoke to matters of "social justice." And though they rejected the New Deal, disparaging social welfare as "handouts," they nevertheless insisted that the party had to offer *something* to address racial inequality and the economic needs of the American public, in a viable and empathetic way.[10] Their notions were both race conscious and, in some respects, class conscious. For the next forty-four years, black Republicans would repeat some variation of this argument, over and over. Their approach was far from perfect, as we have seen; they often discriminated along the lines of class and gender, offering paternalistic and moralistic criticisms steeped in the respectability politics of the black elite and failing to consider the full implications of their proposed policy solutions.

Theirs was a strategy, nonetheless, that recognized the significance of black voters and sought to address African Americans' unique racial history and experience in a distinctly Republican way. But this racial liberalism made their ideological conservatism messy and unwieldy, as their beliefs defied categorization, moving beyond the boundaries of both liberalism and conservatism—overlapping in some places and clashing in others. Black Republicans' philosophy was an amalgamation, taking race into account from the perspective of someone who had lived through inequality and lacked the privilege of whiteness upon which to rest; yet their liberalism also was distinct from that of black Democrats. Moreover, they were acutely aware that many white Republicans did not fully understand the reality and persistence of racial inequality. "I am perhaps more militant than most . . . for the rights of black people," William O. Walker once stated. "Black Republicans realize that there are some reactionaries, some conservatives in the Republican Party. Our job is to convince them to be liberal on Black causes."[11] In essence, black Republicans' ideology was flexible and pragmatic, adjusting to account for the reality of African Americans' lived experiences.

Equally important, in spite of this elastic approach, black Republicans also embraced many of the tenets of mainstream conservatism, in varying degrees, reflecting the subtle philosophical nuances among them. Black Republicans emphasized private industry, distained social welfare, and preached the moral virtues of respectability; some of them accepted government intervention, while others advocated for public-private partnerships. Likewise, many of them advocated a kind of rhetorical colorblindness, exemplified by Edward Brooke's "non-Negro politics," which they balanced with race-conscious appeals to African Americans. Moreover, a strain of right-wing black conservatism thrived within organizations like the National Black Silent Majority Committee and the Lincoln Institute for Research and Education. In fact, despite the hard ideological lines that emerged after 1980, this nuanced and interconnected historical context nevertheless gives rise not only to contemporary moderate and liberal black Republicanism but also to modern black neoconservatism.

This is not to suggest that the messiness of the historical context and its influence on present-day black Republican politics invalidate the hard lines that crystallized after 1980; to the contrary, the starkness of the divide makes black Republicans' dilemmas all the more significant. That ideological chasm is thrown into even harsher focus when we consider that African Americans have become *more* conservative over the decades (now composing almost a third of black communities); their ideological orientation, however, has not translated into Republican affiliation. Between 1984 and 2012, black identification with the GOP reached no higher than 15 percent; similarly, black support for Republican presidential candidates peaked at 12 percent during that period.[12] In short, although their moral, religious, and economic conservatism may align with the GOP, African Americans still experience a political dissonance when it comes to the Republican Party.

There are many reasons for this disconnect: African Americans' exhibit an "everyday" kind of conservatism that is apolitical; poor and working-class blacks continue to see the GOP as the party of the wealthy and the Democratic Party as the party of the "common man"; and, perhaps most relevant, African Americans see Republicans as *racially conservative*, understanding the party's colorblind language as coded antiblack antagonisms. One study, for instance, found that even the most conservative of black respondents resisted messages that dismissed persistent racial discrimination and failed to show a "sensitivity to the specificities of racial struggle." Such findings acknowledge not only African Americans' frustrations with the GOP but also those of black Republicans. A Joint Center survey from the late 1980s, for example, found that only 17 percent of blacks and about half of black Republicans believed that the GOP cared about African Americans' problems.[13]

That half of the party's black members felt as though the GOP was indifferent or actively hostile to black issues is both shocking and unsurprising, epitomizing some of black Republicans ever-present "loneliness." Since 1936, they had complained of being isolated because of their small numbers; and while they developed strategies to address that isolation, all too often, their suggestions were either ignored or neglected. They championed a strategy of two-party competition, hoping to rectify their solitary stature and subvert one-party politics, arguing that blacks could leverage their vote for racially progressive gains and economic uplift. However, this was a flawed philosophy, at least for national contests. The party's equivocation over race and its various dalliances with covert and overt antiblack stances negated any genuine displays of colorblind inclusion and meant that most African Americans refused to risk voting for a Republican candidate, even when disenchanted with the Democratic Party. Without an African American voting bloc, black Republicans had little with which to bargain; but even if black voters had decided to endorse the party en masse, GOP leaders and strategists would have weighed African Americans' demands against those of white voters, who represented the vast majority of the electorate.[14]

Given their minority status within the GOP, black Republican leaders and groups were often dependent on mainstream party organizations. Autonomous splinter groups like the National Negro Republican Assembly struggled to institute their agenda because they eschewed the pragmatic approach of black centrists. However, organizations such as the BSMC and later the LIRE saw their prominence rise among white Republicans because their ideas were analogous to those of the party's right wing.

Moreover, in their push to have their voices heard, black Republicans often made concessions, complicated by their middle-class biases. Although some of them had "bootstrapped" their way out of poverty, and all professed to care about the black poor, they nevertheless underestimated or minimized (or both) the difficulty in escaping poverty; thus, they often offered classist agendas that excluded the most vulnerable members of the community, thereby further alienating African American voters. Black Republicans' attempts to neutralize the black vote were perhaps the most cynical manifestation of such an agenda.

African American members of the GOP constantly bemoaned their outsider status from both their political party and racial community; and for some, this frustration was enough to bid farewell to the Republican Party. For the many who stayed, they did so because they rejected third-party politics as unfeasible; just as crucial, their conservatism, as malleable as it may have been, was still too conservative for the Democratic Party.[15]

And yet, since black Republicans played a significant role in the modern Republican Party, there is an irony to their "loneliness." At various points over the course of forty-four years, the GOP strategically instituted some of African American party members' ideas, initiatives, and policies, acting not only on black conservatives' proposals but also on those of moderate and liberal black Republicans. Their thoughts and approaches sometimes garnered support from outside the GOP, as well, especially among the black press, black Democrats, and black constituents—all audiences who could be just as quick to criticize black Republicans. In particular, those who struck a balance between a colorblind outlook and a race-conscious perspective, like Edward Brooke, were the most successful at finding widespread bipartisan support among diverse audiences.

Many of these philosophies found their way into contemporary black politics, readily apparent among contemporary black Republican officials, and occasionally they even show up among the most conservative of black party officials.[16] A less obvious comparison, however, is the way in which the historical figures addressed in this book influenced the neoliberalism articulated by a sizable number of high-profile black politicians, ranging from New Jersey senator Cory Booker, to former Virginia governor Doug Wilder, to President Barack Obama.[17] As scholars have suggested, the "black neoliberal turn" reflects an ideological departure from black liberalism's emphasis on collective action and government intervention and draws a "direct relationship between economic success . . . hard work," personal responsibility, and self-reliance and celebrates capitalism as a powerful mode of uplift; though black neoliberalism emphasizes individualism, the "collective race" is not forgotten; instead, adherents urge *individual* African Americans to bootstrap their way to equality, through the creation of personal wealth. In its most "progressive" form, the ideology suggests that the government has a responsibility to address the plight of the poor; nevertheless, black neoliberals also argue that the welfare state fosters dependency, preferring instead to advocate for public-private "workfare" partnerships wherein African Americans are reimagined as producers. In short, the mainstream of contemporary black politics, when compared to the Democratic liberalism of the 1960s and 1970s, has shifted to the right.[18]

That black neoliberalism *appears* not unlike historical black Republicanism is unsurprising, given that both philosophies are rooted in a black respectability tradition; a crucial aspect of contemporary black neoliberal ideology is the "adoption of a race-neutral language" that is nearly identical to the rhetoric espoused by the black Republicans discussed within this book. Examples abound but an especially salient comparison is that of Edward Brooke and Barack Obama. In May 2013, for example, the president delivered Morehouse College's commencement address, a speech that veered between entreaties for collective action and appeals to personal responsibility, walking a tightrope between a colorblind perspective and a race-conscious outlook. He told the audience of black men that "nobody is going to give you anything you haven't earned," arguing "nobody cares if you suffered through" racism; "If you stay hungry," Obama declared, "nobody can stop you." He closed by calling on the black graduates to go out into the world and earn money *and* "care about justice," as a means of ensuring that "everyone has a voice" and "gets a chance to walk through those doors of opportunity if they are willing to work hard enough."[19] Here was a vision of American meritocracy that subtly touched on institutional discrimination but suggested that it was up to the *individual* to overcome inequality—through economic uplift—with *measured* help from the government; certainly, the president's talk offered a position that blended liberal and conservative elements, while both emphasizing and decentralizing the significance of race—an argument that undoubtedly looks familiar to the reader, by this point in this study.[20]

• • •

One lingering question that this book hopes to address has been a topic of regular debate and discussion since the political realignment of black voters in the 1936 presidential election: Are black voters irrevocably lost to the Republican Party? The short answer is no, at least not at the local level. This study has demonstrated that black voters were willing to support the *right* Republican candidate, so long as he or she (and the supporting state and local party organizations) demonstrated a genuine empathy toward African Americans, conducted sincere and aggressive outreach, and presented solutions that addressed issues of black concern; local politics undoubtedly offers a level of nuance that allows *individual* politicians to sidestep the rancor between African Americans and the GOP.[21] In 1998, for instance, 48 percent of black voters supported Arkansas governor Mike Huckabee in his successful reelection bid; apparently they did so because he spent "considerable" years establishing trust with black communities, held town halls for black constituents to voice their concerns, and then acted on those concerns—creating, for example, a health care program for poor African American children. Additionally, he played up his Baptist background and avoided discussing controversial issues like affirmative action.[22]

Moreover, the significance of black voters is unmistakable in state and local politics, a reality that Republicans have long understood; in 1986 and in 1998, for example, party officials and leaders attributed their losses in Congress and state legislatures to their inability to earn black support. As we know, this is an old problem; whenever Republicans fall out of power, the party turns inward, debating the demographic composition of a winning strategy. Inevitably, the GOP finds itself divided, roughly split between those who believe the minority vote is unwinnable and those who endorse a more inclusive outreach strategy, aimed not only at disaffected white voters but also at African American and Latino voters. The latter group understands the significance of minority voters, a constituency that has grown rapidly in the past three decades, affecting the racial makeup of the electorate.[23]

This dynamic is more pronounced at the national level; for example, in 2012 President Obama won reelection with the help of a coalition of black, Latino, and white voters.[24] Republican challenger Mitt Romney lost the election despite winning 59 percent of the white vote; indeed, he would have needed upwards of 70 percent of the white vote to win the presidential contest.[25] Exclusively focusing on white voters, while ignoring racial minorities, is an unsustainable strategy; likewise, symbolic short-term outreach efforts to these marginalized racial groups will not work because such appeals feel disingenuous given the contradictory positions of the GOP's mainstream coupled with the reactionary and extremist behaviors of the party's fringe.[26]

The fundamental dilemma for the Republican Party in winning black voters at the national level boils down to issues of politics and policy. To put it another way, African Americans interpret the GOP's "colorblind" approach as insensitive to their history and lived experience—a disconnect that is sorely exacerbated by the fact that Republicans rarely consider race except to use it as an antagonism. More to the point, colorblindness as a political strategy presents a quandary, because it presumes that everyone shares the same set of problems, histories, and racial experiences; it sees the nation as a meritocracy, assumes equality, and sidesteps the complexities of race. Certainly there are commonalities that cross racial lines, like economics and religion. Appealing to African Americans solely on these merits, though, does not work because the country, even as it professes to be race neutral, is in fact, race conscious. As we have seen in this study, not only did black Republicans understand this truth, but white Republicans often did as well; yet many of the latter group shied away from this approach, out of fear of alienating white voters.

It has taken more than half a century to get where we are today; accordingly, any solution for winning the black vote will involve yeoman work, and hard, grueling outreach efforts at the local, state, and national level. It must repair the party's image through genuine displays of empathy; equally important, the party has to propose *and* create viable solutions that meet the needs of the black electorate, moving beyond a singular focus on the black middle class. This is not to suggest that the GOP "become" the Democratic Party; instead, it means that the party has to be willing to commit to forging a broad-based message that takes into account conservatism and the perspectives of racial minorities and does not pit them against one another. Such suggestions may feel clichéd. After all, Ralph Bunche gave the Republican Party the "playbook" to win back black voters in 1939; since then, the GOP has occasionally acted on those recommendations but not in any transformative way. Perhaps one of the final lessons of this history is that the GOP needs to demonstrate an unwavering and sweeping commitment to an evolving American public. What remains to be seen is whether the party has the wherewithal to change.

Appendix

TABLE 1.
Black Vote in Presidential Elections, 1936–1980

Year	Democratic Party	Republican Party	Other/Independent
1936	71	28	1
1940	67	32	
1944	68	32	—
1948	77	23	
1952	76	21	
1956	61	39	—
1960	68	32	
1964	94	6	
1968	85	10	
1972	87	13	
1976	87	8	
1980	86	14	

Sources: David A. Bositis, *Blacks and the 2008 Republican National Convention* (Washington, D.C.: Joint Center for Political and Economic Studies, 2008), 10; Charles D. Hadley and Everett Carll Ladd Jr., *Transformations of the American Party System: Political Coalitions from the New Deal to the 1970s* (New York: W. W. Norton, 1978), 60, 112; *Black Politics, 1980: A Guide to the Republican National Convention* (Washington, D.C.: Joint Center for Political and Economic Studies, 1980); David A. Bositis, *Blacks and the 2012 Republican National Convention* (Washington, D.C.: Joint Center for Political and Economic Studies, 2012); RNC, "Campaign Plan: A Strategy for the Development of the Black Vote in 1972," Mar. 15, 1972, box 5, folder Black Vote 1972, SSS Papers.

Note: Numbers may not equal 100 percent due to rounding.

TABLE 2
Black Vote for GOP in Midterm Elections, 1954–1978

Year	GOP Black Vote (%)
1954	22
1958	31
1962	26
1966	19
1970	8
1974	8
1978	15

Sources: RNC, "Campaign Plan 1972," Mar. 1972, box 5, Folder Black Vote, SSS Papers; "Election in Retrospect," *NBRN* 1, no. 1, (Nov.–Dec. 1974), box 30, MLS Papers; Wright-McNeill to Ben Cotton, Memo on 1979–1980 GOP Black Vote Plan, Jan. 12, 1979, box 40, Brock Papers; "Apples, Oranges and Votes," *NYT*, Nov. 24, 1980; Adam Clymer, "Displeasure with Carter Turned Many to Reagan," *NYT*, Nov. 9, 1980; "Survey Finds Some Blacks Helped Ronald Reagan Win," *OP*, Nov. 26, 1980; Joe Cooper to Craig King, Memo, Aug. 6, 1980; JC to Eleanor Callahan, Memo, Aug. 13, 1980, box 317, Hugel Files.

TABLE 3
Black Delegates at the Republican National Conventions, 1936–1980

Year	Delegates	Delegates (%)	Alternatives
1936	45	4.5	34
1940	32	3.2	53
1944	18	1.7	27
1948	41	3.7	34
1952	29	2.4	34
1956	36	2.7	41
1960	22	1.6	28
1964	14	1.0	29
1968	26	1.9	52
1972	56	4.2	84
1976	76	3.4	74
1980	55	2.7	66

Source: David A. Bositis, *Blacks and the 2008 Republican National Convention* (Washington, D.C.: Joint Center for Political and Economic Studies, 2008), 17.

TABLE 4
Black Vote in 1966 Election: State Examples

Location	Candidate	Position	1966
Arkansas	Winthrop Rockefeller	Governor	96.0
Massachusetts	Edward Brooke	Senator	85.6
Maryland	Spiro T. Agnew	Governor	79.0
Kentucky	John Sherman Cooper	Senator	54.0
New Jersey	Clifford Case	Senator	36.0
Michigan	George Romney	Governor	35.0
New York	Nelson Rockefeller	Governor	35.0
Tennessee	Howard Baker	Senator	20.0
California	Ronald Reagan	Governor	6.0

Sources: Minorities Division, Republican National Committee, Election Report: Republicans and the Black Vote 1966, [1967], folder Republican Party—RNC—Correspondence, 1967; Minorities Division, RNC, "Election Analysis: 1968 and the Black American Voter," Jan. 1969, folder Election Analysis, 1968, Black Vote, both in CLT Papers; Al Sweeney, "LBJ Receives Five Million Negro Votes," *CP*, Nov. 7, 1964; "Romney Is Re-elected Michigan Governor," *WP*, Nov. 9, 1966.

TABLE 5
Black Vote in 1966 Election: City Examples

Location	Candidate	Position	1966
Boston	John Volpe	Governor	63.1
Cincinnati	James A. Rhodes	Governor	47.0
Atlanta	Fletcher Thompson	Congressman	30.0
Houston	George H. W. Bush	Congressman	30.0
Philadelphia	Raymond Shafer	Governor	26.0
Cleveland	James Rhodes	Governor	25.6
Detroit	George Romney	Governor	21.6
Chicago	Charles Percy	Senator	17.2

Sources: Minorities Division, Republican National Committee, Election Report: Republicans and the Black Vote 1966, [1967], Folder Republican Party—RNC—Correspondence, 1967; Minorities Division, RNC, "Election Analysis: 1968 and the Black American Voter," Jan. 1969, folder Election Analysis, 1968, Black Vote, both in CLT Papers; Sweeney, "LBJ Receives Five Million Negro Votes," *CP*, Nov. 7, 1964; "Romney Is Re-elected Michigan Governor," *WP*, Nov. 9, 1966.

TABLE 6

States Where Black Vote Exceeded Carter's Winning Margin in 1976 Election

State	Electoral Votes	Total Winning Margin	Black Vote for Carter	Percent of Black Vote for Carter
Alabama	9	155,100	182,517	86.4
Florida	17	166,469	261,797	94.9
Louisiana	10	73,919	264,615	93.6
Maryland	10	86,951	149,794	91.5
Mississippi	7	14,463	122,819	87.4
Missouri	12	70,944	125,678	91.4
New York	41	288,767	610,015	89.5
North Carolina	13	185,405	204,782	92.8
Ohio	25	11,116	243,273	80.0
Pennsylvania	27	123,073	256,849	87.2
South Carolina	8	104,658	166,907	90.4
Texas	26	129,019	259,202	96.8
Wisconsin	11	35,245	40,854	93.4

Source: Charles W. Hucker, "Blacks and the GOP: A Cautious Courtship," CQ, Apr. 29, 1978, box 24, folder Republicans—Blacks, Civil Rights & Justice, Malson Files.

Notes

Introduction: The Paradox of the Black Republican

1. "In Search of the Negro Republican," *Saturday Night Live Transcripts*, Dec. 5, 1980, accessed July 2013, http://snltranscripts.jt.org/80/80bnegro.phtml.

2. "Find Blacks, Republicans Compatible," *CD*, May 10, 1975.

3. David A. Bositis, *Blacks and the 2012 Republican National Convention* (Washington, D.C.: Joint Center for Political and Economic Studies, 2012).

4. Michael C. Dawson, *Behind the Mule: Race and Class in African-American Politics* (Princeton: Princeton University Press, 1994), 106; Robert C. Smith and Hanes Walton, "U-Turn: Martin Kilson and Black Conservatism," *Transition*, no. 62 (1993): 211. See also Harvard Sitkoff, *A New Deal for Blacks: The Emergence of Civil Rights as a National Issue* (New York: Oxford University Press, 1978); Nancy Weiss, *Farewell to the Party of Lincoln: Black Politics in the Age of FDR* (Princeton: Princeton University Press, 1983); Nikhil Pal Singh, *Black Is a Country: Race and the Unfinished Struggle for Democracy* (Cambridge: Harvard University Press, 2004; Paul Frymer, *Black and Blue: African Americans, the Labor Movement and the Decline of the Democratic Party* (Princeton: Princeton University Press, 2007); Katherine Tate, *From Protest to Politics: The New Black Voters in American Elections* (Cambridge: Harvard University Press, 1998); Ronald Walters, *Black Presidential Politics in America: A Strategic Approach* (Albany: State University of New York Press, 1988); Paul Frymer, *Uneasy Alliances: Race and Party Competition in America* (Princeton: Princeton University Press, 1999); Michael C. Dawson, *Black Visions: The Roots of Contemporary African-American Political Ideologies* (Chicago: University of Chicago Press, 2003).

5. In 2004, Ron Paul (R-TX) was the only congressman to vote against a bill celebrating the fortieth anniversary of the 1964 Civil Rights Act. "This law unconstitutionally expanded federal power, thus reducing liberty," Paul stated in his congressional remarks on July 3. "By prompting race-based quotas, this law undermined efforts to achieve a color-blind society and increased racial strife." Ron Paul, "Remarks," Ron Paul Online, n.d., accessed July 2013: www.ronpaul.com/on-the-issues/civil-rights-act.

6. Smith and Walton, "U-Turn," *Transition*, 1993, 211.

7. Ibid.

8. James Strong, "Malcolm Could Not Be a Black Republican," *PC*, Apr. 25, 1992; Robert W. Robinson, Letter to the Editor, *BE*, Aug. 1993.

9. A recent example of accusations of "bought votes" comes from the 2012 presidential election; as the *New York Times* noted, Mitt Romney "attributed his defeat in part to what he called big policy 'gifts' that the president had bestowed" on "young voters, African-Americans and Hispanics." Ashley Parker, "Romney Attributes Obama Win to 'Gifts,'" *NYT*, Nov. 15, 2012; Timothy N. Thurber, *Republicans and Race: The GOP's Frayed Relationship with African Americans, 1945–1974* (Lawrence: University Press of Kansas, 2013), 388–389. For more on Pat Buchanan and Herman Cain, see Lee A. Daniels, "Black Voters

and the Black (and White) Conservative Shuffle," *New York Beacon*, Oct. 6, 2011; "Nixon Says No Clean Sweep of Blacks," *Jet*, Nov. 7, 1968; George Schuyler, "Views and Reviews," *PC*, Feb. 20, 1965.

10. Julian Zelizer, "What Political Science Can Learn from the New Political History," *Annual Review of Political Science* 13 (June 2010): 25–36; "Conservatism: A Round Table," *Journal of American History* 98, no. 3 (2011); Alan Brinkley, "The Problem of American Conservatism," *American Historical Review* 99 (Apr. 1994): 409–429; Ronald P. Formisano, *Boston against Busing: Race, Class, and Ethnicity in the 1960s and 1970s* (Chapel Hill: University of North Carolina Press, 1991); Dan T. Carter, *The Politics of Rage: George Wallace, the Origins of the New Conservatism, and the Transformation of American Politics* (New York: Simon & Schuster, 1995); Dan T. Carter, *From George Wallace to Newt Gingrich: Race in the Conservative Counterrevolution, 1963–1994* (Baton Rouge: Louisiana State University Press, 1996); Matthew D. Lassiter, *The Silent Majority: Suburban Politics in the Sunbelt South* (Princeton: Princeton University Press, 2007); Robert Mason, *The Republican Party and American Politics from Hoover to Reagan* (New York: Cambridge University Press, 2012); Hugh Davis Graham, "Richard Nixon and Civil Rights: Explaining an Enigma," *Presidential Studies Quarterly* 26, no. 1 (Winter 1996): 93–106; Kevin M. Kruse, *White Flight: Atlanta and the Making of Modern Conservatism* (Princeton: Princeton University Press, 2005); Joseph Crespino, *Strom Thurmond's America* (New York: Hill and Wang, 2012); Nadine Cohodas, *Strom Thurmond and the Politics of Southern Change* (Macon: Mercer University Press, 1995); Devin Fergus, *Liberalism, Black Power, and the Making of American Politics, 1965–1980* (Athens: University of Georgia Press, 2009); Thomas B. Edsall and Mary Edsall, *Chain Reaction: The Impact of Race, Rights, and Taxes on American Politics* (New York: W. W. Norton, 1992).

11. Angela Dillard, *Guess Who's Coming to Dinner Now? Multi-cultural Conservatism in America* (New York: New York University Press, 2002); Lewis Randolph and Gayle T. Tate, eds., *Dimensions of Black Conservatism: Made in America* (New York: Palgrave Macmillan, 2002); Peter Eisenstadt, ed., *Black Conservatism: Essays in Intellectual and Political History* (New York: Routledge, 1998); Christopher Alan Bracey, *Saviors or Sellouts: The Promise and Peril of Black Conservatism, from Booker T. Washington to Condoleezza Rice* (Boston: Beacon, 2008); Michael L. Ondaatje, *Black Conservative Intellectuals in Modern America* (Philadelphia: University of Pennsylvania Press, 2010); Angela K. Lewis, *Conservatism in the Black Community: To the Right and Misunderstood* (New York: Routledge, 2013); Oscar Renal Williams, *George S. Schuyler: Portrait of a Black Conservative* (Nashville: University of Tennessee Press, 2007). See also Tasha S. Philpot, *Race, Republicans, and the Return of the Party of Lincoln* (Ann Arbor: University of Michigan Press, 2007); Michael K. Fauntroy, *Republicans and the Black Vote* (Boulder: Lynne Rienner, 2006).

12. Simon D. Topping, *Lincoln's Lost Legacy: The Republican Party and the African American Vote, 1928–1952* (Gainesville: University Press of Florida, 2008); Geoffrey Kabaserice, *Rule and Ruin: The Downfall of Moderation and the Destruction of the Republican Party; From Eisenhower to the Tea Party* (New York: Oxford University Press, 2012); Thurber, *Republicans and Race.*

13. Ronald Walters, *Black Presidential Politics in America* (Albany: State University of New York Press, 1988), 47–48.

14. See Frymer, *Uneasy Alliances.*

15. Kim Phillips-Fein suggests that over the past two decades, scholars have agreed on a tacit, if not explicit, understanding that American conservatism means "anticommunism, a laissez-faire approach to economics, opposition to the civil rights movement, and a commitment to traditional sexual norms." See Kim Phillips-Fein, "Conservatism: A State of the Field," *Journal of American History* 98, no. 3 (2011): 723–743.

16. As George Nash writes in the introduction to his seminal book *The Conservative Intellectual Movement in America since 1945*, there was no "agreed upon definition" of conservatism among American conservatives. Rather, the "very quest for self-definition has been one of the most notable motifs of their thought since World War II." For the record, Nash has a particular view of the conservative movement, one that sees conservatism as a tradition of anticommunists, traditionalists, libertarians, and religious rightists. But he is very specific in making the argument that his narrative is but *one* representative example of an intellectual movement at a particular point in time and in no way inclusive of every conservative in America. See George Nash, *The Conservative Intellectual Movement in America since 1945* (Wilmington: Intercollegiate Studies Institute, 1996), introduction.

17. Peter Eisenstadt, introduction to *Black Conservatism*.

18. See, for example, Evelyn Brooks Higginbotham, *Righteous Discontent: The Women's Movement in the Black Baptist Church, 1880–1920* (Cambridge: Harvard University Press, 1993), and Kevin Gaines, *Uplifting the Race: Black Leadership, Politics, and Culture in the Twentieth Century* (Chapel Hill: University of North Carolina Press, 1996.

19. Jesse Jackson, "Jesse Jackson on the GOP—Speech," *CT*, Feb. 6, 1978.

20. Tali Mendelberg, *The Race Card: Campaign Strategy, Implicit Messages, and the Norm of Equality* (Princeton: Princeton University Press, 2001); Cornel West, "Demystifying the New Black Conservatism," *Praxis International* 2 (1987): 143–151.

21. Whenever possible, I try to use the words employed by black Republicans and the political culture that surrounded them. Likewise, though "black" refers to a race and "African American" refers to an ethnicity, I use the two terms interchangeably, for stylistic purposes.

CHAPTER 1. RUNNING WITH HARES AND HUNTING WITH HOUNDS

1. St. Clair Drake, *Black Metropolis: A Study of Negro Life in a Northern City* (New York: Harcourt, Brace, 1945), 371–375.

2. Nancy Weiss, *Farewell to the Party of Lincoln: Black Politics in the Age of FDR* (Princeton: Princeton University Press, 1983); Sitkoff, *A New Deal for Blacks*; Hanes Walton Jr., *Black Republicans: The Politics of the Black and Tans* (Metuchen: Scarecrow Press, 1975).

3. Marc Sullivan, "Races: Black Game," *Time*, Aug. 17, 1936; Drake, *Black Metropolis*, 372.

4. Weiss, *Farewell*, 29–33.

5. Drake, *Black Metropolis*, 352.

6. Charles D. Hadley and Everett Carll Ladd Jr., *Transformations of the American Party System: Political Coalitions from the New Deal to the 1970s* (New York: W.W. Norton, 1978), 9, 60, 112.

7. Weiss, *Farewell*, xiii–xiv.

8. Ibid., 4–6, 15–18, 20–28, 269; Charles H. Martin, "Negro Leaders, the Republican Party, and the Election of 1932," *Phylon* 32, no. 1 (1971): 85–93.

9. Walter F. White, *A Man Called White: The Autobiography of Walter White* (New York: Viking Press, 1948), 104.

10. "Illinois Election Statistics, 1934," *Office of the Clerk of the U.S. House of Representatives*, n.d., accessed Apr. 1, 2012, http://clerk.house.gov/member_info/electionInfo/index.aspx.

11. Sullivan, "Races," *Time*, Aug. 1936.

12. Michael K. Brown, *Race, Money, and the American Welfare State* (Ithaca: Cornell University Press, 1999), 65.

13. Weiss, *Farewell*, 236–240; Brown, *Race*, 77–81.

14. Weiss, *Farewell*, 136–156; William Leuchtenburg, *The FDR Years: On Roosevelt and His Legacy* (New York: Columbia University Press, 1997), 130–146.

15. JCPS, *Black Politics 1980: A Guide to the Republican National Convention* (Washington, D.C.: Joint Center for Political and Economic Studies, 1980), 16–26.

16. Hadley and Ladd, *Transformations*, 114.

17. Quoted in Weiss, *Farewell*, 230–231. See also Gerald H. Gamm, *The Making of the New Deal Democrats: Voting Behavior and Realignment in Boston, 1920–1940* (Chicago: University of Chicago Press, 1989), chap. 4.

18. "Ohioans Vote Leaning Away from Parties," *NYAN*, Dec. 5, 1936.

19. Drake, *Black Metropolis*, 375.

20. Richard B. Sherman, *The Republican Party and Black America from McKinley to Hoover, 1896–1933* (Charlottesville: University Press of Virginia, 1973), 255–256.

21. In 1936, black southern voters were largely disenfranchised. In 1940, for example, black voter registration across the South was on average, 3 percent. With the passage of civil rights legislation in the 1940s and 1950s, black voter registration gradually started to increase, and by 1964 30 percent of African Americans across the South were registered to vote. U.S. Census Bureau, 2000 Census, Current Population Survey, Documents P20–504, P20–542, http://www.census.gov/hhes/www/socdemo/voting/publications/p20/index.html and http://www.census.gov/hhes/www/socdemo/voting/publications/historical/index.html; Steven F. Lawson, *Black Ballots: Voting Rights in the South, 1944–1969* (New York: Lexington Books, 1999); George Eaton Simpson and J. Milton Yinger, *Racial and Cultural Minorities: An Analysis of Prejudice and Discrimination* (New York: Springer, 1985), 230–231.

22. "Voted for Roosevelt," *Pittsburgh Courier*, Nov. 7, 1936; Drake, *Black Metropolis*, 353–354.

23. Sullivan, "Races," *Time*, Aug. 1936; "Big Negro Vote Backs F.D.R. as New Deal Sweeps Nation," *NYAN*, Nov. 7, 1936.

24. Drake, *Black Metropolis*, 352–353.

25. "Committee Okays Dropping Old Rule," *Evening Independent*, June 25, 1936; Sullivan, "Races," *Time*, Aug. 1936; "Delicate Aspect," *Time*, Sept. 19, 1938.

26. White, *White*, 171–173; Weiss, *Farewell*, 243–246; "Roosevelt's 'Mum Policy' Kills Lynch Bill," *CD*, Feb. 26, 1938; "Delicate," *Time*, Sept. 1938. See also Kevin J. McMahon, *Reconsidering Roosevelt on Race: How the Presidency Paved the Road to Brown* (Chicago: University of Chicago Press, 2003), 114–120.

27. Drake, *Black Metropolis*, 355; "Cong. Wadsworth under Fire in New York; Voted 'No' on Lynch Bill," *PC*, Sept. 17, 1938.

28. Sullivan, "Races," *Time*, Aug. 1936. See also James J. Kenneally, "Black Republicans during the New Deal: The Role of Joseph W. Martin, Jr.," *Review of Politics* 55, no. 1 (Winter 1993): 117–139; James J. Kenneally, *A Compassionate Conservative: A Political Biography of Joseph W. Martin, Jr., Speaker of the U.S. House of Representatives* (Lanham: Lexington Books, 2003).

29. Drake, *Black Metropolis*, 354.

30. Owens received financial incentives to support both the Democratic and Republican parties. Both believed that employing a high-profile black figure would assist in making significant inroads among African American voters. See Kenneally, *Compassionate*, 24; "National Affairs: Owens for Landon," *Time*, Sept. 14, 1936; "Jesse Owens to Stump in 7 Cities," *NYAN*, Sept. 26, 1936.

31. "Owens for Landon," *Time*, Sept. 1936.

32. Kenneally, *Compassionate*, 68–69; "Democrats: Stumped Stumper," *Time*, Oct. 12, 1936.

33. "Landon and Knox Win Praise from Leaders of Negroes in G.O.P.," *NYAN*, June 27, 1936; "G.O.P. Maps Fight Front for Negroes," *NYAN*, Aug. 22, 1936.

34. Kenneally, *Compassionate*, 23–24, 68–69.

35. Weiss, *Farewell*, 206–207, 268.

36. Kenneally, "Black Republicans," 125–131; JCPS, *Black Politics 1980: RNC*, 10; Hadley and Ladd, *Transformations*, 60.

37. Joseph V. Baker, "Meetings Planned by G.O.P. Negroes: Effects of New Deal to Be Theme of First Conference Saturday," [1940], box 60, folder 21, Ralph J. Bunche Papers, 1927–1971 (Collection 2051), Department of Special Collections, Charles E. Young Research Library, University of California, Los Angeles (hereinafter called RJB Papers; all documents from box 60, folder 21).

38. RJB, "Report on the Needs of the Negro, for Republican Party," unpublished report for Republican Program Committee, June 1939 (hereinafter called RPC Report); Thomas Reed to RJB, Letter, Feb. 19, 1939, both in RJB Papers.

39. RJB to TR, Letter, Feb. 21, 1939; TR to RJB, Letter, Feb. 28, 1939. See also TR to RJB, Letter, Mar. 8, 1939; TR to RJB, Letter, Mar. 6, 1939, RJB Papers.

40. Jonathan Holloway, *Confronting the Veil: Abram Harris, Jr., E. Franklin Frazier, and Ralph Bunche* (Chapel Hill: University of North Carolina Press, 2001), 184, 186–188.

41. RJB to TR, Letter, Mar. 7, 1939, RJB Papers.

42. RJB, "Negro Political Laboratories," in *Ralph J. Bunche: Selected Speeches and Writings*, ed. Charles P. Henry (Ann Arbor: University of Michigan Press, 1996), 33–34.

43. TR to RJB, Letter, Mar. 29, 1939; TR to RJB, Letter, Apr. 3, 1939, RJB Papers.

44. RJB to TR Letter, Apr. 1, 1939; Doris Darmstadter to RJB, Letter, Aug. 30, 1939; RJB to DD, Letter, Sept. 5, 1939; DD to RJB Letter, Sept. 9, 1939; DD to RJB, Letter, Sept. 9, 1939, RJB Papers. See also Holloway, *Confronting*, 187.

45. RJB to TR, Letter, May 20, 1939; RJB, Letter & Final Report, June 12, 1939, RJB Papers.

46. Bunche, RPC Report.

47. Ibid.

48. Ibid; "Dr. Bunche's Report," *NYAN*, Sept. 9, 1939.

49. Bunche, RPC Report.

50. Ibid.

51. TR to RJB, Letter, June 15, 1939, RJB Papers.

52. RJB to DD, Letter, June 16, 1939; DD to RJB, Letter, June 21, 1939; RJB to DD, Letter, June 23, 1939; RJB to DD, Letter, July 5, 1939; RJB to DD, Letter, July 10, 1939; DD, Letter, July 12, 1939, RJB Papers.

53. TR to RJB, Telegram, June 15, 1939. See also TR to RJB, Letter, June 15, 1939; RJB to TR, Letter, June 17, 1939; RJB to TR, Letter & Report, June 20, 1939, all in RJB Papers.

54. DD to RJB, Letter, July 12, 1939; RJB to DD, Letter, July 18, 193, RJB Papers.

55. Henry, *Bunche*, 85; Holloway, *Confronting*, 186.

56. Weiss, *Farewell*, 269–270.

57. Emmett J. Scott, "Along the Political Front," *CD*, Feb. 24, 1940; Kenneally, "Black Republicans," 126.

58. Statistics on the black vote are notoriously inconsistent, especially data generated before 1980. Hadley and Ladd, for example, argue that 32 percent of African Americans supported Wendell Wilkie in 1940, while Kenneally suggests that 50 percent supported the Republican presidential nominee. Hadley and Ladd, *Transformations*, 60, 112; Kenneally, "Black Republicans," 133–134.

59. The GOP's 1940 platform pledged to incorporate blacks into the economic and political life of the nation, rejected discrimination in the military and the federal government, promised to protect the voting rights of African Americans, and condemned mob violence, promising to enact legislation to "curb this evil." Rawn James Jr., *The Double V: How Wars, Protest, and Harry Truman Desegregated America* (New York: Bloomsbury Press, 2013), 100; "Official Election Returns Show Negro Has Strong Claims on Both Parties," *NYAN*, Dec. 14, 1940; Republican Party, "Republican Party Platform of 1940," June 24, 1940, The American Presidency Project, University Of California, Santa Barbara (hereinafter called *APP*, UCSB); Hadley and Ladd, *Transformations*, 60, 112.

60. "A Word of Warning!" *CD*, Feb. 26, 1944; Deton J. Brooks Jr., "Pointing Fingers at Chicago GOP Parlay," *CD*, Feb. 19, 1944; Richard Durham, "Convention Highlights," *CD*, July 8, 1944.

61. In 1945, the RNC followed suit, establishing the National Council of Negro Republicans (NCNR), which also lobbied Republicans to support FEPC legislation. Simon Topping, "'Never Argue with the Gallup Poll'; Thomas Dewey, Civil Rights and the Election of 1948," *Journal of American Studies* 38, no. 2 (Aug. 2004): 185–190. See also "Negro Republicans Ask Full Employment," *CD*, Sept. 1, 1945; "Form National Council of Negro Republicans," *ADW*, Oct. 9, 1945; "Unity Republican Conference Drafts National Organization," *NYAN*, Sept. 1, 1945; "Action on Full Employment Bill Urged by Republicans," *ADW*, Oct. 4, 1945; "Calls Depriest Ouster Blunder," *ADW*, Sept. 3, 1946; "Republicans Taken to Task for Failure to Pass 1944 Platform," *ADW*, Sept. 3, 1947; "Negro GOP Leaders Split Over Bypass of Race Aid Laws," *CD*, Sept. 27, 1947; "GOP Leaders Tell Wherry Party Must Push FEP Vote," *ADW*, Dec. 1, 1949; "The Elephant's Memory," *Baltimore Afro-American*, Aug. 16, 1949; "Does the Republican Party Really Want Our Vote?" *Baltimore Afro-American*, Jan. 3, 1950. See also Thurber, *Republicans and Race*, 8–23, 28–30.

62. Harry S. Truman, "The President's Committee on Civil Rights," Executive Order 9808, Dec. 5, 1946; President's Committee on Civil Rights, "To Secure These Rights," Report, Oct. 1947, Harry S. Truman Presidential Library, Independence, Missouri, http://www.trumanlibrary.org/civilrights/srights1.htm.

63. Carl Rowan, "Harry Truman and the Negro," *Ebony*, Nov. 1959. See also Harvard Sitkoff, "Harry Truman and the Election of 1948: The Coming of Age of Civil Rights in America Politics," *Journal of Southern History* 37, no. 4 (Nov. 1971): 597–616.

64. Harry S. Truman, "Executive Order 9981—Establishing the President's Committee on Equality of Treatment and Opportunity in the Armed Services," July 26, 1948, *APP*, UCSB. See also Topping, "Thomas Dewey."

65. JCPS, *Black Politics 1980: RNC*, 10; Hadley and Ladd, *Transformations*, 60; Ronald Walters, *Black Presidential Politics in America: A Strategic Approach* (Albany: State University of New York Press, 1988), 23–26; Rowan, "Harry Truman," *Ebony*, 1959.

66. JCPS, *Black Politics 1980: RNC*, 10; Hadley and Ladd, *Transformations*, 60.

67. Rowan, "Harry Truman," *Ebony*, 1959; Hadley and Ladd, *Transformations*, 112–114; Matthew R. Rees, *From the Deck to the Sea: Blacks and the Republican Party* (Wakefield: Longwood Academic, 1991), 175–185.

68. "Republicans, What Now?" *PC*, Jan. 15, 1949.

69. "GOP Bosses Meet; Negroes Left Out," *PC*, Dec. 24, 1949.

70. "Our Opinions," *CD*, Aug. 13, 1949. See also "Loss of Negro Vote Blamed on Top G.O.P. Rule," *CT*, Feb. 6, 1949; "Republican Leaders Hit GOP Deal on Gag Rule," *NYAN*, Mar. 26, 1949.

71. Lucius C. Harper, "What a Love Match: The Skunk and the Elephant," *CD*, Apr. 9, 1949; Walter White, "Should GOP Be Called 'Gone Old Party' Now?" *CD* Apr. 23, 1949; "GOP Bosses Meet," *PC*, Dec. 1949.

72. Robert Mason and Iwan Morgan, eds., *Seeking a New Majority: The Republican Party and American Politics, 1960–1980* (Nashville: Vanderbilt University Press, 2013), 35–38.

73. W.O. Walker, "Down the Big Road," *CP*, Apr. 16, 1949.

74. Mason and Morgan, *Seeking a New Majority*, 35–38.

75. As Earl and Merle Black note, Eisenhower's campaign divided the South. He won four southern states, but lost Arkansas, North Carolina, and all five of the Deep South states. The president did best in areas with low black populations; in areas with a higher ratio of blacks, white southerners voted for Democrats. Earl Black and Merle Black, *Rise of Southern Republicans* (Cambridge: Belknap Press, 2003), 62–65. See also "Black Voters Increase Support," *St. Louis Sentinel*, Mar. 16, 1968, folder Republican Party Newspaper Clippings, 1965–1971, Special Collections and Archives, James Branch Cabell Library, Virginia Commonwealth University, Richmond (hereinafter called CLT Papers).

76. Rowan, "Harry Truman," *Ebony*, 1959.

77. Black and Black, *Southern*, 62.

78. David A. Nichols, *A Matter of Justice: Eisenhower and the Beginning of the Civil Rights Revolution* (New York: Simon & Schuster), 273–274; Rowan, "Harry Truman," *Ebony*, 1959; Ethel L. Payne, "Ike's Advocacy of Patience Fails to Impress Leaders," *CD*, May 31, 1958.

79. Harold F. Gosnell and Robert E. Martin, "The Negro as Voter and Officeholder," *Journal of Negro Education* 32, no. 4 (Autumn 1963): 420.

80. "With Mixed Emotions: Negro Voters Accept Republican Triumph," *CP*, Nov. 8, 1952.

81. "NAACP Pledges Full Support of Ike, GOP," *CD*, Nov. 22, 1952.

82. For a discussion of the civil rights accomplishments and failures of the Eisenhower administration, see Nichols, *Matter of Justice*; Robert F. Burk, *The Eisenhower Administration and Black Civil Rights* (Knoxville: University of Tennessee Press, 1984).

83. E. Frederic Morrow, *Black Man in the White House: A Diary of the Eisenhower Years by the Administrative Officer for Special Projects, The White House, 1955–1961* (New York: MacFadden Books, 1963); Milton S. Katz, "E. Frederic Morrow and Civil Rights in the Eisenhower Administration," *Phylon* 42, no. 2 (1981); Simeon Booker, "Black Man in the White House: Eisenhower Aide Weathers Abuse, Criticism," *Ebony*, Apr. 1961.

84. Morrow, *Black Man*, 33.

85. Ibid., 158.

86. Ibid., 33–34, 41, 175–176, 189–190.

87. Ibid., 188; Booker, "Black Man," *Ebony*, 1961.

88. In August 1955, fourteen-year-old Emmett Till of Chicago, Illinois, was kidnapped and lynched in Mississippi, while visiting relatives. His murder (and the subsequent acquittal of his attackers) outraged African Americans and spurred a national outcry against southern violence. By January 1956, the administration had received more than three thousand letters, telegrams, and petitions on the case. See *CD* to Dwight D. Eisenhower, Telegram, Sept. 1, 1955; Max Rabb to Andrew Goodpaster, Memo on Emmett Till, Jan. 6, 1956, all in box 3113, folder Emmett Till; W. Beverly Carter [publisher, *PC*] to EFM, Letter on Emmett Till, Sept. 29, 1955; EFM, Memo on Emmett Till, Nov. 22, 1955, all in box 10, folder Civil Rights Official Memoranda, 1955–56, E. Frederic Morrow Records, all in Papers of Dwight D. Eisenhower as President, 1953–61, Dwight D. Eisenhower Presidential Library, Abilene, Kansas (hereinafter called EFM Papers). See also Nichols, *Matter of Justice*, 116–118.

89. EFM, Memo on Emmett Till, Nov. 1955, EFM Papers. See also Morrow, *Black Man*, 18–20.

90. WBC to Morrow, Letter, Sept. 1955, EFM Papers.

91. Morrow, *Black Man*, 85–86.

92. Harvard Sitkoff, *The Struggle for Black Equality* (New York: Hill and Wang, 2008), 30; Katz, "Morrow."

93. Morrow, *Black Man*, 60.

94. Ibid., 33–34; Nichols, *Matter of Justice*, 120.

95. Morrow, *Black Man*, 60–64, 73–75; JCPS, *Black Politics 1980: RNC*, 10; Hadley and Ladd, *Transformations*, 60, 112.

96. Approximately one million black southerners, or 20 percent, were registered to vote by 1952. The numbers marked an important shift of seventeen percentage points from 1940 and highlighted the painstaking, often dangerous, political work of civil rights advocates and organizations throughout South. Earl Black and Merle Black, *Politics and Society in the South* (Cambridge: Harvard University Press, 1989), 112. See also Lawson, *Black Ballots*.

97. Carroll Kilpatrick, "Eisenhower-Nixon Ticket Made Gains among Negro Voters in All Sections," *WP* Nov. 10, 1956; Walter Trohan, "Negro Voters thruout U.S. Swing to G.O.P.," *CT*, Nov. 12, 1956; "Courier Staff Observers Report on 'Big Switch' of Negro Voters," *PC*, Nov. 17, 1956.

98. Henry Lee Moon, "Editorial Comment: The Negro Vote in the Presidential Election of 1956," *Journal of Negro Education* 26, no. 3 (Summer 1957): 219–230.

99. Morrow, *Black Man*, 60–64, 73–75.

100. Moon, "Editorial Comment," 219–230; Gosnell and Martin, "The Negro," 420.

101. Hadley and Ladd, *Transformations* 60, 112; "Negro Voters Shift to GOP," *CP*, Nov. 10, 1956.

102. Sitkoff, *Black Equality*, 31; James H. Meriwether, "'Worth a Lot of Negro Votes': Black Voters, Africa, and the 1960 Presidential Campaign," *Journal of American History* 95, no. 3 (Dec. 2008): 737–763.

103. In a private conversation with Morrow, *Chicago Defender* editor Louis Martin (who would later become head of black outreach for the Democratic National Committee) suggested that the administration could quickly win back disgruntled blacks if it could finalize "some kind of effective legislation that will protect the Negro's right to vote in the South." Morrow, *Black Man*, 118–122; "President Pushes Civil Rights Plan at G.O.P. Parlay," *NYT*, Jan. 1, 1957.

104. In its final form, the bill passed in the Senate on August 7, 1957, with the support of forty-three Republicans and twenty-nine Democrats—eighteen Democrats opposed it. For a detailed discussion of the congressional debate surrounding the bill and the subsequent limited impact of the act, see Thurber, *Republicans and Race*, 99–108. See also Morrow, *Black Man*, 121; Nichols, *Matter of Justice*, 143–168; Sitkoff, *Black Equality*, 31–36; Katz, "E. Frederic Morrow."

105. Sitkoff, *Black Equality*, 20–31; Nichols, *Matter of Justice*, 170–179, 184–213.

106. Gloster B. Current, "Why Nixon Lost the Negro Vote," *Crisis*, Jan. 1961.

107. The Reminiscences of E. Frederic Morrow, Jan. 31, 1968, pp. 30–33, in the Columbia University Oral History Research Collection, Columbia University Libraries, New York.

108. Morrow, *Black Man*, 266.

109. Ibid., 179, 183–184.

110. Ibid., 165–166, 169–170.

111. Layhmond Robinson, "Survey Shows Negro Voter Displeased by Both Parties," *NYT*, Oct. 17, 1958.

112. Booker, "Black Man," *Ebony*, 1961; Nichols, *Matter of Justice*, 220–222.

113. Morrow, *Black Man*, 66–67.

114. Ibid., 173.

115. Morrow, *Black Man*, 188; Booker, "Black Man," *Ebony*, 1961.

116. Morrow, *Black Man*, 203–204. See also Louis Lautier, "In the Nation's Capitol: Long Past Due," *ADW*, Apr. 28, 1959; Marie Smith, "GOP Needs Negro Vote to Win, Conference Told," *WP*, Apr. 15, 1959; "GOP Neglects Negroes, White House Aide Says," *LAT*, Apr. 15, 1959; Alice A. Dunnigan, "'GOP Needs the Negro Vote' Declares Morrow," *LAS*, Apr. 23, 1959; "Negro Vote Vital, G.O.P. Women Told," *NYT*, Apr. 5, 1959.

117. Morrow, *Black Man*, 173–175.

118. Meriwether, "Worth," 741. See also "Blast Ike's Rights Plan: Seven Points on President's List," *CD*, Feb. 14, 1959.

119. "Nixon Is Popular with Negro Voters," *ADW*, Aug. 28, 1959.

120. Meriwether, "Worth," 737.

121. Republican Party, "The Republican Party Platform 1960," July 25, 1960, *APP*, UCSB.

122. "Nixon Wins Civil Rights Plank Battle" and "Text of GOP Civil Rights Plank," both in *CP*, July 30, 1960. See also "The Drama of the Issues," *Life* 49, no. 12 (Sept. 19, 1960).

123. Morrow, *Black Man*, 210–214.

124. Mattie Smith Colin, "Jewel Rogers Praises Nixon's Rights Record," *CD*, July 28, 1960; Edward Barry, "Mother with a Mission," *CT*, Oct. 9, 1960; "Jewel Rogers Campaign Aide," *CD*, Sept. 24, 1960.

125. Morrow, *Black Man*, 210–214.

126. "National Affairs: A Negro in the Cabinet," *Time*, Oct. 24, 1960.

127. Simeon Booker, "Richard Nixon Tells: What Republicans Must Do to Regain the Negro Vote," *Ebony*, Apr. 1962. See also "Swift Deliverance," *Time*, November 7, 1960.

128. Morrow, *Black Man*, 213–214; JCPS, *Black Politics 1980: RNC*, 10; Layhmond Robinson, "Negro Vote Gave Kennedy Big Push," *NY*, Nov. 11, 1960; "Mayor Tells How Kennedy Aided King," *CSM*, Dec. 16, 1960.

129. Robert Novak, "The Negro Vote," *WSJ*, Oct. 25, 1960.

130. Morrow, *Black Man*, 214. See also Nichols, *Matter of Justice*, 265.

131. Novak, "Negro Vote," *WSJ*, Oct. 1960.

132. Ibid.; Layhmond Robinson, "Baltimore Study Uncovers Apathy," *NYT*, Oct. 23, 1960.

133. Anthony Lewis, "Negro Vote Held Vital to Kennedy," *NYT*, Nov. 27, 1960. See also Thurber, *Republicans and Race*, 40; "Southern Images of Political Parties: An Analysis of White and Negro Attitudes," *Journal of Politics*. 26 (1964): 89–91; "Crisis for the GOP?" *Public Opinion News Service*, May 28, 1958, box 38, DNC Records, Lyndon Baines Johnson Presidential Library, University of Texas at Austin (hereinafter called DNC Papers).

134. Robert Novak, "The Negro Vote," *WSJ*, Oct. 25, 1960; Layhmond Robinson, "Baltimore Study Uncovers Apathy," *NYT*, Oct. 23, 1960; Current, "Nixon," *Crisis*, 1961; "Johnson, Goldwater Records on Civil Rights Reveal Divergence," *Star-News*, Aug. 11, 1964.

135. Kenneally, "Black Republicans," 139.

136. George H. Nash, *The Conservative Intellectual Movement in America since 1945* (Wilmington: Intercollegiate Studies Institute, 1996), xv–xvi.

137. R. L. Ouffus, "One Senator's Manifest," *NYT*, June 26, 1960.

138. Barry Goldwater, *With No Apologies: The Personal and Political Memoirs of United States Senator Barry M. Goldwater* (New York: William Morrow, 1979), 98–100; Robert Alan Goldberg, *Barry Goldwater* (New Haven: Yale University Press, 1995), 138–139.

139. Nash, *Conservative Intellectual*, 191–192; Goldwater, *With No Apologies*, 96–99; Rick Perlstein, *Before the Storm: Barry Goldwater and the Unmaking of the American Consensus* (New York: Hill and Wang, 2001), 61–68; Barry Goldwater, *The Conscience of a Conservative* (Shepherdsville: Victory Publishing, 1960), 5–22; Goldberg, *Goldwater*, 139; Barry Goldwater, "The Dime Store New Deal," Senate Speech, May 5, 1960, box 553,

folder 40, Barry M. Goldwater Papers, Arizona Historical Foundation, Tempe (hereinafter called BMG Papers).

140. George E. Sokolsky, "These Days . . ." *WP*, Apr. 6, 1960; Donald T. Critchlow, *The Conservative Ascendancy: How the GOP Right Made Political History* (Cambridge: Harvard University Press, 2007), 43–54.

141. Robert D. Novak, "Goldwater's Image: Conservative Senator Softens Views, Offers a Plan to Build GOP," *WSJ*, Jan. 11, 1961, folder Civil Rights Files, BMG Papers.

142. "The Highlights of Sen. Goldwater's Manifesto," *WSJ*, Jan. 11, 1961; Novak, "Goldwater's Image," *WSJ*, Jan. 1961, both in ibid. Barry Goldwater, "The Forgotten American/A Statement of Proposed Republican Principles, Programs and Objectives" (Washington, D.C.: Human Events, 1961), box 31–3, folder Republican Party Political Figures: Important Candidates, 1961–1980, Rita Crocker Clements Personal Papers, 1932–2001, Texas A&M University, College Station.

143. Novak, "Goldwater's Image," *WSJ*, Jan. 1961, folder Civil Rights Files, BMG Papers.

144. David Froder. "Face Facts of Politics, Goldwater Tells GOP," Mar. 18, 1961, folder Civil Rights Files, BMG Papers.

145. "Wanted: A Voice," *Time*, Mar. 10, 1961; Goldwater, "Rocky Clash Over Strategy," *CT*, Dec. 28, 1962; Ben W. Gilbert, "GOP Turning Lily-White under Goldwater Brush," *WP*, July 15, 1964; "Goldwater Finds Lag on Defense under Democrats," *NYT*, Aug. 16, 1964.

146. "Novak, "Goldwater's Image," *WSJ*, Jan. 1961, BMG Papers. See also Raymond Lahr, "GOP Rejects 'Forget the Negro' Proposal," *ADW*, Mar. 18, 1961; "Republicans Seek to Woo Negro Votes," *Spokesman-Review*, Mar. 18, 1961; "Fowler Heading GOP Vote Drive," *NYAN*, Mar. 25, 1961; "Morton Favors a G.O.P. Drive to Cultivate Votes of Negroes," *NYT*, Mar. 18, 1961.

147. Booker, "Richard Nixon," *Ebony*, 1962.

148. Ibid. See also "Nixon Says 5 Pct. More Negro Vote," *St. Petersburg Times*, Mar. 29, 1962; "Negro Vote Write-off an Error, Nixon Says," *Milwaukee Sentinel*, Mar. 27, 1962; "Nixon Cites Failure to Win Negro Vote," *NYT*, Mar. 27, 1962; Thurber, *Republicans and Race*, 133.

149. Carl Rowan, "The GOP's Uphill Fight for the Negro Vote," *Sunday Star*, Mar. 6, 1966, box 51, folder Republican Party—1965 Negro Vote, the South, etc., DNC Papers.

150. "GOP Task Force to Analyze Vote," *NYT*, Mar. 17, 1961; "Rockefeller's Political Advisor Warns GOP 'Go After Negro' Vote," *ADW*, Apr. 4, 1961; " Woo Negro Votes," *Spokesman-Review*, Mar. 1961; "David Broden, "G.O.P. Chiefs Hit Goldwater," *Star*, Mar 17, 1961, BMG Papers; Ray C. Bliss, "Report to the Big City Committee 1961," [Jan. 1962], Clarence L. Townes Papers, 1944–1988, CLT Papers. Also see Carl Rowan, "The GOP's Uphill Fight for the Negro Vote," *Sunday Star*, Mar. 6, 1966; Richard L. Strout, "New Coalition? There Aren't Enough Republicans to Win Election without Help," *CSM*, both in box 51, folder Republican Party—1965 Negro Vote, the South, etc., DNC Papers.

151. Prominent committee members included Bernard Newman, coordinator of New York City GOP activities; George H. Fowler, New York deputy labor commissioner; Samuel P. Singletary, African American head of the United Young Republican Club; and Rodman Rockefeller, son of Nelson Rockefeller and head of the 1960 Negro and Puerto Rican divisions of the New York Republican state campaign. "Fowler," *NYAN*, Mar. 1961.

152. While Rockefeller's speech and appearance were well received, he made a bit of a blunder, criticizing the Kennedy administration's recent appointment of Robert C. Weaver as secretary of Housing and Urban Development (HUD) as a "public relations gimmick." His statement was met with stony silence; some audience members later complained that it was rude of Rockefeller to attack a "distinguished Negro public servant." "The Rockefeller Shift," *CD*, Feb. 7, 1962.

153. Warren Weaver, "Chamber in Capital Is Warmer to Rockefeller than Goldwater," *NYT*, Feb. 6, 1964; "Dr. King, at Rockefeller Estate, Addresses Urban League Rally," *NYT*, Mar. 1, 1964.

154. "Russell Says Image of Lincoln Is Not Enough," *BAA*, May 6, 1961.

155. "Scull Urges Republicans," *BAA*, Apr. 7, 1962.

156. Goldwater, *With No Apologies*, 162–188.

157. Goldwater, *Conscience*, 17–23.

158. Ibid., 25–31.

159. Another example of this can be found in the 1962 University of Mississippi incident. After Mississippi governor Ross Barnett, an avowed segregationist, blocked James Meredith's access to attend the state university, President Kennedy sent federal troops to intervene. In response, Goldwater issued statement after statement declaring: "I am totally opposed to segregation of any sort . . . but I don't believe the Supreme Court finding is the supreme law of the land. I disagree with Governor Barnett and think what he has done is distasteful, but I think he has a constitutional right to do it." See "Barnett Action Is Distasteful, Goldwater Says," *Free-Lance Star*, Oct. 5, 1962; "Gov. Barnett's Role Defended by Goldwater," *St. Petersburg Times*, Oct. 6, 1962.

160. "Let the South Handle the Negro," *PC*, Dec. 2, 1961.

161. Claude Sitton, "GOP Parley Charts Campaign for a 2 Party System in South," *NYT*, Nov. 19, 1961; "Lt. Lee Gives the G.O.P. Sound Advice," *ADW*, Dec. 13, 1961; "Goldwater Solicits G.O.P. Votes from Southern Segregationists," *NYT*, Nov. 19, 1961.

162. "The New Breed," *Time*, July 13, 1962.

163. As historian John Andrew indicates, the efforts of Young Americans for Freedom (YAF) played an instrumental role in boosting Goldwater's popularity. Founded in 1960, YAF embodied a new kind of conservatism that leaned toward radical interpretations; the group wanted to use the GOP as a vehicle for change; consequently, it took an aggressive role in the promotion of Goldwater and his subsequent presidential campaign. Also worth noting: YAF had a few black members, most notably J. A. Parker, who joined the organization in 1961 and became chair of the Philadelphia County chapter in 1965, rapidly emerging as a spokesperson for the national group. See John A. Andrew, *The Other Side of the Sixties: Young Americans for Freedom and the Rise of Conservative Politics* (New Brunswick: Rutgers University Press, 1997); David W. Tyson and J. A. Parker, *Courage to Put Country above Color: The J. A. Parker Story* (Washington, D.C.: Lincoln Institute for Research and Education, 2009), 43.

164. P. L. Prattis, "Horizon," *PC*, Dec. 2, 1961.

165. Joseph Alsop, "Matter of Fact . . ." *WP*, Jan. 4, 1962.

166. Jackie Robinson, "The President and the Housing Order," *NYAN*, Dec. 1, 1962; Gertrude Wilson, "A Year's Summary," *NYAN*, Jan. 5, 1962.

167. "Rockefeller Woos Negro Vote as He Carries Presidential Ball for GOP," *CD*, Mar. 23, 1963.

168. Rowland Evans and Robert Novak, "Future 'White Man's' Party," *St. Petersburg Times*, June 24, 1963.

169. Homer Bigart, "Goldwater Fills Rally at Garden," *NYT*, May 13, 1964; Joseph Zullo, "Goldwater in New York," *CT*, May 13, 1964; Earl Mazo, "Goldwater Sees New Race Strife unless G.O.P. Wins," *NYT*, May 13, 1964; Malcolm Nash, "Goldwaterites Won't Hear the Choir Again," *NYAN*, May 23, 1964.

170. Goldwater and his supporters specifically rejected the public accommodations and equal employment provisions of the 1964 Civil Rights Act, labeling both measures unconstitutional. "Text of Goldwater Speech on Rights," *NYT*, June 19, 1964; E. W. Kenworthy, "Goldwater Joins in Futile Effort to Kill Key Part of Rights Bill," June 16, 1964, folder

Goldwater 1964 Presidential Campaign Speeches, Civil Rights, Positions Notebook, 1963–1964, BMG Papers; "Civil Rights Bill Passes Senate by 73–27 Vote," *LAT*, June 20, 1964. See also Everett Dirksen, "A Conservative Speaks in Favor of Civil Rights," *CR*, June 1964, in Donald T. Critchlow and Nancy MacLean, eds. *Debating the American Conservative Movement: 1945 to the Present* (New York: Rowman & Littlefield, 2009), 77–82.

171. "Senator Goldwater's 'No,'" *NYT*, June 20, 1964.

172. "Southern Images of Political Parties: An Analysis of White and Negro Attitudes," *Journal of Politics* 26 (1964): 89–91; "Crisis?" *PONS*, May 1958 in DNC Papers.

173. Joseph E. Lowndes, *From the New Deal to the New Right: Race and the Southern Origins of Modern Conservatism* (New Haven: Yale University Press, 2009), 47–48; Louis Lautier, "Says GOP Stupidity Lost Negro Voters," *CP*, Apr. 11, 1959; "A GOP Tug-of-War," *Eugene Register-Guard*, Oct. 8, 1963; "Backers of Goldwater Now Hold Key Posts in GOP Apparatus," *WP*, Oct. 7, 1963.

174. George H. W. Bush to Albertine E. Bowie, Letter, Mar. 11, 1963; Bonnie Hazelrigg to AEB, Letter, May 28, 1963; GHWB to Gene Crossman, Letter, Apr. 30, 1963; GHWB to Susie Cunningham, Letter, Aug. 30, 1963; SC to GHWB, Letter, Sept. 1, 1963; GHWB to Albert B. Fay, Letter, May 3, 1963; GHWB to W. R. Fuller, Letter, Apr. 29, 1963; Harris County Republicans, Expenditure Budget, [1963]; Letter, Aug. 30, 1963; HCR, Expenditure Budget, [1963], GHWB to F. L. Williams, Letter, Mar. 18, 1963; Bob Rowland to GHWB, Letter, June 22, 1963; Barry Goldwater to Leonard J. Nadasdy, Letter, Mar. 15, 1963; Robert A. Long, "Harris County GOP Resolutions on Civil Rights Bill," June 28, 1963, all in Series: Zapata Oil Files, George Bush Personal Papers, George H. W. Bush Presidential Library, College Station, Texas (hereinafter called GHWB Papers).

175. Nat D. Williams, "Dark Shadows," *Tri-State Defender*, Mar. 16, 1963; "The GOP and Negro Vote," *CD*, May 9, 1963.

176. Kabaserice, *Rule and Ruin*, 78–83. See also Clayton Knowles, "Javits Declares G.O.P. Right Wing Is Peril to Party," *NYT*, Feb. 13, 1962; "Rocky Speaks His Mind," *Deseret News*, July 20, 1963; James Reston, "Deeper Split in G.O.P.," *NYT*, June 19, 1964; Wallace Turner, "Romney Supports Civil Rights Bill," *NYT*, Jan. 18, 1964; McCandlish Phillips, "Nixon Bids G.O.P. Move to Center," *NYT*, Nov. 11, 1964; "Percy Lashes Antirighters Joining G.O.P.," *CT*, Dec. 5, 1964.

177. "A Dismal Outlook," *CD*, June 27, 1964.

178. Benjamin Mays, "My View," *PC*, Mar. 14, 1964.

Chapter 2. A Thorn in the Flesh of the GOP

1. Hadley and Ladd, *Transformations*, 60, 112.

2. "Election Result: Political Action for Rights in Dixie to Increase," *CD*, Nov. 7, 1964. See also "Two Million Negroes Registered in South; They're for Johnson," *CD*, Oct. 13, 1964; U.S. Census Bureau. 2000 Census, Current Population Survey, Documents P20–504, P20–542.

3. "Goldwater Won't Get Votes from Negroes," *LAS*, Sept. 26, 1963.

4. "G.O.P. Negroes Form Clique within Party," *CT*, Aug. 24, 1964. See also Goldwater, *With No Apologies*, 180; Goldberg, *Goldwater*, 140.

5. Paul W. McBride, Letter, *Wichita Eagle*, Nov. 1, 1964, folder Civil Rights Files, BMG Papers.

6. Theodore Jones, "Negro Republicans in 5 Major Cities Are Turning to Johnson," *NYT*, Sept. 27, 1964.

7. "Goldwater's GOP Ousts Negro," *Jet*, Sept. 17, 1964; "Conn. Negro Leaders Angry; 'Won't Vote for Goldwater,'" *CD*, July 18, 1964; "Negro Presidential Elector Says 'I Can't Go Goldwater,'" *NYAN*, Sept. 5, 1964.

8. Wallace Turner, "Negroes Parade on Coast Today," *NYT*, July 12, 1964.

9. Jackson R. Champion, "GOP Please Note," *NYAN*, Aug. 1, 1964.

10. Junius Griffin, "GOP in Harlem Favors Scranton," *NYT*, July 9, 1964.

11. "Top GOP Leader Quits Republicans," *NYAN*, Aug. 1, 1964.

12. Bill Lane, "The Inside Story," *LAS*, Dec. 31, 1964.

13. "The Cornerstone," *NYAN*, Nov. 21, 1964.

14. "Republican Splinters," *CT*, Sept. 5, 1966.

15. William H. Chafe, *Civilities and Civil Rights: Greensboro, North Carolina, and the Black Struggle for Freedom* (New York: Oxford University Press, 1980), 172–174.

16. George G. Fleming to Negro Republican Convention, Aug. 22, 1964, folder on National Negro Republican Assembly 1964–1966, CLT Papers.

17. GGF, "A Call to Statesmanship, A Challenge to Greatness," Aug. 22, 1964, in ibid.

18. NNRA, "Statement of Principles and Policies," Aug. 22, 23, 1964, in ibid.

19. John H. Averill, "Negro Group Won't Vote for Goldwater," *LAT*, July 18, 1964.

20. Ibid.; William Chapman, "Core Shifts Focus of Rights Drive to Democratic Parlay," *WP*, July 17, 1964; William O. Walker, "Republican Convention Notes," *CP*, July 25, 1964. See also Ben Gilbert, "GOP Turning Lily White under Goldwater Brush," *WP*, July 15, 1964; John D. Morris, "Negro Fails in Bid to Upset Seating," *NYT*, July 14, 1964.

21. John H. Clay and William C. Nunn, July 13–16, CLT Papers; author-conducted telephone interview with Clarence L. Townes Jr., July 23, 2008; "Goldwater Show Is Jolting," *PC*, July 25, 1964. See also Simeon Booker, "What Republican Victory Means to the Negro," *Ebony*, Feb. 1967.

22. "A Negro Delegate Sobs," *NYT*, July 16, 1964.

23. "Goldwater's Negro Supporter, Jackie Robinson Have Words," *Jet*, July 30, 1964; "Goldwater's Right-Hand Negro a Mystery," *CP*, Aug. 1, 1964. See also "Biographical Sketch of Edward Banks," n.d. [draft op-ed on Edward Banks Endorsement of Barry Goldwater, *Arizona Tribune*, 1964], both in box 2, folder 2—Correspondence; Banks, Edward, Stephen Shadegg Collection, Arizona Historical Foundation, Tempe (hereinafter called Shadegg Papers).

24. Tom Wicker, "Scranton Beaten on Rights Move," *NYT*, July 14, 1964.

25. JHC and WCN, "Resume of Activities, Republican National Convention," July 13–16, 1964, CLT Papers.

26. John H. Averill, "GOP Negroes May Walk out of Convention," *LAT*, July 13, 1964; John Morris, "Negro Republicans Challenge Goldwater's Fitness to Enforce Civil Rights," *NYT*, July 15, 1964; "GOP Negro Delegates: The Dilemma," *NYAN*, July 15, 1964; Rosemarie Tyler Brooks, "GOP Negroes Bar Walkout," *CD*, July 15, 1964. JHC and WCN, "Resume," July 1964, CLT Papers.

27. Author interview with CLT, 2008.

28. JHC and WCN, "Resume," July 1964, CLT Papers.

29. Elsie Carper, "Negro Republicans Form Anti Barry Unit," *WP*, July 13, 1964; "Text of Anti-Goldwater Position of Tan GOPers," *CP*, July 25, 1964; Gilbert, "GOP Turning Lily-White under Goldwater Brush," *WP*, July 1964;"Negro Delegates Reported Ready to Walk Out if Goldwater Wins," *WP*, July 15, 1964; Nicholas C. Chriss, "Negroes Call off Convention Walkout," *WP*, July 16, 1964; Layhmond Robinson, "City Negro Chiefs of G.O.P. in Revolt," *NYT*, Sept. 14, 1964.

30. Goldwater, *No Apologies*, 188–191.

31. "Negro Delegates," *WP*, July 1964; John D. Morris, "Delegates Disconsolate," *NYT*, July 17, 1964. "Negroes Plot GOP Walkout," *CD*, July 16, 1964; "Negroes to Withhold Support of Nominee," *LAT*, July 16, 1964; Chriss, "Negroes," *WP*, July 1964. See also "Johnson to Make Issue of Rights," *PC*, Aug. 1, 1964; "Jackie Robinson Calls on Gold-water's Defeat," *CP*, Aug. 1, 1964; Jackie Robinson, "Jackie Robinson Says," *Tri-State Defender*, Sept. 5, 1964; Robinson, "It's the Principle, Not the Party," *CD*, Sept. 19, 1964.

32. Four white representatives to the national convention also resigned from the Washington, D.C., delegation. As self-identified Eisenhower Republicans, they found Barry Goldwater's brand of conservatism too extreme to support. Carl Shipley dubbed them "Sunshine" and "Cocktail" Republicans, accusing them of being more interested in socializing than in working for the GOP. If it were possible, he groused, he would permanently excommunicate them from the party. See Elsie Carper, "Some Quit GOP Posts after D.C. Ultimatum," *WP*, July 1964.

33. Carper, "Negro Republicans," *WP*, July 1964; Carper, "Some Quit," *WP*, July 1964; Averill, "Negro Group," *LAT*, July 1964; Ben A. Franklin, "Negroes Bolting Maryland G.O.P.," *NYT*, Sept. 20, 1964.

34. JHC to CLT, Letter, July 27, 1964; JHC to Negro Republican Convention, Letter, Aug. 17, 1964, both in CLT Papers.

35. Representatives came from Alaska, Ohio, New Jersey, New York, Colorado, Indiana, Illinois, Kansas, Virginia, Pennsylvania, Maryland, Tennessee, Florida, Michigan, California, Georgia, Washington, D.C., Texas, and Washington. NNRA, Membership Files, CLT Papers.

36. GGF, NNRA Constitution & Bylaws, Aug.–Sept. 1964, CLT Papers.

37. "Minutes of the National Negro Republican Convention Workshop, 1:00 P.M." Aug. 22, 1964; "Sub-Committee Report on Voter Registration," Aug. 22, 1964- JHC WCN, "Resume," Aug. 22, 1964, all in CLT Papers.

38. "Minutes of the National Negro Republican Convention Workshop, 8:30 P.M.," Aug. 22, 1964; "Minutes of the National Negro Republican Convention Workshop, 2:00 P.M," Aug. 23, 1964; "National Negro Republican Convention: News Release," Aug. 22, 23, 1964; CLT to GGF, Letter, Aug. 25, 1964, all in CLT Papers. See also "Goldwater Threat Cited by Politico," *AA*, Oct. 3, 1964.

39. "Proposed Constitution and Bylaws of the National Negro Republican Assembly," Aug.–Sept. 1964; "NNRA Press Release," Sept. 21, 1964, all in CLT Papers.

40. JHC to NNRA Member, Letter, Sept. 8, 1964, CLT Papers.

41. "NNRA Press Release," Sept. 1964, CLT Papers.

42. "Report of the Political Action Committee to the General Assembly, Sept. 19, 1964, CLT Papers.

43. Ibid.

44. Grant Reynolds to NNRA Members, Letter, Oct. 15, 1964, CLT Papers.

45. Author interview with CLT, 2008; "NNRA Press Release," Nov. 1, 1964, CLT Papers. See also Willard Edwards, "Young Conservatives Inspired by G.O.P. Defeat," *CT*, Dec. 13, 1964.

46. NNRA, Press Release, Nov. 1964, CLT Papers.

47. Ripon Society, *From Disaster to Distinction: A Republican Rebirth* (New York: Pocket Books, 1966), 48–49. See also Louis H. Bean and Roscoe Drummond, "How Many Votes Does Goldwater Own?" *Look*, Mar. 23, 1965; Ben A. Franklin. "G.O.P. Seeks Clues to Party Future in Study of Vote," *NYT*, Nov. 8, 1964; "Election Results," *NYT*, Dec. 18, 1964; "Few Real Barrymen," *BG*, Jan. 11, 1965; Robert E. Baker. "Negro Vote Is Revived in the South," *WP*, Nov. 8, 1964; Walter Trohan, "Beats Goldwater by Big Electoral Vote," *CT*, Nov. 4, 1964; Walter Trohan, "Johnson Gets 61.4 PCT. of U.S. Popular Vote," *CT*, Nov. 5, 1964; "Lyndon Lashes Backlash—It's a Landslide!" *CT*, Nov. 4, 1964; Theodore H. White,

The Making of the President, 1968 (New York: Pocket Books, 1970), 37; Kabaservice, *Rule and Ruin*, 121.

48. Ibid.

49. Theodore H. White, *The Making of the President, 1968*, rev. ed. (New York: Harper Perennial, 2010), 37. See also Theodore H. White, *The Making of the President, 1964*, rev. ed. (New York: Harper Perennial, 2010).

50. Kabaservice, *Rule and Ruin*, 121; Richard L. Strout. "New Coalition? There Aren't Enough Republicans to Win Election without Help," *CSM*, Aug. 6, 1968.

51. C.L. Townes Sr. to GR, JHC, and GGF, Letter, Nov. 5, 1964, CLT Papers.

52. "Negro Republicans Demand Ouster of Goldwater Forces," *NYT*, Nov. 14, 1964; "GOP Moderates to Meet Governors," *NYAN*, Nov. 28, 1964.

53. "Harrisburg Windmill," *PC*, Dec. 26, 1964.

54. "Goldwater's GOP Ousts Negro," *Jet*, Sept. 17, 1964.

55. Editorial, *CT*, Apr. 3, 1965.

56. "Negro GOP Assembly," *CD*, Feb. 13, 1965.

57. Ralph Koger, "Howell Prods Republicans on Closer Ties to Negro," *PC*, Dec. 12, 1964.

58. Ralph Koger, "Hits Bloc Voting and Sectionalism," *PC*, Nov. 28, 1964.

59. "Eisenhower Backs G.O.P. Unity Move," *NYT*, Nov. 22, 1964; "Moderates Form New G.O.P. Group," *NYT*, Feb. 4, 1965; "Reynolds Joins New GOP Group," *NYAN*, Feb. 20, 1965.

60. "GOP Moderates to Meet Governors," *NYAN*, Nov. 28, 1964; Richard L. Strout, "GOP Seeks New Image," *CSM*, Dec. 7, 1964; Ripon, *Disaster*, 78–80, 86–87; Kabaservice, *Rule and Ruin*, 129.

61. Roy Wilkins. "The GOP Seems to Have Learned Its Lesson," *LAT*, Feb. 8, 1965.

62. Strout, "New Image," *CSM*, Dec. 1964; Charles Writeford, "Governors Want to Break Negro Animus against GOP," *Baltimore Sun*, Dec. 5, 1964, box 47, DNC Papers.

63. Earl Mazo. "How Republicans View Their Party Now," *NYT*, Nov. 8, 1964.

64. Earl Mazo, "G.O.P. Urged to Bid for Negro Voters," *NYT*, Jan. 19, 1965; *The 1964 Elections: A Summary Report with Supporting Tables* (Washington, D.C.: The Republican National Committee, 1965).

65. Ripon, *Disaster*, 95–124; Ripon Society, *The Lessons of Victory* (New York: Dial Press, 1969), 173–184.

66. Joseph A. Loftus, "G.O.P. Rebuilding to Try Comeback," *NYT*, Jan. 18, 1965; "Urge GOP Woo Back Negro Vote," *NYAN*, Jan. 23, 1965;"Bliss Rules out Doctrinal Feuds," *NYT*, Jan. 23, 1965.

67. "Negro GOP Assembly," *CD*, Feb. 13, 1965; Charles Bartlett, "Chicago GOP Meeting Evidenced Desire to Seek Better Ground," *LAT*, Jan. 28, 1965; Roscoe Drummond, "Republican Woes," *Deseret News*, Feb. 25, 1965; "GOP and the Negro," *CD*, Feb. 27, 1965; "Woo Back Negro Vote," *NYAN*, Jan. 1965; "Demand Deputy," *NYAN*, Jan. 23, 1965; "Press Demands on National GOP Commit," *NYAN*, Jan. 30, 1965.

68. Joseph A. Loftus. "G.O.P. Is Divided on Negro Voters," *NYT*, Feb. 25, 1965; George Goodman, "The Negro and the GOP," *LAS*, Feb. 25, 1965.

69. Loftus, "Divided," *NYT*, Feb. 1965; Frank C. Porter, "Wilkins Calls Hoover 'Good Public Servant,'" *WP*, Nov. 23, 1964. See also Kabaservice, *Rule and Ruin*, 126; "Southern Negroes and the Political Parties," box 37, Office Files of Fred Panzer, Lyndon Baines Johnson Presidential Library (hereinafter called Panzer Files). See also Black and Black, *Southern Republicans*.

70. Charles Bartlett, "Most Southern Republicans Are Aware of Need to Woo Negro Vote," *LAT*, Mar. 11, 1965; Rowland Evans and Robert Novak, "Inside Report . . . Southern Republican Shift," *WP*, Mar. 25, 1965.

71. Glenn Engle, "Conservatives Hunt Negro for GOP Post," *Detroit News*, Feb. 20, 1965; Glenn Engle, "State GOP Picks 1st Negro for High Post," *Detroit News*, Dec. 5, 1965, box 51, DNC Papers.

72. James Booker, "Fowler in Race for Mayor?" *NYAN*, Apr. 3, 1965; James Booker, "Republicans to Launch Drive Here on Negroes," *NYAN*, Dec. 12, 1965.

73. Booker, "Fowler," *NYAN*, Apr. 1965.

74. "Echoes of Selma," *NYAN*, Apr. 3, 1965; George H. Fowler, "Fowler's Own Story of Montgomery March," *NYAN* Apr. 3, 1965; Malcolm Nash, "Where Do We Go from Montgomery?" *NYAN*, Apr. 3, 1965; GHF, "Where Do We Go from Montgomery? Part II," *NYAN*, Apr. 17, 1965; "NAACP Advertisement," *NYAN*, Apr. 17, 1965.

75. Booker, "Fowler" *NYAN*, Apr. 1965; "GOP's Launch Drive for Negro Mayor," *CD*, Apr. 10, 1965; Leslie Carpenter "Washington Beat," *WP*, Apr. 10, 1965.

76. "Negro GOPers Give Fowler Nod in Bid for Mayoralty," *PC*, May 1, 1965.

77. "Jackie, Lefky to Get Awards," *NYAN*, Apr. 24, 1965; "Fowler Considers Running for Mayor," *NYT*, Apr. 24, 1965; "Events Today," *NYT*, Apr. 24, 1965; Michael G. Long, ed., *First Class Citizenship: The Civil Rights Letters of Jackie Robinson* (New York: Times Books, 2007); James Booker, "Fowler Serious in Bid," *NYAN*, May 1, 1965; "Reynolds Blasts Ray Bliss, Pushes Fowler for NY Mayor," *CD*, May 4, 1965.

78. Major Robinson, "If GOP Doesn't OK Fowler for Mayor Race, He'll Run as Independent Candidate," *PC*, May 15, 1965.

79. Long, *Jackie Robinson*, 129.

80. "Powell Hedges on Support," *NYAN*, May 8, 1965; Thomas P. Ronan, "G.O.P. List for Mayor Cut to 3; Fusion Ticket Also Considered," *NYT*, May 8, 1965.

81. Kabarservice, *Rule and Ruin*, 150; Vincent Cannato. *The Ungovernable City: John Lindsay and His Struggle to Save New York* (New York: Basic Books, 2001), 47–50.

82. Joyce Gelb, "Black Republicans in New York," *Urban Affairs Quarterly* 5, no. 4 (June 1970): 463–465.

83. Thomas Ronan, "Lindsay and Aides Sift Issues to Develop Campaign Strategy," *NYT*, May 16, 1965; Major Robinson, "Negro Vote Is Key to Lindsay's Campaign," *PC*, May 22, 1965; "Rev. Walker Endorses Lindsay," *PC*, Oct. 30, 1965; "Harlem Lindsay Rally Headed by Sammy Davis," *PC*, Sept. 18, 1965. See also JR, "Next New York Mayor," *CD*, Aug. 21, 1965; JR, "All-Out for Lindsay," *CD*, Sept. 25, 1965; JR, "Why Is Buckley Running?" *CD*, Oct. 30, 1965; "Lindsay in Final Harlem Rally," *NYAN*, Oct. 30, 1965.

84. Rowland Evans and Robert Novak, "Inside Report . . . Republican Bobble," *WP*, Apr. 30, 1965; "GOP Salons Attack Charge of Misconduct in Selma," *CD*, May 8, 1965.

85. Author interview with Clarence Townes, 2008.

86. Lyndon B. Johnson, Message on Voting Rights, text of speech, text of bill, text of talking points, Mar. 13, 1965, box 80, DNC Papers.

87. "Unanimity on Voting Rights Bill," *CD*, July 14, 1965; J. A. Rogers. "History Shows: Negro Vote Is a Force against Bigots," *PC*, July 24, 1965.

88. Donald Rumsfeld, "Voting Rights Act—HR 6400," comments and statement, [1965], Congressional Documents, Congressional Voting Record, Donald Rumsfeld Papers, n.d., accessed June 12, 2013, http://papers.rumsfeld.com/library/. See also Joseph Hearst, "G.O.P. Leaders Demand Negro Voting Rights: Ask Why Johnson Does Not Reply to King," *NYT*, Feb. 24, 1965; "GOP and Voting Rights," *CD*, Mar. 6, 1965; Thomas W. Ottendad, "Republicans Look for Ways to Regain Negro Confidence, Erase 'Lily-White' Party Image," *St. Louis Post-Dispatch*, Apr. 11, 1965; "Ohio's McCulloch to Head GOP Voting Rights Crusade," *CP*, Mar. 6, 1965; "Senate OKs Vote Bill," *CD*, May 27, 1965; Kabaservice, *Rule and Ruin*, 139–144.

89. Frank Eleazer, "Rap Johnson for Stand on Rights," *CD* July 13, 1965; Joseph W. Sullivan, "Stands on Voting Equality Bill Point Up GOP Schizophrenia," *WSJ*, July 15, 1965; "Voting Rights Bill May Reach LBJ This Week," *CD*, Aug. 2, 1965; Arnold B. Sawislak, "Civil Rights Bill Passed By House," *CD*, Aug. 4, 1965.

90. Rowland Evans and Robert Novak, "Ohio GOP's Task: Draw Negroes without Scaring the Old Guard," *LAT*, June 18, 1965.

91. JR, "Jackie Robinson Says: Sincerity the Only Hope for the GOP," *PC*, July 3, 1965.

92. Editorial, *NYAN*, July 17, 1965.

93. JR, "Before You Can Say Jackie Robinson," *NYAN*, Dec 11, 1965.

94. "Civil Rights: Your Future Depends on It," *Time*, Aug. 13, 1965; LBJ, "Remarks in the Capitol Rotunda at the Signing of the Voting Rights Act," Aug. 6, 1965, *APP*, UCSB.

95. In a summer 1965 *New York Amsterdam News* editorial, Ed Brooke lauded the efforts of Illinois senator Everett Dirksen, Ohio congressman William McCulloch, and Michigan congressman Gerald Ford in pushing the voting measure through Congress. By the end of May, the Senate approved Lyndon Johnson's version of the act with 30 Republicans and 47 Democrats voting for the bill. Only 2 Republicans, Senators Strom Thurmond of South Carolina and John Tower of Texas, joined with 17 Democrats to vote against the bill. The House approved the bill by the end of July: 112 Republicans and 222 Democrats voted in favor, while 24 Republicans and 61 Democrats rejected it. It is worth noting that Brooke went out of his way to publish a pro-GOP op-ed in a black periodical, in a clear attempt to reassure African Americans that Republicans were progressive on matters of civil rights, despite the right wing of the party. Edward Brooke, "To Be Equal: After the Fall," *NYAN*, June 19, 1965; Dan Day, "Solid South Fading Away," *CP*, Aug. 7, 1965; Hugh Davis Graham. *Civil Rights Era: Origins and Development of National Policy, 1960–1972* (New York: Oxford University Press, 1990).

96. "Why the Rioting" *LAS*, Aug. 19, 1965.

97. JR, "Beware of 'Barry,'" *CD*, Aug. 7, 1965; JR, "Out of the Ashes," *CD*, Aug. 28, 1965.

98. "New Law Spurs Negro Vote Rolls," *NYT*, Aug. 5, 1965; David S. Broder, "Liberal Republicans Urge Past to Appeal to Negro and Punish 'Lily-Whites,'" *NYT*, Apr. 13, 1966; Jack Nelson, "GOP Groups Deplore Bias by Part in South," *LAT*, Apr. 13, 1966.

99. "Bliss Will Select Top Negro GOP Aide," *NYAN*, Sept. 4, 1965.

100. "N.Y. Vote Thriller," *LAT*, Nov. 3, 1965; Raymond Lahr, "Recent Election Shows Strength of Negro Vote," *CD*, Nov. 6, 1965; Major Robinson, "The Harlem Election 'Week That Is,'" *PC*, Nov. 6, 1965; "Why Beame Lost," *NYAN*, Nov. 6, 1965; Jesse H. Walker, "How Negroes Voted," *NYAN*, Nov. 6, 1965; James Farmer, "The Core of It!" *NYAN*, Nov. 13, 1965; "The Negro Vote," *CD*, Nov. 15, 1965.

101. JR, "Jackie Robinson," July 1965; Long, *Jackie Robinson*, 229–230.

102. Daryl E. Lembke, "N. California Drive Started by Reagan," *LAT*, Jan. 23, 1966; "Reagan Visits Ghetto Areas; Lauds Self-Help," *LAS*, Feb. 3, 1966; Paul Beck, "Reagan Strives to Win Support of Negro Voter," *LAT*, June 2, 1966.

103. "The Eleventh Commandment," *Ripon Forum* 2, no. 4 (June 1966), in CLT Papers.

104. "Ronald Reagan for Real," *Time*, Oct. 7, 1966.

105. Paul Beck, "Reagan Storms from Meeting of Negro GOP Unit," *LAT*, Mar. 6, 1966; "Reagan's Exit Stirs Negro G.O.P. Parley," *NYT*, Mar. 7, 1966; Carl Greenberg, "Reagan Walkout Laid to Ire at Christopher," *LAT*, Mar. 10, 1966; "Registrars Withdrawal Brings Dixie Protests," *CD*, Mar. 19, 1966; "Reagan Says Inaccuracies on Walk-Out," *LAS*, Mar. 17, 1966; "Reagan Tells Why He Left Negro Parley," *CT*, Mar. 7, 1966; "Reagan 'Insulted,' Stages Stormy Exit," *WP*, Mar. 7, 1966; Lou Cannon. *Governor Reagan: His Rise to Power*

(New York: Public Affairs, 2003), 142–143; Matthew Dallek, *The Right Moment: Ronald Reagan's First Victory and the Decisive Turning Point in American Politics* (New York: Oxford University Press, 2004), 200; Bill Robertson, "Republican Confab Endorses Vaughn," *LAS*, Mar. 10, 1966.

106. Long, *Jackie Robinson*, 227; Gelb, "Black Republicans," *Urban Affairs Quarterly*, 1969; "Walker Says No to Lindsay," *NYAN*, Jan. 29, 1966.

107. "He Dared Be Republican," *LAS*, Jan. 5, 1967; "Elect Reynolds G.O.P. Council's Chairman," *CT*, Feb. 12, 1966; "Reynolds Gets Nod as Chairman of Council," *CP*, Feb. 26, 1966; Charles Dumas, "Robinson to Join Rocky Team," *Evening News*, Feb. 7, 1966.

108. JR, "Reagan's Victory in California," *NYAN*, June 18, 1966; JR, "Rocky Balance to Reagan," *NYAN*, Nov. 19, 1966; "He Dared Be Republican," *LAS*, Jan. 5, 1967.

109. Jack Steele, "Bliss Aide under Fire," *Washington Daily News*, May 30, 1966, CLT Papers.

110. "Winning Negro Support for the GOP," *New York Herald Tribune*, [1965], box 51, DNC Papers.

111. Carl T. Rowan, "'Irritant' May Help," *Spokane Daily Chronicle*, Mar. 7, 1966; "Bliss and the Negroes: The Drama of Detroit," *Ripon Forum* 2, no. 4 (June 1966), in CLT Papers.

112. Rowan, "'Irritant,'" *Spokane Daily Chronicle*, Mar. 1966; "Bliss," *Ripon Forum*, June 1966.

113. Long, *Jackie Robinson*, 229–230.

114. Arthur L. Peterson to Myron H. Wahls, Letter, Apr. 21, 1966, CLT Papers. See also MHW to CLT, Letter, May 4, 1966, CLT Papers.

115. Alfred Duckett Press Release, CLT Papers.

116. "Bliss," *Ripon Forum*, June 1966.

117. Ibid. See also Long, *Jackie Robinson*, 230–231; JR, "A Trip to Detroit," *Herald-Advance*, June 4, 1966, in CLT Papers. See also "'Keep Parties Guessing,' Romney Tells Negroes," *Jet*, June 16, 1966.

118. NNRA, Press Release and Statement of Proposals, June 1, 1966, CLT Papers.

119. Ibid.

120. In February 1966, the LDF petitioned the Department of Health, Education and Welfare to hold hearings on "substitute parent" policies, arguing that southern states used the measures to deny public assistance to black families with dependent children. For example, at the time Georgia welfare law considered a man who lived with a woman a "substitute father" for any of the women's children, which made him accountable for the "support and care of his and her children, regardless of whether he is married to another woman," thus revoking welfare benefits for the household. "NAACP Hits Racial Bias in Welfare," *PC*, Feb. 19, 1966; Press Release, June 1966, CLT Papers.

121. "Whites Welcome, Negroes Must Lead," *Jet*, June 2, 1969; "Words of the Week," *Jet*, June 16, 1966.

122. "Power and Color," *St. Joseph News-Press*, Aug. 24, 1966; JR, "Let's Have a Real Riot," *CD*, Sept. 4, 1965. See also JR, "Sailing Upstream without a Paddle," *CD*, July 30, 1966.

123. Alfred Duckett Associates, NNRA Press Release, [1966]; "National Committee Charged with Attempt to Dictate to Negro Republican Assembly," [1966], both in NNRA 1966 folder, CLT Papers.

124. ADA, Press Release, [1966]; "National Committee Charged," [1966].

125. Long, *Jackie Robinson*, 230–231; Jack Steele, "Bliss Aide under Fire," *Washington Daily News*, May 30, 1966, in CLT Papers. See also "Ticker," *Jet*, July 7, 1966.

126. JR, "Reagan's Victory in California," *NYAN*, June 18, 1966; "Reagan Please Note: Laws Aid Civil Rights," *LAS*, June 23, 1966.

127. JR, "Famed Jackie Robinson Joins Brown's Campaign," *LAS*, Oct. 27, 1966.

128. JR, "Re-election Bid of Rockefeller," *NYAN*, Aug. 13, 1966; JR, "Racial Team Gets Results in N.Y.," *CD*, Nov. 19, 1966. See also Long, *Jackie Robinson*, 230.

129. "What's Happening in Westchester," *NYAN*, Aug. 13, 1966; "GOP Negroes Honor Rocky at Fund Raiser," *NYAN*, Oct. 8, 1966; "Negro GOP Assembly Aids Rocky," *NYAN*, Oct. 15, 1966; "Negro Republicans Support Governor," *NYT*, Oct. 15, 1966; "What's Happening in Westchester," *NYAN*, Oct. 22, 1966; James Booker, "Roping in Rights Leaders," *NYAN*, Nov. 5, 1966; "Display Advertisement," *NYAN*, Nov. 5, 1966; New York NNRA, "Rockefeller Advertisement," *Jet*, Nov. 10, 1966; "The Year They Stayed In," *Time*, Nov. 18, 1966.

130. Long, *Jackie Robinson*, 232.

131. NNRA, Press Release, Nov. 7, 1966, Organizations File, Manuscript Division, Library of Congress, Washington, D.C.; "Negro GOP Unit Snubs Reagan, Other Foes," *CD*, Nov. 8, 1966.

132. "A Party for All," *Time*, Nov. 18, 1966; "Stayed In," *Time*, Nov. 1966; Simeon Booker, "Election Conclusion: Negroes," *Jet*, Nov. 24, 1966.

133. Rowan, "Irritant," *SDC*, Mar. 1966.

134. JR, "Don't Let it Happen Again," *NYAN*, May 27, 1967; "G.O.P. Is Warned of Negro Switch," *NYT*, May 14, 1967.

135. "Afro-American Republicans Issue Their Position Paper," *NYAN*, May 20, 1967. See also Mary McGrory, "In 1968: Romney-Nixon or Fight," *Evening Independent*, Oct. 24, 1968.

136. "Black Michigan Republicans Endorse Nixon," *CD*, Oct. 15, 1968; "Race Issue Hits Dems and GOP," *NYAN*, July 13, 1968; Gertrude Wilson, "Not 'Anybody's Black Man,'" *NYAN*, Aug. 10, 1968.

137. JR, "The GOP Party and the Negro Vote," *CD*, Mar. 18, 1968; "Unhappy with GOP Ticket Jackie Robinson Bolts Republican Party," *Windsor Star*, Aug. 10, 1968.

Chapter 3. The Challenge of Change

1. The Mississippi legislature appointed two black senators in the nineteenth century: Hiram Rhodes (1870–1871) and Blanche Kelso (1875–1881). See Poppy Cannon White, "Poppy's Notes: History and Brooke," *NYAN*, Nov. 26, 1966; Judson L. Jeffries, "U.S. Senator Edward W. Brooke and Governor L. Douglas Wilder Tell Political Scientists How Blacks Can Win High-Profile Statewide Office," *PS: Political Science and Politics* 32, no. 3 (Sept. 1999): 583; Edward W. Brooke, *Bridging the Divide: My Life* (New Brunswick: Rutgers University Press, 2007), 140–146; "Politics and the Backlash," *CSM*, Nov. 12, 1966.

2. Miscellaneous Headline Clippings, n.d., box 625, folder Press—Clippings, Edward William Brooke Papers, Manuscript Division, Library of Congress, Washington, D.C. (hereinafter called EWB Papers); James P. Murphy to EWB, Letter, Nov. 16, 1972, box 214, folder Brooke for President, EWB Papers; W.E. Barnett, "Tribute to Sen. Brooke," *LAT*, Jan. 15, 1967; Edward Brooke Editorial, *Life*, Oct. 28, 1966, box 214, folder Brooke for President, EWB Papers; Keith Wheeler, "An Off-Year Election with a Difference," *Life*, Nov. 4, 1966; Susanna McBee, "A Long Void Is Filled at Last," *Life*, Jan. 13, 1967; "Edward Brooke: Jet Profile," *Jet*, Nov. 24, 1966.

3. Brooke, *Bridging the Divide*, 187.

4. "The First," *Time*, Jan. 25, 1963.

5. In 1950 Brooke cross-filed with both political parties—a practice not uncommon at the time—seeking a seat in the state legislature. The Democratic Party rejected his bid,

whereas the Republican Party accepted his candidacy. The parties respective decisions reinforced his preexisting beliefs about Democrats and Republicans in Massachusetts. In 1952 he registered as a Republican, attributing his decision to "loyalty, leadership, admiration, and potential," and a belief in traditional conservatism. See "Massachusetts GOP Choice: Nation's Eyes on Candidacy of Brooke for Secretary of State," *PC*, Sept. 24, 1960; "Maturity," *PC*, November 1962; Edward R.F. Sheehan, "Brooke of Massachusetts: A Negro Governor on Beacon Hill?" *Harper's Magazine* 228, no. 1369 (June 1, 1964); "Brooke Sworn in as Mass. Official," *BAA*, Jan. 19, 1963; "Ted Kennedy Wins Senate Seat in Lopsided Fashion," *Ocala Star-Banner*, Nov. 7, 1962.

6. "Maturity," *PC*, Nov. 1962.

7. "Malden Elects First Colored City Officer," *AA*, Nov. 24, 1945; "Elected to City Council by Massachusetts Town's 99% White District," *CD*, Mar. 23, 1946; "Boston Suburb's Council Headed by 'Son of Slave,'" *NYT*, Dec. 29, 1949; "Five in Massachusetts Win GOP Primaries," *CD*, Oct. 4, 1952.

8. It is worth noting that Brooke and Grant Reynolds (NNRA) were friends, having met while serving in the same segregated unit during World War II. Brooke, *Bridging the Divide*, 4–5, 21–38, 43–48, 278; Sheehan, "Beacon Hill?" *Harper's Magazine*, June 1964.

9. Brooke, *Bridging the Divide*, 55–61, 108.

10. Ibid.

11. Ibid., 107–108; "Noisy, but Not Numerous," *BAA*, Nov. 10, 1964.

12. Dan Day, "Edward W. Brooke, Man on Tight Rope," *CP*, July 25, 1964; "GOP Unit Hears Edward Brooke," *WP*, Oct. 19, 1964; "Brooke's Refusal to Back Goldwater Hurts Funds," *CP*, Sept. 26, 1964; "Edward Brooke: Mass. Attorney General Will Not Introduce Goldwater," *PC*, Oct. 10, 1964.

13. "The Figures," *Time*, Nov13, 1964; "Top Elected Negro Official Scores 2nd Win," *CD*, Nov. 5, 1964; "56 Negroes Win Election Races," *CP*, Nov. 14, 1964; EWB, campaign materials, attorney general, final draft script for commercial, Sept. 30,1924, EWB Papers; Elinor C. Hartshorn, "The Quiet Campaigner: Edward W. Brooke in Massachusetts" (Ph.D. dissertation, University of Massachusetts, Amherst, 1973), 97; Brooke, *Bridging the Divide*, 109.

14. EWB, interview on Goldwater and 1964 Election, 1965, box 607, folder Writings, EWB Papers.

15. Ibid.; EWB, Address to the National Press Club, Apr. 28, 1965, box 607, in ibid.

16. EWB, Goldwater Interview, 1965; EWB, "The Republican Crisis," *Washingtonian*, Apr. 1966, both in ibid; "Edward Brooke Is Making History," *St. Petersburg Times*, Feb. 22, 1966.

17. For example, see Evans Tyree Young to EWB, Letter, Nov. 16, 1964; Charles A. Wilson to EWB, Letter, Nov. 9, 1964; E. A. Shmied to EWB, Letter, Nov. 12, 1964; John C. Love to John Lindsay, Letter on Brooke, Nov. 9, 1964, all in box 619, folder "Press," Public Response, EWB Papers.

18. "News at a Glance," *PC*, Nov. 21, 1964; Russell Freeburg, "Negro Leader Scores G.O.P. Race Policy," *CT*, Feb. 21, 1965; "Edward Brooke Counsels: 'GOP Must be Peoples' Party,'" *PC*, Mar. 6, 1965; "Part of Checks, Balances System: Brooke Tells Press Club GOP Needs Off-Year Meet to Unify Role as Critic," *PC*, May 29, 1965. See also EWB on *Meet the Press*, [Nov. 1964], box 619, folder "Meet the Press," Public Response to Brooke Appearance, EWB Papers; Brooke, *Bridging the Divide*, 55–61.

19. "Peoples' Party," *PC*, Mar. 1965; "2,000 Brave Blizzard to Hear Edward Brooke," *CP*, Mar. 6, 1965.

20. Russell Freeburg, "Negro Leader Scores G.O.P. Race Policy," *CT*, Feb. 21, 1965; EWB, Goldwater interview, 1965, box 607, EWB Papers.

21. "An Individual Who Happens to Be a Negro," *Time*, Feb. 17, 1967.

22. Chuck Stone, "Non-Negro Politics," in *Black Political Power in America* (New York: Dell, 1968); Jeffries, "Brooke and Wilder," *PS*, Sept. 1999; "Edward Brooke Is Making His History," *St. Petersburg Times*, Feb. 22, 1966. See also Chuck Stone, "Black Politics: Third Force, Third Party or Third-Class Influence," *Black Scholar* 1, no. 2 (Dec. 1969): 10; Tom Nolan, "Edward Brooke May Be First Negro in U.S. Senate Since Reconstruction," *Victoria Advocate*, Oct. 12, 1966; "Negro," *Time*, Feb. 1967; Isabell McCaig, "Liberals, Conservatives Court Sen. Brooke," *Middlesboro Daily News*, Mar. 29, 1967; Roscoe Drummond, "Big Change in Race Relations," *St. Joseph Gazette*, June 19, 1967.

23. Day, "Tight Rope," *CP*, July 1964.

24. Joseph M. Russin, "7500 Protest Birmingham Atrocities, White House Orders Troops to Area," *Harvard Crimson*, May 13, 1963; "Mass. Atty. Gen. to Enforce Anti-bias," *ADW*, July 21, 1963; "Negro Official Cautions Race Demonstrators," *LAT*, July 29, 1963; "Freedom Now," *Time*, May 17, 1963.

25. Sheehan, "Beacon Hill?" *Harper's Magazine*, June 1964.

26. Victor Lasky, "Brooke's Ideas May Come As a Shock to Liberals," *Virgin Island Daily News*, Dec. 14, 1966; John Skow, "The Black Man Leading a G.O.P. March on Washington," *Saturday Evening Post*, Sept. 10, 1966; "School Boycott Protests Slow Boston Mixing," *Ocala Star-Banner*, Feb. 25, 1964; Hartshorn, "Quiet Campaigner," 101.

27. Sheehan, "Beacon Hill?" *Harper's Magazine*, June 1964.

28. John Henry Cutler, *Ed Brooke: Biography of a Senator* (New York: Bobbs Merrill, 1972), 113–120.

29. In her study of Brooke's 1966 campaign, political scientist Elinor Hartshorn noted that a few studies from the mid- to late 1960s demonstrated that whites from every region of the country still "expressed fear or disgust at having to even touch Negroes, shake hands with them, eat out of the same dishes or use the same facilities" and viewed African Americans as promiscuous with "looser morals," unclean, lazy, unintelligent, carefree and happy (but prone to violence), and dependent on government "handouts." Hartshorn, "Quiet Campaigner," 77–78. See also Angus Campbell and Howard Schuman, *Racial Attitudes in Fifteen American Cities* (Ann Arbor: University of Michigan Institute for Social Research, 1968).

30. EWB, Goldwater interview, 1965, box 607; Brooke for US Senator Committee, "News from Brooke," Press Release, Oct. 21, 1966, both in EWB Papers; "A Negro Leader's Advice to Republicans," *U.S. News & World Report*, Feb. 1, 1965.

31. Stone, "Black Politics," *Black Scholar*, Dec. 1969; Boisfeuillet Jones Jr., "Edward Brooke: Silhouette," *Harvard Crimson*, May 18, 1966.

32. Hartshorn, "Quiet Campaigner," 116–118.

33. Leslie Carpenter, "Washington Beat," *WP*, Mar. 13, 1965; "Work to Get Negro Vote, Burch Urges," *CT*, Feb. 18, 1965; "Burch Asks G.O.P. to Reject Racism," *NYT*, Feb. 18, 1965; "Most Southern Republicans Are Aware of Need to Woo Negro Vote," *LAT*, Mar. 11, 1965.

34. Loftus, "Divided," *NYT*, Feb. 1965; "Nixon Urges Voter Drive for Negroes," *CT*, Feb. 27, 1965; "Brooke Enlisted in GOP Image Rebuilding Effort," *LAS*, Mar. 18, 1965; "GOP Begins Drive for Negro Vote," *NYAN*, Mar. 13, 1965; "Ed Brooke Boosted for Veep," *PC*, Mar. 20, 1965; "Fowler Nod," *PC*, May 1965; "GOP Considering Bay State Negro to Head Minority Policies Panel," *WP*, Mar. 5, 1965; Martin F. Nolan, "Saltonstall's Successor," *New Republic*, Jan. 22, 1966.

35. Brooke often cowrote his policy reports and white papers, relying on advice from a broad spectrum of advisers—for the April 1965 National Press Club speech, he enlisted the help of the liberal Republican Ripon Society. In general, Brooke's advisers were a colorful

lot, ranging from "right of center, pro-business, conservative Republicans" to "left of center, liberal academic Democrats." This also included Albert Gammal, Brooke's 1966 senatorial campaign manager, whom the black official characterized as a Goldwater Republican. Hartshorn, "Quiet Campaigner," 138–148.

36. Ripon Society and EWB, "Att. Gen. Brooke's Speech to National Press Club," outline and notes, Misc. Office File, Roger Woodsworth, Speeches and Speech Material, Misc. in EWB Papers. See also Dan Day, "Brooke Explores Future of Republican Party," *CP*, May 8, 1965.

37. "Says Republican Party Wants Negroes to Return," *Call*, Apr. 23, 1965, folder RNC Correspondence 1966, CLT Papers.

38. Lillian S. Calhoun, "Confetti," *CD*, Apr. 13, 1965.

39. Brooke used "progressive conservatism" interchangeably with "progressive Republicanism" (leaning toward the latter phrase as he became more liberal). Interestingly, in a November 1965 column, Ralph McGill asserted that extremist Republicans had "whittled down the great rock of honest, progressive conservatism" by rejecting civil rights and embracing states' rights—an argument nearly identical to that which Brooke would advance a few months later in his *The Challenge of Change: Crisis in Our Two-Party System* (Boston: Little, Brown, 1966). Ralph McGill, "No Freedom or Rights Are Lost," *HC*, Nov. 30, 1965.

40. Political scientist Elinor Hartshorn's interviews with Brooke's advisers revealed that the attorney general wrote *Challenge* without any help—an unusual decision given that nearly all of his white papers and talks, before the 1970s, were co-written by his staff. All of his advisers objected to him publishing the book, arguing that its topic was far too risky and would alienate his moderate, liberal, and conservative supporters. Hartshorn, "Quiet Campaigner," 138–148.

See also miscellaneous book reviews, n.d.; Little, Brown & Company's editor notes, *Challenge* by EWB, Nov. 4, 1965, all in box 607, folders: *Challenge* (Boston 1966), Book File, Critiques, Draft Chapters, EWB Papers; Wendell H. Woodman, review of *Challenge of Change*, *News-Tribune*, Apr. 7, 1966; William H. Rentschler, "Seeds of Republican Renaissance," *CT*, Apr. 10, 1966; Marion Campfield, "World of Books," *CP*, May 7, 1966; JR, "We Can Be Proud of Edward Brooke," *CD*, Dec. 3, 1966; Elizabeth A. McSherry, "Authors and Critics," *HC*, Mar. 27, 1966; Gertrude Wilson, "Ed Brooke Takes His Stand," *NYAN*, Apr. 9, 1966.

41. Brooke, *Challenge of Change*, 23, 37, 41–47.

42. Ibid., 77–121, 243–255.

43. Rentschler, "Seeds of Republican Renaissance," *CT*, Apr. 966; Jean M. White, "Leaders Not Reflecting GOP Aims, Brooke Says," *LAT*, Feb. 14, 1966.

44. Hartshorn, "Quiet Campaigner," 132–137; Robert Schuettinger, review of 'The Challenge of Change by Edward W. Brooke, *New Leader* 49, no. 11 (May 5, 1966).

45. Brooke, *Challenge of Change*, 159, 243–258; White, "Leaders Not Reflecting GOP Aims, Brooke Says," *LAT*, Feb. 1966; Rentschler, "Seeds of Republican Renaissance," *CT*, Apr. 1966; Gertrude Wilson, "Ed Brooke Takes His Stand," *NYAN*, Apr. 9, 1966; Schuettinger, review, May 1966.

46. Jacob Javits, *Congressional Record* reprint of "Negroes and Open Society" Aug. 2, 1966, box 654, folder Articles about EWB 1962–1967, EWB Papers; Jean Dietz, "Brooke Raps LBJ, Offers Own Poverty War Plan," [1966], Campaign Materials, US Senate, 1966, News Clippings, both in EWB Papers; EWB, "Paying a 350 Year Old Debt: Blueprint for an Open Society," *Negro Digest* 16, no. 1 (Nov. 1966); "Edward Brooke Sounds Off," *Jet*, Aug. 18, 1966; Simeon Booker, "'I'm a Soul Brother'—Senator Edward Brooke," *Ebony*, Apr. 1967.

47. "GOP Probing Switch in N.Y. Negro Votes," *WP*, Nov. 18, 1965; JR, "Report Tells GOP Some Truths," *CD*, Jan. 29, 1966.

48. "The National Hotline," *CD*, Jan. 10, 1967.

49. Rosemarie Tyler Brookes, "Goldwater!" *CD*, July 16, 1964.

50. RNC, "Bliss Names Negro Advisory Committee," Press Release, Feb. 25, 1966; "12 Negroes Chosen as G.O.P. Advisors," *NYT*, Feb. 27, 1966; "Winning Negro Support for the GOP," *New York Herald Tribune*, Feb. 27, 1966; Carl T. Rowan, "The GOP's Uphill Fight for the Negro Vote," *Sunday Star*, Mar. 6, 1966; John C. O'Brien, "GOP to Try Again for Negro Voters," *Philadelphia Inquirer*, Mar. 15, 1966, all in box 51, DNC Papers; Paul Hope "12 Negroes Name[d]," *Washington Star*, Feb. 25, 1966, in RNC Correspondence, CLT Papers; "GOP Probing Switch in N.Y. Negro Votes," *WP*, Nov. 18, 1965; "GOP to Woo Negro Vote," *CSM*, Feb. 28, 1966; Julia Duscha, "Party's Winners Tell GOP How to Go After City Votes," *WP*, Jan. 26, 1966; "Pick 12 Negro Leaders for GOP Advisory Panel," *CD*, Mar. 5, 1966; "Negroes to Give GOP Advice on Race Vote Lures," *WP*, Feb. 26, 1966; Adolph J. Slaughter, "GOP Moves to Change Image," *CD*, May 7, 1966; Alan L. Otten, "Restless Negro Voters: Their Democratic Loyalty Wanes, Yet GOP Fails to Act," *WP*, Feb. 23, 1966; David S. Broder, "Negro to Get Post on Top G.O.P. Unit," *NYT*, Mar. 12, 1966; "A New State Political Organization Is Born," *CP*, Feb. 1, 1958; "12 Negroes Chosen as G.O.P. Advisers," *NYT*, Feb. 27, 1967; "W.O. Walker Is Member of GOP Advisory Committee," *CP*, Mar. 5, 1966; "Negro GOP Advisors," *CD*, Mar. 2, 1966.

51. John Herbers, "G.O.P Aide 'Starts From Scratch,'" *NYT*, May 31, 1966; Major Robinson, "Tan Stalwarts Buck GOP Drive to Regain Support," *PC*, Aug. 6, 1966; Cabell Phillips, "Negro Leaflet Ruse Charged to G.O.P.," *NYT*, Nov. 3, 1964; "Negro Blamed for King Write-In," *NYAN*, Nov. 7, 1964; "G.O.P. Aide Indicted on Leaflet Charge," *NYT*, Nov. 20, 1964; "Indicted G.O.P. Aide Faces Court Today," *NYT*, Nov. 21, 1964; "Claiborne Freed in Write-In," *NYAN*, June 11, 1966; "Claiborne Faces Trial for Write-In Election Activity," *CD*, Feb. 5, 1966; David S. Broder, "Bliss Appealing to '64 Defectors," *NYT*, Aug. 24, 1965. See also "Negro GOPers Censure Claiborne for Write-In Plot," *Jet*, Dec. 3, 1964.

52. CLT, Speech and Report to the Negro Advisory Committee, Mar. 1966, folder Republican Party, RNC, Speeches by Townes, 1966–1969, CLT Papers; author interview with CLT, 2008.

53. Townes, Speech to NAC, Mar. 1966, CLT Papers. See also Carl T. Rowan, "Uphill Pull for Negro Vote Stands before Republicans," *Spokane Daily Chronicle*, Aug. 7, 1968.

54. RNC, "Townes Named Special Assistant to Chairman Bliss," Press Release, Apr. 25, 1966, in folder Republican Correspondence, CLT Papers; Paul Hope, "GOP Committee Hires Negro as Aide in Bid for Support," *Washington Star*, Apr. 25, 1966, box 51, DNC Papers.

55. Carl T. Rowan, "The GOP's Uphill Fight for the Negro Vote," *Sunday Star*, Mar. 6, 1966, box 51, DNC Papers.

56. "Fowler Nod," *PC*, May 1965; George S. Schuyler, "Reagan-Brooke Ticket in 1968," North American Newspaper Alliance Press Release, Jan. 7–8, 1967, box 2/3, NANA News Releases, George S. Schuyler Papers, Special Collections Research Center, Syracuse University Libraries, Syracuse New York.

57. "Washington Beat," *WP*, [Jan. 1966], EWB Papers.

58. "Memo from Washington," *Milwaukee Sentinel*, Mar. 7, 1966.

59. "Brooke Announcement Sets of National Repercussions," *NYAN*, Jan. 29, 1966.

60. CLT, Statement on Virginia House of Delegates, Apr. 5, 1965, CLT Papers; author interview with CLT, 2008; Mary Brinkerhff, "Southern GOP Negro Questions Demos' Role," *Dallas Morning News*, Apr. 14, 1965, CLT Papers; Carl Shires, "House Seat Here Sought by Townes," *State News*, Apr. 5, 1965.

61. "Virginia Contest Adds Dimension," *NYT*, June 20, 1965; "Write-In Ballots Defeat Negro for Virginia House," *WP*, Nov. 3, 1965.

62. Vera Glaser, "Goldwater Offers Money to Put Brooke in Senate," *Virgin Island Daily News*, Feb. 15, 1966; "Goldwater Aids Brooke, Who Didn't Support Him," *NYT*, June 25, 1966; "Brooke Wins Endorsement," *St. Petersburg Times*, June 26, 1966; John Fenton, "Brooke Is Endorsed by Senate by Massachusetts Republicans," *NYT*, June 26, 1966; WBZ, "Transcript from Newsmakers: 1966," Oct. 30, 1966, 1966 Campaign Materials. See also box 415, folder Blacks Misc. 1967–76, all in EWB Papers; Hartshorn, "Quiet Campaigner," 166–170; "Mass. GOP Brooke," *CD*, July 9, 1966.

63. See, for example, "The Black Man Leading a G.O.P. March on Washington," and "Edward Brooke . . . Vote-Getter," and other miscellaneous headlines in box 654, folder Articles about EWB 1962–67, EWB Papers; "Seeks Saltonstall Seat," *Newark Sunday News*, Feb. 2, 1966; Hartshorn, "Quiet Campaigner," 158–164, 170.

64. "A Negro for All the People," *Age*, Jan. 16, 1967.

65. Relman Morin, "White Backlash—How Important Is It?" *Freelance Star*, Nov. 5, 1966; Joseph Alsop, "Matter of Fact," *WP*, Nov. 7, 1966.

66. "Innocent Victim?" editorial cartoon, [James Dobbins], [Oct.–Nov. 1966], box 654, EWB Papers; "A Negro for All the People," *Age*, Jan. 16, 1967; Don Irwin, "Race Issue Emerges in Massachusetts Primary," *LAT*, Sept. 13, 1966; "Threat to Brooke's Bid to U.S. Senate," *CD*, Sept. 24, 1966; Cal Brumley, "Bay State Backlash," *WSJ*, Oct. 20, 1966; "Massachusetts: Brooke Will Test the White Backlash," *NYT*, Oct. 23, 1966; "Peabody, Brooke Close in Bay State Race," *HC*, Oct. 17, 1966; Thomas J. Foley, "White Backlash Slices Brooke's Senate Lead," *LAT*, Oct. 19, 1966; John H. Fenton, "Backlash Enters Bay State Race," *NYT*, Oct. 23, 1966; "Brooke Moving Ahead as Backlash Subsides," *WP*, Oct. 30, 1966; Marianne Means, "Brooke, Peabody Battle," *Tuscaloosa News*, Oct. 11, 1966; John F. Becker and Eugene E. Heaton Jr., "The Election of Senator Edward W. Brooke," *Public Opinion Quarterly* 31, no. 3 (Autumn 1967): 356.

67. Richard Harwood, "White Backlash Reported as Failing to Materialize," *Spokesman-Review*, Nov. 8, 1966; Relman Morin, "White Backlash: How Important is It?" *Free-Lance Star*, Nov. 5, 1966; "Mrs. Hicks Raps Bay State Racial Imbalance Law," *HC*, Mar. 9, 1966.

68. WBZ Radio interview Oct. 1966; George J. Marder, ""Edward Brooke Articulates Viewpoints," *WAA*, Nov. 1, 1966.

69. Becker and Heaton, "Election of EWB," *Public Opinion Quarterly*, 1967, 346–358; EWB, "Statement before the Platform Committee of the 1966 Republican State Convention," June 15, 1966, EWB Papers.

70. Tim Taylor, "Brooke Assails Rights Violence," [1966], folder Campaign Clippings, Press, EWB Papers; "Brooke Says Black Power's Failed, Makes Plea for Negro Moderation," *Harvard Crimson*, Oct. 8, 1966; Lloyd Shearer, "Polls . . . Pollsters—and How They Work," *St. Petersburg Times*, Apr. 28, 1968.

71. David B. Wilson, "Brooke Sets Senate Goals," [1966], EWB 1966 Campaign, EWB Papers; "Negro," *Time*, Feb. 1967. See also Becker and Heaton, "Brooke," *Public Opinion Quarterly*, 1967; Brooke for US Senator Committee, "News from Brooke for U.S. Senator Committee," Press Release, November 6–7, 1966, box 654, EWB Papers.

72. "Jackie Robinson Hails Republican Revival in Ohio," *CP*, Mar. 5, 1966; EWB, transcript: *Issues and Answers*, Sept. 4, 1966, in folder Campaign Materials, TV-Radio Appearances, 1966, EWB Papers.

73. Brooke's campaign manager later expanded on why he was "violently opposed to the slogan: "Proud of what? That Ed was a Negro?" he stated in a 1973 interview. Carl Stokes would use the phrase "Let's Do Cleveland Proud," in his successful 1967 mayoral campaign—his white opponent seized on this immediately, accusing the black politician of "race pride" and racism. Hartshorn, "Quiet Campaigner," 175–176; EWB, WBZ interview, Oct. 1966.

74. "Bay State's Color-Blind Candidate," *Life*, Apr. 8, 1966.

75. Published in the September edition of the *Saturday Evening Post*, John Skow's article reached about 6.5 million subscribers. Within Massachusetts, more than 200,000 people received it. The magazine was shared widely—people read it in their homes, waiting rooms, corporate offices, and schools. The *Post* also ran advertisements about the article in many of the major black newspapers, including the *PC*, *CP*, *LAS*, *NYAN*, and *CD* (Sept. 3, 1966 editions). A postelection study found that Brooke benefited enormously from the publicly, in ways that Peabody was unable to duplicate. Skow, "Black Man Leading," *Saturday Evening Post*, Sept. 1966. See also Hartshorn, "Quiet Campaigner."

76. Roy Wilkins, "Whither 'Black Power'?" *Crisis*, Aug.–Sept. 1966; Manning Marable, *Race, Reform, and Rebellion: The Second Reconstruction in Black America, 1945–1990 (Jackson: University Press of Mississippi, 1990)*, 92–93.

77. The signees included Roy Wilkins of the NAACP, Whitney M. Young Jr. of the NUL, A. Philip Randolph of the Brotherhood of Sleeping Car Porters, Dorothy Height of the National Council of Negro Women, Bayard Rustin of the A. Philip Randolph Institute, Amos T. Hall of the Masons of America, and Hobson Reynolds of the Order of Elks of the World. "A Negro 'No' to Black Power," EWB Papers; Thomas A. Johnson, "Negro Leaders Issue a Statement of Principles Repudiating 'Black Power' Concepts," *NYT*, Oct. 14, 1966.

78. Johnson, "Negro Leaders," *NYT*, OCT. 1966; EWB, transcript, *IA*, Sept. 1966, EWB Papers.

79. See, for example, Evelyn Brooks Higginbotham, *Righteous Discontent: The Women's Movement in the Black Baptist Church, 1880–1920* (Cambridge: Harvard University Press, 1993); Cathy J. Cohen, *The Boundaries of Blackness: AIDS and the Breakdown of Black Politics* (Chicago: University of Chicago Press, 1999), 71–74; Kevin Gaines, *Uplifting the Race: Black Leadership, Politics, and Culture in the Twentieth Century* (Chapel Hill: University of North Carolina Press, 1996); Frederick Harris, *The Price of the Ticket: Barack Obama and the Rise and Decline of Black Politics* (New York: Oxford University Press, 2012), 100–136; Tomiko Brown-Nagin, *Courage to Dissent: Atlanta and the Long History of the Civil Rights Movement* (New York: Oxford University Press, 2012), 32–38.

80. Hugh Scott, "Senator's Report with Hugh Scott and Joseph Clark," transcript, [1966]; EWB, transcript, *Issues and Answers*, Sept. 1966; EWB, WBZ Radio interview, Oct. 1966, all in box 46, EWB Papers; "Brooke," *Harvard Crimson*, Oct. 1966.

81. "Climax Due in Brooke-Peabody Race," *Spokesman-Review*, Nov. 7, 1966; "Carmichael Scoffs at Brooke Win," *Boston Globe*, Nov. 12, 1966.

82. "6 Negro Congressmen Sure of Election," *Chicago Defender*, Nov. 5, 1966.

83. In their first senatorial attempts, Leverett Saltonstall received 64.8 percent of the vote (1944), John F. Kennedy earned 51.5 percent (1952), and Edward M. Kennedy garnered 57 percent (1962). Hartshorn, "Quiet Campaigner," 191–210, 214–224.

84. Richard Harwood, "White Backlash Reported as Failing to Materialize," *Spokesman-Review*, Nov. 8, 1966; "White Backlash No Big Factor," *CT*, Nov. 10, 1966; Chas Loeb, "Ed Brooke Tames Backlash," *CP*, Nov. 12, 1966; Malcolm Nash, "Brooke's Win Answers Backlash," *NYAN*, Nov. 12, 1966; W. O. Walker, "Republicans Open Another Door for Negroes," *CP*, Nov. 19, 1966; "Clevelanders [Applaud] Brooke's Election," *CP*, Nov. 19, 1966; "Senator-Elect Edward W. Brooke," *Crisis*, Nov. 1966; JR, "We Can Be Proud . . . ," *CD*, Dec. 3, 1966.

85. "Mary Peabody: A Hug From Chub," *Newsweek* 63, no. 2 (1964).

86. "Heavy Negro Voting Offsets Effects of Expected 'Backlash,'" *CP*, Nov. 12, 1966; "Eleven Negroes Will Serve in Legislature," *CP*, Nov. 12, 1966.

87. Richard Harwood, "White Backlash Reported as Failing to Materialize," *Spokesman-Review*, Nov. 8, 1966; Robert D. Byrnes, "GOP Cuts Margin in Congress," *HC*, Nov. 9,

1966; Richard Bergholz, "Reagan Triumphs," *LAT*, Nov. 9, 1966; "Heavy Negro Voting," *CP*, Nov. 12, 1966.

88. "Republican Resurgence: Cover," *Time*, Nov. 18, 1966. See also "The Individualist Voters," *Pittsburgh Post-Gazette*, Nov. 11, 1966; Gene Grove, "New Team for the GOP: Bliss & Townes," *Tuesday Magazine*, Feb. 1967, folder Republican Party—RNC—Correspondence, 1967, CLT Papers; "Edward Brooke" cover, and "Happens," *Time*, Feb. 1967.

89. "Entering Quietly," *Time*, Jan. 20, 1967; "A Negro for All the People," *Age*, Jan. 16, 1967; "Teens in Jeans Vie with Matrons in Mink to Greet Brooke," *Jet*, Feb. 2, 1967; "Happens," *Time*, Feb. 1967.

90. Jean Burton, "Letters," *Time*, Feb. 24, 1967; Elizabeth Whitney Willis and Jerry Leaphart, both in "Letters," *Time*, Mar. 3, 1967; Simeon Booker, "I'm a Soul Brother'— Senator Edward Brooke," *Ebony*, Apr. 1967; George Gallup, "Johnson 'Most Admired,'" *LAT*, Jan. 4, 1967; Kenneth J. Cooper, "First Black U.S. Senator Elected by Popular Vote Tells His Story," *Crisis*, Jan.–Feb. 2007.

91. "A Party for All," *Time*, Nov. 18, 1966.

92. Ibid.

93. Kabaservice, *Rule and Ruin*, chaps. 6 and 7; Thurber, *Republicans and Race*, chap. 8.

94. Almena Lomax, "Negro and Nov. 8: All Is Not Lost," *LAT*, Nov. 20, 1966; "Party for All," *Time*, Nov. 1966.

95. Minorities Division, RNC, "Election Analysis: 1968 and the Black American Voter," Jan. 1969, folder Election Analysis, 1968, Black Vote, CLT Papers; "Gallup Poll Cites 8 Negroes among 'Most Admired,'" *Jet*, Jan. 19, 1967.

96. Grove, "Bliss & Townes," *TM*, Feb. 1967, CLT Papers; Simeon Booker, "What Republican Victory Means to the Negro," *Ebony*, Feb. 1967; "Negro 'Frontlash' Held More Sophisticated and Selective than White Backlash," *NYT*, Nov. 10, 1966; George Tagge, "Waner Gets G.O.P. Race Expert's Aid," *CT*, Jan. 21, 1967.

97. "Maryland: The Backlash Issue Divides the Democrats," *NYT*, Oct. 16, 1966; Max Johnson, "Historic Agnew Switchover," *BAA*, Nov. 12, 1966; "The Least You Can Do Is Vote for Agnew," *BAA*, Nov. 1, 1966; "Fear Revival of Hate Groups in City, State under Mahoney," *BAA*, Nov. 1, 1966.

98. "Romney Is Re-elected Michigan Governor," *WP*, Nov. 9, 1966; Grove, "New Team," *TM*, Feb. 1967; Neil Sanders, "Frustrated with the Great Society," *New Orleans States—Item*, [1967]; Sal Perrotta, "Swing to GOP by Negro Voters Seen in '68 Election," *Los Angeles Herald Examiner*, Feb. 9, 1967; CLT, Minorities Division Report Black Vote 1966, [1967], all in folder Correspondence 1967, CLT Papers; Roy Reed, "Negro Vote Held Vital in Key Contests," *NYT*, Nov. 27, 1966.

99. David S. Broder, "Negroes Gained Despite 'Backlash,'" *WP*, Nov. 11, 1967; "Negroes Widen Political Power," *CSM*, November 4, 1967, both in box 387, folder Negro Politics, Panzer Files; Booker, "Republican Victory," *Ebony*, Feb. 1967; "Negro 'Frontlash,'" *NYT*, Nov. 1966; "Who's for Whom," *Time*, Oct. 28, 1966; "Some Random Post-Mortem Thoughts," *Eugene Register-Guard*, Nov. 10, 1966.

100. James Booker, "Here's How Harlem Voted in Election," *NYAN*, Dec. 20, 1958; Layhmond Robinson, "Negroes Widen Political Role," *NYT*, Nov. 8, 1962.

101. "The Drive Is On to Woo Negro Voters in 1968," *Ocala Star-Banner*, June 21, 1967; RNC Minorities Division, *New Directions '68* 1, no. 1 (Oct. 1967), CLT Papers; William T. Peacock, "Parties Woo Negro Voters," *Free-Lance Star*, June 21, 1967; Woody Taylor, "It Happened in Ohio: Why a Democrat Voted for Jim Rhodes," *CP*, Nov. 26, 1966.

102. "GOP Given Plan to Regain Negro Vote," *CP*, Feb. 4, 1967.

103. "GOP Is After 30 Percent of US Negro Vote," *Columbus News*, Feb. 4, 1967.

104. "National News," *St. Petersburg Times*, Jan. 14, 1967; "Ex-SCLC Aide Now with GOP Minorities Division," *Jet*, Jan. 19, 1967; George Tagge, "Politics Photograph," *Miami Times*, Jan. 20, 1967; "Waner Gets G.O.P. Race Expert's Aide," *CT*, Jan. 21, 1967; Betty Granger Reed, "Conversation Piece," *PC*, Jan. 28, 1967.

105. Booker, "Republican Victory," *Ebony*, Feb. 1967.

106. Minorities Division RNC, Memo on Negro Outreach and Self-Help Programs, [1967]; Gilda Manning to CLT, Letter on Minorities, July 12, 1967; GM to Gene Taylor, Letter, July 12, 1967; GT to Ray C. Bliss, Letter on Negro Communities, July 17, 1967; Johnny Lang to CLT, Letter, July 26, 1967; RNC Minorities Division, Office Memorandum on Kansas City, [July 1967]; George Thiss to RCB, Letter, July 26, 1967; Arthur S. Brinkley Jr. to Robert Corber, Letter, July 28, 1967; I. Lee Potter to RCB, Letter, Aug. 3, 1967; "Rights Movement Must 'Wed' Politics: Townes," *CD*, Mar. 21, 1967; "Republicans Improve the Black Vote," *St. Louis Sentinel*, Mar. 16, 1968, all in folder Fieldwork 1967, CLT Papers. See also "Negroes and the Republican," *CSM*, June 7, 1966; "Top Republicans Hold Advisory Planning Session in Washington," *CP*, Sept. 9, 1967.

107. Minorities Division, "Negro Outreach," [1967]; "Improve the Black Vote," *SLS*, Mar. 1968; Minorities Division, *nd Newsletter*, Oct. 1967; RNC Women's Division, Brochure on Community Involvement, [1967–1969], folder RNC Notes, 1968–1970, CLT Papers.

108. Minorities Division, *ND Newsletter*, Oct. 1967, folder RNC Notes, 1968–1970, CLT Papers.

109. "Negroes Widen Political Power," *CSM*, Nov. 4, 1967.

110. Paul Hathaway, "Elected Negro Hones Skills," *Washington Evening Star*, Oct. 10, 1967, box 387; Paul Hathaway, "Revolt of Negro Democrats Is Hinted," *Washington Evening Star*, Oct. 2, 1967, box 351, both in folder Negro Politics, Panzer Files.

111. Black Republicans consistently sidestepped discussions about the Vietnam War, an issue of great importance to African Americans, who were overrepresented in combat roles in the military. In 1972, for instance, surveys revealed that black Republican leaders believed that civil rights rather than the war should be the central issue of the campaign; prominent black Democrats, in contrast, believed that Vietnam was of primary significance, followed by civil rights. There were moments, certainly, when black party leaders attempted to use the war to the advantage. During the 1972 campaign, Jerome Green, a Malcolm X College student and Purple Heart Winner, attempted to mobilize veterans on behalf of the GOP, using Vietnam as a wedge issue. The Black Council of Republican Politics would revisit this strategy, briefly, in 1974. Nevertheless, Brooke did, in fact, wrestle with Vietnam. During 1966, he campaigned as a "peace" candidate, accusing Johnson's foreign policy of bankrupting the country and arguing that military spending should be put into domestic racial and poverty issues. After joining Congress in 1967, he abruptly became a war hawk; by 1972, he again favored withdrawal. See "2,500 Republicans Give $200,000 for Campaign," *CP*, June 17, 1972; Black Council of Republican Politics, Inc., "Blacks and the Republican Party," Survey and Report, July 3, 1974, box 118, folder National Black Republican Council, Gwen Anderson Files 1974, Ford Vice Presidential Papers, Gerald R. Ford Presidential Library (hereinafter called GAA Files and GRF Library); Mark Goldman, "A Study of Message-Change and Reaction in Senator Edward W. Brooke's Views on the Vietnam War," *Today's Speech* 13, no. 3 (1969): 60–62.

112. Godfrey Sperling Jr., "Johnson Losing Negro Support," *CSM*, Oct. 6, 1967; "Negroes Widen Political Power," *CSM*, Nov. 4, 1967; "Reagan Vetoes Poverty Grant," *CT*, Oct. 4, 1967; "Housing Bias Ban Fought on Coast," *NYT*, Apr. 16, 1967; Seymour Korman, "Vote to Modify Housing Law in California," *CT*, Aug. 3, 1967.

113. "Detroit—An Aftermath," *CD*, Aug. 12, 1967; "Racial Justice," *CD*, July 24, 1967; Kabaservice, *Rule and Ruin*, 214; Vernon M. Briggs Jr., "Review Article: Report of the

National Advisory Commission on Civil Disorders," *Journal of Economic Issues* 2, no. 2 (June 1968): 200–210.

114. "Nixon Scores Panel for 'Undue' Stress on White Racism," *NYT*, Mar. 7, 1968.

115. Cutler, *Edward Brooke*, 311; Thomas A. Johnson, "Alienating the Negro Vote," *NYT*, Aug. 18, 1968.

116. "This Law Won't Stop Riots," *NYT*, July 19, 1967; "CRISIS: Ominous Riots Touch Off Partisan Quarrels among Leaders," *LAT*, July 30, 1967; "Low-Income Unit in HUD Proposed," *WP*, Aug. 8, 1967; Hollie I. West, "Rocky Pledges Aid to Restive Buffalo," *WP*, July 1, 1967; "Jackie Robinson Gets Task of Calming Buffalo Youths," *HC*, July 1, 1967.

117. "Economics, Social Facts Urged in Riot Inquiries," *Toledo Blade*, Aug. 3, 1967; "Brooke, Wilkins Rap Anti-riot Bill," *BAA*, Dec. 9, 1967.

118. Aug. 24, 1967, News from EWB, Press Release, NUL Speech. See also "Brooke Gets [Spingarn]," *CP*, July 22, 1967; W. O. Walker, "Senator Brooke Lays It on Line before NAACP," *CP*, July 29, 1967; Ethel Payne and Doris Saunders, "Rights Giving Will Stop U.S. Riots'— Brooke," *CD*, July 15, 1967; "Brooke Accuses FHA of Housing Delays," *LAT*, Aug. 8, 1967.

119. "GOP and the Urban Vote," *LAT*, July 26, 1967; "Brooke to Ask Senate to Look Into Race Riots," *NYT*, July 20, 1967; "Sen. Brooke Calls [Money] a Major Cause of Rioting," *CD*, July 24, 1967; Robert J. Donovan, "GOP Leaders Charge Johnson Racial Failure," *LAT*, July 25, 1967; John Herbers, "Johnson Accused by G.O.P. in Rioting," *NYT*, July 25, 1967;"Brooke Asks for Riot Probe," *Bay State Banner*, July 27, 1967.

120. Simeon Booker, "How Senator Brooke Sparks Civil Rights," *Jet*, Feb. 22, 1968; Neil MacNeil, "How Old Ev Foiled the Filibuster," *Life*, Mar. 15, 1968; "Report Middle-Class Negroes Saved Rights Bill," *Jet*, Mar. 14, 1968.

121. The National Advisory Commission on Civil Disorders, *Report of the National Advisory Commission on Civil Disorders* (New York: Bantam Books, 1968). See also "Johnson Unit Assails Whites in Negro Riots," *NYT*, Feb. 25, 1968;"White Community Blamed for Riots," *LAS*, Feb. 29, 1968; "Text of Summary of Report by National Advisory Commission on Civil Disorders," *NYT*, Mar. 1, 1968; "Riot Report Gets Wide Praise; Brooke Sees Hope for Action," *NYT*, Mar. 1, 1968; William Kling, ""Why, What, When of Riots," *NYT*, Mar. 1, 1968; Richard B. Lyons, "Riot Report Sends Out Sharp Shock Waves," *WP*, Mar. 2, 1968; Sidney E. Zion, "Rights Leaders Support Criticism of Whites," *NYT*, Mar. 2, 1968; Robert B. Semple Jr., "On Reading the Riot Report," *NYT*, Mar. 21, 1968; "White May Find 'Racist' Tag Difficult One to Accept," *Rochester Sentinel*, Mar. 6, 1968. See also "Commission Report" and "Civil Rights," *Brooke Report*, Apr. 1968, folder Newsletters 1968, EWB Papers.

122. "Brooke Saves Rights Bill from Filibuster," *BAA*, Mar. 5, 1968; John H. Averill, "Even Dirksen Himself Can't Explain Flip-Flop," *LAT*, Feb. 28, 1968; John Herbers, "Dirksen Explains Rights Shift," *NYT*, Feb. 28, 1968.

123. Clarence Mitchell to EWB, Telegram, Mar. 11, 1968, Correspondence, NAACP, EWB Papers.

124. "Martin Luther King," *Brooke Report*, Apr. 1968, folder Newsletters 1968, EWB Papers.

125. Dean J. Kotlowski, *Nixon's Civil Rights: Politics, Principle, and Policy* (Cambridge: Harvard University Press, 2002), 47–48; Douglas S. Massey and Nancy A. Denton, *American Apartheid: Segregation and the Making of the Underclass* (Cambridge: Harvard University Press, 1998), 193–199; John M. Quigley, Michael A. Stegman, and William C. Wheaton, "A Decent Home: Housing Policy in Perspective," *Brookings-Wharton Papers on Urban Affairs* (2000), 57.

126. Author interview with EWB, 2008.

127. Brooke, *Bridging the Divide*, 179–180; John Chamberlain, "Trouble-Makers in Nixon," *Evening Independent*, July 1, 1967; John Herbers, "G.O.P. Moderates Consider Revolt," *NYT*, Jan. 29, 1967; "GOP Club Provides Administration Idea," *Rome News-Tribune*, Apr. 17, 1968.

128. "What a Difference 4 Years Makes," *NYAN*, Aug. 10, 1968; Minorities Division RNC, "Forward Together: Election Analysis: 1968 and the Black American Voter," Jan. 1969, CLT Papers.

129. Skow, "Black Man," *Saturday Evening Post*, Sept. 1966; Brooke, *Bridging the Divide*, 187; Kabaservice, *Rule and Ruin*, 202.

130. "Nixon Considering Negro on Ticket," *St. Petersburg Times*, Aug. 5, 1968. See also "Negro Vote Eyed, Moderates Talk Possibility of Brooke for Vice President," *Spokane Daily Chronicle*, Apr. 1, 1968.

131. Booker, "Republican Victory," *Ebony*, Feb. 1967.

132. Charles L. Sanders, "King, Senator Brooke's Views Clash in Geneva," *Jet*, June 15, 1967; "U.S. Moves toward Peace in Vietnam War: Brooke," *Jet*, Feb. 23, 1967; "Senate's Leaders Differ over Sentiment of War," *Spokesman-Review*, Jan. 10, 1967; "First One Is the Toughest," *Bulletin*, Mar. 23, 1967; "Brooke Reverses Stand on Vietnam," *St. Petersburg Times*, Mar. 24, 1967; "That Feeling," *St. Petersburg Times*, Mar. 25, 1967. For example, see "Letters to the Editor: Elephants 'R' in Season," *Time*, Nov. 18, 1966; Drew Pearson, "Romney Seen as No. 1 Candidate," *Free-Lance Star*, Nov. 12, 1966; Mary McGrory, "Romney Is Now on Center Stage," *Evening Independent*, Nov. 17, 1966; "Move to Block Romney Denied by Goldwater," *Rome News-Tribune*, Nov. 14, 1966; Russell Kirk, "Nixon Was a Victor," *Ocala Star-Banner*, Nov. 14, 1966; Neil Sheehan, "Romney Says Republican Gains Assure Party's Victory in 1968," *NYT*, Nov. 14, 1966; "The Future of Goldwater," *Spokesman-Review*, Feb. 10, 1967.

133. Peter Lucas, "Brooke Raps Nixon, Daley, Pushes Rocky as Republican to Unite Nation," *Boston Herald Traveller*, Apr. 17, 1968, box 351, Panzer Files.

134. "Temporary Chairman," *WP*, Aug. 4, 1968, box 351, folder Brooke, Panzer Files.

135. "Can the GOP Win the Black Vote?" cover story, *Jet*, Aug. 22, 1968.

136. JCPS, *Black Politics 1980: RNC*; "Brooke to Call GOP to Order," *NYAN*, June 15, 1968; "Brooke Named Temporary GOP Chairman," *CP*, Aug. 3, 1968.

137. "Nixon Faces Dilemma," *WSJ*, Aug. 7, 1968; Thomas A. Johnson, "Alienating the Negro Vote," *NYT*, Aug. 18, 1968; Lerone Bennett Jr., "The Martyrdom of Martin Luther King, Jr.," *Ebony*, May 1968; Simeon Booker, "What Blacks Can Expect from Nixon," *Ebony*, Jan. 1969.

138. "Spiro Agnew: The King's Taster," *Time*, Nov. 14, 1969; Garry Wills, *Nixon Agonistes: The Crisis of the Self-Made Man* (New York: Houghton Mifflin Harcourt, 2002), 280–291; Rhonda Y. Williams, "Black Women, Urban Politics, and Engendering Black Power," in *The Black Power Movement: Rethinking the Civil Rights–Black Power Era*, ed. Peniel E. Joseph (New York: Routledge, 2006), 91–92, 307; Robert J. Donovan, "Nixon's Selection of Agnew for No. 2 Spot Astounds Politicians," *LAT*, Aug. 9, 1968. For black Republican opinions on Nixon, see Nicholas Horrock, "Area GOP Negroes: 'Ouch,'" *Washington Daily*, Aug. 8, 1968.

139. "Negroes Not Wanted," *CD*, Aug. 12, 1968. See also Ralph de Toledano, "Nixon-Agnew and Negro Defections," *Human Events* 28, no. 35 (Aug. 31, 1968): 14; Roy Wilkins, "Action, Not More Politics," *LAT*, Mar. 18, 1968; Raymond Moley, "Report on Civil Disorders Spurs Wallace's Growth," *LAT*, Mar. 13, 1968; Jackie Robinson, "Nixon Nomination Called Disaster," *NYAN*, Mar. 23, 1968; "Poll Shows Most Feel GOP Dumped Blacks for South," *NYAN*, Aug. 17, 1968.

140. Matthew D. Lassiter, "Suburban Strategies," in *The Democratic Experiment: New Directions in American Political History*, ed. Meg Jacobs, William Novak, and Julian Zelizer (Princeton: Princeton University Press, 2003), 330–332.

141. "Brooke Reaffirms His Support of Nixon," *NYT*, Sept. 8, 1968; "Republican Efforts to Gain Support among Negroes Appear to Have Failed," *NYT*, Oct. 6, 1968.

142. Charles Bartlett, "George Cuts into Both Parties," *Miami News*, Sept. 13, 1968.

143. Jackie Robinson, Is Nixon Using Sen. Ed Brooke?" *PC*, Oct. 5, 1968.

144. "Brooke Not in Total Agreement," *NYAN*, Sept. 14, 1968; "Nixon and Brooke," *CD*, Sept. 16, 1968; "Brooke Rejoins Nixon but Is Upset by Stands," *LAT*, Sept. 14, 1968.

145. Minorities Division, "Forward Together 1968," Jan. 1969, CLT Papers.

146. Ibid; "Widen Political Power," *CSM*, Nov. 1967.

147. CM to EWB, Letter, Oct. 19, 1973, General Correspondence, Clarence Mitchell, EWB Papers.

148. Aldo Beckman, "Rep. Conyers Fills Shoes of Idled Idol Powell," *CT*, Aug. 13, 1967; "Edward Brooke Addresses Democratic Black Caucus," *Bay State Banner*, Oct. 18, 1973; Shirley Chisholm, "Chisholm Urges President Nixon to Nominate Brooke," Press Release, Oct. 12, 1973; Charles B. Rangel, "Rangel Urges President Ford to Name Brooke as Vice-President," Press Release, Aug. 13, 1974, both in box 637, folder Brooke for Vice President, 1971–76, EWB Papers; author interview with EWB, 2008.

149. Walters, *Black Presidential Politics*, 45–47.

Chapter 4. Richard Nixon's Black Cabinet

1. "Message from Dick Gregory," and "Citizens for Humphrey-Muskie," paid political advertisements, *Jet*, Nov. 7, 1968.

2. "Nixon-Agnew Campaign Committee," paid political advertisement, *Jet*, Nov. 7, 1968.

3. "The Birth Pangs of Black Capitalism," *Time*, Oct. 18, 1968.

4. Dean Kotlowski, *Nixon's Civil Rights*, 132; "Nixon and Black Power: An Editorial," *CD*, May 11, 1968; "Nixon & Core," *NYAN*, Sept. 28, 1968; Monroe W. Karmin, "The Negro Vote," *WSJ*, Oct. 4, 1968; Earl Caldwell, "2 Negro Militants See Serious Split," *NYT*, Oct. 2, 1967; Connie Woodruff, "On The Scene," *NYAN*, Nov. 2, 1968; "Negro Baptists Go Republican for the First Time," Oct. 24, 1968; "Clerics Attack Dr. Jackson for Backing Nixon," *CD*, Oct. 29, 1968; "Nixon-Backer J. H. Jackson in Hot Water," *CD*, Oct. 30, 1968; Donald Janson, "Nixon Discerns a New Coalition," May 17, 1968.

5. "Nixon Says No Clean Sweep of Blacks," *Jet*, Nov. 7, 1968; Doris E. Saunders, "Confetti," *CD*, Nov. 18, 1968.

6. See, for example, "Negro Businesses in Harlem Rising," *NYT*, Apr. 28, 1967.

7. For more on Hubert Humphrey's proposed black economic plan, see historian Timothy Thurber, *The Politics of Equality: Hubert H. Humphrey and the African American Freedom Struggle* (New York: Columbia University Press, 1999). See also Robert E. Weems Jr. with Lewis A. Randolph, *Business in Black and White: American Presidents and Black Entrepreneurs in the Twentieth Century* (New York: New York University Press, 2009), 89–109.

8. "In the 'New' Politics," *Time*, June 7, 1968.

9. Richard M. Nixon, "Bridges to Human Dignity," Apr. 25, 1968, reprinted in *HE* 28, no. 21 (May 25, 1968).

10. Ibid.; W. O. Walker, "Down the Big Road," *CP*, Nov. 2, 1968.

11. "Poll Shows Most Feel GOP Dumped Blacks for South," *NYAN*, Aug. 17, 1968.

12. Voter Strategy Reports of the Republican National Committee, 1961–1971, in Stanley S. Scott Papers, Gerald Ford Presidential Library, University of Michigan—Ann Arbor (hereinafter called SSS Papers and GRF Library) and CLT Papers. See also "Poll Shows Most Feel GOP Dumped Blacks for South," *NYAN*, Aug. 17, 1968.

13. Long, *Jackie Robinson*, 282–284.

14. Most sources record Nixon as winning 12 percent of the "nonwhite vote." For the Minorities Division of the RNC, this translated into the president-elect winning 10 percent of the black vote, with the rest coming from other racial minority groups. Between 1969 and 1972, the RNC began to devote more attention to parsing out the racial and ethnic differences among nonwhite voters. Ripon Society, *Jaws of Victory: The Game-Plan Politics of 1972; The Crisis of the Republican Party and the Future of the Constitution* (Boston: Little, Brown, 1974), 173–174; Minorities Division, "Election Analysis: 1968 and the Black American Voter," 1969, CLT Papers.

15. "Gop Given Plan," *CP*, Feb. 1967.

16. "Blacks Have Mixed Reaction to Nixon," *NYAN*, Nov. 16, 1968.

17. Irving A. Williamson, "Secretary Fletcher Goes to the White House," unknown newspaper article [St. Louis, Missouri], June 4, 1970, box 88, folder Arthur Fletcher, WHCF SMOF Leonard Garment, Richard Nixon Presidential Library, National Archives and Records Administration, College Park, Maryland (hereinafter called Garment Files and RN Library).

18. "Black GOP Group Raps Nixon on Cabinet Picks," *CD*, Dec. 17, 1968; "Negro G.O.P. Group Scores Nixon on Aide Appointments," *NYT*, Dec. 16, 1968.

19. "What Blacks Can Expect from Nixon," *Ebony*, Jan. 1969.

20. "A New Administration Takes Shape," *Time*, Dec. 20, 1968; Brooke, *Bridging the Divide*, 199; John Wesley Dean, *The Rehnquist Choice: The Untold Story of the Nixon Appointment that Redefined the Supreme Court* (New York: Simon and Schuster, 2002), 53–54; White House Tapes Nos. 576-11, 577-3, 9–93, RN Library.

21. "Black Lawmakers in Congress," *Ebony*, Feb. 1971, box 137, folder 3, Minorities Activities, Garment Files.

22. "Nixon and Brooke," *Chicago Defender*, Dec. 4, 1968; "Cabinet Post Declined by Sen. Brooke," *New Journal and Guide*, Dec. 7, 1968; "Senate Holds Brooke, He Rejects Cabinet HUD Offer of Nixon," *PC*, Dec. 7, 1968; Robert B. Semple Jr., "Brooke Rejects Post on Housing in Nixon Cabinet; Other Options Also Studied as Two Confer—Senator Prefers His Present Job," *NYT*, Nov. 28, 1968; Stan Benjamin, "Nixon Is Giving More Top Jobs to Nonwhites," *New Observer*, May 2, 1970; "Black Lawmakers in Congress," unknown article, [1968], box 137, folder 3, Minorities Activities, Garment Files.

23. Simeon Booker, "Uneasiness in Nixon Camp," *Jet*, Dec. 5, 1968; Diggs Datrooth, "National Hotline," *PC*, Dec. 21, 1968.

24. "Negro, 'Man of the Year,'" *PC*, Feb. 6, 1965; Ethel Payne, "A Neat Go-Getter Is the Description for Brown, Nixon's Ghetto Aid Man," *CD*, Dec. 16, 1968; Gloria Wolford, "Black Businessman, Is Nixon's Appointee," *CD*, Dec. 10, 1968; "Meet First Black Nixon Staffer," *CD*, Dec. 11, 1968; "New Man in White House," *NYAN*, Dec. 14, 1968; James K. Batten and Dwayne Walls, "Nixon Aide Has Murky Past," *St. Petersburg Times*, Apr. 5, 1969; "Aldo Beckman, "Black Nixon Aide Points to Civil Rights Progress," *CT*, Apr. 18, 1971.

25. Guian A. McKee, *The Problem of Jobs: Liberalism, Race, and Deindustrialization in Philadelphia* (Chicago: University of Chicago Press, 2008).

26. Wolford, "Businessman" *CD*, Dec. 1968; "Black Nixon *CD*, Dec. 1968; "New Man," *NYAN*, Dec. 1968; Batten and Walls, "Murky Past," *SPT*, Apr. 1969.

27. Simeon Booker, "What Nixon Plans for Blacks," *Jet*, Dec. 26, 1968. "Nixon Keeps Black D.C. Mayor, Names All-White Cabinet," *CD*, Dec. 12, 1968; Batten and Walls, "Nixon Aide," *SPT*, Apr. 1969.

28. "Takes Shape," *Time*, Dec. 1968.

29. "'Tom' Tag Fear Made Blacks Reject Nixon Posts," *Jet*, Feb. 6, 1969.

30. Harry S. Dent, *The Prodigal South Returns to Power* (New York: John Wiley & Sons, 1978), 176–177.

31. "President's Eulogy Seen as a Promise to Work toward Young's Goal," *Jet*, Apr. 1, 1971.

32. Whitney Young to Leonard Garment, Letter, Dec. 21, 1968; LG to WY, Letter, Jan. 6, 1969; WY to LG, Letter, Jan. 7, 1969; LG to George Shultz, Memo, Jan. 9, 1969; LG to Winston Blount, Letter, Jan. 9, 1969; LG to Clifford Hardin, Letter, Jan. 9, 1969; LG to Peter Flannigan, Memo, Jan. 9, 1969, all in box 171, folder Whitney Young, Garment Files. See also "Nixon Set for Black Appointees," *PC*, Dec. 28, 1968. See also "Grant Reynolds Gets Regional HUD Post," *NYAN*, Nov. 28, 1970.

33. "New Administration," *Time*, Dec. 1968; "Tom Tag," *Jet*, Feb. 1969. See also Whitney Young, "To Be Equal," *Sacramento Observer*, Nov. 14, 1968; "Negro Leaders See Hope with Nixon on Race Issues," *HC*, Nov. 18, 1968; "AP Finds Negroes Skeptical," *Oakland Post*, Dec. 11, 1968; "All-White Cabinet A Forecast of Black Role in the Next 4 Years," *CD*, Dec. 21, 1968; "Brooke, Young Critical but Undismayed," *NYAN*, Dec. 28, 1968; "Young Rips Nixon for Failure to Appoint Blacks to Cabinet," *CD*, Jan. 9, 1969; Whitney Young, "Welfare Reforms Overdue," *NYAN*, Mar. 22, 1969.

34. In the 1950s and 1960s, the press anointed Farmer, Martin Luther King Jr., Whitney Young, and Roy Wilkins, the "Big Four" civil rights leaders. As CORE's national director in 1961, he helped organize and lead the Freedom Rides, a nonviolent push to desegregate interstate transportation; likewise, he mobilized black voters in the South in the mid-1960s, and played a crucial role in bringing national attention to the horrific conditions of racial inequality and disenfranchisement. It is worth noting that Farmer changed his affiliation to "independent" in 1972; by 1983, he was a registered Democrat. See James Farmer, *Lay Bare the Heart: An Autobiography of the Civil Rights Movement* (Forth Worth: Texas Christian University Press, 1998), 104–106, 196–257, 301–309, 339; "GOP Selects CORE Leader to Enter Race," *LAT*, May 21, 1968; "Liberals and Republicans Endorse James Farmer," *NYAN*, May 25, 1968; Rowland Evans and Robert Novak, "James Farmers's GOP Candidacy Born at Kenyon College Conference," *WP*, July 22, 1968; "Pioneer Leader James Farmer, Last of Civil Rights Movement's 'Big Four,'" *Jet*, July 26, 1999; Steven F. Lawson, *Civil Rights Crossroads: Nation, Community, and the Black Freedom Struggle* (Lexington: University Press of Kentucky, 2003), 73–77.

35. "Working from Within," *Time*, Feb. 21, 1969; "Let's Give Him a Chance," *Ebony*, Apr. 1969. James Farmer interview, in Gerald S. Strober and Deborah H. Strober, *The Nixon Presidency: An Oral History of His Presidency* (New York: Harper Perennial), 59–60; Farmer, *Lay Bare the Heart*, 315–317.

36. "Working," *Time*, Feb. 1969; Farmer, *Lay Bare the Heart*, 316, 330.

37. "Blacks Play Key Roles in Keeping Tight Inaugural Security," *Jet*, Feb. 2, 1969; Wills, *Nixon Agonistes*, 403.

38. "Black Senator Tosses Big Bash for Nixon White Men," *Jet*, Feb. 6, 1969; "Changing of the Guard: Nixon Inaugural," *Ebony*, Mar. 1969; Cathy W. Aldridge, "PS: Inaugural Guests Manage to Party Together," *NYAN*, Feb. 1, 1969.

39. "Changing," *Ebony*, Mar. 1969.

40. "James Brown, Lionel Hampton Headline Inaugural Gala," *Jet*, Jan. 23, 1969; "Hamp's Harlem, Brown's Soul Score!" and "Words of the Week," *Jet*, Feb. 6, 1969; "Changing," *Ebony*, Mar. 1969.

41. D.C. mayor Walter Washington and seven of the nine black members of the House of Representatives were seated on the main dais, as well.

42. Richard Nixon, Inaugural Address, Jan. 20, 1969, *APP*, UCSB; "What Nixon Said to Blacks at the Inauguration," *Jet*, Feb. 6, 1969.

43. Harry Dent to John Mitchell, Memo on Black Voters, Feb. 11, 1971, in Dent, *Prodigal South*, 179; Republican National Committee, Research Division, "Report on the Polls: Blacks," [1971], box 5, Black Vote, SSS Papers. See also "Poll Shows Blacks Favor Nixon Less than Whites," *Jet*, Oct. 9, 1969; Joe Chaney, "View from Inside: Black Republicans," *Sun Reporter*, Jan. 25, 1969.

44. Nixon would ultimately appoint more than thirty African Americans to high-ranking positions in the federal government—the highest tally of any president up until that point. Robert Charles Smith, *We Have No Leaders: African American in the Post-Civil Rights Era* (Albany: State University of New York, 1996), 140; "Top People," *CD*, May 24, 1969.

45. "Let's Give Him a Chance," *Ebony*, Apr. 1969.

46. Sandra Lee, Letter to the Editor, *Ebony*, July 1969.

47. Chaney, "Black Republicans," *SR*, Jan. 1969.

48. James M. Naughton, "Civil Rights: 'The Quiet Way to Get Things Done," *St. Petersburg Times*, Sept. 30, 1969.

49. Kotlowski, *Nixon's Civil Rights*, 133–140; Weems and Randolph, *Business in Black and White*, 127.

50. Ethel Payne, "President Nixon Creates Minorities' Business Unit," *CD*, Mar. 6, 1969.

51. "Nixon Creates Office That's Keyed to Minority Business," *NYAN*, Mar. 15, 1969.

52. Richard Nixon, "Prescribing Arrangements for Developing and Coordination a National Program for Minority Business Enterprise," Mar. 5, 1969, in *APP*, UCSB; "Nixon Sets Up Agency to Help Blacks Own, Manage Businesses," *Jet*, Mar. 20, 1969; "Nixon Creates New Office to Help Minority Business, *BAA*, Mar. 15, 1969; "Taking Care of Business," *Ebony*, Sept. 1978; Ethel Payne, "President Nixon Creates Minorities' Business Unit," *CD*, Mar. 6, 1969; "Minority Capitalists Get Nixon Push," *HC*, Mar. 6, 1969; "Aide Says Nixon to Help Bolster Black Economy," *CD*, Mar. 24, 1969; Walter Rugaber, "Stans to Promote a Minority Business Enterprise," *NYT*, Mar. 6, 1969. See also Devin Fergus, "Black Power, Soft Power: Floyd McKissick, Soul City, and the Death of Moderate Black Republicanism," *Journal of Policy History* 22, no. 2 (2010): 155; Jonathan Bean, *Big Government and Affirmative Action: The Scandalous History of the Small Business Administration* (Lexington: University Press of Kentucky, 2001), 72–73.

53. As the black middle class expanded, the number of African Americans living under the poverty line increased as well. Despite the economic upturn in 1970, for example, about a third of blacks were poor, while unemployment and underemployment also grew. Adolph Holmes, "Blacks and Poor Share Burden of Continuing Recession," *LAS*, July 1, 1971; "More Blacks Enter $10,000-Year Bracket," *HC*, June 4, 1969; "America's Rising Black Middle Class," *Time*, June 17, 1974.

54. William J. Drummond, "Anderson in Battle for 17th District Seat," *LAT*, Nov. 6, 1968.

55. Minorities Division, "Election Analysis: 1968," Jan. 1969, CLT Papers; "Election 1970: Political Report," *1970 CQ Almanac*, Nov. 6, 1970, 1095.

56. Rowland Evans and Robert Novak, "Submerging Dr. Allen," *Day*, Jan. 20, 1969.

57. "Nixon Offers Solution to Urban Problem," *CT*, Apr. 26, 1968; author interview with EWB, 2008.

58. Author interview with EWB, 2008.

59. EWB, Speech to the National Insurance Association, July 1967, CLT Papers.

60. "Scorecard for the Cities," *Time*, Sept. 13, 1968.

61. Hugh Davis Graham, *Collision Course: The Strange Convergence of Affirmative Action and Immigration Policy in America* (New York: Oxford University Press, 2003), 70; Kotlowski, *Nixon's Civil Rights*, 176.

62. Ellen Boneparth, "Black Businessmen and Community Responsibility," *Phylon* 37, no. 1 (1976).

63. Jackie Robinson and black Republican Samuel Pierce were among the founders of Freedom National Bank. Launched in 1964, FNB was created as a black-owned and operated alternative to mainstream banks, which often discriminated against African Americans. As Robinson explained, financial institutions could serve as civil rights vehicles if blacks "put their capital to work locally, in their own neighborhoods." The same year that FNB was founded, Martin Luther King Jr. deposited his Nobel Peace Prize winnings in the bank; likewise, the NAACP deposited $75,000 in 1968. By 1969, FNB was the biggest black bank in the country. Arnold Rampersad, *Jackie Robinson: A Biography* (New York: Ballantine Books, 1997), 392–395; Mary Kay Linge, *Jackie Robinson: A Biography* (Santa Barbara: Greenwood Publishing Group, 2007), 138; "Negroes Not Seeking Handouts Only Want to Help Themselves," *CP*, Oct. 12, 1968.

64. "Nixon Names Negro to Post in Labor Department," *CT*, Mar. 15, 1969; "Fletcher Gets Key Labor Job," *BAA*, Mar. 22, 1969; "Nixon Appoints Negro Asst. Labor Secretary," *CP*, Mar. 22, 1969; Virginia Olds, "Fletcher Spells Plan," *Ellensburg Daily Record*, Mar. 27, 1969; "New Office for Poor Businesses," *AA*, May 31, 1969; Ethel L. Payne, "So This Is Washington," *CD*, May 10, 1969.

65. "Negro Wins Primary in Wash. State," *WP*, Sept. 19, 1968; Michael Flynn, "Negro Running for Lt. Governor," *WP*, Sept. 26, 1968; "Choice of GOP Incumbent Gov. Carries State," *PC*, Oct. 5, 1968. See also "GOP Black Runs Strong for Washington State's No. 2 Office," *CSM*, Sept. 16, 1968; "Gov. Evans Renominated," *NYT*, Sept. 18, 1968; "Black Man Wins GOP Slot for Lt. Governor," *CD*, Sept. 19, 1968; "Nominated for Lt. Governor; Republicans Pick Negro in State of Washington," *New Journal and Guide*, Sept. 28, 1968; Daryl E. Lembke, "Negro Pressing Hard in Washington Contest," *LAT*, Oct. 9, 1968; Daryl E. Lembke, "Negro Loses Election but Hails Big Vote," *LAT*, Nov. 8, 1968. See also Sam Reed, "Two Mainstream Republican Leaders Who Made History," *Washington Mainstream* 15, no. 2 (Sept. 2005).

66. *CT*, Mar. 22, 1969; *AA*, Mar. 22, 1969; *CP*, Mar. 22, 1969.

67. As a condition of his appointment, Fletcher was allowed to select the head of the Office of Federal Contract Compliance (OFCC). He selected John Wilks, a black Republican, as the deputy head of the OFCC. Smith, *We Have No Leaders*, 145.

68. "Fletcher: Time to Put Up," *Sacramento Observer*, Apr. 30, 1970; Virna M. Cason to Arthur Fletcher, Letter, May 25, 1970, box 88, folder Arthur Fletcher, Garment Files.

69. Ernest C. Cooper to AF, Letter and Attachments, Feb. 10, 1970; "End to Job Discrimination by '80 Urged as Goal by Fletcher," *St. Louis Globe-Democrat*, May 28, 1970; Irving A. Williamson, "Secretary Fletcher Goes to the White House," unknown newspaper article [St. Louis, Missouri], June 4, 1970, all in box 88, folder Arthur Fletcher, Garment Files; Arthur Fletcher, *The Silent Sell-Out: Government Betrayal of Blacks to the Craft Unions* (New York: Third Press, 1974).

70. Lyndon B. Johnson, Commencement Address at Howard University, "To Fulfill These Rights," June 4, 1965, Presidential Speeches and Messages, LBJ Library.

71. "What Unions Are and Are Not Doing for Blacks," *Time*, Sept. 26, 1969; Theophilus Green, "The Man Behind Pittsburgh Labor Plan That Becomes Model for Nation," *Jet*, Mar. 11, 1971.

72. Thomas J. Sugrue, "Affirmative Action from Below: Civil Rights, the Building Trades, and the Politics of Racial Equality in the Urban North, 1945–1969," *Journal of American History* 91, no. 1 (June 2004): 145–173; Thomas J. Sugrue, *Sweet Land of Liberty: The Forgotten Struggle for Civil Rights in the North* (New York: Random House, 2008), 363–364; Smith, *We Have No Leaders*, 145–160.

73. "What Unions Are and Are Not Doing for Blacks," *Time*, Sept. 969; "A Narrow Victory for Blacks," *Time*, Jan. 5, 1970; "The Philadelphia Problem," *Time*, Aug. 17, 1970; Graham, *Collision Course*, 65–70; Paul Frymer and John David Skrentny, "Coalition-Building and the Politics of Electoral Capture during the Nixon Administration: African Americans, Labor, Latinos," *Studies in American Political Development* 12 (Spring 1998): 146.

74. Graham, *Collision Course*, 67–68; Sugrue, *Sweet Land of Liberty*, 364–365; Joan Hoff, *Nixon Reconsidered* (New York: Basic Books), 92–93; Kotlowski, *Nixon's Civil Rights*, 109–115. See also "PR Man Named to Lead Labor's Compliance," *Jet*, Aug. 21, 1969; Smith, *We Have No Leaders*, 145.

75. Arthur Fletcher, "Remarks on the Philadelphia Plan," [June 26, 1969], from *America in the Sixties—Right, Left, and Center: A Documentary History*, ed. Peter b. Levy (Westport: Greenwood Press, 1998), 101–104; "US to Order Minority Quotas for Contractors," *LAT*, June 28, 1969.

76. John David Skrentny, *Ironies of Affirmative Action: Politics, Culture, and Justice in America* (Chicago: University of Chicago Press, 1996), 177–221; Hugh Davis Graham, *The Civil Rights Era: Origins and Development of National Policy, 1960–1972* (New York: Oxford University Press, 1990), 326–343; Graham, *Collision Course*, 65–77.

77. "Whites Battle Blacks, Police," *Bryan Times*, Sept. 26, 1969; Seth S. King, "Whites in Chicago Disrupt Hearing; 5 Hurt and 9 Arrested in Dispute," *NYT*, Sept. 26, 1969; Seth S. King, "Whites in Chicago Continue Protest; Plan to Take More Blacks into Building Union Scored," *NYT*, Sept. 27, 1969.

78. The February 1970 announcement of Order No. 4 highlights a key shift in affirmative action policies; the measure required federal contractors, across all industries, receiving federal funds of more than $50,000 and more than fifty workers to submit detailed affirmative action plans with goals, timetables, and proposed remedies for "underutilization" of minorities. "Watchdog for U.S. Labor," *Ebony*, Apr. 1971. GS to RN, Memo on Progress in Civil Rights, May 18, 1971, box 3, folder Black Caucus Demands and Responses, WHCF SMOF Robert Finch, Nixon Library (hereinafter called Finch Files); Skrentny, *Ironies*, 286n; Graham, *Collision Course*, 74; Kotlowski, *Nixon's Civil Rights*, 109–112; David Hamilton Gollard, *Constructing Affirmative Action: The Struggle for Equal Employment Opportunity* (Lexington: University Press of Kentucky, 2011), 225–230.

79. "Black Americans," *CSM*, Apr. 1970.

80. "End to Job Discrimination by '80 Urged as Goal by Fletcher," *St. Louis Globe-Democrat*, May 28, 1970; Irving A. Williamson, "Secretary Fletcher Goes to the White House," unknown newspaper article [St. Louis, Missouri], June 4, 1970), box 88, folder AF, Garment Files.

81. Richard Nixon, "Statement on Executive Order 11478," Aug. 8, 1969, *APP*, UCSB; Robert P. Turner, *Up to the Front of the Line: Blacks in the Political System* (Port Washington: Kennikat Press, 1975), 127–129.

82. Victor Riesel, "High Pay Jobs Open for Blacks," *Rome News-Tribune*, Feb. 13, 1970.

83. "Report Cites Some Gains," *Oakland Post*, Aug. 5, 1971.

84. "Minority Firms Hope for U.S. Contracts," *Jet*, Apr. 9, 1970.

85. Boneparth, "Black Businessmen," *Phylon*, 1976.

86. "Black Capitalism," *NYT*, Aug. 24, 1969; Stephen MacDonald, "What Happened to 'Black Capitalism'?" *WSJ*, Mar. 9, 1970; "Black Capitalism Critics," *SR*, Jan. 17, 1970;

Edward Jones, "Black Capitalism: A Redefinition," *OP*, Oct. 21, 1971; "Article by Angela Davis Says Black Capitalism Is a Ploy against Blacks," *OP*, July 15, 1971; "Black Capitalism All Talk," *Bulletin*, Apr. 7, 1970; Evans and Novak, "Black Capitalism Doom Feared," *St. Petersburg Times*, Oct. 31, 1969; Evans and Novak, "Black Capitalism Show Going on Road," *Toledo Blade*, Oct. 14, 1969; Ethel Payne, "So This Is Washington," *CD*, Jan. 17, 1970; Weems and Randolph, *Business in Black and White*, 127–156; Boneparth, "Black Businessmen," *Phylon*, 1976.

87. Boneparth, "Black Businessmen," *Phylon*, 1976.

88. "Nixon and Black Americans—Two Views," *CSM*, Apr. 23, 1970; Arthur Fletcher, U.S. Delegation to the General Assembly, Press Release and Report, Oct. 26, 1971, box 14, Miscellaneous 1971, SSS Papers; Devin Fergus, "Black Power, Soft Power," *JPH*, 2010, 155.

89. "Black Capitalism," *NYT*, Aug. 24, 1969. See also "Sharp Focus on Black Capitalism," *LAT*, July 6, 1969; Paul Delaney, "Black Capitalism Program Falling Far Sort of Goals," *NYT*, June 29, 1970.

90. Bean, *Small Business Administration*, 71–75; Kotlowski, *Nixon's Civil Rights*, 141–145; "All Talk," *Bulletin*, Apr. 1970; "1969: A Year of Marking Time," *Ebony*, Jan. 1970.

91. "Black Capitalism Is Called a Myth," *CP*, Nov. 22, 1969.

92. "Black Leaders Tell Nixon of Urgent Needs," *Jet*, Jan. 9, 1969.

93. Robert Brown, "The Nixon Administration," *American Visions*, Feb.–Mar. 1995; "Black College Presidents Tell Nixon of Repression Fears" and Theophilus E. Green, "Name-Calling and Racial Hatred Cited Possible Reasons," *Jet*, June 4, 1970; Robert J. Brown to LG, Memo on Black College Presidents, Dec. 11, 1970, box 137, folder Minority Activities, Garment Files; "The Presidency and the Press," *Bulletin of the American Academy of Arts and Sciences* 24, no. 8 (May 1971): 12–14; AF, General Assembly, Oct. 1971, box 14, Miscellaneous 1971, SSS Papers; "Good News, Bad News," *Time*, July 31, 1972; "America's Rising Black Middle Class," *Time*, June 17, 1974.

94. "Black College Presidents Tell Nixon of Repression Fears" and Theophilus E. Green "Name-Calling and Racial Hatred Cited Possible Reasons," *Jet*, June 4, 1970; Brown to Garment, Memo on Black College Presidents, Dec. 1970, box 137, Garment Files.

95. Robert H. Finch and RJB, Press Conference on the Heard Report on Campus Conditions and a report on Federal Agencies and Black Colleges, *Weekly Compilation of Presidential Documents* 6 (July 23, 1970): 978–981.

96. "The Presidency and the Press," *Bulletin of the American Academy of Arts and Sciences*, May 1971; "Letters to the Editor," *NYT*, Sept. 1970; Brown to Garment, Memo on Black College Presidents, Dec. 1970, Garment Files.

97. SSS, Memo and Attachments, July 14, 1972, box 1, Administration Receiving Top Coverage on Minorities 1/4/72–7/14/72, in SSS Papers; GS to RN, Memo on Progress CR, May 1971, box 3, CBC Demands, Finch Files; Memo on Civil Rights Accomplishments, Apr. 15, 1971, box 133, Minority Business Enterprise and Other Minority Programs, and LG to RN, Memo, Nov. 23, 1970, box 137, Minority Oriented Activities, both in Garment Files; Brown, "Nixon," 1995; Kotlowski, *Nixon's Civil Rights*, 152–154.

98. Farmer, *Lay Bare the Heart*, 318–321.

99. GS to RN, Memo on Progress CR, May 1971, box 3, CBC Demands, Finch Files; Memo on Civil Rights Accomplishments, Apr. 15, 1971, box 133, Minority Business Enterprise and Other Minority Programs and LG to RN, Memo, Nov. 23, 1970, box 137, Minority Oriented Activities, both in Garment Files.

100. "America's Rising Black Middle Class," *Time*, June 17, 1974.

101. "Watchdog of U.S. Labor," *Ebony*, Apr. 1971.

102. "The Beginnings of Black Capitalism," *Time*, Apr. 6, 1970; Turner, *Front of the Line*, 128–129; "Statement on Civil Rights," Memo, [1970–1971], box 49, Black Congressmen,

Garment Files; GS to RN, Memo on Progress CR, May 1971, box 3, CBC Demands, Finch Files; Memo on Civil Rights Accomplishments, Apr. 15, 1971, box 133, Minority Business Enterprise and Other Minority Programs, and LG to RN, Memo, Nov. 23, 1970, box 137, Minority Oriented Activities, both in Garment Files; "With Loss of $704,530, Harlem Bank Tops Others," *Jet*, Aug. 31, 1972; Bean, *Small Business Administration*, 76–78, 90–92.

103. List of Black Elected Republican Officials' Proposals, [Mar. 1970], box I: 115, Black Elected Republicans 1970, folder Leadership Conference on Civil Rights, Part I: Subject File, 1951–80, Manuscript Division, Library of Congress (hereinafter called BERO Papers). See also Kotlowski, *Civil Rights*, 145.

104. "U.S. Aid: Blacks, $119 Million; Whites, Billions," *Jet*, Aug. 6, 1970; "Robert Brown Puts Black Consciousness in the White House," *Jet*, Mar. 4, 1971.

105. Timothy Bates, "Government as Financial Intermediary for Minority Entrepreneurs: An Evaluation," *Journal of Business* 48, no. 4 (Oct. 1975): 541–557. See also Bean, *Small Business Administration*, 90–92; Manning Marable, *How Capitalism Underdeveloped Black America* (Boston: South End Press, 1999), 151–173, 190–243.

106. Draft White House Statement on Civil Rights, [1971], box 49, folder Black Congressmen, Garment Files.

107. "Birth Pangs," *Time*, Oct. 1968; "A Disappointing Start," *Time*, Aug. 15, 1969; RJB, Memo on Jim Brown, Aug. 10, 1972; Robert J. Brown to Richard Nixon, Memo on Gale E. Sayers' Meeting [10/17/72], Dec. 5, 1972, both in box 18, folder Presidential Meetings 1972–1973, SSS Papers. See also "Into the Big Leagues," *Time*, July 25, 1969; "Is Black Capitalism a Mistake?" *Time* Jan. 12, 1970.

108. See, for example, "The 100 Most Influential Black Americans," *Ebony*, Apr. 1971. See also "The 100 Most Influential Black Americans," *Ebony* in May 1972, May 1973, and May 1974 issues. See also Stanley Scott, Memo on Minority Media, Nov. 3, 1971, box 1, folder Administration Initiative Minority Publishers 11/3/1971, SSS Papers.

109. Jennifer Delton, *Racial Integration and Corporate America, 1940–1990* (Cambridge: Cambridge University Press, 2009).

110. "Board of Advisors," *BE*, Aug. 1970.

111. Eventually, Nixon would appoint William Rehnquist and Lewis F. Powell to the Supreme Court in 1971; African Americans, in particular, were critical of the Rehnquist nomination. Henry Lee Moon, "The Haynsworth Rejection," *Crisis*, Dec. 1969; Robert M. Smith, "Brooke Opposes Carswell," *NYT*, Feb. 26, 1970; "Judge Carswell," *Bay State Banner*, Mar. 5, 1970; "[Brooke] against Carswell," *CD*, Mar. 5, 1970; "Against Carswell," *NYAN*, Mar. 7, 1970; "Brooke Says Carswell Hasn't Changed Attitude," *HC*, Mar. 20, 1970; Philip Warden, "Carswell Bid Turned Down," *CT*, Apr. 9, 1970; Audrey Weaver, "Dixie Quote Rates Nixon a Racist," *CD*, Apr. 18, 1970; "Rehnquist Softens Civil Rights Stand in Testimony to Senators," *LAT*, Nov. 4, 1971; "Blacks 'Cautious' on Nixon's Court Nominees," *Sacramento Observer*, Oct. 28, 1971.

112. RNC Research Division, Report on Black Political Participation, [1971], box 5, Black Vote 1972, SSS Papers.

113. Milton Viorst, "The Blacks Who Work for Nixon," *NYT*, Nov. 29, 1970; "Ticker," *Jet*, Aug. 27, 1970; "Robert Brown Puts Black Consciousness in the White House," *Jet*, Mar. 4, 1971; SSS, Memo on Minority Media, Nov. 1971, box 1, SSS Papers.

114. "Man and Woman of the Year: The Middle Americans," *Time*, Jan. 5, 1970; Editorial, *Time*, Jan. 5, 1970. See also Richard Nixon, "Address to the Nation on the War in Vietnam," Nov. 3, 1969, APP, UCSB; "Excerpts from Transcript of Nixon Speech," *NYT*, Oct. 31, 1970.

115. Matthew D. Lassiter, *The Silent Majority: Suburban Politics in the Sunbelt South* (Princeton: Princeton University Press, 2007), introduction and 232–237, 254; Lassiter,

"Suburban Strategies," in Jacobs et al., *The Democratic Experiment*, 327–343. See also Carter, *The Politics of Rage*; Carter, *From George Wallace to Newt Gingrich*.

116. As Joel Olsen highlights, white radicals, campus activists, protestors, and the like also were depicted as "permissive," dangerous, disorderly, criminal, and immoral. See Olsen, "Whiteness and the Polarization of American Politics," *Political Research Quarterly* 61, no. 4 (Dec. 2008): 709–712.

117. Dov Weinryb Grohsgal, "Southern Strategies: The Politics of School Desegregation and the Nixon White House" (Ph.D. dissertation, Princeton University, 2013), 205–206; Kotlowski, *Nixon's Civil Rights*, 97–157; Lassiter, *The Silent Majority*, 263; Frymer and Skrentny, "Coalition-Building," 1998, 149–150. See *chapter 5* of this book for more on the black silent majority.

118. "Where Do We Go from Here?" *Ebony*, Jan. 1973; Ethel L. Payne, "1972—A Reflection," *Chicago Defender*, Jan. 6, 1973.

119. Daphne Sheppard, "Nixon's Black Appointees Urged to Resign in Protest," *CD*, Oct. 18, 1969; "Nixon Accused of Lies on Black Appointees," *LAT*, Aug. 2, 1970; William Raspberry, "Nixon Woos the Racists," *WP*, Oct. 20, 1971.

120. Farmer, *Lay Bare the Heart*, 325–326.

121. Paul Delaney, "Black Aides Prod Nixon on Rights," *NYT*, Mar. 7, 1970; "Civil Rights," *St. Petersburg Times*, Mar. 12, 1970.

122. Statement by Black Elected Republican Officials, Mar. 20, 1970; John W. Kellogg to Rogers C. B. Morton, Letter, Mar. 21, 1970; JWK to RN, Letter, Mar. 21, 1970; CLT to Yvonne Price, Letter, Mar. 31, 1970; BERO Proposals, Mar. 1970; RNC, Black Media Monitor, Mar. 28, 1970, all in box I: 115, BERO Papers; "Nixon Talks Hour with Brooke before Speech," *Jet*, Apr. 9, 1970; Ethel Payne, "GOP Blacks Hit Judge Carswell in D.C. Parley," *CD*, Mar. 23, 1970; "Nixon Calls in Critic Brooke for a Chat," *Boston Globe*, Mar. 20, 1970; "School Segregation Message Disappoints Dixie Senators," *Observer-Reporter*, Mar. 25, 1970; Kotlowski, *Nixon's Civil Rights*, 32–37, 174; Audrey Weaver, "Dixie Quote Rates Nixon a Racist," *CD*, Apr. 18, 1970.

123. Don Irwin, "Nixon Requests Funds to Speed Desegregation," *LAT*, May 22, 1970.

124. Lassiter, *The Silent Majority*, 246–252, 263–266; "Gap between Nixon, Blacks, Called Wide," *CT*, May 19, 1970; "Young Hits Nixon Administration," Aug. 6, 1970; "The Phillips Strategy," *Daytona Beach Morning Journal*, Sept. 27, 1969. See also Kevin P. Phillips, *The Emerging Republican Majority* (St. Paul: Arlington House, 1969).

125. Viorst, "Blacks," *NYT*, Nov. 1970.

126. Kotlowski, *Nixon's Civil Rights*; 175; Robert Mason, *Richard Nixon and the Quest for a New Majority* (Chapel Hill: University of North Carolina Press, 2003), 169.

127. Viorst, "Blacks," *NYT*, Nov. 1970.

128. Kabaservice, *Ruin and Rule*, 323; Lassiter, *The Silent Majority*, 271–275; Charles P. Lucas, "Speaking Out," *CP*, Nov. 28, 1970; Dec. 26, 1970.

129. Kotlowski, *Nixon's Civil Rights*, 180.

130. GZ, Address to the National Urban League Conference, July 26, 1971, box 70, folder Urban League, WHCF SMOF Bradley H. Patterson Files, Nixon Library (hereinafter called Patterson Files); GZ to RN, Memo on Progress CR, May 1970, box 3, CBC, Finch Files; Whitney Young, "To Be Equal," *CD*, Jan. 9, 1971.

131. LG, Memo on Urban League and Attachments, Dec. 22, 1970; LG to RN, Memo, Jan. 25, 1971, box 70, NUL, Patterson Files; Tom Buckley, "Whitney Young: Black Leader or 'Oreo Cookie,'" *NYT*, Sept. 20, 1970.

132. LG to RN, Memo, Jan. 1971, Patterson Files; Les Payne, "Vernon E. Jordan: In the Footsteps of Whitney Young," *Ebony*, July 1972.

133. RJB to James D. Hodgson, Memo, June 2, 1971; RJB to John D. Ehrlichman, Memo, June 25, 1971; RJB to RN, Memo, June 25, 1971, all in box 70, NUL, Patterson Files.

134. Dennis C. Dickerson, *Militant Mediator: Whitney M. Young, Jr.* (Lexington: University Press of Kentucky, 2004), 315–317; Richard Nixon, Statement on the Death of Whitney M. Young Jr., Mar. 11, 1971, *APP*, UCSB; "Million-Dollar Center in Whitney Young's Memory Announced by Nixon," *Jet*, Apr. 8, 1971; Simeon Booker, "America Mourns Whitney M. Young Jr.," *Ebony*, May 1971; "Nixon Eulogy," *Jet*, Apr. 1, 1971.

135. Review of NUL Proposals, Sept. 17, 1971, box 88, folder NUL, Garment Files.

136. RJB to JDE, Memo, June 1971; RJB to RN, Memo, June 1971, both in box 88, NUL, Garment Files.

137. Les Payne, "Vernon E. Jordan: In the Footsteps of Whitney Young," *Ebony*, July 1972; GZ, NUL Address, July 1971, box 70, NUL, Patterson Files.

138. "NAACP Judges Nixon More Fairly," [July 1971]; SSS to Herbert Klein, Confidential Memo on NAACP, July 9, 1971, both in box 14, folder NAACP, SSS Papers. See also "Education, Jobs" *Jet*, July 1971.

139. "Getting It Together in Jobs," *Crisis*, Sept. 1971.

140. Quoted in Trevor Griffey, "'The Blacks Should Not Be Administering the Philadelphia Plan," in *Black Power at Work: Community Control, Affirmative Action, and the Construction Industry*, ed. David Goldberg and Trevor Griffey (Ithaca: Cornell University Press, 2010), 137–138, 148–158; Gollard, *Constructing Affirmative Action*, chap. 4; Stacy Kinlock Sewell, "Left on the Bench: The New York Construction Trades and Racial Integration, 1960–1972," *New York History* 83, no. 2 (Spring 2002): 208–214.

141. Robert C. Maynard, "Six Top Black Officials Defend Nixon's Record," *WP*, July 26, 1971.

142. Weinryb Grohsgal, "Southern Strategies," 2013, 258–260; "President Nixon Asks Congress for Moratorium on Busing," *Bryan Times*, Mar. 17, 1972.

143. John Herbers, "Nixon's Top Black Officials Assail His Antibusing Policy," *NYT*, Apr. 27, 1972; Eric Wentworth, "Black Appointees Assail Busing Curbs," *WP*, Apr. 27, 1972; "Nixon Losing Credibility on Busing Stand," *CP*, May 6, 1972; Ethel Payne, "Black Appointees Advise Nixon on Busing," *PC*, Feb. 26, 1972; Robert C. Toth, "Black Appointees Tell President They Oppose Antibus Amendment," *LAT*, Mar. 7, 1972; "Negro Leaders in Government Hit Bus Curbs," *LAT*, Mar. 21, 1972; "Black Officials Concerned," *NYT*, Mar. 21, 1972; Eric Wentworth, "Black Aides Hit Nixon's Busing Plan," *WP*, Mar. 21, 1972; "GOP Blacks on Busing Plan," *CD*, Apr. 27, 1972; "Nixon Antibusing Plan Opposed by Blacks in Administration," *HC*, Apr. 27, 1972.

144. Viorst, "Blacks," *NYT*, Nov. 1970.

145. Carlos E. Russell, "The Black Believers and Richard Nixon," *NYAN*, Feb. 26, 1972; "Vote for Nixon Seen Melting Away as Art Fletcher Quits Republicans," *AA*, Dec. 18, 1971.

146. "News Roundup," *NYAN*, Dec. 25, 1971; Paul Delaney, "Dinner Nets Black Caucus $250,000," *NYT*, June 20, 1971; "Time for Assessment," *St. Louis Sentinel*, July 1, 1971.

CHAPTER 5. EXORCISING THE GHOST OF RICHARD NIXON

1. Gelb, "Black Republicans," *Urban Affairs Quarterly*, June 1970, 463–468, 470–471.

2. Ibid. See also NCAAR, "Can Black Republicans Work Together for National & Local Respect by the Republican Party," Press Release, [1971]; Curtis T. Perkins to Tom Evans,

Letter, Mar. 15, 1971; CTP to RN, Letter, [1971], all in box 37, folder Black Republican Project—Curtis T. Perkins, Robert T. Hartmann Papers, Gerald R. Ford Presidential Library (hereinafter called RTH Papers); Joseph L. Searless and Willie L. Leftwich, "Alternative for Change: Securing the Black Vote for Nixon in 1972," WH Strategy Proposal, September 1971, box 5, folder Black Vote, SSS Papers.

3. "Grant Reynolds Gets Regional HUD Post," *NYAN*, Nov. 28, 1970; "Black GOP Unit Marks Anniversary," *NYAN*, May 31, 1969; Simon Anekwe, "Black Republicans Want Power: Sue!" *NYAN*, Mar.18, 1972; "Black GOP Conclave," Mar. 30, 1972; CTP to RN, Letter, 1971, box 37, RTH Papers.

4. NCAAR, "Some Urgent Goals for All Black Republicans Nationwide," Survey & Report, [1971]; CTP to RN, Letter, 1971; NCAAR, "Can Black Republicans Work Together for National & Local Respect by the Republican Party," Press Release, [1971], all in box 37, RTH Papers.

5. CTP to TE, Letter, Mar. 15, 1971, in ibid.

6. NCAAR, "Black Republicans Work Together," 1971, in ibid.

7. CTP to RN, Letter, 1971; CTP to TE, Letter, Mar. 15, 1971, in ibid.

8. NCAAR, "Urgent Goals," 1971, in ibid.

9. NCAAR, Amended Budget, [1971]; Rogers C. B. Morton, Letter, Jan. 22, 1971, both in ibid.

10. SS to Herbert G. Klein, Memo, Dec. 10, 1971; M. H Media, Inc. to Stan Scott, Proposal, [1971]; SS to HGK, Memo, Oct. 19, 1971, all in box 5, SSS Papers.

11. JLS and WLL, "Alternative for Change," 1971, box 5, SSS Papers.

12. The data on black voter identification are contradictory. For example, the JCPES currently suggests that between 1968 and 1972 black identification with the GOP increased from 3 to 5 percent; in contrast, polls from Gallup and the Michigan Survey Research Center in 1972 place black GOP affiliation at between 6 to 9 percent. The discrepancies among these sources provides evidence of the flaws inherent to historical data on black voting patterns and partisan affiliations. Since Republican and Democratic strategists relied heavily on the Harris, Gallup, and Michigan surveys, at the time, I have chosen to use those figures in this chapter. RNC Research Division, *Report on the Polls: Blacks*, [1971], in box 5, SSS Papers; Bositis, *Blacks and the RNC*, 2012; "Mexican American Analysis of Survey Taken in Orange and Los Angeles Counties," Survey, Oct. 1971, in Select Committee on Presidential Campaign Activities, Executive Session Hearings, Ninety-Third Congress, Second Session, Watergate and Related Activities, Book 19 (Washington, D.C.: U.S. Government Printing Office, 1974), 8678 (hereinafter called Watergate Hearings).

13. RNC Research Division, *Report on the Polls: Blacks*, [1971]; RNC, Research Division, *Report on Black Political Participation*, [1971]; George Gallup, "Nixon and Republican Party Still Rejected by Nation's Blacks," [Feb. 1971], all in box 5, SSS Papers.

14. [Black Vote Division of CREEP], *Campaign Plan: A Strategy for the Development of the Black Vote in 1972*, Mar. 15, 1972; Jeb S. Magruder, Memo on the 1972 Black Vote, Dec. 3, 1971, both in box 5, SSS Papers. See also Watergate Hearings, 8713.

15. RB, "Proposal for the Organization of a Network of Young Black Friends for the Reelection of the President," [Apr. 1972]; Paul R. Jones to Fred Malek, Memo, Apr. 17, 1972; Paul A. Lavrakas to RB, Memo on Young Black Vote Strategy, May 4, 1972; RB, Strategy Memo, [1971–1972], in box 5, SSS Papers. See also Watergate Hearings.

16. FM to John Mitchell, Memo on Black Vote, June 2, 1972; PRJ to Robert C. Odle, Memo, Jan. 10, 1972, both in Watergate Hearings, 8859–8860, 8870.

17. Jack Crawford to Robert Mardian, "Black Re-election Campaign Effort," June 23, 1972; RM to FM, Memo, June 26, 1972; PRJ to FM, Memo, Apr. 18, 1972; Charles Miller to Samuel Dash, Letter on James Farmer, Mar. 8, 1974; JF to SD, Letter, Apr. 23, 1974;

"Affidavit of James Farmer," June 26, 1974; Charles Wallace, Letter, Sept. 12, 1972; RN to CW, Letter, Sept. 14, 1971; "Affidavit of Charles Wallace," Apr. 13, 1974; PRJ to RO Memo, Apr. 4, 1972; PRJ to RO, Memo, [Sept. 1972]; PRJ to Jeb Magruder, Memo on OIC/ Opportunities Industrialization Centers, Feb. 18, 1972; PRJ to FM, Memo, July 21, 1972, all in Watergate Hearings, 8742–8747, 8838–8847, 8850–8860, 8864–8868, 9342–9343.

18. "White House Team Courting Black Republicans in the South," *WP*, Oct. 23, 1971; "White House Woos Blacks," *WP*, Oct. 23, 1971; "Nixon Woos Dixie Blacks," *CD*, Nov. 3, 1971; HSD to H. R. Haldeman, Memo, Oct. 27, 1971, in Watergate Hearings, 8613.

19. Ethel L. Payne, "Blacks Seek GOP Reform, Greater Policy Voice," *CD*, Nov. 13, 1971.

20. "Black G.O.P., Dem Women Zero in on 1 Objective: Influence," *CT*, Nov. 14, 1971.

21. Warren Weaver Jr., "1972 Black Drive for Nixon Mapped," *NYT*, Dec. 17, 1971; "Nixon Organizes Blacks for Campaign Fodder," *PC*, Dec. 25, 1971.

22. "Blacks Polled on Possible Presidential Candidates," *Bay State Banner*, Nov. 25, 1971; "Black Demos Split between Muskie and Kennedy," *Sacramento Observer*, Nov. 25, 1971.

23. "Black Republicans Demand More Representation," *CD*, Feb. 21, 1972; Anekwe, "Sue!" *NYAN*, Mar. 1972; Anekwe, "Black Republican Suing Pres. Ford and GOP Natl. Committee," *NYAN*, Sept. 4, 1976; "Unhappy GOP Blacks," *Tri-State Defender*, Oct. 2, 1976.

24. "Black Republicans Show Strength, Elect Three," *Tri-State Defender*, Feb. 26, 1972.

25. Katherine Tate, *From Protest to Politics: The New Black Voters in American Elections* (Cambridge: Harvard University Press, 1998), 55–60.

26. Thomas A. Johnson, "Parley Shows Complexity and Vitality of Black America," *NYT*, Mar. 14, 1972; Thomas A. Johnson, "Blacks at Parley Divided on Basic Role in Politics," *NYT*, Mar. 12, 1972.

27. "National Black Political Agenda. The Gary Declaration: Black Politics at the Crossroads," Mar. 1972, in *Let Nobody Turn Us Around: Voices of Resistance, Reform, and Renewal; An African American Anthology*, ed. Manning Marable and Leith Mullings (Lanham: Rowman & Littlefield, 2009), 469–472.

28. Stephen Curwood, "Local Figures Assess Convention," *Bay State Banner*, Mar. 23, 1972; Bill Robinson, "Political Roundup," *LAS*, Mar. 16, 1972; Johnson, "Shows Complexity," *NYT*, Mar. 1972; Johnson, "Blacks at Parley," *NYT*, Mar. 1972; Roger Wilkins, "Gary Convention Points to a Black Political Party," *WP*, Mar. 18, 1972; William Greider, "Blacks Meet in Quest of United Vote," *WP*, Mar. 10, 1972; William Greider, "Discord Is the Keynote for Black Convention," *WP*, Mar. 11, 1972; "Black Convention Adopts Compromise," *HC*, Mar. 13, 1972; Herbert H. Denton, "Black Convention Votes Opposition to Busing Students," *WP*, Mar. 13, 1972; "Black Convention Revealed Dissent," *HC*, Mar. 14, 1972; "The Gary Convention," *ADW*, Mar. 16, 1972; "Convention Lost Its Chance," *CD*, Mar. 16, 1972; Eric Wentworth, "Black Caucus Affirms Its Support for Busing," *WP*, Mar. 16, 1972; "Did Nixon Aides Pull Gary Coup?" *CD*, Mar. 28, 1972. See also Walters, *Presidential Politics*, 86–93.

29. "Campaign Plan A Strategy for the Development of the Black Vote in 1972," Mar. 15, 1972, in Watergate Hearings.

30. NCAAR Press Release, 1971, in box 37, RTH Papers; Paul Delaney, "Blacks Parleys in Capital Hail Nixon and Thurmond," *NYT*, June 12, 1972.

31. Betty Granger Reid, "Conversation Piece," *NYAN*, June 24, 1972; "Blacks Polled on Possible Presidential Candidates," *Bay State Banner*, Nov. 25, 1971.

32. "Black GOP for Nixon," *CD*, June 20, 1972; Von Blaine, "Knives & Forks," *Daily Challenge*, June 23, 1972; "Introduce the New Dance," picture and caption, *ADW*, June 2,

1972; "Washington Black Strategy Session: 'Getting Ourselves Together,'" *Chicago South Suburban News*, June 10, 1972; "Atlantans at Dinner for Pres. Nixon," picture and caption, *ADW*, July 6, 1972; "Blacks Meet in DC to Pledge Support to Nixon," *Cincinnati Herald*, June 24, 1972, all in folder Top Coverage on Minorities, box 1, SSS Papers.

33. Launched by Floyd McKissick in 1969, Soul City was designed as a "black-owned-and-operated town" in North Carolina. Relying on funds from HUD's model cities program, it was supported by grants from both the Johnson and Nixon administrations. The city became one of the "models" for black capitalism in the early 1970s, but indifference by the Ford and Carter administrations, combined with McKissick's mismanagement, effectively killed Soul City by 1979. As Devin Fergus suggests, McKissick's effort and his embrace of the GOP highlight the complex ways in which Black Power advocates and Republicans tried to use each other for mutual gain in the 1960s and 1970s. In particular, McKissick was one of the more effective black Republican campaigners (later involved in both the NBRC and Council of 100); and yet Richard Nixon kept McKissick at arm's length throughout 1972 because of the black leader's affiliation with the Black Power movement and his opposition to the president's Vietnam policy; likewise, while Republicans in North Carolina were receptive to McKissick during this period, by 1975 national party officials gave him the cold shoulder, especially after Senator Jesse Helms launched a federal audit and investigation of Soul City. Fergus, "Black Power, Soft Power," *JPH*, 2010, 148–192. For more on Ethel Allen and black independent politics in Philadelphia, see Matthew J. Countryman, "'From Protest to Politics': Community Control and Black Independent Politics in Philadelphia, 1965–1984," *Journal of Urban History* 32 (2006): 839–840.

34. "2500 Black Republican Leaders Attend a $100-a-Plate Re-elect Nixon Dinner," *PC*, July 1, 1972; Lee R. Heidhues, "One Man Recalls Why He Decided to Work for 'The President' in '72," *Sun Reporter*, July 21, 1972.

35. "Black GOP for Nixon," *CD*, June 20, 1972.

36. "Blacks for Nixon," *New Republic*, Oct. 7, 1972.

37. "Black GOP Conclave," *CD*, Mar. 30, 1972; "Black GOP Cohorts Asked to Assess Role in Their Party," *PC*, June 3 1972; Ronald Taylor, "Two Black Units Plan Aid to GOP," *WP*, June 9, 1972; "2,500 Republicans Give $200,000 for Campaign," *CP*, June 17, 1972.

38. Bositis, *Blacks and the RNC*, 2012; Ethel L. Payne, "Sen. Brooke Praises Nixon Peace Efforts," *CD*, Aug. 23, 1972; "The Republican Show," *CD* Aug. 21, 1972; "Symbolism Strong in GOP Delegates," *WAA*, Aug. 21, 1972; "Hard Sell Back Home for GOP Blacks," *Miami News*, Aug. 23, 1972; "Black Republicans May Form Caucus," *HC*, Aug. 21, 1972.

39. Hanes Walton Jr. and C. Vernon Gray, "Black Politics at the National Republican and Democratic Conventions, 1868–1972," *Phylon* 36, no. 3 (1975): 269.

40. Vernon Jarrett, "A Futile Search for G.O.P. Blacks," *CT*, Aug. 23, 1972.

41. Ron Taylor, "Blacks at GOP's Convention Voice Criticism of Party's Shortcomings," *WP*, Aug. 22, 1972.

42. Vernon Jarrett, "Blacks Decry Role in Republican Party Activities," *CT*, Aug. 22, 1972; "A New Majority for Four More Years?" *Time*, Sept. 4, 1972.

43. Jarrett, "Blacks Decry Role," *CT*, Aug. 1972.

44. The Democratic Party reformed its delegate selection process in 1972, instituting an affirmative action policy to achieve proportional representation among state delegations. Consequently, black delegates composed 15 percent of the representative body to the 1972 Democratic National Convention—the highest tally the party had witnessed. In 1976, the party amended the rule, resulting in a 15 percent drop in black delegate strength. See Hanes Walton, *Invisible Politics: Black Political Behavior* (Albany: State University of New York, 1985), 161–162.

45. "Virginia Delegates," photo caption, *WAA*, Aug. 29, 1972; Paul H. Wyche Jr., "Rules Change Bid Ends in Failure," *WAA*, Aug. 29, 1972.

46. "Caucus," *HC*, Aug. 1972.

47. "Virginia Delegates," *WAA*, Aug. 1972; Wyche, "Rules Change," *WAA*, Aug. 29, 1972; Taylor, "Shortcomings," *WP*, Aug. 1972; Diggs Datrooth, "National Hotline," *CD*, Sept. 2, 1972.

48. Moses J. Newson, "Symbolism Strong in GOP Delegates," *WAA*, Aug. 29, 1972.

49. "Caucus," *HC*, Aug. 1972; Taylor, "Shortcomings," *WP*, Aug. 1972.

50. Jackson R. Champion, "Black Power at Miami Beach," *Grass Roots News*, Sept. 1972; Champion, "Black Participation in Miami Beach," *Grass Roots News*, Sept. 1972, all in box 5, SSS Papers.

51. Vernon Jarrett, "Black Republicans Throw a Big Party," *CT*, Aug. 24, 1972; "Sammy Davis, College President to Testify before GOP Platform Committee," *Jet*, Aug. 24, 1972; Simeon Booker, "Blacks at GOP Convention Hard to Get Together for Special Caucus Sessions," *Jet*, Sept. 7, 1972; "Black GOP Leaders Push to Increase Party Membership," *ADW*, Aug. 27, 1972; "Black Republicans Plan for Campaign," *CP*, Sept. 2, 1972.

52. Jessie Mae Beavers, "Black Participants at GOP Convention," *LAS*, Sept. 7, 1972. See also Ethel Payne, "Blacks Split on GOP Strategy," *CD*, Aug. 26, 1972.

53. Charles Kenyatta, "Where I'm Comin' From: Viewpoint," *NYAN*, Sept. 9, 1972.

54. Simon Anekwe, "Republican Women Organize for Nixon," *NYAN*, Oct. 7, 1972.

55. Arthur A. Fletcher, "The Black Dilemma if Nixon Wins," *WSJ*, Sept. 25, 1972.

56. Frank Starr, "McGovern Hit by Landslide," *CT*, Nov. 8, 1972; Phillip Warden and Brenda Stone, "Democrats Win 16 Seats Keep Control of Senate," *CT*, Nov. 8, 1972; "McGovern Wins Bay State, Brooke Regains Senate Seat," *CT*, Nov. 8, 1972; Max Frankel, "President Won 49 States and 521 Electoral Votes," *NYT*, Nov. 9, 1972; Stephen Isaacs, "Surveys See New Pattern of Voting," *WP*, Nov. 9, 1972; Lou Cannon, "Victory Bittersweet for GOP," *WP*, Nov. 9, 1972.

57. Ripon Society, *Jaws of Victory: The Game-Plan Politics of 1972, the Crisis of the Republican Party and the Future of the Constitution* (Boston: Little & Brown, 1974), 193–199; Thurber, *Republicans and Race*, 358–359.

58. John L. Wilks to Ed Sexton, Campaign Wind-Up Report, Nov. 14, 1972, in folder DeBolt Subject File—Blacks, GRF Library (hereinafter called DeBolt Files).

59. Ibid.

60. ES to FM, 1972 Black Voter Analysis Memo and Report, Dec. 12, 1972, in DeBolt Files.

61. JLW to ES, Wind-Up Report, Nov. 1972, in DeBolt Files.

62. Sy Williams, Overall Objectives—Black Vote Division, [Dec. 1972]; Ed Sexton to Fred Malek, Memo on 1972 Black Voter Analysis, Dec. 12, 1972, both in DeBolt Files.

63. "Blacks Backed McGovern," *PC*, Nov. 25, 1972.

64. Celeste Durant, "Appeal to Self-Interest Cited," *LAT*, Oct. 29, 1972.

65. Julian Bond, Letter, *CD*, Aug. 21, 1972; Paul Delaney, "Blacks for Nixon Sharply Rebuked," *NYT*, Aug. 10, 1972.

66. Ripon, *Jaws*, 197.

67. "Dole Names Black to RNC Executive Unit," *CD*, Jan. 20, 1973; "RNC Bush Meets with Henry Lucas," *Bay State Banner*, May 24, 1973.

68. "Davis and Brown Prod President Nixon to Help Blacks," *Jet*, Nov. 23, 1972; Paul Delaney, "Blacks for Nixon Form G.O.P. Group," *NYT*, Jan. 20, 1973; "Blacks Continue to Await Call from Nixon for Jobs," *Jet*, Apr. 19, 1973; "McKissick Tells Blacks Forget OEO Dismantling," *Jet*, May 31, 1973.

69. RNC Minorities Division, Memo on Negro Outreach and Self-Help Programs, [1967], folder Fieldwork, 1967, CLT Papers.

70. GHWB to William N. Michels, Letter, July 29, 1963, in GHWB Papers. See also "In Our Opinion: Meeting Our Destiny," *CD*, Aug. 4, 1973.

71. The RNC tasked the Rule 29 Committee with transforming the GOP into an "Open Door" party and dismantling the party's "traditional image of the rich and exclusive." Chaired by Wisconsin Congressman William Steiger, the fifty-eight-member committee represented a broad spectrum of Republican ideologies but was chiefly propelled by liberal and moderate party reformers. Among them were three black Republicans—moderate Bob Brown, liberal Ed Brooke, and conservative Henry Lucas of California. See "People in Politics," *National Black Republican News* 1, no. 1 (Jan. 1974), in box 19, SSS Papers; "Opening Up the GOP," *Focus* 3, no. 3 (Jan. 1975), in box 30, folder Chairman Political Files, Mary Louise Smith Papers, Iowa Women's Archives, University of Iowa Libraries (hereinafter called MLS Papers); "Widen Minority Participation," *Southeast Missourian*, June 17, 1974; Robert J. Huckshorn and John F. Bibby, "National Party Rules and Delegate Selection in the Republican Party," *PS* 16, no. 4 (Autumn 1983): 658–659.

72. "New Majority Workshops Held in Three Cities," *NBRN*, Jan. 1974, box 19, SSS Papers.

73. "Black GOP Leaders in Meeting," *NYAN*, Sept. 22, 1973.

74. "Black Discontent," *CD*, Sept. 17, 1973; "Black GOPers: Unhappy Republicans," *Tri-State Defender*, Sept. 22, 1973.

75. Ibid. See also "Nixon Blacks in Quander," *CD*, Jan. 27, 1973; Paul Delaney, "Nixon Is Expected to Appoint Blacks," *NYT*, Feb. 25, 1973; Thurber, *Republicans and Race*, 362–367.

76. "Black on Black," *Bay Banner State*, Nov. 9, 1972; Smith, *We Have No Leaders*, 140.

77. RB to FM, Memo, Jan. 2, 1973, in box 15, folder OMBE—General 1973, SSS Papers; Weinryb Grohsgal, "Southern Strategies," 2013, 298–302; Simeon Booker, "Ticker Tape U.S.A.," *Jet*, Mar. 1, 1973; Charlie Cherokee, "Charlie Cherokee Says," *CD*, May 7, 1973. "Black Republicans Meet Laird on Nixon's Yacht," *Jet*, Nov. 1, 1973.

78. "In Our Opinion: Black Comedy of Errors," *CD*, Jan. 13, 1973; Payne, "So This Is Washington," *PC*, Dec. 16, 1972.

79. Paul Delaney, "Nixon Is Expected to Appoint Blacks," *NYT*, Feb. 25, 1973; "Jenkins Out at OMBE," *NYAN*, Mar. 3, 1973; "Black GOP Ask Meeting with Nixon," *NYAN*, June 30, 1973.

80. "Black Republicans Revitalized," *NBRN*, Jan. 1974, in box 19, SSS Papers. See also AF to Edmund E. Pendleton, Letter on NBRC, Dec. 4, 1973; RNC Black Political Division to State RNC Chairmen, Memo on NBRC, Dec. 21, 1973, all in box 118, folder National Black Republican Council, GAA Files; "Fletcher Says the Move Is On for Black Candidates," *Jet*, Oct. 25, 1973.

81. NBRC, Constitution and Bylaws, 1974, box 5, folder Black Republicans 1972, SSS Papers.

82. "Affidavit of Robert Carter," Oct. 14, 1976, in Black Republican Lawsuit, box 30, MLS Papers; "Revitalized," *NBRN*, Jan. 1974; NBRC, Organizational Manual, [1973–1974], both in box 5, folder Black Republicans 1972, SSS Papers.

83. Jackson R. Champion, *Blacks in the Republican Party? The Story of a Revolutionary, Conservative Black Republican* (Washington, D.C.: LenChamps Publishers, 1976), 26–27.

84. NBRC, Constitution, 1974; NBRC, Manual, 1974, both in box 5, SSS Papers.

85. NBRC, Constitution, 1974; NBRC, Manual, 1974, box 19, SSS Papers.

86. NBRC, Registration and Minutes from NBRC Steering Committee Meeting, Feb. 24, 1974; NBRC, NBRC Special Report, Press Release, vol. 1, no. 2 (Mar. 8, 1974), both in box 19, SSS Papers.

87. "People in Politics," *NBRN*, [Aug. 1974], in box 18, folder Presidential Meetings, SSS Papers.

88. "Goals of the National Coordinating Council of Black Republicans," [1974], SSS Papers; Samuel C. Jackson to GRF, Letter from the NCCBR, Aug. 21, 1974; SCJ to GRF, Telegram, [Aug. 1974], all in box 5, folder Black Republicans, SSS Papers.

89. Champion, *Blacks in the Republican Party*, 19–32.

90. "Black Republicans Say 'Watergate' No Burden," *BAA*, July 2, 1974.

91. During the early 1970s, a number of black Republicans applauded the guaranteed minimum income and work incentive provisions in Nixon's failed Family Assistance Plan (FAP). Introduced by Nixon in August 1969, FAP proposed a minimum income of $2,000 for a family of four, paid directly to the recipients, and required beneficiaries to work or undergo job training (if physically able, with the exception of women with young children). The bill passed in the House in 1970 but stalled in the Senate, dying out by 1972. Mitchell K. Hall, *Historical Dictionary of the Nixon-Ford Era* (New York: Scarecrow Press, 2008), 78; RN, "The Present Welfare System Has to be Judged a Colossal Failure," Speech, Aug. 8, 1969, in *Richard Nixon: Speeches, Writings, Documents*, ed. Rick Perlstein (Princeton: Princeton University Press, 2008), 163–169; Kotlowski, *Nixon's Civil Rights*, 248–249. See also "Black Nixon Appointees Hope to Help President Set Domestic Priorities," *Jet*, Jan. 16, 1973; Black Council of Republican Politics, Inc. (formerly NCAAR), "Blacks and the Republican Party," *Survey & Report*, July 3, 1974, box 118, folder NBRC, GAA Files.

92. Champion, *Blacks in the Republican Party*, 31.

93. NBRC, Manual, 1974, box 5; NBRC Steering Committee Meeting, box 5, both in SSS Papers.

94. "Revitalized," *NBRN*, Jan. 1974, box 19, SSS Papers.

95. NBRC, Constitution, 1974; NBRC Manual, 1974, box 5, SSS Papers.

96. NBRC, Constitution, 1974; NBRC Manual, 1974, box 5, SSS Papers.

97. EWB, "Watergate . . . How and Why?" *Brooke Report*, Newsletter, June 1973; EWB, "The Crisis of Confidence . . . The Agonizing Alternatives," *Brooke Report*, Newsletter, Nov. 1973, folder Newsletters 1974, EWB Papers; RN, "Address to the Nation Announcing Decision to Resign the Office of President of the United States," Aug. 8, 1974, *APP*, USCB; "2nd GOP Senator Breaks with Nixon," *LAT*, Nov. 5, 1973; "Brooke Appeals to Nixon to Resign for Nation's Sake: He Is First G.O.P. Senator to Urge Step," *NYT*, Nov. 5, 1973; Don Irwin, "Brooke Tells Nixon—Face-to-Face—He Should Resign," *LAT*, Nov. 10, 1973.

98. "Breaks with Nixon," *LAT*, Nov. 1973; "Brooke Appeals to Nixon to Resign," *NYT*, Nov. 1973; Irwin, "Brooke Tells Nixon," *LAT*, Nov. 1973.

99. BCRP, Addendum "President Nixon, Watergate, Reform," [1974]; BCRP, "Blacks," July 1974, box 118, GAA Files; Carl T. Rowan, "Court GOP Blacks, Too," *Washington Star-News*, Aug. 16, 1974.

100. BCRP, Addendum "Watergate, Reform," [1974], box 118, GAA Files. See also "Nixon Quits," *Jet*, Aug. 22, 1974; "Scandal Hurts Blacks Less, Fletcher Says," *Portsmouth Times*, Mar. 27, 1974; "Black Republicans Say 'Watergate' No Burden," *BAA*, July 2, 1974; "Blacks Supports GOP as Good for Business," *HC*, Aug. 29, 1976.

101. Paul Delaney, "Aid to Minority Business a Lever for Nixon in '72," *NYT*, Nov. 18, 1973; "Watergate Panel Call[s] Nixon's Black 'Team,'" *NYAN*, Nov. 17, 1973; Ethel Payne, "Quiz Black Nixon Aides," *CD*, Nov. 12, 1973; Barbara Bright-Sagnier, "The Fall of a Black Capitalist: Nixon Supporter Faces Prison in Funds Case," *WP*, Feb. 10, 1974; Simeon Booker, "Ticker Tape U.S.A.," *Jet*, May 30, 1974; Kotlowski, *Nixon's Civil Rights*, 147–148. See also Watergate Hearings.

102. BCRP, Survey, 1974, box 118, GAA Files.

103. Council of 100, Fact Sheet, [1974–1975]; Council of 100, "Council of 100: An Organization of Black Republicans," [1974–1975], both in box 8, folder Fund for a Representative Congress, Sheila Weidenfeld Files, First Lady's Staff, GRF Library (hereinafter referred to as SW Papers); SCJ to GRF, Letter, Aug. 1974; NCCBR, Goals, 1974, box 5, SSS Papers; "Blacks Back Rocky," CD, Nov. 12, 1974;"Black GOP Group Pushes for Extension of Voting Act," ADW, Mar. 11, 1975.

104. SCJ, Appeal Letter #3 for Fund for a Representative Congress, [1974–75], in box 30, MLS Papers.

105. "Rocky," CD, Nov. 1974; "Voting Act," ADW, Mar. 11, 1975.

106. Philip Shandler, "Black Silent Majority Plans Crusade," Evening Star, May 13, 1971; "Negro 'Patriots' Promote Crusade," [May 1971]; Guest Editorial, Washington Monday, [May 1971]; Black Silent Majority Statement of Beliefs, [1971], all in box 9, Nixon WHCF SMOF, Finch, CFOA 327 BSMC; Guest Editorials, "Black Silent Majority," CT, July 22, 1970; "Silent Majority of Blacks Formed; National Group Given Funds by G.O.P. for Recruiting," NYT, July 12, 1970; "Form Black Silent Majority, Law, Order Group in D.C.," Jet, Oct. 29, 1970. See also "Silent Majority Urged to Speak Out against Radicals," WAA, Sept. 7, 1971.

107. BSMC, Statement of Beliefs, [1970]; "A Call to Black Conscience: Patriotism or Militancy?" Black Silent Majority Committee Newsletter, Jan. 1971, both in the Wilcox Collection of Contemporary Political Movements, Kenneth Spencer Research Library, University of Kansas Archives (hereinafter called BSMC Papers).

108. BSMC, Statement of Beliefs [1970]; "Patriotism or Militancy," BSMC Newsletter, in BSMC Papers. See also "Silent Majority of Blacks Formed," NYT, July 1970; "Form Black Silent Majority," JET, Oct. 1970.

109. Tom Tiede, "'Black Silent Majority Speaks for Democracy," Rome News-Tribune, Oct. 29, 1970; Henry Cathcart, "Inside Washington," Times, Nov. 19, 1970.

110. Such accusations stemmed from the fact that the Republican Congressional Committee (RCC) had provided $10,000 in start-up costs for the BSMC in 1970. Moreover, in a 1970 article, the Pittsburgh Courier insinuated that the RCC may have even paid African Americans to join the BSMC, an accusation vehemently denied by both groups. And while such allegations are fascinating, sufficient evidence has yet to emerge that would either prove or disprove the "blacks for hire" accusations. "Black Group Is GOP Sponsored," PC, July 18, 1970. See also "National Black Silent Majority Committee," Aug. 1, 1970, box 62, folder 6—BSMC, Shadegg Papers; William Raspberry, "GOP Theme: Building, Not Burning," WP, Nov. 14, 1970. See also Ethel L. Payne, "Negro Group Called GOP Hoax," PC, July 25, 1970; "Most Black Parents Oppose Busing Leader of Group Claims," Avalanche Journal, Apr. 15, 1977.

111. BSMC, BSMC Newsletter, Jan. 1971, BSMC Papers.

112. Ibid.

113. "The Silent Black Majority," Ludington Daily News, Nov. 15, 1971; Tiede, "'Black Silent Majority Speaks for Democracy," Rome News-Tribune, Oct. 1970; "Black Silent Majority Maps Patriotism Crusade," Victoria Advocate, Apr. 12, 1971.

114. "Rev. Searcy to Talk on Crime Tonight," ADW, Apr. 19, 1973; "Majority Group to Fight Crime," ADW, June 10, 1973; "A Welcome Move," ADW, Oct. 13, 1974; "Black Silent Majority Committee Will Be Reactivated in Atlanta," ADW, Mar. 18, 1973; "Let's All Join the Attack," ADW, Mar. 22, 1973.

115. Clay Claiborne, Form Letter for BSMC, Aug. 6, 1971, box 62, Shadegg Papers; "GOP Women Hear Former Democrat," ADW, Nov. 3, 1972; "Young Negroes Say Nixon is 'The Man' for Them," ADW, Oct. 10, 1972; Henry Cathcart, "Inside Washington," Times, Nov. 19, 1970. See also Philip Shandler, "Black Silent Majority Plans Crusade," Eve-

ning Star, May 13, 1971. See also "Negro 'Patriots' Promote Crusade," [May 1971]; Guest Editorial, *Washington Monday*, [May 1971]; Black Silent Majority Statement of Beliefs, [1971], all in Nixon WHCF SMOF Finch, box 9, CFOA 327 BSMC.

116. Lewis, *Conservatism*.

117. Reprint from *RCC Newsletter*, [1974], BSMC Papers; Federal Election Commission, "The Flinns Conciliation Agreement," Audit Report, July 11, 1977, accessed June 13, 2013, http://www.fec.gov/audits/1978/Unauthorized/78BlackVotersforRepublicanCongress.pdf.

118. BSMC, *BSMC Newsletter*, Jan. 1971, BSMC Papers; William Raspberry, "Clay Claiborne: Leader or Dupe," *WP*, Nov. 12, 1970; "Black Group Is GOP Sponsored," *PC*, July 18, 1970.

119. White Republican politicians also attended BSMC meetings; for instance, a gathering in 1970 drew participation from Hugh Scott, California congressman Bob Wilson (chair of the RCC), and Ronald Reagan. Strom Thurmond, "Remarks," *Congressional Record* 116, no. 115 (July 9, 1970), reprinted in full in BSMC, *BSMC Newsletter*, Jan. 1971, BSMC Papers.

120. RN to CC, Letter, Oct. 7, 1970; GRF to CC, Letter, Apr. 23, 1975, both in BSMC Papers.

121. "Ford: President of all People," *NBRN* 1, no. 7 (Aug. 1974), box 30, MLS Papers. See also EWB, "New Economic Initiatives," folder Newsletters 1974, EWB Papers.

122. "Ford," *NBRN*, Aug. 1974, box 30, MLS Papers; "Rocky," *CD*, Nov. 12, 1974; "Black Organization Endorses Rockefeller," *ADW*, Nov. 14, 1974.

123. Simeon Booker, "The Untold Side of President Ford," *Jet*, Aug. 28, 1974.

124. SS to RTH, Memo, Aug. 12, 1974, box 3, folder Black Caucus 1974–75, SSS Papers.

125. "Black Republicans Meet with President Ford," *NBRN* 1, no. 8 (Sept.–Oct. 1974), box 30, MLS Papers.

126. "Meeting with Key Black Republicans," List, Sept.13, 1974, in ibid. See also SS to Anne Armstrong, Memo, Sept. 12, 1974, box 18, folder Presidential Meeting 1974; "'Open Door' Maintained: President Ford Meets Blacks on Domestic Minority Concerns," Press Release, [Sept. 1974], in box 19, both in SSS Papers; MLS, Handwritten Notes from BR Meeting with Ford, Sept. 13, 1975, box 30, MLS Papers.

127. Booker, "Untold Side," *Jet*, Aug. 1974; Hal Gulliver, "Stan Scott's Input at High Levels," *Atlanta Constitution*, Oct. 6, 1976, in box F13, People for Ford Office: Robert Keyes Files, President Ford Committee Records, 1975–76, GRF Library (hereinafter called Keyes Files); "Ford," *NBRN*, Aug. 1974, box 30, MLS Papers.

128. AF, "Profile of a Campaign," *NBRN* 1, no. 6 (June–July 1974); "Spotlight on Black GOP Candidates," *NBRN* 1, no. 5 (May 1974), box 30, MLS Papers.

129. AF, "Profile," *NBRN* (June–July 1974); "Spotlight," *NBRN* (Aug. 1974), box 30, MLS Papers. See also MLS to James B. Morris, Letter to MLS, Sept. 26, 1974, in box 30, MLS Papers; "Republican Leader to Speak Tonight," *ADW*, Oct. 11, 1974; W. O. Walker, "Down the Big Road," *CP*, Oct. 19, 1974; "Black Republican Candidates Running," *ADW*, May 31, 1974; "Black GOP Candidates," *Sacramento Observer*, May 29, 1974. See also "Black Officeholders Increase Nationally," *ADW*, Nov. 5, 1974; Charles E. Price, "Blacks and Republicans: A Feasible Coalition," *ADW*, Nov. 10, 1974.

130. "Election in Retrospect," *NBRN* 1, no. 1 (Nov.–Dec, 1974), box 30, MLS Papers.

131. "T. A. Garrett Jr., 51, Urban Affairs Expert," *NYT*, Nov. 15, 1999.

132. Capitol City Republican Club, *CCRC Newsletter* 1, no. 1 (July 1, 1974), box 2, folder CCRC, Andre M. Buckles 1974–75, Domestic Council, GRF Library.

133. "Retrospect," *NBRN*, Nov.–Dec., 1974, box 30, MLS Papers.

134. Ibid.; JBM to AF, Letter, Oct. 7, 1974; "For the Record . . . Campaign '74," *NBRN* 1, no. 8 (Sept.–Oct. 1974), both in MLS Papers. See also Jack Zaiman, "Rep. Brannen Seeks GOP Nod for Senate," *HC*, June 2, 1974.

135. "Retrospect," *NBRN*, Nov.–Dec., 1974; JBM to AF, Letter, Oct. 1974; "For the Record," *NBRN*, Sept.–Oct. 1974, all in MLS Papers.

136. "NBRC: One Year Old," *NBRN* 1, no. 10 (Nov.–Dec. 1974), box 30, MLS Papers; Barbara Reynolds, "G.O.P. Black Gets No Party Funding," *CT*, Dec. 23, 1974.

137. "One Year Old," *NBRC*, Nov.–Dec. 1974, box 30, MLS Papers.

138. Council of 100, Press Release, Fund for a Representative Congress, Nov. 21, 1975; Council of 100, "Why the Council of 100?" [1974–1975], both in box 8, SW Papers; Council of 100, News Release, Oct. 28, 1975, in box 30, MLS Papers; "Rocky to Address Council Banquet in D.C. Nov. 19," *ADW*, Nov. 4, 1975; "Black Republicans," *NYAN*, Nov. 26, 1975; Julian Bond, "Bond-at-Large," *CD*, Dec. 20, 1975.

139. "Text of Rockefeller's Speech November 19," *ADW*, Nov. 30, 1975; "Please be Seated," *NYAN*, Dec. 3, 1975; "Rocky Promises to Help Elect Black Republicans," *NYAN*, Dec. 3, 1975; "Rocky Pushes GOP Blacks," *CD*, Nov. 27, 1975.

140. "Rocky Promises," *NYAN*, Dec. 1975.

141. As Joseph Crespino suggests, by 1972 Strom Thurmond was attempting to redefine his "racial politics," by tempering and "softening" his segregationist image. In fact, throughout the 1970s, he integrated his staff and campaigned among African American communities in South Carolina, attracting support from black Republicans nationally and from some African Americans on the state and local level, irrespective of partisan affiliation, who argued that the senator had pumped federal funds into South Carolina's black communities. Still, his philosophy only shifted so much; in Congress, his votes against extensions for the Voting Rights Act and his support for antibusing legislation led *A Black Voter's Guide to the 1978 Elections* to suggest that he was one of the twenty-four "people in Congress hostile to black interests." Likewise, as Crespino also suggests, Thurmond's strategy was rooted in his desire not to "antagonize black voters, which would drive up black turnout," to defeat the politician, as most blacks in the state were still wary of him. See Joseph Crespino, *Strom Thurmond's America* (New York: Hill and Wang, 2012), 253, 282; Nadine Cohodas, *Strom Thurmond and the Politics of Southern Change* (Macon: Mercer University Press, 1995), 448–449; Council of 100 "Why?" box 30, MLS Papers.

142. Vernon Jarrett, "Blacks No Longer Tied to Democrats," *CT*, Apr. 23, 1976.

143. Crespino, *Strom Thurmond*, 253–254.

144. NBRC, Manual, 1974, box 5, SSS Papers.

CHAPTER 6. MORE SHADOW THAN SUBSTANCE

1. National Newspaper Publishers Association, "Congratulations to President Ford," *Sun Reporter*, Jan. 18, 1975; Louis Martin, "Gerald Ford Scores Touchdown," *CD*, Jan. 18, 1975.

2. William T. Coleman, *Counsel for the Situation: Shaping the Law to Realize America's Promise* (Washington, D.C.: Brookings Institute Press, 2010), 218. See also "Senate Unanimously OKs Coleman for Cabinet Post," *ADW*, Mar. 6, 1975; "Secretary Coleman Begins Duties," *ADW*, Mar. 13, 1975; "Secretary Coleman," *CD*, Mar. 18, 1975; "Ford Names Black to Cabinet," *CD*, Jan. 13, 1975; Vernon E. Jordan, "To Be Equal," *CD*, Feb. 1, 1975; "Find Blacks, Republicans Compatible," *CD*, May 10, 1975.

3. NNPA, "Congratulations," *SR*, Jan. 18, 1975.

4. "Black Secretary of Transportation," *CP*, Feb. 1, 1975; "The Cabinet: A Quiet Activist," *Newsweek*, Jan. 27, 1975.

5. "Coleman Sworn as Cabinet Member," *NYAN*, Mar. 15, 1975.

6. Counterexamples to black Republicans' claims clearly exist. For example, Council of 100 cochair Willie Williams of South Carolina was appointed to a two-year term to the U.S. Civil Rights Commission in 1975. Likewise, Judge Henry Bramwell was appointed to the federal bench in 1975, making him the first black federal judge in the history of the eastern district of New York. That being said, these counterexamples are few and far between, reflecting a lack of institutional change within the party. See "Civil Rights, Appointee," *NYAN*, Mar. 22, 1975; "Brooklyn Political Scene," *NYAN*, Mar. 29, 1975.

7. Champion, *Blacks in the Republican Party*, 33–34.

8. HGE to Jan Milliken, Letter, Aug. 25, 1975, box 925, WHCF Name File, folder Edmonds, Helen G., GRF Library.

9. Ethel L. Payne, "In Snub of Lafontant," *CD*, Feb. 4, 1974; "ABA Didn't Dump Her," *CD*, Feb. 5, 1974; "Jewel Lafontant," *CD*, Feb. 9, 1974; "Percy on Spot in Choosing Judge," *CD*, Sept. 8, 1975; George Emmett, "Bar Group Revives Drive for Black Federal Judge," *CT*, Aug. 25, 1975.

10. "Ford Met with More Blacks than Any Other President," *ADW*, Apr. 24 1975.

11. "The Outlook for Ford," *CD*, July 14, 1975.

12. During the summer of 1975, the RNC produced three half-hour infomercials entitled, "Republicans Are People Too." The show featured "everyday Republicans" including farmers, students, mechanics, and women discussing why they belonged to the GOP. The RNC spent a considerable amount on the advertisements as part a rehabilitation overhaul; the first one, for example, cost $124,000. Historian Suzanne O'Dea suggests that the commercials were a financial and critical failure, generating approximately $11,000 in contributions and reaching only three million homes. Likewise, the infomercials revealed the party's desperation and confusion in the post-Watergate period; yet while they had little impact on the general population, the commercials "motivated the faithful to action." In total, the GOP spent about $700,000 on its reform program during the early and mid-1970s. Suzanne O'Dea, *Madam Chairman: Mary Louise Smith and the Republican Revival after Watergate* (Columbia: University of Missouri Press, 2012), chap. 7; "Image of the Republican Party Needs Changing," *Wellsville Daily Reporter*, June 30, 1975; Robert Shogan, "Parlay Gives Ringside View of GOP Struggle," *LAT*, Mar. 9, 1975.

13. "Black GOP Leader in Washington," *NYAN*, Mar. 8, 1975; Elaine Jenkins to MLS, Letter, Feb. 24, 1975; MLS to EJ, Letter, Feb. 25, 1975, both in box 30, MLS Papers.

14. John L. Wilks, "Opening Up the GOP," *Focus* (Joint Center for Political Studies) 3, no. 3 (Jan. 1975): 3, box 30, MLS Papers; "Nat'l Black GOP Council Chairman Lashes Demos," *ADW*, Mar. 6, 1975. See also Catherine E. Rymph, *Republican Women: Feminism and Conservatives from Suffrage through the Rise of the New Right* (Chapel Hill: University of North Carolina Press, 2006), chaps. 7 and 8; Mason and Morgan, *Seeking a New Majority*, 76–83.

15. Chas H. Loeb, "World on View: Revamped Republicans?" *CP*, Mar. 15, 1975.

16. M. Stanton Evans, "McGovernizing the GOP," *HE*, 35, no. 8 (Feb. 22, 1975); Lou Cannon, "GOP to Debate Plan to Attract Women, Young, Minorities," *WP*, Mar. 5, 1975; Bill Anderson, "A Republican Resuscitation Squad," *CT*, Mar. 6, 1975.

17. "Reagan's Party Concept," *CD*, Apr. 12, 1975.

18. Jon Margolis, "G.O.P. Yields on '76 Rules," *CT*, Mar. 7, 1975; R. W. Apple Jr., "GOP Chiefs Vote Softened Reform," *NYT*, Mar. 7, 1975. See also R. W. Apple Jr., "G.O.P. Panel Splits on Party Reform," *NYT*, Mar. 5, 1975; Robert Shogan, "Compromise on GOP Minority Delegates OKd," *LAT*, Mar. 7, 1975.

19. MLS to Betty Andujar, Letter, Dec. 20, 1974, box 65, folder Minorities, MLS Papers.

20. Roosevelt Montgomery to MLS, Letter, Mar. 11, 1975; MLS to RM, Letter, Mar. 14, 1975; William M. Smith to GRF, Letter, Mar. 10, 1975, both in box 30, MLS Papers.

21. Phill Trevillion to MLS, Letter, Mar. 5, 1976, box 30, MLS Papers.

22. Charles G. Hurst, "Black Focus," *CD*, Apr. 12, 1975.

23. Chuck Stone, "Color the White House Unequal," Apr. 28, 1975, in box 30, MLS Papers.

24. Gloria Toote, "The U in Housing," *OP*, Mar. 27, 1974; Gloria Toote, "The U in Housing," *OP*, Apr. 28, 1974; Gloria Toote, "The U in Housing: Individual Rights," *ADW*, Oct. 15, 1974.

25. "Can Blacks Serve Equal Rights and a Republican Administration?" *SR*, Mar. 22, 1975; Simeon Booker, "Ticker Tape U.S.A.," *Jet*, Mar. 13, 1976; "Gloria Toote Out as Asst. HUD Secretary," *Jet*, Mar. 27, 1975; Simon Anekwe, "Blacks Ask: Where Was Women's Lib?" *NYAN*, Mar. 22, 1975; "Blacks Support Dr. Toote," *NYAN*, Mar. 29, 1975.

26. Maurice A. Dawkins, "EEOC Chairman Appointment Process: A Black Republican Viewpoint," position paper, [Apr. 1975], in box 30, MLS Papers.

27. William Raspberry, "Discrimination at Transportation," *WP*, May 9, 1975.

28. "An Interview with William T. Coleman," *BE* 5, no. 11 (June 1, 1975): 124–128, 147.

29. Ibid.

30. "$16 Million for Airport Expressway Is Approved," *ADW*, May 1, 1975; Louis Martin, "'Big M' Tells How to Get Action," *CD*, Aug. 2, 1975; "Coretta King to Talk at UL Meet," *CD*, July 23, 1975; "Plight of Minorities and Poor Theme of Urban League Confab," *NYAN*, July 9, 1975; William T. Coleman, *Counsel for the Situation: Shaping the Law to Realize America's Promise* (Washington, D.C.: Brookings Institution Press, 2010), 256–257.

31. Ed Brooke, "Speech before the Annual National Urban League Conference," July 28, 1975, box 30, MLS Papers; Charles E. Price, "Full Employment, A Worthwhile Goal," *ADW*, July 31, 1975. See also "Brooke Pushes Nat'l Health Insurance for Tots, Mothers," *ADW*, Nov. 4, 1976. See also "Congress Hears Clay Talk on New Black Politics," *OP*, Feb. 25, 1971.

32. "Launching Program to Aid Black Republicans," *NYAN*, Mar. 15, 1975; "John Wilks top Black in GOP Nat. Committee," *NYAN*, Apr. 16, 1975.

33. William Torrey, "State-Wide Effort Role for Black GOP Council," *ADW*, Aug. 28, 1975; "Black GOP in Florida Organized," *ADW*, July 18, 1975; "Black Republicans Form New Group In Manhattan," *NYAN*, Dec. 6, 1975.

34. "BRAC Buttons," *CD*, Aug. 11, 1975; "Black GOP Group Hosts D.C. Bicentennial Trip," *ADW*, Aug. 12, 1975; "Buttons, Buttons, Who Has the Buttons," [1975—1976], Black Republican Appointees Council, "Press Release: 'Spirit of '76' Cruise," Aug. 5, 1975, all in box A12, folder: Blacks—Voter Background, President Ford Campaign Records, DeBolt Files, GRF Library (hereinafter called PFC Records).

35. SSS to Helen G. Edmonds, Letter, Sept. 14, 1975, box 925, WHCF Name File, folder Edmonds, Helen G., GRF Library.

36. "Scott on Way Out at White House?" *WAA*, Aug. 2, 1975; "Scott and Fratricide," *AA*, Aug. 9, 1975; John W. Lewis Jr., "54 White House Aides, 1 Black," *PC*, July 19, 1975; "Stan Scott Still at White House, Ford Commends Him," *CP*, Aug. 30, 1975.

37. "GOP Struggle for Power," *PC*, Aug. 30, 1975.

38. Bo Callaway, Memo for the Record, Aug. 28, 1975, box 19, folder Lincoln Day, Gwen A. Anderson Files, 1974–77, GRF Library (hereinafter called GAA Files).

39. Kruse, *White Flight*, 230–231, 252–253.

40. "Stan Scott Out at White House," *CP*, Aug. 9, 1975; Bill Anderson, "Foes Fail to 'Get' Ford's Black Aide," *CT*, Aug. 12, 1975; "Callaway Rules Our 'Southern Strategy,'" *WP*, July 3, 1975.

41. "Mr. Ford's Opinions," *The Crisis*, Nov. 1975, 333.

42. "Ford's First Year," *CD*, Aug. 13, 1975; "Anti-Busing Ford," *CD*, Sept. 17, 1975; Helen Thomas, "Laud Ford for Rapping Busing," *CD*, Sept. 18, 1975.

43. "'Bo' Updates Ga. GOP on Ford Campaign," *ADW*, Aug. 22, 1975.

44. Brooke worked to defeat a number of antibusing measures. In early 1975, for example, Brooke—with the support of the NAACP—helped defeat the Holt Amendment, a proposal introduced by Republican congresswoman Marjorie Holt of Maryland. The amendment would have prohibited the federal government from instituting financial sanctions against public schools that ignored desegregation orders including busing. That same year, he also defeated an amendment proposed by Republican senator Jesse Helms of North Carolina that would have prevented HEW from keeping any "records, files, reporters, or statistics" necessary to "identify segregated school systems." Brooke, however, was unsuccessful in preventing a 1975 amendment proposed by Democratic senator Joseph Biden of Delaware, which required that no funds from $36 billion appropriations bill "shall be used to require any school, school system, or other educational institution, as a condition for receiving funds, grants, or other benefits from the federal government, to assign students or teachers by race." Likewise, Brooke was unsuccessful in securing the passage of an amendment that would have nullified antibusing amendments; the "Brooke Amendment" fell apart due to technical errors in the fall of 1975. "Brooke Opposes Busing Bill," *Virgin Islands Daily News*, May 16, 1974; "Senate Crushes Bid to Nullify Busing Bill," *Star-News*, Sept. 26, 1975. See also "Brooke Rips Plan for Law to Bar Busing," *CD*, Nov. 13, 1975; "NAACP and Brooke Lead in Holt Amendment Defeat," *NYAN*, Jan. 11, 1975; "Senators Act to Bar Busing," *CD*, Sept. 18, 1975; EWB, "Busing—Fact and Fiction," *The Brooke Report*, [1971], folder Newsletter 1971; EWB, "Busing: Myths & Realities," *The Brooke Report*, Sept.–Oct. 1974, folder Newsletters 1974, both documents in EWB Papers.

45. Gerald Ford to Clay Claiborne, Letter, Apr. 23, 1975, BSMC Papers.

46. A Harris poll from 1971 found that, though 45 percent of African Americans favored busing, 47 percent opposed it and 8 percent had no opinion. Gallup polls from 1974 and 1976 found near-identical results; however, other sources contradict this information. Earl and Merle Black, for example, argue that polls from 1974 showed that 75 percent of African Americans supported busing. Untitled Harris Survey, [1971–1973], box 14, folder Black Survey 1973, Patterson Files; Gary Orfield and Susan E. Eaton, *Dismantling Desegregation: The Quiet Reversal of Brown v. Board of Education* (New York: New Press, 1997), 108; Black and Black, *Politics and Society*, 158.

47. BSMC, *BSMC Newsletter*, [1978], BSMC Papers; "Most Black Parents Oppose Busing Leader of Group Claims," *Avalanche Journal*, Apr. 15, 1977; Caren Marcus, "Busing Hurts Blacks, School Official [Tells?] Board," *Pittsburgh Press*, Oct. 25, 1979.

48. Bob Wilson, "Remarks in Congressional Record," *CR*, 121, no. 157 (Oct. 28, 1975), reprint in BSMC Papers. See also Dawson, *Black Visions*.

49. John B. Combs, "Capital Comment," *CP*, May 24, 1975.

50. Lin Hilburn, "Who Needs Black Silent Majority," *LAS*, May 29, 1975.

51. Wilson, "Congressional Record," Oct. 1975; BSMC, Form Letter, [1975], BSMC Papers; Simeon Booker, "Ticker Tape U.S.A.," *Jet*, June 22, 1972.

52. "Brooke Opposes," *VIDN*, May 1974; "Busing Bill," *SN*, Sept. 1975; "Brooke Rips," *CD*, Nov. 1975; "NAACP and Brooke," *NYAN*, Jan. 1975; "Bar Busing," *CD*, Sept. 1975.

53. The *ADW* called for an "interracial citizens committee to work with the school board and other parties in helping to formulate a plan which will meet the approval of the courts." "A Timely Move," *ADW*, Jan. 9, 1976.

54. Gregory Simms, "Baptists Give Ford Hearty 'Amen' at 95th Annual Confab," *Jet*, Oct. 2, 1975.

55. "Mr. Ford's Opinions," *The Crisis*, Nov. 1975, 333.

56. "Black GOP Council Meets in Raleigh," *PC*, Sept. 27, 1975.

57. John B. Combs, "Capital Comment: Blacks Won't Buy Reagan," *CP*, Dec. 6, 1975; "Important Press Conferences," *ADW*, Nov. 13, 1975.

58. Sadie Feddoes, "Please be Seated," *NYAN*, Dec. 20, 1975; Billy Rowe, "Billy Rowe's Notebook," *NYAN*, Dec. 3, 1975.

59. John C. Calhoun to James T. Lynn, Memo, Dec. 8, 1975, box 1, White House Operations, Foster Chanock Files, 1975–76, GRF Library.

60. CTP to AF, Mailgram, Feb. 26, 1976, box 3, folder Arthur A. Fletcher, Arthur A. Fletcher Files, GRF Library.

61. SCJ to Robert Marik, Letter, Feb. 5, 1976, box A12, DeBolt Files.

62. Larnie Horton and Floyd McKissick, members of the Council of 100, were both involved in this effort; however, the campaign dropped McKissick after they learned that he was being investigated for federal contract violations. Larnie Horton to Mimi Austin, Memo, Dec. 5, 1975; Bo Callaway, Memo for the Record, Jan. 5. 1976, both in box A12, DeBolt Files.

63. BC, Meeting Outline, Dec. 19, 1975, in ibid.

64. BC to Dick Cheney, Memo, Nov. 7, 1975, in ibid.

65. MA to BC, "Black Citizens Program Memo," Nov. 7, 1975; Larnie Horton LGH to RM, Letter, Mar. 10, 1976; Black Citizens for the Election of President Ford, Steering Committee List, [1975–1976], all in ibid.

66. BC, Outline, Dec. 1975, in ibid.

67. [Larnie Horton] to Stu Spencer, Letter, Feb. 10, 1976, in ibid.

68. John L. Keenan, "Address to Black Americans by Gerald R. Ford," Sample Speech, [1976], in ibid.

69. Undated Press Release and Caption on BRAC [1975–76]; Bob Visser to RM, Memo, Feb. 6, 1976, both in ibid.

70. BC to Ulysses W. Boykin, Letter, Aug. 26, 1975; BC, Memo for the Record, Aug. 28, 1975, David M. Spark, to BC, Letter, Dec. 3, 1975; BC to Jack E. Robinson, Letter, Dec. 3, 1975; Robert St. Clair to BC, Letter, Feb. 3, 1976; Montgomery Beard to RM, Letter and Resume, Nov. 21, 1975; BC Memo for the Record, Jan. 1976; John Calhoun to Bill Baroody, Memo, Feb. 25, 1976; LGH to RM, Letter, Feb. 26, 1976; Carolyn Booth to Bill Low, Memo and Resume for Sarah Jenkins, Jan. 23, 1976; LGH to RM, Letter, Mar. 2, 1976; LGH to RM, Letter, Mar. 10, 1976; L. P. Lewis to Nola Haerle, Mar. 10, 1976, all in ibid.

71. Simon Anekwe, "Blacks Had Little Impact on Republican Convention," *NYAN*, Aug. 28, 1976; Warren Brown, "A Right-Wing Reactionary? No, A Black GOP Member," *WP*, Aug. 15, 1976.

72. By Mar. 1976, PFC was very active in three special voter group areas: Senior Citizens, Business and Professional Volunteers, and Youth. Robert Marik noted that the campaign needed to move quickly to establish groups for Ethnic, Farm, Labor, and Hispanic Voters. Interestingly, "Women" seemed to occupy the same liminal space as "Black Voters," as Marik appeared unsure as to how best to incorporate women into the campaign, although he recognized it was necessary. Bob Marik, Memo on Special Voter Groups, Mar. 5, 1976, box A15, DeBolt Files.

73. NH to RM, Memo, Mar. 22, 1976; [PFC], Press Release, [Oct. 1976], box A12, in ibid.

74. John C. Calhoun to Bill Baroody, Memo, May 27, 1976, box B10, PFC Records, Hughes Subject File, GRF Library.

75. See, for example, the field reports of the Black Citizens Program: RM to Bob Visser, Memo, Dec. 30, 1975; LGH to RM, Letter, Mar. 2, 1976; George J. Despot to JCC, Letter, Feb. 24, 1976, both in box A12, DeBolt Files.

76. Nathan Wright Jr., "Representing the People," *CP*, Feb. 28, 1976.

77. Robert L. Mitchell to GRF, Letter Re: Florida NBRC Support for GRF, Feb. 24, 1976; U. W. Boykin, Press Release, Jan. 5, 1976; LPL to NH, Letter, Mar. 1976; LPL to Rogers C. Morton, Apr. 7, 1976; GRF to RLM, Letter, Apr. 13, 1976; UWB to Ed Sexton, Letter,

June 18, 1975, all in box A12, DeBolt Files; "Black Republicans to Hold Issues Conference in L.A.," *SR*, May 14, 1976.

78. "Blacks Unwanted in GOP," *PC*, Apr. 3, 1976; Vernon Jarrett, "Blacks No Longer Tied to Democrats," *CT*, Apr. 23, 1976.

79. Vernon Jarrett, "Blacks No Longer Tied to Democrats," *CT*, Apr. 23, 1976.

80. Wm. M. Smith to JCC, Letter, July 13, 1976; JCC to WMS, Letter, Aug. 31, 1976, box 19, folder Volunteer Offers, GAA Files.

81. Edith M. Austin, "Sen. Brooke Sparkles Black Republicans: Endorses Ford, Turns Thumb Down on Vice-Presidency," May 22, 1976; "Black Republicans to Hold Issues Conference in L.A.," *SR*, May 15, 1976; "Brooke Speaks Here," *LAS*, May 6, 1976; Eddye K. Wells, "Social Activities," *LAS*, June 3, 1976.

82. Carlton Jones, "Black Republicans: Looking for an Alternative," *SR*, July 31, 1976.

83. NBR, "From Douglass to Brooke: First National Convention, NBRC," Convention Program, Aug. 13, 1976, Ulysses W. Boykin Papers, 1974–1976, Burton Historical Collection, Detroit Public Library (hereinafter called UWB Papers).

84. Ibid; Brown, "A Right-Wing Reactionary?" *WP*, Aug. 1976; "Benefit for Black GOP Rep. Draws Anger—From Blacks," *Jet*, Nov. 27, 1975.

85. B. Drummond Ayres Jr., "Schweiker Bids for Votes of the 76 Black Delegates," *NYT*, Aug. 15, 1976; "Cummings Cops Black Republican Chair Nod," *Jet*, Sept. 2, 1976.

86. Nathaniel Wright, "Black Empowerment: Black Republican Rumblings," *Scanner*, Aug. 26, 1976.

87. Brown, "A Right-Wing Reactionary?" *WP*, Aug. 1976; "Platform Pressure by Black Republicans," *SR*, Aug. 28, 1976; Ayres, "Schweiker Bids," *NYT*, Aug. 1976.

88. "Cummings Cops Black Republican Chair Nod," *Jet*, Sept. 2, 1976; JLW to MLS, Memo, Sept. 3, 1976, box 6, folder National Black Republican Council Lawsuit, Bobbie Greene Kilberg 1974–77, GRF Library.

89. Champion, *Blacks in the Republican Party*, 26–27.

90. Henry Lucas, "NBRC Issues Statement," NBRC Platform, Aug. 10, 1976, box 19, folder Lincoln Day, GAA Files.

91. Vernon Jarrett, "Dr. Henry Lucas: Black Conservative Speaks Out," *CT*, Aug. 21, 1976; Champion, *Blacks in the Republican Party*, 31.

92. Timothy L. Jenkins to AF, Proposal on the "Development of Constructive Alternatives to Compulsory Busing," Apr. 22, 1976; AF to James Cannon, Memo, May 11, 1976, box 1, folder Match Institution, Domestic Council, Arthur A. Fletcher Files 1976, GRF Library; "Integration Minus Busing Sought by President Ford," *ADW*, June 15, 1976.

93. Lucas, "NBRC Issues," Platform, Aug. 1976, box 19, GAA Files; Henry Lucas, "Outgoing GOP Comment," *The Skanner*, Aug. 26, 1976; "Platform Pressure by Black Republicans," *SR*, Aug. 28, 1976; Brown, "A Right-Wing Reactionary?" *WP*, Aug. 1976; Champion, *Blacks in the Republican Party*, 31.

94. When compared to the 1972 GOP convention, black Republicans success was mixed. The percentage of black delegates and alternates decreased in twenty-two states; seven states that had black delegates in 1972 had none in 1976. In 1972, 38 percent of the black delegates were women, whereas in 1976 only 29 percent were women. "Record Number of Blacks at GOP Convention," *OP*, Aug. 18, 1976.

95. "Plummer Addresses Republican Blacks," *The Skanner*, Aug. 19, 1976; Simeon Booker, "Black Delegates Bolster Ford; Help Him Triumph," *Jet*, Sept. 2, 1976; Wright, "Rumblings," *Scanner*, Aug. 1976.

96. Douglas E. Kneeland, "Reagan Wooing Delegates and Arguing Rule Change," *NYT*, Aug. 17, 1976; Major Robinson, "'Why I Voted for Ronald Reagan!—Gloria Toote," *NYAN*, Sept. 4, 1976.

97. B. Drummond Ayres Jr., "Schweiker Bids for Votes of the 76 Black Delegates," *NYT*, Aug. 15, 1976.

98. Just as important was Reagan's selection of Richard Schweiker as a running mate. His presence reassured Toote, allowing her to comfortably endorse Reagan as the party's nominee. In fact, Schweiker's "stunning selection" was designed to do exactly that. As the conservative *National Review* remarked, Reagan's vice presidential choice was an acknowledgment of the "practical limits" of Goldwater conservatism. That the majority of Americans, the *Review* wrote, had rejected federal intervention on issues like busing did not necessarily mean that they craved "limited government." Schweiker, affiliated with the liberal wing of the Republican Party and favoring an interventionist approach, was thus an acknowledgment that dogmatic conservatism would not win presidential elections. It was a strategy that the Reagan would adopt again four years later, when moderate Republican George H. W. Bush joined him on the ticket as the vice presidential nominee. "Tex Harris' Roving Camera," *NYAN*, Aug. 7, 1976. See also "Republicans: 1976," *National Review*, Sept. 3, 1976.

99. In 1974 Gerald Ford placed Ed Brooke on a confidential short list for potential vice presidential candidates, alongside Anne Armstrong, Howard Baker, George H. W. Bush, Barry Goldwater, Charles Percy, Ronald Reagan, and Nelson Rockefeller. The New York governor eventually became vice president; when he announced he would not seek reelection as vice president, Ford again considered Brooke, among others. Choosing Brooke, or so strategists thought, would balance Ford's moderate-to-conservative philosophy and attract black voters, white liberals and moderates, and independents of all races. Jim Goodwin, "Black Reflects on GOP Parley," *PC*, Aug. 26, 1976; "Brooke Backed as Veep," *NYAN*, Aug. 14, 1976; "Ford: Brooke in Race as Mate," *Palm Beach Post*, Nov. 15, 1975.

100. Wright, "Rumblings," *Scanner* Aug. 26, 1976.

101. Eddie N. Williams, "Black Delegates: The Deciding Factor?" *WP*, Aug. 14, 1976.

102. Simeon Booker, "Black Delegates Bolster Ford; Help Him Triumph," *Jet*, Sept. 2, 1976; Wright, "Rumblings," *Scanner* Aug. 26, 1976.

103. Vernon Jarrett, "Why GOP Blacks Would Buy a Ford," *CT*, Aug. 27, 1976.

104. Ibid.

105. Vernon Jarrett, "Could Reagan Be Sold to Blacks?" *CT*, Aug. 15, 1976; MD to Ronald Reagan, Letter, Dec. 3, 1975, box 45, folder Dawkins, Maurice A., General Correspondence, Robert T. Hartmann 1974–77, GRF Library.

106. "Gloria Toote Lights Fire under Black GOP Delegates," *Jet*, Sept. 2, 1976.

107. Gloria Toote, "Ronald Reagan Seconding Speech," [1976], box 58, folder 14, Citizens for Reagan Records 1975–1986, Hoover Institution Archives, Stanford University. See also Candace Williams, "Black Republicans Maneuver to Solidify Their Interests," *Core Magazine*, Fall 1976, box F15, People for Ford Office: Black Desk Files, President Ford Committee Records, 1975–76, GRF Library.

108. Major Robinson, "'Why I Voted for Ronald Reagan!—Gloria Toote," *NYAN*, Sept. 4, 1976; Hazel Garland, "Video Vignettes," *PC*, Aug. 26, 1976; Margot Hornblower, "Reagan to Delegates: The Choice Is Yours," *WP*, Aug. 18, 1976; Joseph Lelyveld, "Wavering Delegates Find a Place in Sun," *NYT*, Aug. 18, 1976; Frank Lynn, "New York and New Jersey Uncommitted Face Pressure," *NYT*, Aug. 12, 1976; "Say It Isn't So . . . Gloria!" *NYAN*, Aug. 28, 1976; "'Why I Voted for Ronald Reagan!'—Gloria Toote," *NYAN*, Sept. 4, 1976; "Republicans: 1976," *NR*, Sept. 1976.

109. "Education Plank" in the Republican Party Platform of 1976, Aug. 18, 1976, *APP*, UCSB.

110. Alan Sverdlik, "A Black Aftermath of the GOP Convention," *NYAN*, Sept. 5, 1976; Brown, "A Right-Wing Reactionary?" *WP*, Aug. 1976; "Conservatives Show Platform Strength," *HE* 36, no. 34 (Aug. 21, 1976): 5.

111. Sverdlik, "Black Aftermath," *NYAN*, Sept. 1976.

112. William O. Walker, "Down the Big Road: Negro and the 1976 Campaign," *CP*, Sept. 4, 1976.

113. Simeon Booker, "Black Delegates Bolster Ford; Help Him Triumph," *Jet*, Sept. 2, 1976.

114. Jarrett, "Buy a Ford," *CT*, Aug. 1976.

115. Simeon Booker, "Black Delegates," *Jet*, Sept. 1976; Ethel L. Payne, "By the GOP Door," *PC*, Sept. 4, 1976; Vernon Jarrett, "Blacks Didn't Use Balance of Power," *CT*, Aug. 20, 1976.

116. Booker, "Black Delegates," *Jet*, Sept. 1976; Payne, "GOP Door," *PC*, Sept. 1976; Jarrett, "Didn't Use," *CT*, Aug. 1976.

117. In the fall of 1976, Curtis Perkins of the Black Council for Republican Politics, Inc. (formerly NCAAR) also sued the RNC, charging the national committee with racial discrimination. Simon Anekwe, "Black Republican Suing Pres. Ford and GOP Natl. Committee," *NYAN*, Sept. 4, 1976.

118. "Affidavit of John L. Wilks," Oct. 18, 1976, in *Ed Bivens, et al. v. Republican National Committee, et al.* in United States District Court for the District of Columbia, box 64, folder NBRC Lawsuit, MLS Papers; "Bivens Challenges Black Republican Council Election," *Jet*, Sept. 9, 1976; "Cummings Sworn in as Black GOP Group Chief," *Jet*, Sept. 30, 1976.

119. "Black Republicans," *NYAN*, Nov. 26, 1975. ; "Advisors Not Consulted in Boston Issue," *Ocala Star-Banner*, May 19, 1976; "Charlie Cherokee Says," *CD*, Sept. 20, 1976. See also Martin Dinkins, Telegram on Earl Butz Issue, Oct. 4, 1976, box F15, Black Desk Files.

120. Robert Keyes to Elly Peterson, Letter, July 23, 1976, box F12, PFC Records, Keyes Files; "Reagan's Last Gamble," *Newsweek*, Aug. 9, 1976.

121. SCJ to JCC, Letter, Aug. 24, 1976, box F14; NBRC, "A Proposal: Participation of the NBRC in 1976 Campaign for Re-election of GRF," [1976], and NBRC, "Top Level Briefings for Blacks," Proposal, Sept. 29, 1976; Memo to RK Re: Lionel Hampton Suggestions, [1976], box F15, all documents in Black Desk Files.

122. James Cummings, "Report: National Black Republican Council Activities in Support of Re-election of President Gerald R. Ford," Sept. 30, 1976, box F15, Black Desk Files; The Winning Edge Invitation and Program, Oct. 1976, box F13, Keyes Files.

123. NBRC, News Release, Sept. 15, 1976; JC to GRF, Letter, Sept. 14, 1976; JC to EP, Letter, Sept. 13, 1976, box F15, Black Desk Files.

124. NBRC, Press Release, Oct. 15, 1976, box F13, Keyes Files; "Republican Council Activities in Support of Re-election of President Gerald R. Ford," Sept. 30, 1976, box F15, Black Desk Files.

125. James A. Baker to JC, Letter, Oct. 13, 1976, in Ford Disc 2; EP to JC, Letter, Sept. 19, 1976; John Calhoun to Bobbie Kilberg, Memo, Sept. 21, 1976; Robert S. Carter to JC, Letter, Sept. 8, 1976; James Cummings to Robert Keyes, Letter, Oct. 8, 1976; JC to PFC, "Proposed Budget," Oct. 8, 1976, all in box B15, Black Desk Files.

126. Martin Dinkins to Ulysses Boykin, Letter, Sept. 28, 1976, box 65, UWB Papers; National Advisory Committee, People for Ford, Member List, [1976], box F12, Keyes Files; No Author to Royston C. Hughes, handwritten note, [1976], box B4, PFC Records, Hughes Subject File, GRF Library.

127. RK to John T. Dunlop, Letter, Nov. 14, 1975; [Martin Dinkins], Memo, Sept. 19, 1976, both in box F12, Keyes Files, folder Calhoun, John and Minority Issues.

128. RK to JTD, Letter, Nov. 1975; Dinkins, Memo, Sept. 19, 1976, box F12, Keyes Files.

129. PFC Member List, [1976]; Lionel Hampton, Form Letter, [1976]; EP, Memo, [1976], all in box F12, Keyes Files.

130. Black Desk Budget & Goals 1976; EP, Memo, Aug. 8 [1976], both in box F12, Keyes Files.

131. MD to RK, Memo on Black Ministers, Oct. 6, 1976; MD, Status Report People for Ford—Black Desk, Oct. 7, 1976, both in box F12, Keyes Files; Rev. James H. Mims to GRF, Letter, Sept. 17, 1975, both in box F13, folder Notes, Keyes Files. See also U. W. Boykin to Members of NBRC, Campaign Letter, Oct. 7, 1976, UWB Papers; "Pledging Support to the President," Picture Caption," ADW, Aug. 19, 1976; Picture Caption, "Rev. Maddox Joins Ford," Savannah Tribune, Sept. 1, 1976; "Carter First since 1968 to Campaign in Harlem," Jet, Nov. 4, 1976.

132. William Seawright to GRF, Mailgram, Oct. 13, 1976; Jim Field to JCC, Memo, Oct. 15, 1976, box 1, Office of White House Operations, H. James Field Jr., Staff Assistant: Files 1976, GRF Library; Rev. E. T. Henry to Black Desk, Request for Black Speakers, [Oct. 1976] in Black Desk—Status Report, box B15, Black Desk Files.

133. MD to RK, Memo, Oct. 4, 1976, box F12, Keyes Files.

134. MD, Status Report People for Ford—Black Desk, Oct. 7, 1976, in ibid.

135. Jim Cleaver, "Political Potpourri," LAS, Sept. 23, 1976; "Black GOPs, Demos to Debate Issues on PBS TV Oct. 3," ADW, Oct. 1, 1976. See also John Calhoun, "Calhoun Reviews Ford's Priorities," ADW, Oct. 22, 1976; John Calhoun, "Promises, Promises," ADW, Nov. 2, 1976.

136. AAF, "Progress Made by Blacks in Politics," draft speech, 1976; Outline for AAF Speech, Oct. 1976, both in box 3, folder Speeches, Arthur A. Fletcher Files 1976, GRF Library; Yvonne Shinhoster, "Ford's Job for Blacks Hailed as 'Outstanding,'" ADW, Oct. 28, 1976.

137. Ethel Payne, "Profile: Ford, Dole," PC, Sept. 18, 1976.

138. Jack Bass, "Southern Republicans: Their Plight Is Getting Worse," WP, July 12, 1977; Ronald W. Walters, Freedom Is Not Enough: Black Voters, Black Candidates, and American Presidential Politics (Lanham: Rowan & Littlefield, 2005), 89–90. See also "Splitting Tickets by Blacks Elected GOP Congressman in Va.," ADW, Nov. 11, 1976. See also Kabaservice, Rule and Ruin, 348–349; "How Various Groups Voted in Presidential Election," chart, CT, Nov. 7, 1976.

139. Ibid. See also "Out of the Cocoon," Time, Sept. 27, 1976; Carroll Kilpatrick, "Nixon Tells Editors, 'I'm Not a Crook,'" WP, Nov. 17, 1973.

140. There is no historical or contemporary consensus on Gerald Ford's share of the black vote in 1976. Sources offer contradictory numbers, ranging from a low of 6 percent to a high of 17 percent. As of 2012, the JCPES estimates that Ford received 15 percent of the black vote; however, in 1976, the nonpartisan think tank claimed that the president only received 6 percent, a figure that was widely used by the press. By 1980, the JCPES stated that Ford had garnered slightly less than 8 percent; to compare, that same year, the New York Times stated that the former president had received 16 percent. All of these figures are highly contentious and flawed; for the purposes of this book, I use the 8 percent estimate because it was the figure used consistently by the RNC, DNC, NBRC, and Ronald Reagan's presidential campaign. Bositis, Blacks and the RNC, 2012; Austin Scott, "Study Puts Carter's Share of the Black Vote at 94 Per Cent," WP, Nov. 5, 1976; "Survey Finds Some Blacks Helped Ronald Reagan Win," OP, Nov. 26, 1980; Adam Clymer, "The Collapse of a Coalition," NYT, Nov. 5, 1980.

141. "Carter Is Our Choice," NYAN, Oct. 30, 1976; "Black Vote Is Heaviest in Years," NYAN, Nov. 6, 1976. See also "Sentinel's Choice: Jimmy Carter," LAS, Oct. 28, 1976; "Why President Ford Deserves Election," ADW, Oct. 22, 1976.

142. W. O. Walker, "Southern Strategy Sinks Republicans," CP, Nov. 6, 1976; A. S. Doc Young, "Awkward Time for a Column," CP, Nov. 4, 1976; A. S. Doc Young, "A Political

Platform," *CP*, Nov. 18, 1976. See also "GOP Facing Bleak Future," *CP*, Nov. 20, 1976; W. O. Walker, "Down the Big Road," *CP*, Nov. 20, 1976; W. O. Walker, "Down the Big Road," *CP*, Nov. 13, 1976.

143. Champion, *Blacks in the Republican Party*, 83.

144. Tom Ruffin, "Analysis of People for Ford Operation," n.d., box 15, General Subject File NRCC, Robert P. Visser Papers 1972–78, GRF Library.

145. BK to EP, Letter, Nov. 10, 1976, in ibid.

146. Simeon Booker, "Ticker Tape, U.S.A.," *Jet*, Dec. 16, 1976.

147. BK to EP, Letter, Nov. 1976, box 15, General Subject File NRCC, Robert P. Visser Papers 1972–78, GRF Library.

148. "Unhappy GOP Blacks," *PC*, Oct. 9, 1976; Alex Poinsett, "1975: Another Year of Erosion," *Ebony*, Jan. 1976.

149. Champion, *Blacks in the Republican Party*, 83–84.

150. NBRC Congressional Relations Committee, "A Report to the NBRC Executive Committee," Report, Mar. 17, 1978, EWB Papers; "Black Council Meets," *Prescott Courier*, Oct. 9, 1977.

151. Nathan Wright, "Opinion," *NYAN*, Feb. 7, 1976.

CHAPTER 7. THE TIME OF THE BLACK ELEPHANT

1. Jesse Jackson, "Jesse Jackson on the GOP—Speech," *CT*, Feb. 6, 1978; Mary Mc-Grory, "GOP Discovers Black Message," *HC*, Jan. 20, 1978; Mary McGrory, "Jesse in the Promised Land," *CT*, Jan. 25, 1978; Eleanor Randolph, "Jackson to GOP: Blacks May Be Key in '80," *CT*, Jan. 21, 1978; Robert Shogan, "Blacks and GOP Need Each Other," *LAT*, Jan. 21, 1978; "Jesse's Chance," *CT*, Jan. 11, 1978; William Claiborne, "Jackson Urges GOP to Appeal to Blacks," *WP*, Jan. 21, 1978; Adam Clymer, "Jesse Jackson Tells Receptive G.O.P. It Can Pick up Votes of Blacks," *NYT*, Jan. 21, 1978; "Wooing the Black Vote," *Time*, Jan. 30, 1978; Benjamin Hooks, "Blacks and the GOP," *NYAN*, Aug. 27, 1978; William Brock, Letters to Howard H. Baker, John Rhodes et al., Jan. 10, 1978, all in box 56, folder 33, William H. Brock Papers, James D. Hoskins Library, University of Tennessee, Knoxville (hereinafter called Brock Papers). See also "Jesse Jackson Urges Blacks to Terminate 'One Party Allegiance,'" *ADW*, May 29, 1977.

2. Charles W. Hucker, "Blacks and the GOP: A Cautious Courtship," *Congressional Quarterly*, Apr. 29, 1978, box 24, folder Republicans—Blacks, Civil Rights & Justice, Staff Offices Domestic Policy Staff, Bob Malson, Presidential Papers of Jimmy Carter (hereinafter called Malson Files).

3. "Politicians—Part of the Problem," *HC*, Feb. 26, 1976; James M. Naughton, "Some Republicans Fearful Party Is on Its Last Legs," *NYT*, May 31, 1976.

4. Robert Shogan, "Blacks and GOP Need Each Other—Jesse Jackson," *LAT*, Jan. 21, 1978; "Black Vote," *Time*, Jan. 1978. See also "Cocoon," *Time*, Sept. 1976; Simeon Booker, "Ticker Tape U.S.A.," *Jet*, Nov. 25, 1976.

5. Hucker, "Blacks and the GOP," *CQ*, Apr. 1978.

6. Hooks, "Blacks and the GOP," *NYAN*, Aug. 1978; Godfrey Sperling Jr., "Republican Aim: Increasing Their Percentage of the Black Vote," *CSM*, Jan. 25, 1977; Walters, *Black Presidential Politics*, 34.

7. Jack Bass, "Southern Republicans: Their Plight is Getting Worse," *WP*, July 12, 1977.

8. Ibid. There are a few interesting cases from 1976 where black voters provided the margin of victory in state and local GOP victories: Ohio congressman Charles Whalen, for

instance, received more than 49 percent of the black vote, while Virginia congressman Paul Trible captured 25 percent. After the election, Trible continued to make overtures to African Americans by endorsing a legislative effort to make Martin Luther King Jr.'s birthday a federal holiday, establishing a black college scholarship fund, and hiring black employees on staff. However, as *Congressional Quarterly* observed, the congressman also voted against the Congressional Black Caucus (CBC) on all of its key issues in 1977. Hucker, "Blacks and the GOP," *CQ*, Apr. 1978; "Splitting Tickets by Blacks Elected GOP Congressman in Va.," *ADW*, Nov. 11, 1976.

9. Joseph A. Sanders to WHB, Letter, Feb. 25, 1977; WHB to Joseph Sanders, Letter, Mar. 9, 1977, both in box 58, Brock Papers; Bass, "Southern Republicans," *WP*, July 1977.

10. Howell Raines, "Republicans Courting Black Voters in South after Years of Inactivity," *NYT*, Aug. 1, 1978.

11. John J. Rhodes, "The GOP and Black America," *Congress Today! The Magazine of the National Republican Congressional Committee*, SESS. 1, no. 5. (May 1977).

12. Hucker, "Blacks and the GOP," *CQ*, Apr. 1978.

13. Author interview with EWB, 2008.

14. Paul S. Clark, "Carefully Planned, Executed Campaign Helps Black Republican Win in Georgia," *Congress Today!*, May 1977, in box 58, Brock Papers.

15. Warren Weaver Jr., "Republicans Select Brock as Party Head," *NYT*, Jan. 15, 1977; author phone interview with William H. Brock, May 29, 2013.

16. Waver, "Brock as Party Head," *NYT*, Jan. 1977; author interview with WHB, 2013. See also "Tennessee's William Brock," *Time*, Nov. 16, 1970; Glen Ford, interview of H. John Heinz, 1977, box 43, Senate Papers, Series Surety Bonding, H. John Heinz III Archives, Carnegie Mellon University, Pittsburgh (hereinafter called HJH Papers).

17. Sperling "Republican Aim," *CSM*, Jan. 1977.

18. Ibid. See also author interview with WHB, 2013.

19. Don Campbell, untitled article, [Gannett Syndicated News Service], [June 1978], box 58, Brock Papers. See also Hanes Walton, *Invisible Politics: Black Political Behavior* (Albany: State University of New York Press, 1985), 138; Pearl T. Robinson, "Whither the Future of Blacks in the Republican Party?" *Political Science Quarterly* 97, no. 2 (Summer 1982): 207–231.

20. "GOP Map Plans to Bring Blacks into Fold," *NYAN*, Mar. 25, 1978; "GOP to Spend $250,000 to Attract Blacks to Party," *WP*, July 12, 1977; James M. Perry, "The GOP and Black Voters," *WSJ*, Dec. 7, 1977; National Black Republican Council to HJH, Letter, Jan. 26, 1979; NBRC to RNC Executive Committee Members, Letter, Jan. 17, 1979, both in box 265, Senate Papers, Party Leadership Files, HJH Papers.

21. Robert Wright to WHB, Assessment of Wright-McNeill Activities 1977–1980, Feb. 1, 1979, box 40, folder 24, Brock Papers.

22. Robert Dole to Robert Wright and John McNeill, Letter, May 12, 1977; Phyllis Berry, Notes on Senator Bob Dole, May 12, 1977; RW to RD, Letter on Wright-McNeill, May 13, 1977, box 40, folder 24, Brock Papers; Simeon Booker, "Ticker Tape U.S.A.," *Jet*, Nov. 25, 1976. For an extensive list of letters and requests for assistance, see box 40, folders 23 and 24, Brock Papers.

23. PB to Barbara Bailey, Letter and Information on Wright-McNeill & Associates, May 13, 1977, box 40, folder 24, Brock Papers.

24. Perry, "Black Voters," *WSJ*, Dec. 1977; "Hunt on for Black Republicans," *WAA*, June 14, 1977.

25. "Conservatives Gaining Black Votes," *HE* 37, no. 51 (Dec. 17, 1977): 3; Sverdlik, "Black Aftermath," *NYAN*, Sept. 1976. For more on tax credits, massive resistance, and integration, see Kruse, *White Flight*, chap. 5.

26. "Black Votes," *HE*, Dec. 1977.

27. RD to RW and JM, Letter, May 1977; Berry, Notes on Dole, 1977, box 40, folder 24; Guy Vander Jagt to WHB, Sept. 11, 1978, box 58, both documents in Brock Papers.

28. On average, candidates assisted by Wright-McNeill & Associates received between 30 and 45 percent of the black vote in 1977. On their own, this same group of politicians earned between 3 and 5 percent in the 1976 elections. During the special 1977 races, the consulting group also assisted candidates in Kentucky, Virginia, Mississippi, Georgia, Washington, North Carolina, and Oklahoma. For example, the Tulsa, Oklahoma, mayor received 22 percent of the black vote, the Virginia attorney general amassed 35 percent, and the Charlotte, North Carolina, mayor earned 43 percent. Hucker, "Blacks and the GOP," *CQ*, Apr. 1978.

29. Simeon Booker, "Republican Comeback among Blacks," No Source, Oct. 3, 1977, box 57, Brock Papers; Peter E. Teeley to HJH, Memo on Black Progress, Dec. 7, 1977, box 245, Senate Papers, HJH Files.

30. Booker, "Republican Comeback," Oct. 1977, box 57, Brock Papers; PET to HJH, Memo, Dec. 7, 1977, box 245, Senate Papers, HJH Files; Wright-McNeill, State Plan, Apr. 20, 1979, box 40, Brock Papers.

31. Hucker, "Blacks and the GOP," *CQ*, Apr. 1978.

32. Wright to Brock, Assessment 1977–1980, Feb. 1979, box 40, Brock Papers.

33. "Jesse's Chance," *CT*, Jan. 1978; Hucker, "Blacks and the GOP," *CQ*, Apr. 1978; Joint Republican Leadership, Press Release, Apr. 26, 1978, box 265, Senate Papers, Party Leadership Files, HJH Papers.

34. Wright-McNeill & Associates, Brochure on Responsibilities for the RNC, n.d., box 58, Brock Papers.

35. Thelma Duggin, Field Report Form—Texas, Apr. 6, 1978, box 40, folder 23, Brock Papers.

36. Wright-McNeill, Communications Plan for Black Community Memo," [1978–79], box 40, folder 23, Brock Papers. See also Wright to Brock, Assessment 1977–1980, Feb. 1979, Brock Papers.

37. Between 1977 and 1980, Jesse Jackson wrote a number of articles encouraging African Americans to consider the Republican Party to maximize "freedom of choice" and broader political leverage. See, for example, JLJ, "Blacks' Votes Can Decide a National Election," *Milwaukee Sentinel*, Feb. 20, 1978.

38. RW and JM, Confidential Campaign Plan for Maurice Holman 34th District of Kansas, [1978]; Edward Dawson, Field Report Form, Pennsylvania, July 20–28, 1978, both in box 40, Brock Papers.

39. It is worth noting that Maurice Holman and Ben Andrews lost their respective elections, although both received a portion of the black vote. The Connecticut politician, for example, won 40 percent of the black vote in his race. Wright-McNeill, Confidential Campaign Plan for Maurice Holman 34th District of Kansas, [1978]; ED, Field Report PA July 1978, both in box 40, Brock Papers. See also "Norman E. Justice," in *Shaping Kansas Politics: The African American Legislators, the African American Experience*, Collections of the Kenneth Spencer Research Library, University of Kansas Libraries, Lawrence; "1st District Candidates," *HC*, Oct. 15, 1978; Senate Vote Supports Larger Tax Cuts, *HC*, Oct. 7, 1978.

40. Author interview with WHB, 2013.

41. "Brooke Cites Economics as Basis to Woo Blacks," *Jet*, Mar. 16, 1978; Jerry Solomon to Tim Hetz, Memo and Attachments on Black Outreach and Shirley Chisholm, June 16, 1978, box 40, Brock Papers.

42. JS to TH, Chisholm Memo, June 1978, box 40, Brock Papers.

43. Ibid.; "Jesse's Chance," *CT*, Jan. 1978; "GOP Map Plans to Bring Blacks into Fold," *NYAN*, Mar. 25, 1978; Andy Cooper, "One Man's Opinion," *NYAN*, Feb. 4, 1978.

44. McGrory, "Promised Land," *CT*, Jan. 1978; Rowland Evans and Robert Novak, "The GOP's Curious Quest for Black Votes," *WP*, Jan. 26, 1978; Patrick Buchanan, "Jesse, GOP Still Far Apart," *CT*, Feb. 7, 1978.

45. EWB, "Brooke Says Quality Is Issue, Not Money," *Bay State Banner*, Oct. 26, 1978; Michael Fields, "Brooke Faces the Fight of His Life," *Bay State Banner*, Sept. 14, 1978.

46. Terence Smith, "Republicans End Conference in Optimistic Mood on '78 Elections," *NYT*, Nov. 20, 1977.

47. JS to TH, Chisholm Memo, June 1978, box 40, Brock Papers; Hucker, "Blacks and the GOP," *CQ*, Apr. 1978.

48. Terence Smith, "Republicans End Conference in Optimistic Mood on '78 Elections," *NYT*, Nov. 20, 1977.

49. Hucker, "Blacks and the GOP," *CQ*, Apr. 1978.

50. William Safire, "Black Republicans," *NYT*, Feb. 21, 1977; Vernon E. Jordan Jr., "Blacks and the G.O.P.," [*NYT*], Mar. 29, 1977, box 24, folder Republicans—Blacks, Malson Files; Buchanan, "Jesse, GOP," *CT*, Feb. 1978.

51. James M. Perry, "The GOP and Black Voters," *WSJ*, Dec. 7, 1977; Evans and Novak, "Curious Quest," *WP*, Jan. 1978.

52. Claiborne, "Jackson Urges GOP," *WP*, Jan. 1978.

53. Ibid.

54. Ibid. See also "Campaign 1972," Mar. 1972, box 5, SSS Papers.

55. Edward Walsh, "NAACP Opposition to Carter Policies Cited by Reagan," *WP*, Jan. 22, 1978.

56. Ibid.

57. Hucker, "Joint Center Data," in "Blacks and the GOP," *CQ*, Apr. 1978, Malson Files; JCPS, *Black Politics 1980: RNC*, 18–20.

58. Wright to Brock, Assessment of Wright-McNeill, Feb. 1979, box 24, Brock Papers; "1977: Year of Hope and Despair," *Ebony*, Jan. 1978; Simeon Booker, "Washington Notebook," *Ebony*, Oct. 1979.

59. "Jesse Hits Carter Plan," *CT*, Nov. 29, 1978. See also "Black Voices Speak Up," *Time*, Dec. 18, 1978; Robert Wright to Bill Brock, Assessment of Wright-McNeill Activities 1977–1980, Feb. 1, 1979; "Blacks Buy Carter Symbols, Get No Substance," *Washington Star*, Jan. 19, 1979, box 40, folder 24, Brock Papers; Marable, *How Capitalism Underdeveloped Black America*, 222–223.

60. "Are Blacks Too Democratic?" *BE*, July 1980.

61. David Gergen, "Wanted: A GOP Program: A Minority Party with a Majority Philosophy," *WP*, Nov. 19, 1978.

62. Safire, "Black Republicans," *NYT*, Feb. 1977; Jordan, "Blacks and the G.O.P.," *NYT*, Mar. 1977, box 24, folder Republicans—Blacks, Malson Files.

63. JCPS Study in Hucker, "Blacks and the GOP," *CQ*, Apr. 1978; Safire, "Black Republicans," *NYT*, Feb. 1977.

64. JCPS Study in Hucker, "Blacks and the GOP," *CQ*, Apr. 1978; Safire, "Black Republicans," *NYT*, Feb. 1977.

65. "G.O.P. Drive to Woo Blacks, Intellectuals" *NYT*, Mar. 13, 1977; Andy Cooper, "One Man's Opinion," *NYAN*, Feb. 4, 1978; Wright-McNeill & Associates, Brochure on Responsibilities for the Republican National Committee, n.d., box 58, folder 1, Brock Papers.

66. Jordan, "Blacks and the G.O.P.," *NYT*, Mar. 1977, box 24, Malson Files; Adam Clymer, "Jesse Jackson Tells Receptive G.O.P., It Can Pick up Votes of Blacks," *NYT*, Jan. 21, 1978; William Claiborne, "Jackson Urges GOP to Appeal to Blacks," *WP*, Jan. 21, 1978.

67. Unknown article, June 1978, box 58, Brock Papers.

68. JCPS, *Black Politics 1980: RNC*, 21.

69. Ibid., 19; JS to TH, Chisholm Memo, June 1978, box 40, Brock Papers.

70. JCPS, *Black Politics 1980: RNC*, 18; Wright-McNeill to Ben Cotton, Memo on 1979–1980 GOP Black Vote Plan, Jan. 12, 1979, box 40, Brock Papers; Gergen, "A GOP Program," *WP*, Nov. 1978; "Massive Black Support for Conservative Republican," *HE*, Nov. 18, 1978, 3.

71. Andy Cooper, "One Man's Opinion," *NYAN*, Feb. 4, 1978.

72. Bayard Rustin, "The Sadness of Black Political Defeats," *LAS*, Nov. 30, 1978.

73. "Brooke Gains Support of Women Leaders," *Bay State Banner*, Nov. 2, 1978; "Brooke Loses in Bid for 3rd Senate Term," *CT*, Nov. 8, 1978; Michael Knight, "Brooke Loses Race for 3rd Senate Term," *NYT*, Nov. 8, 1978; "The Defeat of Sen. Brooke," *WP*, Nov. 10, 1978; "Ted Kennedy Blamed for Brooke's Defeat," *CP*, Nov. 18, 1978; "Brooke's Loss Hurts Many," *Jet*, Nov. 23, 1978; Dee Primm, "What Does Brooke's Defeat Signify Locally, Nationally?" *Bay State Banner*, Nov. 9, 1978; Aldo Beckman "Brooke Loses in Bid for 3rd Senate Term," *CT*, Nov. 8, 1978; Sally Jacobs, "The Unfinished Chapter," *Boston Globe*, Mar. 5, 2000; Emmett George, "Bouncing Back from Defeat," *Sepia*, Feb. 1979.

74. Lincoln Institute for Research and Education, "Breakfast Forum: U.S. Senator Orrin Hatch," Feb. 2007: www.lincolnreview.com.

75. Jay Parker, "A Message from President Jay Parker: Freeing Black Americans from the Liberal Plantation since 1978," n.d.; "The Lincoln Institute: About Us," n.d., www.lincolnreview.com; "Conservative Forum," *HE* 39, no. 1 (Jan. 6, 1979): 22; David W. Tyson and J. A. Parker, *Courage to Put Country Above Color: The J. A. Parker Story* (Washington, D.C.: LIRE, 2009), 42–55.

76. See for example, *Lincoln Review* 1, no. 2 (Summer 1979); "Review and Outlook: The *Lincoln Review*," *WSJ*, June 12, 1979.

77. "*Lincoln Review*," *WSJ*, June 1979; "Conservative Forum," *HE* 39, no. 1 (Jan. 6, 1979): 22.

78. The BSMC and LIRE shared similar beliefs on issues as varied as busing, apartheid, communism, economics, abortion, and religion; nevertheless, the leaders of the two groups did not get along. In 1982 Clay Claiborne issued a letter publicizing his grievances with Parker and his "Lincoln Institute fellows," writing, "During our long years of work there have been BLACK ORGANIZATIONS that appear on the scene describing themselves as black conservatives, but when a united public appearance is needed, wanted, and necessary we can never find them. . . . These organizations, encouraged by whites, do little with their contributions to enhance the conservative cause among Black Americans. They copy our methods for contributions, but we find no traces of a creditable use of the money." Of course, Claiborne's critics had offered similar accusations of the furtive dealings of the BSMC leader throughout the better part of two decades. BSMC, "End of the Year Report," [Dec. 1982], BSMC Papers.

79. Clay Perry, "Black Middle Class Focus of Magazine," *Milwaukee Journal*, June 4, 1979, Legislative Assistants' Files, box 256, HJH Files; Louis Rukeyser, "Here Come the Free-Enterprise Blacks," *New York Daily News*, June 29, 1979, box 256, Senate Papers, Legislative Assistants' Files, HJH Papers.

80. Parker, "A Message from President Jay Parker," n.d.; "Conservative Forum," *HE* 39, no. 1 (Jan. 6, 1979): 22; "Exclusive Interview with Walter Williams," *HE* 41, no. 5 (Jan. 31, 1981): 10. See also Marva Collins, *Black Education and the Inner City* (Washington, D.C.: Lincoln Institute for Research and Education, 1981); "Black America under the Reagan Administration: A Symposium of Black Conservatives," conference proceedings, *Policy Review* 34 (Fall 1985): 27–41.

81. Andrew Cooper, Wayne J. Dawkins, and Soraya Elcock, "Black[s] Invisible with Presidential Candidates," *NYAN*, Nov. 3, 1979; Allan C. Brownfeld, "Black Conservatives: A Growing Force," *HE* 51, no . 38 (Sept. 21, 1991): 10.

82. Cooper, Dawkins, and Elcock, "Presidential Candidates," *NYAN*, Nov. 1979.

83. "Some Initial Strategic and Tactical Considerations for the 1980 Presidential Campaign," Mar. 28, 1980; Lorelei Kinder to Ed Meese, Voter Programs Structure and Organization of Blacks and Hispanics, Apr. 29, 1980, both in box 104, Ed Meese Files, Ronald Reagan 1980 Presidential Campaign Papers 1964–1980, Ronald Reagan Presidential Library (hereinafter called RRPC Papers, RR Library); "Putting Color in the GOP," *BE*, July 1980.

84. Keith Richburg, "Black Delegates from D.C. Lead on GOP Issues," *WP*, July 16, 1980; James H. Cleaver, "Black Republicans Support Reagan—and Woo Other Blacks," *LAS*, July 24, 1980; Colorado Black Republicans for Reagan, "Governor Reagan's Plans," advertisement, n.d., box 318, folder Voter Groups-Blacks-Advertising, Max Hugel Files, RRPC Papers, RR Library (hereinafter called Hugel Files).

85. Art Teele, Memo on Activities, [Oct. 1980], box 305; AT, Memo on Activities, Sept. 18, 1980, and Art Teele to MH, Handwritten Note, Oct. 2, 1980; Handwritten Note, [Sept. 1980], box 317, all documents in ibid; "Blacks Form Nat'L Comm. for Reagan," *ADW*, Oct. 3, 1980.

86. Joe Cooper to Craig King, Memo, Aug. 6, 1980; JC to Eleanor Callahan, Memo, Aug. 13, 1980, box 317, Hugel Files. See also Luix Overbea, "Reagan Campaign Goal among Blacks: At least 12 percent of vote," *CSM*, Aug. 1980.

87. "Campaign Strategy," n.d., box 229, Promotional and Advertising and Martin Tubridy to JC, Memo on Black Media, Sept. 23, 1980; Data on Newspaper Insertion Orders, [Sept. 1980], box 234, Promotional Department, all documents in Peter Dailey Files, RRPC Papers; Stan Anderson, Memo on Additional Funds, Oct. 21, 80, box 318, Hugel Files.

88. AT, Memo, Oct. 1980, box 305; AT, Memo, Sept. 18, 1980, and AT to MX, Note, Oct. 1980; Note, [Sept. 1980], box 317, all documents in Hugel Files.

89. Angela Wright to Mike Baroody, Memo, Mar. 24, 1980, RRPC Papers, box 317.

90. RW to Drew Lewis, Memo, Sept. 5, 1980; Henry Lucas and Dan Smith, Transcript of Phone Message, Aug. 15, 1980. See also Max Hugel to Elizabeth Dole, Memo, Aug. 15, 1980, all in box 318, Hugel Files.

91. Barbara W. Miles, "Ronald Reagan Wins a Half Vote," *NYAN*, Aug. 16, 1980; "Reagan, in South Bronx, Says Carter Broke Vow," *NYT*, Aug. 6, 1980; "Reagan Booed in Bronx Slum," *LAT*, Aug. 5, 1980; "And South Bronx Cheer," *WP*, Aug. 8, 1980.

92. Miles, "Half Vote," *NYAN*, Aug. 1980; "Broke Vow," *NYT*, Aug. 1980; "Reagan Booed," *LAT*, Aug. 1980; "Cheer," *WP*, Aug. 1980.

93. Richard Wirthlin and Jim Brady to Ronald Reagan, Memo, Aug. 11, 1980, box 126, Subject Files Blacks, Ed Meese Files, RRPC Papers, RR Library.

94. "Inflation," radio advertisement transcript, Oct. 2, 1980, box 317; "Jobs, Employment," Black radio advertisement, Oct. 2, 1980, and Reagan Bush Committee, "Jobs, Jobs, Jobs," newspaper advertisement, [Oct. 1980], and Reagan Bush Committee, "Jobs, Jobs, Jobs," Advertisement, [1980], box 305, all documents in Hugel Files.

95. "Where They Stand: Reagan," *BE*, Nov. 1980.

96. Barry Paris, "Reagan Boost," *Pittsburgh Post-Gazette*, Oct. 17, 1980; "Evers of Fayette for Reagan," *ADW*, Nov. 4, 1980; "Carter Drive Jolted as 3 Top Blacks Back Reagan," *LAT*, Oct. 16, 1980; Vernon Jarrett, "Why Blacks Must Weigh Their Votes," *CT*, Nov. 2, 1980.

97. "Reaction Mixed over Abernathy," *Prescott Courier*, Oct. 17, 1980; "Some Black Leaders Upset by Endorsement of Reagan," *Toledo Blade*, Oct. 16, 1980; David Espo,

"Black Leader Surprises Reagan," *Leger*, Oct. 17, 1980; "Reagan Buoyed by Two Black Leaders' Support," *St. Petersburg Times*, Oct. 17, 1980.

98. Bob Wright to Art Teele, Memo on Roy Innis and CORE, Oct. 22, 1980, box 40, Brock Papers; Vernon Jarrett, "Democrats Kept Loyalty of Blacks," *CT*, Nov. 9, 1980.

99. GOP congressman John Anderson ran as an independent in the presidential election, winning less than 10 percent of the popular vote; half of his supporters were Republicans, while half were Democrats.

100. Jeff Prugh, "Split Dixie Vote Called Anti-Washington Reaction"" *LAT*, Nov. 22, 1980; Adam Clymer, "Displeasure with Carter Turned Many to Reagan," *NYT*, Nov. 9, 1980; "Apples, Oranges and Votes," *NYT*, Nov. 24, 1980; Adam Clymer, "Displeasure with Carter Turned Many to Reagan," *NYT*, Nov. 9, 1980; "Survey Finds Some Blacks Helped Ronald Reagan Win," *OP*, Nov. 26, 1980; Julian C. Dixon, "Blacks Find Gains, Losses," *LAS*, Nov. 27, 1980.

101. At the time, political observers agreed that Reagan performed better among black voters in 1980 than Ford did four years earlier; nevertheless, there was disagreement over what percentage of the black vote Reagan won. The RNC, Wright-McNeill, Reagan campaign, the *NYT*, and CBS placed the figure at 14–16 percent, whereas the NUL, DNC, Gallup, and JCPS placed it at 6–10 percent. By 2012, the JCPS had amended the number to 14 percent. For the purposes of this chapter, I use the 14 percent approximation, since that is what most GOP strategists used. Bositis, *Blacks and the RNC, 2012*; Vernon Jarrett, "Blacks' Loyalty to Democrats Unbroken by Reagan's Victory," *Evening Independent*, Nov. 12, 1980; "Joint Center Releases Results of the Black Vote," *ADW*, Nov. 23, 1980.

102. Editorial, *CP*, Nov. 8, 1980; "Bill Brock: Architect of Republican Revival," *WP*, Nov. 20, 1980.

103. Gilbert H. Caldwell, "Black Needs—Regardless of Party," *WP*, Nov. 16, 1980; Simon Anekwe, "They Swear by Reagan," *NYAN*, Nov. 15, 1980; Robinson, "Whither the Future," *PS*, 1982, 225.

104. Anekwe "Swear by Reagan," *NYAN*, Nov. 1980.

105. Jarrett, "Blacks' Loyalty," *Evening Independent*, Nov. 1980.

106. Billy Rowe, "Quiet Black Republicans Getting Noisy," *NYAN*, Nov. 20, 1980; Anekwe, "Swear by Reagan," *NYAN*, Nov. 1980; Reagan Transition Team Flowchart, [1980–1981], box 240, Senate Papers, Executive Branch, HJH Files; Herbert Denton, "A Prominent New York Lawyer with Blue-Chip Credentials," *WP*, Dec. 23, 1980.

107. "Top Black Appointees Honored at Reception," *Washington Informer*, May 21, 1981; Denton, "Blue-Chip Credentials," *WP*, Dec. 1980. See also Mary McGrory, "Blacks to Great Communicator: Good Riddance," *Eugene Register-Guard*, Jan. 18, 1989.

108. Leon Wynter, "The 'Black Elephant:' Growth for the GOP," *WP*, June 25, 1981.

109. Ibid.

110. Juan Williams, "Black Conservatives, Center Stage," *WP*, Dec. 16, 1980.

111. Herbert Denton, "A Different Look at Old Problems," *WP*, Dec. 15, 1980; *The Fairmont Papers: Black Alternatives Conference* (San Francisco: Institute for Contemporary Studies, 1981), xi.

112. During his presentation, Charles Hamilton, who coauthored *Black Power: The Politics of Liberation in America* in 1967 with Kwame Toure, argued that black politics was no longer a "matter of party labels—Democrats, Republicans, or even [a] . . . national black political party." He also suggested that it was not about "ideological identification—liberals, conservatives, integrationists, nationalists." Charles Hamilton, "Joining the Political Process," *Fairmont Papers*, 122.

113. Denton, "Old Problems," *WP*, Dec. 1980; "Blacks and Mr. Reagan," *WP*, Dec. 15, 1980; Charles V. Hamilton and Dona Cooper Hamilton, *The Dual Agenda: Race and*

Social Welfare Policies of Civil Rights Organizations (New York: Columbia University Press, 1997), 226–227; *Fairmont Papers*, 163–167.

114. "Blacks," *WP*, Dec. 1980; "Blacks and Reagan," *International Herald Tribune*, Dec. 16, 1980.

115. Henry Lucas, *Fairmont Papers*, 92.

116. Thomas Sowell, "Politics and Opportunity," *Fairmont Papers*, 5–12.

117. Ibid. See also Lisa McGirr, *Suburban Warriors: The Origins of the new American Right* (Princeton: Princeton University Press, 2001), 238–239; Robert O. Self, "Prelude to the Tax Revolt: The Politics of the 'Tax Dollar' in Postwar California," in *The New Suburban History*, ed. Kevin M. Kruse and Thomas J. Sugrue (Chicago: University of Chicago Press, 2006), 144–160; Dan J. Smith, "Response to Thomas Sowell," *Fairmont Papers*, 12–15.

118. Oscar Wright, "Response to Thomas Sowell," *Fairmont Papers*, 16–18. See also "Watson Opponent Outlines Platform," *LAS*, Apr. 29, 1982.

119. Chuck Stone, "Introduction to Politics: Goals and Strategies," *Fairmont Papers*, 117–119.

120. Martin Kilson, "Widening Our Reach," *Fairmont Papers*, 134–136.

121. Ibid. See also Martin Kilson, "The Gang That Couldn't Shoot Straight," *Transition*, no. 62 (1993): 222; Martin Kilson, "From Civil Rights to Party Politics: The Black Political Transition," *Current History* 67, no. 399 (Nov. 1974): 193–199.

122. Juan Williams, "Black Conservatives," *WP*, Dec. 1980; Clarence Thomas, "Being Educated Black," *Fairmont Papers*, 81–83.

123. Williams, "Black Conservatives," *WP*, Dec. 1980.

124. Denton, "Old Problems," *WP*, Dec. 1980.

125. Sutton, "A Skeptic Persuaded," *Fairmont Papers*, 156–157.

126. Edwin Meese, "A Significant Beginning," *Fairmont Papers*, 159–160. See also "Blacks and Reagan," *INT*, Dec. 1980; "Blacks and Mr. Reagan," *WP*, Dec. 15, 1980; "Black Republicans Meet Reagan Aides," *NYT*, Dec. 15, 1980.

127. *Fairmont Papers*, xii, 116.

128. Williams, "Black Conservatives," *WP*, Dec. 1980.

129. J. Clay Smith Jr., "A Black Lawyer's Response to the Fairmont Papers," *Howard Law Journal* 26, no. 7 (1983): 195–225.

130. Williams, "Black Conservatives," *WP*, Dec. 1980.

131. Simon Anekwe, "Chuck Stone Probes Black Conservatives," *NYAN*, Mar. 7, 1981; "Views from Two Sides on How to Vault the Color Bar," *NYT*, Apr. 12, 1981; Lee A. Daniels, "The New Black Conservatives," *NYT*, Oct. 4, 1981; "On the Move: Robert Wright," *NYAM*, July 11, 1981; Leon Wynter, "The 'Black Elephant:' Growth for the GOP," *WP*, June 25, 1981; Norman Hill, "The New Black Conservatives," *NYAN*, Jan. 17, 1981; Williams, "Black Conservatives," *WP*, Dec. 1980.

132. Robinson, "Whither the Future," *PS*, 1982, 224–226.

133. Ibid., 227–231.

CONCLUSION: NO ROOM AT THE INN

1. Thomas's speech was originally entitled "Why Black Americans Should Look to Conservative Politics." In 1991, in the midst of Thomas's controversial Supreme Court nomination process, *Policy Review* reprinted it as "No Room at the Inn: The Loneliness of the Black Conservative." Seven years later, black conservative writer Shelby Steele would borrow the title for a speech and a chapter in his book *A Dream Deferred*. Clarence Thomas,

"Why Black Americans Should Look to Conservative Policies," *Heritage Lecture*, no. 119, June 18, 1987 (Washington, D.C.: Heritage Foundation, 1987); Clarence Thomas, "No Room at the Inn: The Loneliness of the Black Conservative," *Policy Review* 58 (Fall 1991): 72–78; Shelby Steele, "The Loneliness of the 'Black Conservative,'" in *The Second Betrayal of Black Freedom in America* (New York: HarperCollins, 1998), 1–114.

2. "Lasting Stigma: Affirmative Action and Clarence Thomas's Prisoners' Rights Jurisprudence," *Harvard Law Review* 112, no. 6 (Apr. 1999): 1331–1348.

3. "Things Thomas Has Written and Said," *Free Lance Star*, Sept. 9, 1991.

4. Thomas, "Black Americans," June 1987. See also "The GOP's Black Eye," *NR*, Jan. 30, 1987.

5. Robert Pear, "Blacks and the Elitist Stereotype," *NYT*, Sept. 29, 1987. See also Frederick Harris, *The Price of the Ticket: Barack Obama and the Rise and Decline of Black Politics* (New York: Oxford University Press, 2012), 157; "Black America under the Reagan Administration," Forum, *Policy Review* 34 (Fall 1985).

6. See, for example, T. R. Reid, "Black Republicans Charge Party's Rules Exclude Minorities," *WP*, Aug. 12, 1988; John Eligon, "Young, Black and Republican in New York, Blogging against the Tide," *NYT*, Oct. 9, 2008; Don Terry, "'Our Party, Too,' Black Republicans Say," *NYT*, Mar. 16, 1996; Raynard Jackson, "A Brand New Problem for Republicans," *Philadelphia Tribune*, Aug. 23, 2013; Zenitha Prince, "Republican Robert J. Brown Known as Maverick in Politics and Business," *AA*, Sept. 28, 2013; "In Outreach to Blacks, a GOP Credibility Gap," *WP*, June 13, 2000; Faye Anderson, "Why I Left the Republican Party," *Afro-American Red Star*, Apr. 15, 2000; Kevin Merida, "Capital Scene: Politicians Fumble over Matters of Race," *Emerge*, June 1999.

7. Thomas, "Black Americans," June 1987; Paul Delaney, "The Nation: 'Black and Conservative' Takes Many Different Tones," *NYT*, Dec. 22, 1991.

8. Census documents suggest that between 1979 and 1987, the percentage of African Americans living under poverty rose from 31 to 33 percent; the result was "distinct societies," within black communities—one an "affluent middle class" and "the other a jobless or working-poor" group that struggled to pull itself out of poverty. The latter group was hit hard by economic recession and the Reagan administration's cuts to social welfare programs including "food stamps, public service jobs, job-training programs, [and] housing subsidies." Moreover, the president's African American critics, bristled at Reagan's "lax enforcement of civil rights laws" and rejected his and other conservatives' insistence that affirmative action was a "needless intrusion into the marketplace" that repressed individual rights. Luix Overbea, "Black Middle Class Moves Up US Economic Ladder," *CSM*, July 31, 1987; John Ehrman and Michael W. Flamm, *Debating the Reagan Presidency* (Lanham: Rowman & Littlefield, 2009), 50–51; Bureau of the Census, U.S. Department of Commerce, "Poverty in the United States 1987," *Current Population Reports: Consumer Income*, Series P-60, no. 163 (Washington, D.C.: U.S. Department of Commerce, 1989), 2.

9. "Divide and Conquer Is Still at Work," *Gainesville Sun*, Feb. 23, 1986. See also Joseph G. Conti and Brad Stetson, *Challenging the Civil Rights Establishment: Profiles of a New Black Vanguard* (Westport: Praeger Publishers, 1993); Hanes Walton Jr., "Defending the Indefensible: The African American Conservative Client, Spokesperson of the Reagan-Bush Era," *Black Scholar* 24, no. 4 (Fall 1994): 46–49.

10. "Republicans Summon Negroes to Support of 'Party of Lincoln,'" *NYAN*, Apr. 25, 1936.

11. "Do Black Republicans Speak for Black America?" *NYAN*, June 27, 1981.

12. Bositis, *Blacks and the RNC*, 2012.

13. Michael K. Frisby, "The Republican Convention, 1966," *WSJ*, Aug. 13, 1996; C. H. Gibbs, "Study Released on Blacks, GOP," *LAS*, Nov. 26, 1987.

14. Political scientist Paul Frymer covers the flaws of two-party competition as it relates to the Democratic Party in his book, *Uneasy Alliances*, suggesting that African Americans are "captured" by the Democratic Party, as they have no choice but to abstain from voting, join "suicidal" third-party movements, or remain in the party given that most view the Republican alternative as hostile to their interests. As a result, African Americans find their interests "muted" by the Democratic Party, which takes their votes for granted. Moreover, Frymer argues that *both* parties avoid race-conscious appeals to minorities out of fear of alienating white swing voters. Frymer, *Uneasy Alliances*, 8–10, 15–22, 125–131.

15. Ibid.

16. See, for example, Colin L. Powell, *My American Journey* (New York: Ballantine Books, 2003); Condoleezza Rice, *No Higher Honor: A Memoir of My Years in Washington* (New York: Broadway Paperbacks, 2011); Clarence Thomas, *My Grandfather's Son: A Memoir* (New York: Harper Perennial, 2008). See also Bracey, *Saviors or Sellouts*, 189–196.

17. Jon F. Hale, "The Making of the New Democrats," *Political Science Quarterly* 110, no. 2 (Summer 1995): 207–232; Robin D. G. Kelley, "Neoliberalism's Challenge," Forum: The Future of Black Politics, *Boston Review*, Jan. 11, 2012: www.bostonreview.net/chal lenge-neoliberalism; Lester Spence, "The Neoliberal Turn in Black Politics," paper presented at the annual meeting of the Western Political Science Association, Mar. 3, 2009, Vancouver.

18. Megan Ming Francis and Michael C. Dawson, "Black Politics and the Neoliberal Racial Order," 2013, 7–12, 28–36, unpublished manuscript, Pepperdine University and University of Chicago. See also Michael Dawson, *Not in Our Lifetimes* (Chicago: University of Chicago Press, 2011). There are many more aspects of black neoliberal politics that are well covered in the scholarly literature and are beyond the scope of this study. See, for example, Dawson, *Black Visions*; Hanes Walton, *African American Power and Politics: The Political Context Variable* (New York: Columbia University Press, 1997).

19. "Transcript: Obama's Commencement Speech at Morehouse College," *WSJ*, May 20, 2013. See also Jeffries, "Brooke and Wilder," *PS*, Sept. 1999; Dennis S. Nordin, *From Edward Brooke to Barack Obama: African American Political Issues, 1966–2008* (Columbia: University of Missouri Press, 2012); Francis and Dawson, "Black Politics," 2013, 6.

20. Fredrick Harris, *The Price of the Ticket: Barack Obama and the Rise and Decline of Black Politics*, chap. 4; Gabrielle Dunkley, "Obama Would Have Been a 'Moderate Republican' Several Decades Ago," *Huffington Post*, Feb. 1, 2013; "Transcript: Obama's Commencement Speech at Morehouse College," *WSJ*, May 20, 2013; "For Black Conservatives, Obama Raises a Conflict," *Bay State Banner*, June 18, 2008.

21. As the JCPES notes, since 1998 a small but important group of state and local Republican elected officials has garnered support from at least 20 percent of African Americans: some of the more prominent figures among this group are Governor George W. Bush (Texas, 27 percent, 1998); Governor George Voinovich (Ohio, 32 percent, 1998); Congresswoman Kay Bailey Hutchinson (Texas, 26 percent, 2006); and Senator LaMar Alexander (Tennessee, 26 percent, 2008). Bositis, *Blacks and RNC, 2012*.

22. Matthew Streb points out that there were a number of unique conditions at play in Huckabee's win, including low voter turnout and both candidates' deliberate avoidance of controversial issues, like affirmative action (which they both opposed). Nevertheless, Streb concludes that "Republicans may be able to win African American votes by reaching out . . . emphasizing religion," without discussing politically charged topics like abortion, and "providing economic programs targeted at least partially at Blacks." Matthew J. Streb, "A New Message: Compassionate Conservatism, African Americans, and the Republican Party," *Politics & Policy* 29, no. 4 (Dec. 2001): 676–682. See also Bositis, *Blacks and RNC, 2012*, 7–9. For more on black increases in the black GOP vote in midterm elections, see Tate, *From Protest to Politics*, 137.

23. Thomas Edsall provides an excellent broad overview of where various party leaders and strategists stand in the debate in a *New York Times* column from July 3, 2013, http://opinionator.blogs.nytimes.com/2013/07/03/should-republicans-just-focus-on-white-voters/. Thomas Edsall, "Should Republicans Just Focus on White Voters?" *NYT*, July 3, 2013. See also George E. Curry, "Black Republicans: Who They Are, What They Want," *Emerge*, Mar. 1990; Ramesh Ponnuru, "Minority Party," *NR* 50, no. 24 (Dec. 21, 1998): 24–25; Ross Douthat, "Republicans, White Voters and Racial Polarization," *NYT*, Aug. 6, 2013; Louis Bolce, Gerald De Maio, and Douglas Muzzio, "Blacks and the Republican Party: The 20 Percent Solution," *Political Science Quarterly* 107, no. 1 (Spring 1992): 63–79; Louis Bolce, Gerald De Maio, and Douglas Muzzio, "The 1992 Republican 'Tent': No Blacks Walked In," *PSQ* 108, no. 2 (Summer 1993): 255–270.

24. Nonwhite voters composed 28 percent of the electorate in the 2012 presidential election. Barack Obama won more than 70 percent of the Asian and Latino votes, and more than 90 percent of the black vote. "Latino Voters in the 2012 Election," Hispanic Trends Project, Pew Research Center, Nov. 7, 2012, http://www.pewhispanic.org/2012/11/07/latino-voters-in-the-2012-election/; Paul Taylor, "The Growing Electoral Clout of Blacks is Driven by Turnout, Not Demographics," Social & Demographic Trends, Pew Research Center, Dec. 26, 2012, http://www.pewsocialtrends.org/2012/12/26/the-growing-electoral-clout-of-blacks-is-driven-by-turnout-not-demographics/.

25. Thomas Edsall, "Should Republicans Just Focus on White Voters?" *NYT*, July 3, 2013.

26. Since 1980, the Republican Party has continued to dabble in black outreach, vacillating back and forth in both national and state and local elections; likewise, several GOP administrations have continued policies like the minority set-aside program that benefit the black middle class. But, as Tim Thurber highlights, many of their efforts have been undercut by a laundry list of misdeeds and racial blunders (deliberate or otherwise) that negate their outreach appeals; this includes everything from accusations of black voter fraud to real and "rhetorical attacks on affirmative action" to implicit racist appeals to white voters. For specific details on contemporary racial antagonisms between the Republican Party and blacks and information on black outreach, see Thurber, *Republicans and Race*, 379–389; Philpot, *Race, Republicans*, 1–5; Bolce, Maio, and Muzzio, "20 Percent Solution," *PSQ*, 1992, 63–79; Bolce, Maio, and Muzzio "1992 Republican 'Tent,'" *PSQ*, 1993; "How Blacks Participated in the Republican Convention," *Jet*, Sept. 2, 1996.

Index